# THE NEW PHYSICAL
# ANTHROPOLOGY

# THE NEW PHYSICAL ANTHROPOLOGY

## Science, Humanism, and Critical Reflection

*Edited by*
**Shirley C. Strum**
**Donald G. Lindburg**
**David Hamburg**

*ADVANCES IN HUMAN EVOLUTION SERIES*

PRENTICE HALL, UPPER SADDLE RIVER, NEW JERSEY 07458

**Library of Congress Cataloging-in-Publication Data**

The new physical anthropology / edited by Shirley C. Strum, Donald G.
    Lindburg, David Hamburg.
        p.   cm. — (Advances in human evolution series)
    Includes bibliographical references.
    ISBN 0-13-206517-7
    1. Physical anthropology.   I. Strum, Shirley C. (Shirley Carol),
19XX–   .  II. Lindburg, Donald G., 19XX–   .   III. Hamburg, David
A., (date).  IV. Series.
GN60.N45   1999
599.0—dc21
                                                    98-37467
                                                    CIP

Editorial Director: Charlyce Jones Owen
Editor-in-Chief: Nancy Roberts
Managing Editor: Sharon Chambliss
Marketing Manager: Christopher DeJohn
Editorial/production supervision
    and interior design: Serena Hoffman
Line Art Coordinator: Guy Ruggiero
Buyer: Mary Ann Gloriande
Cover Art Director: Jayne Conte
Cover Designer: Bruce Kenselaar
Cover Art: "Face from Fish to Man,"
    American Museum of Natural History

This book was set in 10/12 Palatino by BookMasters, Inc.,
and was printed and bound by Courier Companies, Inc.
The cover was printed by Phoenix Color Corp.

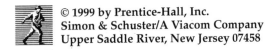

© 1999 by Prentice-Hall, Inc.
**Simon & Schuster/A Viacom Company**
**Upper Saddle River, New Jersey 07458**

Printed in the United States of America

10   9   8   7   6   5   4   3   2   1

ISBN 0-13-206517-7

Prentice-Hall International (UK) Limited, *London*
Prentice-Hall of Australia Pty. Limited, *Sydney*
Prentice-Hall Canada Inc., *Toronto*
Prentice-Hall Hispanoamericana, S.A., *Mexico*
Prentice-Hall of India Private Limited, *New Delhi*
Prentice-Hall of Japan, Inc., *Tokyo*
Simon & Schuster Asia Pte. Ltd., *Singapore*
Editora Prentice-Hall do Brasil, Ltda., *Rio de Janeiro*

# CONTENTS

# PREFACE

Shirley C. Strum
Donald G. Lindburg

Why a book of this nature? In some ways this volume is a historical document. It "re-presents" Washburn's new physical anthropology for those who may have forgotten one of the most important influences on the development of modern physical anthropology in the United States and for those who, entering the field today, may never have been exposed to these seminal works. But it goes beyond history to tell the story of the practice of the field, showing through the work of his "descendants" how the framework has been articulated and expanded over the years. The book is as much about science as it is about physical anthropology because Washburn never separated the two in his vision.

Washburn was not a prolific writer. To assess his influence based on his list of papers and even the citations to his work would be inaccurate and inappropriate. We leave it to historians to write about Washburn's place in the intellectual enterprises of half a century (Haraway 1989). Here we try to convey the vision and why it was so inspiring and so productive. Because he traveled and lectured widely and was such an articulate and charismatic speaker, he was probably the most influential physical anthropologist in the United States from the 1950s to the 1970s. He touched others in related fields, was the spokesman for the new physical anthropology to the public, to the government, to hundreds of thousands of students, and to critical funding agencies like the Wenner Gren Foundation, NSF, NIMH, NIH and later the Leakey Foundation. During his tenure as "dean" of physical anthropology, the field grew from about 100 scientists to more than 1,000 (Washburn 1983). When he began, few departments had one physical anthropologist. By the time he retired in 1979, most departments had one and many had several. His graduate students have populated most of the important anthropology departments in the country. His legacy is most visible today through them. Those in this volume are a representative but not inclusive list. They appear in these pages because of serendipity, dedication, and love. The compendium of his students or those he supported reads like a "who's who" of anthropology. Upon examination, they all share independent mindedness, integrative thinking, a concern for better evidence, better theory, better method—in short, better science. A large number also share his commitment to creating a better society.

Each section of the book illustrates part of the new agenda he set for the "new physical anthropology." Each part of the book begins with a key or representative Washburn paper. The papers that follow are original contributions by those who are part of his legacy. They consider the current status of specific issues illustrating the direction the new physical anthropology has taken. Some discuss the prospects for the future. Washburn strove to increase the complexity of approaches and interpretations, to increase the links between previously segregated sources of evidence and disciplines, and to improve the connection between science and society. Thus the various themes of the papers, such as using the evolutionary perspective as a scientific tool, comparative functional anatomy, the potential of primatology, reconstructions of primate and human evolution, and the problems and challenges of the science of human evolution, are therefore not isolated or encapsulated in only one paper. They recur in other papers and in the variety of work carried out by his students. Thus the sentiments expressed in the introductory Washburn paper of one section may apply equally well to other sections.

Throughout all of his papers, the reader will find not just the important perspective of the new physical anthropology but the integration of the perspectives of science, humanism, and critical reflection that made Washburn's vision of the field unique for his time. Only recently have these issues become part of the enterprise of anthropology and of science.

### References

Harraway, D. (1989). Remodeling the human way of life: Sherwood Washburn and the new physical anthropology. In D. Haraway, *Primate Visions: Gender, Race and Nature in the World of Modern Science.* New York: Routledge, pp. 186–230.

Washburn, S. L. (1983). Evolution of a Teacher. *Annual Review of Anthropology.* 12: 1–24.

Dr. Sherwood L. Washburn

The publisher and editors would like to thank Carnegie Corporation of New York and The L. S. B. Leakey Foundation for their generosity in making funds available for the production of this text.

# LIST OF CONTRIBUTORS

**Dr. Alan Almquist**
Dept. of Anthropology & Geography
California State University
Hayward, CA 94542-3039

**Dr. John V. Basmajian**
Rehabilitation Centre
Chedoke Hospitals
Hamilton, Ontario
Canada L8N 3L6

**Dr. Claud Bramblett**
Dept. of Anthropology
University of Texas
Austin, TX 78712

**Dr. Anthony M. Coelho, Jr.**
National Institutes of Health
NHLB/Review Branch

**Dr. Phyllis Dolhinow**
Dept. of Anthropology
University of California
Berkeley, CA 94720

**Dr. Stephen Easley**
Easley and Associates
PO Box 1022
Alamogordo, NM 88311

**Dr. Linda M. Fedigan**
Dept. of Anthropology
University of Alberta
Edmonton, Alberta
T6G 2H4 Canada

**Gordon Getty**
2880 Broadway
San Francisco, CA 94115

**Dr. Theodore Grand**
Department of Zoological Research
National Zoological Park
Washington, DC 20008

**Dr. Benedikt Hallgrimsson**
Department of Anatomy
University of Puerto Rico
San Juan, P.R.

**Dr. David A. Hamburg**
President, Carnegie Corporation
437 Madison Avenue
New York, NY 10022

**Dr. Richard B. Lee**
Dept. of Anthropology
University of Toronto
Toronto, Ontario
Canada M5S 1A1

**Dr. Donald G. Lindburg**
Zoological Society of San Diego
PO Box 120551
San Diego, CA 92112-0551

**Dr. Jerold M. Lowenstein**
Nuclear Medicine
2333 Buchanan St.
San Francisco, CA 94115

**Dr. David Matsuda**
Dept. of Anthropology and Geography
California State University
Hayward, CA 94542-3039

**Dr. Mary Ellen Morbeck**
Dept. of Anthropology
University of Arizona
Tucson, AZ 85721

**Dr. Dieter Steklis**
Dept. of Anthropology
Rutgers University
New Brunswick, NJ 08903

**Dr. Shirley Strum**
Dept. of Anthropology
University of California
La Jolla, CA 92093
or
PO Box 62844
Nairobi, Kenya

**Dr. Trudy R. Turner**
Department of Anthropology
University of Wisconsin-Milwaukee
Milwaukee, WI 53201

**Dr. Russell Tuttle**
Dept. of Anthropology
University of Chicago
1126 E. 59th St.
Chicago, IL 60637

**Dr. Mark L. Weiss**
Department of Anthropology
Wayne State University
Detroit, MI 48202

**Dr. Adrienne Zihlman**
Clark Kerr Hall
University of California
Santa Cruz, CA 95064

# INTRODUCTION

## David Hamburg

Late in 1956, on my first day at the Center for Advanced Study in the Behavioral Sciences, a wiry man knocked on my door and introduced himself: Sherry Washburn. He had noted in the center's summary of Fellows' interests that I was concerned with biology and behavior—so was he. In no time at all, we were engaged in a lively discourse that has never ended. During the intervening 40-some years, we have discussed an evolutionary approach to many topics, including relations of anatomy and behavior, stress, emotions, aggression, the social group, and growth and development.

When we met, he had just returned from Africa, where he had been instrumental in launching the new wave of primate field studies. In this, as in so much else, he had great vision. His foresight and contagious enthusiasm did so much to bring others into the field—not least his own students.

In his judicious way, he sorted out different approaches, noting that animal behavior may be investigated in the laboratory, in artificial colonies, or under natural conditions. The kinds of knowledge gained from these different approaches complement each other and are all necessary if the complex roots of behavior are to be understood.

In the 1950s, Washburn pointed out the great opportunities of research in the natural habitat. Substantial studies of free-ranging primates were then few and far between. For a long time, the incidental observations of hunters and travelers were widely accepted and influential in their simplistic vision of primates. The emerging studies stimulated by Washburn quickly revealed that the situation was complex. Adaptations of different primate species were locally variable, and individual animals also differed in temperament, experience, and social roles. Thus Washburn began to formulate desiderata for reliable and informative field studies that necessarily meant methodological improvements. He was confident that it would be possible to obtain detailed continuous observations and to recognize individual animals so that, for instance, the role of personality in social structure could be clarified. So too could the interrelations of different species be observed. In this respect, his stimulating observations and suggestions in the 1950s foreshadowed later, long-term studies such as those of Jane Goodall and her colleagues at the Gombe Research Center in Tanzania.

Washburn emphasized that individuals must be set in their social context, pointing out that the group is the locus of knowledge and experience, far exceeding that of any individual member. It is in the group that experience is pooled and the generations linked. The adaptive function of prolonged biological immaturity is that it gives the primate time to learn. During this period, while the young organism learns from other members of the group, it is protected by them.

Washburn's fundamental argument for the importance of field studies was that monkeys and apes evolved under natural conditions as the result of selection pressures. Thus field studies are essential to understanding the way that structure and behavior are adapted to the variety of environmental circumstances. In fact, many topics can only be investigated in the field; for example, ranging, troop size, predation, social structure, aspects of communication, and competitive relations with other species. Yet careful description of behavior in the wild raises many problems of interpretation that can be settled only by experiments. Thus he advocated an interplay of naturalistic observation and careful experimentation.

Washburn's framework extended to every topic he considered. Structure, physiology, social life—all to be seen as the result of selection and the structure-physiology-behavior complex of populations of primates—are adapted ways of life. He argued that behavior should also be adaptable to a wide variety of circumstances. What is inherited is an "ease of learning" more than fixed instinctive patterns, for primates seem readily to learn the behaviors that are essential for their survival and have difficulty learning others.

Washburn and I shared an enduring interest in problems of aggression. Here too he applied his evolutionary framework, his intense curiosity, and his wide-ranging intellect to make prescient comments that foreshadowed future discoveries—for example, in the 1970s, of intercommunity aggression among Gombe chimpanzees. In 1968, we wrote:

> It is our belief that intertroop aggression in primates has been greatly underestimated. No field study has yet been undertaken with this problem as a focus, and no effort has been made to study situations in which conflict is likely to be frequent. More important, the groups of species are normally spaced well apart, and the observer sees the long-term results of aggression and avoidance, not the events causing it.
>
> (Washburn and Hamburg 1968)

His interest in aggression, as in many other issues (race, emotions, language, brain and behavior, learning) was enhanced by the gravity of contemporary problems. Washburn's strong conviction was that an evolutionary perspective could illuminate our approaches to current predicaments. For example, if we could take into account human aggressive propensities in light of their origins and the circumstances in which these propensities are now expressed, we could make realistic appraisals and take corrective actions.

Even when he had no preexisting interest in a subject, his evolutionary approach and his insightful help were always stimulating. For instance, I had an interest in the evolution of emotions that followed naturally from my background in psychobiology and psychiatry. He was intrigued with the subject, my subject. We discussed emotions, and he contributed important concepts and passages to a paper that became widely cited and evidently useful (Hamburg 1963). Our work on emotions marked a widening of Washburn's horizons, a process that characterizes his whole career.

> Society is not composed of neutral actors but of emotional beings—whether we speak of baboons, chimpanzees, or man, emotion lies at the core of the social process. We fear for ourselves, a few loved ones, and the infants of the species. We are positively bound deeply by a few relations. Threat to these relations is equivalent to an attack on life itself. From the standpoint of the species, these are the critical relations for survival. The physiology of emotion insures the fundamental acts of survival: the desire for sex, the extraordinary interest in the infant, the day to day reinforcement of interindividual bonds.

When we consider the profound changes in human environmental conditions within very recent evolutionary times, it becomes entirely conceivable that some of the mechanisms which evolved over the millions of years of mammalian primate, primate, and human evolution may now be less useful than they once were. Since cultural change has moved much more rapidly than genetic change, the emotional response tendencies that have been built into us through their suitability for a long succession of past environments may be less suitable for the very different present environment.

Conquest of the outer world does not free the species from the inner world which made its evolution possible. Social life is rooted in emotion and is basic to survival.

These vignettes only begin to convey the essence of the person. Part of that essence was his immense intellectual generosity toward his students and colleagues. This book is a labor of love by people who have had the privilege of knowing him, being stimulated, challenged, and rewarded by him. We share a common view of his remarkable attributes: integrative and incisive intellect; restless, searching curiosity; honesty, candor, integrity; boundless energy; contagious enthusiasm; kindness and generosity; vision and courage. In short, Sherry Washburn has been an authentic inspiration for us. He represents the best of a life in science—and indeed of life itself.

## References

Hamburg, D. (1963). Emotions in the perspective of human evolution. In P. Knapp (ed.), *Expression of the Emotions in Man*. New York: International University Press.

Washburn, S. L., and Hamburg, D. (1968). Aggressive behavior in Old World monkeys and apes. In P. C. Jay (ed.), *Primates: Studies in Adaptation and Variability*. New York: Holt, Rinehart and Winston.

When I was first learning about human origins in the early 1970s, Sherry Washburn was the foremost anthropologist in the land. Luckily, he taught at Berkeley, which meant that we early-man buffs and Leakey Foundation supporters saw a good deal of him. Washburn was a free thinker and a category-buster, and still is. No one has done more for the science.

Gordon Getty
San Francisco

# THE NEW PHYSICAL
# ANTHROPOLOGY

*Washburn's new physical anthropology proposed progressive and innovative ways to approach the traditional subjects of physical anthropology. He wanted to change the focus from measurement and classification to the processes and mechanisms of evolutionary change as it occurred during primate and human evolution. "But suggestions of adaptations are not enough. It is easy to guess that a form (anatomical or behavioral) is adaptive, but the real problem is to determine the precise nature of a particular adaptation." The immediate result of Washburn's injection of the "new synthesis," as the then current revolution in evolutionary theory was called, was a revolution also in anatomy and in the study of behavior, the development of a comparative, functional anatomy of adaptive complexes, and the resuscitation of naturalistic studies of primate behavior.*

*For Washburn, new methods went hand in hand with the new theory. Better techniques were necessary to achieve his five goals for physical anthropology:*

1. *Diagnose evolutionary complexes (adaptations).*
2. *Describe variations in adaptations.*
3. *Determine the underlying biology and genetics of each adaptive complex.*
4. *Identify the conditions that would have selected for the adaptation.*
5. *Improve the quality of phylogenetic reconstructions.*

*Washburn's most critical tool was the comparative method. But he emphasized the need for the productive interaction between naturalistic data, whether it was the fossils or the behavior of primates, and controlled experimentation in order to tease apart cause and effect. His sensitivity to techniques made him a champion of better dating techniques, better statistical samples, and new forms of evidence.*

*The new physical anthropology had to be multidisciplinary and interdisciplinary. Already embedded in this position paper is a very modern sense of what science is, a theme that weaves itself throughout the subsequent four decades of his work. "There is nothing we do today which will not be done better tomorrow." He believed that and constantly tried to put that lesson into practice by being receptive to new ideas and new approaches and by continually revising his own positions.*

# 1 The New Physical Anthropology (1951)

## S. L. Washburn

What are the dynamic connections between muscles and bones, or between one body segment and another? What actually is the anthropologist measuring when he puts his calipers to a skull? Static bone structure or dynamic processes that resulted in the varying and different kinds of body shapes and complexes? The new physical anthropology is turning its attention to the forces that shaped the phenotypes.

Recently, evolutionary studies have been revitalized and revolutionized by an infusion of genetics into

From *Transactions of the New York Academy of Sciences,* Series II, Vol. 13, No. 7 (1951), pp. 298–304. Reprinted by permission of the author and publishers.

paleontology and systematics. The change is fundamentally one of point of view, which is made possible by an understanding of the way the genetic constitution of populations changes. The new systematics is concerned primarily with process and with the mechanism of evolutionary change, whereas the older point of view was chiefly concerned with sorting the results of evolution. Physical anthropology is now undergoing the same sort of change. Population genetics presents the anthropologist with a clearly formulated, experimentally verified, conceptual scheme. The application of this theory to the primates is the immediate task of physical anthropology.

In the past, physical anthropology has been considered primarily as a technique. Training consisted in learning to take carefully defined measurements and in computing indices and statistics. The methods of observation, measurement, and comparison were essentially the same, whether the object of the study was the description of evolution, races, growth, criminals, constitutional types, or army personnel. Measurements were adjusted for various purposes, but measurement of the outside of the body, classification, and correlation remained the anthropologist's primary tools. The techniques of physical anthropology were applied to a limited group of problems and any definition or statement of traditional anthropology must include both the metrical methods and the problems for which the methods were used. Further, anthropology was characterized by theories, or rather by a group of attitudes and assumptions.

There has been almost no development of theory in physical anthropology itself, but the dominant attitude may be described as static, with emphasis on classification based on types. Any such characterization is oversimplified, and is intended only to give an indication of the dominant techniques, interests, and attitudes of the physical anthropologist. Except for emphasis on particular animals, physical anthropology shared much with the zoology of the times when it developed. Much of the method was developed before the acceptance of the idea of evolution, and all of it before the science of genetics.

Physical anthropology should change, just as systematic zoology has changed. The difficulties which accompany the necessary modifications can be greatly reduced if their nature is clearly understood. Naturally, in a time of rapid flux there will be numerous doubts and disagreements as to what should be done. This is natural, and what I have to offer is a tentative outline to indicate how parts of the new physical anthropology may differ from the old.

The old physical anthropology was primarily a technique. The common core of the science was measurement of external form with calipers. The new physical anthropology is primarily an area of interest, the desire to understand the process of primate evolution and human variation by the most efficient techniques available.

The process of evolution, as understood by the geneticist, is the same for all mammals. The genetic composition of a population may be described in terms of gene frequencies. The modification of these frequencies results in evolution which is caused by selection, mutations, drift, and migrations. Mutations and migrations introduce new genetic elements into the population. But selection on the phenotype, adapting animals to their environment, is the primary cause of alteration in gene frequencies.

This is essentially a return to Darwinism, but with this important difference: Darwin wrote in a pregenetic era. Therefore, he did not understand the mechanism which makes possible the production of variation and the possibility of selection. Since Darwin's ideas could not be proved in detail by the techniques available in his time, the concept of selection did not become fully effective. Therefore, some pre-evolutionary ideas continued in full force. More Linnaean species were described from types after Darwin than before. The idea of evolution created interest in species, but the species were described in pre-evolutionary terms. Further, it is possible for people to hold a variety of theories in place of, or in addition to, Darwin's. For example, Lamarckian ideas have continued right down to today. Orthogenesis has been widely believed and irreversibility has been regarded as a law.

It has been claimed that evolution should be described in terms of nonadaptive traits, yet this is impossible if evolution is largely due to selection. The first great achievement of the synthesis of genetics, paleontology, and systematics is in clearing away a mass of antiquated theories and attitudes which permeate the writings of the older students of evolution. Further, the new evolutionary theory shows which aspects of past work are worth using, extending, and strengthening. This is possible because much of the mechanism of evolutionary change is now understood, clearly formulated, and *experimentally verified*. The logic of Darwin's great theory could only become fully effective when techniques had been developed to prove that selection was right and that other ideas of evolution were wrong. A change in theory, no matter how popular, is not enough. The new ideas must be implemented by effective techniques.

If a new physical anthropology is to differ effectively from the old, it must be more than the adoption of a little genetic terminology. It must change its ways of doing things to conform with the implications of modern evolutionary theory. For example, races must be based on the study of populations. There is no way to justify the division of a breeding population into a series of racial types. It is not enough to state that races should be based on genetic traits; races which can not be reconciled with genetics should be removed from consideration. If we consider the causes of changes in gene frequency as outlined above, and if we are concerned with the process of evolution, the task of the anthropologist becomes clear. He has nothing to offer on mutation, but can make contributions with regard to migration, drift, and selection.

The migrations of man made possible by culture have vastly confused the genetic picture. Before selection can be investigated, it is necessary to know how long a people has been in an area and under what conditions they have been living. For example, the spread of European people, of Bantu speakers, or of Eskimo all have changed the distribution of the blood groups. The interpretation of the genetic situation demands an understanding of history. Whether people became adapted to cold by selection or by change in their way of life completely alters the interpretation of the distribution of physical traits. This has been widely recognized by anthropologists, and the solution of this difficulty requires the active collaboration of archeologists, ethnologists, linguists, and students of the physical man.

Drift is related to population size, and this depends on the way of life. Again, as in the case of migration, the situation in which drift may have taken place cannot be specified by the physical anthropologist alone, but requires the active collaboration of many specialists. The adoption of modern evolutionary theory will force a far closer and more realistic collaboration between the branches of anthropology than ever before.

Although much of the present distribution of races may be explained by migration and although drift probably accounts for some differences, selection must be the explanation of long-term evolutionary trends and of many patterned variations as well. Anthropologists have always stressed the importance of adaptation in accounting for the differences between apes and men, and sometimes have used the idea in interpreting racial divergences. But suggestions of adaptations are not enough. It is easy to guess that a form is adaptive, but the real problem is to determine the precise nature of a particular adaptation. The work I have been interested in is designed to demonstrate the relation of form to function. My feeling has been that it is impossible to do more than guess about this matter using traditional anthropological measurements, and that the literature is already too full of uncontrolled speculations. Therefore, I would like to take this opportunity to present an outline, a beginning, of an analysis of the human body into complexes which may vary independently.

In this work, the guiding principle has been that the major force in evolution is selection of functional complexes. A variety of methods has been used to demonstrate the adaptive complexes. The four major methods for factoring complexes out of the body are: (1) comparison and evolution; (2) development; (3) variability; and (4) experiment. All these have been used by numerous investigators, but, to the best of my knowledge, they have not been combined into a working system. All must be used to gain an understanding of the human body.

Figure 1 shows the body divided into the major regions, which seem to have had remarkable indepen-

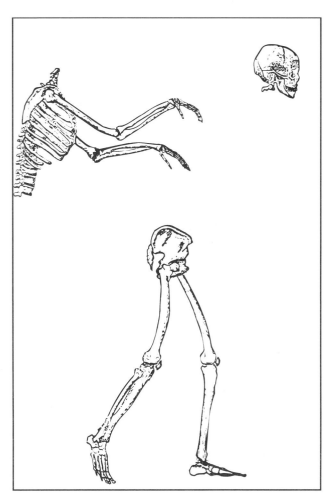

FIGURE 1. *Major regions of the human body (after Washburn). Each of the three areas appears to have had an independent evolution. Thorax and arms were the first to attain modern form, followed by pelvis, legs, and feet. The head and brain were the last to evolve fully. (From Titiev, The Science of Man, Holt, 1954.)*

dence in recent evolutionary history. The complex to attain its present pattern first is that of the arms and thorax. This complex is associated with arm swinging in the trees, the way of life called "brachiation." It is associated with a reduction in the deep back muscles and in the number of lumbar vertebrae and consequent shortening of the trunk and elongation of all parts of the upper extremity, adaptation of the joints and muscles to greater pronation, supination in the forearm, and flexion and abduction at the shoulder. Many changes in the positions of viscera are associated with the shorter trunk. We share this complex with the living gibbons and apes. The bipedal complex was the next to develop and seems to have been fundamentally human in the South African man-apes. The major changes are in the ilium and in the gluteal muscles. Just as in the arm, the change is in a bone-muscle complex, which makes a different way of life possible. The head seems to have attained essentially its present form during the fourth glacial advance, perhaps 50,000 years ago. The brain continued to enlarge until the end of the last interglacial period, and the face decreased in size for some time after that. The great increase in the size of the brain and decrease in the face was after the use of tools.

Evolution, in a sense, has dissected the body for us, and has shown that great changes may occur in arms and trunk, pelvis and legs, and brain case, or face, accompanied by little change in the rest of the body. The first two complexes to change are related to brachiation and bipedal locomotion. The final changes in the head may well be related to changed selection after the use of tools.

To carry the analysis further, it is necessary to deal with one of the areas suggested by this preliminary dividing of the body. Let us consider the face, and especially the lower jaw. Figure 2 shows a lower jaw divided into regions which can be shown to vary independently by all the methods of analysis suggested before. The coronoid process varies with the temporal muscle. The angle of the jaw varies with the masseter and internal pterygoid muscle. The tooth-supporting area varies with the teeth. The main core of the jaw is affected by hormones which do not affect the other parts, as shown in acromegaly. Alizarin dye, which stains the growing bone, reveals the pattern of growth. The split-line technique (Benninghoff) shows the mechanical arrangement.

After making an analysis of this kind, comparisons of a different sort are possible. The simple statement, that a trait is or is not there, is replaced by the attempt to understand under what conditions it might be present. For example, if the simian shelf is developed in monkeys and apes when the jaws are long and the anterior teeth large, then the South African man-apes and

other fossil men would not be expected to have such a shelf. The dental characters necessary to bring out the expression of the shelf are absent in all, except the Piltdown jaw. It can be argued that we have the potential for a simian shelf but that we do not have the necessary tooth and jaw size to make it evident. Trying to understand the process which produces a trait leads to very different evaluations than does a listing of presence or absence.

In the light of this sort of information, let us look at the skull of an Eocene lemur, *Notharctus*. The jaw is long, in conformity with the length of the teeth. It is low, and there is a large angular region. This region has been described as lemuroid. If this angle has remained there for 50 million years, however, over countless generations of lemurs, it must have more of a function than to mark the jaw as primitive or to help us in identifying lemur jaws. If the mandible of a remarkably similar modern lemur (genus *Lemur*) is examined, it is found that the internal pterygoid muscle inserts at the end of the angle, but that the masseter muscle inserts only on the lateral side of the ascending ramus, leaving the angle bare of muscle. An internal pterygoid muscle inserting in this position is a protruder of the jaw. The function of the angle of the lemur jaw is to provide insertion for a large, functionally important muscle. The dependence of the angular process on the internal pterygoid and the exact function of the internal pterygoid need to be experimentally verified.

The only point to be stressed now is that the theory that such a process is of adaptive significance, and that it is maintained by selection, leads one to look for a functional complex. If such a process is regarded simply as a taxonomic aid, or as nonfunctional, no guide is available for research or future understanding.

The post-orbital bar of this same lemur again illustrates the advantage of assuming, until it is proved otherwise, that a part is functionally important. Originally, the complete bony ring around the orbit may have been for protection or for some other unknown function. Once the ring is established, however, the skeletal framework for radical modification of the skull is present. The change from the lemur skull, with a wide interorbital region, to the monkey skull, with reduced olfactory mechanism and reduced interorbital space, is mechanically possible because pressure, tension, and buttressing of the sides of the face is provided by the complete rings of bone around the orbits. Structures which probably developed as part of a protective mechanism were pre-adaptive for a reorganization of the face.

Classic Neandertal man differs from other fossil men in that the angle of the lower jaw is poorly developed, the part of the malar bone associated with the ori-

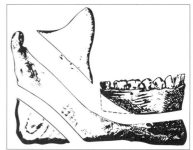

FIGURE 2.   *Human mandible divided into independently evolving regions. (Adapted by Inez Thompson.)*

gin of the largest part of the masseter muscle is small, and the lateral part of the brow ridge is less sharply demarcated. All these differences may be related, and certainly the association of the small angle and malar suggest that the masseter muscle was small compared to the temporal muscle. Differences of this sort should be described in terms of the variation in the groups being compared. Since similar differences may be found in living men, the development of appropriate quantitative, descriptive methods is merely a matter of time and technique. The procedure is: (1) diagnose the complex; (2) develop methods appropriate to describe variations in it; and (3) try to discover the genetic background of these variations.

So far, we are still engaged in finding the complexes, but even at this level it is possible to make suggestions about fossil men. Probably some Mongoloid groups will have the highest frequency of the big masseter complex, and some of the Negro groups the lowest. This is merely stating some traditional physical anthropology in a somewhat different way by relating statements about the face to those on the lower jaw and relating both to a large and important muscle. It differs from the traditional in the technique of analysis and avoids speculation of the sort which says that the characteristics of the Mongoloid face are due to adaptation to cold.

In this preliminary analysis of the lower jaw, the attempt has been made to divide a single bone into relatively independent systems and to show that the differences make sense in terms of differing adaptations. Eventually, it may be possible to understand the genetic mechanisms involved. If this type of analysis is at all correct, it is theoretically impossible to make any progress in genetic understanding by taking the traditional measurements on the mandible. They are all complex resultants of the interrelation of two or more of the variables. The measurements average the anatomy in such a way that it is as futile to look for the mode of inheritance of the length of the jaw as it is to look for the genes of the cephalic index.

The implications for anthropology of this type of analysis may be made clearer by some comparisons of the skulls of monkeys. If the skulls of adult male and adult female vervets are compared, many differences may be seen. The male skull is larger in all dimensions, particularly those of the face. If, however, an adult female is compared to a juvenile male with the same cranial capacity and the same weight of temporal muscle, all the differences disappear, except that in the size of the canine tooth. What would appear to be a very large number of unrelated differences, if traditional methods were used, are only aspects of one fundamental difference in the size of the face. If a large-faced monkey is compared with a small-faced one, both of the genus *Cercopithecus,* there appear to be many differences. Yet again, if animals of the same cranial capacity and the same temporal muscle size are compared, almost all the measurements are the same. The species difference is in quantity of face, although this appears in many different forms. If these two skulls were fossil men, differing in the same way, and if they were treated by the usual anthropological methods, they would be found to differ in numerous observations, measurements, and indices. Yet one may be transformed into the other by a simple reduction in mass of face (including teeth, bones, muscles). Perhaps many fossils are far less different than we have supposed. The methods used created the number of differences, just as a metrical treatment of these monkeys would make the adults appear very distinct.

The purpose of this paper has been to call attention to the changes which are taking place in physical anthropology. Under the influence of modern genetic theory, the field is changing from the form it assumed in the latter part of the nineteenth century into a part of modern science. The change is essentially one of emphasis. If traditional physical anthropology was 80 percent measurement and 20 percent concerned with heredity, process, and anatomy, in the new physical anthropology the proportions may be approximately reversed. I have stressed the impact of genetics on anthropology, but the process need not be all one way. If the form of the human face can be thoroughly analyzed, this will open the way to the understanding of its development and the interpretation of abnormalities and malocclusion, and may lead to advances in genetics, anatomy, and medicine. Although evolution is fascinating in itself, the understanding of the functional anatomy which may be gained from it is of more than philosophical importance. The kind of systemic anatomy in which bones, muscles, ligaments, etc., are treated separately became obsolete with the publication of the *Origin of Species* in 1859. The anatomy of life, of integrated function, does not know the artificial boundaries which still govern the dissection of a corpse. The new physical anthropology has much to offer to anyone interested in the structure or evolution of man, but this is only a beginning. To build it, we must collaborate with social scientists, geneticists, anatomists, and paleontologists. We need new ideas, new methods, new workers. There is nothing we do today which will not be done better tomorrow.

# AN EVOLUTIONARY COMPARATIVE FUNCTIONAL ANATOMY

*Washburn suggests that it is an appropriate time to reconsider human origins because of the new facts (the new South African fossils), the new theories (the synthetic theory of evolution), and the new possibilities of experimental validation of interpretations. The outline of primate and human evolution that he presents discards the old typological thinking and instead considers functional complexes. Central to his argument is that features within functional complexes—and, indeed, different functional complexes—may evolve differentially. Therefore anatomical features are not equally important as markers for the emergence of hominids. Furthermore, he stresses the difference between old style typological classification and new style evolutionary phylogenies. If evolution is about adaptation, fossils (the hard evidence) have their limitations. At minimum, we will need to place the fossil evidence in a comparative framework that includes living forms. Then we can gain a detailed understanding of the precise nature of adaptation and the interrelationship of form and function.*

# 2 The Analysis of Primate Evolution with Particular Reference to the Origin of Man (1951)

**S. L. Washburn**   *Department of Anthropology, University of Chicago*

There are three reasons why this is an appropriate time to discuss the origin of man. The first is the finding of abundant fossils of a new kind of missing link in South Africa. The man-like apes indicate an unanticipated stage in human evolution which radically alters all current theories of human origins. The second reason is that, through the work of numerous geneticists, zoologists, and paleontologists, a theoretical framework is now available which is far superior to any previous evolutionary theories. The third is the fact that evolutionary speculations can be experimentally checked to a far greater extent than has been realized in the past. It is the combination of new facts, new theories, and new hopes of proof which makes this an auspicious moment to reconsider the problems of human origins.

Why the matter needs reconsideration after all the mass of work done on it deserves a word of comment, which may be divided again under the headings of facts, theories, and proof. The facts bearing on human origins were largely collected in the nineteenth century, or according to principles developed at that time, and there has been no "New Comparative Anatomy" comparable to the "New Systematics" or any "Modern Synthesis" as in evolution. The result is that the vast quantity of materials of very unequal value (Zuckerman, 1933; Simpson, 1945) is difficult to use. Each author tends to use only a small part of the easily available information, and the basis for selection is by no means clear. If the papers by Schultz (1936) and Straus (1949) on human origins were examined, it would be hard to tell that the same animals were under discussion, for few facts are mentioned in both papers and their evaluation is totally different. The mere collection of more facts will not advance the understanding of human evolution. Before progress can be made, methods must be outlined for deciding which facts are important.

The evaluation of differences in fossil bones and living primates leads to the question of theory. Certainly the ideas of orthogenesis, irreversibility, and the supreme value of non-adaptive characters have thoroughly blocked the development of effective thinking

From *The Cold Spring Harbor Symposia on Quantitative Biology* (1951), 15: 67–78.

about human evolution. They have been used to rule every known kind of primate out of the line of human evolution. Actually, scholars who specialized in human evolution (and it should be stressed that this includes many human anatomists and others besides physical anthropologists) are in an extremely poor position to develop evolutionary theory. Since they are interested in the origin and classification of a single group of animals, and in actual practice almost entirely with man, there are not enough examples to develop and prove theories. Those interested in human evolution must borrow their general theories and principles from others who have access to wider data and more manageable subjects. The task of the anthropologist is to fit knowledge of the primates into the framework of modern evolutionary theory, as described by numerous authors in "Genetics, Paleontology, and Evolution" (Jepsen, Simpson, Mayr, 1949) and as developed in "The Meaning of Evolution" (Simpson, 1949).

The importance of experiment arises from the nature of the anthropologist's task. If he would demonstrate that one theory is better than another, he must have a method beyond personal opinion of deciding which facts are important. Facts and good theories are important, but people feel strongly on the subject of their own origin and there will be wide disagreement until a modern, experimental comparative anatomy can take its place among the tools of the student of evolution. At the moment, whether man is regarded as derived from an ape in the late Pliocene (Weinert, 1932) or an unknown, unspecialized, tarsioid of Eocene age (Jones, 1948) depends on personal evaluation of the same basic facts.

The origin of man has been studied by so many people, so many different ideas have been expressed, and the nomenclature is in such a complete state of confusion that it will clarify matters if I briefly outline my ideas first, then defend them in some detail and consider a series of problems of general zoological interest.

The earliest primates were distinguished from other primitive mammals by the use of the hands and feet for grasping. This is anatomically a complex adaptation, involving elongation of the digits, flattening of the terminal phalanges and thinning of the nails (Clark, 1936). This basic adaptation has been the foundation of the whole history of the primates, which has been in other ways remarkably diverse. There is no single trend with regard to way of locomotion (which included slow clingers and fast hoppers), or dentition (there are forms with huge incisors, aye aye; or none, Lepilemur; canines may be huge, mandrill; or small, many female Old World forms and hominids), or diet (many primates eat a mixed diet, but one group of lemurs, *Indridae*, and one group of monkeys, *Colobidae*, have specialized in leaf eating and have developed spe-

cialized viscera). It is this great diversity in secondary characters and ways of life which makes primate classification so difficult. Particularly in fossils the hands and feet are usually not preserved, and the main pattern is not reflected in the jaws and teeth. I believe that this accounts for the difficulty in placing many of the Eocene genera (Simpson, 1940).

The early primates took to the trees with the special senses of the primitive mammal. There were tactile hairs, movable ears, and a sense of smell which was predominant. The changes which produced the forms we call monkeys were either present in the advanced lemurs (or tarsiers, I doubt that this is a fundamental distinction) or developed by parallel evolution. For in both New and Old World monkeys active, arboreal forms developed, with reduced external ears and ear muscles, reduced sense of smell, and with stereoscopic, color vision. These arboreal quadrupeds replaced the lemurs, except where the latter remained protected (Madagascar) or by being strictly nocturnal (as the tarsiers, lorises and galagos). The brain greatly increased in size, and Elliot Smith (1924) was the first to appreciate the multitude of differences which came from converting a primitive smell-brain into a sight-brain. Changes at this stage are clearly reflected in the skull by the reduction in parts associated with the olfactory mechanism (reduction in the turbinal bones, interorbital region, and cribriform plate with correlated changes in the anterior fossa).

The origin of the primates was primarily a locomotor adaptation. The first radiation lasted approximately a third of the age of the mammals, perhaps twenty million years. The second was a reorganization of the special senses, making the monkeys successful in the Old World tropical forests by day. The third radiation of Old World primates depended again on a locomotor adaptation. In the apes, a series of modifications in the arms and trunk leads to locomotion of a sort not found in the quadrupedal monkeys. (Spider monkeys brachiate; this is another example of the extensive parallelism in the New and Old Worlds. But spider monkeys also move in typical quadrupedal fashion and have prehensile tails. The combination of brachiation and quadrupedal locomotion is not found in the Old World and shows how the ape type of locomotion may have arisen.) Brachiation involves changes in the motion of the arms and the abandoning of the use of the back in the typical quadrupedal manner. The anatomical changes are in the wrist, elbow, shoulder, and thoracic region. None of these are duplicated in any of the monkeys, and brachiation is an elaborate behavioral and anatomical complex, every essential detail of which is shared by man and the living apes.

Some idea of the profound changes in anatomy which accompany brachiation, as practiced by the apes, is given by the changes in the muscles of the trunk and arm. The scalenes migrate upward; psoas major, rectus abdominis, and the origin of sacrospinalis migrate down; serratus anterior increases in size, as does the deltoid; pectoralis major migrates up, pectoralis minor changes in insertion to the coracoid process; origin and insertion of arm extensors are reduced and the flexors are increased. These are correlated with the changes in the joints previously mentioned. (Loth, 1931, is the best general source of information on the muscles of primates.)

The discovery of the pelves of the South African man-like apes, or small-brained men, has made it possible to outline the basic adaptation which is the foundation of the human radiation. These forms have brains which are in the range of the living apes, and their teeth show both human and ape characters, but the ilia are practically modern-human. Men were bipeds first, and later large-brained, small-faced bipeds. Just as the differences between monkey and ape are in the upper extremity and trunk, so those between ape and man are in the pelvis and foot. To mention but a few differences: in apes gluteus maximus is not maximus, gracilis is not gracile, biceps femoris has one head, and semitendinosus and membranosus are not as the names imply. The bone-muscle-functional complex of the leg distinguishes man from the apes as sharply as the comparable complex of the arms shows their similarity and distinguishes both from the monkeys.

The above outline differs from prevailing theories in several ways. The gibbons are regarded as typical apes and placed in the same family with the living apes and with numerous extinct forms. The South African forms are regarded as in the same family as man, part of the same radiation. However, the arrangement is in the main similar to many others (Hooton, 1946; Simpson, 1949; Zuckerman, 1933). Lemurs, monkeys, apes and men represent a series of radiations. Each is later in time and each is less variable than the one which preceded it.

Among the lemurs there are radically different locomotor, dietary, and dental patterns. At the other extreme man is represented by a single form, being far less variable (even if all fossil forms and the South African man-apes are added) than lorises, galagos, or indris-like lemurs.

Finally, anatomically speaking, man is highly specialized. He represents an extreme and odd form in his way of locomotion. In no other animal can the anatomy of pelvis and foot be matched. His trunk and thorax are very peculiar, their structure being shared only with the great apes. Obviously the brain is a recent and extreme adaptation. This modern, ground-living ape would amount to little without tools. The fact that we number more than a few thousand, ecologically unimportant bipeds living in the Old World tropics is due to the development of tools. And it is important to remember that tools are surely older than Java man. The appearance of all modern forms of men is long after tool using. The origin of the human radiation may be treated just as that of any other mammalian group, but the use of tools brings in a set of factors which progressively modify the evolutionary picture. It is particularly the task of the anthropologist to assess the way the development of culture affected physical evolution.

In defining the major groups of primates the effort has been made to use the most important characters, that is, to use the ones which made the evolutionary radiations possible. In general, characters may be divided into three categories: (1) Primary characters which are responsible for the radiations; (2) secondary characters which are a necessary consequence of the new selection, based on the acquisition of the primary ones; and (3) incidental characters which happen to be selected along with the primary ones. For example, if the group of apes which gave origin to man had a particular type of dentition, this would automatically become part of the original heritage of the hominids. Other features might be due to genetic drift in small groups of early men.

If modern man be examined, he is found to be a mixture of basic primate features, the primary characters of the first or lemuroid radiation. (The hands show a remarkable amount of the primitive grasping adaptation with long digits, nails, etc. It should be remembered that the most perfectly opposable and relatively largest thumbs among all the primates are found in the lorises, and not in man, as often stated. Human feet are a recent modification of the same pattern, fundamentally differing only in a single ligament and the length of the toes.) The next complex is that of the head, brain and special senses which is achieved, except for changes in proportions, in the monkey radiation. Then the arms and trunk become essentially modern. Perhaps then, many millions of years later, the bipedal complex was developed. Finally, the secondary features of the human radiation become general, the small face and the large brain.

Evolution proceeded at different rates in various parts of the body. This is not to suggest that at any time the animals were not functioning wholes adapted to a way of life, but it does mean that there may be a considerable degree of independence of a given part. The eye of monkey, ape, and man are remarkably similar despite major changes in other parts of the body. In spite of a variety of ways of life the same sort of visual mechanism was advantageous and was maintained by selection.

There are three implications of this scheme of evolution for the study of human origins: *First*, different characters are of very unequal taxonomic value at various stages in human evolution. If similarity in trunk and arm show the community of man and ape and if the difference lies primarily in pelvis and legs, a long list of characters in which both features of arm and leg are included may be misleading. Especially is it misleading to say that of so many characters man shares this percent with one form and that percent with another. Similarities in arms, legs, and skull have different meanings. The *second* implication is that there are real changes between ancestors and their descendants. To say that all apes have longer arms or canine teeth than man (Jones, 1948; Weidenreich, 1946) in no way bars them from human ancestry. The ancestors were parts of different radiations and were specialized accordingly. The search for the unspecialized common ancestor becomes either a denial of evolution or a hunt for an illusory, philosophical archetype. The *third* is that there will be many incidental differences at each level which are of no major importance. Even if every ape had one form of pterion and every human another, it would be of no importance. Actually the form varies in both groups and experimental alteration of suture patterns shows that this type of difference does not change the functional pattern of the cranial vault.

It is clear that adaptation to life on the ground is the basis of the human radiation. Many groups of Old World primates have come to the ground at different times and places, but no group of New World monkeys has taken up life on the ground. Two, perhaps three, different groups of baboons, patas monkeys, vervets and macaques have become ground-livers. On the other hand not a single group of the leaf-eating monkeys (*Colobidae*) have taken up life on the ground. The restriction here is clearly diet. The soft leaves and fruits of the tropical forests are not available in plains country, and monkeys adapted to this diet have not become ground-livers, although there seems no reason as far as the locomotor system is concerned why they could not. If the ground-living and tree-living Old World monkeys are contrasted, a series of differences appear which are of the greatest importance for the understanding of human evolution. The ground-living forms, which have far greater ranges, are divided into less distinct varieties than the tree-livers. For example, the vervets, which are only partially ground-livers, still are very similar from Uganda to the Cape. Whereas in the *nictitans* group of cercopiths there are several perfectly distinct varieties in Uganda alone. Or, to take an Asiatic example, macaques of the irus group (long-tail, long face, small size), are distributed throughout South East Asia, while the arboreal leaf-monkeys of the same area are divided into four major groups, three of which are subdivided into numerous species. As far as monkeys are concerned, the sort of difference which Dobzhansky (1950) has shown between the tropical

and temperate forms exists in the tropics between the strictly arboreal forms and those well-adapted to the ground. The great number of forms are in the rain forests. The implication for classification is that the ones well-adapted to life on the ground will not divide up neatly into the sort of localized varieties which the tree-livers do. The attempt has been made repeatedly to divide the baboons into sharply defined groups. The chaos which has resulted is the result of expecting that plains forms, which have vast reaches of similar habitat open to them, will subdivide as the tree-restricted monkeys do.

The implication for human evolution is clear. Once man's ancestors were efficient plains-livers, they probably occupied large ranges with anatomical variation but without separation into distinct forms. In the case of early man-like forms, more difference should be demonstrated before taxonomic groups are set up than in the case of fossil anthropoids believed to have been tree-livers.

Turning from the general implications of efficient ground-living to the anatomy involved, I think that we have every reason to believe that this was fully achieved by the South African man-apes. The pelvis of these forms (known by three specimens, described by Broom, 1950a and b, and Dart, 1949b) is so human in form that some have argued that it must belong to an early hominid which became mixed in the man-ape deposits. Although the ilium is short and broad and of essentially human form (although differing in detail, especially in the shape of the iliac crest) the ischium is ape-like. The muscular attachment area of the ischium is separated from the glenoid cavity by a greater distance than is the case in modern man (Broom, 1950a). The differences are not great but are sufficient to preclude the possibility of the pelves belonging to other animals than the man-apes. The pelvis of a large baboon found in the same deposits is utterly unlike that of the man-apes, being typically baboon. According to all investigators (Broom, 1950a; Dart, 1949c; Camp, 1949; Barbour, 1949) there has been no great change in the climate of South Africa since these forms lived. They are associated with the bones of baboons and numerous antelope, the typical fauna of the African plains, and forest forms are lacking. The man-apes were bipedal, plains-living forms, derived from the forest-living apes. Morphologically they are ideal representatives of a stage in our evolution and chronologically they may be actual ancestors or the first cousins of the same (Clark, 1950). That is, these forms may be representative of populations which were directly ancestral to such humans as Java man.

The derivation of this type from an ape is best regarded as a case of rapid or quantum evolution (Simpson, 1944). It may soon turn out to be one of the best-documented cases. Since the South African materials are abundant and more are being found, and since there are an impressive number of well-preserved human fossils, the main features of the transition should soon be fully known.

Since this is the beginning of the human type of locomotion, the principal problem is to understand the locomotor changes. If an ape stands erect, it can walk, and the gibbon can get along fairly rapidly, but it cannot complete powerful extension of the leg. It should be stressed that it is not the extent of the motion which is different but the ability to finish with a real drive. When walking on a flat surface, the ape goes with a bent-knee gait (Hooton, 1946). In modern man the muscle which finishes swinging back the thigh is gluteus maximus. This is an exceedingly massive and powerful muscle, arising from the posterior part of the ilium and the sacrum. In modern man, if gluteus maximus is paralyzed, the trunk is said to jack-knife. That is, the extreme extension of the thigh necessary for normal human walking is not possible, but a flexed gait, comparable to that of the apes, is perfectly easy. The paralysis of this single muscle makes the human type of very extended bipedal locomotion impossible. It shows that the form and function of this particular muscle is critical in the evolution of man's posture and gait.

In the apes gluteus maximus is a small muscle. In monkeys it is about one-half the size of gluteus medius! Since the ilium of the living apes is long, gluteus maximus lies primarily lateral to the greater trochanter and is an abductor of the thigh. (The relation to the hip joint, and so its function, varies with the position of the leg. A study based on action current is needed to tell when the muscle is really in action.) The primary effect of bending back the ilium is to bring gluteus maximus behind the hip joint, thus making it an extensor. Gluteus

medius now lies lateral to the joint and becomes an abductor, taking over the old function of the maximus. Since selection is for function, it is clear that bending the ilium will change the selection on the gluteal muscles. It is my belief that this single change is the thing which initiates human evolution.

Before continuing to an examination of the circumstances under which such a change might occur, it should be pointed out that the statements above are susceptible to experimental verification. The function of these muscles in man and ape can be checked. This should be done. Further, I believe that it is impossible to reconstruct a gluteus maximus on the pelvis of a man-ape which is anything but an extensor. The importance of gluteus maximus in human locomotion, the effect of bending the ilium on the function of gluteus maximus, and the position of gluteus maximus in the man-apes can all be determined independently by as many people as want to take the trouble. In this sense there can be an experimental and ultimately quantitative study of the critical events in human evolution.

The pelvis has several different functions. It serves to connect the hind limb and the trunk, gives origin to many muscles, and serves as a bony birth canal. If the ilium becomes shorter, it must have a greater angle with the ischium in order to keep the same diameter of the canal. This is illustrated in the accompanying figure (Fig. 1). The figures for apes are from Weidenreich (1913). Many monkeys would be much the same, but in the leaf-monkey (*Presbytis rubicunda*) with a very short ilium the angulation of the ilium, relative to the ischium, is greater. Man and the man-apes are characterized by exceedingly short ilia, far shorter than apes of equivalent size. Without fossils it is impossible to tell whether shortening or bending came first, but a considerable shortening of the ilium (of the sort actually

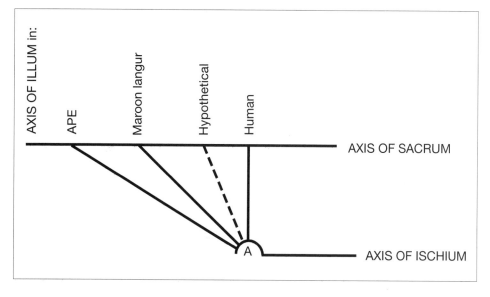

FIGURE 1.   *The effect of shortening the ilium on the angle between the ischium and the ilium. A = the acetabulum.*

seen in other primates) would of necessity result in bending it, which would give the necessary pre-condition to the change in function of gluteus maximus. It should be noted that the difference between the langur and the "hypothetical" form is no greater than that between the hypothetical and the known human extremes. In the Bush race the sciatic notch is extremely wide (Orford, 1934; Washburn, 1949). Comparing an extreme human type to an extreme monkey type gives a totally different idea of the gap than comparing male European to living ape. It should be noted that continued bending, although an advantage from the locomotor point of view, is disadvantageous in females because it narrows the outlet of the birth canal. This accounts for the fact that the bending has been carried further in human males than in females. There is a notable sex difference in the sciatic notch which is directly related to locomotor and postural differences between men and women.

The argument runs as follows: among apes who were living at the edge of the forests and coming to the ground, were some who had shorter ilia. These ilia had to be more bent back for obstetrical reasons and in some this carried gluteus maximus far enough so that it became effective in finishing extension. This started a new selection which favored bigger gluteus muscles and ilia still further bent. The beginning is, of course, supposition, but the functional results can be experimentally checked and the initial shortening and bending is not much beyond the range of known forms.

Characters closely associated with the primary changes in the pelvis are those in the feet and in the muscles of the legs. The feet of the mountain gorilla have approached the human condition in many ways (Schultz, 1934). Changes from a foot of such a sort to the human would not involve any major evolutionary changes. After all, the joining of the first metatarsal to the second by a ligament may well account for a great many of the features which differentiate the feet of apes and men.

Changes in the muscles are extensive but follow a pattern already seen in the monkeys. When a man walks, he straightens the leg primarily with the muscles on the front of the thigh (Q. ex. femoris). This is the same action which an ape or monkey uses in climbing. In running, the apes and monkeys use primarily the muscles in the back of the thigh. If the mass (weight) of the muscles on the front of the thigh is compared to that of those on the back, (quadriceps to the hamstrings), it is found that the relation is 2/1 in man, 1.2/1 in mangabeys, 1/1 in arboreal cercopiths (nictitans), and 1/1.2 in mixed ground-livers (vervets), and 1/2 in baboons. The first and last figures are from Haxton (1947), the others from monkeys obtained in Uganda. Even by such a crude method it is clear that the proportions of the major muscle masses closely follow the habit of the animal. Climbing is pre-adaptive for human walking. Quadrupedal running tends to build a different pattern of muscles. Aside from mass, there are a number of differences in the leg muscles of man and ape, which can best be described as the attenuation of the muscles other than quadriceps, and the migration of the insertions closer to the knee. These changes are of degree only, and the functions are the same. There is no radical alteration of form and function as in the case of gluteus maximus. Once the major change in the pelvis had taken place, these other changes may well have followed rapidly.

It is difficult to determine to what extent these changes had already taken place in the man-apes. There are only fragments of limb bones. However, the ape-like character of the ischium suggests that the hamstrings may not yet have achieved modern human form. The lack of an iliac tuberosity suggests some differences, but many changes in the leg muscles are little, if at all, reflected in the skeleton. The differences between mangabeys and baboons for example, which are functionally important, make no discernible difference in the femur. However, in the man-ape, the distal end of the femur is very large. This is the critical point. If these forms were walking erect, the femur must have borne the weight and given origin and insertion to the enlarged muscles concerned with locomotion. I believe that the argument between Le Gros Clark (1947) and Kern and Straus (1949) over the details of morphology of the femur is irrelevant. Any different group of animals may have somewhat different features of a particular bone. There is no reason why the femora of the man-apes should be identical with man, ape, or monkey. The morphology is of a general primate type and the size is in accord with the idea that these forms were bipeds. Granted a reasonable conformity of shape, the important thing functionally is size.

Considering the arms of the man-apes, the distal end of the humerus has been discovered, and Clark (1947) has claimed that it is of the human type and Straus (1948) that it is catarrhine. However, according to the plan suggested here, one would not expect any fundamental difference in the end of the humerus. The basic ape features, still preserved entirely in modern man, are the great size of the trochlea and conforming width of the proximal ulna and the rounded capitellum. The meaning of these features is that the stability of the elbow joint is determined by the fit between the trochlea and ulna, the radius being freed from stability and support is better adapted for rotation. Naturally, the precise detail of this pattern varies from group to group. These little variations are not of evolutionary significance. The major features and their importance can be easily determined. Cut the annular ligament (which holds the head of the radius in place) in a monkey, and the elbow joint loses its stability. Do the same in man, chimpanzee, or gibbon, and the hinge part of the joint functions nearly normally. The distal fragment of the humerus of the man-apes shows that they were typical members of the ape-human stock. The proximal humerus, clavical, and scapula tell the same story, although detailed study will surely reveal some minor differences from other known forms.

Several authorities have claimed that forms such as the great apes could not be ancestral to man. The reasons given are that the ape's arms are too long and thumbs too small (with the thumb muscles reduced) and that changes in these proportions would break the law of irreversibility of evolution. First, it should be stressed that no one thinks that man is descended from one of the living apes (see Simpson, 1949, for discussion on this point). The question is: could man be descended from a form which had relatively longer arms and smaller thumbs than modern men? Precise differences from living forms are not the issue, but the relations of two kinds of organization. First for the facts: Schultz (1936) has shown that man's arms are, in fact, very long by general primate standards. There is far less difference in length between man and gorilla than between gorilla and orang. The same is true relative to the proportions of the hand. With regard to the thumb muscles, the long flexor is present in all gibbons, over half the chimpanzees, and lesser percentages of gorillas and orangs (Straus, 1949). Once our ancestors had become bipeds, the selection on the arms, hands and associated muscles would have been different from that of tree-living apes. Selection must be quite different for the living gorilla and orang. The issue is, then, could a trend toward long arms and small thumbs in apes be reversed in their descendants when selection pressures were radically changed? That such reversals can and do take place has been recently emphasized by Colbert (1949), Gregory (1949), and Simpson (1949). The idea that such reversals cannot take place seems to be based on the idea that trends are due to orthogenesis, rather than to continued selection of the same sort over a long period. The fact that orthogenesis is not necessary to explain the facts of evolution seems well established and was dealt with at length by several authors in the volume "Genetics, Paleontology, and Evolution," also by Simpson's "Tempo and Mode in Evolution," and more recently by Jepsen (1949). In spite of all this one reads in "Races" published in 1950 (Coon, Garn and Birdsell) that, "Evolution, we are told, is irreversible." Wright (1934) has shown that the missing digits of the foot of the guinea pig may be brought back by mutation. These digits are normally not there at all. It seems that this is precisely the sort of situation in which the cooperation of geneticists, paleontologists and anthropologists is needed. Great knowledge of the proportions and variations of the primate arm and hand is rendered useless by outmoded concepts and by the failure to realize that reversals, far greater than changing the hand of the living chimpanzee into a human-proportioned hand, have actually been produced in the laboratory.

Turning to the skull, the teeth have been most extensively studied and the evidence has been carefully reviewed by Clark (1950). There is nothing in the dentition which would militate against the idea that these forms are direct ancestors of late Pliocene age. The molars of ape, man-ape, fossil man, and modern man form as nearly perfect a morphological record as one could hope to find (Gregory, 1949). There is no gap in the record at all, and, on the basis of molar teeth, one would have an exceedingly difficult time in deciding where apes left off and man began. This gradation is in marked contrast to the pelvis. It supports the idea that there was no sudden moment when selection on the dentition changed, rapidly producing a new type. These molar characters would then be regarded as incidental, useful in sorting, but not fundamental. It should be remembered that some arboreal monkeys have dentitions identical with plains-living ones. There seems to be no reason why the dentition should be different and, in fact, it is not.

The size of the molar teeth is of interest. As Broom (1946) has indicated, the best match for the teeth and jaws of the man-apes outside of Africa is the form named "*Meganthropus*" (Weidenreich, 1945). But the limb bones associated with the African forms are not large, the best match being with a small female Bushman, about the lower limit of size of living humans. This shows that large molars do not necessarily mean giant bodies. After all, a small monkey may have larger molars than a modern man. The correlation of body-size and tooth-size among primates is not high. Of course, if non-primates were considered too, the correlation would be far lower. Think if human standards were used to reconstruct body-size from a wart hog's molar! It is particularly dangerous to reconstruct body-size from the teeth of an unknown form.

The canine teeth offer points of interest. Von Koenigswald (1948) has shown that some at least are not as small as has been claimed. However, they are small compared to those of male apes. Of course, in female apes the canines may be exceedingly small, wearing like incisors and narrower than the first premolar (gorilla). In male monkeys the ground-living forms tend to have larger canines than the tree-livers.

The extremes in canine size are all in male ground-livers (baboons, mandrills, some macaques) (Washburn and Howell, in preparation). The function of these teeth is in the organization and protection of the group. The males dominate in the social organization (Zuckerman, 1932), and no female has a chance in fighting against the great canine teeth of the males. The big males likewise act as sentries and guards. From the evidence of other primates one would expect a male plains-living ape to have at least as large canines as the forest-forms. The fact that they are much smaller in the man-ape suggests that the teeth were less important in protection and fighting than among the living apes. This supports Dart's (1949a) hypothesis that the man-apes were already using tools. However, this cannot be definitely proved at the present time. Differences in the size of the canine teeth should not be overemphasized because there is a complete series in size and form linking man and ape.

At least some of the problems of the dentition can be dealt with experimentally. It would be useful to know to what extent size and pattern of the teeth are independently inherited. The simpler pattern of the molars of some of the small modern domestic pigs suggests that reduction of cusps may be only one aspect of size reduction. Weidenreich (1941) indicated the same in small dogs. This could be checked experimentally. Also, it would be possible to prove the importance of the large canines in the social organization of the monkey. With groups such as those on an island off Puerto Rico, the social organization could be studied, the dominant male trapped and his canines removed. A quantitative, experimental approach is possible so that the significance of the changes shown in the evolutionary record could be documented by fact and raised beyond the level of individual opinion. Tree shrews would be ideal experimental animals for this type of problem. They are small, hardy, and can be raised in the laboratory. If anthropologists and geneticists plan to cooperate in the solution of problems of mutual interest, it will be necessary to develop some new laboratory animals, and tree shrews may well prove to be the most suitable. Some experimental analysis of cranial form has been attempted (Washburn, 1947).

The evolution of the brain has always been of particular interest in the primates. Since the brain of modern man is so big and since man likes to think of himself as a rational animal, there has been a tendency to define man in terms of brain size. (Keith, 1949, defined the border of man and apes as 750 cc.) The idea that mammals as a group have triumphed over the reptiles because of better brains received a set-back from the work of Edinger (1948). She showed that the brain tends to follow in evolution, that the earliest of mammals did not have brains in advance of reptiles, and that at least several of the orders of mammals had established locomotor and dental adaptations prior to having their characteristic brain form. The hominids follow Edinger's pattern perfectly. The range of variation in cranial capacity is:

| | |
|---|---|
| chimpanzee and gorilla | 325–650 |
| man-apes | 450–650 |
| Java man | 750–900 |
| Pekin man | 900–1,200 |
| Neanderthal | 1,100–1,550 |

The range for Java man is too small, because of the small number of specimens. The figure for the man-apes should perhaps be raised because of a later, partially-described find (Broom, 1949). So there is either a complete series or very close to one. There is no doubt that all human fossils described so far have human pelves and limb bones and the man-apes were remarkably human in these features. Therefore, it appears that the differences in the brain between apes and man, just as those in dentition, were attained after full human status had been achieved in the limbs and trunk (Clark, 1950).

If one considers the primates in general, the same pattern seems to hold. The lemurs have bigger brains than the tree shrews, the monkeys than the lemurs, the apes than the monkeys. With each major advance in primate evolution the brain doubled or even tripled its size. If the human brain is viewed from this point of view, the remarkable thing about man is that his ancestors went through three major different locomotor adaptations during the age of mammals and one major reorganization of the special senses. After each of these the brain at least doubled its size. Viewed in this way the remarkable size of the human brain is due to the number of times this organ had to adjust to new ways of life. This is added to the general tendency for mammalian brains to increase in size, and to the fact that at least the last doubling was after the use of tools, which may have greatly increased the selection for large brains.

The final adjustment in brain size seems to have been rapid. If capacities of 800–1000 were common in the early Pleistocene (and they may well have been less in the beginning), and 1200–1400 common in the third inter-glacial, the same rate of change would make the man-ape capacities expected in direct ancestors of the late Pliocene age. If the change in brain size follows the change in locomotion, it might be expected to continue rapidly until a new plateau is reached. If so, there is some justification in projecting the known rate back for at least a short period of time, and even a short prolongation of the known rate would reduce brain size to that of the apes and man-apes. Brains of this size may have been characteristic of apes for many millions of years. There is almost no direct evidence, but the skull found by Leakey (Clark, 1950) would be in accord with such an idea.

In summary, the critical primary adaptation initially responsible for the origin of man as a distinct group is in the pelvis. Efficient, bipedal locomotion of the human type involves primarily the pelvis and gluteus maximus, but a series of secondary changes in thigh, leg, and foot must have followed soon to complete the adaptive complex. This complex may have been further improved by continued selection, but, as far as can be determined from the skeleton, had reached modern form in the early Pleistocene. Changes in the teeth, brain size, and many other parts of the body took place at a much slower rate and continued on into late Pleistocene times. These changes are the result of the secondary selection patterns which followed after the establishment of the primary human pattern. Finally, there are many little differences between any two forms. These incidental features may be due to a variety of causes and should not be allowed to confuse the major patterns.

It is customary to present the results of phylogenetic speculations in the form of a classification. There has been so much overemphasis on classification and names, especially with regard to the primates, that common names have been used here as far as possible. At the moment they are better guides to the identity of living primates than the supposedly scientific ones. Without wishing to stress names or overemphasize their importance, the views expressed in this paper imply a reduction in the number of names of categories among the primates. If the term "family" is reserved for a group of animals representing a major adaptive radiation (such as the Indridae, Lorisidae, or Galagidae), then the gibbons belong in the same family as the great apes. Bipedal man might be put in a separate family. The reasons for granting bipedal man more taxonomic distinction from apes than the ground-living monkeys from the tree-living monkeys, is that there is a much greater series of anatomical changes in the case of man. Within the human family one genus, *homo*, might easily include all the Pleistocene large-brained hominids (Java man, Pekin man, etc.). One other genus, *Australopithecus*, might contain the man-apes (*Australopithecus*, *Plesianthropus*, *Paranthropus*, and perhaps *Meganthropus* and even *Gigantopithecus*). Obviously, since little is known of the time when these forms lived, the extent of their range and how many local forms there may have been, the significance of this category is uncertain. If such forms were widely spread over the Old World in late Pliocene and early Pleistocene times,

probably there were quite distinct local groups. It seems convenient to place these small-brained men in a single genus, at least until there is more evidence to the contrary. The number of names is a function of the kind of interest of the investigator (Broom, 1950). If one is primarily interested in classification, in type specimens and priority, then the less there is known about fossil primates the more names there will be. If one is interested in the mechanics of evolution, in the understanding of process, a cumbersome and constantly changing classification is a great liability and the tendency will be to lump, to leave fragmentary bits unnamed, and to create new groups only when absolutely necessary.

In conclusion, it might be repeated that this is an appropriate time to reconsider the problems of the origin of man; for the traditional phylogenies have been upset by the discovery of new fossils; the old theories of orthogenesis, irreversibility and the supremacy of non-adaptive characters have been proved false; and because experimental procedures offer methods of raising some conclusions beyond the level of individual opinion. Looking to the future, fossils are being found at a rate undreamed of in the past. The cooperation of geneticists and paleontologists has produced a rich evolutionary theory which places the fundamental contribution of Darwin in modern form. Facts are increasing and new theories are challenging, but methods must be developed for proving and checking the importance of particular facts and the fit of any given theory. Such testing requires a knowledge of fossils, of living forms and the application of experimental procedures. All three types of evidence are necessary and a science of human origins can be built only upon this triple foundation.

Without fossils, ancestors can be reconstructed only by what has been called "mental triangulation." With all the vast effort which went into the comparative anatomy of the primates, no one reconstructed an animal with a human ilium and an ape's head. There were attempts in this direction and Weidenreich (1947) recognized that the evolution of the locomotor system preceded that of the head, but before the discovery of the man-apes, and before Edinger's investigations, it remained equally logical to maintain that the brain was the primary and initial factor in human evolution. The actual course of evolution can be determined only from fossils.

But, fossils, at best, constitute a very limited source of information. Adaptations in the digestive, circulatory, reproductive systems, and special senses affect the skeleton little or not at all. The significance of many changes in the skeleton cannot be determined, unless living forms of comparable structure are available for study. Unfortunately, much of the fossil record of primates is limited to teeth and jaws, and the extent to which these parts can be misleading is well-shown by the living lemurs. The skulls of lorises and galagos show not only detailed similarity but comparable trends, yet the whole post-cranial skeleton is different and the animals represent opposite extremes in locomotor adaptations. From the point of view of the comparative anatomist the primates have definite advantages, for there are living representatives of all the major primate radiations, and numerous parallel series offer opportunities for the analysis of the causes of anatomical similarity. Of course, the living forms are not ancestors and will not reveal the detailed anatomy of extinct types, but a far fuller understanding of a lemur can be gained by studying fossils and living forms than by the study of either one alone. Obviously, the chimpanzee is not studied to prove that it is *the* human ancestor but to understand the kind of organization which may have been characteristic of the ancestral forms.

After the study of fossils and living animals, when theories take definite form, then experiments should be planned. Particularly the importance of adaptive complexes and the precise nature of adaptation can be advanced far beyond the level of individual opinion. The fact that gluteus maximus functions differently in man and ape is not a matter of opinion but can be precisely determined. Again, the importance of gluteus in walking can be quantitatively investigated and placed beyond the realm of debate. The study of human origins requires an appreciation of the nature of evolutionary change in animals, an understanding of the specific problems of the primates, and a detailed comprehension of form and function of man and ape. Solution of the problems will require the cooperation of many scientists, and it is hoped that this conference may be the beginning of much close cooperation between anthropologists and others interested in the origin and differentiation of the human stock.

## REFERENCES

Barbour, G. B., 1949, Yearbook of Physical Anthropology, 1948. Edited by G. W. Lasker and F. P. Thieme. The Viking Fund, Inc.

Broom, R., 1949, Discoveries from South Africa. London Illust. News, September 10, p. 378.

1950a, The genera and species of the South African fossil ape-men. Amer. J. Phys. Anthrop., n.s., *8:* 1–13.

1950b, Finding the missing link. London: Watts & Co.

Broom, R., and Schepers, G. W. H., 1946. The South African fossil ape-men, the Australopithecinae. Transvaal Mus. Memoir no. 2, Pretoria.

Camp, C. L., 1949, Yearbook of Physical Anthropology, 1948. Edited by G. W. Lasker and F. P. Thieme.Viking Fund, Inc.

Clark, W. E. Le Gros, 1936, The problem of the claw in primates. Proc. Zool. Soc. Lond. pp. 1–24.

1947, Observations on the anatomy of the fossil Australopithecinae. J. Anat. *81:* 300–334.

1950, New palaeontological evidence bearing on the evolution of the Hominoidea. Quart. J. Geol. Soc. Lon. *105:* 225–264.

Colbert, E. H., 1949, Some paleontological principles significant in human evolution. Studies in Phys. Anthrop. *1:* 103–147.

Coon, C. S., Garn, S. M., and Birdsell, J. B., 1950, Races. Springfield: Charles C. Thomas.

Dart, R. A., 1949a, The predatory implemental technique of *Australopithecus.* Amer. J. Phys. Anthrop. n.s. *7:* 1–38.

1949b, The first pelvic bones of *Australopithecus prometheus.* Amer. J. Phys. Anthrop. n.s. *7:* 255–257.

1949c, Yearbook of Physical Anthropology, 1948. Edited by G. W. Lasker and F. P. Thieme. Viking Fund, Inc.

Dobzhansky, TH., 1950, Evolution in the tropics. Amer. Scientist *38:* 209–221.

Edinger, T., 1948, Evolution of the horse brain. Geol. Soc. Amer. Mem. *25.*

Gregory, W. K., 1949, The bearing of Australopithecinae upon the problem of Man's place in nature. Amer. J. Phys. Anthrop. n.s. *7:* 485–512.

Haxton, H. A., 1947, Muscles of the pelvic limb. A study of the differences between bipeds and quadrupeds. Anat. Rec. *98:* 337–346.

Hooton, E. A., 1946, Up from the ape. Revised edition. New York: Macmillan.

Jepsen, G. L., 1949, Selection, "Orthogenesis" and the fossil record. Proc. Amer. Phil. Soc. *93:* 479–500.

Jepsen, G. L., Simpson, G. G., and Mayr, E., 1949, Genetics, paleontology and evolution. Princeton: Princeton Univ. Press.

Jones, F. W., 1948, Hallmarks of mankind. Baltimore: Williams and Wilkins Co.

Keith, A., 1949, A new theory of human evolution. New York: Philosophical Library.

Kern, H. M., and Straus, W. L., 1949, The femur of *Plesianthropus transvaalensis.* Amer. J. Phys. Anthrop. n.s. *7:* 53–77.

von Koenigswald, G. H. R., 1948, Remarks on the lower canine of *Plesianthropus transvaalensis* Broom. Robert Broom Commemorative Volume, Royal Society of South Africa, Cape Town.

Loth, E., 1931, Anthropologie des parties molles. Paris: Masson & Cie.

Orford, M., 1934, The pelvis of the Bush race. S. Afr. J. Sci., *31:* 586–610.

Schultz, A. H., 1934, Some distinguishing characters of the mountain gorilla. J. Mammal. *15:* 51–61.

1936, Characters common to higher primates and characters specific for man. Quart. Rev. Biol. *11:* 259–283, 429–455.

Simpson, G. G., 1940, Studies on the earliest primates. Bull. Amer. Mus. Nat. Hist. *77:* 185–212.

1944, Tempo and mode in evolution. New York: Columbia Univ. Press.

1945, The principles of classification and a classification of mammals. Bull. Amer. Mus. Nat. Hist. *85.*

1949, The meaning of evolution. New Haven: Yale Univ. Press.

Smith, E. G., 1924, The evolution of man. Essays. Oxford Univ. Press.

Straus, W. L., 1948, The humerus of *Paranthropus robustus.* Amer. J. Phys. Anthrop. n.s. *6:* 285–311.

1949, The riddle of man's ancestry. Quart. Rev. Biol. *24:* 200–223.

Washburn, S. L., 1947, The relation of the temporal muscle to the form of the skull. Anat. Rec. *99:* 239–248.

1949, Sex differences in the pubic bone of Bantu and Bushman. Amer. J. Phys. Anthrop. n.s. *7:* 425–432.

Weidenreich, F., 1941, The brain and its role in the phylogenetic transformation of the human skull. Trans. Amer. Phil. Soc. n.s. *31:* 321–442.

1945, Giant early man from Java and South China. Vol. 40. Anthrop. Papers, Amer. Mus. Nat. Hist., pp. 5–134.

1946, Apes, giants, and men. Chicago: Univ. of Chicago.

1947, The trend of human evolution. Evolution *1*: 221–236.

Weinert, H., 1932, Ursprung der Menschheit. Stuttgart.

Wright, S., 1934, Polydactylous guinea pigs. J. Hered. *25*: 359–362.

Zuckerman, S., 1932, The social life of monkeys and apes. London: Kegan Paul.

1933, Functional affinities of man, monkeys, and apes. New York: Harcourt, Brace and Company.

## DISCUSSION

ANGEL: It seems clear that the bone mass genetically available to cover various sizes of brains must play a major part in both cranial index and details of cranial form. As in the examples you gave, a functional breakdown of head-form into antero-posterior and radial growth of the skull base and bone mass or brain size would, through the principle of relative growth, greatly reduce the number of genic factors apparently needed.

MACDOWELL: Dr. Washburn suggests that genetics can step in after experimental studies, such as those he has just reported on the dependence of certain bone configurations on muscles, have separated traits that are directly inherited from the secondary effects of such traits. It happens that genetics has already stepped in by contributing a mutation.[1] among others that performs a similar experiment. In this case the configuration of a bone, the sternum, is found to be dependent upon the timing of growth of other bones, the ribs. This mutation occurred in a mouse, but it has led to an interpretation of the division of the sternum into segments, or sternebrae, applicable to all mammals including man and the apes. Dr. Schultz showed drawings of several primate sterna varying from broad to narrow, with sternebrae varying in number and degree of separation. It now appears highly probable that all these variations, and countless others, are expressions of differences in the ontogenetic timing of rib elongation, and that, in regard to the pattern of this bone, the tissues of the different sterna are intrinsically alike. The anlage of the sternum appears as a pair of diverging bands, which the elongating ribs meet and push together. Differentiation towards cartilage and bone proceeds uniformly in the sternum, except at the points of contact with ribs. At these points, and in a zone radiating from them, differentiation is inhibited. This is the essential point revealed by the mutation. With normal rib growth the inhibited zones for a pair of ribs overlaps, so that differentiation first proceeds only inter-

costally, and, in the mouse, four slender sternebrae, with epiphyses, as in long bones, are formed. The recessive, monogenic mutation, called *screw-tail* from one of its various effects, temporarily retards the elongation of ribs[2] at a time when they would normally be uniting the halves of the sternum. Nevertheless, the halves do unite by cell migration from the inner margins, at the sacrifice of length and thickness. Thus the paired zones of inhibited differentiation do not meet, and at birth, instead of a series of four intercostal bone centers, there is a single elongated bone center. Since the ends of the 6th and 7th ribs are attached side by side, a single zone of inhibition is formed but this is so large that it meets its opposite mate and so the xiphoid process starts with a separate bone center. Subsequently, instead of the inter-sternebral epiphyses lengthening the sternum, the zones of continued growth are lateral and a broad short, shield-shaped sternum is formed, with deep lateral indentations at the ends of the ribs resulting from the inhibition of differentiation. By the time rib-growth is resumed the new pattern of the sternum has been established. The adult ribs give no suggestion of abnormality or of their responsibility for the dramatic appearance of a sternum lacking sternebrae from the beginning.

In other mice, deviations in the position of attachment or growth of individual ribs or single pairs of ribs, which in some cases may fail to join the sternum, have given a wide range of sternal patterns, all in perfect accord with the interpretation that the rib-end induces an inhibition of differentiation of the sternum. The most bizarre of these patterns appeared in a strain in which rib growth was normal, but occasionally all the ribs on one side were attached slightly higher than those on the other, so that each rib-end was opposite an intercostal space, and the zones of inhibited differentiation were staggered and did not overlap. In these cases, at birth, the sternum had a single continuous bone-center, in the form of a wall of troy (meander pattern).

WASHBURN: I want to thank Dr. MacDowell for contributing this excellent example of the way genetics can aid our evolutionary thinking. If many apparently complex morphological changes can be the result of a single change in a process, in this case the slowing of growth of ribs, then it will be far easier to account for the sort of differences seen between various primates. As Dr. Angel points out, studies of relative growth will also help. At present there is a vast quantity of descriptive data, and what we need is more studies of the type recommended by Dr. Angel and so beautifully illustrated by Dr. MacDowell.

[1] MacDowell, E. C., J. S. Potter, T. Laanes, and E. N. Ward, 1942, J. Hered. *33*: 439–449.

[2] Bryson, V., 1945, Anat. Rec. *91*: 119–141.

*This chapter illustrates many of Washburn's concerns. It demonstrates how the comparative, functional, and evolutionary perspective on variation can give us new answers. Morbeck's use of data from a natural population of our closest living relatives, her relatively large sample size, her treatment of bones as part of adaptive complexes that intertwine anatomical, behavioral, ecological, and genetic factors, and her interpretations of the skeleton from the point of view of functional morphology are hallmarks of the new physical anthropology. She carries the perspective further by including detailed data on the life stories of the bones as they were when they were living animals. This broadening of framework permits her to begin to distinguish between species attributes and idiosyncratic outcomes of individual lives in the skeletal variation that she finds.*

# 3 Life History of Gombe Chimpanzees: The Inside View from the Skeleton

**Mary Ellen Morbeck**   *Departments of Anthropology and Cell Biology & Anatomy, University of Arizona*

## ABSTRACT

Chimpanzees from Gombe National Park, Tanzania, have been studied for more than 30 years. *Pan troglodytes* species characters and local population conditions are known. Each individual's sex, age at death, and behaviors during life also are known. In combination with these data, skeletons of Flo and others show us what can—and cannot—be determined from an individual's bones and teeth about its phylogeny, species, population, and sex; sequence and timing of growth, development, reproduction, and aging; locomotion and other social-maintenance activities; nutrition and health, including disease and injury; and unique life experiences. Gombe field records also tell us about females (and, in some cases, males) and their offspring. By studying both skeletal biology and observations of individuals during life, we see what biosocial and ecological factors contribute to individual survival and reproductive outcome, to Gombe chimpanzee population dynamics, and thus to evolution through generational time.

## INTRODUCTION

One of the various features which are [is] unusual about bone is that it exists both as a tissue and as an organ. Bones as organs are exemplified by the skeletons which adorn museums of natural history. The femur, the humerus, or a single rib, each represents an individual organ. Together with all the other bones in the body, they constitute an organ system, the skeleton. Because this is more often the only organ system preserved from the past in a fossilized form, virtually all of our knowledge of the evolution of vertebrate morphology, including that of our own species, is based on bones. (Hall 1988:175)

Fossils, the mineralized bones and teeth of once-living individuals, provide the most important data for testing hypotheses about when, where, how, and under what circumstances humans evolved. All research designs in paleoanthropology confront a major issue: how to interpret skeletal variation among humans, our ancestors, and closest relatives in terms of form, function, and phylogeny.

Because fossils are fragments of an individual's skeleton at one point in its life (i.e., the time of death), they provide only a glimpse of past life ways and life cycles. Inferences about function and phylogeny can never be confirmed with known species characters and lifetime behavioral observations of individuals. Study of a contemporary primate skeletal series of individuals observed when alive, such as that from the Gombe chimpanzee population, allows us to see the nature of variation in bone and tooth size, shape, and structure as related to multifaceted biobehavioral and ecological influences, evolutionary history, and genetics. We can learn to distinguish features associated with species attributes (including sex differences) that reflect the nature of variation among and within populations and those that document unique experiences of individual lives.

## LIFE HISTORY AND GOMBE CHIMPANZEE SKELETONS

A life history approach that integrates life ways and the life cycle to define lifestyle helps to explain skeletal variation. Life histories are evolutionary adaptations. Many behaviors of *Pan troglodytes*—or *Homo sapiens*—contribute to survival throughout the life stages and, as adults, also to mating and rearing of offspring. These behaviors are based on a species-defined body structure and the physiology, bioenergetics, and biomechanics of each individual as the individual grows, matures, reproduces, and ages.

Locomotor, postural, and manipulative abilities and associated social-maintenance behaviors of traveling, feeding, social grooming, communicating, avoidance of predators, and caring for infants are examples of survival characters. These life way features sustain individuals and promote biosocial health. They unfold as part of the life course of females and males as determined by timing of the life cycle. Time-based attributes include age and maturation at birth, weaning, first reproduction, and death. They pattern the life stages of in utero, infancy, childhood, and adulthood and mark the transitions between them. Life history features of species, and of females and males within species, in my view, describe both the nature of life ways and the schedule of growth, development, reproduction, and life span to characterize a species' lifestyle (Morbeck 1991, 1994, 1997a; Smith 1992; Stearns 1992; Zihlman et al. 1990).

This study of *Pan troglodytes schweinfurthii* from Gombe National Park, Tanzania, focuses on recognized individuals throughout the life stages. Many social, biological, and other environmental factors, including chance, influence a female's or male's life and genetic contribution to the population. This unique sequence of experiences and reproductive profile, as expressed within the boundaries of species attributes, is an individual's life story. From the level of the whole organism, we can move "down" or "into" chimpanzee body systems, cells, proteins, genes, and molecules, and we can move "up" from the individual to populations, species, and higher taxa or "out" to environmental interactions within social groups and of populations in ecological communities (Morbeck 1997a).

The Gombe chimpanzee skeletons and the individuals who "owned" them provide a natural experiment.

Quantitative and nonmetric analyses of skeletons and field observations of the same animals when alive give us a rare opportunity to test hypotheses in our closest living relatives about species- and sex-defined attributes, that is, how anatomy and behavior contribute throughout the life stages to functionally integrated individuals; about what events happened to real animals in the course of their lives and how these individual life stories are recorded in teeth and bones; and about how these experiences influenced survival, health, and reproductive outcome.

This "real animals, real lives" perspective allows a more complete understanding of the factors that shape an individual's life and how these affect population demography and shifts in patterns of variation through generational time. Evolution generally is measured in populations as change in diversity from generation to generation. By studying the life stories of Gombe chimpanzees observed over several generations, we see what biosocial and ecological factors contribute to individual survival and reproductive outcome. From the perspective of well-known individuals growing to maturity and living together at Gombe, we also see the many factors that determine population size, composition, and variation. The Gombe chimpanzees, therefore, allow a short-term view of how evolution "works."

## TEETH AND BONES: LIFE HISTORY FEATURES

Teeth and bones preserve information about form, function, and phylogeny. Teeth are the mechanical processors of food—energy for body growth, development, maintenance, and repair. Bones provide a framework for body support and movement. Bones also protect organs, store minerals, and serve as places for red blood cell and immune system cell production. These hard tissues can be studied during life or long after an individual's death as part of a skeletal series or as fully mineralized fossils.

The anatomy, physiology, and behavior shared by all *Pan troglodytes* represent historical overlays of species life history attributes, built on hominoid, catarrhine, primate, mammal, and vertebrate body plans. Corresponding skeletal features that reveal evolved life ways throughout the life stages of modern species (and fossils) allow broad interpretations of phylogenetic relationships (Morbeck 1994, 1997).

Bones and teeth also record life ways and time-based life cycle experiences in individuals. Size, shape, structure, and composition of bones tell us what animals could do (species features) and actually did do (individual life stories) with their skeletons. The skeleton also documents the sequence and timing of changes in size and shape related to growth, development, reproductive maturity, and aging. Expressions of this species-defined life cycle pattern, combined with many kinds of life-long environmental interactions, result in the skeletal anatomy that underlies survival features as each individual negotiates a unique pathway throughout the life stages.

Life stories preserved in an individual's skeleton document: normal physiological function associated with energy acquisition and activities; environmentally mediated disruptions to growth, tissue maintenance, and repair such as disease, including malnutrition; and other biophysical/biochemical interactions. These life story features allow us to read "osteobiographies" of individuals, their skeletal series, and populations (Morbeck 1997b; Saul and Saul 1989).

## SKELETAL SERIES, MEASUREMENTS, AND OBSERVATIONS

### Gombe Chimpanzees

FIELD OBSERVATIONS   Sex, estimated birth year and age at death, behaviors, and some aspects of biology during life are recorded for each adult in the Gombe chimpanzee skeletal series (Goodall 1971, 1983, 1986, 1990; Morbeck et al. 1993; Zihlman et al. 1990). Live body weights are available for some individuals (Wrangham and Smuts 1980). In addition, female reproductive outcomes are known (Goodall 1986; Morbeck et al. 1992). Comparable field data are not available for individuals in other *Pan* skeletal series.

SKELETAL SERIES   Size, shape, external features, internal structure, and mineral content of teeth and bones describe life ways, life cycles, and individual life stories of 15 free-ranging, adult chimpanzees (Table 1). Individual biological profiles are constructed using information about sex, age and maturational status at death, skeletal measurements, and observed nonmetric effects of life events.

Teeth and bones of many individuals are combined with others to make up the skeletal series. The sample is a cross-sectional view of time slices of many individual life stories that potentially reflect life history features of the local chimpanzee population. Aggregated skeletal data are compared to skeletal measurements of other chimpanzees that represent larger populations, subspecies, and species (Morbeck and Zihlman 1989).

MEASUREMENTS AND OBSERVATIONS   Field researchers retrieve chimpanzee bodies after death, and skeletons are cleaned by natural decomposition at Gombe. Measurements are noninvasive and they include volumetric/weight, linear, and areal dimensions

**TABLE 1.   Gombe Adult Chimpanzee Skeletons of Known Individuals**

| | Year at Birth[1] | Age at Death[1] | Life Stage[2] |
|---|---|---|---|
| **Females** | | | |
| Gilka | 1960 | 19 | Mature |
| Pallas | 1955 | 27 | Mature |
| Madam Bee | 1947 | 28 | Mature |
| Passion | 1951 | 31 | Mature |
| Miff | 1956 | 31 | Mature |
| Melissa | 1950 | 36 | Old age |
| Flo | 1929 | 43+ | Old age |
| Old Female | NA[2] | 40+ | Old age |
| **Males** | | | |
| MacDee | 1953 | 15 | Young |
| Charlie | 1951 | 26 | Prime |
| Jomeo | 1956 | 31 | Middle age |
| Satan[3] | 1955 | 32 | Middle age |
| Humphrey[3] | 1946 | 35 | Old age |
| Hugo | 1936 | 39+ | Old age |
| Mr. McGregor | 1925 | 41+ | Old age |

[1]Year of birth and age at death are estimates from field observations; life stage status is defined by Goodall (1986).
[2]Field observations are not available.
[3]Skeletons are not complete.

of the braincase, face, teeth, forelimb and hindlimb long bones, shoulder and pelvic girdles, and vertebral column to quantify bone size and shape, describe joint movement and weight-bearing, and determine body segment proportions; CT (computer tomography) scans of five equidistant sites on the shafts of the humerus and femur (plus the femoral neck) and one site on the radius to describe distribution of bone tissue in cross sections and indicate biomechanical loading conditions; and SPA (single photon absorptiometry) scans at the same sites to measure bone mineral content. Sex differences, birth year differences, and left/right skeletal asymmetry are evaluated using the percent difference method. Data are analyzed via SPSS statistical programs (SPSS-X 1988).

Life experiences recorded in the skeleton include: growth (e.g., bone size and status of mineralization and epiphyseal sutural closure); load-bearing recorded in the amount of bone mineral, the extent and distribution of cortical bone, and the orientation of trabecular bone; left/right asymmetries possibly associated with behaviors during life (e.g., locomotion, tool use); health, including nutrition (e.g., bone size, shape, structure, and mineralization and condition of teeth), disease (e.g., fungal- or bacteria-caused lesions, effects of limb paralysis, periodontal disease and abscesses); trauma (e.g., fractures, bite wounds, muscle pulls, wear and tear (e.g., degenerative changes in bone and tooth wear and loss); female reproduction (e.g., apparent decrease in bone mineralization but not resorption areas on the pubis or ilium); and cause of death. (For more information, see Galloway and colleagues 1990, 1993; Jurmain 1989; Kilgore 1989; Morbeck and colleagues 1991,

1992, 1994; Morbeck and Zihlman 1989; Sumner et al. 1989; Zihlman et al. 1990 and cited references.)

## Comparative *Pan* Skeletal Series

Skeletons of 50 free-ranging adult *Pan troglodytes* and 22 *Pan paniscus* provide a comparative sample. The *Pan troglodytes* series combines skeletons of individuals derived from all subspecies (with assumed genetic variation; Morin et al. 1994). They represent different geographic localities and dates of collection, access to different environmental resources, and variable social-maintenance activity patterns. The *Pan paniscus* skeletal series represents individuals from a smaller geographic area in Zaire (i.e., probably less genetic variation), presumably less ecological and behavioral variation, and, in addition, a shorter time period for collection of individuals.

Linear dimensions are compared among *Pan* skeletal series. Mean values of pooled-sex and single-sex samples of Gombe chimpanzees and other *Pan troglodytes* and *P. paniscus* skeletal dimensions are used for all comparisons. These data are analyzed with SPSS statistical programs (Morbeck and Zihlman 1989; SPSS-X 1988).

## WHAT DO THE SKELETONS TELL US?

I being and end with individuals. First, I compare the aggregated set of individuals in the Gombe skeletal series to those of other *Pan troglodytes* and to *P. paniscus*. Second, I discuss within population variation associated with sex and, in the Gombe skeletal series, decade of birth. Finally, I emphasize individuals and discuss Gombe chimpanzee skeletal variation in terms of individuals' life stories and their biosocial and reproductive roles in the local chimpanzee population.

## Populations and Species: Comparisons Among Skeletal Series

SKELETAL SIZE AND SHAPE    Average Gombe chimpanzee braincase volume, tooth size, and limb proportions are like those of other *Pan troglodytes*. In contrast, Gombe chimpanzees have shorter limb bones with smaller joints, less broad shoulders, and a shorter, more narrow pelvis (Morbeck and Zihlman 1989).

The pattern of variation between Gombe chimpanzees and *Pan paniscus* differs from that among the *Pan troglodytes* skeletal series. First, Gombe chimpanzee braincase volume and canine/molar tooth sizes, like other *Pan troglodytes*, are larger than *Pan paniscus*. Second, although Gombe skeletons generally have shorter limb bones, their shoulder and acetabular

joint areas are larger and trunk size (i.e., clavicular length, os coxa height, iliac breadth) generally is greater than measured in *Pan paniscus* (Morbeck and Zihlman 1989).

BODY WEIGHT    Live body weights recorded during field studies at Gombe support the skeletal data. These include, but are not limited to, individuals that make up the skeletal series. Gombe chimpanzee average weights (females $\bar{x}$ 29.8 kg; males $\bar{x}$ 39.5 kg) are less that those published for other *Pan troglodytes*, including other *P. t. schweinfurthii*. Mean body weights also are lower than those reported for *Pan paniscus* (reviewed in Morbeck and Zihlman 1989).

SEX DIFFERENCES IN THE POSTCRANIAL SKELETON Postcranial linear measurements show that sex differences are more pronounced, with males larger than females (about 5–7%), in non-Gombe common chimpanzees than those calculated for the Gombe skeletal series (see below). Both Gombe and other *Pan troglodytes* show males to have large trunks relative to those of females. Non-Gombe common chimpanzees reveal slightly greater percent differences in both clavicular length and iliac breadth.

*Pan paniscus* limb bone and os coxae lengths, unlike those of common chimpanzees, are about the same size in males and females (<2%). Male and female upper body size also apparently is similar in *Pan paniscus*. Shoulder breadth, in fact, is slightly greater in females, although clavicles show only a minimal difference in length. Iliac breadth (about 5%), however, shows a more pronounced sex difference than do other linear measurements. This may indicate, as in *Pan troglodytes*, relatively greater upper body/trunk weight bearing in males (Galloway et al. 1993).

SEX DIFFERENCES IN THE BRAINCASE AND TEETH Sex differences in cranial capacity are more pronounced in *Pan troglodytes* than in *Pan paniscus* (Cramer 1977). Cramer's sample (with an unknown amount of overlap with this non-Gombe skeletal series) produces about a 7% difference in braincase volume (males > females). The *Pan paniscus* samples share many of the same individuals; Cramer's results show less than 1% difference. Gombe *Pan troglodytes* males, as discussed below, also have cranial capacities that are only slightly larger than those of Gombe females.

Upper canine buccolingual breadth mean values for different, but overlapping, samples of non-Gombe *Pan troglodytes* and *Pan paniscus* show males are larger. Percent differences between the sexes calculated from published data range from 18 to 24% (see Almquist 1974, Johanson 1974a, b; Shea 1982). The sex differences calculated from Johanson's data on buccolingual breadth of the maxillary second molar are less than 2% in both *P. troglodytes* and *P. paniscus*. Gombe sex differences in tooth size are greater than those of either comparative sample (see below).

## Gombe Population: Variation Within the Skeletal Series

An individual's sex, age at death, year of birth, and unique life story features combine to pattern variation within the Gombe chimpanzee skeletal series. Tracking measurements and observations individual by individual and by sex and age gives a better understanding of statistical analyses at the skeletal series/population level and comparisons with other chimpanzees.

SEX DIFFERENCES IN THE POSTCRANIAL SKELETON Percent differences between male and female averages for volumetric, linear, and areal dimensions, as well as mineral content, vary from 1.4% (humerus length) to about 35% (humerus mineral content, C7 vertebral body area). Female average values are less than those of males, with one exception—pubic length (−5.7% difference).

Postcranial skeletons reflect sex differences in average body weight. Females weigh about 10 kg less than do males (24.6% difference; calculated from Wrangham and Smuts 1980). The upper trunk vertebral body weight-bearing surfaces are larger in males (17–35%). Males also have more calcium in their limb bones (21–35%).

Upper body differences associated with body weight are indicated by shoulder, hip, and vertebral column dimensions. The C7 vertebral body superior surface area, for example, shows a greater difference between the sexes (35%) than do other vertebral joint surfaces (17–21%). Males have longer clavicles and scapulae associated with larger shoulder complexes and upper trunk, as well as indication of greater weight bearing by the upper trunk (i.e., iliac breadth with moderate differences). In addition, shoulder joint areas are about 9–12% larger in males, whereas hip joint areas differ by about 6% in the acetabulum and only 3% in the femoral head.

Although males are heavier and have larger upper bodies, lengths of all limb bones and the os coxa show less than a 4% difference between Gombe male and female means. Forelimb and hindlimb length measurements, especially the proximal long bones (i.e., humerus and femur), are strikingly similar.

SEX DIFFERENCES IN BRAINCASE AND TEETH Cranial volumes show little difference (3%). The teeth tell a different story. Statistically significant differences oc-

cur in upper canine size (MD, 20%; BL, 28%). These maxillary canine and, in addition, second molar buccolingual linear differences are greater than those calculated from data reported in studies of both *Pan troglodytes* and *Pan paniscus*.

AGE AND CONDITION AT DEATH Gombe chimpanzees with estimated ages of 40 years or more exhibit extreme enamel attrition, tooth inflammation, alveolar bone deterioration, and tooth loss compared to younger adults at the time of death (Kilgore 1989; Zihlman et al. 1990). Pathologies associated with trauma, especially fractures, also are more common. External evidence for degenerative disease of the joints of the vertebrae and limb bones, in contrast, is rare (Jurmain 1989; Zihlman et al. 1990).

"Old age" adults at the time of death also show internal changes in geometric and material properties of long bone shafts. Both males and, to a greater extent, females have diminished cortical bone relative to total cross-sectional shaft area and less mineral content at the same scan sites of the humerus and femur when compared to younger adults. In elderly females, long periods of lactation coupled with possible hormonal changes later in life probably affected bone structure and the amount of calcium (Morbeck 1991; Sumner et al. 1989).

YEAR OF BIRTH: A POSSIBLE SECULAR TREND Gombe chimpanzees with estimated birth years and growth to maturity in the 1920s, 1930s, and early 1940s generally have longer limb bones with larger joint areas when compared to individuals born in the late 1940s and 1950s. Although a few individuals born in later decades have large skeletons, percent differences of mean long bone lengths that compare pre-1937 and post-1946 sets of individuals show about a 4–6.5% difference.

Only external measurements hint at a possible secular trend of decreasing limb bone sizes. Individuals born in the earlier decades also are those in the "old age" category at the time of death. The aging process has altered internal dimensions of their limb bones with apparent thinning of cortical bone and decrease in calcium content (see above), but not overall limb bone size.

## Gombe Individuals: Mosaic Variation Within the Skeletal Series

The life story as read in the teeth and bones of each chimpanzee is unique. A mosaic of individual features contributes to a statistical description of the skeletal series. Among Gombe chimpanzees, for example, shoulder, pelvis, and limb bones of Flo, Old Female, Hugo, and Jomeo are long and have large joint areas. Limb bones of Charlie, Madam Bee, Gilka, Passion, and

Melissa are short. However, braincase sizes in Charlie and Madam Bee, as in "big-boned" Gombe adults, are relatively large. In contrast, although Jomeo's bones and teeth are among the largest of Gombe individuals, his braincase volume is relatively small.

Life experiences are preserved in the shapes and internal architecture of bones (Morbeck et al. 1997b; Zihlman et al. 1990). Many biosocial and ecological factors contribute to the condition of the skeleton at death, including life events, cause of death, and the normal aging process. Charlie's right browridge has a small hole indicative of a bite wound that had not healed at the time of his death. Its canine-fitting morphology suggests an encounter with another chimpanzee. He apparently died of injuries. Hugo's right calcaneus and talus show extensive remodeling of the subtalar joint. The bones show that he sustained a compressive fracture of his heel/ankle as an adult; it had healed prior to his death. Flo must have experienced difficulty in moving and bearing weight on her right shoulder and forelimb sometime during adulthood. The lateral aspect of her clavicle shows a healed fracture, as does the acromion process of the corresponding scapula. Hugo and Flo later died of old age. The teeth and bones of Gilka, Madam Bee, and Passion (discussed below) highlight individualized mosaics of skeletal features.

## Individual Skeletal Biology, Health, and Reproductive Outcome and Population Dynamics

Exploring the life stories of chimpanzee individuals via bones and teeth and from the perspective of observed behaviors during life illustrates the mosaic nature of an individual's contribution to population-level features that characterize a skeletal series; the behaviors that can and cannot be determined from the teeth and bones; and the importance of field observations in assessing an individual's role in population dynamics.

GILKA AND MADAM BEE    Gilka apparently died as a result of chronic poor health. Madam Bee died of injuries sustained during intergroup conflicts (Zihlman et al. 1990).

Shoulder and forelimb bones in each female show pronounced left/right asymmetries in external linear and areal measurements, whole bone weights, and internal dimensions of cross-sectional areas and mineralization. Whereas most upper limb variables in other Gombe chimpanzee skeletons show side differences that typically are less than 3%, some features of the skeletons of Gilka and Madam Bee (e.g., mineral content of left and right humeri) exhibit more than 10 times this percent difference. The position and extent of left-

right skeletal asymmetries are a result of changes in bone size, shape, mineralization, and internal structure due to skeletal responses to loss of muscle activity, associated movement abilities, and load-bearing and, in addition, probable increased weight-bearing on the opposite limb. The individualized patterns of side differences show that different muscles (or parts of muscles) were affected at different stages in these females' lives (Morbeck et al. 1991). The bones record that, when alive, Gilka and Madam Bee each experienced long-term, unilateral, partial paralyses of forelimb muscles.

Bones reveal movement and weight-bearing potentials, but field observations confirm actual behaviors and how these affect survival and reproductive outcome. Locomotor, postural, and manipulative abilities are life history attributes and are essential to expressed survival behaviors. They also directly underlie reproductive efforts. Like many other mammals, primate mothers protect, feed, and socialize their infants. But chimpanzees and other nonhuman primates also carry their infants, and they rely on their hands for grooming their youngsters. Their infants, in turn, use well-developed hands and feet to grip their mothers; they go everywhere with her. These interactive behaviors, which are negotiated by both the mother and her offspring, are an important component of the mother's reproductive success and, at the same time, her infant's survival (Morbeck 1994).

Field observations document that paralytic poliomyelitis constrained locomotor/postural/manipulative behaviors (Goodall 1971, 1983, 1986; Morbeck et al. 1991). Gilka had forelimb difficulties as a growing juvenile. She later gave birth to several infants. She was unable to use her right forelimb fully and had difficulty in caring for a newborn infant. Each of her infants died. Although at least two of these infants were killed by Passion and Pom (Goodall 1986, 1990, 1992; see below), they died, in part, as a result of Gilka's disability (Goodall 1986; Zihlman et al. 1990).

Madam Bee's left forelimb became partially paralyzed as an adult after she had reared two daughters. Both infants born after she contracted paralytic poliomyelitis died. Madam Bee's two daughters, however, survived to adulthood and one is known to have offspring of her own (Goodall 1986).

The poliovirus and its paralytic disease affected the neuromusculoskeletal systems of Gilka and Madam Bee in the same way. The timing of the disease during the life cycle, on the other hand, compromised each female's health and contributions to the next generation of chimpanzees at Gombe in different ways. Madam Bee left a direct genetic legacy; Gilka did not (Morbeck et al. 1991).

PASSION  Passion died of an illness that cannot be read in her teeth and bones. Her skeleton is similar to other Gombe chimpanzee females in terms of cranial capacity and tooth size. The postcranial skeleton is distinguished by apparently narrow shoulders and un-usually short limb bones. Bone mineral indices are sub-stantially less than means for the pooled-sex sample but are similar to other "normal" females who died before reaching old age. Left/right side differences in dimensions of forelimb bone lengths and areas lack clearly defined directional asymmetry. Few distinctive nonmetric features of Passion's skeleton can be ex-plained by particular life events.

Field observers described Passion as asocial, lacking close female companions, uneasy and wary of males, an extraordinarily inefficient mother, and Gombe's most notorious character—a "cannibal" (Goodall 1986, 1990). Psychologists characterized her as isolated and aggressive, a "deviant" chimp (Buirski and Plutchik 1991). None of these biosocial behaviors are preserved in her teeth and bones!

Passion was perceived to be a poor mother, but her daughter Pom grew to maturity. Passion later gave birth to two sons who also survived infancy and now have grown. If she still were alive, Passion might have enjoyed grandchildren.

Passion's genetic legacy represents only part of how she influenced local population dynamics. Pas-sion and Pom were observed to attack other females and to steal, kill, and eat at least three (possibly more) chimpanzee infants (Goodall 1983, 1986, 1990). Most of the cohort of individuals born in the mid-1970s did not survive.

Chimpanzees at Gombe and other localities are known to kill and eat infants of their own species. When youngsters are eaten by adult males, as observed by Gombe researchers, the chimpanzees typically have attacked "outsider" females. The initial focus is on the mother; her infant dies as a result of the conflict. Pas-sion and Pom, in contrast, attacked mothers from the same community. Their apparent interest was to obtain infants for meat (Goodall 1986).

Passion's cannibalistic activities had a considerable impact on the Gombe chimpanzee population. After she stopped her attacks, a "baby boom," as described by Goodall, soon followed. Unlike the usual staggering of births within the group, many youngsters now have grown to maturity at about the same time, thus creat-ing an unusual set of social dynamics. Passion's life story shows that even short-term fluctuations in popu-lation size and age-graded structure, such as stimu-lated by her asocial behaviors, can affect long-term group social interactions, mating opportunities, and reproductive outcome of other individuals.

## DESCRIBING AND EXPLAINING VARIATION: WHAT DOES IT ALL MEAN?

Gombe chimpanzees share life history attributes with other members of the genus *Pan*. The skeleton is func-tionally integrated with all aspects of an animal's life from its early development in utero to infancy through old age as an individual interacts with physical, bio-logical, and social environment. It tracks an indi-vidual's life ways and life cycle—both its species capabilities and its own health and experiences throughout the life stages.

Adult tooth and bone size, shape, internal struc-ture, and mineralization are products of a species' ge-netically guided pattern formation and coordinated, timed program of increase in cell number, size, content, and specialization during preadult life stages. The physiology and anatomy of growth and maturation (and later reproductive efforts during adulthood) par-allel changes in biobehavioral survival features during the life course (Morbeck 1994, 1997a, b).

Chimpanzee teeth and the brain, for example, de-velop and grow to maturity well before the postcranial skeleton achieves adult form and size. Growth patterns are similar in all common chimpanzees. But environ-mental factors can affect the times of onset, durations, and rates of change at any stage of an individual's life. Extended periods of gestation, infancy, childhood, ado-lescence, and old age expand the potential for environ-mentally influenced variation (Morbeck and Zihlman 1989; Zihlman et al. 1990). A mosaic of skeletal similari-ties and differences among individuals, females and males, their populations and subspecies, and between species in the genus *Pan* reveals the pattern and range of individual/group interactions with both short- (i.e., lifetime) and long-term (i.e., generational time) multi-faceted adjustments to environmental conditions.

*Pan troglodytes* is distinguished skeletally from *Pan paniscus* by its larger braincase and teeth (and face/jaws that house teeth; Coolidge 1933; see Shea et al. 1993 for a recent discussion). Shoulder, trunk, pelvis, and limb bone dimensions are more variable (Groves 1986; Mor-beck and Zihlman 1989).

The Gombe chimpanzee skeletal series represents a local breeding population of two generations of *Pan troglodytes schweinfurthii* chimpanzees living at the east-ern edge of the species' geographic distribution. Both genetic and environmental factors contribute to the pattern of skeletal variation reported here.

A genetic interpretation of Gombe features empha-sizes the increasing isolation of a small population of slow-growing, late to reproduce, long-lived primates. Every individual is important to survival of the group. This situation potentially enhances genetic drift as a way to alter variation through time. It also may lead to reduction in genetic diversity (see below for a discussion of a test of this hypothesis; see also Korn 1994; Soulé 1987) and possible adverse consequences for production of viable offspring.

An ecological explanation of the patterns of skeletal variation at Gombe, in contrast, highlights the role of natural selection and the evolutionary history of physiological/anatomical adaptability to maintain functioning individuals throughout the life stages (see Goodman et al. 1988; Morbeck 1997). The nature and extent of variation are preserved and can be measured in the skeletons.

The average long bone dimensions of Gombe chimpanzee (and body weights obtained when alive) when compared to those of other *Pan* skeletal series indicate small overall body size. Intrapopulational variation at Gombe further reveals variation associated with sex differences, changing environmental influences on individual growth and maturation as shown by differences associated with decade of birth, and individual expressions of skeletal physiology and anatomy associated with unique life stories.

## Energy, Nutrition, and Skeletal Biology

All individuals require energy to maintain life and to fulfill changing biosocial roles throughout the life stages. In addition to daily life activities, youngsters especially need energy for body systems to grow and develop. Adults invest in maintaining group life, mating, and rearing of offspring.

An adult female, as with all mammals and especially primates with a big-brained, biosocially dependent infant, needs additional energy to give her infant a good start in life. She promotes her infant's growth and well-being by providing food, warmth and protection, transportation, and socialization to become part of the local population. From the young chimpanzee's viewpoint, growth and development during in utero and infancy are tied to its mother's biosocial health/well-being and her access to and use of ecological (and social) resources during pregnancy and lactation. Later, its skills of food acquisition, physical activity, and biomechanical loading conditions, as well as psychosocial and physiological health during the more independent childhood and adolescent years contribute to adult body/skeletal size, proportions, and skeletal health status.

If energy levels are inadequate and the body no longer can adjust to particular environmental conditions, an individual is said to be "stressed." Physiological disruptions usually are responses to disease and malnutrition and injury and can also be stimulated by difficult social situations. Physiological disturbances preserved in skeletal anatomy especially are evident when they occur early in life, are severe, or are long term. Bone growth or tooth development may stop or slow down when a youngster's immune system confronts infection or as a consequence of malnutrition when the digestive system is unable to process adequate energy for normal growth (Martorell 1989; Simmons 1990). In adults, maintenance and repair mechanisms may be compromised.

Teeth and bones record these kinds of continuous biochemical and physical interactions with the environment. Some biological (e.g., genetic diseases) and environmental (e.g., certain kinds of nutritional, mineral, and vitamin deficiencies) conditions are marked clearly in the skeleton. Other acute or chronic health conditions, including less than optimal nutrition, produce systemic physiological adjustments and are read in the skeleton only as generalized responses (Morbeck 1997).

Much of the skeletal variation among individuals reflects nutritionally mediated responses to a variety of environmental conditions. Patterns of variation emerge as individuals are aggregated and analyzed statistically in groups that represent species, geographically different populations within species, and local populations through generational time.

Nutritional status is multifaceted; it relates to quality as well as quantity of food and water, minerals, and vitamins that meet the energetic requirements determined by species life history attributes. An individual's general health status, at any slice of time during its life story, reflects body condition primarily as a result of nutrient intake, absorption, and use.

Malnutrition results from imbalances in species-typical energy needs. It can relate to nutrient excesses in addition to the more common perception of, first, inadequate food or the inability to process and use it and, second, lack of an appropriate mix for a balanced diet. Less than adequate nutrition for growth and/or maintenance can have a cascade effect on many body functions. Undernutrition in humans, for example, is linked to a decrease in energy obtained and used, lowered production of growth hormone, and suppression of the immune system (Goodman et al. 1988; Saunders and Hoppa 1993). These synergistic relationships can result in delayed or truncated maturity of different body systems.

People who grow to maturity in less than ideal environmental conditions for reaching our species' potential size—that is, compromised socioeconomic situations, poor access to natural resources and especially quality food and water, high frequencies of infectious diseases, and so on—respond by "slowing" the processes (i.e., rate changes) including a delay in achievement of reproductive maturity (Tanner 1990). Bone size may be smaller than "average" (standard reference samples often are controversial). In addition, teeth may show disruptions in enamel formation. But exact causes of the expression of bone size or tooth anatomy usually cannot be determined.

Limb bone sizes frequently are compromised. Limbs achieve full adult size late in the growth trajectory and with shorter lengths do not severely impact on survival activities as would, for instance, small and poorly developed brains or teeth. Long bone lengths, in particular, are used by most biologists who work with human skeletal series as nonspecific markers of infant or childhood physiological adjustments (reviewed in Saunders and Hoppa 1993).

Weight and stature, recorded as body size and reflected in skeletal size, also are variable among humans. The extent of differences in "average" size between females and males varies under different environmental conditions (Borgognini-Tarli and Repetto 1997; Hall 1982).

Some researchers characterize small body/skeletal size as an adaptive strategy to cope with fewer available nutrients in resource-deficient environments (Stini 1975). This flexible response is part of the physiology and anatomy of species-defined process of growth and maturation and is critical to growth of subadults, maintenance and repair of body systems in all individuals, and reproduction by adults. From the perspective of natural history and evolution, it is the *extent* of phenotypic plasticity, not small body size itself, that results from natural selection (reviewed in Morbeck 1997).

Study of chimpanzee skeletal biology and life stories shows the same relationships. Chimpanzees, like humans, are long-lived with considerable time for environmental stressors to affect individual lives at different times and in different ways. Variation in growth, development, maintenance, and repair, as observed and measured in adult skeletal features, ultimately relates to, first, an individual's energy acquisition and use and, second, the amount of energy available under particular environmental situations. Understanding the ecological setting at Gombe, including past and current changes in food and availability of other resources necessary for sustaining chimpanzee individuals and their populations, helps to explain the observed patterns of skeletal variation.

## Gombe National Park, Tanzania: Chimpanzees Need Trees

The species-defined needs of *Pan troglodytes* for wet season foods from riverine forests and dry season fruits and seeds from woodlands may determine the distrib-

ution of populations (Kano 1971, 1972; cited in Collins and McGrew 1988). Gombe National Park, a 32-square-kilometer park that lies north of Kigoma on the eastern shore of Lake Tanganyika, provides these resources (Goodall 1986).

The Kasekala community chimpanzees, primary subjects of Goodall's long-term behavioral study and of the Gombe skeletal series, spend most of their time in the forests of the middle portions of the park. Here, rugged hills are cut by permanent streams and steep-sided valleys covered with closed forest ("evergreen" or "semi-evergreen") and open or thicket woodland (Clutton-Brock and Gillett 1979; Collins and McGrew 1988).

Gombe chimpanzees rely on the forests during the day for vertical as well as horizontal travel pathways, water from streams and natural tree holes, and fruit and other food found in trees. More than half of the daily activities of these quadrupedal climbing, knuckle-walking omnivores involves foraging both on the ground and in the trees (Goodall 1986; Wrangham and Smuts 1980; see Hunt 1994 for a review of bipedal posture while feeding and common chimpanzee anatomy associated with arboreality; see also cited references). Trees also are essential for nest making and sleeping at night. In addition, tree cover isolates areas for socialization and other activities, including females giving birth and, in the past, protection from large predators.

Gombe chimpanzees feed primarily on seasonal fruits concentrated in trees (some are human cultigens, see below), but also eat leaves and other plant parts (in some cases, as "medicinal cures" [Wrangham and Goodall 1989]). Animal protein includes termites, birds' eggs, and meat obtained from hunting, killing, and eating monkeys and other mammals (and, as discussed above, infant chimpanzees) (Goodall 1986; Stanford et al. 1994; Teleki 1973; Wrangham and Bergman-Riss 1990).

Gombe chimpanzees also use forest products as tools. They recognize form-function relationships and anticipate the outcomes of toolmaking and tool-using behaviors. Branches, twigs, bark, vines, leaves, and grass are used to probe for insects, soak up water, clean soiled body parts, and accentuate social encounters, including dominance displays (Goodall 1986; McGrew 1992; Morbeck 1994).

Individual and group ranging patterns and food item choices vary with natural fluctuations in the availability and distribution of potential foods or other resources through time and across geographic space (i.e., daily, seasonal, year-to-year variation). For example, strong winds accompanying rainy season storms and natural fires uproot or destroy trees and, with them, food and other resources. These new forest openings encourage growth of different kinds of colonizing vegetation. Grasses, which grow in cleared areas, in particular, cannot substitute for big trees. They offer little food and no cover for chimpanzees (Goodall 1986).

## Gombe Chimpanzees and People

Fishermen, farmers, and their families have lived along the eastern shore of Lake Tanganyika near Kigoma for a long time. People cleared patches of forest to plant crops and to collect wood/charcoal for fuel. Historical data indicate that these activities increased about 1940 (reported from the literature by Collins and McGrew 1988).

From a chimpanzee's viewpoint, cutting of large trees by humans rapidly diminishes, fragments, and alters their preferred closed forest/woodland habitat. Compressed foraging ranges are accompanied by changes in food composition, availability, and distribution. Although human cultigens, such as mangoes and oil palm nuts, have appeared as new foods, the reduction and break up of the forest potentially can limit available food and other forest resources and, in addition, decrease activity levels of chimpanzees.

Furthermore, population density has increased. Large predators have disappeared, primarily as a result of human activities, and since they live in the park, chimpanzees are "protected." With higher densities, insects, intestinal worms, and the smallest predators, that is, bacterial and viral microorganisms—ironically, often with life cycles facilitated by human behaviors—pose an increasing threat (File et al. 1976; Goodall 1983, 1986; McGrew et al. 1989; Morbeck et al. 1991). Field observations suggest that infectious pathogens that can be transmitted from humans (or other primates) to chimpanzees especially affect respiratory and gastrointestinal systems; chimpanzees often die with common cold or pneumonia-like symptoms (Goodall 1983, 1986, 1987/1988, 1988/1989). During a visit to Gombe in 1987, I observed sniffling-sneezing tourists within only a few feet of the chimpanzees. Such close encounters can have long-term effects on chimpanzee individuals, their lives, and their population.

Decrease in habitat also can increase competition for food, cover, or other resources. Health may be diminished. Social and other interactions among individuals may change as well as those between females and males within groups, among various chimpanzee groups (e.g., intergroup conflicts), and among chimpanzees and other species (e.g., baboons and red colobus monkeys) that rely on the same geographic space and forest products (see Goodall 1986 and cited references).

Researchers and field assistants who have observed (and interacted) with chimpanzees at close range for more than 30 years also may have influenced their subjects' lives. The well-known story of Mike kicking kerosene cans to create an unusual noise and intimidate his peers shows use of human material culture integrated within chimpanzee social displays. Another example centers on food distribution. Although the effects of banana-feeding programs during the early years of Goodall's study remain unclear (Power 1991; Teleki et al. 1976; Wrangham 1974), the number of observed aggressive encounters associated with this concentrated food source increased (Goodall 1986). Banana-feeding programs could have affected individuals both in terms of ongoing social interactions and physiological/anatomical features preserved in skeletons (Morbeck unpublished data).

As in the past, people continue to exploit the park's resources. Park employees and their families live in a nearby village. As many as 1000 fishermen move along the lakeshore (Goodall 1988/1989). Scientists spend months or years studying animals and plants. Increasing numbers of tourists and photographers come for short visits to see the chimpanzees.

## Skeletal Responses to a Changing Habitat

Gombe chimpanzee individuals represented in the skeletal series grew to maturity under varying ecological conditions, especially as related to human activities. Overall small body size, expressed skeletally in short limb bones when compared to other *Pan troglodytes*, may reflect long-term, ongoing constraints on vertical/horizontal space and food and other nutrients for a species-typical balanced diet. Skeletal anatomy also may reflect high population density combined with increased chances for infectious diseases, parasite loads, and trauma associated in social-ecological competition, including conflict situations.

Individuals who were youngsters in the 1920s and 1930s prior to the increase in human activities at Gombe about 1940 achieved limb bone sizes that apparently are closer to the *Pan troglodytes* species potential (although still smaller than "average" common chimpanzees). Most chimpanzees born in later decades seem to have grown to maturity under more difficult ecological conditions. Yet the details of their lives cannot be fully reconstructed.

The small amount of difference in long bone lengths and braincase size between male and female Gombe chimpanzees is difficult to explain since males exhibit greater body weight, especially in the trunk (also species features of canine size and bone mineral content). The answer may be in the nature of individual variation and the importance of understanding each chimpanzee's life story as it responds to particular environments. Ecogeographic variation as a source of similarities and differences in craniodental, body size, and body proportion features in nonhuman primates only recently has been investigated in detail (e.g., see Albrecht et al. 1990; Albrecht and Miller 1993; Ravosa et al. 1993; see also Wainwright and Reilly 1994). In addition, as illustrated by Gombe chimpanzees, events during an individual's life that occur by chance in addition to more obvious factors associated with socio-ecological interactions especially may be important. This is highlighted by the life stories of Gilka, Madam Bee, and Passion.

### More Changes at Gombe

Today Gombe National Park and its inhabitants have become an almost isolated ecological community. Once-forested hillsides adjacent to park boundaries mostly are bare—a result of an increasing human population's need for fuel wood and food via farming (McGrew et al. 1989). Houses and cultivation "surround" (along with the lake) the park (Goodall 1988/1989, 1992). LAND-SAT 1984 images and recent on-site observations in the Kigoma region show that deforested land characterizes 20–60% of drainage areas next to the lake (Cohen et al. 1993). It is unlikely that the forest ecosystem will recover. Regionally, primary forest has disappeared and soils have been degraded by use of fires to create fields (sometimes becoming uncontrolled), by abandonment of cultivated plots, and by severe erosion resulting from poor conservation methods (e.g., lack of terracing on hillsides) (Cohen et al. 1993). From the perspective of chimpanzees, survival behaviors are altered, reproductive potential is compromised, and continuation of the population is threatened.

Censused at the end of 1991 (Stanford et al. 1994), the Kasakela community included only 42 chimpanzees with a home range of 18 square kilometers. Chimpanzee population replacement rate, even in the most suitable environments, is slow. Geographic isolation limits mating opportunities. Inbreeding and its genetic consequences also may contribute to compromised health and population decline.

Studies of within-group DNA variation of the current Kasakela community (via recovery of shed hair) show a high degree of relatedness, especially among adult males. This is predicted from field observations; males typically remain in the natal group. *Pan troglodytes* females, as documented in other field studies, generally leave their respective groups at the time of reproductive maturity. Gombe females, in contrast, are closely related. Fewer females may be dispersing to other groups in response to recent habitat

changes (Morin and colleagues 1993, 1994; see also Morin 1993).[1]

## BACK TO BONES, TEETH, AND FOSSILS

Skeletons provide clues about life stories and thus link an individual chimpanzee with population-level phenomena. Studies of a chimpanzee's skeleton, combined with recorded field observations during its life, illustrate how anatomy and behavior affect survival and reproduction in the context of the physical, biological, and social environments at Gombe. Good health/well-being and long lives maximize the potential for successful reproduction. Disease, injury, and earlier-than-expected death can shorten an individual's reproductive span, reduce opportunities to mate successfully, and limit a female's ability to rear an infant. Individuals who die as infants or juveniles never have a chance to contribute directly to their population's gene pool.

Sherry Washburn will appreciate the intertwining of anatomical, behavioral, ecological, and genetic data from a well-known population of our closest living relatives. The advantage of studying bones and teeth of known chimpanzee individuals is that we can confirm our interpretation of form-function relationships and other aspects of skeletal biology with documented species/sex-defined life history characters and, in addition, events during an individual's life that are known to influence anatomy. The Gombe chimpanzee case study helps to determine what the skeletons "meant" to their owners. It shows us how to begin to distinguish the functional and evolutionary significance of skeletal features in fossil remains of our own ancestors.

As we study fossils, we now can begin to ask more appropriate questions about the nature of variation during the life cycle, between females and males among local populations, and among higher taxa. Sherry Washburn showed me, first, how to link bones and anatomy with behaviors as expressed in particular environments; and, second, how to use the comparative, functional, and evolutionary approach to explain both past and present variation among humans and our pri-

---

[1]Long-term field observations of Gombe chimpanzees show family relationships. Females and their offspring are known and we can guess paternity from observations of male/female consort behaviors (Goodall 1986). Studies of nuclear and mitochondrial DNA of chimpanzees living at Gombe now provide data on paternity exclusion (Morin and colleagues 1993, 1994). Future extraction of DNA from bones of individuals that make up the Gombe skeletal series will clarify genetic relationships in the sample (Hagelberg et al. 1991; see also Pääbo 1993).

mate relatives (Washburn 1951, 1982). Now we can combine his theoretical construct with a broader framework and detailed studies of modern primates that record life-long interactions of life history attributes.

## ACKNOWLEDGMENTS

I thank Sherry Washburn for teaching me how to think about what it means to be human and how we got to be the way we are. And I thank him for showing me how primates learn and for encouraging my commitment to teaching (see Washburn 1993).

One of the joys of developing the Gombe chimpanzee skeletal biology and life history project emerges from the nature of multifaceted and multidisciplinary research. Many colleagues contributed to data collection, analyses, and interpretation: W. Birkby, A. Galloway, J. Goodall, R. Jurmain, L. Kilgore, J. Lobick, K. Mowbray, C. Payne, W. A. Stini, D. R. Sumner, J. Weber, A. L. Zihlman, and student assistants at the University of Arizona and the University of California, Santa Cruz.

I also thank the government of Tanzania, and, in particular, the director of the Tanzanian National Parks and director of Wildlife for access to chimpanzee skeletons. J. Goodall, A. Collins, and the Tanzanian Field Staff, Gombe National Park, made skeletons available. Their studies of behaviors of the same individuals when alive give the teeth and bones real-life meaning. The following institutions gave access to comparative skeletal collections: American Museum of Natural History; Musée Royale de l'Afrique Centrale; Museum of Comparative Zoology, Harvard University; and the Smithsonian Institution.

Thanks to J. Olsen, who provided me with incredible "hired hands," and M. Bezanson for everything she is and does. Thanks also to D. Sample and E. Stamp, who produced the manuscript from tape-recorded messages, cut and pasted hard copy, and weird, chicken-scratch writing.

A. Galloway, J. Hoffman, V. Landau, V. Morbeck, J. Underwood, and especially P. Martin and the Desert Laboratory folks continue to provide much-appreciated intellectual stimulation, patience and logistical help, and good humor for all of my endeavors.

Financial support for this research has been provided by the L. S. B. Leakey Foundation, the University of Arizona (Social and Behavioral Sciences Research Institute, Office of the Vice President for Research, Main Campus Biomedical Research Support Grant, and the Department of Anthropology), the University of California, Santa Cruz (Division of Social Sciences and Faculty Research Committee), and the Wenner-Gren Foundation for Anthropological Research.

Finally, thanks to editors S. Strum, D. Lindburg, and D. Hamburg for their good work (and persistence).

## LITERATURE CITED

Albrecht, G. H., Jenkins, P. D., and Godfrey, L. R. (1990). Ecogeographic size variation among the living and subfossil prosimians of Madagascar. *Am. J. Primatol. 22:* 1–50.

Albrecht, G. H., and Miller, J. M. A. (1993). Geographic variation in primates. A review with implications for interpreting fossils. In W. H. Kimbel and L. B. Martin (eds.), *Species, Species Concepts, and Primate Evolution.* New York: Plenum Press, pp. 123–161.

Almquist, A. (1974). Sexual differences in the anterior dentition in African primates. *Amer. J. Phys. Anthropol. 40:* 359–368.

Borgognini-Tarli, S., and Repetto, E. (1997). Sex differences in human populations: Change through time. In M. E. Morbeck, A. Galloway, and A. L. Zihlman (eds.), *The Evolving Female: A Life-History Perspective.* Princeton, NJ: Princeton University Press, pp. 198–208.

Buirski, P., and Plutchik, R. (1991). Measurement of deviant behavior in a Gombe chimpanzee: Relation to later behavior. *Primates 32:* 207–211.

Clutton-Brock, T. H., and Gillett, J. B. (1979). A survey of forest composition in the Gombe National Park, Tanzania, *Afr. J. Ecol. 17:* 131–158.

Cohen, A. S., Bills, R., Cocquyt, C. Z., and Caljon, A. G. (1993). The impact of sediment pollution on biodiversity in Lake Tanganyika. *Conservation Biology 7:* 667–677.

Collins, D. A., and McGrew, W. C. (1988). Habitats of three groups of chimpanzees (*Pan troglodytes*) in western Tanzania. *J. Hum. Evol. 17:* 553–574.

Coolidge, H. (1933). *Pan paniscus.* Pygmy chimpanzee from south of the Congo River. *Am. J. Phys. Anthropol. 18:* 1–57.

Cramer, D. L. (1977). Craniofacial morphology of *Pan paniscus. Contributions to Primatology,* Vol. 10. Basel: S. Karger.

File, S. K., McGrew, W. C., and Tutin, C. E. G. (1976). The intestinal parasites of a community of feral chimpanzees, *Pan troglodytes schweinfurthii. J. Parasit. 62:* 259–261.

Galloway, A., Morbeck, M. E., and Zihlman, A. L. (1993). Sex differences in the vertebral column of Gombe chimpanzees. *Amer. J. Phys. Anthropol.* (Suppl.) *16:* 90–91.

Galloway, A., Stini, W. A., Fox, S. C., and Stein, P. (1990). Stature loss among an older United States population and its relation to bone mineral status. *Amer. J. Phys. Anthropol. 83:* 467–476.

Goodall, J. van Lawick (1971). *In the Shadow of Man.* London: Collins.

Goodall, J. (1983). Population dynamics during a 15-year period in one community of free-living chimpanzees in the Gombe National Park, Tanzania. *Z. Tierpsychol. 61:* 1–60.

Goodall, J. (1986). *The Chimpanzee of Gombe. Patterns of Behavior.* Cambridge, MA: Harvard University Press.

Goodall, J. (1987/1988). *The Jane Goodall Institute Winter Newsletter.* Jane Goodall Institute for Wildlife, Research, Education, and Conservation.

Goodall, J. (1988/1989). *The Jane Goodall Institute Fall/Winter Newsletter.* Jane Goodall Institute for Wildlife, Research, Education, and Conservation.

Goodall, J. (1990). *Through a Window. My Thirty Years with the Chimpanzees of Gombe.* Boston: Houghton Mifflin.

Goodall, J. (1992). *The Chimpanzee: The Living Link Between "Man" and "Beast."* Third Edinburgh Medal Address. Edinburgh: Edinburgh University Press.

Goodman, A. H., Thomas, R. B., Swedlund, A. C., and Armelagos, G. J. (1988). Biocultural perspectives on stress in prehistoric, historic, and contemporary population research. *Yearbk. Phys. Anthropol 31:* 169–202.

Groves, C. P. (1986). Systematics of the great apes. In D. R. Swindler and J. Irwin (eds.), *Comparative Primate Biology, Vol. I: Systematics, Evolution, and Anatomy.* New York: Alan R. Liss, pp. 187–217.

Hagelberg, E., Gray, J. C., and Jeffreys, A. J. (1991). Identification of the skeletal remains of a murder victim by DNA analysis. *Nature.* 352: 427–429.

Hall, B. K. (1988). The embryonic development of bone. *Amer. Sci.* 76: 174–181.

Hall, R. L., ed. (1982). *Sexual Dimorphism in Homo sapiens: A Question of Size.* New York: Praeger.

Hunt, K. D. (1994). The evolution of human bipedality: Ecology and functional morphology. *J. Hum. Evol. 26:* 183–202.

Johanson, D. C. (1974a). *An Odontological Study of the Chimpanzee with Some Implications for Hominoid Evolution.* Ph.D. dissertation, University of Chicago.

Johanson, D. C. (1974b). Some metric aspects of the permanent and deciduous dentition of the pygmy chimpanzee (*Pan paniscus*). *Amer. J. Phys. Anthropol. 41:* 39–48.

Jurmain, R. (1989). Trauma, degenerative disease, and other pathologies among the Gombe chimpanzees. *Amer. J. Phys. Anthropol. 80:* 229–237.

Kano, T. (1971). Distribution of primates on the eastern shore of Lake Tanganyika. *Primates 12:* 281–304.

Kano, T. (1972). Distribution and adaptation of the chimpanzee on the eastern shore of Lake Tanganyika. *Kyoto Univ. Afr. Stud.* 7: 37–129.

Kilgore, L. (1989). Dental pathologies in ten free-ranging chimpanzees from Gombe National Park, Tanzania. *Amer. J. Phys. Anthropol. 80:* 219–227.

Korn, H. (1994). Genetic, demographic, spatial, environmental, and catastrophic effects on the survival probability of small populations of mammals. In H. Remmert (ed.), *Minimum Animal Populations.* New York: Springer-Verlag, pp. 33–49.

Martorell, R. (1989). Body size, adaptation and function. *Hum. Org.* 48: 15–20.

McGrew, W. C. (1992). *Chimpanzee Material Culture: Implications for Human Evolution.* Cambridge: Cambridge University Press.

McGrew, W. C., Tutin, C. E. G., Collins, D. A., and File, S. K. (1989). Intestinal parasites of sympatric *Pan troglodytes* and *Papio* spp. at two sites: Gombe (Tanzania) and Mt. Assirik (Senegal). *Amer. J. Primatol.* 17: 147–155.

Morbeck, M. E. (1991). Bones, gender, and life history. In D. Walde and N. Willows (eds.), *The Archaeology of Gender.* Chacmool, Archaeological Association of the University of Calgary. Calgary: University of Calgary, pp. 39–45.

Morbeck, M. E. (1994). Object manipulation, gestures, posture, and locomotion. In D. Quiatt and J. Itani (eds.), *Hominid Culture in Primate Perspective.* Denver: University Press of Colorado, pp. 117–135.

Morbeck, M. E. (1997a). Life history, the individual, and evolution. In M. E. Morbeck, A. Galloway, and A. L. Zihlman (eds.), *The Evolving Female: A Life-History Perspective.* Princeton, NJ: Princeton Univ. Press, pp. 3–14.

Morbeck, M. E. (1997b). Reading life history in teeth, bones, and fossils. In M. E. Morbeck, A. Galloway, and A. L. Zihlman (eds.), *The Evolving Female: A Life-History Perspective.* Princeton, NJ: Princeton Univ. Press, pp. 117–131.

Morbeck, M. E., Galloway, A., Mowbray, K. M., and Zihlman, A. L. (1994). Skeletal asymmetry and hand preference during termite fishing by Gombe chimpanzees. *Primates 35:* 99–103.

Morbeck, M. E., Galloway, A., and Zihlman, A. L. (1992). Gombe chimpanzee sex differences in the pelvis and observations of pubic and preauricular areas. *Primates 33:* 129–132.

Morbeck, M. E., and Zihlman, A. L. (1989). Body size and proportions in chimpanzees, with special reference to *Pan troglodytes schweinfurthii* from Gombe National Park, Tanzania. *Primates 30:* 369–382.

Morbeck, M. E., Zihlman, A. L., and Galloway, A. (1993). Biographies read in bones: Biology and life history of Gombe chimpanzees. In V. Landau (ed.), *ChimpanZoo Conference Proceedings (1992).* Tucson, AZ: Jane Goodall Institute, pp. 62–88.

Morbeck, M. E., Zihlman, A. L., Sumner, D. R., and Galloway, A. (1991). Poliomyelitis and skeletal asymmetry in Gombe chimpanzees. *Primates 32:* 77–91.

Morin, P. A. (1993). Reproductive strategies in chimpanzees. *Yearbk. Phys. Anthropol. 36:* 179–212.

Morin, P. A., Moore, J. J., Chakraborty, R., Li, J., Goodall, J., and Woodruff, D. S. (1994). Kin selection, social structure, gene flow, and the evolution of chimpanzees. *Science 265:* 1193–1201.

Morin, P. A., Wallis, J., Moore, J. J., Chakraborty, R., and Woodruff, D. A. (1993). Non-invasive sampling and DNA amplification for paternity exclusion, community structure, and phylogeography in wild chimpanzees. *Primates 34:* 347–356.

Pääbo, S. (1993). Ancient DNA. *Sci. Amer.* 269: 86–92.

Power, M. (1991). *The Egalitarians: Human and Chimpanzee. An anthropological view of social organization.* Cambridge: Cambridge University Press.

Ravosa, M. J., Meyers, D. M., and Glander, K. E. (1993). Relative growth of the limbs and trunk in sifakas: Heterochronic, ecological, and functional considerations. *Amer. J. Phys. Anthropol. 92:* 499–520.

Saul, F. P., and Saul, J. M. (1989). Osteobiography: A Maya example. In M. Y. Iscan and K. A. R. Kennedy (eds.), *Reconstruction of Life from the Skeleton.* New York: Alan R. Liss, pp. 287–302.

Saunders, S. R., and Hoppa, R. D. (1993). Growth deficit in survivors and non-survivors: Biological mortality bias in subadult skeletal samples. *Yearbk. Phys. Anthropol. 36:* 127–151.

Shea, B. T. (1982). *Growth and Size Allometry in the African Pongidae: Cranial and Postcranial Analyses.* Ph.D. dissertation. Duke University.

Shea, B. T., Leigh, S. R., and Groves, C. P. (1993). Multivariate craniometric variation in chimpanzees. Implication for species identification in paleoanthropology. In W. H. Kimbel and L. B. Martin (eds.), *Species, Species Concepts, and Primate Evolution.* New York: Plenum Press, pp. 265–296.

Simmons, D. J., ed. (1990). *Nutrition and Bone Development.* New York: Oxford University Press.

Smith, B. H. (1992). Life history and the evolution of human maturation. *Evol. Anthropol. 1:* 134–142.

Soulé, M. E., ed. (1987). *Viable Populations for Conservation.* Cambridge: Cambridge University Press.

SPSS-X (1988). *SPSS-X.* Chicago: SPSS Inc.

Stanford, C. B., Wallis, J., Matama, H., and Goodall, J. (1994). Patterns of predation of chimpanzees on red colobus monkeys in Gombe National Park 1982–1991. *Amer. J. Phys. Anthropol. 94:* 213–228.

Stearns, S. (1992). *The Evolution of Life Histories.* Oxford: Oxford University Press.

Stini, W. A. (1975). Adaptive strategies of human populations under nutritional stress. In E. S. Watts, F. E. Johnston, and G. W. Lasker (eds.), *Biosocial Interrelations in Population Adaptation.* The Hague: Mouton.

Sumner, D. R., Morbeck, M. E., and Lobick, J. J. (1989). Apparent age-related bone loss among adult Gombe chimpanzee females. *Amer. J. Phys. Anthropol. 79:* 225–234.

Tanner, J. M. (1990). *Foetus into Man: Physical Growth from Conception to Maturity.* Cambridge, MA: Harvard University Press.

Teleki, G. (1973). *The Predatory Behavior of Wild Chimpanzees.* Lewisburg, PA: Bucknell University Press.

Teleki, G., Hunt Jr., E. E., and Pfifferling, J. H. (1976). Demographic observations (1963–1973) on the chimpanzees of Gombe National Park, Tanzania. *J. Hum. Evol. 5:* 559–598.

Wainwright, P. C., and Reilly, S. M., eds. (1994). *Ecological Morphology. Integrative Organismal Biology.* Chicago: University of Chicago Press.

Washburn, S. L. (1951). The new physical anthropology. *Trans. NY Acad. Sci. 13:* 298–304.

Washburn, S. L. (1982). Human evolution. *Perspec. Biol. Med. 25:* 583–602.

Washburn, S. L. (1993). Evolution and education. In A. J. Almquist and A. Manyak (eds.), *Milestones in Human Evolution.* Prospect Heights, IL: Waveland Press, pp. 223–240.

Wrangham, R. W. (1974). Artificial feeding of chimpanzees and baboons in their natural habitat. *Anim. Behav. 22:* 83–93.

Wrangham, R. W., and Bergman-Riss, E. (1990). Rates of predation on mammals of Gombe chimpanzees (1972–1975). *Primates 31:* 157–170.

Wrangham, R. W., and Goodall, J. (1989). Chimpanzee use of medicinal leaves. In P. G. Heltne and L. A. Marquadt (eds.), *Understanding Chimpanzees.* Cambridge, MA: Harvard University Press, pp. 22–37.

Wrangham, R. W., and Smuts, B. (1980). Sex differences in the behavioral ecology of chimpanzees in the Gombe National Park, Tanzania. *J. Reprod. Fert.* (Suppl.) *28:* 13–31.

Zihlman, A. L., Morbeck, M. E., and Goodall, J. (1990). Skeletal biology and individual life history of Gombe chimpanzees. *J. Zool., Lond. 221:* 37–61.

*Washburn used comparative anatomy combined with experimentation to produce a truly functional morphology which he then placed in the context of nonhuman primates to generate primate adaptive complexes for the interpretation of hominoids. Tuttle, Hallgrimsson, and Basmajian take up the challenge that was a central part of the new physical anthropology: that the functions of muscles in apes and humans can be checked through experimentation. They use electromyography to better understand the mechanism of knuckle-walking and incorporate these new data to address the questions of whether there is a knuckle-walking complex and, if so, its role in hominoid evolution.*

# 4 Electromyography, Elastic Energy, and Knuckle-walking: A Lesson in Experimental Anthropology

**Russell H. Tuttle**   *Department of Anthropology, The University of Chicago*

**Benedikt Hallgrimsson**   *Department of Anatomy, University of Puerto Rico*

**John V. Basmajian**   *Rehabilitation Centre, Chedoke Hospitals, Hamilton, Ontario*

The functions of . . . muscles in man and ape can be checked. This should be done. (Washburn 1950, p. 71)

The mechanics of Primate locomotion, a subject which has been brought to the fore by the discovery of the Australopithecine fossils, might bear more intensive investigation. Measurements of the size and strength of muscle groups, techniques for recording the weight distribution, cinematographic records of the living animal and possibly electromyography might be able to contribute useful information. (Barnicot 1958, p. 35)

Foretelling future activity was chancy in 1950 and is chancy now. . . . Washburn at that time believed experiment would become important, but it is really not in the nature of physical anthropology to be experimental; . . . work like Tuttle's on muscle performance is representative of what can be done. (Howells 1992, p. 13)

The great challenge of the future will be to move electromyographic, strain gauge and other kinesiological experiments out of the laboratory and into the field or at least to emulate field conditions more fully as one tests arm-swinging, bipedalism, knuckle-walking, vertical climbing and other positional behavior that may have been important in hominoid evolution. (Tuttle et al. 1991, p. 190)

## INTRODUCTION

Sherwood Washburn was a major force in modernizing and humanizing physical anthropology after World War II (Washburn 1950, 1951, 1953, 1963, 1973a; see also Fleagle and Jungers 1982; Haas 1982; Haraway 1988, 1989; Howells 1992; Little 1982; Ribnick 1982). Early in his research career, Washburn, the comparative anatomist, realized that experimentation might open windows to a truly functional morphology, which, combined with knowledge of the naturalistic behavior of primates, might lead to fuller understanding of various primate adaptive complexes and evolutionary careers. And, as an anthropologist, he was particularly interested in detailing the course of human and collateral hominid evolution via strategic functional-morphological interpretations of fossil hominoids.

Although Washburn (1946, 1947; Washburn and Detwiler 1943) was a practicing experimentalist for only a decade, he persistently encouraged students and other colleagues to apply novel biological techniques to evolutionary anthropological problems.

Our pioneering experimental studies of hominoid functional and evolutionary morphology were inspired by Washburn's (1950) remark that questions about the relative functions of muscles in apes and people can be tested experimentally. Having formulated a number of ideas about the functional morphology of pongid and human hands on the basis of numerous dissections (Tuttle 1967, 1969a, b, 1970), we inaugurated the first application of electromyography via indwelling fine-wire electrodes to pongid apes at Yerkes Regional Primate Research Center, in Atlanta, Georgia (Basmajian 1974, 1993; Basmajian and Tuttle 1973; Bourne 1974; Bourne and Cohen 1975; Tuttle and Basmajian 1974 a, b, c, 1975, 1977, 1978 a, b; Tuttle et al. 1972, 1975, 1978, 1979, 1983, 1992). We focused our first series of experiments on the mechanism of knuckle-walking in a young female western gorilla (Tuttle et al. 1972).

## KNUCKLE-WALKING AND KNUCKLE-WALKERS

The African apes *Pan (Gorilla) gorilla, Pan (Pan) troglodytes,* and *Pan (Pan) paniscus,* commonly travel on the ground via a unique quadrupedal positional behavior—knuckle-walking (Tuttle 1965, 1986). Although all healthy gorillas, chimpanzees, and bonobos are obligate knuckle-walkers, individuals variously support their upper body weight on the dorsa of the middle phalanges of digits II, III, IV, and V, which are covered by special pads of friction skin. The metacarpophalangeal joints of load-bearing fingers are overextended moderately to acutely, depending on species and age; metacarpal bones II–V, the carpus and the forearm, are more or less aligned to form a continuous supporting column (Tuttle 1967, 1969a, b). Accordingly, when metacarpophalangeal joints II–V are bearing notable loads, we might expect some support to be provided by one or both of the long digital flexor muscles (*m. flexor digitorum superficialis; m. flexor digitorum profundus*) that pass beneath them (Figure 1).

## ELECTROMYOGRAPHY OF KNUCKLE-WALKING

Despite the efforts of two electromyographic research teams, the supportive role of muscles versus osseoligamentous mechanisms during knuckle-walking is unclear. On the basis of our initial studies with a young female *Pan gorilla,* we concluded the following:

1.  Whereas the flexor carpi radialis muscle acts regularly to support the wrist when the knuckled hand is load-bearing, the flexor carpi ulnaris muscle is either silent or negligibly active

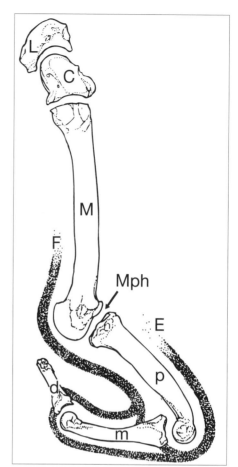

FIGURE 1.    *"Exploded" knuckled third digital ray and associated carpal bones of an adult female chimpanzee. L, lunate; C, capitate; M, metacarpal; Mph, metacarpophalangeal joint; p, proximal phalanx; m, middle phalanx; d, distal phalanx; E, tendon of m. extensor digitorum; F, tendons of mm. flexor digitorum superficialis et profundus.*

during knuckled stances and slow or moderately-paced knuckle-walking. Contraction of the flexor carpi radialis muscle probably resists excessive adduction of the wrist while the knuckled hand is load-bearing (Basmajian and Tuttle 1973; Tuttle and Basmaijian 1974a, 1975; Tuttle and Watts 1985; Tuttle et al. 1972).

2.  Fasciculi of the flexor digitorum superficialis muscle to load-bearing digits (II, III, and sometimes IV) act notably during knuckle-walking progression and stance, while the flexor digitorum profundus muscle is relatively inactive

during knuckling behavior. Accordingly, the flexor digitorum superficialis muscle probably supports the overextended metacar-pophlangeal joints of load-bearing, knuckled digits (Basmajian and Tuttle 1973; Tuttle and Basmajian 1974a, b, 1975; Tuttle and Watts 1985; Tuttle et al 1972).

Susman and Stern (1979, 1980) performed EMG experiments on hand muscles in three subadult *Pan troglodytes* at the State University of New York at Stony Brook (SUNY) and concluded the following:

1. The flexor digitorum superficialis and flexor digitorum profundus muscles of load-bearing digits III and IV are negligibly active during static knuckled postures and slow and moderately paced knuckle-walking, except to clear the floor at the outset of swing phase. They act during the latter half of support phase when chimpanzees knuckle-walk rapidly (Susman and Stern 1979).

2. During knuckle-walking, the interosseous muscles of digits III and IV are variably active during the support phase; and they are generally silent or negligibly active during the swing phase and during quiescent quadrupedal stance. The lumbrical muscle to digit III is negligibly active during knuckling behavior (Susman and Stern 1980).

Recently, Tuttle et al. (1994) presented results of EMG experiments on both *Pan troglodytes and Pan gorilla* that may enable us to explain apparent inconsistencies between the conclusions of the two research teams, particularly regarding the role of the flexor digitorum superficialis muscle during knuckle-walking by chimpanzees.

## Hand Posture During Knuckle-walking

Although differing in detail, during knuckle-walking, the hands of our gorilla and chimpanzee subjects functioned similarly. They pronated their knuckling hands to lie in a coronal plane, with the dorsa facing anteriorly. The chimpanzee occasionally supinated his knuckling hand to varying degrees, but it rarely lay in a sagittal plane, with the dorsum oriented laterally.

The following general description is for the common knuckling posture, with the hand oriented in a coronal plane (Tuttle et al. 1994).

GROUND STRIKE AND FIRST THIRD OF SUPPORT PHASE When the knuckle pads on the dorsa of middle phalanges II–V contact the ground, the proximal phalanges of digits II–V are approximately aligned with

their respective metacarpal bones. As weight falls on the forelimb, the load-bearing metacarpophalangeal joints overextend. The joints remain overextended during the first third of the support phase during knuckled steps that are moderately paced and moderately long. During the first third of support phase, the wrist flexes $\approx 15°–20°$ in the chimpanzee and only slightly in the gorilla.

MID-SUPPORT PHASE As the ape's body moves forward over the knuckling hand, the load-bearing metacarpophalangeal joints flex so that the proximal phalanges are aligned again with the nonpollical metacarpus.

TERMINAL SUPPORT PHASE Toward the end of the support phase, the load-bearing metacarpophalangeal joints flex $\leq 30°$, at which time the knuckles are free of the substrate. Concurrently, the wrist flexes.

SWING PHASE The wrist and load-bearing metacarpophalangeal joints extend during the swing phase, and initially, interphalangeal joints II–V appear also to extend. However, the latter joints flex before the onset of the next support phase.

## Electromyographic Activity (Tuttle et al. 1994)

FLEXOR DIGITORUM SUPERFICIALIS MUSCLE As the chimpanzee and gorilla knuckle-walked with the hand in the coronal plane, fasciculi II, III, and IV of the flexor digitorum superficialis muscle were moderately active immediately before ground contact and throughout the support phase of the step.

During most knuckled steps by the gorilla and during long, rapid steps by the chimpanzee, EMG activity peaks in the first third of support phase and then declines toward the end of support phase. This EMG pattern is much clearer on the oscilloscope displays than on the printouts (Figures 2 and 3) due to dampening of the signals by the penwriter.

When the chimpanzee partially supinated his knuckling hand, EMG in the flexor digitorum superficialis muscle was lower than when his load-bearing hand was in a coronal plane, and there was no peak of EMG activity early in support phase, with tapering toward its termination.

FLEXOR DIGITORUM PROFUNDUS MUSCLE Fasciculi II, III, and IV of the flexor digitorum profundus muscle usually exhibited short, irregular spurts of EMG potentials during swing phase and at the beginning of support phase. This EMG activity is associated with flexion of the distal interphalangeal joints of digits II–IV, which characteristically occurs just before the onset of support phase.

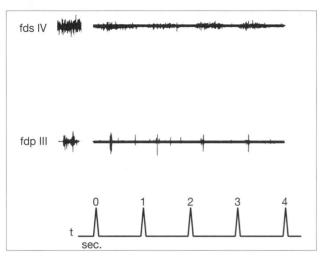

FIGURE 2.    *Electromyograms of fascicle IV of the flexor digitorum superficialis muscle (fds IV) and fascicle III of the flexor digitorum profundus muscle (fdp III) during four relatively rapid knuckle-walking steps by the chimpanzee. Time is in seconds (sec.). The periods of increased EMG activity in fds IV occur during the support phase of the step. In the first step (sec. 0–1), the support phase begins just before 0.25 sec.; the signal peaks shortly thereafter and then tapers to nil at the end of support phase (sec. 1). A similar pattern appears on the oscilloscope for the second and third steps but is not manifest on the printout. The fourth step shows the pattern on both records. The fdp III is most active at the beginning of support phase, with small, irregular bursts at other points in the step.*

Occasionally, fasciculi of the flexor digitorum profundus muscle were active briefly during support phase, which probably prevented contact between their fingernails and the floor and lower edge of the ramp.

**EXTENSOR DIGITORUM MUSCLE**    In the chimpanzee, the extensor digitorum muscle was active during the swing phase and at the beginning of support phase of knuckle-walking; this is associated with extensions of metacarpophalangeal joints II–V and of the wrist, which occurs during swing phase.

## DISCUSSION

Alexander (1991) noted that mammals that are highly adapted for economy of energy in running should have long compliant tendons and muscular fascicles that are short or have low intrinsic speeds. Via elastic stretch and recoil, as forces on them increase and decrease, respectively, tendons conserve energy. Cursorial beasts that have such muscles also can possess more economical—short or slow—force-generating muscular fibers.

In obligate knuckle-walkers, the distal, and even the central and more proximal, regions of many antebrachial flexor muscles appear to be highly tendinous by comparison with their counterparts in orangutans, which are not habitual knuckle-walkers; their muscular segments are characterized by relatively short fibers and pennate architecture (Basmajian and Tuttle 1973; Susman and Stern 1979; Tuttle 1967, 1969a, b, 1970, 1974, 1975a, b, 1977, 1986; Tuttle and Basmajian 1974a, b, 1975; Tuttle and Cortright 1988; Tuttle and Watts 1985; Tuttle et al. 1972, 1979, 1994). Our inference from these observations contrasts with the conclusion of Rauwerdink (1993), who did not study orangutans or gorillas. Ker (1993) did not study pongid ape specimens.

Unlike most other mammals, adult quadrupedal primates support more of their weight on the hind limbs than on the forelimbs (Demes et al. 1994; Kimura et al. 1979; Kimura 1985; Reynolds 1985a, b). In captive chimpanzees, knuckle-walking and hind limb dominance are established by the end of the first year of life (Kimura 1987; Riesen and Kinder 1952), though knuckle-walking is rare among forest-dwelling chimpanzees during the first two years (Doran 1992a). During static quadrupedal posture, a 7-year-old chimpanzee supported 75% of her body weight on the hind limbs. However, according to Reynolds (1985b), "chimpanzees support roughly 55% of their weight on their hindlimbs and also decrease stresses on their forelimbs by other means at higher speed." We propose that a specially adapted flexor digitorum superficialis muscle is one of these mechanisms.

During knuckle-walking, tendons of the flexor digitorum superficialis muscle are loaded in tension. In chimpanzees and gorillas, it is relatively shortened by comparison with its counterparts in other hominoid primates. This is evidenced by the fact that passive extension of the wrist and metacarpophalangeal joints II–V is accompanied by flexion of interphalangeal joints II–V in the African apes but not in the Asian apes or in humans (Tuttle 1967, 1969a, b). Accordingly, the simultaneous extension at the wrist and metacarpophalangeal joints that occur at the beginning of support phase in knuckle-walking must load the flexor digitorum superficialis muscle in tension. The peak in EMG activity early in the support phase, particularly during longer and more rapid steps, increases the tensile load of the flexor digitorum superficialis tendons (Tuttle et al. 1994).

We infer that the potential energy, which is represented by the strain of the superficial long digital flexor tendons when they are loaded by the weight of the subject and muscular stretch and contraction, is released as

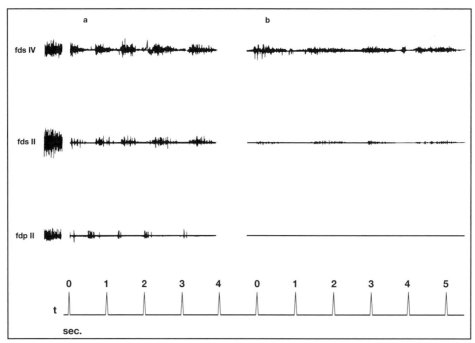

FIGURE 3.  *Electromyograms of fascicles II and IV of the flexor digitorum superficialis muscle (fds II, fds IV) and fascicle II of the flexor digitorum profundus muscle (fdp II) during knuckle-walking steps by the gorilla. Time is in seconds (sec.).*

*(a) The subject knuckle-walks with very short, rapid steps and appears to bounce on her knuckles. Tapering EMGs toward the end of the support phase are manifest for fds IV and fds II in all five knuckled steps. The short bursts of EMG in fdp II occur just before the onset of support phase.*

*(b) At this point in the experiment, only fds IV is producing reliable data. EMGs occur during the support phase. In sec. 0–1, she steps off the side of the ramp at a point ≈ 30 cm above the floor. She takes two steps (secs. 1–4) on the floor, during which EMG activity peaks early in support phase, followed by tapering toward its termination. In the fourth step, she pauses and pivots on her hand in the corner of the room, without complete flexion of her metacarpophalangeal joints, which generally occurs during the latter two-thirds of support phase of knuckle-walking. There is no tapering in EMG activity. Accordingly, we infer that the muscle and its tendon remained taut for the duration of this support phase, which probably indicates that, in contrast to previous steps, their potential energy is not converted to propulsive force via elastic recoil, as would occur were the metacarpophalangeal joint to flex as usual.*

elastic recoil during carpal and metacarophalangeal flexion, which occurs during the latter two-thirds of the support phase. Tapering activity of the flexor digitorum superficialis during the latter two-thirds of the support phase implies release of potential energy by its tendons. Since some, perhaps most, of this potential energy is gained by placement of the upper body weight on the load-bearing forearm, instead of from direct muscular effort, the elastic recoil of the flexor digitorum superficialis muscle probably contributes to mechanical energetic efficiency when gorillas and chimpanzees knuckle-walk (Tuttle et al. 1994).

Although much of the propulsive force to move the body forward during knuckle-walking is provided by the hind limbs, the forelimbs must be coordinated with them if the overall quadrupedal locomotor pattern is to be effective (Demes et al. 1994). The elastic recoil mechanism of the flexor digitorum superficialis muscle may provide energy-efficient propulsion to the hand, and perhaps to the entire forelimb, immediately before swing phase (Tuttle et al. 1994).

### Fist-walking and Other Eccentric Hand Posture

Occasionally, the chimpanzee fist-walked (Tuttle 1967) on the dorsum of proximal phalanges II–V, with his hand oriented in a coronal plane. While fist-walking, the flexor digitorum superficialis muscle was slightly active during the support phase of the step, and it lacked an activity peak. During some fist-walking steps, the flexor digitorum profundus muscle also was active during the support phase and less so during the swing phase. But throughout two fist-walking sequences, fascicle IV of his flexor digitorum profundus muscle was silent.

In one instance, after several knuckle-walking steps, the chimpanzee walked on the dorsum of the metacarpus of the recorded hand and fist-walked on the other hand. The extensor digitorum muscle, which is active during the swing phase of normal knuckle-walking, was active during the support phase, when his hand was eccentrically placed on the dorsum of the metacarpus. Moreover, his flexor digitorum profundus exhibited irregular, slight EMG potentials and his flexor digitorum superficialis was silent.

There is no indication of noteworthy elastic recoil in these muscles during occasional fist-walking and walking with the dorsum of the metacarpus on the ground.

## Comparison of Studies

We suspect that discrepancies in the activities of the flexor digitorum superficialis muscles of the SUNY subjects versus those in our chimpanzees are largely due to different placements of their knuckled hands vis-à-vis the line of movement and perhaps also to conditions of experimental substrates in the two laboratories.

Unfortunately, Susman and Stern (1979, 1980) provide insufficient descriptions of their subjects' positional behavior to resolve this puzzle. They noted that "subject C showed greater variability in hand postures during knuckle-walking than did the wild caught animals" (A and B), but they did not describe their knuckled hand positions relative to lines of movement. They illustrate subject B knuckle-walking with his supportive hand in a sagittal plane and its dorsum oriented laterally (Susman and Stern 1979, p. 567). Further, subject B appears to be supporting a major portion of his weight on hind limbs.

Susman and Stern (1979, p. 566) mention also that their subjects walked on "painted concrete or ceramic tile, sometimes covered with pine shavings," which could cause slippage.

Our subjects walked on clean painted wooden surfaces that did not induce slippage of hands or feet. Recall that they chiefly placed their knuckled hands in a coronal plane and that they appeared to bear notable loads during regular knuckle-walking. Moreover, when our chimpanzee knuckle-walked with his hand partially supinated from a coronal plane, EMG activity was lower in his flexor digitorum superficialis muscle.

Clearly, additional, more naturalistic, and more fully described experiments are required before we can establish the range of actions by the flexor digitorum

superficialis and other muscles among young and fully adult chimpanzees, gorillas, and bonobos. Longitudinal ontogenetic studies would be most revealing. Until then, generalizations about chimpanzees and cross-specifically among African apes will be unreliable.

## Is There a Knuckle-walking Complex?

The obligate knuckle-walking of the African apes suggests that one might profitably search for special manual features that underpin this unique behavior. Tuttle (1965 et seq.) pioneered this investigation after the discovery of hominid hand bones at Olduvai Gorge, Tanzania (Napier 1962 a, b), and particularly after he noted that 30 newly captive orangutans at Yerkes RPRC in Orange Park, Florida, did not knuckle-walk (Tuttle and Rogers 1966). Susman (1978, 1979; Susman and Creel 1979) and several contemporary morphologists (Jenkins and Fleagle 1975; Preuschoft 1965, 1973a) carried the search to finer levels of detail, and a third cohort of evolutionary primatologists has refined our knowledge further via sophisticated quantitative analyses (Inouye 1990, 1991, 1992) and field studies (Doran, 1992a, b, 1993a, b; Hunt 1991a, b, 1992a, b; Susman 1984; Susman et al. 1980; Tuttle and Watts 1985).

The preeminent, incontrovertible morphological feature that links obligate knuckle-walkers is epidermal—knuckle pads of friction skin of the dorsa of manual digits II–V (Ellis and Montagna 1962; Montagna 1965). Osseoligamentous and myological features that predetermine and facilitate knuckle-walking are more variably expressed ontogenetically in and interspecifically among gorillas, chimpanzees, and bonobos (Shea and Inouye 1993; Susman and Creel 1979).

Manipulation of the wrists of gorillas, chimpanzees, orangutans, and gibbons shows that the African apes are particularly limited in dorsiflexion (extension), adduction (ulnar deviation), and abduction (radial deviation). Tuttle (1967, 1969a, b, 1970) documented osseoligamentous mechanisms that limit these carpal movements in gorillas and chimpanzees (Andrews 1987, p. 42). Nevertheless, unless fossil carpal specimens are quite similar to those of adult *Pan gorilla* and *Pan troglodytes,* one probably should not argue dogmatically that their owners were obligate knuckle-walkers. Indeed, we need thoroughgoing analyses of hominoid carpal and distal radial morphology, like those performed on metacarpal bones II–V by Inouye (1990, 1991, 1992), to inform future functional interpretations of fossil carpal bones. Further, we need measurements of potential wrist movement in bonobos to test Doran's (1993a) speculation that bonobo wrists may differ from those of chimpanzees, since bonobos more frequently use palmigrade postures to climb on boughs.

Metacarpal tori (also called dorsal metacarpal ridges and dorsal transverse ridges) on the dorsodistal surfaces of weight-bearing metacarpal bones II-V indicate knuckle-walking, particularly if the articular surface of the metacarpal head extends dorsally, thereby facilitating overextension of the metacarpophalangeal joint (Preuschoft, 1973a, b; Tuttle 1965, 1967; see Figure 4). Unfortunately for paleoprimatologists who would trace the history of knuckle-walking, the metacarpal torus is variably expressed interdigitally and interspecifically in African apes. It develops ontogenetically, probably in response to stresses of knuckle-walking. Metacarpal tori may not be salient on all adult non-pollical metacarpal bones, particularly those of digits V and II, due to disuse during knuckle-walking. Moreover, some adult *Pan paniscus* sport poorly developed metacarpal tori even though, like *Pan troglodytes* and *Pan gorilla*, they commonly traverse the forest via knuckle-walking (Doran 1992a, 1993a; Inouye 1990, 1991, 1992; Susman 1979, 1984; Susman et al. 1980). We have no quantitative datum on overextension of metacarpophalangeal joints II–V in bonobos to compare with those for chimpanzees, gorillas, orangutans and gibbons (Tuttle 1969a, c, 1970, 1972).

In sum, there is an adaptive complex for knuckle-walking in African apes, whose morphological features include knuckle pads on digits II–V; restricted wrist motions vis-à-vis those of Asian apes; enlargement of the dorsal articular surfaces of metacarpal

heads II–V and associated metacarpal tori; and shortened tendons of the flexor digitorum superficialis muscle. Except for knuckle pads, these features are most complete and evident in adult *Pan gorilla* and adult *Pan troglodytes*. Further detailed research is required to document their ontogeny in both species and their manifestation in *Pan paniscus*.

### The Role of Knuckle-walking in Hominoid Evolution

With the current state of knowledge, it is impossible to sketch the phylogeny of knuckle-walking and knuckle-walkers, even at the level of well-informed speculation. Some features of obligate knuckle-walkers—knuckle pads, tendinized long digital flexor muscles, carpal ligaments—are unlikely to be discerned from fossil specimens. The fossil record for ancestry of extant African apes is unknown (Tuttle, 1986, 1988, 1994). There is no unequivocal indication of knuckle-walking in available Miocene, Pliocene and Pleistocene hand bones that are ascribed to the Hominoidea (Tuttle 1992).

Accordingly, all of the following optional scenarios about the role of knuckle-walking in hominoid evolution are reasonable:

1. The adaptive complex of knuckle-walking is basal to the radiation of *Pan* (including *Gorilla*), but it was not a feature of emerging Hominidae (Andrews 1987; Andrews and Martin 1987; Tuttle 1965, 1967, 1969a, b, 1970, 1974, 1975a, b, 1977, 1981).

2. Like *Pan*, ancestors of the Hominidae sensu stricto were knuckle-walkers before the evolution of obligate bipedalism (Begun 1992, 1994; Clark 1970; Conroy and Fleagle 1972; Kortlandt 1972; Leakey 1971; Sarich 1971; Washburn 1967, 1968a, b, c, 1972, 1973a, b; Washburn and Moore 1974; Zihlman 1990).

3. Knuckle-walking evolved in parallel in lineages leading to gorillas, to chimpanzees and bonobos (Boaz 1988; Pilbeam 1972; Simons and Pilbeam 1972) and perhaps to humans (Begun 1992).

It would be overly optimistic to expect that fossils will ever resolve this puzzle. Most proponents of the second scenario are convinced by molecular studies—evidencing greater genetic affinity of humans with chimpanzees and bonobos than among chimpanzees, bonobos, and gorillas—that knuckle-walking was the basal terrestrial locomotor adaptation not only of ancestral African apes but also of the proximate predecessors of bipedal hominids.

Although the second scenario is more parsimonious than the third scenario, there is no compelling reason to

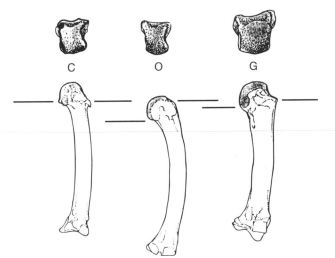

FIGURE 4. *Distal end (upper row) and medial aspect (bottom row) of metacarpal bone III in chimpanzee (C), orangutan (O), and gorilla (G). The distal articular surfaces are shaded. Horizontal lines indicate the anterior and posterior borders of articular areas. Note the greater posterior extension of the articular surface and metacarpal tori in C and G versus O.*

deny that more than one species of relatively large-bodied, long-handed arboreal apes, with high centers of mass, could have adopted knuckle-walking at different times due to selection for quadrupedal terrestrial locomotion in the forest or in more open areas.

Our preference for the first scenario is precisely that—a preference. We would rather know than to be right about this and other questions of primate evolution. Accordingly, we would abandon the hylobatian model (Tuttle 1974, 1975a, 1981, 1987, 1988, 1994; Tuttle et al. 1991) if the functional meanings of genetic data demonstrated the validity of another scenario.

In the spirit of Sherwood Washburn's long, productive, stimulating career in evolutionary anthropology, we expect that keen naturalistic observations and experimental morphological, molecular, and paleontological studies will provide us with further clues to the locomotor repertoires of ancestral African apes and protohominids and to hominoid phylogeny.

## ACKNOWLEDGMENTS

Our investigation was subsidized by NSF grants GS-3209, SOC75-02478, and BNS 8540290 and by a U.S. Public Health Service Research career development award (1-KO4-GM16347-01) from the National Institutes of Health. It was supported also in part by NIH grant RR-00165 from the Division of Research Resources to the Yerkes Regional Primate Research Center, which is fully accredited by the American Association of Laboratory Animal Care. We are especially grateful for the assistance of J. Malone, E. Regenos, J. Perry, Dr. G. H. Bourne, Dr. F. A. King, R. Pollard, S. Lee, R. Mathis, J. Roberts, Dr. M. Keeling, Dr. M. Vitti, and J. Hudson.

## REFERENCES

Alexander, R. McN. (1991). Elastic mechanisms in primate locomotion. *Zeitschrift für Morphologie und Anthropologie 78:* 315–320.

Andrews, P. (1987). Aspects of hominoid phylogeny. In C. Patterson (ed.), *Molecules and Morphology in Evolution: Conflict or Compromise.* Cambridge: Cambridge University Press, pp. 23–53.

Andrews, P., and Martin, L. (1987). Cladistic relationships of extant and fossil hominoids. *Journal of Human Evolution 16:* 101–118.

Barnicot, N. A. (1958). The experimental approach to physical anthropology. In D. F. Roberts and J. S. Weiner (eds.), *The Scope of Physical Anthropology and Its Place in Academic Studies.* Oxford: Church Army Press, Cowley, pp. 33–41.

Basmajian, J. V. (1974). *Muscles Alive,* 3rd ed. Baltimore: Williams & Wilkins.

Basmajian, J. V. (1993). *I.O.U. Adventures of a Medical Scientist.* Hamilton, Ont.: J. & D. Books.

Basmajian, J. V., and Tuttle, R. (1973). EMG of locomotion in gorilla and man. In R. B. Stein, K. B. Pearson, R. S. Smith, and J. B. Redford (eds.), *Control of Posture and Locomotion.* New York: Plenum Press, pp. 599–609.

Begun, D. R. (1992). Miocene fossil hominids and the chimp-human clade. *Science 257:* 1929–1933.

Begun, D. R. (1994). Relations among the great apes and humans: New interpretations based on the fossil great ape *Dryopithecus. Yearbook of Physical Anthropology 37:* 11–63.

Boaz, N. T. (1988). Status of *Australopithecus afarensis. Yearbook of Physical Anthropology 31:* 85–113.

Bourne, G. H. (1974). *Primate Odyssey.* New York: Putnam's.

Bourne, G. H., and Cohen, M. (1975). *The Gentle Giants.* New York: Putnam's.

Clark, J. D. (1970). *The Prehistory of Africa.* New York: Praeger.

Conroy, G. C., and Fleagle, J. G. (1972). Locomotor behaviour in living and fossil pongids. *Nature 237:* 103–104.

Demes, B., Larson, S. G., Stern, Jr., J. T., Jungers, W. L., Biknevicius, A. R., and Schmitt, D. (1994). The kinetics of primate quadrupedalism: "Hindlimb drive" reconsidered. *Journal of Human Evolution 26:* 353–374.

Doran, D. M. (1992a). The ontogeny of chimpanzee and pygmy chimpanzee locomotor behavior: A case study of paedomorphism and its behavioral correlates. *Journal of Human Evolution 23:* 139–157.

Doran, D. M. (1992b). Comparison of instantaneous and locomotor bout sampling methods: A case study of adult male chimpanzee locomotor behavior and substrate use. *American Journal of Physical Anthropology 89:* 85–99.

Doran, D. M. (1993a). Comparative locomotor behavior of chimpanzees and bonobos: The influence of morphology on locomotion. *American Journal of Physical Anthropology 91:* 83–98.

Doran, D. M. (1993b). Sex differences in adult chimpanzee positional behavior: The influence of body size on locomotion and posture. *American Journal of Physical Anthropology 91:* 99–115.

Ellis, R. A., and Montagna, W. (1962). The skin of primates. VI. The skin of the gorilla (*Gorilla gorilla*). *American Journal of Physical Anthropology 20:* 79–93.

Fleagle, J. G., and Jungers, W. L. (1982). Fifty years of higher primate phylogeny. In F. Spencer (ed.), *A History of American Physical Anthropology, 1930–1980.* New York: Academic Press, pp. 187–230.

Haas, J. D. (1982). The development of research strategies for studies of biological variation in living human populations. In F. Spencer (ed.), *A History of American Physical Anthropology, 1930–1980.* New York: Academic Press, pp. 435–446.

Haraway, D. J. (1988). Remodeling the human way of life. In G. W. Stocking, Jr. (ed.), *Bones, Bodies, Behavior.* Madison: University of Wisconsin Press, pp. 206–259.

Haraway, D. J. (1989). *Primate Visions.* New York: Routledge.

Howells, W. W. (1992). Yesterday, today and tomorrow. *Annual Review of Anthropology 21:* 1–17.

Hunt, K. D. (1991a). Positional behavior in the Hominoidea. *International Journal of Primatology 12:* 95–118.

Hunt, K. D. (1991b). Mechanical implications of chimpanzee positional behavior. *American Journal of Physical Anthropology 86:* 521–536.

Hunt, K. D. (1992a). Positional behavior of *Pan troglodytes* in the Mahale Mountains and Gombe Stream National Parks, Tanzania. *American Journal of Physical Anthropology 87:* 83–105.

Hunt, K. D. (1992b). Social rank and body size as determinants of positional behavior in *Pan troglodytes. Primates 33:* 347–357.

Inouye, S. E. (1990). Variation in the presence and development of the dorsal ridge of the metacarpal head in African apes. *American Journal of Physical Anthropology 81:* 243.

Inouye, S. E. (1991). Ontogeny and allometry in African ape fingers. In A. Ehara, T. Kimura, O. Takenaka, and M. Iwamoto (eds.), *Primatology Today.* Amsterdam: Elsevier, pp. 537–538.

Inouye, S. E. (1992). Ontogeny and allometry of African ape manual rays. *Journal of Human Evolution 23:* 107–138.

Jenkins, Jr., F. A., and Fleagle, J. G. (1975). Knuckle-walking and the functional anatomy of the wrists in living apes. In R. H. Tuttle (ed.), *Primate Functional Morphology and Evolution.* The Hague: Mouton, pp. 213–227.

Ker, R. F. (1993). Elasticity of hand and forefoot tendons. In H. Preuschoft and D. J. Chivers (eds.), *Hands of Primates.* Vienna: Springer-Verlag, pp. 257–269.

Kimura, T. (1985). Bipedal and quadrupedal walking of primates: Comparative dynamics. In S. Kondo (ed.), *Primate Morphophysiology, Locomotor Analyses and Human Bipedalism.* Tokyo: University of Tokyo Press, pp. 81–104.

Kimura, T. (1987). Development of chimpanzee locomotion on level surfaces. *Human Evolution 2:* 107–119.

Kimura, T., Okada, M., and Ishida, H. (1979). Kinesiological characteristics of primate walking: Its significance for human walking. In M. E. Morbeck, H. Preuschoft, and N. Gomberg (eds.), *Environment, Behavior, and Morphology: Dynamic Interactions in Primates.* Stuttgart: Gustav Fischer, pp. 297–311.

Kortlandt, A. (1972). *New Perspectives on Ape and Human Evolution.* Amsterdam: Stichting voor Psychobiologie.

Leakey, R. E. F. (1971). Further evidence of Lower Pleistocene hominids from East Rudolf, North Kenya. *Nature 231:* 241–245.

Little, M. A. (1982). The development of ideas on human ecology and adaptation. In F. Spencer (ed.), *A History of American Physical Anthropology, 1930–1980.* New York: Academic Press, pp. 405–433.

Montagna, W. (1965). The skin. *Scientific American 212:* 56–66.

Napier, J. R. (1962a). Fossil hand bones from Olduvai Gorge. *Nature 196:* 409–411.

Napier, J. R. (1962b). The evolution of the hand. *Scientific American 207:* 56–62.

Pilbeam, D. R. (1972). *The Ascent of Man.* New York: Macmillan.

Preuschoft, H. (1965). Muskeln und Gelenke der Vorderextremität des Gorillas (*Gorilla gorilla* Savage et Wyman, 1847). *Morphologisches Jahrbuch 107:* 99–183.

Preuschoft, H. (1973a). Functional anatomy of the upper extremity. In G. H. Bourne (ed.), *The Chimpanzee,* Vol. 6. Basel: Karger, pp. 34–120.

Preuschoft, H. (1973b). Body posture and locomotion in some East African Miocene Dryopithecinae. In M. H. Day (ed.), *Human Evolution.* London: Taylor and Francis, pp. 13–46.

Rauwerdink, G. P. (1993). Muscle fibre and tendon lengths in primate extremities. In H. Preuschoft and D. J. Chivers (eds.), *Hands of Primates.* Vienna: Springer-Verlag, pp. 207–223.

Reynolds, T. R. (1985a). Mechanics of increased support of weight by the hindlimbs in primates. *American Journal of Physical Anthropology 67:* 335–349.

Reynolds, T. R. (1985b). Stresses on the limbs of quadrupedal primates. *American Journal of Physical Anthropology 67:* 251–262.

Ribnick, R. (1982). A short history of primate field studies: Old World monkeys and apes. In F. Spencer (ed.), *A History of American Physical Anthropology, 1930–1980.* New York: Academic Press, pp. 49–73.

Riesen, A. H., and Kinder, E. F. (1952). *Postural Development of Infant Chimpanzees.* New Haven, CT: Yale University Press.

Sarich, V. M. (1971). A molecular approach to the question of human origins. In P. Dolhinow and V. M. Sarich (eds.), *Background for Man: Readings in Physical Anthropology.* Boston: Little, Brown, pp. 60–81.

Shea, B. T., and Inouye, S. E. (1993). Knuckle-walking ancestors. *Science 259:* 293–294.

Simons, E. L., and Pilbeam, D. R. (1972). Hominoid paleoprimatology. In R. H. Tuttle (ed.), *The Functional and Evolutionary Biology of Primates.* Chicago: Aldine-Atherton, pp. 36–62.

Susman, R. L. (1978). Functional morphology of hominoid metacarpals. In D. J. Chivers and K. A. Joysey (eds.), *Recent Advances in Primatology.* Vol. 3, *Evolution.* London: Academic Press, pp. 77–80.

Susman, R. L. (1979). Comparative and functional morphology of hominoid fingers. *American Journal of Physical Anthropology 50:* 215–236.

Susman, R. L. (1984). The locomotor behavior of *Pan paniscus* in the Lomako forest. In R. L. Susman (ed.), *The Pygmy Chimpanzee,* New York: Plenum Press, pp. 369–394.

Susman, R. L., Badrian, N. L., and Badrian, A. J. (1980). Locomotor behavior of *Pan paniscus* in Zaire. *American Journal of Physical Anthropology 53:* 69–80.

Susman, R. L., and Creel, N. (1979). Functional and morphological affinities of the subadult hand (O.H. 7) from Olduvai Gorge. *American Journal of Physical Anthropology 51:* 311–332.

Susman, R. L., and Stern, Jr., J. T. (1979). Telemetered electromyography of flexor digitorum profundus and flexor digitorum superficialis in *Pan troglodytes* and implications for interpretation of the O.H. 7 hand. *American Journal of Physical Anthropology 50:* 565–574.

Susman, R. L. and Stern, Jr., J. T. (1980). EMG of the interosseous and lumbrical muscles in the chimpanzee (*Pan troglodytes*) hand during locomotion. *American Journal of Anatomy 157:* 389–397.

Tuttle, R. H. (1965). *A Study of the Chimpanzee Hand with Comments on Hominoid Evolution.* Ph.D. thesis, University of California, Berkeley.

Tuttle, R. H. (1967). Knuckle-walking and the evolution of hominoid hands. *American Journal of Physical Anthropology 26:* 171–206.

Tuttle, R. H. (1969a). Quantitative and functional studies on the hands of the Anthropoidea. I. The Hominoidea. *Journal of Morphology 128:* 309–364.

Tuttle, R. H. (1969b). Knuckle-walking and the problem of human origins. *Science 166:* 953–961.

Tuttle, R. H. (1969c). Terrestrial trends in the hands of the Anthropoidea: A preliminary report. In H. Hofer (ed.), *Proceedings of the 2nd International Congress of Primatology, Atlanta, GA,* Vol. 2. Basel: Karger, pp. 192–200.

Tuttle, R. H. (1970). Postural, propulsive, and prehensile capabilities in the cheiridia of chimpanzees and other great apes. In G. H. Bourne (ed.), *The Chimpanzee,* Vol. 2. Basel: Karger, pp. 167–253.

Tuttle, R. H. (1972). Functional and evolutionary biology of hylobatid hands and feet. In D. Rumbaugh (ed.), *Gibbon and Siamang,* Vol. I. Basel: Karger, pp. 136–206.

Tuttle, R. H. (1974). Darwin's apes, dental apes, and the descent of man: Normal science in evolutionary anthropology. *Current Anthropology 15:* 389–426.

Tuttle, R. H. (1975a). Parallelism, brachiation and hominoid phylogeny. In W. P. Luckett and F. S. Szalay (eds.), *Phylogeny of the Primates. A Multidisciplinary Approach,* New York: Plenum Press, pp. 447–480.

Tuttle, R. H. (1975b). Knuckle-walking and knuckle-walkers: A commentary on some recent perspectives on hominoid evolution. In R. H. Tuttle (ed.), *Primate Functional Morphology and Evolution.* The Hague: Mouton, pp. 203–212.

Tuttle, R. H. (1977). Naturalistic positional behavior of apes and models of hominid evolution, 1929–1976. In G. H. Bourne (ed.), *Progress in Ape Research.* New York: Academic Press, pp. 277–296.

Tuttle, R. H. (1981). Evolution of hominid bipedalism and prehensile capabilities. *Philosophical Transactions of the Royal Society. London B-292:* 89–94.

Tuttle, R. H. (1986). *Apes of the World. Their Social Behavior, Communication, Mentality and Ecology.* Park Ridge, NJ: Noyes.

Tuttle, R. H. (1987). Kinesiological inferences and evolutionary implications from Laetoli bipedal trails G-1, G-2/3, and A. In M. D. Leakey and J. M. Harris (eds.), *Laetoli, a Pliocene Site in Northern Tanzania.* Oxford: Clarendon, pp. 503–523.

Tuttle, R. H. (1988). What's new in African paleoanthropology? *Annual Review of Anthropology 17:* 391–426.

Tuttle, R. H. (1992). Hands from newt to Napier. In S. Matano, R. H. Tuttle, H. Ishida, and M. Goodman (eds.), *Topics in Primatology.* Vol. 3, *Evolutionary Biology, Reproductive Endocrinology and Virology.* Tokyo: University of Tokyo Press, pp. 3–20.

Tuttle, R. H. (1994). Up from electromyography. Primate energetics and the evolution of human bipedalism. In R. S. Corruccini and

R. L. Ciochon (eds.), *Integrative Paths to the Past.* Englewood Cliffs, NJ: Prentice Hall, pp. 269–284.

Tuttle, R. H., and Basmajian, J. V. (1974a). Electromyography of forearm musculature in gorilla and problems related to knuckle-walking. In F. A. Jenkins, Jr. (ed.), *Primate Locomotion.* New York: Academic Press, pp. 293–347.

Tuttle, R. H. and Basmajian, J. V. (1974b). Electromyography of the long digital flexor muscles in gorilla. In F. Barnosell (ed.), *Proceedings of the 6th Congreso Internacional de Medicina Fisica, Vol. II, 1972.* Madrid: Ministerio de Trabajo, Instituto Nacional de Prevision, pp. 311–315.

Tuttle, R. H., and Basmajian, J. V. (1974c). Electromyography of brachial muscles in *Pan gorilla* and hominoid evolution. *American Journal of Physical Anthropology 41:* 71–90.

Tuttle, R. H. and Basmajian, J. V. (1975). Electromyography of *Pan gorilla:* An experimental approach to the problem of hominization. In S. Kondo, M. Kawai, A. Ehara, and S. Kawamura (eds.), *Proceedings from the Symposia of the 5th International Primatological Society, 1974.* Tokyo: Japan Science Press, pp. 303–314.

Tuttle, R. H., and Basmajian, J. V. (1977). Electromyography of pongid shoulder muscles and hominoid evolution. I. Retractors of the humerus and "rotators" of the scapula. *Yearbook of Physical Anthropology—1976 20:* 491–497.

Tuttle, R. H., and Basmajian, J. V. (1978a). Electromyography of pongid shoulder muscles. II. Deltoid, Rhomboid and "Rotator Cuff." *American Journal of Physical Anthropology 49:* 47–56.

Tuttle, R. H., and Basmajian, J. V. (1978b). Electromyography of pongid shoulder muscles. III. Quadrupedal positional Behavior. *American Journal of Physical Anthropology 49:* 57–70.

Tuttle, R. H., Basmajian, J. V., and Ishida, H. (1975). Electromyography of the gluteus maximus muscle in gorilla and the evolution of hominid bipedalism. In R. H. Tuttle (ed.), *Primate Functional Morphology and Evolution.* The Hague: Mouton, pp. 253–369.

Tuttle, R. H., Basmajian, J. V., and Ishida, H. (1978). Electromyography of pongid gluteal muscles and hominid evolution. In D. J. Chivers and K. A. Joysey (eds.), *Recent Advances in Primatology.* Vol. 3, *Evolution.* London: Academic Press, pp. 463–468.

Tuttle, R. H., Basmajian, J. V., and Ishida, H. (1979). Activities of pongid thigh muscles during bipedal behavior. *American Journal of Physical Anthropology 50:* 123–136.

Tuttle, R. H., Basmajian, J. V., Regenos, E., and Shine, G. (1972). Electromyography of knuckle-walking: Results of four experiments on the forearm of *Pan gorilla. American Journal of Physical Anthropology 37:* 255–266.

Tuttle, R. H., and Cortright, G. W. (1988). The positional behavior, adaptive complexes and evolution of *Pongo pygmaeus.* In J. H. Schwartz (ed.) *Orang-utan Biology.* Oxford: Oxford University Press, pp. 311–330.

Tuttle, R. H., Cortright, G. W. and Buxhoeveden, D. P. (1979). Anthropology on the move: Progress in experimental studies of nonhuman primate positional behavior. *Yearbook of Physical Anthropology 22:* 187–214.

Tuttle, R. H., Hallgrimsson, B., and Basmajian, J. V. (1994). Electromyography and elastic mechanisms in knuckle-walking *Pan gorilla* and *Pan troglodytes.* In B. Thierry, J. R. Anderson, J. J. Roeder, and N. Herrenschmidt (eds.), *Current Primatology.* Vol. I, *Ecology and Evolution.* Strasbourg: Université Louis Pasteur, pp. 215–222.

Tuttle, R. H., Hollowed, J. R., and Basmajian, J. V. (1992). Electromyography of pronators and supinators in great apes. *American Journal of Physical Anthropology 87:* 215–226.

Tuttle, R. H., and Rogers, C. M. (1966). Genetic and selective factors in reduction of the hallux in *Pongo pygmaeus. American Journal of Physical Anthropology 24:* 191–198.

Tuttle, R. H., Velte, M. J., and Basmajian, J. V. (1983). Electromyography of brachial muscles in *Pan troglodytes* and *Pongo pygmaeus. American Journal of Physical Anthropology 61:* 75–83.

Tuttle, R. H., and Watts, D. P. (1985). The positional behavior and adaptive complexes of *Pan gorilla.* In S. Kondo (ed.), *Primate Morphophysiology, Locomotor Analyses and Human Bipedalism.* Tokyo: University of Tokyo Press, pp. 261–288.

Tuttle, R. H., Webb, D. M., and Tuttle, N. I. (1991). Laetoli footprint trails and the evolution of bipedalism. In Y. Coppens and B. Senut (eds.), *Origines de la Bipédie chez les Hominidés. Cahiers de Paléonathropologie.* Paris: Editions du CNRS, pp. 203–218.

Washburn, S. L. (1946). The effect of facial paralysis on the growth of the skull of rat and rabbit. *American Journal of Anatomy 94:* 163–168.

Washburn, S. L. (1947). The relation of the temporal muscle to the form of the skull. *Anatomical Record 99:* 239–248.

Washburn, S. L. (1950). The analysis of primate evolution with particular reference to the origin of man. *Cold Spring Harbor Symposia on Quantitative Biology 15:* 67–78.

Washburn, S. L. (1951). The new physical anthropology. *Transactions of the New York Academy of Sciences 13:* 298–304.

Washburn, S. L. (1953). The strategy of physical anthropology. In A. L. Kroeber (ed.), *Anthropology Today.* Chicago: University of Chicago Press, pp. 714–727.

Washburn, S. L. (1963). The study of race. *American Anthropologist 65:* 521–531.

Washburn, S. L. (1967). Behaviour and the origin of man. *Proceedings of the Royal Anthropological Institute of Great Britain and Ireland 1967,* pp. 21–27.

Washburn, S. L. (1968a). The study of human evolution. *Condon Lectures.* Eugene: University of Oregon Books.

Washburn, S. L. (1968b). Speculations on the problem of man's coming to the ground. In B. Rothblatt (ed.), *Changing Perspectives on Man.* Chicago: University of Chicago Press, pp. 193–206.

Washburn, S. L. (1968c). One hundred years of biological anthropology. In J. O. Brew (ed.), *One Hundred Years of Anthropology.* Cambridge, MA: Harvard University Press, pp. 97–115, 242–248.

Washburn, S. L. (1972). Human evolution. In T. Dobzhansky, M. K. Hecht, and W. C. Steere (eds.), *Evolutionary Biology,* Vol. 6. New York: Appleton-Century-Crofts, pp. 349–361.

Washburn, S. L. (1973a). Primate studies and human evolution. In G. H. Bourne (ed.), *Nonhuman Primates and Medical Research.* New York: Academic Press, pp. 467–485.

Washburn, S. L. (1973b). Human evolution: Science or game? *Yearbook of Physical Anthropology 17:* 67–70.

Washburn, S. L., and Detwiler, S. R. (1943). An experiment bearing on the problems of physical anthropology. *American Journal of Physical Anthropology 1:* 171–190.

Washburn, S. L., and Moore, R. (1974). *Ape in to Man.* Boston: Little, Brown.

Zihlman, A. L. (1990). Knuckling under: Controversy over hominid origins. In G. H. Sperber (ed.), *Apes to Angels: Essays in Anthropology in Honor of Phillip V. Tobias.* New York: Wiley-Liss, pp. 185–196.

*Science, according to Washburn, is deeply immersed in a particular European history. Cultural biases affect the way we do science and the interpretations we make about the "nature of man." The promise of primatology is that it could become a science "not limited by the past" that may help us understand human nature in a new way. Primatology embodies the tenets of the new physical anthropology. It is cross-disciplinary and multidisciplinary, animal-oriented, problem-oriented and experimental. In short, it breaks the traditional divisions of knowledge. Washburn uses traditional ideas about "mind" and new data about brain to illustrate why the old way of doing research no longer works. He also highlights the importance of experimentation (in addition to description) to produce a rigorous framework within which to compare human and nonhuman primates. Washburn suggests that the major contributions of primatology will be to challenge the notion that the social should be studied without reference to the biological, to demonstrate that the study of behavior must include an understanding of the internal mechanisms, including emotions, and to explore the brain as an organ of adaptation. Seeing ourselves as primates with brains and minds that are the result of evolutionary history will have major implications for how we think about truth, about science, and about ourselves.*

# 5 The Promise of Primatology (1973)

**Sherwood L. Washburn**  *Professor, Department of Anthropology, University of California, Berkeley*

Primatology is coming of age. Starting as a minor interest in a dozen different sciences, it now has its own journals and an international association. Stimulated by the needs of medical research, interest in animal behavior, and the fascination of monkeys and apes, primatology has grown into the beginning of a science and a profession.

The purpose of this paper is to suggest that primatology may become much more than the study of man's nearest relatives. After all, man is a primate, and it is my belief that the study of the nonhuman primates may be used to illuminate the nature of man.

It is easy to speak of the science of primatology, but science is a very peculiar business. Parts are highly developed and technically efficient. Other parts are relics of the 19th century. The whole is embedded in

From *American Journal of Physical Anthropology 38:* 177–182. Reprinted by permission of Wiley-Liss, Inc., a division of John Wiley & Sons, Inc. This paper is part of a program on primate behavior supported by the National Science Foundation (grant GS-31943X). I wish to thank Dr. William Montagna for the invitation to speak on the occasion of the Fourth International Congress of Primatology and Mrs. Alice Davis for editorial assistance.

a prescientific and primitive social system, much of which is based on the illusion that man is a rational animal.

For example, take the name applied to the monkeys. Particularly in the early 19th century, when scientists were describing and naming the monkeys, it often happened that the same species was given several different names. Since at that time naming was one of the most important aspects of science, giving the name gave an illusion of understanding. Because the scientist received his social rewards for describing and naming, customs which slowed the process would have been unacceptable to the scientific community. And so a set of rules was established to enable one to decide which of the competing names was correct. The most important rule was priority—which name was given first. Granted that the scientists were to receive satisfaction and social reward from the discovery of new species (thus motivating the "discovery" and naming of a vastly inflated number of species), some such guide was necessary. It was not possible for the scientist in one museum to know whether the specimen before him was really the type of a new species or not, and, since his reputation depended on discovery, description, and naming, all the pressures were to name.

Although the whole intellectual setting has been changed for more than 100 years, there are still those who burrow in the early papers to gain personal credit by changing the names—which in many cases have been stable for many years. I am not talking about taxonomy, about the effort to understand the varieties of primates. I am talking about museum moles (to use Malinowski's happy phrase) who make it difficult for the rest of us to work. What kind of activity is it in which the reward is to keep the taxonomy in turmoil? Obviously, as the so-called scientific names change from *Macaca cynomolgus* to *M. irus* to *M. fascicularis*, the common name offers a more useful and stable guide to the crab-eating macaque, particularly if this form is not a species and all these names are wrong.

It is likely that the easiest way out of the dilemma is to use the common names, as listed in Napier and Napier ('67). Many of these names have been in existence for years, far longer than the supposedly scientific terms. Actually, most medical research involves only a small number of species, and it might not be too difficult to agree on common names for these few. For example, most of us find gorilla, chimpanzee, and pygmy chimpanzee, plus a geographical qualification, an adequate way to refer to the African apes. There is no agreement on the proper scientific names. In this paper, however, I am not really concerned with the names of primates as such, but with the climate of opinion in which the controversies over names can thrive. An individual interested in classification cannot go to his departmental chairman and say, "I have done a great thing. I have gone to the international commission. I have prevented several names from being changed. I have written no papers because the correct judgments were made in 1824."

What is involved is not only science in some absolute sense, but human customs carried out by human beings, by primates, in a particular kind of society. The history of taxonomy is not only the story of a part of biological science, but a revelation of the peculiarities of human beings.

Primatology is not something over there. It is not a logically conceived body of knowledge and techniques. Primatology is us, and we are deeply immersed in a particular European history. That history determined our education and set our social rewards; the greatest contribution of the study of the nonhuman primates might be to free us from some of the traditional limitations and points of view.

Consider the division of the university into departments. Most of these divisions have their roots in the European elitist university of the 19th century, or ear-

lier. Suppose that one of the goals of education is to gain some understanding of ourselves, of mankind. The necessary knowledge is apportioned out among more than a dozen different departments. The university is divided for the convenience of professors, and it is assumed that the knowledge of the present and of the future will fall into the intellectual patterns of the past. Primatology knows no such limitations. Look at our program of the Fourth International Congress of Primatology (IPC). It begins with behavior, reproduction, anatomy, genetics, and computers. It continues with evolution, special senses, physiology, pathology, and communication. Primatology offers the possibility of the development of a science which is not limited by the past.

No one underestimates the difficulty of maximizing both technical advance and communication among the specialists. But one way to work toward the goal is through an interest in a group of animals, rather than in a technique. Although the development of effective techniques is essential for modern science, the techniques must be used in ways which are useful in the service of human understanding. The traditional department is not only not used for technical advance, it may actively oppose the advance of useful knowledge.

Let me give an example of such active opposition which is deeply rooted in the social sciences. There is an illusion in our culture, in the European intellectual tradition, that knowledge can be divided into levels: the physical, the biological, and the social. The social sciences have as an article of faith that social problems cannot be reduced to the biological. But in the study of the nonhuman primates, we assume that behaviors are the result of the biology of the species, the ecology, the particular individual, and local history. The behavior of gibbons, for example, is based on a pattern in which such factors as feeding, locomotion, territory, psychology, and reproduction are all interrelated. A gibbon's biology is not at one level and its social life at another.

Studies of the nonhuman primates clearly show that the behaviors of a species are determined by such factors as genetic prenatal environment, early experiences, peers, ecology, and the realities of adult life. Yet in our schools intelligence tests are still used as if they offered direct clues to the genes. The way the tests are used assumes that man is less adaptable, less intelligent than monkeys—or even rats. Treating man as a primate immediately brings a large amount of information to bear on human problems.

The animal and the social system develop in a complex feedback relationship and neither aspect can be understood without the other. And since the reality is complex, it cannot be unraveled by the unaided human mind. In the studies of the nonhuman primates, we assume that the relative roles of particular genes, hormones, or experiences are to be understood through experiments. The social sciences and humanities specifically outlaw experimentation, although this is the only way to reliable knowledge and scientific progress.

The assumptions which lie behind the way the behaviors of the nonhuman primates are studied constitute an assault on the compartmentalization of the university and, particularly, on the social sciences.

For a moment let us consider human behavior. In the tribal world, in the small society, the human mind regards the world as flat, where things fall unless held up. Nature is personified and origins and causes are simple and personal—other people, spirits, or gods. Times are short, spaces small, and only a few people are important. Other people are barbarians at best, but usually are not even regarded as human. Words have meanings of inherent, often magical, significance.

It is not my purpose to catalog all the peculiarities of the human mind, but to call your attention to certain universal human mistakes that lie hidden in the customs of mankind. The personification of nature is an essential prerequisite to religions. The idea of simple, human causes lies at the root of our law and politics and is embodied in the notion that social science can be built on questionnaires.

The human mind evolved in the small, primitive world, and it is adapted to those conditions. For example, it seemed obvious to mankind that diseases were caused by spirits, objects, magic, ill will, etc. For the most part, primitive medicine is concerned with dealing with illness in those ways. The human mind adapted by remarkably similar customs all over the world: everyone believed in spontaneous generation. The change from the primitive view of diseases to modern medicine has taken place for the most part in less than 100 years. It is small wonder that the prescientific ideas still hold sway in much of the world. But the point is that it was technical advances which have made the difference, not the human minds. The brain adapted to the knowledge of its time. With technical advances, perceptions changed. But at each stage there was an illusion that the brain did more than adapt, an illusion that man had found truth in some much more ultimate sense.

This illusion is still with us, motivating much of culture and feeding the flames of scientific controversy. Let me illustrate the issues with the study of anatomy, particularly human gross anatomy. The detailed dissection of the human body used to be required as a necessary basis for the practice of medicine. The course occupied two years of the medical curriculum. Emphasis was on description and parts of the body were named after people, honoring the name and, hopefully,

earning good will and promotion for the namer. With the loss of interest in this kind of anatomy, the number of names was reduced from 50,000 to about 5,000.

Not only had the acceptance of the descriptive tradition of gross anatomy caused the waste of countless hours of human time, but the systemic approach of the major anatomical texts blocks the study of function. Most of traditional gross anatomy is best regarded as an intellectual mistake, an unnecessary block to the development of a functional, experimental anatomical science. The fact that it was regarded as important, pioneering, and essential, that it served as a satisfying career for many successful people, never proved that it was efficient, desirable, or necessary.

What was wrong with gross anatomy was the reliance on a particular descriptive tradition with little attention to purpose. Anatomists assumed that the judgments of highly informed anatomists must have a kind of reality that simply was not the case.

It may be easy to see the mistakes of the past, but the important thing for primatology is to see the complications of the present. It is the tradition of our culture to see the complications as rights and wrongs, as competitions between logical, rational people. What I have been trying to suggest is that this view of science is a product of our culture, our tradition, that it comes from thinking that the brain is an organ of logic and truth, not that it is only an organ of adaptation.

The design of the sciences of taxonomy and gross anatomy was: describe and think, preferably along traditional lines. It was the overemphasis on description and the reliance on thought which brought the downfall of these sciences in their traditional form. Without a clear understanding of purpose, there can be no decision as to when enough information has been collected. Many controversies cannot be settled without the aid of experiments.

In the matter of human speech, the first point to consider is that an extraordinary amount is known about the languages of contemporary peoples. With all this information, and a good deal about the sounds of the nonhuman primates, it might be thought it would be easy to state the universals of human languages, the basic design features, and how these differ from the communication systems of the nonhuman primates. This has not proved to be the case. Even with massive amounts of information and much human thought, the problem remains. The reason lies in the limitations of the human mind. The descriptions of human languages and of the sounds of nonhuman primates does not provide the human brain with the information it needs to clarify what happened in evolution.

The problem has been elucidated somewhat by the experiments of Ploog ('70) and his co-workers and

Robinson ('67). These investigators showed that electrodes implanted in the primitive brain, in the limbic system, will elicit all the normal sounds of the animals. Further, Myers ('69) showed that massive removals of cortex in the rhesus monkey did not affect sounds and had very little effect on facial expression. Both sound and facial expression were primarily under limbic control. In the nonhuman primates, communication is multi-modal (gestures, postures, expressions, and sounds); and what is conveyed is primarily emotional information (Lancaster, '68).

In man, emotions may be conveyed by the same mechanisms, but a new system is added. This is a code, made up of short, contrasting sounds. A small number of sounds in the code may be combined in an almost infinite number of ways, and arbitrary meaning may be connected with the combinations. The cortex on the dominant side of the brain controls the code, and with lesions centering in the area of the angular gyrus, the larger the lesion, the greater the linguistic deficit. The split brain studies settled the problem of lateralization and localization (Gazzaniga, '70).

It was the experiments performed between 1966 and 1970 which shed much light on the fundamental nature of the differences, suggesting that nonhuman primate communication has much in common with the communications of nonprimates, while the human sound code is unique. Obviously, in the evolutionary process, the human system must have been derived from the nonhuman kind, but in spite of many efforts, there is no direct evidence for intermediate stages.

If this view of the differences between the communication systems of human and nonhuman primates is at all correct, there are important implications for the field studies. So far, the tendency has been to look for sounds and for their meanings in social contexts. Struhsaker's ('67) list of 36 sounds and their meanings for vervets is one of the most successful studies of this sort. But if the limbic-emotional interpretation of the sounds is correct, sounds and gestures should fall into a small number of groups. Ploog ('70) found six groupings, and MacLean ('70) describes six main categories of behaviors mediated by the limbic system. Perhaps the goal of the research should be activities categories of behaviors, rather than the human influenced pursuit of the meanings of sounds. For example, perhaps threat should be described as an activity with an intent and an intensity, including both gestures and sounds. In Delgado's ('71) experiments with implanted electrodes, the whole pattern of threat is elicited, not the elements which a human observer describes. In the description of threat, there may be no more reason to separate sound than pilo-erection or motions of the ears. Myers' ('69) work clearly shows that facial expression in man is far more dependent on cortex than is the case in monkeys or chimpanzees.

It appears to be quite reasonable to list monkey sounds and tabulate their meanings. It is also reasonable to say that most of the sounds are only parts of a multimodal system, and considering them in isolation destroys the system. Collection of more data and further reasoning by the human mind will not settle a conflict of this kind, unless the mind has the critical information, the information which comes from experiments.

Consider walking as the activity, rather than communicating. We could agree to divide the activity into many observable, describable segments, but such description would give no information on joints, muscles, center of gravity, or the forces involved. The analysis of the activity of walking requires an understanding of the internal structures and how they work. In my opinion, the same is the case for social activities, and the search for all the items which can be listed in an ethogram will be regarded as useless as is much of traditional systematic anatomy. The fact that the lists can be made does not prove that they are useful or a necessary way of understanding behaviors.

Turning to the subject of human speech, it is the sound code which makes speaking possible. The short, contrasting sounds (phonemes) permit an almost infinite number of combinations. This vocal communication system is controlled by a great deal of cortex, and any conscious thought may be labeled. From an evolutionary point of view, the success of the beginning of such a system led to modification of both the articulatory apparatus and, more importantly, the controlling brain. This point of view stresses the factors of the brain, the phonetic code, the adaptive value of the system, and the rapid communication of knowledge.

But this is not a necessary way of approaching the problem. Hockett ('69) argues that so little is known about the brain that comparisons should be made by using a common frame of reference for both human and nonhuman communication. This view led to the description of design features for primate communication. Altmann ('67) has shown that most, if not all, the design features of human language may be found in the communication systems of monkeys. This indicates the difference in the approaches. Emphasis on the code and the brain leads to seeing the human system as very different and, from an evolutionary point of view, new. Emphasis on sounds and design features makes it hard to demonstrate any differences at all.

My bias is that it is necessary to consider the internal mechanisms and that it is very misleading to use the same design features to describe nonhuman multimodal and human code-dependent communication.

The problem can be illustrated by the studies of the Gardners ('71) and Premack ('71) on chimpanzee communication. Chimpanzees do not speak and cannot be taught to do so but they are highly intelligent animals and, when men arrange matters so they can communicate without using a sound code, the chimpanzees' behaviors may show most of the characteristics of human language. Since the human sound code puts a label on some human thought processes, it should not come as a surprise that the functioning of human brains and chimpanzee brains have a great deal in common.

In our culture there is a deep confusion between language and thought. It is commonly believed that language is necessary for thought, rather than that thinking is an activity of the brain and language the labeling of some of the conscious activities of the brain. It is often said that human languages may refer to the past or future and are not limited to expressing feelings of the moment. But that is just a normal activity of the brain.

Again, it has been constantly averred that man alone can symbolize, and this is one of the reasons that the studies of the Gardners ('71) and Premack ('71) were so astonishing. Obviously the chimpanzees are capable of elaborate use of symbols. Yerkes demonstrated this many years ago, and the point is that it is only one class of symbols, those of the sound code, which are unique to man. In a very real sense, the mammalian brain is a symbolic machine, and the animal acts only on the basis of what the brain has processed.

These matters can now be investigated directly in human beings whose corpus callosum has been sectioned. In the split brain, the sound code is on one side and an otherwise normal human brain on the other. The non-language side thinks and, in some tasks, performs better than the language side. It would be very interesting to use Premack's chimpanzee tests in exploring the non-language side of a human.

The problem of the nature of human language could not be solved by studying languages, no matter how thoroughly and how imaginatively, because the word "language" stands both for the phonetic code and for some functions of the brain. The use of the word "language" builds a fundamental confusion into the problem. This confusion can only be reduced by experiments which keep these two quite different problems separated.

It is here that an eclectic primatology may contribute because it is not bound to find the solutions in a traditional division of knowledge: in a department of linguistics, psychology, philosophy, or anthropology. In primatology, answers may be sought in field studies, in the laboratory, or in the hospital. Clearly, what would help the study of language most is a much better understanding of the brain. The problem cannot be settled at the level it is usually attacked, and it offers a good example of the futility of endless description carried on at one traditional level.

In summary, primatology has the unique opportunity to contribute to the understanding of man. It is not limited by the traditional departmental boundaries which stifle progress in the universities. It is not bound to any particular technique or point of view. As shown in the IPC program, primatology uses the methods of many different sciences. All primatologists should encourage this approach and should discourage parts of the field from becoming intellectually isolated from the rest.

Especially from the point of view of the social sciences, I see three major contributions of primatology:

1.  A fundamental challenge to the notion that there are different levels of knowledge and that the social should be studied without reference to the biological.
2.  A repudiation of the "black box" philosophy, and an insistence that the study of behavior must include an effort to understand internal mechanisms, including emotions.
3.  A repudiation of the thought that man is a rational animal and that the brain offers any simple road to truth. We, too, are primates, carrying the advantages and limitations of our evolutionary history and indoctrinated in a particular primitive culture.

Truth is a very restless thing. The promise of primatology lies in being animal oriented, problem oriented, and experimental. The less we trust the past, the more likely we are to be useful in the present. The more we can borrow techniques which probe far beneath superficial description, the more likely we are to make substantial progress. If we would understand the primates, we cannot accept the view of rational, scientific man which is deeply embedded in our culture. We are primates, products of the evolutionary process, and the promise of primatology is a better understanding of the peculiar creature we call man.

## LITERATURE CITED

Altmann, S. A. (ed.). 1967 Social Communication among Primates. University of Chicago Press, Chicago, pp. 325–362.

Delgado, J. M. R. 1971 Brain research and behavioural activity. In: Background for Man. P. Dolhinow and V. M. Sarich, eds. Little, Brown and Co., Boston, pp. 324–339.

Gardner, B. T., and R. A. Gardner. 1971 Two-way communication with an infant chimpanzee. In: Behavior of Nonhuman Primates. A. M. Schrier and F. Stollnitz, eds. Academic Press, New York, pp. 117–184.

Gazzaniga, M. S. 1970 The Bisected Brain. Appleton-Century-Crofts, New York.

Hockett, C. F. 1969 In: Primate Communication. D. Ploog and T. Melnechuk. eds. Neurosciences Research Program Bulletin, Brookline, Massachusetts. Vol. 7, No. 5, p. 462.

Lancaster, J. B. 1968 Primate communication systems and the emergence of human language. In: Primates: Studies in Adaptation and Variability. P. C. Jay, ed. Holt, Rinehart and Winston, New York, Chap. 16, pp. 439–457.

MacLean, P. D. 1970 The triune brain, emotion and scientific bias. In: The Neurosciences. F. O. Schmitt, ed. Rockefeller University Press, New York, pp. 349–360.

Myers, R. E. 1969 Neurology of social communication in primates. In: Proc. of the 2nd Int. Congr. Primate. Atlanta, Ga. 1968. Vol. 3, H. Hofer, ed. S. Karger, New York, pp. 1–9.

Napier, J. R., and P. N. Napier 1967 A Handbook of Living Primates. Academic Press, New York.

Ploog, D. 1970 Social communication among animals. In: The Neurosciences. F. O Schimitt ed. Rockefeller University Press, New York, pp. 349–360.

Premack, D. 1971 On the assessment of language competence in the chimpanzee. In: Behavior of Nonhuman Primates. A. M. Schrian and F. Stollnitz, eds. Academic Press, New York, pp. 186–228.

Robinson, B. W. 1967 Vocalization evoked from the forebrain in *Macaca mulatta*. Physiol. Behav., 2: 345–354.

Struhsaker, T. T. 1967 Auditory communication among vervet monkeys (*Cercopithecus aethiops*). In: Social Communication among Primates. S. A. Altmann, ed. University of Chicago Press, Chapt. 16, pp. 281–324.

*Washburn insisted that the study of behavior be linked to biology and internal mechanisms. His own interests in brain and behavior made important connections between evolutionary questions, the fossils, and the neurosciences. Steklis uses this approach to consider the evolution of brain and intelligence. Early anomalous findings about the effect of brain lesions on social behavior and cognition led Steklis to reconsider the evolution of primate intelligence. He discusses the history of two current hypotheses integrating perspectives from anthropology, psychology, animal behavior, sociobiology, and neurobiology. This cross-disciplinary framework offers up new questions and an alternative neuromodular view of cognition. Steklis explores what it might mean to say the brain is an organ of adaptation and demonstrates the "promise of primatology" that Washburn had envisioned.*

# 6 The Primate Brain and the Origins of Intelligence

**H. Dieter Steklis**   *Department of Anthropology, Rutgers University*

## INTRODUCTION

The discipline of primatology, Washburn (1973) once argued, could make unique contributions to the social sciences because of its problem-oriented, multidisciplinary approach—its field of inquiry was not stifled by the arbitrary traditional academic departmental boundaries that had promoted the artificial separation of organisms into physical, biological, and social components for study. To Washburn, the elucidation of internal mechanisms was as important as understanding ecological influences on behavior—only in this way could humans, or any other animal, be understood as evolved, integrated wholes. When in the early 1970s the neurosciences were booming, Washburn urged his students, whether in the field or in the laboratory, to take a serious interest in the brain. The study of brain function, he felt, provided important insights into primate social behavior (e.g., especially in the study of communication; see Washburn 1973), which inspired some of his students to conduct pioneering brain-behavior field experiments (Kling, Lancaster, and Benitone 1970) and many to develop an abiding interest in the neurobiology of primate behavior.

I was among those students fortunate to be exposed to Washburn's integrative perspective, and it is no doubt because of this background that this chapter's topic of primate intelligence originally captured my at-

tention. This interest grew out of a puzzling finding we had obtained early in our study of social and cognitive behavioral effects of brain lesions in social groups of nonhuman primates (Kling and Steklis 1976). In brief, removal of certain brain areas led to consistent disturbances in social behavior but spared performance on standard laboratory learning tasks, whereas lesions to other areas impaired learning abilities but spared social behavior. In neurological terms, we had found for some brain areas a "double dissociation" between the general learning ability of monkeys and their ability to maintain normal social relationships. This was certainly perplexing at the time and remained so until recently. Should not social skills tap into the same intellectual capacities that underlie learning in other contexts? After all, I had been taught that primate intelligence likely arose as an adaptation for skillful social action—the hallmark of primate evolution.

And so the matter stood until a few years ago, when primatologists, on the heels of progress in the neurocognitive sciences and sociobiology, with a vengeance took up the topic of the evolution of primate intelligence. From these developments, I believe, emerges an answer to our earlier perplexing findings on the dissociation of cognitive and social skills. However, as I show in this chapter, this answer raises new, significant questions about the nature of primate intelligence and its neural basis that have not been fully appreciated or explored. My plan here is to review briefly the major ideas proposed on the origin of primate intelligence, discuss the nature and neural substrates of different types of intelligence, and finally consider the implications of this discussion for theories of the evolution of social and ecological intelligence and comparative investigations of the brain and intelligence. Along the way, I will place much of this discussion in a historical perspective of primatology and related disciplines.

## SOCIAL VERSUS ECOLOGICAL INTELLIGENCE

There is little disagreement that primates are large-brained, intelligent animals. Though they are neither uniquely intelligent nor uniquely large-brained (see dolphins, for example; Connor et al. 1992), primates as a group do have larger brains than the average expected for terrestrial mammals of corresponding body sizes (Jerison 1973). Moreover, while most prosimian brains fall within the range expected for their body size, the monkeys and apes have brains about two times larger than expected for mammals of their size, and the human brain is three times larger than expected for a primate of similar body size (Passingham 1982).

These differences in relative brain size among primates and between primates and other mammals roughly match our intuitive understanding of differences in intelligence or cognitive abilities, although, as we will see, finding a meaningful measure of "intelligence" across species has proved all but impossible (e.g., Passingham 1982). And on the notion that "bigger is better," it is usually assumed that large brains and high intelligence go together, such that the former can serve as a proxy measure for the latter (e.g., Byrne 1995a). We will examine this claim further in Section 7. In answer to the question of what selection pressures were responsible for the evolution of large primate brains, and thus intelligence, two sets of hypotheses have been proposed. One, which I call the "social intelligence hypothesis" (SIH), in essence proposes that social life itself, that is, the complexity of social interaction, has been the driving force behind the evolution of high intelligence. The second hypothesis, here called the "ecological intelligence hypothesis" (EIH), avers that the demands of foraging for food and the associated development of food extraction and processing skills and technologies promoted the evolution of intelligence.

The SIH was the earlier of the two hypotheses, proposed in the mid-1960s (Jolly 1966). The intervening years have seen formidable advances in our understanding of the structure and function of primate social systems, feeding and foraging ecology, and brain, behavior, and cognition. This progress appears to have provided more support for the SIH, perhaps in large part because of the "paucity of well-developed alternatives" (Byrne 1995a). But I believe it also owes its present wide palatability to a fundamental reorientation to the study of animal social behavior that occurred in the 1970s and 1980s that I will describe briefly below. Indeed, it is easy to see why the SIH appears more appealing and plausible in the light of our growing understanding of the complexity of primate social interaction (e.g., Harcourt 1992). The SIH and EIH are often considered alternative evolutionary explanations of primate intelligence, and there has been surprisingly little discussion of their interrelationship and fit with research on the brain and intelligence (but see Cheney and Seyfarth 1990; Cachel 1994; and Byrne 1995b, for notable exceptions). I will explore this more fully in Section 6, after a closer look at the SIH and EIH.

## THE SOCIAL INTELLIGENCE HYPOTHESIS (SIH)

With the end of World War II came a renaissance of primate field studies that had begun in the 1930s with the work of Clarence Carpenter (Washburn and Hamburg 1965). This resurgence was led mostly by anthropologists and psychologists because study of the complexity and adaptive function of primate social systems promised to elucidate the nature and evolution of human social behavior (e.g., Jay 1968; Washburn 1963). Though much research had been done on primate intelligence in the laboratory, observations of primates in the wild begged the question of the adaptive use, or ecological relevance, of the intellectual capacities demonstrated in captivity. In this intellectual climate, Jolly (1966) set out to study lemurs in Madagascar with the question: "What bearing has primate social behavior on the evolution of intelligence?" Her work led her to propose that, because primates learn most of what they know about their social and natural worlds through social example, it is the use of intelligence in the context of primate social life, what she called "the social use of intelligence," that accounts for the evolution of high intellect in monkeys, apes, and humans (Jolly 1966). Jolly included in her discussion of intelligence "manipulative, object cleverness," whose development she saw as dependent on social learning, particularly social imitation, and consequently as a by-product of social intelligence.

Jolly's paper (1966) was the first explicit formulation of the SIH. A decade later, Humphrey (1976) independently proposed essentially the same idea, but he provided a more detailed discussion of the social uses of intellect. It is easy to see in his discussion the influence of the rise of sociobiology, with its emphasis on individuals in social groups as reproductive competitors. Humphrey thus argues that in a social group composed of individuals with potentially conflicting reproductive interests, social interaction is like a game of chess: Each player must at every turn consider several alternative moves because of the unpredictable nature of the opponent's next move. Life in a social group composed of many social partners spanning several generations would thus place a premium on the development of complex behavioral strategies and the requisite cognitive abilities. To Humphrey, a key function of social intellect is to keep the social group together as a functioning unit in which the young can learn proper social conduct and, ultimately, through which factual knowledge about the environment can be passed from one generation to the next. Like Jolly, he argues it is therefore social intelligence that makes possible the acquisition of knowledge about the habitat (i.e., ecological intelligence) and in humans the development of scientific thought. In short, both Jolly and Humphrey view creative intelligence as a unitary faculty that evolved in response to the cognitive demands of social interaction and gave rise secondarily to forms of intelligent behavior in other contexts, such as problem solving in the laboratory, or scientific reasoning.

The flowering of sociobiological theory in the 1970s and 1980s, and in particular that of one of its successful offspring—behavioral ecology (see Gross 1994)—led to a strong interest in the proximate mechanisms responsible for the complex behavioral decisions of social animals. The result was a renewed interest in the study of animal cognition, including previously eschewed subjective states like intentionality and consciousness (Griffin 1981, 1992) or mental content (e.g., Cheney and Seyfarth 1990). The eventual result of this new interest and the desire to place the study of mental processes on a firm scientific footing was a certain merger between the cognitive neurosciences and animal behavior, whereby animal behaviorists incorporated cognitivist methods (e.g., artificial intelligence models) and concepts (computation, representation) into their analyses of key adaptive behavioral strategies like foraging or mate choice. Indeed, the founding of behavioral ecology's subdiscipline of cognitive ecology (Real 1993) in the 1980s formally reflected and validated these new interdisciplinary interests.

In this intellectual atmosphere in the late 1980s, Byrne and Whiten (1988; Whiten and Byrne 1988) took Jolly's and Humphrey's ideas a step farther by introducing the idea of Machiavellian intelligence. By this they mean that, unlike most animals, including the prosimians, monkeys and apes have evolved minds that are adept at representing socially relevant information about conspecifics and using that information to manipulate the behavior of others to selfish ends. In their view, the great apes surpass monkeys in this capacity by being capable of intentional deception, an ability that requires the modeling of another's mind and the attribution of intentions to others—or "mind reading" (Whiten 1991). Harcourt (1988, 1992) has shown that Machiavellian intelligence is particularly manifest in social coalitions and alliances. Primate coalitions are more complex than those of nonprimates because primates cultivate and use allies opportunistically on the basis of detailed (cognitive) evaluation of a potential ally's usefulness in competitive situations (Harcourt 1992). Byrne (1995a) argues that while the use of Machiavellian intelligence provided the principal selection pressure for the evolution of the primate brain and intelligence, ecological factors may also have contributed: "It is unlikely a single factor was crucial in selecting intelligence over a span of 55 million years—diet must be a part of a full explanation." (I will return to Byrne's view of the interrelationship between ecological and social intelligence in Section 5.)

The Machiavellian version of the SIH thus specifies in far greater detail than could have been done by Jolly or Humphrey what is complex—perhaps uniquely so—about primate social interactions and the mental operations to support them. It is ironic that these mentalistic descriptions of primate social behavior in terms of deception and mind reading, while not unjustly criticized by some (e.g., Kummer et al. 1990), nevertheless owe their wide acceptance today to the foundations laid by sociobiology, a discipline at its emergence ridiculed for espousing a rigid genetic determinism.

## THE ECOLOGICAL INTELLIGENCE HYPOTHESIS (EIH)

I have subsumed under the EIH several ideas about ecological factors responsible for the origin of primate intelligence. These are foraging for food and the extraction of food, including manufacture and use of tools (Parker and Gibson 1977), and what Cachel (1994) has called "natural history intelligence"—the knowledge, internal representation, and manipulation of the nonsocial world. I have lumped these together under the EIH because, despite their emphasis on different components of the nonsocial world, they all focus on the importance of the natural environment or ecology as a stimulus to the evolution of intelligence.

The most powerful challenge to the SIH was by Milton (1981). Based on her fieldwork with howler and spider monkeys in central Panama, she put forward the alternative hypothesis that the problems of finding food in a tropical rain forest selected for large brains and intelligence. Her argument went something like this: In tropical forests, primate plant foods (like young leaves, flowers, and fruit) are patchily distributed in space and time, but their pattern of availability is predictable. As larger primates in particular require absolutely more food and in a patchy environment a more diversified diet, greater intelligence would make this process more efficient by allowing the memorization of the location and timing of preferred foods. Milton predicted that primates dependent on the most "hyper-dispersed" and patchy foods will have greater intelligence (as determined indirectly by relative cranial capacities) than species dependent on more uniformly distributed foods. Milton showed that spider monkeys rely more on fruit than howlers, and forage over an area about 25 times larger, placing a premium on good memory for types and locations of foods. Consistent with her prediction, spider monkey brains are about twice as large as howler monkey brains (taking body weight and gut size differences into account); and indeed among primates generally, frugivore brains are larger than folivore brains (citations in Milton 1981). In contrast to proponents of the SIH, Milton (1981, 1988) suggests that the majority of behavioral differences between spider and howler monkeys (e.g., in social organization and richness of communicative repertoire) are secondary to basic dietary differences, and thus the resultant differences in social complexity secondarily contributed to the evolution of encephalization and intelligence.

As few years prior to Milton, Parker and Gibson (1977, 1979) arrived at the same conclusion, that feeding strategies are the primary cause of primate intelligence from which "intellectual adaptations for social life" are secondarily derived. Indeed, in their discussion of the evolution of human intelligence in relation to subsistence activities, Parker and Gibson (1979) anticipated much of Milton's (1988) ideas on the subject. Parker and Gibson's argument was a recapitulationist one, in which the evolution of primate intelligence is reconstructed from the sequence of the Piagetian stages of human sensorimotor development (as an index of intellectual development). In their scenario, intelligence first evolved as an adaptation for efficient extractive foraging with tools, while highly developed forms of intelligence, including language, in the hominid lineage evolved as adaptations for cooperative hunting, food sharing, stone tool making, and other subsistence-related activities. Milton (1988) similarly suggests (and apparently independently of Parker and Gibson's earlier work) that complex mental abilities and language in hominids evolved for improved food getting and processing abilities (cooperative hunting, food sharing, etc.).

More recently, Cachel (1994) has suggested that an important aspect of "ecological intelligence" is what she calls "natural history intelligence." In essence, she views this as the ability to deduce cause-and-effect relationships from observations of natural events (e.g., inferring the presence of predators from their tracks), "to predict events, and to plan behaviors that anticipate or control these events . . . outside of the social world" (p. 26). Humans, she suggests, are particularly good at this, whereas some other primates virtually lack this ability. Thus, east African vervet monkeys, for example, do not associate python tracks on the ground with the actual presence of pythons, nor the stored carcasses in trees with the dangerous presence of leopards, though one could imagine it would serve the vervets well to make such associations, given that they are preyed upon by both pythons and leopards.

Contrary to some advocates of the SIH, Cachel argues that natural history intelligence is *not* derived from social intelligence because the latter is not transferable to other nonsocial contexts, and that therefore other factors must be identified to explain the high development of natural history intelligence in humans. In fact, Cachel sees an incompatibility between the development of Machiavellian and natural history intelligence predicated on competition between "behavioral, anatomical, and physiological components of the phenotype that relate to sociality . . . (and) phenotypic components that relate to the external environment" (p. 27). Thus natural history intelligence only appears in species that lack or have a reduced Machiavellian mode of social life (e.g., emphasizing social cooperation over status-striving), which according to Cachel characterized the course of hominid evolution.

## DOMAIN-GENERAL OR DOMAIN-SPECIFIC INTELLIGENCE?

I hope it is apparent from this review of the SIH and EIH that their authors present, implicitly if not explicitly, a diversity of viewpoints on the nature of intelligence and therefore its evolutionary course. Simplifying a little, the different viewpoints can be summarized thusly:

1.   Intelligence is a general, unitary faculty that has its primary origins in either the social (Jolly, Humphrey) or ecological (Parker and Gibson, Milton) realm.
2.   Intelligence is a general, unitary faculty that, while primarily derived from Machiavellian social cognition, is likely also the result of ecological problem solving (Byrne).

3.  Social intelligence and ecological intelligence are different, nontransferrable, and antagonistic, with the result that one flourishes at the expense of the other (Cachel).

One major difference between these viewpoints is whether intelligence is seen as some sort of general high capacity for problem solving that is independent of context (i.e., social or ecological) or whether it is a context-specific problem-solving ability. In the parlance of cognitive science, the arguments turn on whether intelligence is "domain-general" or "domain-specific." A second issue concerns the transferability of domain-specific intelligence across domains, such that skills (or intelligence) employed in one domain (e.g., food processing) are of use in another (e.g., social interaction). I will address each of these issues in turn.

Historically, among animal behaviorists the prevailing view has been of intelligence as a unitary (or domain-general) faculty that is derived from general processes of learning (i.e., association and reinforcement) characteristic of most animal species (see Kamil 1994 for review). This view has had its persistent proponents. For example, from his broad survey of learning in vertebrates, Macphail (1982, 1987) concluded that "there are no differences in intellect among non-human vertebrates" and that problem-solving abilities, based in all species on simple processes of association formation, are therefore "independent of niche-specific adaptations" (i.e., ecology).

However, Macphail's strong views are atypical, and as Kamil (1994) has argued, they can hardly be maintained in the light of much research and theoretical development in behavioral ecology and in cognitive ecology especially (e.g., see edited volume by Real 1994). In countering Macphail, Kamil (1994) has argued that on logical grounds alone, intelligence cannot be independent of an animal's niche: From an evolutionary perspective, if animal learning abilities are adaptive, then there must be species differences in learning and intelligence. Different species may well rely on similar basic learning mechanisms (such as association and reinforcement), but the manner and extent to which these are employed and whether entirely new, specialized abilities (e.g., song learning) are called for will depend on the species-specific nature of the adaptive problems to be solved. A unitary cognitive capacity, or some sort of multipurpose problem solver, therefore, is highly unlikely as an effective evolutionary solution to a diversity of social and ecological adaptive problems. In the language of cognitive ecology, each species has evolved a niche-specific set of distinct problem-solving abilities—a "cognitive architecture" (Real 1991)—

rather than more or less of some general problem-solving (or intellectual) capacity.

Much research in cognitive ecology clearly supports this evolutionary logic, but this is not the place to review it. Notably, domain specificity at the cognitive level is undergirded by domain-specific neural specializations, or cognitive modules in several mammalian species (see Francis 1995 for review). Indeed, we can take Harvey and Krebs's (1990) finding that brain components have evolved independently of each other in response to particular environmental demands as strong support of neural modularity.

In humans as well, beginning with the study of language, we have known for some time that higher cognitive processes are largely domain-specific or modular in their functional organization and neural representation (see Fodor 1983; Gardner 1985; Gazzaniga 1989; Hirschfeld and Gelman 1994 for review). It is of interest that historically the modern idea of modularity of function is a reinvention of the old, once dominant school of faculty psychology that fell out of favor because of its detour into phrenology (Fodor 1983). Modern neuroscience, however, has embraced modularity as an efficient organizational principle of the brain: The "encapsulation" of functions in the brain may be a particularly efficient way of packaging a diverse array of "problem solvers." In describing the very different problem-solving aspects of the visual and auditory systems in the brain, for example, Hubel commented on the logical inescapability of regional specialization: "It is difficult to imagine the same neural apparatus dealing with all of these phenomena . . . for the major aspects of the brain's operations, no master solution is likely (quoted in Gardner 1983, p. 51).

Evolutionary psychologists concerned with the evolution of human psychological characteristics perhaps have presented some of the most persuasive arguments for what they call domain-specific adaptive cognitive modules (e.g., Buss 1990; Barkow, Cosmides, and Tooby 1992). Cosmides and Tooby (1994), for example, argue boldly that "the widespread prejudice among cognitive psychologists for theories positing evolved architectures that consist of nothing but general-purpose problem solvers" (p. 87) is wholly unjustified. (I will not repeat here their detailed argument against the plausibility of domain-general mechanisms; see especially Tooby and Cosmides 1992). In brief, they take essentially a cognitive ecological perspective in arguing that human cognitive architecture was designed (by natural selection) to solve specific adaptive problems encountered by ancestral Pleistocene hunter-gatherers. Because many of these adaptive problems (finding food, selecting a mate, parenting, engaging in social exchange) have (fitness) solutions that are different or incompatible, they are each solved most effectively by problem or domain-specific cognitive mechanisms. Any domain-general learning system that had to generate a best course of action in such diverse, sometimes even life-threatening, circumstances, they argue, would fail miserably, being quickly paralyzed by a "combinatorial explosion" of possible courses of action. As a consequence, evolution opted for specialized cognitive modules (also called "algorithms"), that, on the basis of millions of years of "experience," produce statistically reliable, situation-appropriate, and, if necessary, unblinking behavioral results.

It may already be apparent from my description of the evolutionary psychologists' view of the human psyche that what we have been calling "social intelligence" (i.e., cognitive operations employed to solve social problems) in their view cannot serve the diversity of adaptive social problems encountered (Cosmides and Tooby 1992). They argue that social intelligence, or social cognition, is not a unitary domain because social life poses a number of distinct problems that "must involve very different procedures for their solution" (Cosmides and Tooby 1994). Thus these authors would fine-tune social cognition to consist of several modules each with a distinct computational rule structure (i.e., an algorithm) that is inapplicable from one social problem to another (i.e., not transferable across social domains). Cosmides and Tooby (1992) show, for example, that rules of inference for detecting cheaters on social contracts will not be effective in detecting bluffs and double-crosses in situations of threat. If this high degree of computational specificity for the solution of adaptive problems is generally correct, we could easily wind up with several dozen evolved cognitive modules to fill the human psyche—a modern, revitalized phrenology of the mind.

Are these cognitive modules or algorithms of the evolutionary psychologist intelligences? Cosmides and Tooby don't say (in their edited volume on the evolution of the human mind [Barkow, Cosmides, and Tooby 1992], the word "intelligence" does not appear in the index!), but we will assume they are because they fit modularists' definitions of intelligence. These definitions are in fact very general so as not to be specific to the operations of any particular module. Two examples should suffice: Gardner (1983), who has perhaps provided the most in-depth treatment of modular or "multiple intelligences" in humans, eliminates sensory and perceptual processes (like face recognition) by defining intelligence broadly, as entailing "a set of skills of problem solving . . . (as well as of) finding or creating problems" (p. 60). Kamil (1994) similarly provides what he calls a broad, synthetic definition of intelligence that

includes a variety of learning and conditioning processes: "those processes by which animals obtain and retain information about their environments and use that information to make behavioral decisions" (p. 21). To the extent that domain-specific cognitive modules are responsible for such processes and skills, they are each intelligent but in different ways, and what we have been traditionally calling "intelligence" likely reflects a composite of multiple intelligences.

Even if we can agree that there are many, separate cognitive modules, or intelligences, in the brain, and I have argued that the evidence in their favor is very strong, there are nevertheless two related problems that must be addressed. One concerns the functional relationship among the separate intelligences, or what I earlier referred to as the problem of transferability, and whether transferability can give rise to any domain-general intelligent processes. The second issue concerns the evolution of separate intelligences: Might there be antagonisms or incompatibilities as suggested by Cachel?

A strict modular account holds that the separate intelligences are completely autonomous, with no transferability of skills across modules (reviewed in Gardner 1983). For many theorists, however, this strict modularity defeats common understanding of what is a hallmark of intelligent activity, namely, the ability to apply skills or knowledge acquired in one domain to other domains—in other words, a domain-general abstract problem-solving ability. One way out of this apparent modularist straightjacket is to posit a domain-general module nestled amidst, and superordinate to, an array of domain-specific modules (e.g., see Fodor 1983). Another is simply to suggest that modules are not impenetrable but can access each other's processes to make possible generalization across domains. Cosmides and Tooby (1994), understandably, remain dubious about any domain-general devices, granting that to the extent such exist, they are "embedded in a constellation of specialized mechanisms." For Byrne (1995b), transfer between domains is the essence of primate intelligence. He defines intelligence as a set of general-purpose skills that are abstracted from and cut across behavioral domains. According to him, the evolution of (domain-general) primate intelligence thus might well have been built from skills derived in *both* social and ecological contexts: "perhaps the answer is not 'either/or' at all. Social and technical skills are not independent in practice" (Byrne 1995b: 209). In support, he goes on to note that the socially most intelligent primates (chimps) also turn out to be technologically the most sophisticated. Byrne's position here is similar to the one of Cheney and Seyfarth (1990), who also see primate intelligence depending on transfer between modules.

However, in their view, such transfer occurs only in apes and humans, which is why vervet monkeys, for example, who are socially highly intelligent, appear relatively unintelligent in other contexts.

No matter whether we see intelligence (defined as a *general* problem-solving ability) as arising from the operation of a domain-general module or through access between specialized, domain-specific modules, each view faces substantial problems. First of all, the two are not in essence different: If general problem solving occurs through intermodular transfer, then there must be a separate neural network connected to all modules in which abstraction and generalization occur, given that the individual modules are dedicated, domain-specific processors. There is, then, either an identifiable general processor in the brain (which so far has eluded neuroscientists) or else we are left with the scientifically less comfortable notion of intelligence (like consciousness itself) as an emergent property of the identifiable, collective modular activity. This is indeed a central problem in neuropsychology, where we know well, for example, the location and operation of the modular components of the visual system (like color and motion) but have no idea of how an integrated visual image results or "where" it resides. As a result, the existence of a central all-purpose processor, like consciousness or vision, can take on a near mystical quality, as, for example, the locus of the "self" (Gardner 1983) or of "beliefs" (Fodor 1983). Such a processor's very centrality and integrative function also suggest a neural homunculus—unwelcome to most neurophilosophers—who is conscious (or is consciousness itself) and decides (or wills) courses of thought and action (e.g., Gazzaniga's [1992] "interpreter" in the left hemisphere). In short, neither the idea of emergence nor of a homunculus is scientifically appealing because of the neural intractability of each.

Finally, the modularist's version of a domain-general module is still open to the same criticisms leveled at all domain-general modules that we explored earlier. It is therefore hard to imagine such a module playing any significant role in the brain's decision-making hierarchy. (Indeed, if it did play a key role in decision making, then there would be little need for specialized but unempowered modules in the first place!) In short, appealing as the idea of a domain-general module may be from a common-sense view of intelligence, it is hard to accommodate into an evolutionary, modular view of cognition and the brain.

A stricter modular view of intelligence, on the other hand, in which there are multiple domain-specific intelligences offers the positive opportunity of reconceptualizing the evolution of intelligence. For one, it should be immediately apparent that the SIH and EIH need no longer be alternative hypotheses since they address the evolution of different intelligence modules. Second, if intelligence does not depend on domain-general processes, then it is unnecessary to resort to scenarios in which social or ecological pressures at different times in phylogeny contributed to the evolution of (an) intelligence. As described earlier, advocates of the SIH or EIH see either one or the other or a combination of the two selection pressures over time giving rise to a general intellectual faculty. Jolly (1979), for example, in response to Parker and Gibson, suggests (in keeping with her original SIH) that sociality was the key selection pressure in the evolutionary transition of prosimian to anthropoid, whereas foraging became central to the later evolution of hominoid intelligence. And, more recently, in discussing the contributions of social life and foraging techniques to primate intelligence, Jolly (1985) concludes, "I suspect that both contributed to a general capacity for thought." In Cachel's (1994) scenario, a Machiavellian social life was key to the evolution of intelligence throughout most of primate evolution. Only in the course of human evolution, with a reduced need for Machiavellian intelligence, did natural history intelligence flower and prevail.

A modular perspective offers an alternative scenario not previously considered. In the same way that multiple intelligences develop in ontogeny (Gardner 1983), depending on natural talent (or genetic background) and appropriate domain-specific stimulation (or environment), more than one intelligence could have been selected for at any one time in a species' phylogeny. The mix of social and ecological settings encountered by the species would determine the adaptive set of intelligences and the manner in and degree to which each is developed—that is, a species' cognitive architecture. Thus, vervet monkeys, or other nonhuman primates, may not lack natural history intelligence because they have a highly developed Machiavellian intelligence, as Cachel (1994) proposes, but rather because the former has been of relatively less adaptive value to them. (Here we need only assume that the evolution of both faculties was not limited by available brain space—that there was no necessary trade-off; see Section 6.) In any event, by most accounts, humans evidence a high development of both types of intelligence (Macchiavelli was, after all, human), which is consistent with modularity and clearly mitigates against the sort of antagonism between the two faculties posited by Cachel. If I am correct in adopting this modular, cognitive ecological view, then we should be able to identify other primate species that have both highly developed Machiavellian and natural history intelligence. To do this, we will have to examine more closely the content and neural basis of intelligence.

## THE CONTENT AND NEURAL BASIS
## OF INTELLIGENCE

In this section I examine the content of social intelligence, as well as review what is known about its neural basis. This analysis is prerequisite to a comparative and evolutionary investigation of intelligence. As I hope to show, a modular view of intelligence is testable comparatively through predictions about the existence and relative elaboration of intelligences among primate species. I restrict my review to the topic of social intelligence, as there is virtually no information available on the content or neural basis of ecological types of intelligence. As well, my review will have to be highly selective, given the vast experimental and clinical literature pertinent to social intelligence (e.g., a published Primate Information Center bibliography lists over 100 citations between 1965 and 1984 on the topic of neural correlates of social behavior in nonhuman primates). More extensive, systematic reviews of this literature can be found in Steklis and Kling (1985) and in Brothers (1990) and Brothers and Ring (1992).

In examining the proposed separate intelligences more closely, we are naturally led to ask by what criteria one can be distinguished from the other, or what defines a "domain" (or cognitive "module") in the first place. Here there is, unfortunately, little consensus, in part because the high interest in domain-specific cognition is relatively new and because different criteria for isolating domains have been employed (for review, see Hirschfeld and Gelman 1994). Herschfeld and Gelman propose an "uncontroversial characterization" of a domain: "A domain is a body of knowledge that identifies and interprets a class of phenomena assumed to share certain properties and to be of a distinct and general type. A domain functions as a stable response to a set of recurring and complex problems faced by the organism. This response involves difficult-to-access perceptual, encoding, retrieval, and inferential processes dedicated to that solution" (1994: 21). A domain is generally not considered equivalent, for example, to processing in a sensory channel (e.g., visual line detection) or a perceptual process (e.g., face recognition) but, rather, is thought of as a broader, adaptive problem-oriented computational mechanism. Human language comes to mind as most easily fitting this domain characterization (Fodor 1983; Pinker and Bloom 1992).

The question of whether social intelligence, or what is more often referred to as "social cognition," is a unitary domain is not as easily answered. Cosmides and Tooby (1994) don't think so, given that different social problems require distinctly different computational mechanisms for their solution. Brothers (1990), on the other hand, presents a convincing case for a "social cog-nition module," as does Gardner (1983), whose idea of "interpersonal intelligence" as a single domain has much in common with the essence of Brothers' proposal; however, the latter is a more detailed account of this module's content as it relates to the ethologists' theory of Machiavellian intelligence. Briefly, Brothers proposes the following: The module's core function is to establish a "theory of mind," that is, a set of inferences about the dispositions and intentions of others. In primates this is achieved, perhaps uniquely, by linking the processing of social information (e.g., individual identity, posture, facial expression, vocalization, relations between individuals) to affect. By virtue of this intimate tie between perceived social information and affect, another's intention or disposition is experienced as affect:

> The affective coloration of social experience, experienced as lived feeling, is a powerful signal to its possessor. Shame is a social affect, as are triumph, jealousy, parental tenderness, romantic love, and all the hard-to-name affects . . . Complex social life calls for subtle, differentiated and varied feelings, useful as internal signals in environments consisting of mates, offspring, allies, rivals, leaders, in-groups, bullies, and friends. I propose that the human possession of a huge "dictionary" of innate feelings has as its evolutionary origin the demands of social existence. (Brothers 1990: 41)

In apparent agreement with Byrne (1995a), who argues that only the great apes attribute intentionality to others, Brothers and Ring (1992) also see qualitative differences among primates in the construction of a theory of mind. Thus, while macaques have an "understanding of affective display, of basic social interactions occurring between other animals, and perhaps of simple agency" (p. 111), the assignment of social traits or qualities to others, such as "helpful," "generous," "selfish," or "untrustworthy" is evolutionarily more recent.

Some have argued that the human "mind-reading system" consists of a larger complex of four interlinked modules, of which a "theory of mind" module is only one (Baron-Cohen 1994). Whether one or more modules or domains are involved in this "system" remains a matter of active debate (see commentators following Baron-Cohen 1994), and the question may finally turn on interpretations of its neural substrate, inasmuch as neural isolatability constitutes an acid test of modularity (Fodor 1983).

There is considerable evidence, from human and nonhuman primates, pointing to brain structures and processes specialized for social cognition. Brothers (1990) and Brothers and Ring (1992) have reviewed much of this evidence, particularly from the standpoint of its fit with Gardner's (1983) criteria for modularity (e.g., isolation by brain damage, distinctive development, existence of prodigies or of individuals lacking the capacity). The majority of the experimental evidence comes from brain lesion experiments in socially living nonhuman primates, all of which points to three brain areas as critical to the formation and maintenance of normal social relationships—the orbital-frontal cortex, temporal pole cortex, and subcortical amygdaloid nuclei (see Steklis and Kling 1985 for review).

The main results of this earlier ablation work can be summarized as follows. Following bilateral removal of any one of these three brain structures, monkeys (several species of Old World monkeys were examined) in captive groups show reduced and inappropriate social behavior, and in free-ranging settings, they lose contact with their social group and become social isolates. Notably, from the standpoint of the importance of social cognition for the formation of social alliances, vervet monkeys with orbital lesions are impaired in their ability to form alliances, and a drop in dominance status is not an uncommon outcome of lesioning any of these three areas. Since removal of dorsolateral frontal cortex adjacent to orbital cortex, or of inferior temporal cortex exclusive of the temporal pole region, does not result in profound changes in social affect and relationships, early on we were led to conclude that the three, densely interconnected, neural structures—the orbital and temporal pole cortex, and the amygdala—form a special neural circuit that in some way underlies a primate's ability to form and maintain affiliative social relationships (Kling and Steklis 1976).

While these results from lesion experiments identify a set of neural structures critical for social behavior, they tell us little about the actual mechanisms involved or, more specifically, how they might contribute to the processing of social information. Significant insight into the processes that underlie social cognition is provided by more recent experiments involving electrical recording from the amygdala in several primate species (reviewed in Kling and Brothers 1992). Multiunit recordings in freely moving, socially housed subjects have shown that amygdala activation varies with the intensity and socioemotional significance of stimuli, both visual (e.g., facial threat) and auditory (e.g., alarm calls).

These findings have been further refined through recordings from single neurons in the macaque amygdala (Brothers and Ring 1992). In these experiments, monkeys were shown brief film segments of conspecifics engaging in a variety of locomotor and social activities. Amygdala units were most responsive to socially meaningful stimuli, such as filmed movements signaling approach or facial movements indicating mild threat (e.g., staring or raising the eyebrows). Reversed film sequences depicting movements such as "walking or trotting backward," movements unlikely to happen in the real world, or sequences of socially in-

significant facial movements like chewing, were relatively ineffective in exciting amygdala neurons.

Collectively, these results from the amygdala are consistent with the idea of a social cognition module, wherein "the core cognitive operation that underlies the representation of others' intentions and dispositions is exactly the computation of the gesture's significance, which is felt subjectively as a social affect" (Brothers and Ring 1992). With the exception of the work by Perrett (reviewed by Brothers 1990) on specialized face recognition cells in temporal cortex, we have at this time no similarly detailed account of the neural mechanisms serving social cognition outside the amygdala, especially in the orbital or temporal pole cortex.

Clinical evidence, however, provides additional support for the orbital cortex and amygdala forming part of a social cognition module as envisioned by Brothers. Here, again, I rely on reviews of relevant material by Brothers (1990) and Damasio (1994). As is the case with nonhuman primates, when either the orbital cortex or amygdala is surgically removed or becomes damaged bilaterally, patients show profound impairments in their social skills. Such patients' behavior is socially inappropriate, and they appear oblivious to social rules or conventions. These behavioral disturbances are accompanied by emotional and personality changes that often lead to loss of employment and severing of personal relationships. Brothers and Ring (1992) suggest that these deficits are fully in keeping with their proposed functions of a social cognition module: The social difficulties seem to arise from a "failure to accurately assess the character and motivations of other persons"; such patients appear to have "lost access to the internal cues which the behavior of others should generate."

Remarkably, these profound socioemotional impairments are unaccompanied by impairments in other spheres. Patients who are socially unintelligent show no impairments on standard intelligence tests (IQ). For example, Damasio (1994) describes one patient with bilateral orbital damage as "a man with a normal intellect who was unable to decide properly, especially when the decision involved personal or social matters" (p. 43). This patient could even solve social problems when they were presented to him abstractly, but he failed abjectly when faced with the same problems in real-life social situations. Only in cases where damage includes the dorsolateral frontal lobe adjacent to the orbital cortex are impairments in reasoning and decision making no longer confined to the social domain (Damasio 1994).

Recall that in our earlier lesion studies we had obtained similar, then puzzling, dissociations: Monkeys that are impaired socially after temporal pole lesions, for example, show no deficits on standard learning tasks (object or place discrimination and reversal tasks; Steklis and Kling, unpubl. obs.). On the other hand, monkeys with inferior temporal cortex lesions display normal social behavior but are impaired on visual learning tasks (Steklis and Kling 1985). Similar dissociations between social capacities and performance in other cognitive domains have also been observed in autistic children (Brothers 1990) and have long been known in isolation-reared monkeys. In short, what seemed to us when we were doing the lesion work as a nonsensical and certainly counterintuitive dissociation between cognitive domains is no longer bizarre but instead is fully consistent with current views of neuro-cognitive modularity.

Future clinical and experimental studies will have to demarcate the full neural circuitry comprising the social cognition module as well as delineate the computations occurring in each of its neural components. The structures so far identified in the primate brain are ones traditionally considered part of the limbic system (the amygdala) or closely associated limbic cortex (orbital and pole cortex). They all stand in close anatomical relationship, on the one hand, to the brain's emotional machinery—the limbic system and hypothalamus—and, on the other, to the neocortical sensory processing zones. Thus the primate amygdala, for example, receives sensory input from all modalities, and its downstream projections trigger autonomic and somatomotor responses typical of emotional responses, such as rage or fear. Given this neural architecture, much of which is evolutionarily as old as the mammals themselves, it is perhaps unsurprising that these particular cortical and subcortical elements were eventually co-opted into the service of social cognition. In other words, the evolutionary history and anatomical position in the brain of these cortical and subcortical limbic components are highly consistent with their proposed core function—the computation of appropriate affects (feelings) and emotional responses in relation to specific social stimuli (Brothers and Ring 1992).

## IMPLICATIONS FOR THE EVOLUTION OF INTELLIGENCE

In this final section I want to examine the implications of the neuromodular view of cognition I have been describing for evolutionary models of human intelligence and for comparative studies of the brain and intelligence. Specifically, I will revisit the ideas that all human intelligence is derived from social intelligence and that social intelligence and natural history intelligence are incompatible. I will then move on to discuss some of the key comparative studies that have attempted to link differences in brain size or the size of its subcomponents to indices of social intelligence.

As I described earlier (Section 3), Humphrey (1976) advocated the idea that all human intellect, including its "highest" expression—"philosophical and scientific thought"—ultimately derives from its social uses. This line of thinking finds a more recent counterpart in the notion of a "social bias" in all human thought (Goody 1995). What is meant by this is the human tendency to ascribe agency (or intentions) to all things animate and inanimate and to apply forms of reasoning effective in solving social problems—an "interactional" reasoning—to problems in other domains (e.g., Levinson 1995). The trouble is, "interactional" reasoning does not follow rules of logic. The reasoning employed in solving problems of "social exchange," for example, does not follow rules of inference of the propositional calculus (Cosmides and Tooby 1992). Because social reasoning is, strictly speaking, not rational, Levinson (1995) suggests that a "social bias" in all thinking accounts for the well-known result of high error rates in solving virtually any problem whose correct solution requires strict adherence to logical principles. Indeed, this discovery, surprising to many who believed in the fundamental rationality of human thought, has turned opinion toward the view that by standards of logic much, if not all, of human cognition is irrational (Gardner 1985). The social-bias-in-thinking argument, then, is a way to explain the broad tendency toward the irrational in all human cognition.

As appealing as it might seem, in light of an evolutionary, neuromodular view of cognition, there are two problems with the social-bias-in-thinking argument. First, the logician's view of human cognition as irrational must be tempered by evolutionary logic. What the logician considers to be flawed thinking, from an evolutionary standpoint, surely must be at least sufficiently rational. That is, the logician's logic per se is immaterial to evolution; what evolves is reasoning of whatever sort that is reliably effective. Fox (1992) has put this rather succinctly: "rationality cannot be equated with 'logic' as generally understood but rather consists of a series of pragmatic prejudgments of reality that have stood the test of natural selection."

Second, even if we distinguish between an evolutionarily sufficient rationality and the logician's rationality, the fact is we still wind up with two kinds of "rational" thinking. After all, humans *are* capable of "logical-mathematical" thought, which Gardner (1983) considers to be a separate intelligence module. If during the course of our evolutionary history a domain of adaptive problems (yet to be identified) consistently required through that followed formal logical principles, then social intelligence would have provided an unsuitable wellspring for the evolution of rationality, given the proposal that social cognition steers all thought toward illogic (Levinson 1995). There should, then, have been selection against any general "spillover" of social-cognitive algorithms into other domains. There are, unfortunately, no serious proposals I am aware of regarding the evolutionary history of logical-mathematical thought, other than Gardner's (1983) own very sketchy remarks (linking it to primitive calendars and notational systems), which in any case do not address the question of adaptive purpose. A less interesting possibility, of course, is that logical capacity is not a separate, evolved core intelligence at all (a caveat also expressed by Gardner) but is epiphenomenal (or emergent) to the operation of other core intelligences.

As I described earlier, Cachel (1994), who takes an implicitly modular view of human intelligence, also argues against the transferability of Machiavellian intelligence to nonsocial domains, notably to objects and events outside the social group, that is, "natural history intelligence":

> Because it constrains much non-human primate attention and awareness to happenings in the social world, Machiavellian intelligence may militate against the development of natural history intelligence rather than contributing to its appearance. Competitive social life may enhance social intelligence, but unless awareness of and attention to the non-social world occurs, this social intelligence will not be applied to the world outside the social group. (pp. 26–27)

Natural history intelligence, in Cachel's view clearly the dominant intelligence in humans, cannot be derived from Machiavellian intelligence, she suggests, because the two forms of intelligence depend on different components of the phenotype (behavior, anatomy, physiology). Intense natural selection on components related to Machiavellian intelligence would, therefore, compromise the development of components subserving natural history intelligence. As a result, neuroanatomical features that focus awareness and cognition on social dynamics will compete with features that direct awareness and cognition outside the social group. In the course of human evolution, Cachel contends, size changes in components of the limbic system provided effective control of emotions associated with Machiavellian intelligence—for example, sex, aggression—which, pari passu, with "diminishment of dominance hierarchies and positive selection pressure for cooperative behavior" made possible the development of natural history intelligence.

While I am generally sympathetic to Cachel's implicitly modular criticism of the popular view of Machiavellian intelligence as a substrate for other forms of intelligence, I suggest that cognitive modularity mitigates against the sort of antagonism she describes. (Hence my earlier remark that there is no need to take the seemingly controversial position of describing humans as less Machiavellian than their pongid relatives. In other words, the old aphorism "it takes one to know one" applies fully here!) My disagreement is based on taking a stricter modular view of cognition and of emotion, a view closer to Fodor (1983), who distinguishes among "horizontally" and "vertically" organized faculties in the brain. This is to say, specific cognitive domains are not simply "cold" intellects that, as appropriate, draw on nonspecific (i.e., horizontal) attentional or emotional systems to motivate behavior. Rather, memory, attention, and emotion are, at least in a functional sense, also modular in that they are specific (i.e., vertical) to cognitive domains. Much like the ethologist's classic innate releasing mechanism, domain-specific stimuli focus attention and trigger specific emotions and memories. We need only think of the well-known effects of brain stimulation evoked rage compared to predatory aggression in the cat: Two entirely different behavioral, attentional, and emotional responses are obtained from electrodes separated by a few millimeters in hypothalamic tissue (Flynn 1972). Brothers (1990) has well described this type of specific coupling between social stimuli, memory, and emotion elicited in humans by electrical stimulation of the amygdala.

Emotion and cognition are not separate domains; rather, evolution has tied them together in particular configurations to serve domain-specific adaptive functions. Emotion and cognition, thus, are not antagonistic processes, although they are often regarded that way, as a comment by Cachel suggests: "In social species with natural history intelligence, one would expect to find relative enlargement of brain areas to *control* or focus sexual, feeding, or fighting emotions" (emphasis mine; Cachel 1994: 28). The generally known phenomenon of high emotional arousal interfering with cognitive processing might seem supportive, but not when viewed in an evolutionary framework: The kinds of natural situations likely to produce extreme emotional states—attack by a social rival or predator—would leave little time for cognitive reflection (or for solving any of the sorts of cognitive tasks that can be shown to be disrupted by high arousal in a laboratory experiment).

For these reasons, I am not convinced that a fundamental antagonism between the two intelligences is inescapable. The domain specificity of cognition and emotion would ensure that selection for both Machiavellian and natural history intelligence, in principle, need not involve a compromise. While constraints imposed on overall brain size could result in the elaboration of one functional neural circuit at the expense of another, available comparative data show little, if any, evidence of such compromises among brain components (Harvey and Krebs 1990).

I want to turn now to the implications of the modular view of intelligence I have been championing for comparative studies of the brain and intelligence. Specifically, I want to examine how we might direct comparative investigations given what I have sketched out here concerning the content and neural bases of social intelligence. As I indicated at the beginning of this essay, the large relative brain size of primates has traditionally been taken as reflecting selection pressures for increased intelligence. But since it is the neocortex in particular that accounts for most of this increase in overall brain size, and as it can be reasonably considered to play a prominent role in higher cognitive functions—or "thinking"—it is this region on which most recent comparative studies have focused (for review see Byrne 1995b).

Among these comparative studies only a few have really attempted to test the alternative theories—the SIH and EIH—against the data on neocortex size in nonhuman primates. Dunbar's (1992, 1993) work appears to provide the strongest evidence so far in favor of a primary association between neocortical growth and social intelligence. Dunbar used group size as a measure of social complexity, that is, as reflecting the amount of social information a group member must process, while diet, range area, and day journey length served as indices of ecological information processing. After correcting for the influence of body weight on these variables, only group size emerged as highly correlated with neocortex ratio (vs. rest of the brain). Additional analyses showed that extractive foragers do not have larger neocortex ratios than nonextractive foragers (contra Parker and Gibson's theory), and number of reproductive-age females in a group, while significantly correlated with neocortex ratio, explains far less of the variance than does overall group size. Collectively these results suggest to Dunbar that while ecological factors select for optimal group sizes, neocortical size constrains the maximum group size that can be attained by a species. The constraint arises from the limits imposed by the size of neocortex on the number of social relationships that can be attended to. When groups get too large, there is an information overload, and groups become unstable and may split.

These are truly intriguing results, but how definitive are they? There are at least three problems that should direct future research in this area. One concerns our ability, in principle, to separate out ecological from social factors as determinants of brain size and intelligence, given that features of ecology and social organization are themselves correlated. Food abundance and distribution, for example, are associated with variation in group size and the quality of inter- and intragroup social relationships (Isbell 1991). In other words, more complicated social systems arise in relation to solving complex ecological problems. Is it, therefore, reasonable to hold either ecological or social factors constant while assessing variation in the other? How likely are we to find, for example, species that vary significantly in the complexity of their social systems (reflecting the demands for social intelligence), while showing no significant variation in their ecologies (i.e., demands for ecological intelligence)? In the present case, this problem makes it logically difficult to determine if neocortex size or ecological niche primarily constrains group size (Harcourt 1993).

This brings us to the second problem, which is with the measures themselves for social or ecological intelligence. Dunbar (1992) himself bemoans the fact that group size is hardly a sensitive index of social intelligence, but for broad comparisons there are few better options. To test Machiavellian intelligence more directly, Byrne (1993) calculated a "deception index" for different species—amount of tactical deception seen in excess of that expected from how much a species was studied—and when he plotted it against Dunbar's neocortex ratio data, a strong positive correlation emerged. We should expect the development of Machiavellian intelligence to be dependent not so much on group size per se than on the social makeup of groups (e.g., dominance hierarchies, mating competition). Thus, while female group size used by Dunbar is an improvement over group size as a measure of social complexity, it still falls short of the most relevant dimension, namely, not number of females per se but number of philopatric (or bonded) females who form matrilines, dominance hierarchies, alliances, and the like. Similarly, it would be instructive in comparative brain studies to compare male-bonded societies to one male or male-dispersal species rather than simply comparing number of males in groups (e.g., see Sawaguchi 1990; Sawaguchi and Kudo 1990). Employing more relevant social indices would constitute more direct tests of Machiavellian intelligence.

In assessing ecological intelligence, we are in worse straits. This is because this category, as I have noted, is a potential grab bag of heterogeneous behaviors and abilities (e.g., foraging memory, tool use, natural history intelligence, extractive foraging) that such measures as "range," "day journey length," or even diet (e.g., frugivory) only very indirectly tap into. Very few brain studies have compared primate species on more direct measures of the different types of ecological intelligence. To the extent that more direct ecological intelligence indices are uncorrelated with measures of social intelligence, their dissociable effects on brain size and organization will become apparent. Here comparisons involving other mammals that show forms of ecological intelligence in the absence of complex social systems may prove particularly instructive.

A third problem inherent in current studies is the use of neocortex size as a proxy measure of intelligence because of the difficulty in evaluating intelligence cross-specifically (Byrne 1995b). This problem would appear solvable in two ways. First, if we use a modular intelligence approach, then it is possible to compare particular kinds of intelligences across species (e.g., mental foraging maps, toolmaking). Second, if we apply a modular approach to the brain, then different intelligences, where the neural data are available, can be correlated with the relative development of their neural substrates. Social intelligence, for example, as we have seen, is mediated by specific neocortical, paleocortical, and subcortical components, and, in primates hippocampus size correlates with range size, perhaps reflecting, as in food-storing birds, ecological pressures for mental maps (Barton and Purvis, cited in Dunbar 1993). Virtually nothing is known, by comparison, about the neocortical role in different kinds of ecological intellect, though it is likely, as Cachel (1994) suggests, that a distinct neural substrate subserves natural history intelligence. In using the entire neocortex as a measure, we are, therefore, not only measuring social as well as ecological intelligence but also ignoring important subcortical contributions (especially the limbic system; e.g., see Armstrong 1991). As pointed out by some commentators (Falk and Dudek 1993; Holloway 1993) on Dunbar (1993), the primate neocortex is not a functionally homogenous structure, nor did it evolve by simply becoming larger; rather, its subcomponents evolved at different rates.

Finally, we might also focus our attention on differences between the sexes in intelligence and brain organization, given the different selection pressures faced by male and female primates. In some species, for example, males and females may have been under selection for the differential development of social or ecological intelligences (e.g., chimpanzee males may have better social intelligence and females better ecological intelligence, as shown in termiting or nut-cracking). Such sex differences in relation to mating-related male spatial abilities have been established in other mammals (reviewed in Francis 1995). We should thus be able to make predictions about sex differences in neural organization employing the same reasoning for predicting species differences. There is clearly much exciting work to be done at the interface of primate neurobiology and socio-

ecology. Future studies will have to attempt to relate the relative development among primates of different intelligence domains to their respective neural modules, if we are to gain an accurate picture of the selection pressures responsible for the evolution of the primate brain and intellectual capacities.

## ACKNOWLEDGMENTS

I am grateful to my wife and collaborator, C. Netzin Gerald, for her critical reading of the manuscript and for making valuable suggestions for its improvement. I also thank Ms. Wendy Birky for her help in arranging the bibliography. Most of all, I dedicate this article to the late Arthur S. King, to whom I remain deeply indebted for my sustained interest in and much of my knowledge about the primate brain.

## BIBLIOGRAPHY

Armstrong, E. (1991). The limbic system and culture: An allometric analysis of the neocortex and limbic nuclei. *Human Nature* 2(2): 117–136.

Barkow, J. H., Cosmides, L., and Tooby, J., eds. (1992). *The Adapted Mind, Evolutionary Psychology and the Generation of Culture*. New York: Oxford University Press.

Baron-Cohen, S. (1994). How to build a baby that can read minds: Cognitive mechanisms in mind reading. *Current Psychology of Cognition* 13(5): 513–552.

Barton, R. A., and Purvis, A. J. (in press). *Primate Brains and Ecology: Looking Beneath the Surface*. Strasbourg.

Brothers, L. (1990). The social brain: A project for integrating primate behavior and neurophysiology in a new domain. *Concepts in Neuroscience* 1(1): 27–51.

Brothers, L., and Ring, B. (1992). A neuroethological framework for the representation of minds. *Journal of Cognitive Neuroscience* 4(2): 107–118.

Buss, D. M. (1990). Evolutionary social psychology: Prospects and pitfalls. *Motivation and Emotion* 14(4): 265–287.

Byrne, R. W. (1993). Do larger brains mean greater intelligence? *Behavioral and Brain Sciences* 16(4): 696–697.

Byrne, R. W. (1995a). The ape legacy: The evolution of Machiavellian intelligence and anticipatory interactive planning. In E. N. Goody (ed.), *Social Intelligence and Interaction*. Cambridge: Cambridge University Press, pp. 37–52.

Byrne, R. W. (1995b). *The Thinking Ape, Evolutionary Origins of Intelligence*. Oxford: Oxford University Press.

Byrne, R. W., and Whiten, A. (1988). *Machiavellian Intelligence. Social Expertise and the Evolution of Intellect in Monkeys, Apes, and Humans*. Oxford: Clarendon Press.

Cachel, S. (1994). The natural history origin of human intelligence: A new perspective on the origin of human intelligence. *Social Neuroscience Bulletin* 7(1): 25–30.

Cheney, D. L., and Seyfarth, R. M. (1990). *How Monkeys See the World*. Chicago: University of Chicago Press.

Connor, R. C., Smolker, R. A., and Richards, A. F. (1992). Dolphin alliances and coalitions. In A. H. Harcourt and F. B. M. deWaal (eds.), *Coalitions and Alliances in Humans and Other Animals*. Oxford: Oxford University Press, pp. 415–443.

Cosmides, L., and Tooby, J. (1992). Cognitive adaptations for social exchange. In J. H. Barkow, L. Cosmides, and J. Tooby (eds.), *The Adapted Mind, Evolutionary Psychology and the Generation of Culture*. New York: Oxford University Press, pp. 163–228.

Cosmides, L., and Tooby, J. (1994). Origins of domain specificity: The evolution of functional organization. In L. A. Hirschfeld and S. A. Gelman (eds.), *Mapping the Mind, Domain Specificity in Cognition and Culture*. Cambridge: Cambridge University Press, pp. 85–116.

Damasio, A. R. (1994). *Descartes' Error*. New York: Putnam's.

Dunbar, R. I. M. (1992). Neocortex size as a constraint on group size in primates. *Journal of Human Evolution 20*: 469–493.

Dunbar, R. I. M. (1993). Coevolution of neocortical size, group size and language in humans. *Behavioral and Brain Sciences 16*(4): 681–694.

Falk, D., and Dudek, B. (1993). Mosaic evolution of the neocortex. *Behavioral and Brain Sciences 16*(4): 701–702.

Flynn, J. P. (1972). Patterning mechanisms, patterned reflexes, and attack behavior in cats. In J. K. Cole and D. D. Jensen (eds.), *Nebraska Symposium on Motivation 1972*. Lincoln: University of Nebraska Press.

Fodor, J. A. (1983). *The Modularity of Mind, An Essay on Faculty Psychology*. Cambridge, MA: MIT Press.

Fox, R. (1992). Prejudice and the unfinished mind: A new look at an old failing. *Psychological Inquiry 3*(2): 137–152.

Francis, R. C. (1995). Evolutionary neurobiology. *Trends in Ecology and Evolution 10*(7): 276–281.

Gardner, H. (1983). *Frames of Mind*. New York: Basic Books.

Gardner, H. (1985). *The Mind's New Science, A History of the Cognitive Revolution*. New York: Basic Books.

Gazzaniga, M. S. (1989). Organizations of the human brain. *Science 245*: 947–952.

Gazzaniga, M. S. (1992). *Nature's Mind*. New York: Basic Books.

Goody, E. N. (1995). Introduction: Some implications of a social origin of intelligence. In E. N. Goody (ed.), *Social Intelligence and Interaction*. Cambridge: Cambridge University Press, pp. 1–36.

Griffin, D. R. (1981). *The Question of Animal Awareness*, 2nd ed. New York: Rockefeller University Press.

Griffin, D. R. (1992). *Animal Minds*. Chicago: University of Chicago Press.

Gross, M. R. (1994). The evolution of behavioural ecology. *Trends in Ecology and Evolution 9*(10): 358–361.

Harcourt, A. H. (1988). Alliances in contests and social intelligence. In R. W. Byrne and A. Whiten (eds.), *Machiavellian Intelligence. Social Expertise and the Evolution of Intellect in Monkeys, Apes, and Humans*. Oxford: Clarendon Press, pp. 132–152.

Harcourt, A. H. (1992). Coalitions and alliances: Are primates more complex than non-primates? In A. H. Harcourt and F. B. M. de-Waal (eds.), *Coalitions and Alliances in Humans and other Animals*. Oxford: Oxford University Press, pp. 445–471.

Harcourt, A. H. (1993). Brains, grouping and language. *Behavioral and Brain Sciences 16*(4): 706.

Harvey, P. H., and Krebs, J. R. (1990). Comparing brains. *Science 249*: 140–146.

Hirschfeld, L. A., and Gelman, S. A. (1994). Toward a topography of mind: An introduction to domain specificity. In L. A. Hirschfeld and S. A. Gelman (eds.), *Mapping the Mind, Domain Specificity in Cognition and Culture*. Cambridge: Cambridge University Press, pp. 3–35.

Holloway, R. L. (1993). Another primate brain fiction: Brain (cortex) weight and homogeneity. *Behavioral and Brain Sciences 16*(4): 707–708.

Humphrey, N. K. (1976). The social function of intellect. In P. P. G. Bateson and R. A. Hinde (eds.), *Growing Points in Ethology*. Cambridge: Cambridge University Press.

Isbell, L. A. (1991). Contest and scramble competition: Patterns of female aggression and ranging behavior among primates. *Behavioral Ecology 2*(2): 143–155.

Jay, P. (1968). Primate field studies and human evolution. In P. Jay (ed.), *Primates: Studies in Adaptation and Variability*. New York: Holt, Rinehart and Winston, pp. 487–503.

Jerison, H. J. (1973). *Evolution of the Brain and Intelligence*. New York: Academic Press.

Jolly, A. (1966). Lemur social behavior and primate intelligence . *Science 153*: 501–506.

Jolly, A. (1979). Comment on Parker and Gibson. *Behavioral and Brain Sciences 2*:

Jolly, A. (1985). *The Evolution of Primate Behavior*, 2nd ed. New York: Macmillan.

Kamil, A. C. (1994). A synthetic approach to the study of animal intelligence. In L. A. Real (ed.), *Behavioral Mechanisms in Evolutionary Ecology*. Chicago: University of Chicago Press, pp. 11–45.

Kling, A., and Brothers, L. (1992). The amygdala and social behavior. In J. Aggleton (ed.), *The Amygdala*. New York: Wiley, pp. 353–377.

Kling, A., Lancaster, J., and Benitone, J. (1970). Amygdalectomy in the free-ranging vervet (*C. aethiops). Journal of Psychiatric Research 7*: 191–199.

Kling, A., and Steklis, H. D. (1976). A neural substrate for affiliative behavior in non-human primates. *Brain, Behavior, and Evolution 13*: 216–238.

Kummer, H., Dasser, V., and Hoyningen-Huene, P. (1990). Exploring primate social cognition: Some critical remarks. *Behaviour 112* (1–2): 84–98.

Levinson. (1995). Interactional biases in human thinking. In E. N. Goody (ed.), *Social Intelligence and Interaction*. Cambridge: Cambridge University Press, pp. 221–260.

Macphail, E. M. (1982). *Brain and Intelligence in Vertebrates*. Oxford: Clarendon Press.

Macphail, E. M. (1987). The comparative psychology of intelligence. *Behavioral and Brain Sciences 10*: 645–695.

Milton, K. (1981). Distribution patterns of tropical foods as an evolutionary stimulus to primate mental development. *American Anthropologist 83*: 535–543.

Milton, K. (1988). Foraging behavior and the evolution of primate intelligence. In R. W. Byrne and A. Whiten (ed.), *Machiavellian Intelligence. Social Expertise and the Evolution of Intellect in Monkeys, Apes, and Humans*. Oxford: Clarendon Press, pp. 285–305.

Parker, S. T., and Gibson, K. R. (1977). Object manipulation, tool use and sensorimotor intelligence as feeding adaptations in cebus monkeys and great apes. *Journal of Human Evolution 6*: 623–641.

Parker, S. T., and Gibson, K. R. (1979). A developmental model for the evolution of language and intelligence in early hominids. *Behavioral and Brain Sciences 2*: 367–408.

Passingham, R. E. (1982). *The human primate*. San Francisco: Freeman.

Pinker, S., and Bloom, P. (1992). Natural language and natural selection. In J. H. Barkow, L. Cosmides, and J. Tooby (eds.), *The Adapted Mind*. New York: Oxford University Press, pp. 451–493.

Real, L. A. (1991). Animal choice behavior and the evolution of cognitive architecture. *Science 253*: 980–986.

Real, L. A. (1993). Toward a Cognitive Ecology. *Trends in Ecology and Evolution 8*(11): 413–417.

Real, L. A., ed. (1994). *Behavioral Mechanisms in Evolutionary Ecology*. Chicago: University of Chicago Press.

Sawaguchi, T. (1990). Relative brain size, stratification, and social structure in anthropoids. *Primates 31*(2): 257–272.

Sawaguchi, T., and Kudo, H. (1990). Neocortical development and social structure in Primates. *Primates 31*(2): 283–289.

Steklis, H. D., and Kling, A. (1985). Neurobiology of affiliative behavior in nonhuman primates. In M. Reite and T. Field (eds.), *The Psychology of Attachment and Separation*. Academic Press, pp. 93–134.

Tooby, J., and Cosmides, L. (1992). The psychological foundations of culture. In J. H. Barkow, L. Cosmides, and J. Tooby (eds.), *The*

*Adapted Mind, Evolutionary Psychology and the Generation of Culture.* New York: Oxford University Press, pp. 19–136.

Washburn, S. L. (1963). Behavior and human evolution. In S. L. Washburn (ed.), *Classification and Human Evolution.* New York: Wenner-Gren Foundation/Viking Fund Publications in Anthropology, pp. 190–203.

Washburn, S. L. (1973). The promise of primatology. *American Journal of Physical Anthropology 38*(2): 177–182.

Washburn, S. L., and Hamburg, D. A. (1965). The implications of primate research. In I. DeVore (ed.), *Primate Behavior.* New York: Holt, Rinehart, and Winston, pp. 607–622.

Whiten, A. (1991). The emergence of Mindreading: Steps toward an interdisciplinary enterprise. In A. Whiten (ed.), *Natural Theories of Mind; Evolution: Development and Simulation of Everyday Mindreading.* Oxford: Basil Blackwell.

Whiten, A., and Byrne, R. W. (1988). The manipulation of attention in primate tactical deception. In R. W. Byrne and A. Whiten (eds.), *Machiavellian Intelligence. Social Expertise and the Evolution of Intellect in Monkeys, Apes, and Humans.* Oxford: Clarendon Press, pp. 211–223.

*This essay epitomizes the spirit of the new physical anthropology where disciplinary barriers are overcome in the discussion of human evolution. Bramblett, Coelho, and Easley create a new model for representing individual actors and their social affinities by importing a modern statistical technique into a new domain. The authors propose that three-dimensional models could be a more efficient way for the primate brain to represent and handle information on social relationships. They discuss the evolution of this type of neural model, its adaptive advantages, and how it might resolve some persistent controversies about cognition. This essay illustrates the promise of primatology to become a science "not limited by the past" that may help us understand human nature in a new way.*

# 7 Visual-Spatial Neurological Modeling as a Possible Mechanism for Learning and Managing Social Structure

**Claud Bramblett**   *Department of Anthropology, The University of Texas, Austin*

**Anthony M. Coelho, Jr.**   *National Institutes of Health, National Heart, Lung, and Blood Institute, Bethesda, Maryland*

**Stephen P. Easley**   *Department of Sociology and Anthropology, New Mexico State University, Las Cruces, New Mexico*

An important feature of education at the University of California, Berkeley, was the nearly continuous bull sessions among graduate students that occurred in the Gifford Room, the student lounge. On any day one could drop in and be treated to discourse in a topic related to human evolution. Subdiscipline barriers did not exist, and participants were not confined to strict rules of evidence. It was a place where *explanations, what if's,* and *models* were constructed and discussed for the pure joy of exploration. It is in the spirit of the Gifford Rooms around the world that we offer the following essay.

## INTRODUCTION

Application of multidimensional scaling techniques to records of affinitive behaviors in gang-caged captive baboons produced three dimensional models in which each baboon is represented by X, Y, Z coordinates and the relative distance between individuals is proportional to the affinitive social activities between animals (Easley et al. 1990). Such models account for a maximum amount of data variation and are extremely compact. As a model is rotated, an observer sees the relative relationships of all group members.

In comparison, two-dimensional projections are deficient in information. Dyadic descriptions, another two-dimensional approach, are cumbersome because each dyad is represented by a separate mathematical expression. Thus conservatively the total number of such expressions required to represent all possible dyads is $(n^2 - n)^c$, in which $n$ = number of individuals and $c$ = number of behavioral categories. On the other hand, if X, Y, Z coordinates represent the relationships, the number of mathematical values accessed is reduced to $nc$, in which every individual is represented by a X, Y, Z coordinate for each category. Coalitions and correlations between behavioral categories can be incorporated as clusters of related X, Y, Z coordinates.

## PROPOSED MECHANISM

Because three-dimensional models produce an efficient representation of relationships in a social group, we propose that the primate brain uses analogous three-dimensional techniques to estimate and predict behavioral responses and to compute relational information.

Humans have the neural abilities to rotate models and imagine the relative distances between elements (Shepard and Cooper 1982). We utilize complex visual-spatial abilities in commonplace acts such as walking through a crowded mall without bumping into others. But a more interesting example is the way in which a baseball player judges a fly ball, computing very quickly whether the ball is to be on the right or left and distance from him or her to where the ball will drop. Right or left is judged so readily that there is little human variance in this ability. A more difficult task is to predict the drop point of a fly ball that is hit directly at a fielder. Chapman (1968) proposed that a fielder judges the ball by moving his body so that the tangent of the angle of elevation of the ball remains constant, concluding that this was the only computation needed to put the fielder in a position to make the catch. Unfortunately, Chapman's solution assumed flight of the ball occurred in a vacuum. Since a baseball travels only about 60% as far in air as one would expect without air resistance, a more complex computation is required (Brancazio 1984: 304). An interesting feature about this type of visual-spatial computation is that tracking an object in order to judge its landing site requires a projection into the future. The same neural mechanism that predicts the future impact site of a baseball (or prey) can be generalized to other events. Memory of the source provides a "past," the experience a "present," and anticipation of impact a "future."

How did such an ability evolve? It is possible that a neural substratum for topographically mapping images and making vector computations evolved in the context of visual-spatial task in some ancient predecessor, perhaps for the purpose of pursuing prey or recognizing pursuit. Once this type of neural tissue existed, it could be expanded, modified, and/or specialized for other useful computations, such as being aware of one's position in a social situation or construction of a relational map of a home range. If so, the flexible behaviors of vertebrates are partly a consequence of the evolution of their particular visual biology.

Use of neural computation of models to predict social events may account for social "intuition" in humans. Incomplete evidence or lack of experience to form an accurate model may result in making "guesses" about the $X,Y,Z$ coordinates of some individuals and then projecting relationships on a "best estimate" basis. If the predictions are inaccurate, adjustments can be made to the $X,Y,Z$ coordinates. If they prove reliable, then the relational structure of that group has been "learned."

What is the nature of the models? If the computation is a digital process, the watershed evolutionary adaptation would be a biological way to estimate and use trigonometric functions (such as tangent and cosine). However, it is more likely that the neural substratum performs as an analog computer (Georgopoulos et al. 1989). Thus data points are represented as permanent locations in neural tissue and the computation process involves retrieval of measurements of neurological distances between locations—that is, the $X,Y,Z$ coordinates of data points. This analog simulation would allow storage and retrieval of any type of relational data (visual input, estimate of trajectory, maps, social relationships, language, patterning of morphemes, mathematics, etc.) and would be a logical precursor for networks that could perform other types of computations (Allman 1989). There would be no need for computed rotation of models since neural tissue has access to an iconic, albeit analog, representation of the model.

Perhaps formation of subsets (kin groups, political groups) serves to break down very large groups into manageable units that lend themselves to distributed computing. If our hypothesis is plausible, it provides a simple mechanism to explain how human observers can form mental models of their study groups but are not able to judge activity rates reliably. Is it possible that we may gain insight into the way models are internalized by comparing quantitatively documented models with the mental models of the ethologists? Is it possible that the elusive "deep structures" of language and the anthropological "universal structures" of structuralism are artifacts of this type of modeling? If this model is valid, there are only three dimensions plus time available for relational storage. Sets of relationships would be finite, perhaps even very small. Large aggregates would have to be broken down into categories or classes of relationships (matrilines, noun classes). Conceivably the ability that we recognize as "insight" is a consequence of being able to link different sets of relationships.

This neurological model also provides an answer to the question of animal self-awareness. In all useful models that contain information relative to oneself, "self" would have to be included as a data point with its own $X,Y,Z$ coordinates. Phylogenetically, "self" would be almost as ancient as vision.

It seems noteworthy that only two groups in the animal kingdom, the Cephalopoda (nautili, cuttlefish, squids, octopods) and the Vertebrata, have this complex of eye type, neural signals, and visual processing. Details of the eye suggest that the cephalopod and vertebrate eye are not homologous; a common ancestor would precede the development of present anatomy. Nerve signal properties in these two groups contrast with those in other animals. Oscilloscope representations of activity from most invertebrate neurons depict extremely complex and rapidly cycling signals. Cephalapod and vertebrate neurons produce signals that are simpler and cycle more slowly. Sensory processing produces mental representations—cognitive maps (Neisser 1987).

Coincidentally, the Cephalopoda and Vertebrata groups are also the "smart" members of the animal kingdom. Invertebrate behaviors often indicate that they have mental maps of roosts/nests, and resources. The ability of invertebrates to attack prey or to coordinate movements in a swarm reflects a capacity to perform complex actions, but these activities can be managed through a rule-based system that does not utilize mental rotation. An exception is the ability of some invertebrates (such as bees) to take "shortcuts" (more direct routes) between food sources and hives. Though other animals are capable of learning, the so-cieties of Isoptera (termites) and Hymenoptera (ants, bees, wasps) are very different from those of vertebrate social systems. Could this be in part a corollary their type of vision, a consequence of its supporting neuro-biology and limitations on their ability to relate sets of relationships to each other? Perhaps the megabrains of vertebrates are specializations to handle relationships between sets of $X, Y, Z$ coordinates.

## REFERENCES

Allman, W. F. (1989). *Apprentices of Wonder: Inside the Neural Network Revolution.* New York: Bantam.

Brancazio, P. J. (1984). *Sport Science: Physical Laws and Optimum Performance.* New York: Simon & Schuster.

Chapman, S. (1968). Catching a baseball. *Am. J. Phys. 36:* 868.

Easley, S. P., Coelho, Jr., A. M., and Rutenberg, G. W. (1990). Multidimensional scaling of social relationships in baboons. *Int. J. Anthro.* 5(4): 309–324.

Georgopoulous, A. P., Lunto, J. T., Petrides, M., Schwartz, A. B., and Massey, J. T. (1989). Mental rotation of the neuronal population vector. *Science* 243, 234.

Neisser, U. (1987). A sense of where you are: Functions of the spatial module. In *Cognitive Process and Spatial Orientation in Animal and Man,* Vol. II. Dordrecht: Martinus Nijhoff, pp. 293–310.

Shepard, R. N., and Cooper, L. A. (1982). *Mental Images and Their Transformations.* Cambridge, MA: MIT Press.

*Washburn's concern about science and his vision of science as a cultural practice with a particular history presage today's science studies. He suggested the pivotal place that primatology would have (and now has) in what has been called the border zone between nature and culture (Haraway 1989). In the traffic across this zone, there are multiple connections between science and society. Strum and Fedigan address many of Washburn's concerns as they strive to resolve the current controversy about what changed our ideas about primate society. They first establish which ideas have changed, then suggest a comparative framework of closely related disciplines and other national/cultural traditions of primatology to generate new and better data. Their approach also enlists analytic resources from science, feminist, and popular culture studies. The essay illustrates both the new physical anthropology and the promise of primatology by insisting that the controversies be resolved by data, not opinion, and through a comparative approach that integrates disciplines and uses new methods.*

# 8 Theory, Method, Gender, and Culture: What Changed Our Views of Primate Society?

**Shirley C. Strum**   *Department of Anthropology, University of California at San Diego*

**Linda M. Fedigan**   *Department of Anthropology, University of Alberta, Canada*

## INTRODUCTION

The naturalistic study of primate behavior has grown dramatically in the last 75 years. The primary impetus for modern field studies was the belief that knowledge of our closest living relatives could help us understand the origins and evolution of human behavior. As a result there has been widespread interest in the conclusions of these studies both among scientists and the general public.

Images of primate society have changed dramatically during this short history. Simply put, we have moved from a general vision that society revolves around the males and is based on aggression, domination, and hierarchy to a more complex array of options based on phylogeny, ecology, demography, social history, and chance events. The current image of primate society, if we ventured to make generalizations at all, would be a strong counterpoint to the earlier view. It would highlight the importance of females within society, emphasize tactics other than aggression particularly those that rely on social finesse and the management of relationships, and argue that hierarchy may or

may not have a place in primate society but that males and females are equally capable of competition and hierarchical ordering.

Given the origins of primatology, the widespread interest in its conclusions, and the direction of the modifications, there is a great deal of curiosity about what caused these changes in images of primate society. The issue is complex, not least because recently primate studies have also become a resource in the controversy about whether knowledge is socially constructed. Feminists, historians, and those who study the interaction of science and society, and even the popular media, have given special attention to the role of women in building new images of primates and primate society. There are, however, very few comprehensive reviews of the history of the field (Gilmore 1981; Ribnick 1982; Southwick and Smith 1986) and only a few discussions of the impact of specific factors on our ideas about primate society. Theory (Gilmore 1981; Richard 1981; Sperling 1991), methodology (Burton 1994; Mason 1990; Strier 1994a), gender of the scientist (Adams and Burnett 1991; Haraway 1989; Hrdy 1986), and the larger sociocultural context (Asquith 1986, 1994; Haraway

1989; Sperling 1991) have been identified as important, at least at some point.

Our goal in this essay is to create a framework that will help us ask the right questions and will direct our attention to the most appropriate domains in the search for answers. First, we define which ideas have changed by sketching their historical progression through major stages of research from 1920 to the present. To keep the project manageable, we focus on primate field studies and on evolutionary interpretations of behavior and society, primarily by American scientists. This is our point of reference, the "what" and the "how" of our quest (Stages and Issues). The historical review is not exhaustive but we have tried to make it comprehensive. Two representative studies are discussed to illustrate each period.

Second, we suggest a framework for tackling the question of "why" our ideas have changed. Let us state our bias at the start. We agree that knowledge may be socially constructed, yet we believe that there is a knowable "reality" that should provide constraints on what stories can be legitimately told as part of a scientific enterprise. In science, as opposed to myth, some "stories" are more accurate than others (and their accuracy can be tested), some theory is better able to predict and explain, and some methods are more appropriate and reliable when applied to the phenomenon under investigation. In our framework we broaden the scope of previous discussions by including *all* factors that have been suggested as influential in the short history of the field—minimally, the development of new theories, changes in methodology, changing proportion of women scientists, and the larger context of social, cultural, and historical influences. We attempt an assessment of each factor's impact on our ideas about primate society, but our efforts are preliminary. We hope that by extending the previous single-factor analyses and expanding Haraway's (1989) multifaceted sociocultural analysis to include elements intrinsic to the science, we can indicate fruitful directions for further research. This research should be empirical. The history of ideas can be documented and the importance of specific concepts and changes in concepts are both amenable to quantification. Similarly, the question of the relative contribution of various factors to changing images of primate society can be evaluated with "data," given the proper framework, including information about sociocultural influences. The research should also be systematically comparative. By investigating what happened in closely related fields over the same period of time or in other national traditions of primatology, we will be in a better position to assess the relative importance of contributing influences in primate studies.

## STAGES AND ISSUES

In order to document that our ideas of primate society have changed, we must first sketch the historical progression of some of these ideas. To facilitate comparisons, we have divided the period from the 1920s to the present into stages. Using primate field studies as our marker, we have made the following delineations:

Prestage 1: Early Studies Between World Wars I and II
Stage 1: 1950–1965
Stage 2: 1965–1975
Stage 3: 1975–1985
Stage 4: 1985 to present

To some extent, these divisions are arbitrary, and a stage is often characterized by the results of work done in previous years but published later on. However, the stages do have some integrity in terms of conceptual, theoretical, or methodological "rubicons" that act as boundaries. For example, Stage 1 is characterized by the collection of natural history data. Stage 2 encapsulates the discovery of variability and the dilemma it posed for existing theoretical frameworks. Stage 3 is marked by the impact and immediate reaction to sociobiology. Stage 4 witnesses a shift to behavioral ecology, the reemergence of animal "mind" and concerns about conservation.

We also propose that throughout this century's primate studies, scientists have been interested in specific questions and issues about primate societies. Over time, the answer to these questions have changed. As part of our framework for tracing the changing images of primate society, we have extracted 10 key questions that we refer to as "enduring issues":

1. Why do primates live in social groups?
2. What is the social structure of the group, and what holds society together?
3. What is the relationship of the group to its environment?
4. What are the roles of aggression, dominance, sex, and affiliation in primate societies?
5. What is the basic nature of males and females and the relationship between the sexes?
6. What is the pattern of ontogeny, development, and socialization?
7. What are the roles of instinct, learning, and cognition in behavior?
8. What is the pattern of intra- and interspecies variability?
9. What is the evolutionary relationship between different social grouping patterns?
10. What is unique about humans and what is shared with our primate relatives?

We have stated these issues in their original simplistic terms. Later they will be rephrased in a variety of ways (e.g., see Strier 1994a), but each transformation is clearly linked to the original issue.

Space does not allow an extensive review of primate field studies. Therefore, we outline only some of the important influences and trends of each stage, focusing on science in the United States and on field studies of primates. The few exceptions are relevant to the historical comparison. Our objective is not to construct a complete history of the complex web of primate studies but to extract and trace some of the major ideas about primate society as they wind their way through the different stages and are transformed in the process. Although this risks oversimplification of the many views that existed in each stage (see Dunbar 1990), it does allow us to begin our analysis.

For each stage, we compare the descriptions of two of the primate species that were well studied in that time period and briefly discuss the prevailing theory(ies) and method(s) that helped shape the stage. Where possible, we consider the most relevant enduring issues as they were discussed during that stage and address some of the larger issues and context that also influenced the science of the times.

## PreStage 1: Primate Studies Between the World Wars

A variety of studies on the social behavior of primates were initiated in the period between World Wars I and II. These included the establishment of primate colonies and laboratories, experiments in raising apes as part of human families and field expedition and field studies (see Asquith 1986, 1994; Bramblett 1994; Burton 1994; Gilmore 1981; Haraway 1989; Mason 1990; Ribnick 1982; Richard 1981, 1985; Southwick and Smith 1986; and Sperling 1991, for several versions of the history of primate studies). Although they were not part of a unified scheme, these diverse efforts shared a common scientific ethos—that the close biological relationship of nonhuman to human primates would allow us to use them, particularly monkeys and apes, as surrogates or as windows into understanding human behavior and its evolution. This had particular relevance and appeal to investigators from the disciplines of psychology and anthropology, and increasingly, zoologists also became involved.

ZUCKERMAN AND CARPENTER, BABOONS AND HOWLERS  Robert Yerkes was the central figure in primate studies during the 1920s and 1930s. He initiated field expeditions, sponsored behavioral studies, founded the first primate research facility in the United States, and set the explicit and implicit scientific agendas for laboratory and field research. His book, *The Great Apes* (Yerkes and Yerkes 1929), was a landmark, both because it established how little was then known about primates and because it greatly stimulated further research. The scientific issues of Yerkes' time have their own history, which we will not consider here. Instead, we begin with two influential studies of monkey behavior that provided the first clear images of primate society: Solly Zuckerman's study (1932) of hamadryas baboons at the London Zoological Garden and the field study (1934) of howlers by Yerkes' student, Clarence Ray Carpenter.

When Zuckerman conducted his study of the hamadryas baboons at the London Zoo in the late 1920s and early 1930s, the natural behavior patterns and social system of this species were unknown. In 1925, the zoo colony was created with 100 males. By 1927, when 30 females were added, only 56 males remained; the rest had died of injuries incurred during fights. Colony composition continued to change as animals died from stress-related disease or injury and others replaced them. Today we realize that there were too many animals, strangers to each other, put in too small a space and combined in inappropriate sex ratios. Field studies have since documented that hamadryas baboons live in polygynous societies with several females to every male, and that neighboring males establish relationships with one another that inhibit them from fighting over females (e.g., Kummer 1971a, b). However, Zuckerman believed he was watching "normal" behavior and extrapolated from this baboon social catastrophe a general thesis of sexual competition as the basis of hamadryas social life (1932). He concluded that because female primates were continually receptive (an assumption later refuted) and because males fought vigorously over access to females, sex must be the driving force behind primate society. Sex, aggression, competition, and male dominance over both females and each other, expressed through a rigid male hierarchy, were inextricably linked in his model.

Carpenter's study (1934) of howler monkeys on Barro Colorado Island in Panama stands in marked contrast to Zuckerman's work, both in approach and interpretation. Carpenter insisted that data from captive animals could not be properly interpreted without knowledge of that species naturalistic way of life. His naturalistic study of howlers suggested a well-organized, coordinated society that resulted from a network of mutualistic social relationships. The dyadic analysis of relationships he employed helped describe the process of social integration through affiliation. Sexual relations were basically "communal," with females more assertive and sexually motivated during mating than were the males. According to Carpenter, this communality was adaptive. Through multiple matings, females and males became "conditioned" (i.e., bonded) to many partners and thus established important social and emotional ties essential to group cohesion.

Relations within age-sex classes also seemed relaxed in such a communal atmosphere. Competition or aggression between clan (group) males was not seen, and there were no sharp gradients of dominance and submission among either males or females. Antagonism was reserved for intergroup contact, but even aggression between groups appeared highly ritualized, consisting mostly of mutual avoidance.

**THEORY AND METHODS**  The theoretical framework of primate studies was not as explicit at this stage as in later periods. Both Zuckerman and Carpenter considered social behavior to be adaptive. This functionalism was painted with broad biological and evolutionary strokes yet also linked to social "structuralism" (Gilmore 1981) and systems theory (Haraway 1983). The selective advantages of social behavior were couched in terms of benefits accruing to the group and to the species.

While sharing the same interpretive framework, the two investigators diverged dramatically in methodology. Zuckerman's methods and conclusions evinced little appreciation for the difficulties of collecting behavioral data, the complexities of social life, and the limitations of his chosen zoo setting. Still, his approach was representative of the undeveloped state of scientific knowledge and methodology in his era. By contrast, Carpenter set a new and lasting standard in data collection. He clarified and pioneered methods of habituation for wild primates, made explicit the standards for the acceptance of naturalistic observations as facts, and developed a new approach to the analysis of complex social interactions.

**ENDURING ISSUES**  Both Zuckerman and Carpenter were concerned with why primates live in social groups and what holds primate society together, but they resolved these issues quite differently. Zuckerman asserted that sex was the social glue and that male competition, expressed through aggression and dominance, was the organizing principle. Carpenter's communal howlers, in contrast, stayed together through positive conditioning, affect, and affiliation. He saw social relationships as primary and complementary; cooperation was the norm.

**OTHER ISSUES AND LARGER CONTEXT**  Two other issues deserve mention because they became important controversies at later stages. The first is the characterization of female primates. There are already two divergent positions. Zuckerman, who concentrated on the hamadryas male point of view, saw females as mere pawns in male competition. Carpenter, by contrast, carefully described the perspective of both sexes. He characterized howler females as active members of their society with roles equally important and complementary to males.

The second issue is that of animal "mind." The conflict between behaviorist and cognitivist models was not yet explicit in the research of this era, but concepts of mind were embedded in discussions about whether behavior was instinctual or learned. Carpenter, as a psychologist, was very interested in the motivation of behavior. For him, mind was manifested in emotions, and emotions were central to individual behavior and to group structure. Carpenter also emphasized the flexibility of behavior and the important role that learning played in certain behavioral repertoires, implicating mind in a major way. Zuckerman, instead, argued for the importance of instinct (and genetics) in behavior.

The respective fates of these two early models of primate society provide a lesson in science history. While the weight of the evidence did not favor one over the other, Carpenter's image of primate society was more in keeping with the themes and theories running through the biological and social sciences of the 1930s (Haraway 1989). Yet, as the next stage makes clear, it was Zuckerman's vision that prevailed. What was it about the Zuckerman view that proved so powerful? Like Herbert Spencer's view of nature as "red in tooth and claw" some 50 years earlier, did Zuckerman's vision of primate social life in 1932 draw its strength from its resonance with contemporary human society? Certainly, science was increasingly being used to generate or validate a genealogy for human behavior (Haraway 1989; Latour 1987; Latour and Strum 1986). We can speculate that the subsequent history of ideas about primate society would have been very different had Carpenter's version been more influential.

These themes, issues, questions, and currents lay dormant during the period just before and after World War II but reemerged when field studies were revived in the 1950s.

## Stage 1: 1950–1965—The Revival of Primate Field Studies

The first wave of post–World War II field studies by Americans was largely stimulated by Sherwood Washburn's (1951, 1962) insistence that proper interpretation of primate functional anatomy and human behavioral evolution required comparative information from living primates in their naturalistic settings. Many of the influential field studies of this period were carried out by students of Washburn whose fundamental objective was to describe as much social behavior from the wild as possible, particularly that relevant to evolutionary issues (but see also S. Altmann 1962; Collias and Southwick 1962).

Washburn and his students used an evolutionary framework whose underlying argument was straightforward. There were adaptive features shared by all primates, human and nonhuman. This "primate pattern" was believed to vary little across contexts and across species. Therefore scientific generalizations and evolutionary reconstructions could be based on extrapolations from one species to another. Their field studies searched for the characteristics of the primate pattern in the primate group and its constituent parts: the primate male, the primate female, and the primate immature. Investigators tried to delineate the basic dimensions of the primate pattern, including sexual behavior, socialization, infant development, play, social organization, intergroup relations, and daily routine.

The list of primate species studied in the wild grew significantly during Stage 1[1]; some of the more notable were baboons in Kenya, Rhodesia, South Africa, and Uganda; patas monkeys in Uganda; vervets in Kenya; rhesus monkeys in North India and on Cayo Santiago; bonnet macaques in India; and langurs in North India, with some data on populations in South India and in Ceylon. British scientists studied chimpanzees and gorillas in Tanzania and Uganda, the French studied lemurs in Madagascar, Swiss biologists initiated fieldwork on hamadryas baboons in Ethiopia, and the first reports of Japanese studies of macaques appeared in English.

**BABOONS AND LANGURS**   To illustrate the nature of Stage 1 field studies, and as a heuristic device for discussing images of primate society, we will continue to follow research on baboons. However, we will contrast baboons with research on hanuman langurs to show the divergence of views about primate society. Baboons were probably the most studied species of the period. Washburn and his student Irven DeVore studied baboons in Rhodesia and in two places in Kenya, Nairobi Park and Amboseli Reserve (Washburn and DeVore 1961). Later, K. R. L. Hall, an English psychologist, added his data on South African baboons to theirs (DeVore and Hall 1965; Hall and DeVore 1965). Baboon group sizes varied widely, but for ease of observation and data collection, investigators focused on smaller-

sized groups. Baboon society appeared to be remarkably consistent across locations, and investigators argued that this was because baboons everywhere had to solve the same basic problems of survival on the savanna. The many large predators, the lack of trees, and limitations on resources, such as food, water, shade, and sleeping sites, were the main selective pressures.

The evolutionary solution to these problems was seen in baboon anatomy and society. Male anatomy (big size, greater muscle mass, large canines, and an impressive mantle of shoulder hair) was specialized for aggression and male behavior was crafted for competition and defense. Aggression between males created and was modulated by a dominance hierarchy that was then interpreted as the organizing principle of baboon society. The male hierarchy provided structure, stability, and leadership and ensured that the group would be protected from threats and that peace would prevail. As a result, males were the leaders, policers, defenders, and protectors of the group.

Female relationships seemed more difficult to identify. Female status was thought to be more variable and more subtle than that of the males. A female's position improved, no matter what her status, when she was sexually receptive, particularly when she was "consorting" with a dominant male. The female role was assumed to be reproduction and care of infants.

The baboon studies also described details of socialization, communication, mating behavior, ranging, and feeding. These, too, seemed remarkably similar despite variations in ecology and in species. The conclusion was obvious: Baboon behavior fit together to create a cohesive, well-structured and male-centered society specially suited to survival on the savanna. The selective advantage of such a system accrued to the group and, through the group, to the species.

Hanuman langurs were first studied in Stage 1. Phyllis Jay, also a Washburn student, observed these langurs in North India from 1958 to 1960 and surveyed them throughout India in 1964–1965 (Jay 1965). Jay's main study site was woodland habitat, but langurs were found in a wide range of habitats from forests to more open areas. North Indian langurs live in smaller groups than baboons, but, like baboons, the groups are multimale, multifemale. In addition, langur males live in all-male groups whose ranges overlap those of bisexual groups.

Although the baboon and langur studies used similar methods of observation and the same dyadic age-sex class analysis, the results were very different. Jay described langur groups as peaceful and relaxed; the presence of infants was a major cohesive factor. The style of langur mothering was very different from baboons. A new mother was willing to pass her infant to

---

[1] Our understanding of primate studies in this stage is much influenced by the summaries of field studies in *Primate Social Behavior* (Southwick 1963) and *Primate Behavior: Field Studies of Monkeys and Apes* (DeVore 1965). The latter was the result of a nine-month conference held at the Institute for the Advanced Study of the Behavioral Sciences at Stanford in 1962–1963. A number of different primate societies are described, and the volumes also present synopses of important concepts and a vision of what future research would entail.

others almost immediately, and baby-sitting by "aunts" was common. Langur males had a dominance hierarchy, but in most respects the males were peripheral to the group, both spatially and socially. Female langurs policed interactions within the group, defended infants against threats, and acted as socializing agents. The males helped coordinate group movements and were leaders in that sense. However, dominance was not particularly visible or important in langur life. Being a member of the group seemed protection enough against predators; the many alert animals gave ample warning in time for the group to escape to the trees.

The differences between langur society and baboon society were obvious, yet there were similarities as well, particularly in the processes of socialization, communication, play, ranging, foraging, and daily routine. These commonalities lent weight to the idea of an evolutionarily significant primate pattern that transcended species boundaries. But the clear differences reported for langurs and baboons also held a hidden challenge (whose full impact was not to be felt for some time) to the belief in an overarching primate pattern.

The contrasting images of primate society offered by the baboon and the langur studies in Stage 1 show striking parallels to the divergent depictions offered prior to World War II based on hamadryas and howlers. Savanna baboon society, like Zuckerman's hamadryas society, was described as male-centered, competitive, aggressive, rigidly organized, and hierarchical. Like Carpenter's howlers, langur society, at least in North India, was low key, with males and females in complementary roles, and sex, aggression, and dominance relegated to the background of everyday life.

**THEORY AND METHODS** Stage 1 field studies can be called "improved natural history." Like the Boasian phase that had occurred earlier in sociocultural anthropology, the major mandate of this first stage of fieldwork was to collect descriptions of as many primate societies as possible. The difference was that these animal "ethnographies" were couched in a strictly functionalist evolutionary framework.

The evolutionary formulations of Stage 1 were more precise than those prior to World War II. The modern synthesis, developed in the 1940s (e.g., Dobzhansky 1944; Huxley 1942; Mayr 1942; Simpson, 1949), had a powerful impact on physical anthropology by the 1950s (see Washburn 1951, 1962). This modern version of evolutionary theory explicitly acknowledged the importance of behavior in the process of natural selection, and Washburn argued (see also Hooton 1955) that naturalistic studies of primate social behavior would provide the context for understanding human evolution as part of the primate pattern.

During Stage 1, primatologists trained in anthropology also looked to the social sciences for theoretical orientation. According to Gilmore (1981), Richard (1985), and Sperling (1991), many of these primatologists applied the structural-functional model used by British social anthropologists, particularly Radcliffe-Brown, to the interpretation of societies of nonhuman primates. In brief, social behavior is modeled as part of an ordered, integrated system in which individuals play patterned roles that function to fulfill the needs of the group. According to Gilmore (1981), the structural-functional model was congruent with both the prevailing group selectionist view among evolutionary biologists and with Washburn's emphasis on understanding the structural features of societies as adaptive (i.e., functional) mechanisms. Examples of structural-functional approaches from this stage (and the next) in primatology include studies of social roles, of play as practice for adulthood, of socialization as a mechanism to adjust the behavior of the individual to the needs of the group, and of dominance hierarchies as a device to regulate aggression and bring order to social life.

New standards for data collection had also been set. Many studies were still of short duration compared to later stages because practitioners looking for the primate pattern assumed they could find it in a few months. Yet, for the most part, the organization of these field studies was more scientifically rigorous, extensive, and ultimately more comprehensive than previous efforts. "Typical" groups of each species/population were selected and the comparisons were based on age-sex classes, simple food lists, ranging patterns, behavioral ethograms, and social relationships. Individual identification of animals was largely limited to groups of smaller sizes. Carpenter's method of dyadic analysis was employed as the standard entry point into the group's organization. One notable piece of research in terms of methods was Stuart Altmann's (1962) two-year study on Cayo Santiago. Animals in two very large groups of rhesus macaques were individually marked and systematically tracked, presaging the later widespread use of checklists and other quantitative techniques.

**ENDURING ISSUES** Stage 1 inherited a controversy about the basis of primate society and the nature of social relationships from the previous period. In some ways, the ascendancy of the idea of the primate pattern, and specifically the baboon model for primate society, reduced some ambiguities. Why live in a group? The simple answer was that it was adaptive. In fact, the major primate adaptation seemed to be group living both as a means of predator defense and as the basis of learning and reproduction. What holds a group together? Stage 1 field studies dealt a blow to the theory that sex is the basis of primate society. Some primates were found to have breeding seasons and their society still remained together even when no sexual behavior occurred (Lancaster and Lee 1965). Emotional bonds replaced sex as the societal glue because the process of socialization creates bonds between the various group members, especially between mothers and offspring.

Other issues remained unresolved. Were social relationships about power and domination (baboons), or were they based on attraction, affiliation, and cooperation (howlers, langurs)? Was the group structured by a male dominance hierarchy or by a network of attraction and affiliation between all individuals? How flexible was behavior, and what was the relative role of instinct (genetics) and learning? These unanswered questions left a controversy about where behavior could best be investigated, in the field or in captivity?

Despite the added sophistication of our understanding of primates during Stage 1, and despite what appeared to be unresolved issues about the nature of society and of social relationships, a monotypic view of primate society emerged. It was a baboon-based view, a toned-down reincarnation of Zuckerman's model. The male dominance hierarchy was still central, but in addition to providing the structure of the group, it now also provided peace, stability, and coordination. Social roles were still sexually distributed; males were leaders, defenders, and policers, and females cared for infants. But the roles were more elaborate. Competition was no longer the war of all against all witnessed at the London Zoo, because group living necessitated a rudimentary mutualism where individual interests were sometimes subverted to group interests in exchange for the benefits of being a member of the group.

OTHER ISSUES AND LARGER CONTEXT A description of this period would be incomplete without mention of field studies of apes (Goodall 1965; Reynolds and Reynolds 1965; Schaller 1963, 1964, 1965a, b). New findings about the tool-using and hunting behavior of chimpanzees gave them a special position in the study of nonhuman primates for the purposes of understanding human evolution. Yet the "primate pattern" and the baboon model so captured the scientific imagination that the chimp data did not really alter the scientific zeitgeist. The tendency during Stage 1 was to assume, often unconsciously, that baboon society could represent all monkey society and that monkey society could represent all primate society, including that of humans, despite the variability between species. Even Carpenter (1964, 1965) presented a new vision of howler society after a brief restudy. Howlers now seemed much more like the competitive, male-dominated baboons.

The remarkable evolutionary story of the interaction among environment, anatomy, and behavior told by the baboon model may have given it special potency. Added to that was the appropriateness of savanna-living baboons for reconstructing human evolution. This was a rare combination: a species that shared in the primate pattern but also had to face the challenge of life away from the trees.

The baboon vision of primate society did not remain isolated within the scientific community. A spate of popular books about the evolution of human behavior, including Ardrey (1961, 1966), Lorenz (1966), Morris (1967), and Tiger and Fox (1971), drew heavily from the primate data for their interpretations. Haraway (1989) situates this growth in popular interest as part of the historical and cultural currents following World War II. Science became a sociocultural resource where humans could look for answers about their basic nature and the options for the future. This trend, which had begun much earlier in the century, now accelerated, and studies of primates were of central importance.

Stage 1 ends with a resurgence of scientific and popular interest in primates. The interaction between the scientific and public domains probably enhanced the saliency and status of the baboon model, perhaps explaining why an "aggressive" image of a primate society once again triumphed over alternative interpretations. Piggybacked on the view that aggressive competition was central to society was an assumption that males triumphed over females in power and status within society. Put another way, it was the males who were important to the functioning of society, not the females.

### Stage 2: 1965–1975—The Discovery and Enigma of Variability

Stage 2 is best characterized as a period that revealed the extent of variability in primate behavior and society (e.g., see S. Altmann 1967; Jay 1968). Field studies of new species and of the same species in different locations challenged the notion of a unified primate pattern. At the same time existing theory seemed unable to provide a compelling explanation for what this variability meant or how it was generated. Consequently, the rationale for studying nonhuman primates, as it had been previously articulated, faltered. How could we make evolutionary generalizations across species, particularly from nonhuman to human primates, if we could not accurately predict the behavior of the same species in different locations? Some primate researchers turned to other ways of solving the evolutionary puzzle, such as studies of hunter-gatherers (e.g., Lee and DeVore 1968) and ethological studies of children (e.g., Blurton Jones 1967; McGrew 1972).

The number and variety of field studies in Stage 2 are too large to enumerate here. Upwards of 20 new books on primate social behavior were published. Some of these focused on individual species (e.g., Altmann and Altmann 1970; Goodall 1967; Hinde 1974, Jolly 1966a), but many volumes were edited collections of field reports (e.g., S. Altmann 1967; Dolhinow 1972; Holloway 1974; Jay 1968; Morris 1967; Tuttle 1975).

**BABOONS AND LANGURS**   Studies of baboons and langurs continue to be good illustrations of the data, issues, and dilemmas of this era. Hanuman langurs in South India were found to differ from the North Indian populations. They lived at higher densities and in smaller troops and had smaller, defended home ranges than North Indian langurs (Jay 1968; Sugiyama 1965, 1967). In the south, groups contained only one male. According to Sugiyama (1965), the extra males lived in large, roving, all-male bands. The description of South Indian langurs' behavior made them seem like a different species. All-male bands aggressively attacked bisexual groups until they defeated the male leader. Forced out, he took the group's immature males with him when he left. The new leader was thought to subsequently kill the group's infants. Mothers who had lost their infants seemed to become sexually receptive soon thereafter and to mate with the new male.

It was difficult to explain these striking differences in behavior between Jay's langurs in North India and those in South India. Certainly population density was extremely high at the southern sites (220 to 349 langurs per square mile in South India versus 7 to 16 individuals per square mile in North India). Higher densities, smaller groups, smaller home ranges, and daily intergroup encounters all seemed interrelated in some way, but the causal links and adaptive explanations were not yet well formulated.

The South Indian data generated a host of questions. Do langurs form the peaceful, relaxed, multimale society of Jay's description, or do they live in polygynous groups subject to frequent aggressive attacks and subsequent episodes of infanticide? Which pattern was normal? How could the variation be explained? And how could such a range of behaviors occur within one species?

Stage 2 field studies of baboons also documented variability. Females had a stable hierarchy of their own (Hausfater 1975; Ransom 1979; Strum 1975a, b), the baboon social network was complex, including "special relationships" between males and females and between infants and males (Ransom 1979; Ransom and Ransom 1971; Ransom and Rowell 1972; Strum 1975a, b), and the male hierarchy was not so obvious (Rowell 1966; Strum 1975a, b) or so adaptively related to preda-

tor protection as had been assumed (S. Altmann 1979; Rhine 1975; Rowell 1966, 1972). Unlike the langur case, the newly discovered variability among baboons did not yet seriously call into question the prevailing male centric model of baboon society for at least two reasons. Some studies did support the model (Hausfater 1975). Furthermore the new divergent data did not offer a compelling alternative model. The discovery of variability among baboons did contribute to the growing number of anomalies that would eventually bring down the notion of one primate pattern.

**MORE VARIABILITY**   The prevailing image of baboon society and of a baboon-like primate pattern were challenged from another source. New studies of a diversity of monkey species in a variety of habitats offered a range of alternative images. For example, patas monkeys were reported to live successfully on the savanna without aggressive male hierarchies by using a different set of specializations in anatomy, group organization, and sexual division of roles (e.g., Gartlan 1974; Hall 1968); vervets exhibited varying social relations, ranging patterns, and territorial behavior in different habitats (Gartlan and Brain 1968); and rhesus and Japanese macaque societies were found to be based on female genealogical relationships (e.g., Koyama 1967; Sade 1967). Gartlan (1968) and Rowell (1972, 1974) questioned the assumption that dominance hierarchies are a widely and naturally occurring adaptive structure in African monkeys in particular, and primate societies in general.

The troubling aspects of variability were also apparent in the plethora of social systems reported for our closest relatives, the apes (Reynolds 1967). During this stage ape social organization was documented to range from solitary individuals (orangutans, Galdikas 1979) to monogamous pairs (siamangs, Chivers 1974, and gibbons, Ellefson 1974) to age-graded male groups (gorillas, Fossey 1979; Harcourt 1979; Schaller 1972) to fission-fusion communities (chimpanzees, Goodall 1968; Nishida 1968). The existence of such a diversity of social systems among our closest genetic kin also seriously compromised the assumption that we could easily make evolutionary models of human society based on our primate relatives.

**THEORY AND METHODS**   The range of primate behavior and social organization exposed by Stage 2 field studies raised another issue: Were these anomalies real or artifactual. Observer bias was now a recognized shortcoming of a natural history methodology, and a search had begun for better methods to minimize such bias. Jeanne Altmann's (1974) review of sampling options was extremely useful, presenting the various methods that were in use in the study of behavior. Her discussion of the relative strengths and weaknesses of different techniques influenced subsequent generations of primate fieldworkers.

The selection of species for study was another possible bias. Although more than 90% of primate species are arboreal forest dwellers, the primary criterion for the selection of species or study sites had often been convenience and ease of observation. The result was a skew towards terrestrial or semiterrestrial species and a preponderance of baboon/macaque species in the corpus of our knowledge about primates—and thus reason to be concerned about what this might be doing to our ideas about the primate pattern and our understanding of primate society.

Skepticism extended as well to the evolutionary framework. Even if observed differences were "real," were they all adaptive? Could some behavior be random and not necessarily interpretable in evolutionary terms (S. Altmann 1965)? Could some of the variant behavior be "abnormal" rather than "normal" and therefore be excluded from an evolutionary interpretation (e.g., Gartlan 1968)? Or should we think in terms of "species potential" (Kummer 1971a, b), seeing all behavior as part of the range of possible responses under different circumstances?

Although each of these arguments—observer bias, species bias, random variation—could explain some of the reported variability, none was comprehensive. We were left with the problem of variation. If primates are born social and if group living is the main primate adaptation, what brings about different forms of social organization? Arguments took two forms: ecological and phylogenetic. An early ecological approach created "grades" of social organization in relationship to major environmental factors (Crook 1970a, b; Crook and Gartlan 1966; Eisenberg et al. 1972). However, these and subsequent revisions could only account for a portion of the documented variability. More importantly, variability within grades was as great as that between them (Clutton-Brock 1974). Advocates of ecological models admitted that some aspects of social organization were probably phylogenetic (see Struhsaker 1969). Yet phylogenetic analyses were themselves not much more successful, and promising new ideas about the interactions among ecology, mating strategies, and social organization were not yet fully articulated (Goss-Custard et al. 1972). No one theory or model seemed fully able to resolve the growing problem of intra- and interspecific variability, in part because there were so many variables and they were still loosely defined.

**ENDURING ISSUES**  The image of the "primate pattern" that had been handed down from Stage 1 decayed rather slowly, perhaps because of the time lag between studies and their impact. Many old ideas persisted, including stereotypes of male and female primates. However, in Stage 2, the social nexus was enlarged beyond the males to include families, special relationships, and individuals in tripartite (Kummer 1967; Kummer et al. 1974) as well as dyadic perspective. Confusion over the meaning of variability dominated the view of primates at the end of Stage 2. The lack of a good theoretical framework stimulated exploratory efforts in theory, methods, and interpretations that were to bear fruit in subsequent stages.

**OTHER ISSUES AND LARGER CONTEXT**  Carpenter's original interests in the mind as a motivator of behavior lay dormant during Stage 2. Although Chance (1961) and Kummer (1968) expressed interest in the ability of primates to use one another as social tools, Altmann and Altmann (1970) suggested that baboons have mental maps of their ranges, and Jolly (1966b) published a prescient paper speculating that primate intelligence originally evolved to solve social problems, the issues of "animal mind" were largely untouched during this stage.

The tenacity and power of the baboon image of primate society had a particularly profound effect on our ideas about female primates. It created a stereotype of the female role, a specific sexual division of roles and a particular mode of power relations that tended to undervalue females. This distortion and its emphasis on males occurred in the face of evidence from contemporary studies of langurs, patas, Japanese macaques, and chimpanzees (to name only a few species) which implied that female and male primates were equally important social and evolutionary actors in primate societies.

At the end of Stage 2 we ask the now familiar question: Why did a particular image of primate society gain and retain such wide currency despite significant evidence to the contrary? By 1975, the data arrayed against a baboon-based model of society were impressive, including challenges proffered by studies of baboons themselves.

### Stage 3: 1975–1985—The Sociobiological Era

The 10 years between 1975 and 1985 can be called the era of sociobiology because of its crucial impact on primate studies and on images of primate society. But sociobiology was not the only important contributor to ideas during Stage 3. At least four other factors played a significant role: long-term studies of primates, new studies of a diversity of previously unexamined primate species, studies of female primates by female scientists, and the emergence of theories of animal "mind."

**A CHANGE IN THEORY** The impact of sociobiology on primate behavioral research was radical not in its insistence on an evolutionary framework, but because it shifted the unit of selection from the group to the individual and ultimately brought genetics back into the interpretation of behavior. The theoretical framework of "sociobiology" attempts to explain social behavior entirely in terms of self-maximizing, biological processes. The most important of these are self-replication and reproductive success. This had two consequences for primate studies. First, the injection of modern genetics into behavioral explanations breathed new life into the evolutionary approach. Sociobiology promised to resolve the anomalies of Stage 2 through the application of new theoretical models that could explain intra- and interspecific variability. Second, it created a new way to talk about social behavior and generated testable hypotheses about individuals and groups. Space does not permit a complete discussion of the application of sociobiological principles to primate behavior (but see Gray 1985). We will simply highlight some of the most important consequences of this new, powerful theory for interpretations of primate society.

Sociobiology tackled many pressing issues about primate social behavior, often by reframing the questions and by shifting explanatory models to biological interpretations and away from a social science framework. It focused questions of adaptive behavior on the individual rather than the group or species. Sociobiologists discredited group selection as an evolutionary explanation of (primate) behavior by demonstrating that the conditions for group selection were limited and rare. Darwin's "struggle for survival" became much more precisely defined within this sociobiological framework: selfish competition between individuals or between genes for reproductive success under conditions of limited resources. Fitness now had both individual and "inclusive" components. Altruism and cooperation became selfish strategies that could be used to improve reproductive success under certain conditions. For example, kin should help each other but only to the degree that they were related. Kin selection theory (Hamilton 1964) seemed a robust explanation of many social behaviors in primates; reciprocal altruism and parental investment theories (Trivers 1971, 1972) appeared to explain most of the others. Primate sociability emerged in a fresh guise.

The several theories developed under the rubric of sociobiology generated many new hypotheses, some of which were hotly contested. Reproductive strategies, including mating strategies and rearing strategies, assumed center stage. Differences in the costs of reproduction for males and females produced a "battle of the sexes" (Dawkins 1978). Parents and offspring also had

their "battle of the generations" (Dawkins 1978; Trivers 1972). Examples of cooperation were often interpreted as competition in disguise. Behaviors that had seemed strange and abnormal acquired novel and acceptable evolutionary explanations. For example, infanticide and cannibalism were interpreted as evolutionary tactics, ways that individuals could improve their reproductive success at the expense of others. Aggression was also an adaptive tactic, but whether it was advantageous to be aggressive depended on a range of factors, including age, relative rank, and what your opponent did. Evolutionary stable strategies, or ESS (Maynard-Smith 1978), provided a new way to describe the options. Through these avenues, sociobiology addressed and reassessed almost every dimension of primate behavior, including the nature of competition and of cooperation, the importance of family and kinship, and the relationship between parents and offspring, between males, between females, and between males and females.

The language of explanation also changed. Sociobiologists combined economic analysis with game theory to generate metaphors about trade-offs of costs and benefits and about warfare with an arsenal of tactics and strategies. Some of the new terminology carried emotional baggage when applied to animals (e.g., rape, prostitution, infanticide, exploitation, deception, infidelity, coyness) and some was simply more precise than anything previously part of the scientific lexicon (e.g., parent-offspring conflict, reciprocal altruism, evolutionary stable strategies).

Studies of primates flourished in this new intellectual environment; there were more investigations initiated in Stage 3 than in any time before or after (Southwick and Smith 1986). Rather than try to review them all, we will focus on what happened to ideas about baboons and langurs during the sociobiological era.

**LANGURS AND BABOONS** Sarah Hrdy (1977) studied langurs at Mt. Abu in South India intermittently from 1971 to 1975. These langurs lived in all-male or one-male heterosexual groups at exceedingly high densities, and the turnover of leader males resulted in a high incidence of infanticide. One of Hrdy's innovations was to use sociobiological theory to suggest an adaptive explanation for langur infanticide. In her view, the killing of unweaned infants was not abnormal behavior brought on by the stress of high density living but was a male reproductive strategy honed by selective forces. Killing infants improved the new male's reproductive success by making it possible for him to sire infants earlier (and hence more often) than if he waited for females to come into estrus naturally. In addition, by eliminating the offspring of his male rivals, the new male improved the competitive chances of his own future progeny.

Infanticidal males obviously gained at the expense of the females who lost their infants. This made sense because of the asymmetry in parental investment between male and female mammals. The sexes almost seemed like "two different species" (Hrdy 1977). Female langurs were said to have counterstrategies, although these did not appear very effective. Older females risked their lives to protect infants. Reproductive females, whether or not they were already pregnant, copulated with the invading male either to confuse him about paternity and thus protect their infants from future attack or in the hopes that their sons would inherit the winning male reproductive strategy. These counterstrategies were framed in sociobiological terms. For example, the old females who provided aid were thought to be relatives who were already beyond their reproductive prime. By saving the infants of younger female kin, they increased their own inclusive fitness.

Other aspects of langur behavior were also reevaluated. Hrdy and Hrdy (1976) reported that female dominance rank declined with age and suggested that rank was related to a female's reproductive potential. Such a system could occur only in groups of closely related females where both the dominant and subordinant animals would benefit from inequality. Langur infant sharing was interpreted, at least in part, as a tactic for increasing the caretaker's fitness by disrupting the reproductive success of the mother. This was mothering "to death" rather than the earlier mothering "to learn" or "helping" hypotheses (Hrdy 1976).

The sociobiological view of langur society explained many anomalous behaviors. In the process it told an evolutionary story as well integrated and compelling (although controversial) as the baboon scenario proposed during Stage 1. Langur society was a battleground of individuals whose reproductive interests often conflicted. Females were active strategists, as ready to compete, exploit, and make choices as were the males. But male interests dominated, nonetheless, because the inequalities of mammalian reproduction limited female options.

Sociobiology did not create such a radical revision of baboon society. Perhaps the already well-organized adaptationist evolutionary scenario resisted. Or perhaps the large number of baboon studies presented too much data, too much variation, and too much noise to fit neatly into the sociobiological framework. A few studies did try to reassess specific aspects of baboon behavior using sociobiological principles. For example, Joseph Popp (1978), a student of DeVore's who studied baboons in Masai Mara in Kenya, reinterpreted several social patterns, including aggression and agonistic

buffering. He suggested that aggression should be selectively used by males because it carried a high risk of injury. Young males who had the most to lose in terms of future reproductive potential if they were injured should avoid aggressive tactics. By contrast, males nearing the end of their reproductive life should be aggressive because the possible gains were worth the risks. In all populations, baboon males sometimes pick up infants when they are in the midst of an agonistic encounter. A variety of interpretations had been proposed for this behavior. Popp added a new argument to past interpretations by suggesting that "agonistic buffering" was effective because the infant was actually the challenger's offspring. Continuing to be aggressive would be against the challenger's reproductive interests.

Baboon males sometimes form alliances in which two lower-ranking males, acting together, can defeat a more dominant male. Packer's (1977) study of baboons at Gombe Stream Reserve in Tanzania suggested that male coalitions were based on reciprocal altruism, because the assistance was reciprocated at a later date and because coalition partners were more successful together than if they acted alone. Wasser's study of baboons at Mikumi National Park in Tanzania (1983) interpreted female aggression toward pregnant females as a reproductive strategy that often resulted in miscarriages among competitors.

Strum's long-term study of Pumphouse baboons near Gilgil, Kenya, suggested that male investment in "special relationships" with females had greater reproductive payoffs than did a male's rank in an agonistic dominance hierarchy (1982) and that the success of agonistic buffering depended on a system of strategically reciprocating social relationships between males and females and between males and infants (1983a, b). Smuts' study of the Eburru Cliffs troop in the Gilgil baboon population (1983a, b, 1985) applied sociobiological principles to argue that female choice had an impact on male reproductive success through the influence of special relationships on consorting.

Although sociobiological interpretations of baboon behavior tinkered with certain aspects of baboon society, they primarily reinforced rather than changed the previous emphasis on competition and aggression. Yet the picture of baboon society did begin to change, primarily because of perturbations brought by data from long-term studies.

LONG-TERM STUDIES Most long-term studies of primates were not preconceived but began as short-term projects that simply continued. Studies of chimpanzees (Goodall 1965; Nishida 1968) were among the first. Stage 3 witnessed more long-term studies than ever. Longitudinal baboon projects (e.g., Amboseli, Gilgil, Gombe, Mikumi, Okavango) and Japanese studies of Japanese macaques (see Asquith 1994) were the most numerous. These projects share some key characteristics. Foremost is the identification of individuals. Animals become more than just members of age-sex classes, and following them through their lives produces rich detail and essential information on a variety of topics. Long-term studies demonstrate the value of life history data, of demographic data, and of socioecological data to interpretations of behavior. Only within this diachronic perspective could emergent properties of social organization such as dominance, kinship and friendship be assessed. The result was the discovery of a new dimension of primate society: social complexity.

Long-term studies of baboons suggested a similar *structure* to society, one that confirmed the findings of long-term studies of macaques (e.g., Koyama 1967; Sade 1972; see also papers in Fedigan and Asquith 1991). Females, not males, were the stable core of the group since males migrated. Consequently, baboon society was matrilineal, making kinship the key to understanding both the outcome of interactions and the structure of the group. Within their extended families, females performed many of the roles that had been earlier attributed to males: policing, protecting, and leading. Females also had a clear and stable dominance hierarchy not just subtle relationships dependent on association with dominant males as suggested by DeVore, Washburn, and Hall. Jeanne Altmann's (1980) work at Amboseli in Kenya helped to fill in the picture of female baboon daily life. Although time and energy were spent in direct reproductive activities, by far the greatest effort of females was to acquire enough food to sustain themselves and their unweaned young. Simultaneously, females also had to maintain social relationships essential to successful group living. Females were "dual-career" mothers whose knowledge of home range, of group history, and of social relationships ensured female social power. Males were not irrelevant to social life, but the data from a number of studies convincingly argued that baboon society was not as male-focused as it had seemed earlier.

A long-term study at Gilgil (Strum 1975a, 1982, 1983a, b, 1987) reinforced the view that females were central to baboon society and challenged the earlier baboon model in other ways, most notably the role of aggression, the evolutionary significance of the male dominance hierarchy, and the nature of the relationship between males and females. Males in this population did not have a stable dominance hierarchy and male rank did not provide access to limited resources (1975b), particularly when these were receptive females (1975a, 1982). Pumphouse baboons had nonaggressive alternatives, "social strategies" that were less

risky than aggression but just as effective in competition and defense (1982, 1983a, b, 1987).

The existence of baboon social strategies put a new complexion on the relationship between males and females (Strum 1975a, b, 1983a, 1989). Not only was baboon society female-based and female-centered but females could both exert influence over males and successfully compete with them for some limited resources, despite their smaller size. Males needed female cooperation in reproduction and in defense. Females needed male protection and the improved access to resources that they provided. Males and females created, monitored, and carefully managed an unwritten social contract. There was a similar social contract between males and infants (Strum 1983b). These were the "special relationships" that Ransom (1979) had earlier described for Gombe baboons but whose significance was not well understood. Now it seemed that "friendships" were evolutionarily important for both males and females, and that mutual need generated complementary and more balanced power relationships (see also J. Altmann 1980; Seyfarth 1978; Smuts 1983a, b, 1985).

The complexity of baboon social strategies required skillful actors who could dexterously manipulate relationships and situations (Strum 1987; Western and Strum 1983). Later termed "Machiavellian" intelligence (Byrne and Whiten 1988), such social sophistication and skills suggested (but did not yet implement) a reinterpretation of baboon society almost as radical as the sociobiological revision of langur society. Ironically, the movement was in the opposite direction. The new baboon society seemed more egalitarian and more socially flexible, whereas the new langur society seemed less egalitarian with fewer and more biologically determined social options.

**DIVERSITY OF PRIMATE SPECIES AND OTHER THEORY**
Stage 3 saw both the proliferation of studies on a great variety of species and the continuation of studies, particularly on the apes. Only a few of the new findings and interpretations can be mentioned here.

Reports from the long-term study at Gombe were particularly abundant and provocative during this decade. In 1977 Goodall revealed that Gombe chimpanzees had a high rate of beatings, killings, and infanticides. Such violent behavior was later confirmed also among the Mahale chimpanzees by Nishida (1979). Wrangham (1979) and Pusey (1979) now characterized the social organization of chimpanzees as communities of related males with dispersing females. Mating was not entirely promiscuous as previously reported. Gombe chimps formed consort pairs, sometimes initiated by a dominant male (McGinnis 1979) and sometimes by the female (Tutin 1979).

There was a new emphasis on arboreal species in both the Old and the New Worlds to correct the earlier bias toward terrestrial cercopithecoids. But with details of social behavior hard to see among most arboreal species, the focus turned to demography and ecology. Until now, ecological studies of primates lagged behind studies of social behavior. Early primate ecology was rudimentary, often consisting of simple food lists and descriptions of habitats. Socioecology gained prominence at the end of Stage 2 as investigators tried to grapple with the variability of primate behavior. Sociobiological theory predicted that social organizations were the outcome of the interaction of reproductive strategies and such ecological factors as predation, diet, and food distribution, as well as the energetic costs of traveling in groups of different sizes (e.g., Clutton-Brock and Harvey 1977). Socioecology incorporated optimal foraging theory (e.g., Pyke et al. 1977), proposing that feeding strategies optimize or maximize caloric and nutrient intake. These predictions were examined in primates (e.g., J. Altmann 1974; Sussman 1977) with implications for many old issues such as territoriality, sexual dimorphism, and home range size. On the social side of the socioecology equation, Stuart Altmann and Jeanne Altmann (1979) argued for the role of demographic constraints on socioecological patterns, whereas Wrangham (1980) explored the wide-ranging implications of female philopatry for primate society.

Despite the difficulty of obtaining information on social behavior from arboreal species, the new studies on prosimians and New World monkeys yielded some provocative results. For example, prosimians raised the possibility that females can be dominant over males (Jolly 1984) and that even among these supposedly "primitive" primates, a variety of social organizations can exist. Research on New World monkeys demonstrated that some primate societies, such as those of howlers, can function without a reliance on kinship (Clarke and Glander 1984). This decade's studies provided even more evidence of species diversity and in so doing further softened the focus on baboons as *the* primate society.

The growth of primate studies on many fronts in this time period is well exemplified by the series of review chapters commissioned for Smuts et al.'s edited volume *Primate Societies* (1987). Twenty years after the first primate study group convened in 1962–1963 at the Center for Advanced Study in the Behavioral Sciences at Stanford, leading to DeVore's edited volume *Primate Behavior* (1965), a second study group was assembled at Stanford to review the current status of primate field research. The resulting book, with 46 authors and 5 editors, surveys much of the state of the art up to that time. Chapters in *Primate Societies* illustrate a range of perspectives: sociobiology, socioecology, and cognitive ethology, as well as that coming from long-term field studies. The overall emphasis of the book is on the diverse social patterns of both familiar and newly studied species.

METHODS   Sociobiological research broke with the past tradition of natural history and its vague group selectionism. Instead, the new body of theory offered tightly constructed predictions amenable to quantitative testing using behavioral data, particularly from long-term studies where individuals were known and at least matrilineal kinship was certain. Research design was oriented around testing specific hypotheses. Biological data were also critical, stimulating biosocial projects (e.g., Melnick and Kidd 1983; Turner 1981) that took biological samples from wild animals. Blood samples, in particular, were essential to determining relatedness within a group and the genetics of the population.

Ecological research methods changed as well. Optimal foraging theory provided more precise methodology for assessing the physical environment and shifted the emphasis to finer levels of ecological analysis by making predictions about how individuals should interact with their habitat. Studies of primates now also measured substrates and analyzed foods for their nutritional content and for secondary compounds that might limit consumption (e.g., Glander 1978; Oates et al. 1977) as other wildlife research had done for decades. Cost-benefit analyses generated time and activity budgets that potentially could be linked to survival and reproductive success (see studies in Clutton-Brock 1977; Sussman 1979).

**OTHER ISSUES**

*Females Studying Females*   Another factor that contributed to Stage 3 was the impact of female scientists studying female primates. Although females had always been subjects of primate field studies, the disproportionate impact of the baboon model with its focus on males had made it seem as if females were unimportant to primate societies. By the early 1980s, female scientists began to change this view (e.g., J. Altmann 1980; Fedigan 1982; Hrdy 1981; Small 1984).

Studies documented the significance of females and the diversity of their roles and behaviors. These results were synergistic with other Stage 3 trends: Sociobiological theory included an emphasis on female strategies, long-term studies argued that female kin groups were the core structure, providing stability for many primate groups and that females engaged in social manipulation, and the changing view of animal "mind" (see below) implied that both males and females made strategic decisions. The females that were brought back into the evolutionary drama were remade, however, struggling with their own problems of survival amid a myriad of conflicting demands. They were both more cooperative and more competitive than previously portrayed. Female influence extended even to the males whose behavior they could mold through female choice and sexual selection.

*The Emergence of Animal "Mind"* Changing views of the cognitive abilities of animals also contributed to shifts in the image of primate society during Stage 3. Jolly (1966b) had argued for the central importance of social behavior in the evolution of primate intelligence, and Humphrey (1976) had proposed that the large brain of primates was a result of the need to adapt to the complexities of social life. But it was really Griffin (1976) who spearheaded the new movement with his claim that behaviorism had robbed animals of the cognitive abilities that were clearly essential to their survival. He aimed to reverse this bias, making the investigation of animal "mind" part of the study of animal behavior. By the second edition of his book, Griffin's previously "heretical" position was already widely accepted (Griffin 1984) and stimulated the new discipline of cognitive ethology (Griffin 1992).

The rapidity of this change in orientation could be due to several factors. The "cognitive revolution" had triumphed more than a decade earlier among the human behavioral sciences (see Gardner 1985). Studies of captive apes, particularly the language experiments, presented compelling evidence for the human-like abilities of some pongids (e.g., see reviews in Parker and Gibson 1990; Ristau and Robbins 1982). And long-term studies of wild chimpanzees and baboons showed them to be naturally sophisticated tacticians whose negotiation of social complexity seemed to require "mind."

The emerging cognitivist position of active actors conflicted with the sociobiological view of animals as "gene machines." Where were the adaptive strategies? Is it in the genes and subject to the slow march of evolutionary time or in the heads of the animals, flexible and immediately adaptable? This fundamental clash of perspectives was diminished by its timing; the cognitivist view was not strongly articulated until the end of Stage 3, by which time the sociobiological gene strategist position was beginning to weaken.

**ENDURING ISSUES** At the end of Stage 3, the idea that there was one "primate society" had disintegrated. Variability, unmasked over the past 20 years, became enshrined in theory. Now any answer to the question, What is the nature of primate society?, would first have to consider which species, which group, which habitat, and at what point in the group's history.

Although the baboon model lingered, especially in the minds of the public and those in other scientific disciplines, within primatology it had been both transformed and overwhelmed.

During the sociobiological era, many issues were abandoned as irrelevant and others were restated using new language. For example, the focus on inclusive fitness turned family into kin, sex into mating strategies, and weaning into parent-offspring conflict. Novel issues also emerged from the theory: female choice, infanticide, foraging strategies, and life history, to name just a few.

Theory provided some important answers, but it also renewed and generated controversies. Is a group an accidental selfish herd, a cooperating kin group, or an assembly of individuals for whom the benefits of living together outweigh the costs, despite their conflicting interests? Do groups stay together because of genetic calculations, evolutionary stable strategies, evolutionarily based emotions, facultative interactions, or all of these? Theory-generated primate nature seemed to become ever more selfish, competitive, manipulative, and exploitative. Male and female reproductive interests appeared irreconcilable. Yet the sexes sometimes made peace. We were left to wonder whether it was really only the female who had to pay the price of divergent mammalian reproductive physiologies.

Sociobiology brought humans back into the picture after the collapse of the rationale that had been provided by the "primate pattern." If no other species could model humans, then the bridge to understanding human behavior would have to be evolutionary principles. To that end, Wilson (1975) argued that sociobiology, as the unified theory, would absorb all the human social sciences, including anthropology, sociology, and psychology.

**LARGER CONTEXT** Thirty-five years after the resumption of primate field studies, there was an increasingly complex convergence and interaction of trends within the science and between the science and the currents of the larger society. For example, the emphases of long-term studies dovetailed with some sociobiological hypotheses, data on social complexity argued for the presence of animal "mind," and studies of female primates converged with both theory and long-term research. In the larger context, the rise of feminism and the feminist critique of science certainly bolstered efforts by female scientists to study and value female primates. The reaction to sociobiology within society affected its position in science as well. Liberal scientists criticized and rejected sociobiology as a justification for a conservative political agenda (e.g., see discussions in Caplan 1978; Montagu 1980; Ruse 1979;

Sahlins 1976). Even concepts about animal mind were inextricably tied up with the animal rights movement, which was fast becoming a powerful political force (Blum 1994). And soon animals rights would provide its own feedback into the study of primate behavior and images of primate society.

## Stage 4: 1985 to Present—Ecology, Complexity, Cognition, Conservation, Animal Rights, and Beyond

The sociobiological era ended with a multitude of new answers to old questions. Yet despite the unifying evolutionary vision, there were anomalies that presaged the trends in the present period. For example, social complexity in primates implied higher cognitive abilities that were not just gene strategies. Although social strategies included exploitation and competition, they also could involve cooperation and assistance. If we now better understood why relationships between males and females were often adversarial, the instances when relations were complementary became more problematic. As the theory, methods, and data of Stage 3 redefined female options, they also transformed male options.

Stage 4 may be the hardest period to characterize for a number of reasons. The most obvious is that it is our current history and thus still unfinished; trends are easier to discuss retrospectively. But difficulties of depicting the present stage also result from growing fragmentation and specialization within the discipline and an expanding labyrinth of theories, issues, and interaction of factors within the science as well as between the science and its larger context.

The 1985 to present period is perhaps best categorized as an era that has moved away from a strongly reductionist application of sociobiological theory. Crook (1989) has argued that in the history of studies of behavior there has been an oscillation between emphases on genetic and environmental themes in the process of evolution. The focus of classical ethology on innate factors was a reaction to behaviorist environmentalism; then the emergence of socioecology led to a renewed interest in social relations as biotic systems. Next, sociobiology once more emphasized genetic determinism; and most recently behavioral ecology has proposed a more holistic model of adaptation that relates environmental and societal processes to those of genetic selection. In the realm of theory, behavioral ecologists have begun to explore multicausal analyses while placing the focus on evolutionary ecology rather than on isolated behaviors. Researchers have begun to grant individual animals the abilities that were previously denied them by the parsimonious principles of

ethological behaviorism and later by the reductionist model of sociobiological gene machines. When individual primates are perceived as sentient beings, the explanation inevitably becomes more multifactorial.

Even the feedback between science and society has become increasingly dense and complicated. For example, both the primate conservation and animal welfare movements have greater scientific legitimacy because of shifts in societal concerns about the biodiversity crisis and about animal rights. Studies of primates have shifted geographically because of political factors. Many parts of Africa and Asia have been closed to primate research because of growing political unrest while new stability and hospitality in Madagascar and in Latin America have stimulated research on New World monkeys and on lemurs. An emphasis on arboreal species in the past decade has tended to bring ecological and demographic research to the foreground, at least in part because the details of social behavior are often difficult to see in tropical forests. By 1995, the composition and complexion of primate studies had changed markedly from earlier work. Work on Old World terrestrial species such as baboons and macaques continues. But the new excitement is about a plethora of other species: arboreal monkeys of both the neotropics and the Old World, pygmy chimpanzees (bonobos), lowland gorillas, and endangered primates like the lemurs of Madagascar and the muriqui of Brazil.

THEORY: FROM SOCIOBIOLOGY TO BEHAVIORAL ECOLOGY   The scientific pursuit of evolutionary explanations in primatology over the past decade has diverged along several related but distinct lines. Sociobiologists have continued to concentrate on mating and rearing strategies, on sexual selection, and on the variety of social behaviors that determine differential reproductive success. In particular, during Stage 4, the field of human sociobiology has expanded in an attempt to reframe human cultural behavior using evolutionary principles (e.g., Alexander 1986a, b; Barash 1986; Betzig et al. 1988; Mealey et al. 1985; Turke and Betzig 1985). But other investigators (e.g., Dunbar 1988, 1989; Garber 1987; Isbell 1991; Janson 1992; Richard 1985; Terborgh 1983; van Schaik 1989) have gone in a different direction, turning the focus away from the strongly genetic approach of the 1980s toward the perspectives of behavioral ecology.

Behavioral ecology is primarily concerned with how animals find enough food, avoid predators, and balance the conflicting demands that their environment places on them in order to survive and reproduce. Optimal foraging theory and life history theory have been crucial to explicating the foraging strategies of individuals, groups, and species and ways in which animals interact with their living and nonliving environment (e.g., Krebs and Davies 1993). The fact that primates are a slowly reproducing species should have major consequences for primate patterns of fecundity, mortality, and survivorship, and through these, for demographic processes and population dynamics (Clutton-Brock 1988; DeRousseau 1990; Dunbar 1988; Fedigan et al. 1986). Behavioral ecology can be seen as an outgrowth of both socioecology and sociobiology (Crook 1989; Foley 1986). Although it shares with these two schools of thought an interest in applying evolutionary principles to behavior, behavioral ecologists have diverged from both the environmental determinism of early socioecology and the genetic determination of early sociobiology.

The broader perspective embedded in behavioral ecology places greater emphasis on primates as part of larger communities and has widened the ecological context to include a consideration of community structure and dynamics (e.g., Gautier-Hion 1988; Richard 1985; Standen and Foley 1989; Terborgh 1983). This contrasts with previous approaches that treated each species (and sometimes each behavior) separately, that viewed primates as unique, and that interpreted primate adaptations in isolation from the nonprimate ecological context.

Behavioral ecology has also taken a new look at the question of why primates live in groups. During Stage 4, primatologists have pursued a lively debate about the relative importance of enhanced predator protection versus cooperative defense of resources as the ultimate and primary benefits of social living. Although most theorists agree that group living involves a trade-off between increased predator protection and decreased foraging opportunities, some researchers (e.g., Terborgh and Janson 1986; van Schaik 1989) have stressed predator defense strategies as determining the size and composition of primate groups, whereas others have emphasized resource exploitation and defense (e.g., Isbell 1991; Rodman 1988; Wrangham 1987). Obviously, the answer to why primates live in groups is multifaceted, and at a minimum involves predator defense, resource defense, foraging efficiency, and rearing strategies. In each situation the balance of costs and benefits changes with the specifics of evolutionary history, habitat, group size, and group composition.

Less common than behavioral ecology research, but also important in the last decade, has been a reemergence of arguments in favor of phylogenetic analyses of social systems. Some socioecologists have argued that phylogenetic hypotheses should be the last resort, when all attempts to explain social patterns in terms of local ecological circumstances have failed (e.g., Rod-

man 1988). However, others (e.g., Chan 1992, 1993; Di Fiore and Rendall 1994; Garber 1994; see also discussion in Gautier-Hion et al. 1988) have suggested that the distribution of certain behavioral patterns across species is best explained by phylogenetic constraints, or at the very least, that phylogenetic analyses must be integrated into the study of behavioral ecology. Di Fiore and Rendall (1994), for example, performed a cladistic analysis identifying a highly uniform and conservative suite of social organization traits in Old World monkeys that all hinge on female philopatry and male dispersal. The similarity and persistence of these traits in the face of considerable ecological diversity among cercopithecoids suggest that there has been a strong and conservative phylogenetic influence on the social organization of these related species. Ecological adaptations are still important; the cercopithecoid ancestor itself presumably evolved social behaviors in partial response to past environments. But primate societies are not infinitely free to vary in response to contemporary ecological conditions. Social structure is a composite system brought about by evolutionary, historical, epigenetic, and situational factors.

**SOCIAL COMPLEXITY WITHIN GROUPS**  Behavioral ecology has been the broadest current running through Stage 4, but new perspectives on the internal social dynamics of groups have also had significant impact. Research in the past decade has explored social complexity, particularly the implications for competition and cooperation. Earlier, the diversity and complexity of social relationships had been transformed from social "noise" into an important evolutionary resource for individuals. Social strategies quickly became primate "politics," where not only size or strength give individuals a competitive edge but also the ability to assess and manipulate the social situation. The changing context for both competition and cooperation meant that factors like age, temperament, tenure in the group, history of previous interactions, and current social context could be important. Equally significant, social strategies require cognitive as well as social skills. Actors have to perceive the multiple dimensions of social relationships, to predict the combined effects of sequential or simultaneous polyadic interactions, and to plan and manipulate such interactions for their own ends. Research in the past decade has explored social complexity, particularly the implications for competition and cooperation. Work by De Waal (1989), Goodall (1990), Kummer (1988), Strum (1987), and Whiten and Byrne (1988a) provide strong evidence that primates are capable of both social and cognitive skills. As a result, the study of dominance and other aspects of competition has advanced from a rather mechanistic model of brute force to one that finds many parallels to the study of human politics with all its intricacies of motivations, objectives, and manipulations (see discussions in Byrne and Whiten 1988; Chapais 1991; Mason and Mendoza 1993; Schubert and Masters 1991; Silverberg and Gray 1992).

The politics of social strategies have become a subject for study, including alliances and coalitions, reconciliation, and the interaction of aggressive and nonaggressive social strategies. Studies of the value of coalitions and alliances have focused mostly on Old World monkeys and apes (e.g., Datta 1986; De Waal 1984; Dunbar 1984; Harcourt 1988, 1989; Hunte and Horrocks 1987; Moore 1982; Seyfarth and Cheney 1984; Silk 1982; and see especially papers in Harcourt and De Waal 1992). In addition to these largely field observations, Chapais (e.g. 1991) conducted a series of experiments on alliances in Japanese macaques that document the key role of these associations in competitive success, particularly in the acquisition and maintenance of dominance rank. More attention has also been given to the mechanisms by which primates cooperate and maintain their relationships and social systems (see Hinde 1983). De Waal (1986, 1987, 1989), for one, has argued that the earlier strong focus on aggression and competition as evolutionary means and ends has led to the neglect of how conflicts are socially mediated in order for primates to live successfully in social groups. The past decade has seen the blossoming of the study of reconciliation, or "peacemaking," as part of this shift (e.g., Aureli 1992; Cords 1988; De Waal 1993; Judge 1991; Kappeler and van Schaik 1992; York and Rowell 1988). Other work has begun to address how aggressive and nonaggressive options emerge and are integrated during an individual's lifetime (Strum 1994) and how they are implemented according to constraints of space and time during interactions (Forster and Strum 1994).

Another aspect of the study of social dynamics that has also increased in the past decade is the research on mate choice. The priority of access model (reviewed in Bercovitch 1991; Cowlishaw and Dunbar 1991; Fedigan 1983; Shively 1985; Smuts 1987) has been at the center of a long debate. The model assumes, among other things, that dominant males will have greater reproductive success by unilaterally controlling mating. Extensive research and comparative analysis have failed to resolve this controversy (e.g., see recent discussion in volume 44 of *Animal Behavior* 1992). Instead, some investigators have turned their attention to other factors that may influence mate choice for both males and females. Huffman (1991), Janson (1984), Keddy (1986), Manson (1992), and Small (1990), among others, have conducted studies of female mate choice, and Small (1989, 1993) has reviewed the central question for fe-

male choice: What do female primates want from males—resources, parental care, protection from aggression, familiarity, novelty, status, superior genes? Although observational research on female choice in primates is in its infancy, and little experimental work is yet available, primates seem to have preferences for certain sexual partners. Huffman (1991), for example, found that female Japanese macaques, unlike baboons, do not prefer to mate with their friends. While they may repeat consorts with a given male from one year to the next, they begin to avoid mating with these same individuals after a few years. Case histories of individual males suggest that as their consort frequencies decline, even top-ranking males are prone to emigrate. Such findings yield a more dynamic view of what determines individual preferences than does the traditional dominance model, which was insensitive to the history of relations or preferences between individuals.

**ANIMAL COGNITION** Studies of behavioral ecology and social complexity forged new directions for image(s) of primate society(ies), but the recognition of animal mind has created a new kind of actor. First the idea that mind was an important determinant of behavior became orthodoxy in Stage 4. Then social manipulation of strategic partners was transformed into the Machiavellian intelligence hypothesis (Byrne and Whiten 1988). Finally, the growing momentum of this position ignited a controversy over the evolutionary roots of primate intelligence. Although Jolly (1966b) and Humphrey (1976) had earlier presented the case for the social function of intellect, the idea lay dormant. Later, Milton (1981, 1988) revived the discussion by suggesting the importance of ecological intelligence used in mapping and tracking seasonally variable food resources essential to survival. Subsequently, the evolution of cognition among primates has been explored by a variety of investigators (reviewed in Byrne 1995). In general, the social origins hypothesis has had more advocates (cf. Byrne 1995; Parker and Gibson 1990). For example, Seyfarth and Cheney (1988; see also Cheney and Seyfarth 1990) demonstrated that vervets not only recognize other individuals from their calls but can also recognize relationships between other members of the group. When they played back an infant's lost call to the group, the mother oriented toward the hidden speaker and the other group members oriented toward the mother, suggesting that they recognized the relationship between the mother and the distressed infant. Research on rhesus macaques by Gouzoules et al. (1984) demonstrated that the screams of monkeys during conflicts convey information about the relative ranks and level of agonism of the participants, and that listeners act upon this information. These and other studies have shown that primate calls are not just expressions of arousal, a long-standing assumption, but contain and convey specific information about the environment and about the social contingencies of an interaction. By using experimental protocols and sophisticated technology for recording, analyzing, and playing back vocalizations, this research has demonstrated that primates remember past interactions, recognize relationships along kinship and dominance lines (see also Dasser 1988), communicate contextual information, and predict the responses of others on the basis of this knowledge.

An animal's knowledge of social relationships has also led to discussion about whether primates possess a "theory of mind" (see Byrne 1995; Premack 1988; Whiten 1993), that is, whether they respond to what they think another individual might be "believing and desiring." Tactical deception, which occurs when individuals deliberately mislead conspecifics, may provide some of the best evidence for theory of mind among primates (see Byrne 1995; Byrne and Whiten 1988, 1990; Cheney and Seyfarth 1990; Mitchell and Thompson 1986; Snowdon 1990). The issue is still controversial, but some indicative evidence exists among all families of monkeys and apes.

Cognitive issues are a major focus of primate research in Stage 4. While the controversy about the evolutionary origins of primate intelligence continues, we can conclude that any cognitivist stance implies a major shift in images of primate society; individual action has become more intricate, more variable, and less predetermined.

METHODS  The technological developments since 1985 have reinforced and advanced previous methodological innovations in data collection and analysis. Sociobiology, behavioral ecology, and cognitive ethology all generate testable predictions that require quantitative data. New computer and other technologies have made a significant contribution to improving data collection, data analysis, and modeling.

Biological data are increasingly important in resolving many debates in the study of primate society, including controversies about which individuals are more reproductively successful. Among the easily observed baboons and macaques, information on paternity is critical. But biological data also have an important role to play in the newer research projects on the more difficult to study species since these may not even provide basic observational data on maternal kinship. Biomedical samples from these studies provide essential genetic analyses of population and group structure (e.g., Glander et al. 1991, Hildeboltet al. 1993; Melnick and Pearl 1987; Richard et al. 1991; Sussman 1991, 1992). Biologi-

cal samples from free-ranging primates can also be used to study growth, development, physical condition, and the physiological correlates of behavior, such as the relationship between the endocrine stress response and rank in baboons (Sapolsky 1989, 1990, 1993; Stelis 1993).

The development of noninvasive techniques that do not require the capture of animals is also an exciting new source of biological data on the genetic and physiological correlates of behavior. These include DNA analyses from hair follicles (e.g., Morin et al. 1994) and hormonal assays from fecal analyses (e.g., Strier and Ziegler 1994; Wasser et al. 1988, 1991).

Field experimentation, although limited, is an important aspect of Stage 4 methods. This approach combines the controlled environment of a laboratory with the evolutionarily appropriate context of the natural setting. As early as the 1950s, Washburn (1951) argued for experimentation as a way to tease out causal factors. Despite Kortlandt's (1967) early imaginative manipulations with chimpanzees (e.g., dressing up as a chimp, automated leopard), field experimentation was not popular. Later, Kummer's sophisticated series of transplantation experiments with anubis and hamadryas baboons (1973; Kummer et al. 1970, 1974) clearly demonstrated the value of field experimentation, yet not many followed his lead either. Stage 4 field experiments (see references in Cheney and Seyfarth 1990) have tended to focus on cognitive issues, translating captive experimental design into a natural setting and thereby addressing both the criticism leveled at captive studies of cognition and at the anecdotal nature of naturalistic studies of primate cognition.

Ecological methods have become more sophisticated during Stage 4, particularly techniques for monitoring habitats and measuring substrates. Improved technology in remote sensing, in precise location and mapping using GPS (Global Positioning System), and in integration of data using GIS (Geographical Information System) has made geographic and topological data a more important aspect of primate research (e.g., Provost et al. 1994; Sprague 1993; Sussman et al. 1994). Ecological monitoring programs have become routine parts of most field projects, providing essential background data for studies of ranging, foraging, and social behavior. Monitoring has also been crucial to conservation work, since deciding on the long-term viability of primate populations requires, at a minimum, an assessment of habitat quality.

As standardized methodology is increasingly part of social, ecological, and socioecological studies of primates, interdisciplinary boundaries have faded. Zoologists, psychologists, anthropologists and now even cognitive scientists and philosophers seem to be interested in the same issues, not just the same subjects. More than ever, it is the topic not the disciplinary background of the investigator that dictates the methodology.

### BABOONS AND HOWLERS

*Baboons* We return to baboon studies in order to follow the changing images of primate society. It is impossible in Stage 4 to propose one simple model of baboon society. Within the diversity of baboon research no single study can be taken as representative. Yet this diversity of theoretical interests, focused on increasingly specialized topics, does make baboon research typical of work on other species. Nonetheless, baboon studies remain distinct by virtue of their large number, long duration, and exceptional quality of data generated by excellent conditions of observation.

Long-term field sites continue to predominate in Stage 4, including sites in Kenya (Amboseli: J. Altmann et al. 1988; Gilgil/Chololo: Barton et al. 1992; Strum 1987; Masai Mara: Sapolsky 1990; Tana River: Condit and Smith 1994), Tanzania (Gombe: Packer et al. 1995; Mikumi: Norton et al. 1987, Wasser and Wasser 1995), Botswana (Okavango: Bulgar and Hamilton 1988), and Namibia (Brain 1992). Even recently initiated sites (Tana, Kibale, South Africa) are organized as "long-term" projects by piggybacking shorter cross-sectional studies to build up project records. Baboon research now has a strong theoretical grounding in hypotheses from sociobiology, behavioral ecology, and cognitive ethology that includes issues such as life history strategies, reproductive strategies (mating and rearing), social complexity, ontogeny of social skills, animal cognition, communication, reconciliation, foraging strategies, ontogeny of foraging skills, demographic processes, and socioecology. Studies concentrate on both males and females with special interest in sex-related constraints and patterns like those imposed on females by motherhood and on males by life history factors.

Even without a consensus model of baboon society, some characteristics have been widely observed. The group is primarily a multimale unit organized around a core of female matrilines that have their own relatively stable hierarchy. Ecological circumstances determine group size, age structure, and socioeconomic sex ratio. Males are dominant over females by virtue of their larger size, but females are not powerless. They create their own options through social tactics, special relationships, kinship, and the female hierarchy. The male dominance hierarchy is not stable for very long, and as a result each male holds a variety of ranks during his lifetime. Aggression is a basic part of the male repertoire, but so are nonaggressive strategies. The competitive tactics a male uses depend on life history

factors that include age and residency status, as well as size and condition. Sexual competition is part of baboon life for both males and females. Males must compete over access to a limited number of reproductive females, and females must compete over access to preferred males. Female choice can influence male consort success while at the same time, males can play an active role in molding female preferences. Sexual competition is typical of most forms of competition in baboons. It is embedded in a matrix of social relationships that must be created, managed, serviced, and repaired. All competition rests on a foundation of assistance, coordination, and cooperation.

The amount of social complexity within a group depends on its size and its composition, which, in turn, is sensitively tuned to the nature and distribution of key resources like food, water, and sleeping sites. The result is a dynamic set of socioecological relationships in which size, dimorphism, survivorship, age structure, patterns of migration, foraging strategies, and social strategies (to name just a few factors) are inextricably linked in determining individual evolutionary success. By 1998, baboons everywhere had more options than ever before.

*Howlers* What has become of our perception of howler society in the 50 to 60 years since Carpenter's original study? Carpenter's 1934 monograph was long considered the "type" report not just for the mantled howler species but for the entire genus of howlers, and according to Neville et al.'s review (1987), many of Carpenter's original conclusions still stand. However, we do know a good bit more today about dispersal patterns in howlers, intragroup aggression, and foraging patterns. Studies of the behavioral ecology and demographic patterns of howlers are fairly common and indicate that the neotropical forests do not provide the rich smorgasbord that was once assumed. Howlers are selective leaf-eaters, carefully choosing new leaves on individual trees of species that contain lower levels of secondary compounds or toxins (e.g., Glander 1982).

Data from longitudinal studies are now available for mantled howlers in Costa Rica (Clarke and Glander 1984; Glander 1992; Jones 1980) and red howlers in Venezuela (Crockett 1985; Crockett and Eisenberg 1987). From these we know that both sexes disperse from natal groups and that the adults of a group are largely unrelated. Although there are some differences between red and mantled howlers, it is generally true that females disperse a little earlier and more often than males. In mantled howlers, Glander (1992) reports that 96% of females and 79% of males disperse. Some males remain in their natal groups and eventually take over breeding positions from their presumed fathers. Most individuals of both sexes spend from one to four years of their lives as solitaries because it is not easy to emigrate successfully into a new group.

Carpenter found little competition or aggression between group members and no sharp gradient of dominance. Today we know that the picture is more complicated. Males and females can be ranked in a hierarchy by the observer, primarily on the basis of supplantations rather than overt fights. It is easy to see why Carpenter would have concluded that howlers are peaceful animals. Social interactions of any type are rare in howlers compared to other primates, and howlers spend most of their waking hours quietly feeding and resting while digesting their largely folivorous diet. Neville et al. (1987) concluded that competitive interactions between howlers are subtle, often consisting of one animal supplanting another from food or a resting place. Even more common is for one howler to avoid an interaction or move out of the way of another. However, on rare but notable occasions, howlers of both sexes do fight, and then the interactions are very intense, resulting in wounds and falls from high in the canopy. In both Venezuela and Costa Rica, occasional infanticide of young infants by newly resident males also has been reported (Clark and Glander 1984; Crockett and Sekulic 1984).

One of the several ways in which howlers are different from Old World monkeys is that their dominance hierarchies are constituted in reverse order of ages: Younger females rank over older females and younger males rank over older males. This is primarily related to the pattern of bisexual dispersal, in which young individuals of both sexes must fight their way into established groups. According to Glander, a newly emigrated female will either receive some support from one or more of the resident males and fight her way to the top of the female hierarchy, or else leave to try another group. For red howlers, Crockett (1984) has argued that there are a limited number of female breeding positions in the group which are defended by the resident females. Thus a young female must either fight her way in or form an entirely new group with other young emigrants. In both mantled and red howlers, the unrelated resident females of the group may form an alliance to keep the newcomer at a distance, but the emigrant female tries to take on each female one at a time, rising step by step in rank.

Thus howler monkeys, as noted by several of the researchers who study them, raise many challenges to the general assumptions about primate societies, assumptions that have been based largely on studies of ground-dwelling cercopithecines. Strier (1994a) has reviewed how studies of New World monkey species should lead us to rethink the many generalizations in

the "myth of the typical primate." Howlers (Alouattini) and their close relatives, the Atelini (woolly monkeys, spider monkeys, and muriqui) are placed together in the subfamily Atelinae by some taxonomists (e.g., Rosenberger 1979) because these species share many morphological and behavioral features (Rosenberger and Strier 1989). Research on atelines, especially in the past decade, challenges at least the following assumptions about the typical primate social pattern.

1. *The common primate pattern is one of male dispersal and female philopatry.* By contrast to many Old World monkeys, howlers of both sexes disperse, and in muriquis, spiders, and wooly monkeys, the females disperse (Moore 1984, 1992).

2. *Most primate societies are female-bonded, and matrilines/nepotism forms a central structural feature of the social system.* In howlers, unrelated resident females form alliances against emigrant females. In spider monkeys, females disperse to new ranges and different communities from their mothers, whereas males occupy large ranges overlapping those of their mothers (Chapman et al. 1989; Fedigan and Baxter 1984; Fedgan et al. 1988; Symington 1988). In muriquis, patrilineal associations and male affiliation are essential to social structure (Strier 1994; Strier et al. 1993).

3. *Dominance hierarchies are based on inherited rank for females and aggressive interactions for males.* In howlers, the newest emigrants of both sexes usually fight their way to the top rank or leave the group. In muriquis, intergroup relations are largely egalitarian with co-dominance between males and females and no female dominance hierarchies.

4. *Intragroup competition over food is frequent.* In howlers, food competition mainly takes the form of subtle avoidance and supplantation interactions. In the howlers of Santa Rosa, large groups fission in the seasons when food is only available in small patches, and fuse when food is more densely distributed (Chapman 1989; Fedigan 1986). Similarly, muriquis and spider monkeys avoid direct confrontations over food, either by avoiding interactions or through fission-fusion feeding groups (Kinzey and Cunningham 1994; Strier 1990, 1994b).

*Conclusions about Baboons and Howlers* The baboon and howler studies, although very different in their scope and focus, point to some similar conclusions. First, we can no longer talk about "primate society." Primate societies are highly varied and affected by both local circumstances and species' phylogeny. The longer we continue to study the familiar species such as baboons, macaques, and chimpanzees, and the more we branch out to study the lesser known primates such as prosimians, neotropical monkeys, arboreal colobines, and cercopithecines of the African and Asian forest, lowland gorillas, and bonobos, the more apparent it becomes that many of our generalizations about primates have been premature and based on limited and possibly biased data. During Stage 4 we once again confront some Stage 2 issues: What is it that generates diversity among primates, and given this diversity, how can we generalize about primate patterns?

A second conclusion from both sets of studies is about complexity in individuals, in interactions within social and ecological domains, and in the synergism between domains. Such complexity requires more sophisticated and comprehensive ways to model factors and their interactions. This is particularly apparent when we consider the "new actors" in primate societies. They are, regardless of sex or age, smart strategists involved in intricate evolutionary games. Options, choices, and successes depend on a variety of factors, including environment, demography, age, sex, development, personality, biology, and historical accident. What is still unclear is how much flexibility and variability exist in the range of complexity that has been documented over a day, a week, and a lifetime, and how much it matters.

**LARGER CONTEXT: ANIMAL RIGHTS AND CONSERVATION** We have already mentioned the effects of geopolitics on the ability to do primate field research during Stage 4. The current emphasis on New World primates and its resulting research agendas have as much to do with political realities as with scientific design. The convergence of the world inside and outside primate studies is most obvious in two other areas: animal welfare/animal rights and conservation.

The cognitive revolution within primate studies had unintended consequences for social action and for science. If a creature had awareness and mind, it could suffer. Members of the growing animal welfare movement used scientific findings to bolster their position, particularly targeting captive primates. Hotly contested lines were drawn between the welfare of animals and the rights of science, a conflict that became very public and political (see Blum 1994). But by raising their concern in the context of legitimate scientific issues of animal mind and awareness, the movement also convinced some scientists to change their attitudes. Animal welfare is increasingly a consideration in creating the living conditions and research designs for captive primates.

The animal welfare movement was linked to, but was not identical with, the animal rights movement

(Nash 1989; Shabecoff 1993). As early as 1975, Peter Singer had argued for the *rights* of animals in his book, *Animal Liberation*. But the main impetus for animal rights, rather than animal welfare, came later with the rise of environmentalism and its liberal but radical extension of "rights" to nature (Nash 1989). The rights of primates have depended on two different kinds of arguments. In the first, primates are viewed simply as "animals." Since all of nature has an intrinsic right to exist and animals are part of nature, primates share in this intrinsic right. In the second argument, the rights of nonhuman primates come from evidence of their similarity to humans. Cavalieri and Singer (1993) offer the most recent version of this argument. They propose extending the United Nations Charter and basic human "rights" to the great apes because of current evidence on ape cognition, social complexity, and language abilities. They argue that we cannot legitimately draw a line between human and ape experience, and therefore cannot make a distinction between human and ape rights.

Just as the line between science and advocacy is increasingly blurred in the arena of animal welfare and animal rights, the line between basic and applied science has dissolved in the arena of conservation. Primatologists have not been able to ignore the vulnerability of their subjects during Stage 4 (e.g., Galdikas 1995; Goodall 1990; Jolly 1984; Strum 1987). Habitat destruction (particularly of the principal primate habitat, the tropical forest), the impact of medical research on certain primate species, the conflict between people and primate "pests" throughout the developing world, and even the attraction of primates as pets and for exhibition have all spelled doom for already dwindling populations (e.g., Lee et al. 1988). Traditional conservation approaches seem inadequate to safeguard endangered and threatened species (Western et al. 1994). For primates, as for many other taxa, the challenge of conservation has stimulated a search both for new techniques (e.g., Benirschke 1986) like reintroduction (Kleiman et al. 1986) and translocation (Strum and Southwick 1986) and for better and more rapid ways to assess the vulnerability of threatened species (e.g., Mittermeier 1986). Primate conservation has begun to claim larger portions of research effort and journal space, including surveys of populations and habitats of threatened or endangered species, monitoring habitat destruction and population decline, and testing new conservation techniques. Field investigators have also confronted the necessity of going beyond science to become deeply involved in promoting public awareness and advancing human social and economic development as a way to stem the conflict and ultimate destruction of their animals.

ENDURING ISSUES: TRENDS   The preceding discussion of baboons and atelines illustrates some of the Stage 4 answers to our enduring issues. In general, our understanding of primates and primate societies in 1998 is based on more information on more species in more environments. These data are both cross-sectional and longitudinal; they include more ecology and more biology than in any previous period. There have also been refinements in theory. Sociobiology, behavioral ecology, and cognitive ethology present heuristic and intelligible ways for beginning to explain the complexity that has been unearthed. Better methods of data collection, analysis, and modeling have allowed us to agree on what constitutes the data even if we do not always agree on interpretations. And although many questions remain, no one could doubt that in 1998, primatology has a better understanding of the diversity of primate behavior and societies than in the era of Zuckerman and Carpenter.

As a summary to our historical framework of ideas and how they have changed, it may be useful to trace the answers to some of our enduring issues as they wind their way through the stages of primate research we have just reviewed. For the sake of brevity we will summarize only the first five questions but the same could be done for the remaining five.

*Why Do Primates Live in Groups?*   Starting from Zuckerman's conclusion in Pre-Stage 1 that sexual competition is the basis of primate society, we progress to a position more reminiscent of Carpenter's view in Stage 1. Primates live in groups for a variety of reasons. The most important are reproduction and predator defense. The group is also seen as the repository of traditional knowledge that goes beyond the individual and is critical to each animal's socialization and survival. The vague socioecological models of primate groups promoted during Stage 2 are replaced by precise gene-based reproductive arguments offered by sociobiology in Stage 3. Behavioral ecology adds to these a set of integrative socioecological principles which suggest that a number of factors, acting in combination, make the group the prime primate adaptation. But controversy continues over the relative contribution of specific variables and whether groups are primarily for predator protection or for resource-holding power during intergroup competition. Over time the original question has been transformed; it is no longer why live in a group but why live in a group of a particular size and composition. The answer(s) still contain(s) elements that both Zuckerman and Carpenter would recognize.

*What Holds Society Together?*   Zuckerman and Carpenter did not agree. One claimed that sexual instincts were the cement of the group, and the other argued for social conditioning, social attraction, and affiliation. By Stage 1, the argument already implicitly included a distinction between proximate and ultimate levels of causation. Stage 1 investigators agreed with Carpenter on the proximate means of social cohesion. Social emotions were the cement between the bricks of evolutionary payoffs. The group and the species benefited in myriad ways from the existence of society. Natural selection ensures that animals are motivated to do what was essential to their survival in the past—they would want to be "social." The shift of the unit of selection caused by sociobiology during Stage 3 focused attention both on the individual and on the ultimate level of causation but, in the process, also ignored proximate considerations. Society was the result of gene-based individual selfish strategies. When conditions changed, so would the evolutionary outcome. Stage 4 extended this strategic view of society by incorporating more complexity and more active agency on the part of "actors as authors."

*What Is the Nature of Society: Aggression and Dominance, Sex and Affiliation?*   We begin with controversy and end with controversy when we try to consider the basic nature of society. Is society aggressive and competitive or peaceful and cooperative? Zuckerman and Carpenter each championed a different view, but it was Zuckerman's image and the baboon model that took precedence for decades. In its various incarnations this view emphasized aggression, competition, and dominance (primarily over things sexual and primarily by males). Aggressive baboons were briefly replaced by peaceful chimpanzees as the standard society. But sociobiology revived the competitive view, making individuals and their societies even more selfish and exploitative than earlier versions. At about that time, chimpanzees turned to warfare, infanticide, and cannibalism, taking with them the notion of a peaceful society.

After 1985, the situation becomes confusing. There are more and more evolutionary reasons to cooperate, assist, affiliate, and reconcile, as well as to compete and exploit. Meanwhile, at least in some places, the old villains, baboons, turn into social managers who shun aggression and follow the golden rule. Chimpanzees and other species even make peace after they make war.

Who should we believe? Which version is correct? Although the controversy continues, we can reasonably conclude that as there is no longer one basic primate society, there can no longer be one basic nature of primate society.

*What Is the Basic Nature of Males, of Females, and the Relationship Between the Sexes?*   The answers to these questions are intimately related to changes in theory and in model(s) of primate society(ies). Here, too, the Zuckerman/Carpenter contrast is a useful starting point. On one hand, males are central, controlling, and domineering, whereas females are peripheral, submissive, and dominated. On the other hand, both males and females are communal and cooperative, and their relationship and societal roles complementary. For quite a while, there seemed to be little doubt that Zuckerman or a variant of his position was correct.

In Stage 3, sociobiology retooled the role of females, making them competitive and aggressive actors, central to the evolutionary story. Yet sociobiology redefined male and female nature using mammalian physiology in a way that once again made females pawns in the games that males played. At the same time, other voices were heard. Social complexity, primate social strategies, and politics gave both males and females new opportunities and created new constraints on males in some species. Cognitive tactics helped to level the playing field, since smarter weaker animals could win against stronger but dumber opponents.

Perhaps most important, by Stage 4, the diversity of species, of social organizations, and of social relationships suggested that regardless of the basic mammalian nature of males and females, relationships between them could be exploitative, cooperative, complementary, or some combination of all three.

*What Is the Relationship of the Group to the Environment?* Primatologists have moved from largely ignoring and oversimplifying the effects of environmental factors to an integrated socioecology where few social facts exist outside of an ecological context and social considerations mold ecological opportunities. Whereas Zuckerman gave no consideration to the impact of the abnormal social and physical environment in which he observed hamadryas baboons, Carpenter felt it was important to study primates in their naturalistic setting. According to Richard (1981), Carpenter laid the foundations of primate ecology, one of meticulous and almost completely atheoretical description of feeding, ranging, and habitat that stood in isolation from relevant developments in the discipline of ecology. In Stage 1, the pendulum swung to a simplistic form of environmental determinism. The assumption of the early field studies of baboons was that because both baboons and hominids evolved on the East African savannas, baboons would make a good model for humans. This position, that there is one social organization best suited to each habitat and that the environment can unilaterally determine social systems, carried over into the next stage's attempts to explain the variability in social systems between species. The enigma of intra- and interspecific variation in Stage 2 brought environmental issues to the fore. The finding that baboons, vervets, and langurs behaved differently in different locations suggested that variation in local environmental factors, such as food supplies, predation levels, and population densities, might cause intraspecific differences. Variations in social groupings *between* species were also attributed to major ecological features, such as open-country or tropical forest living. Various schemes attempted to categorize all known primate species into a few ecological "grades" or levels. This solution to the puzzle of variation in primate societies was a typological perspective with little theoretical underpinning.

In the 1970s and 1980s, primate socioecology became much more sophisticated, particularly as it drew on formal ideas from the discipline of ecology. Primatologists recognized that social systems are interrelated with many factors such as demographic and life history processes and phylogenetic constraints, as well as the presence of other species and abiotic aspects of the environment. Primates, as part of ecological communities, both affected and were affected by their environments. Simplified adaptive stories were replaced by hypotheses from models developed by theoretical ecologists.

In the most recent decade, the perspective of behavioral ecology has brought the first true integration of studies of social systems and the environments in which they exist. Steklis (1993) notes that Washburn long ago envisioned a holistic discipline of primatology, one that would integrate knowledge of the biology, evolutionary history, social behavior, and ecological context of its study subjects. However, until recently, studies with proximate perspectives and those interested in ultimate causes of behavior have been isolated from each other. Only now are we beginning to realize the potential insights that come from combining levels of causation and from the multiple standpoints of biological, phylogenetic, ecological, and behavioral perspectives.

## THEORY, METHOD, GENDER, AND CULTURE: WHAT CHANGED OUR VIEWS OF PRIMATE SOCIETY?

We have traced the change in images of primate society through the stages of primate field research. In the process, we have also alluded to the factors that played crucial roles in our understanding of primates during each stage and to shifts in our orientations between stages. Now we highlight these factors themselves, to assess their particular contributions to changing images of primate society.

## The Impact of Theory

We cannot legitimately claim to assess the impact that theory had on changing images of primate society without a more rigorous and extensive historical study. However, the review of stages and trends just presented offers some tentative suggestions.

A theoretical "revolution" gave birth to the scientific study of primate behavior. This Darwinian approach created the first image of an evolutionarily adapted society. Since then, an evolutionary framework has been one of the most constant hallmarks of primate studies. But the nature of the evolutionary framework itself has changed. Although the interaction between fact and theory, between image and concept is complex, we feel that changing images of primate society have been influenced by these shifts in evolutionary theory. For example, primate society was first described using a functionalist and group selectionist model. The model, borrowed from the social sciences, cast society in terms of roles instead of individuals and in terms of implicitly homeostatic mechanisms necessary for maintaining social continuity and stability. Washburn's new physical anthropology elaborated issues of behavior and society more clearly within an evolutionary framework. But it went farther. It specified a "primate pattern" and emphasized the universality of an ostensive (Strum and Latour 1987) primate society made up of common parts segmented by sex and role as important as any of the morphological traits that had classically defined the order. The compelling and pervasive search for the "primate pattern" dominated the research agenda until the mid-1970s when sociobiology reframed images of primate society by insisting that the individual/gene was the unit of selection. At the same time, specific subtheories, such as those concerning mating and rearing strategies, changed the nature of the questions about society and remolded individual action. Against the backdrop of sociobiological transformations of primate society(ies), the later theoretical impact of behavioral ecology seems a minor modification. It dampened determinism, introduced complexity, and tried rigorously to integrate the social and the ecological in images of primate society.

So far we have taken only one small step in assessing the role of theory in changing images of primate society. Going farther is both increasingly challenging and perhaps more controversial. Can we really say that one theory was more important than another theory? How might we compare "big" theory against "little" theory? Is there some way to track the interaction of theory with other factors such as methods, gender, and culture during each stage of research? Overall? These are important questions worthy of further empirical research, perhaps within the comparative perspective of other closely related disciplines and other national traditions of primatology.

## The Impact of Methods

Field methods in primatology have advanced considerably in sophistication since the 1930s when Carpenter first laid the foundations for observations of primates in the wild. Nonetheless, his basic approach of naturalistic observation and habituation of animals and a dyadic approach to studying social systems have stood the test of time. In the first stage of primate field studies following World War II, a natural history approach focused on largely qualitative descriptions of the behavior of age/sex classes, the development of ethograms, the study of feeding and ranging patterns, and the nature of social groups and social relations. Stage 2 brought the codification of systematic sampling techniques and other attempts to minimize observer bias and to develop more rigorous quantification of observations. By the mid-1970s, with the explosion of theory in the areas of sociobiology and socioecology, primatology turned from a largely inductive enterprise to one that tested specific predictions and hypotheses generated from theoretical models. Long-term studies of chimpanzees and Old World cercopithecines (a methodological advance) began percolating into general assumptions about all primate species, including those yet to be studied so intensively, and feeding back into theories of primate social life. Technological advances in the use of computers for both the collection and analysis of field observations also made possible the accumulation and interpretation of large amounts of systematic data. The development of techniques for field experimentation and collection of biological samples for genetic and other analyses have helped primatologists explore the causes of social behavior. Stage 4 has seen further technological progress, particularly in the areas of hand-held data loggers, satellite imaging systems, and noninvasive techniques for the collection of biological samples. In the past decade, there have also been more integrative team efforts to study the behavioral ecology of primates.

Thus the primary shifts in methods have been from naturalistic to quantitative research, from handwritten notes to technologically assisted data collection, from short-term, cross-sectional to longitudinal studies, from one-person to team efforts, and from data-driven to theory-driven approaches. At one level, it may seem obvious that changes in theory relate more directly than do changes in methods to our ideas of how and why primates behave socially in the ways they do. However, it is possible to point to several examples where changes or improvements in methods have helped to change significantly our perceptions of our study animals and their society. For one, systematic observation techniques certainly played a role in bringing females, juveniles, and subordinates out of the shadows of early descriptions of the catarrhines, and onto center stage along with the more prepossessing dominant adult males. Systematic sampling of individuals also helped us to recognize the enormous importance of individual variation. Technological advances have made it feasible to research the more difficult to study species (e.g., arboreal, tropical forest dwellers) and the more difficult to study questions (e.g., paternity), and this new information is presently challenging our prior assumptions and generalizations about primate society. Finally, longitudinal research provides a perspective that is essential to understanding animals as long-lived as primates and groups as enduring as primate societies.

We are left with tantalizing hints but no conclusive answers to the questions of how and in what ways changes in methods have influenced our views about primate society.

## The Impact of Gender and of Feminism

In reviewing the literature on feminism and science, it is noteworthy how often feminist scholars have singled out primatology for discussion (e.g., Adams and Burnett 1991; Bleier 1986; Haraway 1989; Harding 1986; Keller 1987a; Morell 1993; Rosser 1986; Sperling 1991). Although these authors are not in full agreement as to whether women have always or only recently played an important role in primate studies, and precisely what this role might be, their analyses largely share a fundamental assertion. This is the idea that primatology today has many women practitioners and therefore incorporates the female point of view, either because women primatologists attend more to female actors and/or because women primatologists have a different vision of their subject matter than do men.

This assumption contains a number of elements that we will attempt to tease apart and address in this section. First, we will distinguish briefly among the feminist *critique* of science, the characteristics of a *"feminine"* science, and images of a *feminist* science. Then we will relate these ideas to changes in primatology by looking briefly at the history of gender representation in primatology and by exploring the distinction between women doing primate studies and the feminist approach to primatology.

*What Is the Feminist Critique of Science?* In the mid-1970s and early 1980s, concerns about how the lives of women are affected by science and technology, especially reproductive technology, led feminist scholars to turn their analytical skills to addressing the production

and application of scientific knowledge. In particular, many of these writers developed critiques of specific theories then current in the biological sciences, ranging from models of human evolution to deterministic explanations of differences between the sexes to endocrinological constructions of ontogeny (e.g., Birke 1986; Bleier 1984; Fausto-Sterling 1985; Haraway 1978, 1981; Hubbard et al. 1982; Keller 1992; Leibowitz 1983; Longino and Doell 1983; Lowe and Hubbard 1983; Sayers 1982; Tanner 1981; Tuana 1989; Zihlman 1978, 1981). Larger critiques of the scientific enterprise as a whole often argued that the history of science in the West is based on assumptions of male domination and patriarchal power (e.g., Harding 1986; Keller 1985, 1992; Longino 1990; Merchant 1980; Tuana 1993), and that at least since the Renaissance, the language and metaphors of science have been those of domination and sexuality (Keller 1992).

Women are thought to have reacted to this male-oriented model of science in various ways, including avoiding science, participating while denying that gender attributes play any role in science, or becoming "nonfeminine" in order to be accorded authority. Others have argued that women should not have to change to become scientists; rather science itself should change, embracing feminine or feminist characteristics.

*How Might We Characterize a Science Carried Out by Women—A "Feminine Science"?* Do women do science differently from men? The answers are far from uniform. If the behavior of women is socially constructed, as some suggest, then the differential history, status, and socialization of women should provide them with a perspective on science that is different from men's. Alternatively, if both women and men scientists have been strongly socialized as scientists, gender differences should be minimal. Finally, some scholars have argued both that there is a biological basis for gender differences and that the gender-based traits of women are superior to those of men and should be espoused in science. In whatever manner feminine traits are seen to be acquired, some feminists (see discussions in Fee 1986; Longino 1990; Rosser 1989; Schiebinger 1987) have argued that women are more likely than men to possess certain characteristics that enable them to understand better the complexities of natural processes, such as a feeling of connectedness to nature; an integrative, holistic, contextual worldview; a disposition to attend to details, complexities, and interactions; a sense of patience and empathy; and a high valuation of pragmatic, experiential knowledge. Fee (1986) has argued that whether consciously articulated or not, women carry the seeds of an alternative epistemology.

One opinion is that this alternative epistemology could constitute the basis for a feminist science. There have been objections to such a move on several grounds. For example, Longino (1989, 1990) points out that a science based on "feminine characteristics" could be a new guise for the old argument that women cannot do real, quantitative, hard science. Harding (1986) and Keller (1987b, 1991) have argued that these traits ascribed to women are socially constructed categories originating in the historical subordination of women and are merely the converse of the culturally dominant "masculine traits." As such, they may be as much characteristics of "outsiders" of the scientific mainstream as characteristics of women. At the very least, it would surely be an oversimplification to suggest that these "feminine" traits reflect the temperaments of all women. Furthermore, Longino (1989) argued that such a characterization of feminist science conflates feminine with feminist.

*How Might We Characterize Feminists Doing Science— A "Feminist Science?"*  At the risk of oversimplification, we will list a few of the features that recur in different depictions of feminist science. The most common trait suggested has to do with bias and reflexivity. Scientists of a feminist science would acknowledge their biases and see themselves and the process of science in context. Such contextual values, related to race, class, gender, and nationality/culture, among other factors, are believed to act as constraints on scientific reasoning and interpretations. In particular, feminists have been concerned that scientists acknowledge the role that gender plays in how they perceive the world, and that scientists explicitly factor gender into their research.

Another trait of feminist science is a move away from dualisms—the lessening of rigid boundaries between the scientist as knower and the object of knowledge, between objectivity and subjectivity, dispassion and empathy. Feminist science would also move away from the language of control and domination, away from a hierarchical and reductionist worldview, toward a language of empowerment, toward a commitment to science working in cooperation with nature, to the use of knowledge as a tool of liberation rather than domination, to humility in the face of the complexity of nature, to a view of nature as active, holistic, dynamic, rather than mechanistic. Finally, most descriptions of feminist science see it as more accessible and egalitarian than the science of today, more culturally diverse, and more geared to humane values.

## The Relationship Between Gender, Feminism, and Primatology

One of the initial impetuses for our joint discussions, and for this chapter, was the attention given to women

in primatology, by both the media and feminist scholars. In particular, a claim has been made that women have had a major influence on the nature of primate studies as practiced over the past few decades and on changing our images of primate society. We have already outlined some of the views that have changed since the 1930s. Here we turn to the question of whether and how our ideas about primate societies may have been altered by increasing proportions of women practitioners, by women approaching this science in their own characteristic way, and by the impact of feminist concerns and critiques of science. We cannot hope to answer these questions definitively, but we can begin to point out directions for future discussions.

*Are There Larger Proportions of Women in Primatology than in Related Sciences, and Have the Proportions of Women in Primate Studies Increased?*  Both Haraway (1986) and Hrdy (1986) carried out preliminary calculations of the proportions of women in primatology societies in the early 1980s, and concluded that women were disproportionately represented among primatologists compared to their representation in other sciences. Today, there is a significantly higher proportion of women in primatology than in analogous biological sciences, such as ornithology, mammalogy, and benthology (Fedigan 1994). In 1991, women made up 48% of the membership of the American Society of Primatologists (ASP) and 38% of the International Primatological Society (IPS), whereas they only made up an average of 20% of the analogous biological disciplines sampled. However, there are *not* significantly more women primatologists than there are women anthropologists, psychologists, and animal behaviorists, all parental disciplines of primatology. Thus the perception that there are larger proportions of women in primatology than in related sciences is valid in a comparison across the biological sciences, but not particularly striking from the perspective of the behavioral sciences. However, during the most recent stage of primatology (1981–1991 in Fedigan's analysis [1994]), there has been a significant increase in the proportion of women members of primatological societies, from 33% to 48% in ASP and from 27% to 38% in IPS. Women seem to be joining the ranks of professional primatologists in ever-increasing proportions.

These findings are only a first step. It would be useful to do further analyses of membership in professional societies over the past several decades, of proportions of women and men receiving doctoral degrees with specializations in primatology, and of other indicators of gender representation and participation.

*Do Women Practice Primatology Differently from Men?* In spite of the uniformity of the scientific method to which practitioners adhere, we can envision several ways in which scientists might differ in their approaches and activities. For example, women might tend to choose different topics from those chosen by men, they might frame different questions about these topics, they might prefer different theories and hypotheses, they might use different methods, and they might favor different interpretations of similar findings.

There has been little research into what female and male primatologists actually do, so there is as yet little evidence to support or reject a hypothesis of sex differences in research. The primary assumption has been that women have tended to focus more on female primates, but a sociometric study of the literature is needed to confirm this. Haraway (1989) provided an impressive list of books and articles published by women on female primates, and many more have appeared since she constructed her list. Small (1984) edited a volume of field studies to showcase the diversity of studies on female primates by women primatologists, and later (1993) argued that it is natural for women primatologists to study females since all scientists study things that have relevance to their own lives. On a similar note, Rowell (1984) commented that women find it easier to empathize with female primates. However, Holmes and Hitchcock's (1997) large multivariate analysis of the research choices of animal behaviorists did not find that women were more likely to study female animals.

Besides choosing different topics of study, women might also frame their questions and develop their interpretations of results differently. Again, Rowell (1984), Haraway (1989), Hrdy (1984), and others have suggested that women are more likely to try to see the social and physical environment from the female animal's point of view. It is clear that in the early days of primate field studies, female animals were seen by scientists almost exclusively as mothers and as sexual partners of males. A change was heralded by Lancaster's (1973) prescient article: "In Praise of the Achieving Female Monkey." In the past two stages of primatology, the image of female primates has been fleshed out to include the significance of their sexual assertiveness, their bonding through female kinship lines, their long-term knowledge of the group's local environment, their social strategies, their cognitive skills, and their competition for reproductive success. That women primatologists have been more responsible for this elaboration has often been suggested but not yet documented. A sociometric study of the literature might begin to answer this question.

The possibility that women primatologists might prefer different theories and methods than men has not been addressed in the literature. Burk (1986, 1993) has found that women are significantly underrepresented in theoretical papers given at animal behavior conferences, but no such analysis has been made of theory papers in primatology. Louis Leakey believed that women's minds were less cluttered with theory than those of men and that women were more patient, more persistent, and made better observers of primate behavior (Hrdy 1986; Montgomery 1991; Morrell 1993). According to Hrdy (1986), it is fairly commonplace to hear among ethologists that women have a better ability to individually identify animals. Also current is the view that women primatologists are more associated with long-term (i.e., decades-long) field studies than are men. Some of these anecdotal assumptions would be difficult to document, whereas others would not. It should be possible to investigate sex differences in the use of certain theories and methods in primatology, or the number of women opposed to men who are principal investigators in long-term field studies. Assessing sex-differentiated observational skills, or the so-called "feminine" characteristics listed earlier, presents a much greater challenge. The task is to operationalize these characteristics in a way that can be tested. One case study analysis of research on baboons (Fedigan and Fedigan 1989) does suggest that women researchers were largely responsible for bringing about changes in our views of baboons and that their significant and distinctive approach to baboon research exemplifies many of the traits cited earlier.

*How Has the Women's Movement and the Feminist Critique of Science Influenced the Discipline of Primatology?* Some have argued that it cannot be a coincidence that a strong shift in the perception of female primates began to occur in the mid-1970s at the same time as the second wave of Western feminism urged scientists to take account of the female point of view (e.g., Haraway 1989; Hrdy 1986; Sperling 1991). Apart from noting this apparent correspondence of historical events, how might we document the impact of feminism on primatology? Few primatologists have identified themselves in print as feminists (see Hrdy 1986, and Smuts in Rosenthal 1991). Yet this does not mean that others were not influenced by feminism. Here, too, we have the challenge of how to obtain reliable information about such complex interactions (but see Larger Context and Conclusions). One could build a circumstantial case by showing that primate studies in the second two stages (1975–1985, 1985–1995) have shifted toward the values and practices outlined earlier as "feminist science" (Fedigan 1997). For example, if primatologists have become more reflexive, if they have moved away from a language of control and domination toward a language of "empowerment," if they have shifted from a hierarchical and reductionist worldview to a perception of their subjects as active, complex, and dynamic rather than mechanistic, if they have made primatology more "accessible" and diverse, then one might argue that feminist ideology has influenced our scientific views of primate societies.

However, other possibilities should be considered if a correlation between feminist goals and shifting practices in primatology were found. One is that the objectives of a feminist science may be similar to those of other alternate approaches to the scientific enterprise. For example, Fee (1986), Haraway (1989), and Montgomery (1991) have noted the parallels between the feminist critique and other epistemologies of science, such as African, Indian, Chinese, Japanese, and Marxist perspectives on natural knowledge. Furthermore, the women's movement in the 1960s and 1970s was part of a larger movement of social liberalization in North America and Europe. Thus we must also consider the possible influence of other societal forces on shifts in primatology over the past few decades.

Finally, it may be that the shifting practices and perceptions of primatology outlined here result from processes intrinsic to the development of any science. In the initial stages, a new science may be more descriptive, make more simplifying assumptions, take a more mechanical, reductionist view, and so on, whereas later, models are more complex, dynamic, and reflexive. If so, the changes of the last several decades in primate studies may reflect the inherent constraints and processes of any evolving science.

## The Impact of the Larger Context: Science and Society

Feminism is certainly part of the larger context of science. We have treated it separately because of the special attention given to women in primatology by scholars and the media. Now we turn to a more general examination of what constitutes the "context" of primatology and its importance to changing scientific images of primate society.

There are many models of science, each with implicit assumptions about the relationship of science and society. At one end of the spectrum is the view that science and society exist independently of each other and that science is (or should be) isolated from societal processes and concerns. This adversarial separation treats the intermingling of politics (or any social issue) with science as "pollution" and "bias." At the other end of the spectrum, science and society are seen to be mutually constituted, two distinct outcomes of the same cultural process. Here, the interest is in how science becomes successful and powerful as a cultural practice, for example, what makes it work, what kind of work is done, what counts as evidence, how are networks—links between people, things, and environment—created and maintained. In this view, history, politics, and economics are not extrinsic and polluting but are as central to the practice of science as they are to any other cultural practice. Although we cannot resolve current controversies in science studies here, we suggest that such issues are central to any attempt at understanding how scientific images of primate society are created, what they represent, and the legitimacy of primatology as a science.

There are tantalizing glimpses into the nature of science in the history of ideas we have just reviewed. For example, the triumph of Zuckerman's model of primate society over Carpenter's version cannot be explained in traditional ways such as the "weight of the evidence," the predictive power of the models, or the appropriateness of the methodology. It seems that from the start, the science of primatology was not narrowly configured.

Our brief history of primate studies also illustrates how the cultural practice of making society and of making science can be similar and connected. We see evidence in the tenacious hold that the baboon model had on the primatological imagination for decades despite mounting counterevidence, and in the increase in the number of female practitioners in primatology as well as their specific concern, both empirically and theoretically, with female primates. An adequate model of science must also find a way to explain why French primatologists rejected sociobiological theory during its North American heyday, why British scientists used behavioral ecology for more than a decade before North Americans, and why the popularity of sociobiological theory declined so suddenly and so precipitously in the United States in the 1980s. The list would also include the sudden reversal of opinion about animal "mind" in the face of half a century of behaviorism and the recent change in the scientific status of animal rights and wildlife conservation.

These questions should be of profound interest to both primatologists and to those who study science since both the notion of primatology as a science and the very idea of what constitutes science are at stake. Take, for instance, the controversy over gendered interpretations of primate society. How does the claim of male bias in earlier studies and the subsequent politicization of the study of female primates affect the scientific standing of primatology? In the past the only option was to choose between science and politics or science as politics by other means (Haraway 1986; Latour 1987). However, primatology may be a special resource in understanding science in the modern context (because of its apparent transparency), one that provides new ways of interpreting the relationship of science and society.

In what follows we highlight some of the most frequently raised questions and most obvious issues concerning the nature of primatology within its larger context. The list is not exhaustive, and the questions we raise, more than in any other section, are currently without answers. We mention them to stimulate future discussions.

### THE SPECIAL "POSITION" OF NONHUMAN PRIMATES

The study of nonhuman primates has a special position both in science and in society. As our closest living relatives, they look and act a lot like us. So what we discover about their behavior and their society adds to our knowledge about ourselves—an example of how society and science are mutually constituted. Human agendas (social, political, and personal) enter into the science as easily as scientific information about primates structures expectations about past, present, and future human action. Certainly the special scientific and social location of nonhuman primates creates problems. For example, we have more difficulty with language in the description of primates than in the study of other animals because of a complex loop in the scientific process. First science imports language about human behavior to describe the behavior and society of nonhuman primates. Then it re-exports the nonhuman primate translation to interpret human action. The traffic in both directions is heavily ladened with extra and often hidden meanings. Because of this, primatology is often caught in a web of contradictory scientific assumptions, as when it treats nonhuman primates as evolutionary mirrors for humans, yet rejects human "identification" with these same animals as a legitimate scientific methodology for understanding "their" behavior.

The history and practice of primatology suggests that we need to reexamine ideas about science and about the process of scientific purification (Latour 1993) that allow us to hold the separatist view of science and society. It would also be interesting to compare the study of primates with other disciplines where the subjects and topics are less cathected and less directly relevant to humans (Shapin and Schaffer 1985).

### THE QUESTION OF BIAS AND EMPATHY

When we study animals so like ourselves, the proper methodology and analytic resources are not self-evident, as we have already seen in the contradictory application of the assumption of "identification." Over its short history, primatology has balanced precariously on several different pivot points. Each cannot be understood in isolation because each was, in part, a reaction to what came before. For example, the ethological anti-anthropomorphism of the 1920s and 1930s reacted against the earlier Victorian sentimentalization and anthropomorphism of animals. The cognitivist anthropomorphism of the 1980s and 1990s was itself a reaction to previous behaviorist and ethological reductionism. Certainly, the current controversy about the use of feminist empathy as a scientific methodology can itself be seen as a response to what has been perceived as past chauvinist biases in the study and interpretation of nonhuman primate behavior and society.

Each shift in orientation raises questions about what constitutes a legitimate scientific methodology and interpretation of data and what processes or set of rules confer this legitimacy. For some, the question is about a simple demarcation: the boundary where science ends and bias begins. But the case studies within primatology illustrate how much more complicated this assessment may be including issues of how far the interpretation can be from the data—what is an acceptable gap and an acceptable bridge—how the interpretation of bias may be related to the use of naturalized and socialized categories or connected to considerations of what is and what is not being socially contested at the time. There is some evidence that when certain human behaviors are seen as "natural," therefore inevitable, the investigation of their origins is more readily seen as free of bias, whereas, by contrast, when the behaviors being investigated are, in humans, socially constructed and currently contested, then accusations of bias flow freely. It is also interesting to consider whether the acceptance and/or naturalization of behaviors changes the perception of the vulnerability of the research. That is, do previously problematic categories lose their stigma within science when they are no longer socially contested, and if so, what role does the practice of science play in moving things across the gradient of what is and is not contested?

We have already mentioned some problems with scientific assumptions as applied to the study of nonhuman primates. A growing controversy surrounds the role of empathy in the collection and interpretation of data on primate behavior and society. Early ethologists, having seen the wildly anthropomorphic claims of the Victorians, declared empathetic knowledge unreliable and therefore inappropriate to science. However, not all scientists have conformed to this standard during the last 60 years. More recently, cognitive ethology has relied heavily on anthropomorphism for guidelines in research into the "minds" of nonhuman primates. Such previously anthropomorphic interpretations of some behaviors appear appropriate given mounting evidence that, at times, nonhuman primates are "almost human." However, the unstable scientific position of empathy is most apparent in the contradictory assumptions held by individual scientists. A scientist might argue at one point for relaxing the tight prohibition against anthropomorphism in the context of cognition but at another point object strongly to the claim that empathy between female scientists and female primates may have played an important role in revisions of female strategies, or the more general suggestion that empathy should be used as a scientific tool. This controversy is a microcosm of the complexity and confusion about the nature of science and the relationship between human scientists and their nonhuman subjects that the history of ideas about primate society illustrates so well. One thing is certain: The outcome of the empathy debate will dramatically influence the future of primate research.

**OPEN VERSUS CLOSED SCIENCE**    The opening up of science is a democratization process that makes scientific information more available and more relevant to nonspecialists and to society at large. During the twentieth century this process has differentially affected scientific disciplines. Primatology is an important case for the study of the rarely examined benefits and costs of "open" science.

The media have enthusiastically responded to, and created, public curiosity about primates. Today, information, interpretations, and implications leap from the wilds into living rooms—and back again—almost instantaneously. Media images feed back into the science in myriad ways, from recruitment of future practitioners to implicit expectations about methodology to explicit notions about the nature of primate society. This broad involvement and interest in primate studies has, in the past, yielded rich sources of funding and, more recently, created a growing constituency for biodiversity conservation. But if primatology is an example of the benefits of opening up science, it also illustrates very clearly that we do not yet know what it means to make the public (for now simplistically homogeneous and ill-defined) and the media (currently totally unaccountable) part of a more broadly distributed scientific enterprise. Of immediate concern is what happens to "facts" and to the scientific process. We take for granted the institutionalized means for granting credibility, checking reliability of data, and holding individuals accountable which is part of traditional "closed" science. Where are these checks and balances in the larger network of actors that are part of the new open science of primatology? The implications are far ranging, including who has the right to speak and what they should be allowed to say, and what happens when the number of steps required in the scientific transformation of information is dramatically short-

ened by the early intervention of the media. Making the public part of a distributed science also puts new obligations and responsibility on scientists, for example, to actively engage nonspecialists, perhaps even creating "corrective" models that take account of what the public already believes in order to present new data most effectively.

Other disciplines may fight hard against the opening up of science, but primatology does not have this option. The processes of open science have already dramatically influenced our images of primate society and it is not an insignificant or unimportant task to figure out how.

**MISSION SCIENCE**    The opening up of science, as has happened in primate studies, and a more critical appraisal of the scientific process, as is happening both in "science studies" and in the publicly waged "science wars," change notions of both science and society. One new direction is "mission science." Using science for advocacy, that is, having a mission, has often been labeled "bad" science. Even the weaker version, admitting the social contributions to scientific processes and social consequences of scientific results, has, in the past, impugned the credentials of science and scientists.

Primatology is not yet classified as a mission science. But the growing involvement of primatologists in both conservation and animal welfare/rights requires that we think carefully about the special position of primatology and the changing nature of science in the modern context. These issues are increasingly relevant to many daily decisions in primatology—decisions about what data to collect, what to do with divergent interpretations, how to apportion professional time, and which set of activities can be considered appropriate to science. Mission science already exists to some extent within primatology. What is interesting, in the current context, is the differential value we assign to various "missions" and the implications of these for our interpretations of primate society. For example, primate conservation, which can be seen as science in the service of saving our environment/biodiversity has recently attained complete legitimacy. Science in the service of animal rights is more controversial, whereas science in the service of feminist rights is the most contested of the three. The fate of ideas about primate society are embedded differently in each mission. Thus conservation foregrounds populations, demography, and ecology and gives questions of "society" low priority. Primate society is important to the fight for animal rights and welfare but very narrowly, as it concerns the basic nature of socialness and the need for appropriate social groupings. By contrast, the scientific issues raised by feminists make the nature of primate society a critical issue, giving it the most attention and generating the greatest controversy.

The history of ideas about primate society and an examination of the larger context of the science of primatology suggest that over the past 70 years a lot has changed. The challenge is to untangle the complex contributions made by a changing world, a changing primatology, and a changing nature of science to our ideas about primate society. This requires careful analysis of the larger context of primatology and of the special position of the study of our closest relatives. It also mandates a reexamination of many of our sacred ideas about science and perhaps even a reformulation of more appropriate criteria for the contemporary context.

## CONCLUSIONS

Our conclusions about who or what changed the views of primate society can only be preliminary. The goal of this exercise was to define which ideas have changed within a restricted domain (field studies done primarily by North Americans) and to identify the minimum set of factors that have played a role in their transformation. This is only a first step; we need to go further. Before outlining how we propose to proceed, we make three claims:

1. Ideas about primates and images of primate society have changed.
2. These changes have been responsive to the effects of theory, methods, gender of the scientist, and cultural/historical/social context.
3. Single factors have influenced changes in images, but factors increasingly interact and multiple factor explanations are likely to have more explanatory power.

We propose two ways to go beyond these conclusions to a more comprehensive understanding of history, of process, and of our views of primate society. The first is the use of a comparative perspective. This involves both an interdisciplinary and a cross-cultural component. Many closely related fields share some, but not always the same, set of characteristics with primatology. If we look at psychology, animal behavior, cultural anthropology, and archaeology, for example, we see variations in configurations of theories, methods, and practitioners. By rotating our lens through these fields, holding some factors constant while letting the others vary, we should be able to perform a very gross but simple experiment that isolates and highlights specific factors. First we can align different fields according to the same historical signposts as a way of gaining some insight into the role of societal trends on scientific interpretations. Then we can compare fields that share all but one factor in order to see the relative contribution of that factor to scientific outcomes. We might expect, for example, to be able to assess the relative contribution of women scientists to interpretations of animal society by comparing primatology with animal behavior since the two fields have shared theoretical and methodological orientations, but primatology has had a much larger proportion of women investigators. Similar contrasts between psychology and primatology, between cultural anthropology and primatology, and between archaeology and primatology highlight fields that have a large proportion of women investigators but do not share the same theoretical orientation, or that share the same theory but use different methods, or that share theory and methods but diverge in terms of demographics of practitioners. We expect that this composite picture will provide better insights into the role of specific factors, and possibly even the manner of their interaction with each other, than the study of any one field in isolation.

Comparing different "national" traditions of primatology provides another lens and another experiment about the cultural, historical, and social determinants of our ideas. The provocative contrast between the Japanese and North American traditions of primatology has already begun to be documented (e.g., Asquith 1986, 1991). The comparison suggests that theory, methods, and scientists are configured differently in the two cultures and that differences have had significant consequences for ideas about primate society. We propose extending the comparison to include other cultural and national traditions of primatology: British, Swiss, Dutch, French, Spanish, Brazilian, and Mexican, to name the most obvious.

Our comparative framework will certainly contribute important facts to our data base. But we also need analytical tools. The special position of primatology raises critical issues about what science is and about the relationship of science and society. This is why we feel the second avenue should be to make use of the perspectives and expertise of science studies and feminist studies. They have developed models of science and ways of looking at the intersection of society and science that are particularly well suited to the issues at hand. This is not to say that those experts agree. But perhaps the range of options that they offer can help us begin to explore the domains that are new to primatology. And perhaps along the way, we will shed light on some of their controversies with data from the study of primates.

Finally, we do not expect that everyone will agree with the "potted" history we have just presented, with our selection of issues, or our line-up of causal factors. What we do claim is that the controversies that surround interpretations about who or what changed our views of primate society can be resolved through the use of heuristic frameworks for the collection and analysis of data. We also strongly suspect that any alternative account would need to consider the minimal set of causal factors we have proposed (theory, method, gender, and culture), and would benefit from the empirical data and insights provided by the comparative and analytic perspectives we have suggested.

## ACKNOWLEDGMENTS

We thank Pam Asquith, Charis Cussins, Mary Pavelka, David Western, and Sandra Zohar for many helpful suggestions that improved the manuscript and Sandra Zohar for excellent editorial assistance. Linda Fedigan's research is funded by an ongoing operating grant (A7723) from the Natural Sciences and Engineering Research Council of Canada (NSERCC).

## BIBLIOGRAPHY

Adams, E. R., and Burnett, G. W. (1991). Scientific vocabulary divergence among female primatologists working in East Africa. *Social Studies of Science 21:* 547–560.

Alexander, R. D. (1986a). Biology and law. *Ethology and Sociobiology 7:* 19–25.

Alexander, R. D. (1986b). Ostracisms and indirect reciprocity: The reproductive significance of humor. *Ethology and Sociobiology 7:* 105–122.

Altmann, J. (1974). Observational study of behaviour: Sampling methods. *Behaviour 49:* 227–267.

Altmann, J. (1980). *Baboon Mothers and Infants.* Cambridge, MA: Harvard University Press.

Altmann, J., Altmann, S. A., and Hausfater, G. (1988). Determinants of reproductive success in savannah baboons (*Papio cynocephalus*). In T. H. Clutton-Brock and P. H. Harvey (eds.), *Reproductive Success: Studies of Individual Variation in Contrasting Breeding Systems.* Chicago: University of Chicago Press.

Altmann, S. A. (1962). A field study of the sociobiology of rhesus monkeys. *Macaca mulatta. Annals of the New York Academy of Sciences 102:* 338–435.

Altmann, S. A. (1965). Sociobiology of rhesus monkeys. II. Stochastics of social communications. *Journal of Theoretical Biology 8:* 490–522.

Altmann, S. A. ed. (1967). *Social Communication Among Primates.* Chicago: University of Chicago Press.

Altmann, S. A. (1974). Baboons, space, time and energy. *American Zoologist 14:* 221–248.

Altmann, S. A. (1979). Baboon progressions, order or chaos? A study of one-dimensional group geometry. *Animal Behaviour 27:* 46–80.

Altmann, S. A., and Altmann, J. (1970). *Baboon Ecology: African Field Research.* Chicago: University of Chicago Press.

Altmann, S. A., and Altmann, J. (1979). Demographic constraints on behavior and social organization. In E. O. Smith and I. S. Bernstein (eds.). *Primate Ecology and Human Origins. Ecological Influences on Social Organization.* New York: Garland Press.

Ardrey, R. (1961). *African Genesis.* London: Collins.

Ardrey, R. (1966). *The Territorial Imperative.* New York: Atheneum.

Asquith, P. (1986). Anthropomorphism and the Japanese and Western traditions in primatology East and West. In J. Else and P. Lee (eds.), *Primate Ontogeny, Cognition and Behavior: Developments in Field and Laboratory Research.* New York: Academic Press.

Asquith, P. (1991). Primate research groups in Japan: Orientations and East-West differences. In L. M. Fedigan and P. J. Asquith (eds.), *The Monkeys of Arashiyama: 35 Years of Research in Japan and the West.* Albany: SUNY Press.

Asquith, P. (1994). The intellectual history of field studies in primatology. In A. Herring and L. Chan (eds.), *Strength in Diversity: A Reader in Anthropology.* Toronto: Canadian Scholars Press.

Aureli, F. (1992). Post-conflict behavior among wild long-tailed macaques (*Macaca fascicularis*). *Behavioral Ecology and Sociobiology 31:* 329–337.

Barash, D. P. (1986). *The Hare and the Tortoise: Culture, Biology, and Human Nature.* New York: Viking.

Barton, R., Whiten, A., Strum, S. C., Byrne, T. W., and Simpson, A. J. (1992). Habitat use and resource availability in baboons. *Animal Behaviour 43:* 831–844.

Benirschke, K., ed. (1986). *Primates: The Road to Self-Sustaining Populations.* New York: Springer-Verlag.

Bercovitch, F. B. (1991). Social stratification, social strategies, and reproductive success in primates. *Ethology and Sociobiology 12:* 315–333.

Betzig, L., Borgerhoof Muder, M., and Turke, P., eds. (1988). *Human Reproductive Behaviour: A Darwinian Perspective.* Cambridge and New York: Cambridge University Press.

Birke, L. (1986). *Women, Feminism and Biology. The Feminist Challenge.* New York: Methuen.

Bleier, R. (1984). *Science and Gender: A Critique of Biology and Its Theories on Women.* New York: Pergamon Press.

Bleier, R. (1986). Introduction. In R. Bleier (ed.), *Feminist Approaches to Science.* New York: Pergamon Press.

Blum, D. (1994). *The Monkey Wars.* New York: Oxford University Press.

Blurton Jones, N. G. (1967). An ethological study of some aspects of social behavior of children in nursery school. In D. Morris (ed.), *Primate Ethology.* London: Weidenfeld & Nicolson.

Brain, C. (1992). Deaths in a desert baboon troop. *International Journal of Primatology 13:* 593–599.

Bramblett, C. A. (1994). *Patterns of Primate Behavior,* 2nd ed. Prospect Heights, IL: Waveland Press.

Bulgar, J., and Hamilton III, W. J. (1988). Inbreeding and reproductive success in a natural chacma baboon, *Papio cynocephalus ursinus,* population. *Animal Behaviour 36:* 574–578.

Burk, T. (1986). Sexual selection, feminism and the behavior of biologists. *Creighton University Faculty Journal 5:* 1–16.

Burk, T. (1993). More Ethology of Ethologists: Further Studies of Animal Behavior Papers, 1953–93. Paper presented at 30th Annual ABS Meeting, Davis, CA.

Burton, F. D. (1994). In the footsteps of Anaximander. Qualitative research in primatology. In A. Herring and L. Chan (eds.), *Strength in Diversity: A Reader in Anthropology.* Toronto: Canadian Scholars Press.

Byrne, R. (1995). *The Thinking Ape. Evolutionary Origins of Intelligence.* Oxford: Oxford University Press.

Byrne, R., and Whiten, A., eds. (1988). *Machiavellian Intelligence. Social Expertise and the Evolution of Intelligence in Monkeys, Apes and Humans.* Oxford: Clarendon Press.

Byrne, R., and Whiten, A. (1990). Tactical deception in primates: The 1990 database. *Primate Report, 27.*

Caplan, A. L., ed. (1978). *The Sociobiology Debate.* New York: Harper & Row.

Carpenter, C. R. (1934). A field study of the behavior and social relations of howling monkeys. *Comparative Psychology Monographs 16:* 59–97.

Carpenter, C. R. (1964). *Naturalistic Behavior of Nonhuman Primates.* University Park: Pennsylvania State University Park.

Carpenter, C. R. (1965). The howlers of Barro Colorado island. In I. DeVore (ed.), *Primate Behavior: Field Studies of Monkeys and Apes.* New York: Holt, Rinehart and Winston.

Cavalieri, P., and Singer, P., eds. (1993). *The Great Ape Project.* London: Fourth Estate.

Chan, L. K. W. (1992). Problems with socioecological explanations of primate social diversity. In F. D. Burton (ed.), *Social Processes and Mental Abilities in Non-Human Primates.* New York: Edwin Mellon Press.

Chan, L. K. W. (1933). A phylogenetic interpretation of reproductive parameters and mating patterns in *Macaca. American Journal of Primatology 30:* 303–304.

Chance, M. (1961). The nature and special features of the instinctive social bond of primates. In S. L. Washburn (ed.), *The Social Life of Early Man. Viking Fund Publications in Anthropology No. 31.* New York: Wenner-Gren Foundation for Anthropological Research and Chicago: Aldine Press.

Chapais, B. (1991). Matrilineal dominance in Japanese macaques: The contribution of an experimental approach. In L. M. Fedigan and P. J. Asquith (eds.), *The Monkeys of Arashiyama.* Albany: SUNY Press.

Chapman, C. (1989). Ecological constraints on group size in three species of neotropical primates. *Folia Primatologica 73:* 1–9.

Chapman, C., Fedigan, L. M., Fedigan, L., and Chapman, L. J. (1989). Post-weaning resource competition and sex ratios in spider monkeys. *Oikos 54:* 315–319.

Cheney, D. L., and Seyfarth, R. M. (1990). *How Monkeys See the World.* Chicago: University of Chicago Press.

Chivers, D. J. (1974). The siamang in Malaya. A field study of a primate in a tropical rain forest. *Contributions to Primatology,* Vol. 4. Basel: S. Karger.

Clarke, M. R., and Glander, K. E. (1984) Female reproductive success in a group of free-ranging howling monkeys (*Alouatta palliata*) in Costa Rica. In M. F. Small (ed.), *Female Primates: Studies by Women Primatologists.* New York: Alan R. Liss.

Clutton-Brock, T. H. (1974). Primate social organization and ecology. *Nature 250:* 539–542.

Clutton-Brock, T. H., and Harvey, P. H. (1977). Primate ecology and social organization. *Journal of Zoology 183:* 1–39.

Clutton-Brock, T. H., and Harvey, P. H., eds. (1988). *Reproductive Success: Studies of Individual Variation in Contrasting Breeding Systems.* Chicago: University of Chicago Press.

Collias, N., and Southwick, C. W. (1952). A field study of population density and social organization in howling monkeys. *Proceedings of the American Philosophical Society 96:* 143–156.

Condit, V. K., and E. O. Smith, Yellow baboon labor and parturition at the Tana River National Primate Reserve, Kenya. *American Journal of Primatology* (1994), 33: 51–55.

Cords, M. (1988). Resolution of aggressive conflicts by immature long-tailed macaques (*Macaca fascicularis*). *Animal Behavior 36:* 1124–1135.

Cowlishaw, G., and Dunbar, R. I. M. (1991). Dominance rank and mating success in primates. *Animal Behavior 41:* 1045–1056.

Crockett, C. M. (1984). Emigration by female red howler monkeys and the case for female competition. In M. F. Small (ed.), *Female Primates: Studies by Women Primatologists.* New York: Alan R. Liss.

Crockett, C. M. (1984). Population studies of red howler monkeys (*Alouatta seniculus*). *National Geographic Research 1:* 264–273.

Crockett, C. M., and Eisenberg, J. F. (1987). Howlers: Variations in group size and demography. In B. B. Smuts et al. (eds.), *Primate Societies.* Chicago: University of Chicago Press.

Crockett, C. M., and Sekulic R. (1984). Infanticide in red howler monkeys (*Alouatta seniculus*). In G. Hausfater and S. B. Hrdy (eds.), *Infanticide: Comparative and Evolutionary Perspectives.* Hawthorne, NY: Aldine.

Crook, J. H. (1970a). Social organization and the environment, aspects of contemporary social ethology. *Animal Behavior 18:* 197–209.

Crook, J. H. (1970b). The socio-ecology of primates. In J. H. Crook (ed.), *Social Behaviour in Birds and Mammals.* London: Academic Press.

Crook, J. H., and Gartlan, J. S. (1966). Evolution of primate societies. *Nature 210:* 1200–1203.

Crook, J. H., and Gartlan, J. S. (1989). Introduction: Socioecological paradigms, evolution and history; perspectives for the 1990s. In V. Standen and R. A. Foley (eds.), *Comparative Socioecology.* Oxford: Blackwell.

Dasser, V. (1988). Mapping social concepts in monkeys. In R. Byrne and A. Whiten (eds.), *Machiavellian Intelligence.* Oxford: Clarendon Press.

Datta, S. B. (1986). The role of alliances in the acquisition of rank. In J. Else and P. Lee (eds.), *Primate Ontogeny.* Cambridge: Cambridge University Press.

Dawkins, R. (1978). *The Selfish Gene.* London: Granada.

DeRousseau, C. J., ed., (1990). *Primate Life History and Evolution. Monographs in Primatology.* Vol 14. New York: Wiley-Liss.

DeVore, I., ed. (1965). *Primate Behavior: Field Studies of Monkeys and Apes.* New York: Holt, Rinehart and Winston.

DeVore, I., and Hall, K. R. L. (1982). Baboon ecology. In I. DeVore (ed.), *Primate Behavior.* New York: Holt, Rinehart and Winston.

de Waal, F. (1982). *Chimpanzee Politics: Power and Sex Among Apes.* London: Unwin.

de Waal, F. (1984). Sex differences in the formation of coalitions among chimpanzees. *Ethology and Sociobiology 5:* 239–255.

de Waal, F. (1986). The integration of dominance and social bonding in primates. *Quarterly Review of Biology 61:* 459–479.

de Waal, F. (1987). Dynamics of social relationships. In B. B. Smuts et al. (eds.), *Primate Societies.* Chicago: University of Chicago Press.

de Waal, F. (1989). *Peace-Making Among Primates.* Cambridge, MA: Harvard University Press.

de Waal, F. (1993). Reconciliation among primates: A review of empirical evidence and theoretical issues. In W. A. Mason and S. P. Mendoza (eds.), *Primate Social Conflict.* Albany: SUNY Press.

Di Fiore, A., and Rendall, D. (1994). Evolution of social organization: A reappraisal for primates by using phylogenetic methods. *Proceedings of the National Academy of Science 91:* 9941–9945.

Dobzhansky, T. (1944). On species and races of living and fossil man. *American Journal of Physical Anthropology 2:* 251–265.

Dolhinow, P. ed. (1972). *Primate Patterns.* New York: Holt, Rinehart and Winston.

Dunbar, R. I. M. (1984). Use of infants by male gelada in agonistic contexts: Agonistic buffering, progeny protection or soliciting support? *Primates 25:* 28–35.

Dunbar, R. I. M. (1988). *Primate Social Systems.* Ithaca, NY: Cornell University Press.

Dunbar, R. I. M. (1989). Social systems as optimal strategy sets: The costs and benefits of sociality. In V. Standen and R. A. Foley (eds.), *Comparative Socioecology.* Oxford: Blackwell.

Dunbar, R. I. M. (1990). The apes as we want to see them. *New York Times Book Review,* Jan. 10.

Eisenberg, J. F., Muckenhirn, N. A., and Rudran, R. (1972). The relation between ecology and social structure in primates. *Science 176:* 863–874.

Ellefson, J. O. (1974). A natural history of white-handed gibbons in the Malayan Peninsula. In D. M. Rumbaugh (ed.), *Gibbon and Siamang,* Vol. 3. Basel: S. Karger.

Fausto-Sterling, A. (1985). *Myths of Gender.* New York: Basic Books.

Fedigan, L. M. (1982). *Primate Paradigms. Sex Roles and Social Bonds.* Montreal: Eden Press.

Fedigan, L. M. (1983). Dominance and reproductive success in primates. *Yearbook of Physical Anthropology 26:* 91–129.

Fedigan, L. M. (1986). Demographic trends in the *Alouatta palliata* and *Cebus capucinus* populations in Santa Rosa Park, Costa Rica. In J. Else and P. Lee (eds.), *Primate Ecology and Conservation.* Cambridge: Cambridge University Press.

Fedigan, L. M. (1994). Science and the successful female: Why there are so many women primatologists. *American Anthropologist 96:* 10–20.

Fedigan, L. M. (in press). Is primatology a feminist science? In Lori Hager (ed.), *Women in Human Evolution.* New York: Routledge Press.

Fedigan, L. M., and Asquith, P. J., eds. (1991). *The Monkeys of Arashiyama: 35 Years of Research in Japan and the West.* Albany: SUNY Press.

Fedigan, L. M., and Baxter, J. (1984). Sex differences and social organization in free-ranging spider monkeys (*Ateles geoffroyi*) at Tikal, Guatemala. *Primates 25:* 279–294.

Fedigan, L. M., and Fedigan, L. (1989). Gender and the study of primates. In S. Morgen (ed.), *Gender and Anthropology. Critical Reviews for Teaching and Research.* Washington, DC: American Anthropology Association.

Fedigan, L. M., Fedigan, L., Chapman, C., and Glander, K. (1988). Spider monkey home ranges: A comparison of radio telemetry and direct observation. *American Journal of Primatology 16:* 19–29.

Fedigan, L. M., Fedigan, L., Gouzoules, H., Gouzoules, S., and Koyama, N. (1986). Lifetime reproductive success in female Japanese macaques. *Folia Primatologica 47:* 143–157.

Fee, E. (1983). Woman's nature and scientific objectivity. In M. Lowe and R. Hubbard (eds.), *Woman's Nature: Rationalizations of Inequality.* New York: Pergamon Press.

Fee, E. (1986). Critiques of modern science: The relationship of feminism to other radical epistemologies. In R. Bleier (ed.), *Feminist Approaches to Science.* New York: Pergamon Press.

Foley, R. (1986). Anthropology and behavioral ecology. *Anthropology Today 2:* 13–15.

Forster, D., and Strum, S. C. (1994). Sleeping near the enemy: Patterns of sexual competition in baboons. *Proceedings of the International Congress of Primatology. Current Primatology,* Vol. II.

Fossey, D. (1979). Development of the mountain gorilla (*Gorilla gorilla beringei*): The first 36 months. In D. A. Hamburg and E. R. McCown (eds.), *The Great Apes. Perspectives on Human Evolution, Vol. 5.* Menlo Park, CA: Benjamin Cummings.

Galdikas, B. M. F. (1979). Orangutan adaptation at Tanjung Puting Reserve: Mating and ecology. In D. A. Hamburg and E. R. McCown (eds.), *The Great Apes: Perspectives on Human Evolution.* Menlo Park, CA: Benjamin Cummings.

Galdikas, B. M. F. (1995). *Reflections of Eden: My Years with the Orangutans of Borneo.* New York: Little, Brown.

Garber, P. A. (1987). Foraging strategies among living primates. *Annual Reviews in Anthropology 16:* 339–364.

Garber, P. A. (1994). Phylogenetic approach to the study of tamarin and marmoset social systems. *American Journal of Primatology 34:* 199–219.

Gardner, H. (1985). *The Mind's New Science.* New York: Basic Books.

Gartlan, J. S. (1968). Structure and function in primate society. *Folia Primatologica 8:* 89–120.

Gartlan, J. S. (1974). Adaptive aspects of social structure in *Erythrocebus patas. Symposium of the 5th Congress of the International Primatological Society,* 161–171.

Gartlan, J. S., and Brain, C. K. (1968). Ecological and social variability in *Cercopithecus aethiops* and *Cercopithecus mitis.* In P. Jay (ed.), *Primates: Studies in Adaptation and Variability.* New York: Holt, Rinehart and Winston.

Gautier-Hion, A. (1988). Polyspecific associations among forest guenons: Ecological, behavioural and evolutionary aspects. In A. Gautier-Hion et al. (eds.), *A Primate Radiation.* Cambridge: Cambridge University Press.

Gautier-Hion, A., Bourliere, F., Gautier, J. P., and Kingdon, J., eds. (1988). *A Primate Radiation. Evolutionary Biology of the African Guenons.* Cambridge: Cambridge University Press.

Gilmore, H. A. (1981). From Radcliffe-Brown to sociobiology: Some aspects of the rise of primatology within physical anthropology. *American Journal of Physical Anthropology 56:* 387–392.

Glander, K. E. (1978). Howling monkey feeding behavior and plant secondary compounds: A study of strategies. In G. C. Montgomery (ed.), *The Ecology of Arboreal Folivores.* Washington, DC: Smithsonian Institute Press.

Glander, K. E. (1982). The impact of plant secondary compounds on primate feeding behavior. *Yearbook of Physical Anthropology 25:* 1–18.

Glander, K. E. (1992). Dispersal patterns in Costa Rican mantled howling monkeys. *International Journal of Primatology 13:* 415–436.

Glander, K. E., Fedigan, L. M., Fedigan, L., and Chapman, C. (1991). Field methods for capture and measurement of three monkey species in Costa Rica. *Folia Primatologica 57:* 70–82.

Goodall, J. (1965). Chimpanzees of the Gombe Stream Reserve. In I. DeVore (ed.), *Primate Behavior.* New York: Holt, Rinehart and Winston.

Goodall, J. (1967). *My Friends the Wild Chimpanzees.* Washington, DC: National Geographic.

Goodall, J. (1968). The behavior of free-living chimpanzees of the Gombe Stream Reserve. *Animal Behaviour Monographs 1:* 161–311.

Goodall, J. (1977). Infant-killing and cannibalism in free-living chimpanzees. *Folia Primatologica 28:* 259–282.

Goodall, J. (1990). *Through a Window. My Thirty Years with the Chimpanzees of Gombe.* Boston: Houghton Mifflin.

Goss-Custard, J. D., Dunbar, R. I. M., and Aldrich-Blake, F. P. G. (1972). Survival, mating and rearing strategies in the evolution of primate social structure. *Folia Primatologica 17:* 1–19.

Gouzoules, S., Gouzoules, H., and Marler, P. (1984). Rhesus monkey (*Macaca mulatta*) screams: Representational signaling in the recruitment of agonistic aid. *Animal Behavior 32:* 182–193.

Gray, J. P. (1985). *Primate Sociobiology.* New Haven, CT: HRAF Press.

Griffin, D. R. (1976). *The Question of Animal Awareness: Evolutionary Continuity of Mental Experience.* New York: Rockefeller University Press.

Griffin, D. R. (1984). *Animal Thinking.* Cambridge, MA: Harvard University Press.

Griffin, D. R. (1992). *Animal Minds.* Chicago: University of Chicago Press.

Hall, K. R. L. (1968). Behaviour and ecology of the wild patas monkeys, *Erythrocebus patas,* in Uganda. In P. Jay (ed.), *Primates: Studies in Adaptation and Variability.* New York: Holt, Rinehart and Winston.

Hall, K. R. L., and DeVore, I. (1965). Baboon social behavior. In I. DeVore (ed.), *Primate Behavior.* New York: Holt, Rinehart and Winston.

Hamilton, W. D. (1964). The genetical evolution of social behavior I and II. *Journal of Theoretical Biology 7:* 1–52.

Haraway, D. (1978). Animal sociology and a natural economy of the body politic. *Signs 4:* 21–60.

Haraway, D. N. (1981). In the beginning was the word: The genesis of biological theory. *Signs 6:* 469–481.

Haraway, D. (1983). Signs of dominance: From physiology to a cybernetics of primate society, C. R. Carpenter 1930–70. *Studies in the History of Biology 6:* 129–219.

Haraway, D. (1986). Primatology is politics by other means. In R. Bleier (ed.), *Feminist Approaches to Science.* New York: Pergamon Press.

Haraway, D. (1989). *Primate Visions. Gender, Race and Nature in the World of Modern Science.* New York: Routledge.

Harcourt. A. H. (1979). The social relations and group structure of wild mountain gorillas. In D. A. Hamburg and E. R. McCown (eds.), *The Great Apes: Perspectives on Human Evolution.* Menlo Park, CA: Benjamin Cummings.

Harcourt, A. H. (1988). Alliances in contests and social intelligence. In R. Byrne and A. Whiten (eds.), *Machiavellian Intelligence.* Oxford: Clarendon Press.

Harcourt, A. H. (1989). Social influences on competitive ability: Alliances and their consequences. In V. Standen and R. A. Foley (eds.), *Comparative Socioecology.* Oxford: Blackwell.

Harcourt, A. H., and De Waal, F. B. M. (1992). *Coalitions and Alliances in Humans and Other Animals.* Oxford: Oxford University Press.

Harding, S. (1986). *The Science Question in Feminism*. Ithaca, NY: Cornell University Press.

Harding, S. (1989). Is there a feminist method? In N. Tuana (ed.), *Feminism and Science*. Bloomington: Indiana University Press.

Harding, S. (1991). *Whose Science? Whose Knowledge?* Ithaca, NY: Cornell University Press.

Hausfater, G. (1975). *Dominance and Reproduction in Baboons (Papio cynocephalus): A Quantitative Analysis. Contributions to Primatology No. 7*. Basel: S. Karger.

Hildebolt, C. F., Phillips-Conroy, J. E., and Jolly, C. J. (1993). Alveolar bone loss in wild baboons. *American Journal of Physical Anthropology 29*: 61–72.

Hinde, R. A. (1974). *Biological Bases of Human Social Behaviour*. New York: McGraw-Hill.

Hinde, R. A., ed. (1983). *Primate Social Relationships: An Integrated Approach*. Oxford: Blackwell.

Holloway, R. L. (1974). *Primate Aggression, Territoriality and Xenophobia. A Comparative Perspective*. New York: Academic Press.

Holmes, D. J., and Hitchcock, C. L. (1997). A feeling for the organism? An empirical look at gender and research choices of animal behaviorists. In P. Gowaty (ed.), *Feminism and Evolutionary Biology*. New York: Chapman and Hall.

Hooton, E. E. (1955). The importance of primate studies in anthropology. In James A. Gavan (ed.), *The Nonhuman Primates in Human Evolution*. Detroit: Wayne University Press.

Hrdy, S. B. (1976). Case and exploitation of nonhuman primate infants by conspecifics other than the mother. In D. S. Lehrman, R. A. Hinde, and E. Shaw (eds.), *Advances in the Study of Behavior*, Vol. 6. New York: Academic Press.

Hrdy, S. B. (1977). *The Langurs of Abu. Male and Female Strategies of Reproduction*. Cambridge, MA: Harvard University Press.

Hrdy, S. B. (1981). *The Woman That Never Evolved*. Cambridge, MA: Harvard University Press.

Hrdy, S. B. (1984). Introduction. Section II. Female reproductive strategies. In M. F. Small (ed.), *Female Primates*. New York: Alan R. Liss.

Hrdy, S. B. (1986). Empathy, polyandry, and the myth of the coy female. In R. Bleier (ed.), *Feminist Approaches to Science*. New York: Pergamon Press.

Hrdy, S. B., and Hrdy D.B. (1976). Hierarchical relations among female Hanuman langurs. *Science 193*: 913–915.

Hubbard, R., Henefin, M. S., and Fried, B., eds. (1982). *Biological Woman: The Convenient Myth*. Cambridge, MA: Schenkman Press.

Huffman, M. A. (1981). Mate selection and partner preferences in female Japanese macaques. In L. M. Fedigan and P. J. Asquith (eds.), *The Monkeys of Arashiyama*. Albany: SUNY Press.

Humphrey, N. (1976). The social function of intellect. In P. P. G. Bateson and R. A. Hinde (eds.), *Growing Points in Ethology*. Cambridge: Cambridge University Press.

Hunte, W., and Horrocks, J. A. (1987). Kin and non-kin interventions in the aggressive disputes of vervet monkeys. *Behavioral Ecology and Sociobiology 20*: 257–263.

Huxley, J. S. (1942). *Evolution, the Modern Synthesis*. London: Allen and Unwin.

Isbell, L. A. (1991). Contest and scramble competition: Patterns of female aggression and ranging behavior among primates. *Behavioral Ecology 2*: 143–155.

Janson, C. H. (1984). Female choice and mating system in the brown capuchin monkey, *Cebus apella. Zeitschrift fur Tierpsychologie 65*: 177–200.

Janson, C. H. (1992). Evolutionary ecology of primate social structure. In E. A. Smith and B. Winterhalder (eds.), *Evolutionary Ecology and Human Behavior*. New York: Aldine.

Jay, P. (1965). The common langurs of north India. In I. DeVore (ed.), *Primate Behavior*. New York: Holt, Rinehart and Winston.

Jay, P., ed. (1968). *Primates: Studies in Adaptation and Variability*. New York: Holt, Rinehart and Winston.

Jolly, A. (1966a). *Lemur Behavior*. Chicago: Chicago University Press.

Jolly, A. (1966b). Lemur social behavior and primate intelligence. *Science 153*: 501–506.

Jolly, A. (1984). The puzzle of female feeding priority. In M. F. Small (ed.), *Female Primates*. New York: Alan R. Liss.

Jolly, A., Oberle, P., and Albignac, R., eds. (1984). *Madagascar*. New York: Pergamon Press.

Jones, C. B. (1980). Seasonal parturition, mortality, and dispersal in the mantled howler monkey, *Alouatta palliata. Brenesia 17*: 1–10.

Judge, P. J. (1991). Dyadic and triadic reconciliation in pigtail macaques. *American Journal of Primatology 23*: 225–237.

Kappeler, P. M., and van Schaik, C. P. (1992). Methodological and evolutionary aspects of reconciliation research among primates. *Ethology 92*: 51–69.

Keddy, A. C. (1986). Female mate choice in vervet monkeys (*Cercopithecus aethiops sabeus*). *American Journal of Primatology 10*: 125–134.

Keller, E. F. (1985). *Reflections on Gender and Science*. New Haven, CT: Yale University Press.

Keller, E. F. (1987a). Feminism and science. In Sandra Harding and Jean F. Barr (eds.), *Sex and Scientific Inquiry*. Chicago: University of Chicago Press.

Keller, E. F. (1987b). Women scientists and feminist critics of science. *Daedalus 116*: 77–91.

Keller, E. F. (1991). The wo/man scientist: Issues of sex and gender in the pursuit of science. In H. Zuckerman, J. R. Cole, and J. T. Bruer (eds.), *The Outer Circle. Women in the Scientific Community*. New York: Norton.

Keller, E. F. (1992). *Secrets of Life. Secrets of Death. Essays on Language, Gender and Science*. New York: Routledge.

Kinzey, W. (1986). New World primate field studies: What's in it for anthropology? *Annual Reviews in Anthropology 15*: 121–148.

Kinzey, W. and Cunningham, E. P. (1994). Variability in Platyrrhine social organization. *American Journal of Primatology 34*: 185–198.

Kleiman, D., Beck, B., Dietz, J., Dietz, L., Ballow, J., and Coimbra-Filho, A. (1986). Conservation program for the golden lion tamarin. In K. Benirschke (ed.), *Primates: The Road to Self-Sustaining Populations*. New York: Springer-Verlag.

Kortlandt, A. (1967). Experimentation with chimpanzees in the wild. In D. Starck, R. Schneider, and H.-J. Kuhn (eds.), *Neue Ergebnisse der Primatologie*. Stuttgart: Gustau Fischer Verlag.

Koyama, N. (1967). On dominance rank and kinship of a wild Japanese monkey troop in Arashiyama. *Primates 8*: 189–216.

Krebs, J. R., and Davies, N. B. (1993). *An Introduction to Behavioural Ecology*. Oxford: Blackwell.

Kummer, H. (1968). *Social Organization of Hamadryas Baboons*. Chicago: University of Chicago Press.

Kummer, H. (1971a). Immediate causes of primate social systems. In *Proceedings of the Third International Congress of Primatology, Zurich, 1970*. Basel: S. Karger.

Kummer, H. (1971b). *Primate Societies: Group Techniques of Ecological Adaptation*. Chicago: Aldine.

Kummer, H. (1973). Dominance versus possession. An experiment on hamadryas baboons. In J. R. Napier and P. R. Napier (eds.), *Old World Monkeys. Evolution, Systematics and Behavior*. London: Academic Press.

Kummer, H. (1988). Tripartite relations in hamadryas baboons. In R. Byrne and A. Whiten (eds.), *Machiavellian Intelligence: Social Expertise and the Evolution of Intellect in Monkeys, Apes, and Humans*. Oxford: Clarendon Press.

Kummer, H., Goetz, W., and Angst, W. (1970). Cross-species modifications of social behavior in baboons. *Behavior 49*: 62–87.

Kummer, H., Goetz, W., and Angst, W. (1974). Triadic differentiation: An inhibitory process protecting pair bonds in baboons. *Behaviour 49*: 62–87.

Lancaster, J. (1973). In praise of the achieving female monkey. *Psychology Today*, September.

Lancaster, J., and Lee, R. B. (1965). The annual reproductive cycle in monkeys and apes. In I. DeVore (ed.), *Primate Behaviour*. New York: Holt, Rinehart and Winston.

Latour, B. (1987). *Science in Action: How to Follow Scientists and Engineers Through Society*. Cambridge, MA: Harvard University Press.

Latour, B. (1993). *We Have Never Been Modern*, trans. Catherine Porter. Cambridge, MA: Harvard University Press.

Latour, B., and Strum, S. C. (1986). Human social origins: Please tell us another story. *Journal of Social and Biological Structures 9:* 167–187.

Lee, P., Thornback, J., and Bennet, E. (1988). *Threatened Primates of Africa. The IUCN Data Book*. Cambridge: IUCN Gland.

Lee, R. and DeVore, I., eds. (1968). *Man the Hunter*. Chicago: Aldine.

Leibowitz, L. (1983). Origins of the sexual division of labor. In M. Lowe and R. Hubbard (eds.), *Woman's Nature: Rationalizations of Inequality*. New York: Pergamon Press.

Longino, H. (1989). Can there be a feminist science? In Nancy Tuana (ed.), *Feminism and Science*. Bloomington: Indiana University Press.

Longino, H. (1990). *Science as Social Knowledge*. Princeton, NJ: Princeton University Press.

Longino, H., and Doell, R. (1983). Body, bias, and behavior: A comparative analysis of reasoning in two areas of biological science. *Signs 9:* 206–227.

Lorenz, K. (1966). *On Aggression*, trans. M. K. Wilson. New York: Harcourt, Brace & World.

Lowe, M., and Hubbard, R. (1983). *Woman's Nature. Rationalizations of Inequality*. New York: Pergamon Press.

Manson, J. H. (1992). Measuring female mate choice in Cayo Santiago rhesus macaques. *Animal Behaviour 44:* 405–416.

Mason, W. A. (1990). Premises, promises and problems of primatology. *American Journal of Primatology 22:* 123–138.

Mason, W. A., and Mendoza, S. P., eds. (1993). *Primate Social Conflict*. Albany: SUNY Press.

Maynard-Smith, J. (1978). Evolution and the theory of games. In T. H. Clutton-Brock and P. H. Harvey (eds.), *Readings in Sociobiology*. San Francisco: Freeman.

Mayr, E. (1942). *Systematics and the Origin of Species*. New York: Columbia University Press.

McGinnis, P. R. (1979). Sexual behavior in free-ranging chimpanzees: Consort relationships. In D. A. Hamburg and E. R. McCown (eds.), *The Great Apes: Perspectives on Human Evolution*. Menlo Park, CA: Benjamin Cummings.

McGrew, W. C. (1972). *An Ethological Study of Children's Behavior*. New York: Academic Press.

Mealey, L., Young, R. K., and Betzig, L. L. (1985). Comment on: Despotism and differential reproduction by L. L. Betzig. *Ethology and Sociobiology 6:* 75–76.

Melnick, D. J., and Kidd, K. K. (1983). The genetic consequences of social groups fission in a wild population of rhesus monkeys (*Macaca mulatta*). *Behavioral Ecology and Sociobiology 12:* 229–236.

Melnick, D. J., Kidd, K. K., and Pearl, M. C. (1987). *Cercopithecus* in multimale groups: Genetic diversity and population structure. In B. B. Smuts, D. L. Cheney, R. M. Seyfarth, R. W. Wrangham, and T. T. Struhsaker (eds.), *Primate Societies*. Chicago: University of Chicago Press.

Merchant, C. (1980). *The Death of Nature: Women, Ecology and the Scientific Revolution*. New York: Harper & Row.

Milton, K. (1981). Distribution patterns of tropical plant foods as an evolutionary stimulus to primate mental development. *American Anthropologist 83:* 534–548.

Milton, K. (1988). Foraging behaviour and the evolution of primate intelligence. In R. Byrne and A. Whiten (eds.), *Machiavellian Intelligence*. Oxford: Clarendon Press.

Mitchell, R. W., and Thompson, N. S. (1986). *Deception: Perspectives on Human and Nonhuman Deceit*. Albany: SUNY Press.

Mittermeier, R. (1986). Strategies for the conservation of highly endangered primates. In K. Benirschke (ed.), *Primates: The Road to Self-Sustaining Populations*. New York: Springer-Verlag.

Montagu, A., ed. (1980). *Sociobiology Examined*. New York: Oxford University Press.

Montgomery, S. (1991). *Walking with the Great Apes*. Boston: Houghton Mifflin.

Moore, J. (1982). Coalitions in langur all-male bands. *International Journal of Primatology 3:* 314.

Moore, J. (1984). Female transfer in primates. *International Journal of Primatology 5:* 537–589.

Moore, J. (1992). Dispersal, nepotism, and primate social behavior. *International Journal of Primatology 13:* 361–378.

Morin, P. A., Moore, J. J., Chakraborty, R., Jin, L., Goodall, J., and Woodruff, D. S. (1994). Kin selection, social structure, gene flow, and the evolution of chimpanzees. *Science 265:* 1193–1201.

Morrell, V. (1993). Called "trimates," three bold women shaped their field. *Science 260:* 420–425.

Morris, D., ed. (1967). *Primate Ethology*. London: Weidenfeld & Nicolson.

Nash, R. (1989). *The Rights of Nature: A History of Environmental Ethics*. Madison: University of Wisconsin Press.

Neville, M. K., Glander, K. E., Braza, F., and Rylands, A. B. (1987). The howling monkeys, Genus *Alouatta*. In G. A. B. de Fonseca, A. B. Rylands, R. A. Mittermeier, and A. F. Coimbra-Filho (eds.), *Ecology and Behavior of Neotropical Primates*, Vol. 2. Rio de Janeiro: Academie Brasil Ciencias.

Nishida, T. (1968). The social group of wild chimpanzees in the Mahale Mountains. *Primates 9:* 167–224.

Nishida, T. (1979). The social group of chimpanzees of the Mahale Mountains. In D. A. Hamburg and E. R. McCown (eds.), *The Great Apes: Perspectives on Human Evolution*. Menlo Park, CA: Benjamin Cummings.

Norton, G., Rhine, R. J., Wynn, G. W., and Wynn, R. D. (1987). Baboon diet: A five year study of stability and variability in the plant feeding and habitat of yellow baboons (*Papio cynocephalus*) of Mikumi National Park, Tanzania. *Folia Primatologica 48:* 78–120.

Oates, J. F., Swain, T., and Zantovska, J. (1977). Secondary compounds and food selection by colobus monkeys. *Biochemical Systematics and Ecology 5:* 317–321.

Packer, C. (1977). Reciprocal altruism in *Papio anubis*. *Nature 265:* 441–443.

Packer, C., Collins, D. A., Sindimwo, A., and Goodall, J. (1995). Reproductive constraints on aggressive competition in female baboons. *Nature 373:* 60–63.

Parker, S. T., and Gibson, K., eds. (1990). *"Language" and Intelligence in Monkeys and Apes*. Cambridge: Cambridge University Press.

Popp, J. L. (1978). Male Baboons and Evolutionary Principles. Ph.D. thesis, Harvard University.

Premack, D. (1988). Does the chimpanzee have a theory of mind? Revisited. In R. Byrne and A. Whiten (eds.), *Machiavellian Intelligence*. Oxford: Clarendon Press.

Provost, M., Wynn, T. G., Huber, T. P., and McGrew, W. C. (1993). Seasonal and sex differences in Gombe chimpanzee ranging. Paper presented at the 63rd Annual Meeting of the American Association of Physical Anthropologists, Denver.

Pusey, A. (1979). Intercommunity transfer of chimpanzees in Gombe National Park. In D. A. Hamburg and E. R. McCown (eds.), *The Great Apes: Perspectives on Human Evolution*. Menlo Park, CA: Benjamin Cummings.

Pyke, G. H., Pulliam, H. R., and Charnov, E. L. (1977). Optimal foraging: A selective review of theories and tests. *Quarterly Review of Biology 52:* 137–154.

Ransom, T. W. (1979). *The Beach Troop of Gombe*. Lewisburg, PA: Bucknell University Press.

Ransom, T. W., and Ransom, B. S. (1971). Adult male-infant relations among baboons, *Papio anubis*. *Folia Primatologica 16:* 179–195.

Ransom, T. W., and Rowell, T. (1972). Early social development of feral baboons. In F. E. Poirier (ed.), *Primate Socialization*. New York: Random House.

Reynolds, V. (1967). *The Apes. The Gorilla, Chimpanzee, Orangutan and Gibbon, Their History and Their World*. New York: Harper & Row.

Reynolds, V., and Reynolds, F. (1965). Chimpanzees in the Budongo Forest. In I. DeVore (ed.), *Primate Behavior*. New York: Holt, Rinehart and Winston.

Rhine, R. J. (1975). The order of movement of yellow baboons (*Papio cynocephalus*). *Folia Primatologica 23:* 72–104.

Ribnick, R. (1982). A short history of primate field studies: Old World monkeys and apes. In F. Spencer (ed.), *A History of Physical Anthropology 1930–1980*. New York: Academic Press.

Richard, A. F. (1981). Changing assumptions in primate ecology. *American Anthropologist 83:* 517–533.

Richard, A. F. (1985). *Primates in Nature*. New York: Freeman.

Richard, A. F., Rakotomanga, P., and Schwartz, M. (1991). Demography of *Propithecus verreauxi* at Beza Mahafaly, Madagascar: Sex ratio, survival, and fertility 1984–88. *American Journal of Physical Anthropology 84:* 307–322.

Ristau, C. A., and Robbins, D. (1982). Language in great apes: A critical review. In J. S. Rosenblatt, R. A. Hinde, C. Beer, and M. C. Busnel (eds.), *Advances in the Study of Behavior*. New York: Plenum Press.

Rodman, P. (1988). Resources and group sizes in primates. In C. N. Slobodchikoff (ed.), *The Ecology of Social Behavior*. New York: Academic Press.

Rosenberger, A. L. (1979). Phylogeny, Evolution and Classification of New World Monkeys (Platyrrhini, Primates). Ph.D. thesis, City University of New York.

Rosenberger, A. L., and Strier, K. B. (1989). Adaptive radiation of the ateline primates. *Journal of Human Evolution 18:* 717–750.

Rosenthal, E. (1991). The forgotten female. *Discover 12:* 22–27.

Rosser, S. (1986). The relationship between women's studies and women in science. In R. Bleier (ed.), *Feminist Approaches to Science*. New York: Pergamon Press.

Rosser, S. (1989). Feminist scholarship in the sciences: Where are we now and when can we expect a theoretical breakthrough? Nancy Tuana (ed.), *Feminism and Science*. Bloomington: Indiana University Press.

Rowell, T. (1966). Forest living baboons in Uganda. *Journal of Zoology 149:* 344–364.

Rowell, T. (1972). *The Social Behavior of Monkeys*. Middlesex, England: Penguin.

Rowell, T. (1974). The concept of dominance. *Behavioural Biology 11:* 131–154.

Rowell, T. (1984). Introduction. Section I. Mothers, infants and adolescents. In M. F. Small (ed.), *Female Primates*. New York: Alan R. Liss.

Ruse, M. (1979). *Sociobiology: Sense or Nonsense?* Holland: D. Reidel.

Sade, D. (1967). Determinants of dominance in a group of free-ranging rhesus monkeys. In S. A. Altmann (ed.), *Social Communication Among Primates*. Chicago: University of Chicago Press.

Sade, D. (1972). A longitudinal study of social relations of rhesus monkeys. In R. H. Tuttle (ed.), *Functional and Evolutionary Biology of Primates*. Chicago: Aldine-Atherton.

Sahlins, M. (1976). *The Use and Abuse of Biology*. Ann Arbor: University of Michigan Press.

Sapolsky, R. (1989). Hypercortisolism among socially-subordinate wild baboons originates at the CNS level. *Archives of General Psychiatry 46:* 1047–1051.

Sapolsky, R. (1990). Adrenocortical function, social rank, and personality among wild baboons. *Biological Psychiatry 28:* 862–879.

Sapolsky, R. (1993). The physiology of dominance in stable versus unstable social hierarchies. In W. A. Mason and S. P. Mendoza (eds.), *Primate Social Conflict*. Albany: SUNY Press.

Sayers, J. (1982). *Biological Politics: Feminist and Anti-feminist Perspectives*. New York: Tavistock.

Schaik, C. P. van (1989). The ecology of social relationships amongst female primates. In V. Standen and R. A. Foley (eds.), *Comparative Sociology*. Oxford: Blackwell.

Schaller, G. B. (1963). *The Mountain Gorilla*. Chicago: University of Chicago Press.

Schaller, G. B. (1964). *The Year of the Gorilla*. Chicago: University of Chicago Press.

Schaller, G. B. (1965a). The behavior of the mountain gorilla. In I. DeVore (ed.), *Primate Behavior*. New York: Holt, Rinehart and Winston.

Schaller, G. B. (1965b). Behavioral comparisons of the apes. In I. DeVore (ed.), *Primate Behavior*. New York: Holt, Rinehart and Winston.

Schaller, G. B. (1972). The behavior of the mountain gorilla. In P. Dolhinow (ed.), *Primate Patterns*. New York: Holt, Rinehart and Winston.

Schiebinger, L. (1987). The history and philosophy of women in science: A review essay. In S. Harding and J. Barr (eds.), *Sex and Scientific Inquiry*. Chicago: University of Chicago Press.

Schubert, G. and Masters, R. D. (eds.) (1991). *Primate Politics*. Carbondale: Southern Illinois University Press.

Seyfarth, R. M. (1978). Social relationships among adult male and female baboons. II. Behaviour throughout the female reproductive cycle. *Behaviour 64:* 227–247.

Seyfarth, R. M., and Cheney, D. (1984). Grooming, alliances and reciprocal altruism in vervet monkeys. *Nature 308:* 541–543.

Seyfarth, R. M., and Cheney, D. (1988). Do monkeys understand their relations? In R. Byrne and A. Whiten (eds.), *Machiavellian Intelligence*. Oxford: Clarendon Press.

Shabecoff, P. (1993). *The Fierce Green Fire*. New York: Hill and Wang.

Shapin, S., and Schaffer, S. (1985). *The Leviathan and the Air Pump: Hobbes, Boyle, and the Experimental Life*. Princeton, NJ: Princeton University Press.

Shively, C. (1985). The evolution of dominance hierarchies in nonhuman primate society. In S. Ellyson and I. Davido (eds.), *Power, Dominance, and Nonverbal Behavior*. Berlin: Springer-Verlag.

Silk, J. B. (1982). Altruism among female *Macaca radiata*: Explanations and analysis of patterns of grooming and coalition formation. *Behaviour 79:* 162–187.

Silverberg, J., and Gray, J. P. (1992). *Aggression and Peacefulness in Humans and Other Primates*. Oxford: Oxford University Press.

Simpson, G. G. (1949). *The Meaning of Evolution*. New Haven, CT: Yale University Press.

Singer, P. (1975). *Animal Liberation: A New Ethics for Our Treatment of Animals*. New York: Random House.

Small, M. F., ed. (1984). *Female Primates: Studies by Women Primatologists*. New York: Alan R. Liss.

Small, M. F. (1989). Female choice in nonhuman primates. *Yearbook of Physical Anthropology 32:* 103–127.

Small, M. F. (1990). Promiscuity in Barbary macaques (*Macaca sylvanus*). *American Journal of Primatology 20:* 267–282.

Small, M. F. (1993). *Female Choices. Sexual Behavior of Female Primates*. Ithaca, NY: Cornell University Press.

Smuts, B. B. (1983a). Dynamics of social relationships between adult male and female olive baboons: Selective advantages. In R. A. Hinde (ed.), *Primate Social Relationships*. Oxford: Blackwell.

Smuts, B. B. (1983b). Special relationships between adult male and female baboons. In R. A. Hinde (ed.), *Primate Social Relationships*. Oxford: Blackwell.

Smuts, B. B. (1985). *Sex and Friendship in Baboons*. New York: Aldine.

Smuts, B. B. (1987). Sexual competition and mate choice. In B. B. Smuts, D. L. Cheney, R. M. Seyfarth, R. W. Wrangham, and T. T. Struhsaker (eds.), *Primate Societies*. Chicago: University of Chicago Press.

Smuts, B. B., Cheney, D. L., Seyfarth, R. M., Wrangham, R. W., and Struhsaker, T. T., eds. (1987). *Primate Societies*. Chicago: University of Chicago Press.

Snowdon, C. T. (1990). Language capacities of nonhuman primates. *Yearbook of Physical Anthropology 33*: 215–243.

Southwick, C. H., ed. (1963). *Primate Social Behavior*. Princeton, NJ: Van Nostrand Reinhold.

Southwick, C. H., and Smith, R. B. (1986). The growth of primate field studies. In G. Mitchell and J. Erwin (eds.), *Comparative Primate Biology*, Vol. 2A, *Behavior, Conservation and Ecology*. New York: Alan R. Liss.

Sperling, S. (1991). Baboons with briefcases vs. langurs in lipstick. Feminism and functionalism in primate studies. In M. di Leonardo (ed.), *Gender at the Crossroads of Knowledge. Feminist Anthropology in the Postmodern Era*. Berkeley: University of California Press.

Sprague, D. S. (1993). Applying GIS and remote sensing to wildlife management: Assessing habitat quality for the Japanese monkey (*Macaca fuscata*). *Research Reports*, Vol. 3. Division of Changing Earth and Agroenvironment, National Institute of Agroenvironmental Sciences.

Standen, V. and Foley, R. A., eds. (1989). *Comparative Socioecology. The Behavioural Ecology of Humans and Other Mammals*. Oxford: Blackwell.

Steklis, H. (1993). Primate socioecology from the bottom up. In A. J. Almquist and A. Manyak (eds.), *Milestones in Human Evolution*. Prospect Heights, IL: Waveland Press.

Strier, K. B. (1990). New World primates, new frontiers: Insights from the wooly spider monkey, or muriqui (*Brachyteles arachnoides*). *International Journal of Primatology 11*: 7–19.

Strier, K. B. (1994a). Myth of the typical primate. *Yearbook of Physical Anthropology 37*: 233–271.

Strier, K. B. (1994b). Brotherhoods among atelines: Kinship, affiliation, and competition. *Behaviour 130*: 151–167.

Strier, K. B., Mendes, F. D. C., Rimoli, J., and Rimoli, A. O. (1993). Demography and social structure in one group of muriquis (*Brachyteles arachnoides*). *International Journal of Primatology 14*: 513–526.

Strier, K. B., and Ziegler, T. E. (1994). Insights into ovarian function in wild muriqui monkeys (*Brachyteles arachnoides*). *American Journal of Primatology 32*: 31–40.

Struhsaker, T. T. (1969). Correlates of ecology and social organization among African cercopithecines. *Folia Primatologica 9*: 123–134.

Strum, S. C. (1975a). Life with the Pumphouse Gang: New insights into baboon behavior. *National Geographic Magazine 147*: 672–691.

Strum, S. C. (1975b). Primate predation: Interim report on the development of a tradition in a troop of olive baboons. *Science 187*: 755–757.

Strum, S. C. (1982). Agonistic dominance in male baboons: An alternate view. *International Journal of Primatology 3*: 175–202.

Strum, S. C. (1983a). Use of females by male olive baboons (*Papio anubis*). *American Journal of Primatology 5*: 93–109.

Strum, S. C. (1983b). Why males use infants. In D. M. Taub (ed.), *Primate Paternalism*. New York: Van Nostrand.

Strum, S. C. (1987). *Almost Human: A Journey into the World of Baboons*. New York: Random House.

Strum, S. C. (1989). Longitudinal data on patterns of consorting among male olive baboons. *American Journal of Physical Anthropology 78*: 310.

Strum, S. C. (1994). Reconciling aggression and social manipulation as means of competition. Pt. 1: Life history perspective. *International Journal of Primatology 91*: 387–389.

Strum, S. C. and Latour, B. (1987). Redefining the social link: From baboons to humans. *Social Science Information 26*: 783–802.

Strum, S. C. and Southwick, C. (1986). Translocation of primates. In K. Benirsche (ed.), *Primates*. New York: Springer-Verlag.

Sugiyama, Y. (1965). On the social change of hanuman langurs (*Presbytis entellus*) in their natural condition. *Primates 6*: 381–418.

Sugiyama, Y. (1967). Social organization of hanuman langurs. In S. A. Altmann (ed.), *Social Communication Among Primates*. Chicago: University of Chicago Press.

Sussman, R. W. (1977). Feeding behavior of *Lemur catta* and *Lemur fulvus*. In T. H. Clutton-Brock (ed.), *Primate Ecology: Studies of Feeding and Ranging Behavior in Lemurs, Monkeys, and Apes*. London: Academic Press.

Sussman, R. W., ed. (1979). *Primate Ecology: Problem-Oriented Field Studies*. New York: Wiley.

Sussman, R. W. (1991). Demography and social organization of free-ranging *Lemur catta* in the Beza Mahafaly Reserve, Madagascar. *American Journal of Physical Anthropology 84*: 43–58.

Sussman, R. W. (1992). Male life history and intergroup mobility among ringtailed lemurs (*Lemur catta*). *International Journal of Primatology 13*: 395–413.

Sussman, R. W., Green, G. M., and Sussman, L. (1994). Satellite imagery, human ecology, anthropology, and deforestation in Madagascar. *Human Ecology 22*: 333–354.

Symington, M. M. (1988). Demography, ranging patterns, and activity budgets of black spider monkeys (*Ateles paniscus chamek*) in the Manu National Park, Peru. *American Journal of Primatology 15*: 45–67.

Tanner, N. (1981). *On Becoming Human*. Cambridge: Cambridge University Press.

Terborgh, J. (1983). *Five New World Primates. A Study in Comparative Ecology*. Princeton, NJ: Princeton University Press, 1983.

Terborgh, J., and Janson, C. H. (1986). The socioecology of primate groups. *Annual Review of Ecology and Systematics 17*: 11–135.

Tiger, L., and Fox, R. (1971). *The Imperial Animal*. New York: Holt, Rinehart and Winston.

Trivers, R. L. (1971). The evolution of reciprocal altruism. *Quarterly Review of Biology 46*: 35–57.

Trivers, R. L. (1972). Parental investment and sexual selection. In B. Campbell (ed.), *Sexual Selection and the Descent of Man*. Chicago: Aldine.

Tuana, N. (1989). The weaker seed: The sexist bias of reproductive theory. In N. Tuana (ed.), *Feminism and Science*. Bloomington: Indiana University Press.

Tuana, N. (1993). *The Less Noble Sex. Scientific, Religious, and Philosophical Conceptions of Woman's Nature*. Bloomington: Indiana University Press.

Turke, P. W., and Betzig, L. L. (1985). Those who can do: Wealth, status, and reproductive success on Ifaluk. *Ethology and Sociobiology 6*: 79–87.

Turner, T. (1981). Blood protein variation in a population of Ethiopian vervet monkeys. *American Journal of Physical Anthropology 55*: 225–232.

Tutin, C. E. G. (1979). Mating patterns and reproductive strategies in a community of wild chimpanzees. *Behavioral Ecology and Sociobiology 6*: 29–38.

Tuttle, R. H., ed. (1975). *Socioecology and Psychology of Primates*. Paris: Mouton.

Washburn, S. L. (1951). The new physical anthropology. *Transactions of the New York Academy of Sciences*, Ser. II *13*: 298–304.

Washburn, S. (1962). The analysis of primate evolution with particular reference to the origin of man. *Cold Spring Harbor Symposia on Quantitative Biology* (1951). In W. W. Howells (ed.), *Ideas on Evolution: Selected Essays, 1949–61*. Cambridge, MA: Harvard University Press.

Washburn, S., and DeVore, I. (1961). Social behavior of baboon and early man. In S. L. Washburn (ed.), *The Social Life of Early Man. Viking Fund Publication in Anthropology No. 31*. New York: Wenner-Gren Foundation for Anthropological Research.

Wasser, L. M., and Wasser, S. K. (1995). Environmental variation and development among free ranging yellow baboon (*Papio cynocephalus*). *American Journal of Primatology 35*: 15–30.

Wasser, S. K. (1983). Reproductive competition and cooperation among female yellow baboons. In S. K. Wasser (ed.), *Social Behavior of Female Vertebrates*. New York: Academic Press.

Wasser, S. K., Risler, L., and Steiner, R. A. (1988). Excreted steroids in primate feces over the menstrual cycle and pregnancy. *Biology of Reproduction 39:* 862–872.

Wasser, S. K., Monfort, S. L., and Wildt, D. E. (1991). Rapid extraction of fecal steroids for measuring reproductive cyclicity and early pregnancy in free-ranging yellow baboons (*Papio cynocephalus cynocephalus*). *Journal of Reproductive Fertility 92:* 415–423.

Western, J. D. and Strum, S. C. (1983). Sex, kinship and the evolution of social manipulation. *Ethology and Sociobiology 4:* 19–28.

Western, J. D., Wright, M., and Strum, S., eds. (1994). *Natural Connections: Perspectives on Community Based Conservation*. Washington, DC: Island Press.

Whiten, A., ed. (1993). *Natural Theories of Mind: Evolution, Development and Simulation of Everyday Mindreading*. Cambridge: Blackwell.

Whiten, A., and Byrne, R. (1988a). The Machiavellian intelligence hypotheses: editorial. In R. Byrne and A. Whiten (eds.), *Machiavellian Intelligence*. Oxford: Clarendon Press.

Whiten, A. (1988b). Tactical deception in primates. *Behavioral and Brain Sciences 11:* 233–244.

Wilson, E. O. (1975). *Sociobiology: The New Synthesis*. Cambridge, MA: Harvard University Press.

Wong, Y., Barash, D. P., Boyden, S., Falger, V. S. E., Wapner, P. K., and Weimer, D. L. (1994). Impotence and intransigence: State behavior in the throes of deepening global crisis. *Politics and the Life Sciences 13:* 3–14.

Wrangham, R. W. (1979). Sex differences in chimpanzee dispersal. In D. A. Hamburg and E. R. McCown (eds.), *The Great Apes: Perspectives on Human Evolution*. Menlo Park, CA: Benjamin Cummings.

Wrangham, R. W. (1980). An ecological model of female-bonded primate groups. *Behaviour 75:* 262–300.

Wrangham, R. W. (1987). Evolution of social structure. In B. B. Smuts, D. L. Cheney, R. M. Seyfarth, R. W. Wrangham, and T. T. Struhsaker (eds), *Primate Societies*. Chicago: University of Chicago Press.

Yerkes, R. M., and Yerkes, A. W. (1929). *The Great Apes*. New Haven, CT: Yale University Press.

York, A. D., and Rowell, T. E. (1988). Reconciliation following aggression in patas monkeys, *Erythrocebus patas*. *Animal Behaviour 36:* 502–509.

Zihlman, A. (1978). Women in evolution. Pt. II. Subsistence and social organization among early hominids. *Signs 4:* 4–20.

Zihlman, A. (1981). Women as shapers of human adaptation. In Frances Dahlberg (ed.), *Woman the Gatherer*. New Haven, CT: Yale University Press.

Zuckerman, S. (1932). *The Social Life of Monkeys and Apes*. London: Routledge & Kegan Paul.

*Washburn and Hamburg use the problem of aggression to illustrate how scientifically valuable an evolutionary perspective can be to the understanding of behavior. Aggressive behavior is an adaptive complex with its own evolutionary history. The scientific challenge is to identify the elements of the adaptation and then to create scientifically rigorous evolutionary reconstructions. There are several steps in diagnosing an evolutionary complex: The biological basis of the behavior must be understood. This usually requires laboratory research and experimentation. The frequencies and functions of the behavior also have to be determined. This is properly done in a naturalistic setting through observation. Biology and behavior, experimentation and observation can then be combined and interpretations about the nature of the behavioral adaptation made within an evolutionary perspective. Washburn and Hamburg discuss the biological basis of aggression as evidenced in hormones, the brain, and anatomical structures, as well as the patterning of aggression between individuals and between groups among Old World monkeys and apes. They suggest that all parts of this primate adaptive complex evolved together and that it is only by viewing human aggression in this evolutionary context that we can understand the problems of aggression in modern humans.*

# 9 Aggressive Behavior in Old World Monkeys and Apes (1968)

*S. L. Washburn and D. A. Hamburg*

In this essay we hope to use the problem of aggression as an example of evolutionary perspective as a scientific tool. We are interested in the way the behavior of the nonhuman primates may be useful in increasing our understanding of man. Study of the forces and situations that produced man is one way of attempting to understand human nature, of seeing ourselves in evolutionary perspective. Because the use of man's closest relatives in the laboratory is the nearest approach to experimenting on man himself, the use of primates as laboratory animals is increasing rapidly. As in so much of science, there is no boundary between the pure and the applied, and the answers to our questions lie in the domain of many different disciplines. Since no one could

possibly master all the relevant information, we wish to clarify our objectives before proceeding to the main topic of the paper. In discussions at the conference a series of general questions emerged, many of which we have encountered before—since the beginning of our collaboration at the Center for Advanced Study in the Behavioral Sciences in 1957. We propose to deal with these recurrent, general questions first.

Field studies in a comparative evolutionary framework do not permit the manipulation of variables and the precision of measurement that are possible in laboratory experiments. They are, however, likely to give new perspectives which suggest fruitful directions for experiments and for deeper analysis of problems of living organisms. Field studies do not replace other methods of investigation, nor do studies on animals substitute for the direct study of man. For example, Prechtl (1965) has pointed out that much of the behavior of the human newborn is understandable only in phylogenetic perspective. This does not mean that comparison is the only way to approach the study of behavior in the newborn but only that inclusion of some comparison enriches the understanding of what

From Phyllis C. Jay, ed., *Primates: Studies in Adaptation and Variability*, pp. 458–478. Copyright © 1968 by Holt, Rinehart and Winston. Reprinted by permission of the publisher.

[1] This paper is part of a program on primate behavior supported by the United States Public Health Service (Grant No. MH 08623) and aided by a Research Professorship in the Miller Institute for Basic Research in Science at the University of California at Berkeley. We particularly want to thank Dr. Jack Barchas, Dr. Phyllis C. Jay, Dr. Donald Lunde, and Mrs. Jane B. Lancaster for advice and help in the preparation of this paper.

is being observed. In advocating the use of the evolutionary approach, we are not suggesting that it is the only method or that it is always relevant. We are suggesting, however, that the comparative, evolutionary study of behavior offers many insights that are unlikely to come from other sources. We believe that the combination of the evolutionary perspective with experimental science provides a powerful approach to biological problems including those of behavior, and we echo Simpson's 1964 statement "100 years without Darwin are enough."

A central problem in the study of the evolution of behavior is that contemporary monkeys and apes are not the equivalents of human ancestors. To what extent their behaviors may be used as indicators of the behaviors of long-extinct fossil forms is debatable. Obviously this is not a simple question, and the possibility of reconstruction differs with each particular behavior. Each answer is a matter of probability, and there is great variation in the adequacy of evidence bearing on different questions. For example, in all the nonhuman primates females have brief, clearly limited periods of estrus. Since this state is universal and highly adaptive, it is virtually certain that this condition was present in our ancestors. Although the time of the loss of estrus cannot be dated, the comparison calls attention to the significance of the loss. The physiology of human females is quite different from that of any other primate, and many specifically human customs and problems are directly related to continuing receptivity in the human female. The human family is based upon a female physiology different from that of any other primate, and the physiology may well be the result of selection for stable male-female relations. The close similarity in much reproductive physiology permitted the use of the rhesus monkey as the most important laboratory animal in working out the human female's reproductive cycle (Corner 1942), but the behavioral approach emphasizes the significance of the differences. Our understanding benefits from seeing the nature of both the similarity and the difference. The problems of reconstructing behavior are discussed more fully in Washburn and Jay (1965).[2]

Estrus has been used as an example of a problem of the reconstruction of behavior when there is no direct fossil evidence. The same kind of logical reconstruction from indirect evidence can be applied to many other behaviors. We have indirect evidence, for example, that our remote ancestors probably matured more rapidly than we do, lived in small areas, were very aggressive, and hunted little, if any. Let us consider this first statement: If the infant is to cling to the mother, as does the infant monkey and ape, then the infant must be born able to cling. A human infant born with this ability would need far too large a brain at the time of birth, and the adaptation of the mother's holding the immature infant may be looked on as an adaptation to the evolution of the brain. Monkeys are born with more highly developed nervous and motor capabilities than those of apes at birth. A gorilla mother must help her baby for approximately six weeks before it can cling entirely unaided (Schaller 1963). In *Homo erectus* (Java man, Pekin man, and comparable forms) the brain was approximately twice the size of a gorilla, and the infant's behavior must have been much more like that of modern man than like that of an ape.

The implication of the clinging of the nonhuman primate infant can be generalized that biology guarantees the infant monkey or ape a far greater chance of appropriate treatment than it does the human infant. So far as early experience is important in determining later performance, man should show by far the greatest variability of all primates. The study of comparative behavior calls attention to the uniqueness of the human condition, the importance of early events, and of the human mother's need to acquire complex skills of child care.

In addition to the reconstruction of behavior, another problem that has arisen repeatedly in discussions of the comparison of behavior is the extent to which behaviors in different groups of animals are comparable. The issue is whether behaviors labeled, for example, "aggression" or "play" are comparable enough so that comparisons are useful, or whether these are simply subjective human words used to symbolize collection of noncomparable behaviors. There are four important considerations.

The first is that the words are least likely to be misleading when animals, whose behaviors are being compared, are closely related. For example, we think there would be little disagreement as to which behaviors should be called "play" or "aggression" in Old World monkeys and apes, but the problem is very different if the behaviors of monkeys and birds are to be compared.

The second point is that in the observation of the behavior we are not limited to the view of a single animal or to one occasion. An observer sees repeated interac-

[2] After this paper was in nearly final form we received *Adaptation et Agressivité* (1965), edited by Kourilsky, Soulairac, and Grapin, and *On Aggression* (1966), by Konrad Lorenz. *Conflict in Society* (de Reuck 1966) also appeared, although we had access to part of that data in prepublication. We find ourselves in general agreement with these new sources, and only wish that we had had them a year ago. We have found J. Altman's *Organic Foundations of Animal Behavior* (1966) exceedingly valuable, and it too would have been very useful if it had been available earlier. None of these references would have led us to different conclusions, and we hope that the point of view presented in the introduction to this paper may help to bridge the gap between the thinking of the students of animal behavior and the social scientists.

tions of animals in the social group or groups. The judgment that an action is threatening, for example, is based on the repeated specifiable response of the other animals. The response to biting in play and in aggression is very different, and the difference is unmistakable in the response of the bitten animals, although it would often be hard for the human observer to perceive the difference in the actual bite.

The third point is that in classifying and labeling behavior we are not limited to the external view of the actions. For example, Delgado (1963) has shown that stimulation of certain brain areas elicits threat behavior in rhesus monkeys. Although present evidence is limited, we think it likely that the same brain areas are concerned with rage in man. If it can be shown that the behaviors that are classified together are mediated by comparable structures, then the classification is much more likely to be useful. This is best exemplified by the category "sexual," in which the interrelations of behaviors, nervous system, hormones, and experience have been thoroughly investigated (Beach 1965b). This takes us back to our first point: One reason that labeling categories of behavior is less likely to be misleading when the animals are closely related is that the internal biological mechanisms on which these actions are based are more likely to be similar.

The fourth point is that the human observer is most likely to detect relevant cues when observing the behavior of animals closely related to himself. We do not underestimate the formidable problems of observation and the need for experimental clarification of what is being observed in the behavior of monkeys and apes, but at least the special senses and central nervous system of the observer are highly similar to those of the animals being observed. Even within the primates the interpretation of observations becomes much more difficult with the prosimians. Since the sense of smell is important in prosimians and the animals have special tactile hairs that we lack, in many situations there is no assurance that the human observer has access to information of importance to the animal being observed. The human can see a dog in the act of smelling, but simple observation gives no knowledge of the information received by the dog. Viewed in this way, the human observer is more likely to be able to see and record the actions that are important in the analysis of behavior when studying monkeys and apes than he is when watching any other animal.

This does not mean that observations are necessarily easy or correct, but it does mean that man is potentially able to see, describe, and interpret actions made by a close relative, especially in a mode that approximates the judgments the animals themselves are making. The more distantly the animal is related to man, the less the human perception of the situation is likely

to correspond to that of the animal's. For example, a human observer can learn the facial expressions, gestures, and sounds that express threat in a species of monkey, with some assurance that the signals are seen in the same way a monkey sees them. It is possible to play back their recorded sound to monkeys and most sounds without gestures produce no response. Some monkey gestures can be learned by man, and the human face is sufficiently similar that a monkey interprets certain human expressions as threats and responds with appropriate actions. Without experiment a human observer would hardly have expected that a male turkey would display to the isolated head of a female (Schein and Hale 1959; reprinted in McGill 1965). Even when a bird and a mammal are responding to the same sense, vision, in this case, the internal organization of perception is so different that comparison can be made only on the basis of experiments. In monkey, ape, and man the internal organizations are highly similar, and the use of a word such as aggression carries far more comparable meaning than when the same word is used to describe a category of behavior in vertebrates in general. We are not belittling the importance of the study of behavior in a wide variety of animals, but we are emphasizing that the problems of comparison in such studies are more complex than they are in these comparing a very few of man's closest relatives.

We are writing on aggression in certain monkeys and apes because we think that there is enough information to make such an essay useful. The word "aggression" only indicates the area of our interest and our use of it does not mean that we think the area is fully understood or precisely defined. Accurate definition often comes at the end of research; initially, definitions serve only to clarify the general nature of the subject to be explored. For the purpose of opening the area for exploration and discussion we find that the definition of Carthy and Ebling (1964: 1) is useful. They state that "An animal acts aggressively when it inflicts, attempts to inflict, or threatens to inflict damage on another animal. The act is accompanied by recognizable behavioral symptoms and definable physiological changes." Carthy and Ebling recognize the displacement of aggression against self or an inanimate object, but rule out predation as a form of aggression. For our analysis, it is not useful to accept this limitation; if one is concerned with aggressive behavior in man, the degree to which human carnivorous and predatory activity is related to human aggressiveness should be kept open for investigation and not ruled out by definition.

In discussing aggression it is important to consider both the individual actor and the social system in which he is participating. In the social systems of monkeys and apes evolution has produced a close correlation between the nature of the social system and the nature of the actors in the system. Societies of gibbons, langurs, and macaques represent different sociobiological adaptations, and, as will be developed later, the form and function of aggressive behaviors are different in these groups (Jay 1965a). Through selection, evolution has produced a fit between social system and the biology of the actors in the system. Aggression is between individuals or very small groups, and individual animals must be able to make the appropriate decisions and fight or flee. Rapoport (1966), in particular, has argued that war between modern nations has nothing to do with the aggressiveness of individuals, but rather is a question of culture, of human institutions. Although agreeing that it is very important to understand the cultural factors in war, we think that it is important to understand the human actors too. It is still individuals who make decisions, and it is our belief that the limitations and peculiarities of human biology play an important part in these decisions. We will return to this issue later; at this point we only want to emphasize that it is necessary, particularly in the case of man, to think both of the social system and the actors. It was not long ago that human war was carried out on a person-to-person basis, and our present customs go back to those times.

Finally, we return to a point of view which we have discussed elsewhere (Washburn and Hamburg 1965a), but which needs emphasis and clarification particularly in the context of aggression. The result of evolution is that behaviors that have been adaptive in the past history of the species, which led to reproductive success, are easy to learn and hard to extinguish. As Hinde and Tinbergen have put it: "This exemplifies a principle of great importance: many of the differences between species do not lie in the first instance in stereotyped behavior sequences but consist in the possession of a propensity to learn" (1958: 255, reprinted in McGill 1965). It is particularly important to consider ease of learning, or the propensity to learn, when we are discussing monkeys and apes. These forms mature slowly and there is strong reason to suppose that the main function of this period of protected youth is to allow learning and hence adaptation to a wide variety of local situations.

There is a feedback relation between structure and function starting in the early embryo. Structure sets limits and gives opportunities. Apes cannot learn to talk because they lack the neurological base. Man can easily learn to be aggressive because the biological base is present, is always used to some degree, and is frequently reinforced by individual success and major social reward. The biological nature of man, now far more amenable to scientific analysis than ever before, is thus relevant to aggressive behavior in ways that include learning and social interaction.

## THE BIOLOGICAL BASIS OF AGGRESSION

Collias (1944) in a major review of aggressive behavior in vertebrates concluded that the function of the behavior was control of food and reproduction through the control of territory and the maintenance of hierarchy and that males were responsible for most of the aggressive behavior. Scott (1958, 1962) supported these main conclusions, and emphasized the importance of learning in the development of aggressive behavior. Breeds of dogs differ greatly in aggressiveness, but the expression of these differences is greatly modified by learning and the social situation. Recently, Wynne-Edwards (1965) has stressed the role of social behavior in control of territory, hierarchy, and reproduction as mechanisms of species dispersion and population control. In general, the biological studies indicate that aggression is one of the principal adaptive mechanisms, that it has been of major importance in the evolution of the vertebrates (Lorenz 1966).

We think that these major conclusions will apply to the primates, although adequate data are available on only a few forms and these will be discussed later. Order within most primate groups is maintained by a hierarchy, which depends ultimately primarily on the power of the males. Groups are separated by habit and conflict. Aggressive individuals are essential actors in the social system and competition between groups is necessary for species dispersal and control of local populations. In view of the wide distribution of these behaviors and their fundamental importance to the evolutionary process, it is not surprising to discover that the biological basis for aggressive behavior is similar in a wide variety of vertebrates. As presently understood, the essential structures are in the phylogenetically oldest parts of the brain, and the principal male sex hormone testosterone is significant for aggression. In general, motivational-emotional patterns essential to survival and reproductive success in mammals find their main structural base in the older parts of the brain, particularly in hypothalamus and limbic system. In the higher primates this mammalian "common denominator" is linked to a remarkable development of newer parts of the brain. These are mainly concerned with increasing storage (learning), more complex discrimination, and motor skills; they function in a complex feedback relationship with the older parts (Noback and Moskowitz 1963; MacLean 1963). This interrelation of the older and newer parts of the brain is especially important to remember when monkeys and apes are considered because the expression of the brain-hormone-behavior paradigm may be greatly modified by learning in a social environment. A simple release of a complicated emotion-motor pattern in aggression is not to be expected in such species.

The recognition of a biological factor in aggressive behavior long antedates modern science: stock breeders certainly recognized differences in individuals, in breeds, and in the effects of castration. Comparison of the behaviors of ox and bull, as well as experiments such as those of Beeman (1947) on mice, show that a part of the difference in aggressive behavior between males and females is due to the sex hormones. Testosterone makes it easier to stimulate animals to fight, and aggressive behavior in males tends to be more frequent, more intense, and of longer duration than in females. Experimental studies fully support the conclusions of Collias' (1944) survey of vertebrate behavior, and are in agreement with the field studies of primate behavior. It would be extremely interesting to trap a male baboon from a troop that had been carefully studied, castrate him, and release him back into the same troop. The effects of the operation could then be studied relative to hierarchy, predators, and participation in troop life in general.

However, the relation of the hormone to the behavior is not simple, for androgen stimulates protein anabolism in many animals (Nalbandov 1964), and this is one of the factors accounting for the greater size of males. Skeletal muscles of castrated males and females grow less rapidly than those of intact animals, and androgen administration increases the number and thickness of fibers. The sex hormones affect the growth of the brain, and appear to act in an inductive way to organize certain circuits into male and female patterns (Harris 1964; Levine and Mullins 1966). This effect is comparable to that on the undifferentiated genital tract. There is then an interplay, a feedback, among hormones, structure, and behavior, and the nature of this relation changes during development. Testosterone is first a factor in influencing the structure of the brain (especially the hypothalamus) and of the genitals. Later it is a factor in influencing both muscle size and the more aggressive play of males. Finally, it is important in influencing both aggressive and sexual behavior in adults. We stress the complex interplay between hormones, structures, and behavior throughout the life of the individual. It can be seen at once that the concept of a system of coadapted genes is so important because such a developmental and functional pattern depends on the interaction of many different biological entities: variation in any of these may affect the final result. It is probably the primary methodological difficulty in the science of behavior genetics that even apparently simple behaviors are often built from very complex biological bases.

Two groups of experiments yield what seems to be particularly important information regarding factors influencing male aggression. Harris and Levine have studied the sexual behavior patterns in female rats that had received early androgen treatment; treatment of newborn rats with testosterone results in abolition of estrous behavior combined with an exaggeration of male patterns, particularly in the aggressive sphere. Young, Goy, and Phoenix (1964) and Goy (personal communication) gave testosterone to pregnant rhesus monkeys during approximately the second quarter of gestation. In addition to producing pseudohermaphroditic females, the behavior of the prenatally treated females was modified in the male direction. Rosenblum (1961) has shown that there are marked sexual differences in the play of infant rhesus monkeys. The masculinized females were allowed to play for 20 minutes per day, five days a week, from the age of two months: this continued for more than two years (at the time of writing). They threatened, initiated play, and engaged in rough play more than did the controls. Like the males studied by Rosenblum, the masculinized females withdrew less often than did untreated females from initiations, threats, and approaches of other animals. They also showed a greater tendency to mounting: evidently there is a general tendency toward male behavioral repertoire. Treatment changed the whole brain-hormone-behavior complex, and the results of the prenatal treatment persisted into the third year of life.

However, it should be stressed that the expression of the pattern depended on social learning. The infant monkeys were allowed to play, and Harlow and Harlow (1965) have shown that gross behavioral deficits in behavior result from early social isolation. It is also important to remember that these testosterone-treated monkeys were protected. In a free-ranging troop of rhesus, subject to human harassment, predation, intertroop conflict, and intratroop aggression (Jay, personal communication: Southwick et al. 1965), such an animal would probably be punished for inappropriate behavior. The experimentally masculinized female does not have the large canine teeth, jaw muscles, or body size to be successfully aggressive against males under natural conditions. A similar point is well illustrated in an experiment by Delgado (1965). A monkey in whose brain an electrode had been implanted so that threat behavior could be stimulated at the experimenter's will, was put in a cage with four other monkeys. In the test where the experimental animal was dominant over the other four, stimulation led him to threaten and immediately attack. But when the experimental animal was subordinate to all four of the other monkeys, stimulation led to his being attacked and cowering. Even when there is a restricted biological base for a behavior, the expression of the behavior will be affected by socio-environmental factors.

This brings us to a closer examination of the brain in relation to aggressive behavior. Perhaps, the most thorough work has been done on cats and this is summarized by Brown and Hunsperger (1965). Their experiments show several areas in which electrical stimulation will elicit threat and escape behavior. They have been able to elicit such behavior by stimulation in portions of the midbrain, hypothalamus, and amygdala. Although, just as in monkeys, threat can be elicited from only a very small part of the brain, it is not a single or simple area. The threat behaviors are multiple and it is especially interesting that escape is closely related to threat. Brown and Hunsperger relate the anatomical facts to the behavioral fact that following threat an animal may either attack or escape. Certainly this is frequently seen in monkeys; whether threat ends in attack or flight depends on the participating animal's appraisal of the situation. In the laboratory, the direction and intensity of the attack resulting from stimulation of the brain depends on what is available for attack, and may be changed by offering the cat a dummy or a real rat.

In man the same parts of the brain are believed to be involved in rage reactions. Obviously, the same kind of detailed stimulation cannot be undertaken on man, but clinical evidence including neurological studies suggests that the limbic system and hypothalamus are very important in mediation of emotional experiences, positive and negative, including anger.

## AGGRESSION IN FREE-RANGING APES AND MONKEYS

Just as the biological basis of aggression that we have been discussing can only be seen and analyzed in the laboratory, so the functions and frequencies of aggressive behaviors can only be determined by field studies. The field studies have recently been reviewed by Hall (1964) and Washburn (1966), and here we will call attention only to a few of the major points of interest from an evolutionary point of view.

Conflict between different species is infrequent, even when the species are competing for the same food. Places where the general situation can be most easily observed are at water holes in the large African game reserves. Particularly at the end of the dry season, hundreds of animals of many species may be seen in close proximity in South Africa. Rhodesia, or Tanzania. The

Ngorongoro crater affords magnificent views over vast numbers of animals, and from this vantage point it becomes clear that the human notion of "wild," that is, that animals normally flee, is the result of human hunting. In Amboseli it is not uncommon to see various combinations of baboons, vervet monkeys, warthogs, impala, gazelle of two species, zebra, wildebeest (gnu), giraffe, elephant, and rhinoceros around one water hole. Even carnivores, when they are not hunting, attract surprisingly little attention. When elephants walk through a troop of baboons the monkeys move out of the way in a leisurely manner at the last second, and the same indifference was observed when impala males were fighting among the baboons or when a rhinoceros ran through the troop. On one occasion two baboons chased a giraffe, but, except where hunting carnivores are concerned, interspecies aggression is rare. Most animals under most conditions do not show interest in animals of other species, even when eating the same food—warthogs and baboons frequently eat side by side. The whole notion of escape distance is predicted on the presence of a hunter.

Although the general situation seems to be great tolerance for other species (Hall 1964), there are exceptions. Gibbons usually drive monkeys from fruit trees (Ellefson, this vol.). Goodall has shown remarkable motion pictures of baboons and chimpanzees in aggressive encounters. Baboons have been seen trying to drive vervets (*Cercopithecus aethiops*) from fruit trees in which the baboons had been feeding. There is some deliberate hunting by monkeys and apes. DeVore (personal communication) and Struhsaker (1965) have seen baboons catch and eat vervets. Goodall (1965) records chimpanzees' hunting and eating red colobus monkeys. Nestling birds and eggs are probably eaten by most monkeys, but the majority of interspecific encounters among the primates appear to be neutral, causing little or no reaction among the species.

Monkeys and apes certainly take aggressive action against predators, and this has been particularly well described by Struhsaker (1965) for vervets. Vervet alarm calls distinguish among snakes, ground predators, and birds, and the monkeys respond with different appropriate actions. Baboons have been seen to chase cheetahs and dogs. Monkeys and apes make agonistic displays against predators, including man, and these behaviors have been reviewed by Hall (1964; this vol.) and Washburn (1966). The amount of this agonistic behavior leads us to think that predation and interspecies conflict may have been underestimated in the field studies so far available. The problem is that although the primates may have become conditioned to the observer's presence, he is likely to disturb the predator. A fuller picture of interspecies conflict requires field studies of a nonprimate species involved in conflict with primates.

Relations among groups of the same species range from avoidance to agonistic display and actual fighting. In marked contrast to the normally neutral relations with other species, animals of the same species evoke interest and action. This can be seen when strange animals of the same species are artificially introduced (Gartlan and Brain, this vol.; Kummer, this vol.; Hall 1964; Washburn 1966), on the occasions when an animal changes troops, and when troops meet. We think these behaviors suggest that intertroop conflict is an important mechanism for species spacing. The spacing represents a part of the adjustments of the species to the local food supply. The quantity of food is a very important factor in determining the density of primate populations. It has been shown in both Japan and a small island off Puerto Rico where rhesus monkeys were introduced that population expands at a rate of more than 15 percent per year if food is supplied ad libitum (Koford 1966). Intertroop aggression either leads to one group's having the resources of an area at its exclusive disposal, or at least creates a situation in which one group is much more likely to obtain the food in one area. The clearest description of extreme territorial defense is Ellefson's account (Chap. 6) of gibbons. The relation of food supply to population size is considered by Hall (this vol.). A very clear case of the relation of food supply to territorial defense is given by Gartlan and Brain (Chap. 10): Where food was abundant and there was a high density of vervets, the monkeys showed territorial marking and defense. These behaviors were absent in an area of poor food supply and low population density. From this and other examples (rhesus, langurs) it is clear that one cannot describe a primate species as "territorial" in the same sense the word has been used for species of birds. In monkeys and apes the behavior of a part of a species will depend both on biology (perhaps best shown by the gibbon) and on the local conditions. The intertroop fighting of city rhesus monkeys appears to depend both on high density and on the great overlap of living areas that is a product of the city environment (Southwick *et al.* 1965). The intertroop conflict of langurs described by Yoshiba (this vol.) also occurred in an area in which the population is estimated at possibly more than 300 langurs per square mile.

It is our belief that intertroop aggression in primates has been greatly underestimated. No field study has yet been undertaken with this problem as a focus, and no effort has been made to study situations in which conflict is likely to be frequent. More important, the groups of a species are normally spaced well apart, and the observer sees the long-term results of aggression and avoidance, not the events causing it. (In this regard, as in so many others, gibbons are exceptional.) A further complication is that the groups of monkeys which are likely to meet have seen each other before. The relations among groups has been established in previous encounters, and one is exceedingly unlikely to see strange troops meet or some major event change the relative strength of the troops. Carpenter (1964), particularly, has called attention to the importance of sounds in species spacing, and, in species in which this mechanism is important, group avoidance does not even require that the animals see each other. The importance of both sounds and gestures in intertroop relations is discussed by Marler (this vol.). Lorenz (1964, 1966) has stressed the ritualistic nature of the vast majority of aggressive encounters.

In evaluating the amount of intertroop aggression in Old World monkeys and apes, it is important to keep in mind that the data have increased very rapidly. In Scott's (1962) review on aggression in animals the only major sources of information on primates were Carpenter's studies of the howling monkey (1934) and of the gibbon (1940). In Hall's review of aggression in primate society (this vol.) the data are chiefly from publications in 1962 or later. We stress the frequency and importance of aggressive behavior more than Hall does, in part because of our greater emphasis on the biological importance of aggression in species spacing, but more importantly because there is much more information available in recent accounts. Aggression in langurs is described by Ripley (1965) and Yoshiba (this vol.). Many more observations of aggressive encounters in rhesus, including intertroop fighting in forest troops, are now available (Jay, personal communication). Shirek (personal communication) has observed a complex pattern of intertroop fighting in *Macaca irus*. Ellefson (this vol.) has given a much more complete account of intertroop encounters, including actual fighting, in gibbons. For vervets, Gartlan and Brain (this vol.) and Struhsaker (1965) have provided descriptions of intertroop encounters and of the settings that increase their frequency.

## AGGRESSION WITHIN THE LOCAL GROUP

Conflict between individuals within the local group or aggregation is far more frequent than intergroup or interspecies conflicts. It is impossible to watch monkeys and apes for any long period without seeing conflict over food or in interpersonal relations. Scott (1962) has emphasized the importance of learning in the development of aggressive behaviors and Hall (this vol.) has shown that most learning in monkeys takes place in a group and is appropriate to the group's social structure, individual biology, and ecology. In the societies of nonhuman primates aggression is constantly rewarded. In baboons (DeVore and Hall 1965; Hall and DeVore 1965) the most dominant male can do what he wants (within the limits of the traditions of the troop), and he takes precedence in social situations. As DeVore first emphasized, the dominant male is attractive to the other members of the troop. When he sits in the shade, others come to him to sit beside him and groom him. When the troop moves, it is the behavior of the dominant males in the center of the troop that ultimately decides the direction the troop will follow. The whole social structure of the troop rewards the dominant animal, or animals, and when a dominant animal is sick or injured and loses position the change can be seen in the behavior of the other animals. No longer is precedence granted to him for social position, grooming, food, sex, or leadership. Thus, monkeys not only have the biological basis for aggressive behavior, but also use this equipment frequently, and success is highly rewarded.

There are marked species differences in aggressive behavior and in the dominance hierarchies that result from it. Baboons and macaques are probably the most aggressive of the monkeys, but even here there are species differences. *M. radiata* is far less aggressive than *M. mulatta* (Simonds 1965). The behavior of *Papio hamadryas* is certainly different from that of other baboons (Kummer, this vol.). But *interindividual conflict is important in all species described so far.* Even in chimpanzees with their very open social organization (Goodall 1965; Reynolds and Reynolds 1965) some males are dominant. Goodall had to make elaborate arrangements to prevent a few large males from taking all the food when bananas were provided.

The position of the individual animal relative to other animals in the group is learned, and this process starts with the mother and her support of her infant in aggressive encounters (Yamada 1963; Sade 1965, 1966). Sons of dominant females are more likely to be dominant. The passing of the infant langur from one female to another may be one of the factors in the lack of development of clearly defined dominance hierarchies in this species (Jay 1965).

Since the animals in a local group know one another, the dominance order is understood, is normally maintained by threat, and usually serves to preserve a relatively peaceful situation. For example, a small group of crab-eating macaques (*M. irus*) kept in a runway (16 by 75 feet) at Berkeley was dominated by one male. For more than two years there had not been a single serious bite by any member of the group. When the dominant animal was removed, no change occurred for two weeks; the social habits continued. Then the formerly number two animal asserted his power, and four adult animals received deep canine bites. (These bite are quite different from incisor nipping, which hurts the other animal but does not do serious damage. Incisor nipping is the normal mode of biting when an animal gives mild punishment.) Two infants were killed in the encounters. This incident clearly shows the role of dominance in preventing fighting. It also shows another characteristic of dominance behavior in macaques. In the runway all animals had access to ample food; they had comfortable social position including opportunities for grooming; and the dominant animal, although he copulated more than the others, did not prevent them from access to females. Being dominant appears to be its own reward—to be highly satisfying and to be sought, regardless of whether it is accompanied by advantage in food, sex, or grooming. In the long run, position guarantees reward, but in the short run, position itself is the reward, as this monkey's actions suggest: satisfaction apparently comes from others being unable to challenge effectively, as well as from more tangible rewards.

**Evolution of Conflict**

The aggressive behaviors that are the basis of dominance within the group, that are a factor in spacing groups, and that may result in some predation are rooted in the biology of the species and are learned in the social group. As noted earlier, the biological roots of these behaviors are complex, and the individual animal, which carries out the threat or other aggressive action, must have the necessary structure, physiology, and temperament. For example, males tend to be more aggressive than females, and this difference depends on testosterone and is altered by castration of the male or prenatal treatment of the female. The aggressive actions are practiced and brought to a high level of skill in play. Then, as the male monkey becomes fully adult, the canine teeth erupt. Notice that the whole practiced, skillful, aggressive complex is present before the canine teeth erupt. The really dangerous weapon is not present until the male monkey is a fully adult, experienced member of the social group. As the canine teeth erupt, the temporal muscles more than double in size, and the male changes from a roughly playing juvenile to an adult that can inflict a very serious wound, even death, with a single bite.

All the parts of this aggressive complex evolve, and this is best shown by the differences between species. The differences between baboons and patas monkeys give an example of very different ways of adapting to savanna life (Hall, this vol.; DeVore and Hall 1965; Hall and DeVore 1965). Differences between *Cercopithecus aethiops* and *C. mitis* are noted by Gartlan and Brain (this vol.). Since selection is for reproductive success, it is clear that there must be a balance between all the different structural and physiological factors that make aggressive actions adaptive; although the biological elements seem remarkably similar in primates, the pattern and degree of development may be very different in various species. It is no accident that the differences between male and female monkeys are in body size, tooth form, neck muscles, hormones, brain, play patterns, and adult behavior, and this whole pattern of sexual differentiation may result in sex difference that is extreme (as in baboons and macaques) or very minor (as in *Presbytis rubicunda* or *Cercopithecus nictitans*). But as these species have evolved, the process has been slow enough so that selection has modified the whole complex of the adapting aggressive behaviors and their biological base. In man, however, the whole technical-social scene has changed so rapidly that human biological evolution has had no opportunity to keep pace. Throughout most of human history societies have depended on young adult males to hunt, to fight, and to maintain the social order with violence. Even when the individual was cooperating, his social role could be executed only by extremely aggressive action that was learned in play, was socially approved, and was personally gratifying.

In the remainder of this paper we wish to consider human aggression, and the problems created by the nature of man.

As Lorenz (1964, 1966) has stressed, most conflict between animals is ritualized. Gestures and sounds convey threats and greatly reduce the amount of actual fighting. This is certainly true for the primates, and many structures are understandable only as the basis for displays. Dramatic structures of this kind, such as the laryngeal sac of the siamang gibbon, have long been recognized, but many less noticeable (from a human point of view) should be included—for example, the pads of connective tissue on the head of the male gorilla or those of the male orangutan's cheeks. Motions of the ears, scalp, eyelids, are important in gesture. The posture, or the position of the tail, may signal social status. Hair, particularly on the shoulders and neck, erects, signaling aggressive intent, and the manes of many male primates probably are to be interpreted as structural adaptations for agonistic display. Man lacks the kind of structures that the other primates use in threat and agonistic display. Although the structures used in display may differ to some extent from species to species, it is remarkable that man has none—no erecting hair,

colored skin, callosities, or dramatic actions of ears or scalp. The kinds of gesture that communicate threat in the nonhuman primates have been shifted to the hand (freed by bipedalism and made important by tools) and to language. The evolution of language as a more efficient method of social communication, including the communication of threat, changed the pressures on a wide variety of other structures that must have functioned in agonistic display, unless it is postulated that our ancestors were unique among mammals and lacked all such adaptations. For example, only about one-half of the behavioral items that Brown and Hunsperger (1965) list as indicating agonistic behavior are anatomically possible in man. It is particularly the kind of structures that signal threat at a distance that have been lost. But even the structures that serve in close, face-to-face social communication may have been simplified. Human facial muscles have been described as more complex than those of the apes, making more elaborate expressions possible, but this is surely a misreading of the anatomical evidence and there is no evidence that the facial muscles of a chimpanzee are less complicated than those of man. Certainly the chimpanzee's mouth is more mobile and expressive, and a much wider variety of mouth expressions are possible in an ape than in man.

If we read the evidence correctly, in man language replaces the agonistic displays of nonhuman primates, and it opens the way to the existence of a social system in which aggressive behavior is not constantly rewarded. As noted earlier, in the societies of monkeys and apes dominance is the key to social order. Even if the dominance system of a group is not a rigid one, individuals in protecting young, gaining access to food, sex, grooming, or social position often threaten, and the threat—or, rarely, actual aggression—is rewarded with the acquisition of the desired goal. Agonistic behavior is an essential element in the day-to-day behavior of monkeys and apes, and language removes the necessity of rewarding this kind of aggressive behavior.

Just as the changed selection that came with tools led to increase in the parts of the brain controlling manual skills and to reduction in the whole tooth-fighting complex, so the origin of language led to changes in parts of the brain (Lancaster, this vol.) and to a reduction or loss of most structures concerned with displays. In this sense the human body is in part a product of language and of the complex social life that language made possible. Similarly, the emotions of man have evolved in a way that permits him to participate in complex social life (Hamburg 1963). We think it is probable that individuals with uncontrollable rage reactions were killed and that, over many thousands of years, there was selection for temperaments compatible with moderately complex social situations. This process may have been somewhat like the early stages of domestication that involved the removal of socially impossible individuals, rather than the breeding of animals according to any plan. It is a fact that the human adrenals are relatively small compared to those of nonhuman primates and in this way man differs from the ape as domestic rats do from wild rats.

The expression of the emotions in man is more complex than in nonhuman primates, and, although emphasizing the continuity of the biological nature of aggressive behavior, we do not forget the remarkable differences. Compared with the ape or monkey, all the association areas of the human brain have undergone a three-fold increase in size. These are the areas particularly concerned with the ability to remember, to plan, and to inhibit inappropriate action. The increase in these areas is probably the result of new selection pressures that came with the evolution of more complex forms of social life, and is probably highly related to the evolution of language which made the new ways of life possible. Taken together the new parts of the association areas and the parts of the brain making language possible might be thought of as the "social brain"—the parts of the brain that (from an evolutionary point of view) evolved in response to social pressures and the parts that today mediate appropriate social action. This concept is consistent with the fact that degeneration in these parts leads to senile dementia, the inability of some old people to continue normal social life—to remember, to plan, and to keep actions appropriate to time and place. However, the social world in which the human brain and emotions evolved was very different from the present one.

Throughout most of human history (at least 600,000 years, if by "man" we mean the genus *Homo,* large-brained creatures who made complex tools, hunted big animals, and at least some of whom used fire), our ancestors lived in small groups, and (as evidenced by the ethnographic literature, archeology, and the behavior of the nonhuman primates) males were expected to hunt and to fight, and to find these activities pleasurable. Freeman (1964) has given us an anthropological perspective on aggression; the record of war, torture, and planned destruction is exceedingly impressive. Most of the behaviors are so repugnant to our present beliefs and values that people do not want to consider them; in spite of the vast number of courses offered in the modern university, usually there is none on war, and aggression is treated only incidentally in a few courses. As ordinarily taught, history is expurgated, and the historian considers the treaties that were never kept rather than the actual experiences of war.

The situation relative to human aggression can be briefly stated under three headings. First, man has been a predator for a long time and his nature is such that he easily learns to enjoy killing other animals. Hunting is still considered a sport, and millions of dollars are spent annually to provide birds, mammals, and fish to be killed for the amusement of sportsmen. In many cultures animals are killed for the amusement of human observers (in bullfighting, cockfighting, bear baiting, and so forth). Second, man easily learns to enjoy torturing and killing other human beings. Whether one considers the Roman arena, public tortures and executions, or the sport of boxing, it is clear that humans have developed means to enjoy the sight of others being subjected to punishment. Third, war has been regarded as glorious and, whether one considers recent data from tribes in New Guinea or the behavior of the most civilized nations, until very recently war was a normal instrument of national policy and there was no revulsion from the events of victorious warfare, no matter how destructive. Aggression between man and animals, between man and man and between groups of men has been encouraged by custom, learned in play, and rewarded by society. Man's nature evolved under those conditions, and many men still seek personal dominance and national territory through aggression.

The consequence of this evolutionary history is that large-scale human destruction may appear at any time social controls break down; recent examples are Nazi Germany, Algeria, the Congo, Vietnam. Further, it must be remembered that the customs governing our lives evolved in the era when killing animals for fun, the brutal torture of human beings, and war were opposed by few. It is not only our bodies that are primitive, but also our customs, which are not adapted to the crowded and technical world that is dominated by a fantastic acceleration of scientific knowledge. Traditional customs nurtured aggression and frequently continue to do so.

The view that man is aggressive because of his evolutionary past, because of his biological nature, seems pessimistic to some, but we agree with Freeman that if aggression is to be controlled in a way compatible with survival and the realities of the new world of science, "it is only by facing the realities of man's nature and of our extraordinary history as a genus that we shall be able to evolve methods likely, in some measure, to succeed." (1964:116)

The situation might be compared to that of a bank. It is desirable to have employees who are honest people who will abide by the bank's customs. But no bank would rely solely on the honesty of its employees. The best auditing and accounting devices are used to make it virtually impossible for the human element to disrupt the functions of the institution. But on the international scene no comparable institutions for accounting and auditing exist, and reliance is still placed on the judgment of leaders and the customs of states. But these states have used war as a normal instrument of policy, their customs have glorified war, and all history shows that nothing in the human leader will necessarily restrain him from war if he sees success as probable. There is a fundamental difficulty in the fact that contemporary human groups are led by primates whose evolutionary history dictates, through both biological and social transmission, a strong dominance orientation. Attempts to build interindividual relations, or international relations, on the wishful basis that people will not be aggressive is as futile as it would be to try to build the institution of banking with no auditing on the basis that all employees will be honest.

In summary, in Old World monkeys and apes aggression is an essential adaptive mechanism. It is an important factor in determining interindividual relations; it is frequent; and successful aggression is highly rewarded. It is a major factor in intergroup relations, and the importance of aggression as a species-spacing mechanism means that aggression is most frequent between groups of the same species. Both within groups and between groups aggression is an integral part of dominance, feeding, and reproduction. The biological basis of aggressive behaviors is complex, including pasts of the brain, hormones, muscles-teeth-jaws, and structures of display; successful aggression has been a major factor in primate evolution.

Man inherits the biological base, modified by the great development of the social brain and language. Aggression may be increased by early experience, play, and the rewards of the social system. The individual's aggressive actions are determined by biology and experience. But an aggressive species living by prescientific customs in a scientifically advanced world will pay a tremendous price in interindividual conflict and international war.

## REFERENCES

Altman, J., 1966, *Organic Foundations of Animal Behavior.* New York: Holt, Rinehart and Winston, Inc.

Beach, F., 1965*b*, *Sex and Behavior.* New York: Wiley.

Brown, J. L., and R. W. Hunsperger, 1965, "Neuroethology and the Motivation of Agonistic Behavior," *Readings in Animal Behavior,* T. E. McGill, ed. New York: Holt, Rinehart and Winston, Inc., pp. 148–161.

Carpenter, C. R., 1934, "A Field Study of the Behavior and Social Relations of Howling Monkeys (*Alouatta palliata*)," *Comp. Psychol. Monogr.,* 10(2):1–168.

——— , 1940, "A Field Study in Siam of the Behavior and Social Relations of the Gibbon (*Hylobates lar*)," *Comp. Psychol. Monogr.,* 16(5):1–212.

——— , 1964, *Naturalistic Behavior of Nonhuman Primates.* University Park, Pa.: Pennsylvania State University Press.

Carthy, J. D., and F. J. Ebling, eds., 1964, *The Natural History of Aggression.* New York: Academic Press.

Collies, N. E., 1944, "Aggressive Behavior among Vertebrate Animals," *Physio. Zool.,* 17:83–123.

de Reuck, A., and J. Knight, eds., 1966. *Conflict in Society.* Boston: Little, Brown.

DeVore, I., and K. R. L. Hall, 1965, "Baboon Ecology," *Primate Behavior: Field Studies of Monkeys and Apes,* I. DeVore, ed. New York: Holt, Rinehart and Winston, Inc., pp. 20–52.

Freeman, D., 1964, "Human Aggression in Anthropological Perspective," *The Natural History of Aggression,* J. D. Carthy and F. J. Ebling, eds. New York: Academic Press, pp. 109–119.

Goodall, J., 1965, "Chimpanzees of the Gombe Stream Reserve," *Primate Behavior: Field Studies of Monkeys and Apes,* I. DeVore, ed. New York: Holt, Rinehart and Winston, Inc., pp. 425–473.

Hall, K. R. L., 1964, "Aggression in Monkey and Ape Societies," *The Natural History of Aggression,* J. D. Carthy and F. J. Ebling, eds. New York: Academic Press, pp. 51–64.

Hall, K. R. L., and I. DeVore, 1965, "Baboon Social Behavior," *Primate Behavior: Field Studies of Monkeys and Apes,* I. DeVore, ed. New York: Holt, Rinehart and Winston, Inc., pp. 53–110.

Hamburg, D. A., 1963, "Emotion in the Perspective of Human Evolution," *Expression of the Emotions in Man,* P. Knapp, ed. New York: International Universities, pp. 300–317.

Harlow, H. F., 1962, "The Development of Affectional Patterns in Infant Monkeys," *Determinants of Infant Behavior,* B. M. Foss, ed. New York: Wiley, pp. 75–97.

Harris, G., 1964, "Sex Hormones, Brain Development and Brain Function," *Endocrin.,* 75:627–648.

Hinde, R. A., and N. Tinbergen, 1958, "The Comparative Study of Species-Specific Behavior," *Behavior and Evolution,* A. Roe and G. G. Simpson, eds. New Haven: Yale University Press, pp. 251–268.

Jay, P., 1965*a*, "Field Studies," *Behavior of Nonhuman Primates,* A. M. Schrier, H. F. Harlow, and F. Stollnitz, eds. New York: Academic Press, pp. 525–591.

Jay, P., 1965*b*, "The Common Langur of North India," *Primate Behavior: Field Studies of Monkeys and Apes,* I. DeVore, ed. New York: Holt, Rinehart and Winston, Inc., pp. 197–249.

Koford, C., 1966, "Population Changes in Rhesus Monkeys, 1960–1965," *Tul. Studies in Zool.,* 13:1–7.

Kourilsky, R., A. Soulairac, and P. Grapin, 1965, *Adaptation et Agressivité.* Paris: Presses Universitaires de France.

Levine, S., and R. F. Mullins, Jr., 1966, "Hormonal Influences on Brain Organization in Infant Rats," *Science,* 152:1585–1592.

Lorenz, K., 1964, "Ritualized Fighting," *The Natural History of Aggression,* J. D. Carthy and F. J. Ebling, eds. New York: Academic Press, pp. 39–50.

——— , 1966, *On Aggression.* New York: Harcourt.

MacLean, P. D., 1963, "Phylogenesis," *Expression of the Emotions in Man,* P. Knapp, ed. New York: International Universities, pp. 16–35.

McGill, T. E., ed., 1965, *Readings in Animal Behavior.* New York: Holt, Rinehart and Winston, Inc.

Nalbandov, A. V., 1964, *Reproductive Physiology.* San Francisco: W. H. Freeman.

Noback, C. R., and N. Moskowitz, 1963, "The Primate Nervous System: Functional and Structural Aspects in Phylogeny," *Evolutionary and Genetic Biology of Primates,* Vol. I, J. Buettner-Janusch, ed. New York: Academic Press, pp. 131–177.

Prechtl, H. F. R., 1965, "Problems of Behavioral Studies in the Newborn Infant," *Advances in the Study of Behavior,* D. S. Lehrman, R. A. Hinde, and E. Shaw, eds. New York: Academic Press, pp. 75–98.

Rapoport, A., 1966, "Models of Conflict: Cataclysmic and Strategic," *Conflict in Society,* A. de Reuck and J. Knight, eds. Boston: Little, Brown, pp. 259–287.

Reynolds, V., and F. Reynolds, 1965, "Chimpanzees in the Budongo Forest, *Primate Behavior: Field Studies of Monkeys and Apes,* I. DeVore, ed. New York: Holt, Rinehart and Winston, Inc., pp. 368–424.

Rosenblum, L. A., 1961, "The Development of Social Behavior in the Rhesus Monkey," unpublished doctoral thesis, University of Wisconsin.

Sade, D. S., 1965, "Some Aspects of Parent-Offspring and Sibling Relations in a Group of Rhesus Monkeys, with a Discussion of Grooming," *Amer. J. Phys. Anthrop.,* 23:1–17.

Sade, D. S., 1966, "Ontogeny of Social Relations in a Free-ranging Group of Rhesus Monkeys," unpublished Ph.D. thesis, University of California, Berkeley.

Schaller, G. B., 1963, *The Mountain Gorilla: Ecology and Behavior.* Chicago: University of Chicago Press.

Schein, M. W., and E. B. Hale, 1965, "The Effect of Early Social Experience on Male Sexual Behaviour of Androgen Injected Turkeys," *Readings in Animal Behavior,* T. E. McGill, ed. New York: Holt, Rinehart and Winston, Inc., pp. 314–329.

Scott, J. P., 1958, *Aggression.* Chicago: University of Chicago Press.

Scott, J. P., 1962, "Hostility and Aggression in Animals," *Roots of Behavior,* E. L. Bliss, ed. New York: Harper, pp. 167–178.

Simonds, P. E., 1965, "The Bonnet Macaque in South India," *Primate Behavior: Field Studies of Monkeys and Apes,* I. DeVore, ed. New York: Holt, Rinehart and Winston, Inc., pp. 175–196.

Simpson, G. G., 1964, *This View of Life,* New York: Harcourt.

Southwick, C. H., M. A. Beg, and M. R. Siddiqi, 1965, "Rhesus Monkeys in North India," *Primate Behavior: Field Studies of Monkeys and Apes,* I. DeVore, ed., New York: Holt, Rinehart and Winston, Inc., pp. 111–159.

Washburn, S. L., 1966, "Conflict in Primate Society," *Conflict in Society,* A. de Reuck and J. Knight, eds. Boston: Little, Brown, pp. 3–15.

Washburn, S. L., and D. A. Hamburg, 1965a, "The Implications of Primate Research," *Primate Behavior: Field Studies of Monkeys and Apes,* I. DeVore, ed. New York: Holt, Rinehart and Winston, Inc., pp. 607–622.

Washburn, S. L., and P. Jay, 1965, "The Evolution of Human Nature," unpub. paper presented at the Amer. Anthrop. Assoc. Meeting, Denver, Nov. 19, 1965.

Wynne-Edwards, V. C., 1965, "Selfregulating Systems in Populations of Animals," *Science,* 147:1543–1548.

Yamada, M., 1957, "A Case of Acculturation in a Subhuman Society of Japanese Monkeys," *Primates* 1(1):30–46.

Young, W., R. Goy, and C. Phoenix, 1964, "Hormones and Sexual Behavior," *Science,* 143:212–218.

*Dolhinow reexamines a behavioral complex that has recently been interpreted as adaptive: infant death by aggression. In particular, she discusses the case of langur infanticide asking whether the existing evidence is strong enough to support an interpretation of infanticide as an adaptation. As Washburn and Hamburg suggest for aggression, the behavior needs to be considered from as many perspectives of its biology and expression as possible. Dolhinow does this by looking at it from the immature's point of view and from long-term data on langur ontogeny and life history. She also considers the difficulty of using loaded words such as infanticide as the basis for scientific interpretations. How do we measure adaptation? An evolutionary perspective is essential, but we must also keep in mind that a behavior that we isolate for examination may not always have a function or that it might function differently in ordinary and in extraordinary circumstances. Scientific rigor and caution should be applied to this as to other attempts to interpret adaptation.*

# 10    A Mystery: Explaining Behavior

**Phyllis Dolhinow**    *Department of Anthropology, University of California, Berkeley, California*

This is an investigation into a "mystery," a supposed globally widespread complex of behaviors that lead to infant death by aggression. The case we will examine is set in India and Berkeley, California. Our evidence comes from observations of the perpetrators, victims, and innocent bystanders, all Indian "Hanuman," or gray langur monkeys. Langurs, like many primate species, show different patterns of social behavior from one habitat to another as well as over time. In different regions, langur populations differ in density, group size and composition, male transfer from group to group, and levels of aggression. Included in levels of aggression are violent deaths of immatures, labeled by many investigators, prematurely as it turns out, as "infanticides." These are our victims. We have viewed these deaths in oversimple terms as either the product of an adult male evolved reproductive strategy or, in contrast, as events stimulated by stressful living conditions. The purpose of reopening the case is to reconsider old and introduce new evidence—to view the "who done it" from a new perspective. To explore this mystery we need to do more than reidentify what has conventionally been assumed to be the motive, means, and opportunity that lie behind these langur monkey acts of violence.

The reopened case includes evidence derived from a detailed study of generations of langur development, an epigenetic study of langur life course. There are immense numbers of facets to the behavior patterns that characterize the nature of all kinds of primate, and each wrinkle is to a large extent constructed by the magnificently complex processes of development, of nurture (Oyama 1989). By taking a close look at the experiences of infants and juveniles that are undoubtedly important in the construction of adult life, as well as ensuring survival as an immature, we may be able to avoid explaining infanticide, a remarkable adult behavior, only by reference to infant death, which is its presumed effect.

Behaviors may increase fitness and have adaptive value in some contexts but need not have been shaped by evolution (Colwell and King 1983; Jamieson 1986). Under average circumstances the behavior of an immature does not endanger it, but given another set of circumstances, identical actions could prove fatal. In explaining the case of infant death by aggression, infanticide, using an adaptive metaphor, that it is an evolved male reproductive strategy based solely upon benefit for adults, may have restricted our search for information that would allow us to understand the cause of these deaths. Rather than invoking hypothetical and untestable evolutionary explanations, we will learn more about the dead or missing immatures by looking at the behavior of the young langurs, the victims, in the context of the special events of group life.

We will now consider the roles immatures play in fatal outcomes.

## THE CASE OF THE DEAD AND MISSING INFANTS: THE CRIME

There is a mystery afoot, and this is the story of that mystery. In many respects our tale resembles a traditional who done it: We will look for motives, means, and opportunity in an attempt to understand the "crime." However, in the course of our investigation as to *why* it happened, we are going to raise the crucial first question as to whether, in fact, a crime *has* been committed. It has been decades since the first headline in the primatological news media broadcast a startling report of the brutal murders of young langur monkeys by stranger adult males that forced their way into established social groups. The purpose of these assertedly goal-directed, violent "takeovers" by outsider males was said to have been to gain control of the group, do away with all young fathered by other males, inseminate adult females, and in relatively short order, become "father" to the next generation (Hrdy 1977a,b, 1979). "Hanuman langurs (are) a species in which adult males routinely resolve their conflicting interests with females by killing the females' offspring" (Hrdy 1977a). The body count of immatures grew rapidly as every infant and juvenile that went missing was "presumed" to have been slain by infanticidal males. It wasn't long before reports of infanticide were coming in from primate studies in locations around the world. Then, low and behold, more and more nonprimate creatures, invertebrates and vertebrates, furred, feathered, or finned, were added to the ranks of perpetrators. As the lists lengthened, so did the numbers and kinds of explanations for the phenomenon.

For the primates on the list it was asserted that the killings, infanticides, were the result of behavior firmly embedded in and directed by the genes. The slayings represented "evolved reproductive strategies" and eventually even attained the status of being a major reason for primate sociality. Infanticide had become part of the popular discourse of the discipline. The only dissenting suggestion, that the fatal attacks might reflect social pathology, generally was dismissed as unlikely, with mutterings of ineffable twaddle. It is highly likely that when we get around to looking closely at the myriad cases from many orders of animals we will discover the phenomenon, labeled so quickly as infanticide, is not the same everywhere, but is exceedingly complicated and has many causes in a vast array of settings. However, where better to begin this inquiry but with the Indian langur monkey where it first began? As for langur monkeys, do we have a case of mayhem and murder, of infanticide? Have we a solved set of murders, complete with motive, means, and opportunity? Is it the case that these brutish males were acting out a scenario built into their "natures" by the stern dictates of genes? Or perhaps we are mistaken in our interpretation of the events, most of which, do not forget, were unwitnessed. Is there another as yet unconsidered body of evidence to help us understand what happened when these young langurs suffered grievous and sometimes fatal harm? It will become clear that how you study behavior, your questions, assumptions, and methods, will guide your definition of evidence and thereby shape your interpretations of why animals act the way they do. Nowhere is this clearer than in the case of the dead and missing infants.

## HISTORY: EVIDENCE

> Facts are stubborn things; and whatever may be our wishes, our inclinations, or the dictates of our passions, they cannot alter the state of facts and evidence. (John Adams, 1770)

The earliest reports of infant killing by langur monkeys appeared in the 1960s, but they did not capture the attention of the primatological community until Hrdy's 1974 presentation of infant death by aggression as a sexual selection hypothesis (see Boggess 1979 and 1984 for reviews). The data to support her thesis were drawn from three locations in India: Abu, Jodhpur, and Dharwar. It was not long before reports of presumed infant killing in other kinds of monkeys began to appear (Wolfe & Fleagle 1977; Poirer and Kanner 1989), reports that were at times a reinterpretation of events recorded earlier or, for example, a reevaluation of the meaning of immature disappearances that occurred when adult males moved in and out of groups (Leland et al. 1984).

A major but glossed-over troublesomeness with many of these reports was the fact that very seldom were there eyewitnesses to presumed infanticides, and the bodies often were not recovered. Although the numbers of presumed deaths by adult male aggression grew, the evidence remained, in sum, less than compelling. This was the situation in spite of the fact that a bibliography on infanticide in the nonhuman primates containing 245 references was published in 1991 by the Primate Information Center (Williams 1991). Bartlett et al. (1993) recently reviewed infant killing in primates and stated that the number of well-documented cases of infant death as a result of adult males attack is surprisingly small. In 13 primate species, of 48 cases in which the death was actually observed, half, 21, were by Indian langur monkeys; and more than half of langur deaths were from one site: Jodhpur (Bartlett et al. 1993; Sommer 1993). They note that this single location accounted for 27 percent of the total number of cases reviewed for all the nonhuman primates.

In retrospect it is, to say the least, puzzling why such modest evidence was assumed to be sufficient to serve as proof for an evolved reproductive strategy. This strategy, the sexual selection hypothesis, asserts that infanticidal males gain reproductive advantage over other males by selectively killing the latter's immature offspring. These fatal attacks accomplish two things. One is to eliminate a rival's progeny, and the second is to shorten the interbirth intervals of the dead infants' mothers so that the new adult male might inseminate the females to produce infants. Hrdy and Hausfater assert, "In the case of sexually selected infanticide among primates, for example, it is predicted that (1) infanticidal behavior is heritable; (2) that an infanticidal male will typically not be the father of any infant he kills: (3) that on average the killer will gain sexual access to the mother sooner than if the infant had lived: and (4) that the reproductive gain to the killer will be a function of the average tenure length and age of the infant at death" (1984: xix) More on these predictions later in this paper, but for now let it be sufficient to note that they assumed these behaviors were written in the genes. It was a short step from there to the construction of mathematical models of the impact of infanticide as it was to an extension of the definition of infanticide to incorporate "any form of lethal curtailment of parental investment in offspring brought about by conspecifics," including destruction of gametes or reabsorption of a fetus (Hrdy and Hausfater 1984: xix)!

At first, observers described infanticide as harmful, but as time passed infant deaths by aggression were gradually wrapped in a cloak of normalcy, and eventually they came to be considered adaptive behavior on the part of the killer adult males. From there it was but a short step to regarding the then assumed ever-present threat of infanticide to be a prime mover in the construction of primate sociality (Dunbar 1984; van Schaik and Dunbar 1990; van Schaik and Kappeler 1992). A few investigators went on record interpreting the mayhem of male takeovers and subsequent deaths as nonadaptive and definitely not what it seemed to those arguing an evolved reproductive strategy (Boggess 1979, 1980, 1982; Curtin 1977; Curtin and Dolhinow 1978; Dolhinow 1977; Schubert 1982). More than a decade ago Schubert provided a strong challenge to conventional thinking on infanticidal behavior and described it as academic mythology in which data were unabashedly manipulated to fit a model. " . . . the stretching of the evidence said to be in favor of the sexual selection hypothesis cannot be justified; and hence,

in view of the conspicuous notoriety of Hrdy's model, it must be understood to be a myth of our contemporary academic culture rather than to be a scientific fact" (1982: 201).

## WORDS

Let's pause before going further into reopening the case of langur infanticide to reflect on how our use of words, such as "murder" and "infanticide," might have colored our thinking from the time we first identified the phenomenon. It is always sound practice to define all terms at the outset of any investigation. Doing so sets the parameters of the problem and thereby helps adjudge what evidence is required in the study. It is particularly important in the case under consideration to make clear the full meanings popular culture places on some of the key words used in this investigation. When we read in the morning paper that someone has murdered an infant, committed infanticide, we are outraged–our society condemns this act and metes its strongest punishment to the perpetrator. We do this from an informed position because we understand the nature of the biological and social ties that exist between generations. We assign through law and custom a value to and a responsibility for the young life, and define a harsh penalty for breaking the convention of safety guaranteed our children.

According to the Oxford American Dictionary, infanticide is "murder of an infant soon after its birth" (1980: 337). Black's Law Dictionary defines it as "the murder or killing of an infant soon after its birth. The fact of the birth distinguishes this act from 'feticide' or 'procuring abortion' which terms denote the destruction of the *fetus* in the womb" (1990: 778). Murder in the Oxford American Dictionary is "the intentional and unlawful killing of one person by another" (1980: 438), and in Black's is "the unlawful killing of a human being by another with malice aforethought, either express or implied" (1990: 1019). Part and parcel of our understanding of infanticide is the intentional and unlawful killing of a young infant with malice aforethought.

How has infanticide been defined and used by those who have diagnosed it among the nonhuman primates? Quite variably. To promote ease of comprehension over a number disciplines, one definition has been "any behavior that makes a direct and significant contribution to the immediate death of an embryo or newly hatched or born member of the perpetrator's own species" (Hausfater and Hrdy 1984: xiv). To make the definition include "any form of lethal curtailment of a parental investment in offspring brought about by conspecifics," Hrdy and Hausfater (1984) broaden it to include destruction of gametes or reabsorption of a fetus. "Only by viewing foeticide-infanticide-pedicide in the context of the whole range of possible manipulations of the reproductive continuum can we make meaningful statements about the selective value of infanticidal behavior in cost-benefit terms" (p. xv). They continue by "recommending the use, at least over the next few years, of such a broad definition . . . to avoid at this early stage in research narrowing of focus to the point that we arbitrarily exclude from consideration any of the remarkably diverse array of intraspecific social behaviors which lead to decreased survival of immature" (p. xv).

It is wonderfully convenient to think that words may mean what we want them to mean; indeed, nothing prevents us from redefining any term—it happens regularly in the literature. However, there are consequences when a term such as "infanticide" is defined so expansively that it encompasses many ages and all manner of insult from lethal to merely an inconvenience. It lumps occurrences willy-nilly, behaviors with many different causes and contexts as though dealing with one kind of occurrence. Using the same identification leads a person to assume that there is a uniformity to the items so labeled, but when we review the examples from many different kinds of animals, vertebrates and invertebrates, all designated victims of infanticide, we see that this is not the case. The net effect of a hippopotamic definition has been to trivialize the search for understanding of the cases that originally stimulated the investigation and those reported since that time. In addition to muddling the events that have happened in a large number of dissimilar creatures, it also, unfortunately, makes it remarkably easy to commit the error of affirming the consequent (Estling 1983). The very existence of a presumed effect, a dead or missing infant, is taken as proof of an ostensible cause, an infanticide. Furthermore, the infanticide then becomes the proof of an evolved reproductive strategy. While minds may work this way, science does not.

## THE CAST OF CHARACTERS: INCLUDING SUSPECTS AND VICTIMS

The common langur monkey lives from Nepal, throughout India, to Sri Lanka in an extensive range of habitats, including desert margins, cultivated fields, city centers, and many types of forest. Langur population density varies enormously, from less than 20 animals per square mile at Orcha to more than 340 at Dharwar. Efforts to measure the effects of humans on the habitats of South Asian monkeys have met with mixed success because of the great complexity of environments and the almost insurmountable difficulties of comparing vicinities (e.g., Bishop et al. 1981). Throughout their distribution langurs live in three kinds of groups: females and young with one adult male (one-male group), females and young with more than one adult male (multimale group), and groups containing only males. The three group types are found in every population, though the proportion of each type differs from one locality to another. Field studies from many sites have constructed a clear picture of the remarkable adaptability of langur monkey social organization and its high degree of behavioral variability (Curtin and Dolhinow 1978; Jay 1965).

Although the ecological and social contexts of life vary widely, there are universal elements to a langur monkey's life wherever it is born (Dolhinow 1972). The conspicuous newborn, with bare pink hands, feet, and face and dark brown fur, is a center of interest for young and old females alike. It may be passed among the females for hours on the first and each succeeding day of life for weeks (Dolhinow 1991; Jay 1962, 1963a). Passing infants among members of the group usually involves little stress to the immature, although at times it may be traumatic and costly for the infant as when, for example, a holder does not wish to give it up or a rambunctious tug-of-war centers on the infant (Dolhinow and Murphy 1982; Hrdy 1977b). But very young infants are far from helpless—they are active, persistent, opportunistic manipulators of their social world (Dolhinow 1991; Dolhinow and DeMay 1982). When the infant is about 5 weeks old, and is first able to struggle free from its holder, the frequency of passing infants from one female to another declines to almost zero. The rapidly maturing infant concentrates on exploring an expanding physical and social world, as free from maternal restrictions as possible. Weaning is a process that culminates toward the end of the first or the beginning of the second year of life and it heralds increasing independence for the young langur.

Although they have much more in common than not, male and female langurs follow somewhat divergent paths of development soon after the first year of life. The young female usually associates with adult females and manifests great interest in new infants, whereas the young male tends to spend more time away from the adult females, whom they often annoy, in other activities such as roughhousing play. The spheres of their activity gradually diverge, and males as young as 15 months may leave the natal group to join an all-male band (Mohnot 1978; Sommer, personal communication). Leaving the group of birth appears to be usual for male langurs and they may live apart from females for years at a time. The female, on the other hand, remains in her original group, perhaps for her entire lifetime. She reaches sexual maturity and then has her first infant when she is about 4 years old. Males of that age who are still in their birth group are far from being adults and they will not take a place in the adult ranks until they are mature.

The adult females in a group are held together within a network of relations based on rank and personality. There is seldom a tidy linear rank order. Instead, there are clusters or layers of more or less controlling or dominant females with, in larger groups, clearly delineated hierarchies among some of the females. Young adult females are often ranked highly and have their way in conflicts over places, things, and individuals; however, there are notable exceptions, and most females change ranks over the course of maturity with events in the life cycle such as pregnancies, births, and health-related events including sickness or injury affecting female social status. One female with a newborn might go out of her way to remain at the greatest distance possible from aggression, while another might, without a nanosecond of hesitation, plunge into the midst of a fierce fight with her infant clinging to her ventrum. In short, the observer may rank many, if not most, adult females in a group with respect to specific situations, but there are a number of exceptions, and rankings change due to many factors in normal life. A major confounding variable is personality or individual style. There are adult females best characterized as aggressive, determined, "won't take no for an answer" individuals. Others may get what or go where they want with a minimum of fanfare and a seeming propensity to avoid agonistic interactions. Our ranking of some females might reflect the topography of the tip of the iceberg with her motivations the unknown and perhaps unknowable major portion out of sight. A female's rank and relations change over the decade or more during which she survives as an adult, perhaps very slowly or relatively little, but in some cases before she dies she will have occupied positions from top to bottom in the human conception of hierarchy. The only thing we ought to assume about our assessment of a female langur's rank or status is that our evaluation might be partially correct and only under certain circumstances.

We see a different pattern in males. It is likely that all male langurs leave their natal group, some rather early in life. Reasons for departure may include aggravated relations with adults, as large juveniles and young subadults become very annoying with their boisterous activity and insolent challenges to and sometimes apparent disregard for established social order. Perhaps more often than being kicked out, the cause for leaving is curiosity and the ever-present opportunity to join a nearby all-male group that might include relatives and/or familiar males. Their motivation for leaving isn't readily apparent, but it is important that leaving is not necessarily preceded by heightened aggression with others in the group. We know little about the relations of males in all-male groups in the field (Moore 1984), but in the Berkeley colony we have extensive information about the very complex relations that build and wane among males (Curtin 1981; Dolhinow and Taff 1993; Moorhouse 1980; Taff 1990).

Adult males in reproductive groups with females and young can be ranked relative to many activities. There is usually a clearly defined priority of access among the males when it comes to food, sleeping or resting places, and, sometimes to a lesser degree, copulations with receptive females. Attempts at linear rankings are confounded in many instances by alliances between males, but the important point is that regardless of whether males act alone or in concert, there is normally little conflict and rarely serious fighting. While these rankings usually enable the observer to predict which males will consort with sexually receptive females, there are notable exceptions, as when female choice taps a middle- or low-ranking male in a total shutout of higher ranking males. As one might expect, this creates a difficult situation for the male of choice, especially when the adult female persists in expressing her preference in the face, so to speak, of the higher ranked male (Jay 1963b; personal observation).

Relations between adult males and females are extremely variable, depending on the individual. Some adults show strong preferences for association and interaction and may consistently seek out a specific individual to be near. Other adults avoid one another. These patterns of preferential interaction can remain constant for years or change slowly or very quickly, depending on events in the group and a host of other factors relating to one or both members of the pair. The birth of an infant often does not change association patterns that have developed between an adult male and the mother.

Relations among males are typically characterized by cooperation, accommodation, and give-and-take. Avoidance is used often as a means of preventing confrontation, and coalitions, however temporary or shifting, effectively serve to dampen a langur's temper when coordinated action is directed toward an aggressor. Motor strength and agility, competitiveness, problem-solving ability, and social savvy are among the many intervening variables influencing male competitive and affiliative interactions. Although it is possible to anticipate the outcome of many conflict situations, there are consequential times when it is not possible to predict what will happen because we do not know the variables an individual male uses to make choices of action or inaction—options are always available.

Male mobility from one group to another is typical of this species, but the results of this movement vary. When female langurs are sexually receptive, and this can be concentrated in a few weeks, males from nearby all-male groups enter the multimale group to copulate. As Laws and Vonder Haar Laws note for Rajaji, "Relations between bisexual troops and all-male bands are characterized by relatively low levels of aggression, and members of all-male bands are able to associate with bisexual troops for prolonged periods during the mating season. As a result of these associations, non troop males are about as successful as troop males in achieving reproductive access to troop females. These associations between bisexual troops and all-male bands occurred with a minimal amount of agonistic behavior and without mortality or injury to troop females or immatures" (1984: 31).

This is in stark contrast with the "takeover" scenario described by Hrdy for the langurs at Abu (1977a, b) and by Sommer and other for Jodhpur (Agoramoorthy and Mohnot 1988; Sommer 1993). At both of these locations the result of forced and strongly disputed entry is carnage. Young are killed or disappear at a frightful cost to the group. Sommer estimates that 22% of immatures are killed by infanticidal males (p. 154, ms). This is, of course, in addition to death from common causes, such as congenital defects, inadequate care, disease, predation, or injury. It does not require complex computations to realize that local populations could not withstand such devastation for more than a few generations before collapsing.

If we plot the occurrence of aggression, of intense male conflict throughout langur populations, what we have appears to be less a normal distribution than an "$n$-dimensional" hypervolume (Hutchinson 1957). In addition to peacekeeping cooperation, coordination, and compromise, it is clear that bickering, conflict, clash, competition, disagreement, resistance, and coercion are also common elements of daily social life wherever langurs have been observed. This normal range of agonistic behavior is extended by leaps and bounds by the conflict in a few other locations where the results of aggression are staggering. It is clear that langur monkeys are capable of behaving in exceedingly different ways, depending on many aspects of their living conditions.

## A FOCUS ON IMMATURITY

So far the interest researchers have shown in young assault victims has been limited almost entirely to whether they are genetically related to the attacking male and, if so, how closely. Young langurs have been tokens or pawns in a much larger evolutionary game whose final reckoning presumes to decide reproductive success for adults and particular males. Reminded of the venerable adage "I wouldn't have seen it if I hadn't believed it," it is not surprising that attention was seldom directed to the actions of the infants and juveniles because they were not considered "first-string" players in the action. Attention was directed toward those animals the observers were certain would be important. Fatal attacks, or attacks of any kind, usually happen quickly and invariably are quite unpredictable. They are seldom witnessed from start to finish; and it is no wonder we lack records of all of the adult participants, let alone detailed observations of what befalls immatures that become involved. This is not a criticism of the observers, it is a simple statement of regrettable human limitations in predicting and/or following all that happens in times of prodigious activity. But perhaps our attention on the adults has led us to overlook key aspects of the infants' disappearances, injuries, and deaths. Thus it is time to concentrate on young langurs, the class of animals providing victims to fuel the so-called evolved reproductive strategies of infanticidal males.

After having observed more than 20 years of five generations of langurs maturing in stable social groups constituted as they would be in the field in their native India, it is impossible to think about infants, and certainly not small juveniles, mainly as dependent or helpless. Of course, the very young infant would not survive without constant and considerable care (Dolhinow and Murphy 1982); and its need for support, although becoming less and less continues long after close ties with the mother are lessened. Whereas the tactics of adulthood, the choices and maneuvers leading to success or fitness, could fill volumes, the tactics that structure daily life activities for the young have been given short shrift if considered at all. Young langurs are sensitive to the smallest details of their surroundings, they make choices, broadcast their feelings, pleasures and displeasure, and endeavor to attain what they want. They are quick to learn the best ways, or at times the only possible ways, to manipulate the animals around them. It isn't an easy task, learning by trial and error. There is a tremendous range in how quickly these skills are acquired and at what cost, and once possessed, how effectively they are employed (Dolhinow 1991).

A critical component of the infant's environment is its mother, and it is impossible at this stage of our investigation to know the full extent to which her attributes and relations facilitate and limit her offspring's life course. Maternal "style," for lack of a better term, is exceedingly difficult to delineate and measure in scientifically approved units, but it exists. The most perceptive and well-organized infant accomplishes naught if its mother isn't a supportive, or at least a cooperating, part of the calculus. Her attributes—tolerances, tensions, preferences, health, experiences, friends, enemies, to name but a few—interact to make her, among many possibilities, permissive, restrictive, gentle, punishing, ignoring, attentive—and ever-changing combinations of these attributes depending on what is happening in her life (Dolhinow and Krusko 1984). The details of a mother's behavior are not givens. Mothers respond differently in adversity: Some move instantly to retrieve or protect their infant, whereas others may pay little or no heed to the infant regardless of the source or nature of the problem. Most mothers monitor their infants well, although they may do so very unobtrusively, seeming almost by radar to know when intervention or assistance is appropriate. Maternal vigilance wanes as the young langur grows older and becomes more adept at managing its own affairs. To complicate things, a female's treatment of successive offspring may vary pronouncedly.

With this as the setting, no matter what type of mother the infant draws, all healthy infants typically demonstrate intense interest in what goes on around them. This is notably the case when there is action and excitement, whether of a routine nature such as harassments or copulations, or more serious as the jockeying accompanying the introduction of a new animal into the group. Not only does the young langur stare fixedly at the action, it goes to investigate. After monitoring visually for a short time, the infant or juvenile approaches, follows, and often actually contacts the animal or animals it was focusing on. The attention of infants as young as 4 or 5 months, both males and females, is riveted to whatever action is going on, and the youngster apparently does not hesitate to approach and become interactive with adults. This is true even when the adult is a male and new to the social group. During times of group excitement it is important to realize that mothers differ greatly in the extent to which they restrict, retrieve, carry, or attempt to control their infants. Some mothers seem preoccupied with interactions and are apparently unaware of the whereabouts of an offspring, especially when the latter is an older infant. It is fascinating that some infants seek out specific adolescent or adult females other than the mother for contact or protection in stressful times.

On rare occasions during the colony's 20 years it has been necessary to replace the adult male or males in a group with new and sometimes unfamiliar males because of, for example, death or the need to avoid inbreeding (Moorhouse 1980; Taff 1990). In every instance the group contained infants and usually juveniles when the new male or males were introduced. Never did one of these new males attack or injure an infant or a juvenile. There were no attacks and no infanticides, and it is very important to note that the new adult males were not the fathers of any of the immatures in the group. The following examples, drawn from records made during introductions, illustrate typical patterns of behavior among group members of all ages during introductions.

Following the introduction of a young adult male into an established social group after the group's adult male was removed, the new male's interactions with two large male juveniles were the most important determinants of his aggression. Relations between the adult male and juveniles were tense and involved interactions initiated by each. Although the adult sometimes approached the juveniles spontaneously, they also approached him. Constant staring by the juveniles frequently stimulated the male's approach. Regardless of which animal was responsible, as soon as they got near one another, it lead to avoidance by the young langurs and then following by the adult male. These follows quickly became chases, and the adult did not appear to try to make contact with the young langurs, although he could easily have done so. Adult females frequently became involved, either as they avoided the adult or as they intervened on behalf of the juveniles. Twenty-seven of 40 aggressive acts directed by adult females to the male were in response to the adult males' attentions toward the juveniles, usually his following them, but sometimes it only required his moving in their direction. Six of 13 aggressive acts by the male were toward the females in response to their interventions on behalf of the immatures. Within about two weeks, relations in the group were once again mainly calm; as with the previous adult male, aggression was infrequent and observed only in normal circumstances, such as occasional mild disputes over food or perches.

Recently, two adult males, aged 11 and 14 years, were placed in a group where the adult male died suddenly. The new males had lived together for years in an all-male group and knew each other exceedingly well. They had established a very well defined ranking between them with one male more controlling in every circumstance. There was not a trace of doubt in the human observers' minds that they would get along well with each other and that the dominant one from the all-male group would make a splendid top-ranking male in the group with females and young. What follows will come as no surprise to the seasoned primate observer, and, in retrospect, it certainly would have been on the list of all possible outcomes had we written such a document.

There was a rank reversal on day one and it has lasted to the present. It must be emphasized that the switch was not the result of any visible contest between the males. Complex, rapid, untidy, confused interactions filled the hours after the introduction, all recorded but requiring months of work to analyze in detail. One thing is certain, however; it was the adult females that clearly served as catalyst for the males' rank flip-flop. The most retiring, low ranking, picked-upon adult female in the group, the one we would have voted unanimously as the least likely even to raise her head to watch a chase, was the most aggressive, interactive, determined, furious animal in the group by what seemed a factor of 10. She exploded into action and tirelessly chased, slapped, bit, and harassed both adult males until they panted and sought a place out of sight to escape her wrath. When the harridan attacked, the other three adult females in the group often quickly followed suit with resulting periods of intense and chaotic activity. All that it would take to ignite her fury seemed to be the mere sight of one of the two males moving from one place to another.

This high-pitched action lasted intermittently for several days and then gradually decreased to only an occasional brief chase or threat. During the entire time, days of high action, the only visible blood was a slight bit from some of the patches of hair that had been pulled from one of the adult males. Remarkably, neither adult male returned the females' attack in kind, but rather chose to run, or at most, to stop abruptly and turn to face the harassers. The quick stop seemed to startle the chasing females and made them desist, at least temporarily. Throughout the period of the females' harassment of the new adult males the ranking between the latter remained constant in a position of reversal from their previous years together.

When the two adult males were introduced, the group contained three infants, two males, and a female, all approximately 1½ years of age and unrelated to either male. From the moment the adult males entered the group the attention of the three infants was riveted on them and the ensuing action. The three were old enough that they were not always carried by their mothers, and hence were not directly involved in most chases. In fact, the female infant spent most of her time near and in contact with one of the adult females, not her mother, when the stress levels were high and the infant wanted comfort from an adult. This choice reflected a waning relationship with the mother who tended to be rather punitive and rejecting.

The infants were responsible for all interactions that occurred between them and the adult males. If contact was gained and then maintained for short periods it was due to the infant's initiative. Variability among the three infants in their interactions with the males depended on a number of factors, including the mother's behavior and her interactions with the males. Although the three infants had approached and interacted with the previous group adult male, it was done much less frequently than their similar attentions to the new males. Neither of the new adult males behaved aggressively to any of the infants, regardless of the latter's behavior. This included when one or more of the young langurs would watch and then be attracted to the moving or running males and dash up, squealing loudly, and attempt to touch the male, often getting right in the path of the rapidly moving adult. This required some fancy footwork on the male's part to avoid stepping on or tripping over the infant. It was always the obviously curious, although at times cautious, infant that was responsible for interaction with the males. In fact, the attitude of both males generally seemed to be utter indifference toward the infants.

As was often the case when the adult females were acting aggressively toward the new adult males, there were times when the females' actions placed the infants clinging to their ventrums at risk. This risk included, for example, falling off when the mother runs flat out and jumps up, or down, 10 or more feet, or of getting slammed into a branch, or on the ground, because of a hard, fast landing. Perhaps even more important than the bumps and lumps from getting rammed into a branch during rushing about, a mother's behavior can put her infant at risk of being in the middle, literally, of the action between herself and another animal during a skirmish that involves aggressive physical contact. Adult females were often quick to threaten infants, even their own, when the latter got in the way during a chase or a scuffle. If an infant got nipped or slapped, it was far more often by the female than by an adult male.

In the above example of the two adult males entering an established social group, it was the human observers' strong unanimous conviction that the mere possibility of coordinated adult female attack kept the adult males from provoking any of the young monkeys whenever it was in their power to avoid doing so. Fear of attack is a powerful motivater, even when it is fear of attack by a single female, but certainly when it is by several females. I suspect this is a much more important factor in male-female relations than has been given credit in most field studies. The only times in India when I witnessed one or more females attacking an adult male occurred immediately after a male inadvertently frightened an infant. It does not require much imagination to picture females responding aggressively to males even in circumstances when the females' agonism might place them and their infants in greater jeopardy than they were already.

The infant female presented to each of the new males on many occasions during their first few days in the group. She would approach noisily, squealing, and when within a few feet of the male, she would present repeatedly, dropping her tail and looking over her small shoulder toward him, just as an adult female would. Curtin saw similar behavior in a female less than 8 months of age (1984). Invariably the response of the male was to ignore her completely, though he might look at her briefly as she approached. If he were to dash in her direction, because he was chased, he carefully avoided stepping on her even when this required breaking his stride and made him careen into a branch or against a wall. Later, after some days when the group settled down, the infant female began to approach and groom the males.

A different set of experiences and interaction typical of immature male-adult male relations is observed in the colony and in some, but not all, field locations. Jay first noted that infant and juvenile males often approached and touched or tried to contact adult and subadult males when the latter walked or ran past them (Jay 1963b; and personal observation). The young male races up to the adult, while squealing or screeching, stares at the adult intensely, and tries to touch, embrace, or stay in contact with him. Usually there are no negative repercussions for the immature as the adult is not aggressive and ignores the young male's actions, even his contact. When there is tension, and the adult might be fighting or chasing animals, the young males continue to approach as when the group is calm. Even when occupied in strenuous interaction, the adult male seems unaware of the youngster and may run into or over him if he gets in the way. It is obvious that the young males do not avoid adult males when there is fighting even when proximity to the action places them at risk. An approach and contact that normally carries no penalty for the juvenile can come at a gravely high price if it is done at the wrong time, as it might be in some Indian locations when males are fighting seriously during a "takeover" or entry into a new group.

Lest it be thought that no comparable situation exists between immatures and adult females, infants approach adult females when there is excitement and/or fighting. In fact infants are almost certain to try to gain contact with the mother in times of stress and fighting, even when she is a major actor in the mayhem. Many adult females in the field and some in the colony have been seen to reject an infant that is trying to cling or be carried when she is in the midst of a fray, and the form of this rejection can be severe. Boggess recorded considerable redirected aggression toward infants by adult females in Nepal (1979), and McKenna noted accidental harm to immatures during periods of upheaval in a colony group of langurs (1982). One female in India was seen to tear her infant from her ventrum in her attempt to flee from an opponent. She was high in a tree at the time and it remained for an adult male to dash to the ground and retrieve the stunned fallen infant (personal observation). There is no reason to doubt that females kill infants, intentionally directing aggression to the young as well as unintentionally or accidentally. Certainly having an infant on the ventrum does not stop an adult female from serious fighting. Placing blame for unobserved instances of infant wounding or death solely on adult males is an act of faith based on assumption rather than evidence.

## PLOTS AND SOLUTIONS

Langur monkeys have been studied in many locations, including captivity, during the last four decades. Primarily because of the diversity of environments in which the animals live, patterns of group life vary dramatically, from minimally aggressive to regular periods of mayhem and fighting with fatal results. Locations such as Jodhpur, Abu, and Dharwar present puzzling different behavior profiles than observed at, for example, Orcha, Kaukori, Rajaji, and Junbesi (see Bartlett et al. 1993 for summary of these sites). At the former set of sites sometimes astonishingly high rates of infant and juvenile disappearance and death accompanied takeovers when adult males forced their way into groups replacing resident males. Missing infants, presumed killed, as well as the young whose bodies were recovered were labeled victims of infanticide and the killing described as the inevitable result of an evolved male reproductive strategy. This sexual selection hypothesis quickly gained ground in the interpretive accounts of injury in a majority of primate study locations, but our concern here is only with langurs. Almost as an afterthought, other elaborate and evolved strategies were then identified for langur females to help them balance the dreadful costs of losing their offspring to selfish infanticidal males. Her strategies ranged from tricking a potentially killer male by pretending to be sexually receptive so that he could not determine paternity to deserting a wounded infant because its chances of survival were low.

An evolutionary strategy does not refer to the day-to-day behavior of individuals, it is an abstraction representing generalized schema of populational properties. To qualify as an evolved reproductive strategy, as certain researchers claim infanticide to be, it must have a genetic basis and be heritable, increase the fitness of the animals possessing the trait, and have come about as the result of natural selection. We have reviewed some of the data on which the sexual selection model was based; now let us see what claims were made when infanticide was granted the status of an evolved reproductive strategy. Hrdy and Hausfater asserted that "in the case of sexually selected infanticide among primates, for e.g., it is predicted that (1) Infanticide behavior is heritable; (2) that an infanticidal male will typically not be the father of any infant he kills; (3) that on average the killer will gain sexual access to the mother sooner than if the infant had lived; and (4) that the reproductive gain to the killer will be a function of the average tenure length and age of the infant at death" (1984: xix). Predictions are fine, they are legitimate steps in understanding, but they do not become fact simply by assertion or repetition.

Look closely at some at these predictions, starting with the assertion that infanticidal behavior is heritable. Sons of infant killer fathers must be more likely to kill infants than will sons of other males in the population. When we review all available information there is no evidence to support the assertion that this behavior is heritable. The error here is in assuming that there was a correlation between the phenotype and reproductive success and that this assumed correlation meant that natural selection was operating on genetically transmitted differences. Genetic transmission of the trait infanticide was assumed, not demonstrated, to have reproductive advantage as the result of natural selection, a classic example of the Sower's Fallacy (Colwell and King 1983).

The adaptive significance of any behavior can only be measured in the future and cannot be part of the calculus of the behavior's origin. Neither langurs nor genes are prescient, a fact that should have instilled caution in the originators of the "explanation" of infanticide for events at a few locations in India. It was clear then as it is now what we need to know to test the hypothesis that males killed other males' infants to bring mothers into sexual receptivity and thereby to be able to inseminate them. For a starter, the kin relations of all actors must be known, and this includes paternity for the infants that are killed as well as, of course, of the infants to be born. Infant death must shorten the interbirth interval for a mother. The lifetime reproduction records for all males must be known to determine whether males that killed did better in the long run than males that did not.

And what is it that langur males presumably are able to calculate to bring on line their reproductive strategy? Before committing infanticide the male taking over the group must evaluate his potential victim's age and then perform a computation; he must in some way count back the $6\frac{1}{2}$-month time of a langur gestation to the date of conception. For a 1-year-old infant this would mean going back approximately 18 months. The adult male must be certain he did not copulate with the infant's mother at that time or he will lose his advantage and kill his own offspring. Before an image of a langur with pencil and calendar makes the argument more trivial than it already is, be aware that no mechanism has been offered to explain how an animal comes to know what he needs to know. Necessary information includes both a concept of time and an understanding that copulations lead to conception, to pregnancy, to birth, to infant—biological events not fully understood by many modern humans. It appears that the sexual selection model was not generated as a result of observations; rather, it was a creation of assumptions.

In only 8 of 48 cases is there convincing evidence that the infanticidal male fathered the next infant of those females that had lost their last offspring by aggression (Bartlett et al. 1993). In other instances it appears that the victim may have been an infant or juvenile fathered by the killer. Often an attack does not result in death for hours or days, and to call the attack a killing is premature and inaccurate. All that the attacker can experience is having wounded a young langur, if in fact the attacker is conscious that its actions had any effect. Boggess noted that because infanticidal attacks regularly occurred in an atmosphere of generalized aggression within and among the sexes, it was not possible to identify the main target of the attack. "If an infant is injured in an atmosphere of aggressive dominance displays, is it not more parsimonious to suggest that the infant's death is an incidental consequence of high aggression levels—particularly when infanticide is so rare? Ultimately, infanticide may be the occasional outcome of even "normal" levels of aggression" (1979: 977). This view of infanticide as an epiphenomenon of elevated levels of aggression, an artifact of males attempting to establish themselves in a new social group, rather than an evolved reproductive strategy, fits the existing data.

What, then, are the alternatives to a sexual selection explanation for the deaths and disappearances of langur infants and juveniles? Perhaps we may understand many of the fatalities if we add our richly detailed records of development during the first years of life to our review of the information on male rivalry and movement among groups in India. Traditionally in human society when a crime such as murder is committed, the unlawful killing of a human being by another with malice aforethought, we may start to discover the perpetrator by considering who might have motive, opportunity, and means. Let us ask this of our nonhuman primate langur suspects.

Motive? This is legally defined as "cause or reason that moved the will and induces action. An idea, belief or emotion that impels or incites one to act in accordance with his state of mind or emotion" (Black's 1990: 1014). In law, a distinction is drawn between motive and intent, although in common usage the two are frequently regarded as one and the same thing. "'Motive' is said to be the moving course, the impulse, the desire that induces criminal action on part of the accused: it is distinguished from 'intent' which is the purpose or design with which the act is done, the purpose to make the means adopted effective" (Black's 1990: 1014). To ask for motive or intent in a monkey killing (we shall not call it murder) implies a reason for the killing, an intentionality and a plan of some sort for the accomplishment of the deed.

The sexual selection hypothesis, which was offered as an explanation of the adult male's motivation to kill unrelated young langurs, is not supported by the great majority of evidence from the field. So after rejecting the sexual selection hypothesis of infanticide as a reproductive strategy, what can we suggest? Let us look at a reconstruction of what might have happened to bring about infant fatality. In many of the accounts of the action preceding attacks that resulted in injury, it seems there are very high levels of aggression often involving a number of animals, both male and female. Adult males enter a social group, a "takeover" in Hrdy's terms (1977a), and fight with the resident males, and it seems with the females as well when the latter resist contact. When an adult male acts aggressively for more than a brief time, the level of tension usually escalates in proportion to the resistance he encounters as well as the length of time spent fighting. Some, but by no means all or even the majority of adult males appear to go into an "attack mode" when experiencing very high arousal. At that point they do not modulate their aggression, or control which animal becomes the target. An adult male normally does not attack an immature, and seldom attacks an adult female unless she persistently acts to provoke him, and then often not even with provocation (personal observation). It is possible that judgment during the heat of an aggressive takeover may be clouded by excitement or arousal. It is also possible that the few males that do kill young are those least able to control aggression under stress, for whatever physiological or psychological reasons—unknown to us.

Of course, this is assuming that the attacks are by adult males. It is by no means known in most of the cases of missing or dead infants which animal committed the act responsible for the loss. As noted, the possession of a very young infant does not deter an adult female, the mother, from fighting, with other females and with males. During times of female aggression, infants may become involved, either because they happen to be on a female's ventrum or because they insert themselves into the action by trying to approach and contact one or more of the interacting females. If an infant is in the way or gets in the way, it is vulnerable to injury. It may also become the direct focus of aggression by an adult female—she may clearly intend to strike or bite it, no mistake. The tolerance of individual females for noisy, pushy young langurs varies enormously, not only from female to female but from one time to another (Dolhinow and Krusko 1984). In the heat of a squabble about something as seemingly inconsequential (human judgment) as who is to get a specific fallen mango, even though there may be several dozen nearby, a usually permissive female may bite an infant that gets between her and the female grabbing the fruit she wants. When serious fighting or harassment involving males and females takes place, a female may push away her infant, which in turn may frantically try to regain contact only to be dealt with more harshly than with a shove. Females racing to follow another animal or escape from danger may not stop to pick up an infant and carry it with her. The distressed youngster has to fend for itself under possibly very dangerous circumstances. When the mother is racing to escape a predator and does not pause to grab her infant, the latter may become lunch (personal observation). There are a number of situations that can lead to, or increase, the likelihood of infant damage or death.

Is the infant the object of the attack or an accidental victim? When it is on the mother's ventrum, it is difficult, if not impossible, to determine whether the mother or her offspring is the intended receiver of aggression. What is directed toward the mother may unavoidably affect the infant, and it is much easier to damage an infant than an adult. A three-inch wound may prove fatal to an infant but not to the mother.

Opportunity? The opportunity for any individual langur, adult or subadult, male or female, to harm a young langur is always present as long as there are infants in the group. However, if a mother is alert and actively protects her infant when she perceives a threat of danger, for example, by avoiding conflict, the opportunity for damage decreases. The higher and more pervasive the level of tension and aggression the more likely any animal is to be wounded. Infant deaths have been high in a few locations in India where adult males must force their way into a social group and meet with resistance by the resident male and/or females. In most other areas of India males enter and leave groups during mating periods with little or no fighting and no infant disappearance or death. When infants and juveniles actively approach and contact adults that are being aggressive, it is very possible that under the unusual situations at a few locations such as at Jodhpur, it is the immature itself that increases or creates the opportunity for its own damage or destruction. "In fact, as the database for infanticide has grown, evidence has become available to show that in some cases lone infants are clearly the express targets of infanticidal attacks. In particular, six of the attacks described here were directed toward infants that were foraging or moving independently of their mothers at the time of the attack" (Bartlett et al. 1993: 976).

Means? As with opportunity, all adults and subadults, male and female, have the teeth and body strength to wound or kill infants and juveniles. Consider, too, that even a lucky push by just about any animal, even a large juvenile, or an accidental hit might result in a fatal fall or injury that might later become infected and kill.

## UNDERSTANDING BEHAVIOR: THE VERDICT

When you have eliminated the impossible, whatever remains, *however improbable,* must be the truth. (Doyle 1890, ch. 6)

Infant mortality is relatively high in nonhuman primates regardless of where the animals live, whether in virginal forest or in the center of a large city, and there are many causes of death, including aggression, even under the best living conditions. This is the case with langur monkeys as well as for every other monkey or ape included in the list of species whose adult males have been accused of infanticide. Typically the male langur moves about from group to group during his lifetime and this may begin when he is as young as $1\frac{1}{2}$ years of age. Males leave their natal group to live in all-male groups, and it is from the ranks of these all-male groups that they eventually move into groups with females and young, especially during the times when females are sexually receptive. Normally this movement is accomplished with little aggression, and it is rare that fighting produces wounds. However, in a few locations in India the picture is very different. When adult males from an all-male group enter a group with females and young, presumably to mate with the females, pitched battles ensue with high levels of aggression and the disappearance or death of infants and juveniles. In these few places the attacks and subsequent fatalities sometimes do not occur until weeks after the entrance of the new adult males, and, in many instances, the attacks are not witnessed, so it is not known which animal is responsible for the damage. Females may or may not be impregnated by the killer males, and the paternity of subsequent offspring is not known; neither in many instances was the paternity of the missing or dead young. We ought to have heeded the advice of Joe Friday when he said, "Just the facts, ma'am."

In addition to not knowing who killed whom, or the reproductive results of the loss for the mothers and for the adult males involved, the critical role of the immature in stimulating the attacks was never considered, if, in fact, it had been observed at all. Infants too often are overlooked as important actors in group life, and their visual monitoring, approaches, harassment, vocalizations, and general intense interest in activities have been ignored as a factor in shaping their fates. It is all too likely that they may have been responsible for doing, at the worst possible time, the common approaches and investigations so central to their social development, in what would normally be a safe and acceptable situation—with disastrous results. No infant or juvenile exists that can slow, stop, or escape a blindly attacking adult male whose focus either does not discriminate among the objects of his wrath or places on hold the normal restraints against harming immatures.

On the strength of reports of violent male takeovers at a few locations, it was asserted that we were witnessing an evolved male reproductive strategy. No hypothesis, including that of sexual selection, should be dismissed without cause, but to be evaluated as credible it must be supported with evidence. It has not been upheld by the data derived from observation of Indian langurs. Most unfortunately, even without legitimacy for langurs, infanticide has been widely accepted as an explanatory mechanism to interpret the significance of infant disappearance and death in a number of other nonhuman primates. An ostensible teleological cause, a male-evolved reproductive strategy, was demonstrated by its presumed effects, infanticides—a posteriori thinking by any definition. Quite remarkably, the absence of infanticide is assumed to result from actively avoiding infanticide and has been granted a totally undeserved place as a major factor in some theories of primate sociality and social evolution.

How is it that so many have come to view the unusual as typical? In the case of the langur monkey, it seems that aggression by males too often has been taken as the only language of adult male interaction, when, in reality, relations among males, as well as between the sexes, are characterized by a give and take, an accommodation, a constant flow of compromise as well as often of cooperation. Recent considerations of social order have wisely focused on the many aspects of conflict rather than the single strand of aggression (Mason and Mendoza 1993) and offer a far more sensitive and insightful set of measures of how primates live with one another. Langurs are no exception: Conflict in its many forms, from mild and subtle to strong, is an integral part of daily social life. So, too, is cooperation and compromise, of monitoring all that goes on in the group, and then, as often as not, modulating behavior to maximize gains (Dolhinow and Taff 1993; Taff 1990).

But what does a living nonhuman primate know? Fatherhood, the concept, is well beyond the comprehension of any monkey or ape, and, for that matter, of our immediate ancestors until very recently. Copulation, insemination, and pregnancy are biological facts that remain unclearly related by many modern humans. Why might we think that these events and conditions possibly could be part of a monkey's calculations let alone thinking? It has even been suggested that abortions, identified as a form of infanticide, may represent an evolved female reproductive strategy to avoid giving birth to an infant that may be killed once it is born (Agoramoorthy et al. 1988). Quite aside from the implications in this equation as to what a female must know about her "condition," what mechanisms could possibly affect such a deliberately willed end to a normal pregnancy?

As mentioned at the outset of this essay, part of the reason we are in such a muddle about whether or not behaviors have been incorporated into evolved strategies has to do with our initial careless use of language in framing the problem. This poor selection of words directed inquiry along paths that were almost guaranteed to reveal wrong or partial answers—conclusions have been driven in part by the way the problems were formulated. Calling the results of a presumed attack murder did not encourage looking closely into the matter or the motives behind the actions. The term "infanticide" was loaded with emotional meanings and assumptions of deliberation and goal directedness far beyond what was merited in identifying an act resulting in the death of an immature. Casual use of labels not only encouraged careless interpretation, it also discouraged further investigation and search for the mechanisms responsible for what was observed.

Our goal is to understand behavior, and to this end we must consider all the evidence and identify the gaps in our knowledge. We must remember that a behavior may not have a function in the sense that it exists for a specific purpose and is the result of natural selection (Jamieson 1986). Furthermore, actions serving important purposes in one context can be disastrous in a different one. The infant's powerful relationship with its mother is expressed by seeking contact with her at all costs when either of them is frightened or threatened. The infant is also intensely curious and attracted by action—normally with no risk of harm. But when ordinary conditions are replaced by extraordinary ones, when violent fighting accompanies male movement from one group to another, different rules pertain and normal attachments and attractions become endangering. We are, without a doubt, getting closer to solving our who-done-it, the case of the dead and missing infants, and that will include answering the question

"why," at least for langur monkeys. It remains for us to turn our attention to other reported cases of presumed infanticide to discover whether or not we are on the trail of an evolved strategy requiring death. In any event, "the game is afoot" (Doyle 1904).

## ACKNOWLEDGMENTS

Many people have contributed to the contents of this essay, including a long list of individuals who have taken part in our research with the langur colony over the last 20-some years. To each and every one of them I offer my appreciation. I especially acknowledge the insights I have gained from countless lively discussions with Dr. Mark Taff, whose research on the langurs helped provide us with a new framework for understanding male behavior. Agustin Fuentis set aside precious time from the completion of a major manuscript to offer his thoughts on this paper; and Elsworth Ray, Allisa Neves, and Melissa Panger added the task of critiquing my thoughts to schedules crammed with preparation for a major rite of passage. I give my thanks to all.

## BIBLIOGRAPHY

Agoramoorthy, G., and Mohnot, S. M. (1988). Infanticide and juvenilicide in Hanuman langurs (*Presbytis entellus*) around Jodhpur, India. *J. Hum. Evol. 3*(4): 279–296.

Agoramoorthy, G., Mohnot, S. M., Sommer, V., and Srivastava, A. (1988). Abortions in free ranging Hanuman langurs (*Presbytis entellus*): A male induced strategy? *Human Evolution 3*(4): 297–308.

Bartlett, T. Q., Sussman, R. W., and Cheverud, J. M. (1993). Infant killing in primates: A review of observed cases with specific reference to the sexual selection hypothesis. *American Anthrop. 95*: 958–990.

Bishop, N. H., Hrdy, S. B., Teas, J., and Moore, J. (1981). Measures of human influence in habitats of South Asian monkeys. *Int. J. Primatol. 2*: 153–167.

Black's Law Dictionary. (1990). 6th ed. St. Paul, MN: West.

Boggess, J. (1979). Troop male membership changes and infant killing in langurs (*Presbytis entellus*). *Folia Primatol. 32*: 65–107.

Boggess, J. (1980). Intermale relations and troop male membership changes in langurs (*Presbytis entellus*) in Nepal. *Int. J. Primatol. 1*(3): 233–274.

Boggess, J. (1982). Immature male and adult male interactions in bisexual langur (*Presbytis entellus*) groups. *Folia Primatol. 38*: 19–38.

Boggess, J. (1984). Infant killing and male reproductive strategies in langurs (*Presbytis entellus*). In G. Hausfater and S. B. Hrdy (eds.), *Infanticide: Comparative and Evolutionary Perspectives*. New York: Aldine, pp. 283–310.

Colwell, R., and King, M. (1983). Disentangling genetic and cultural influences on human behavior: Problems and prospects. In D. W. Rajecki (ed.), *Comparing Behavior: Studying Man Studying Animals*. Hillsdale, NY: Lawrence Erlbaum Associates, pp. 227–249.

Curtin, R. A. (1977). Langur social behavior and infant mortality. *Kroeber Anthro. Soc. Papers 50*: 27–36.

Curtin, R. A. (1981). Strategy and tactics in male gray langur competition. *J. Hum. Evol. 10:* 245–253.

Curtin, R. A. (1984). Play, practice and predictability in nonhuman primates: A study of the langur (*Presbytis entellus*). In M. I. Roonwal, S. M. Mohnot, and N. S. Rathor (eds.), *Current Primate Researches.* Jodhpur: S. K. Enterprises, pp. 287–293.

Curtin, R. A., and Dolhinow, P. (1978). Primate social behavior in a changing world. *Amer. Scientist 66:* 468–475.

Dolhinow, P. (1972). The north Indian langur. In P. Dolhinow (ed.), *Primate Patterns.* New York: Holt, Rinehart, and Winston, pp. 181–238.

Dolhinow, P. (1977). Normal monkeys? *Amer. Scientist 6:* 266.

Dolhinow, P. (1991). Tactics of primate immaturity. In M. H. Robinson and L. Tiger (eds.), *Man and Beast Revisited.* Washington, DC: Smithsonian Institution Press, pp. 139–240.

Dolhinow, P., and DeMay, M. G. (1982). Adoption: The importance of infant choice. *J. Hum. Evol. 11:* 392–420.

Dolhinow, P., and Murphy, G. (1982). Langur monkey (*Presbytis entellus*) development. *Folia Primatol. 39:* 305–331.

Dolhinow, P., and Krusko, N. (1984). Langur monkey females and infants: The female's point of view. In M. F. Small (ed.), *Female Primates.* New York: Alan R. Liss, pp. 37–57.

Dolhinow, P., and Taff, M. A. (1993). Rivalry, resolution, and the individual: Cooperation among male langur monkeys. In A. J. Almquist and A. Manyak (eds.), *Milestones in Human Evolution.* Prospect Heights, IL: Waveland Press, pp. 75–92.

Doyle, A. C. (1890). *The Sign of Four.* London: Lippencott's Magazine.

Doyle, A. C. (1904). *Adventure at Abby Grange.* London: Strand Magazine.

Dunbar, R. I. M. (1984). *Reproductive Decisions: An Economic Analysis of Gelada Baboon Social Strategies.* Princeton, NJ: Princeton University Press.

Ehrlich, E., Flexner, S. B., Carruth, G., and Hawkins, J. M. (1980). *Oxford American Dictionary.* New York: Oxford University Press.

Estling, R. (1983). The trouble with thinking backwards. *New Scientist 2:* 619–621.

Hausfater, G., and Hrdy, S. B., eds. (1984). *Infanticide: Comparative and Evolutionary Perspectives.* New York: Aldine.

Hrdy, S. B. (1974). Male-male competition and infanticide among the langurs (*Presbytis entellus*) of Abu, Rajasthan. *Folia Primatol. 22:* 19–58.

Hrdy, S. B. (1977a). Infanticide as a primate reproductive strategy. *American Scientist 65:* 40–49.

Hrdy, S. B. (1977b). *The Langurs of Abu: Female and Male Strategies of Reproduction.* Cambridge, MA: Harvard University Press.

Hrdy, S. B. (1979). Infanticide among animals: A review, classification, and examination of the implications for the reproductive strategies of females. *Ethology and Sociobiology 1:* 13–40.

Hrdy, S. B., and Hausfater, G. (1984). In G. Hausfater and S. B. Hrdy (eds.), *Infanticide: Comparative and Evolutionary Perspectives.* New York: Aldine, pp. xiii–xxxix.

Hutchinson, G. E. (1957). Concluding remarks. *Cold Spring Symposium of Quantitative Biology 22:* 415–427.

Jamieson, I. G. (1986). The functional approach to behavior: is it useful? *Amer. Naturalist 127:* 195–208.

Jay, P. (1962). Aspects of maternal behavior among langurs. *Annals of NY Acad. Sci. 102:* 468–478.

Jay, P. (1963a). Mother-infant relations in langurs. In H. L. Rheingold (ed.), *Maternal Behavior in Mammals.* New York: Wiley, pp. 282–304.

Jay, P. (1963b). *The Social Behavior of the Langur Monkey.* Ph. D. thesis, University of Chicago.

Jay, P. (1965). The common langur of north India. In I. DeVore (ed.), *Primate Behavior: Field Studies of Monkeys and Apes.* New York: Holt, Rinehart, and Winston, pp. 114–123.

Laws, J., and Vonder Haar Laws, J. (1984). Social interactions among adult male langurs (*Presbytis entellus*) at Rajaji Wildlife Sanctuary. *Int. J. Primatol. 5:* 31–50.

Leland, L., Strusaker, T. T., and Butynski, T. M. (1984). Infanticide by adult males in three primate species of Kibale forest, Uganda: A test of hypotheses. In G. Hausfater and S. B. Hrdy (eds.), *Infanticide: Comparative and Evolutionary Perspectives.* New York: Aldine, pp. 151–171.

McKenna, J. J. (1982). The evolution of primate societies, reproduction, and parenting. In J. Fobes and J. Kind (eds.), *Primate Behavior.* New York: Academic Press, pp. 87–133.

Mason, W. A., and Mendoza, S. P., eds. (1993). *Primate Social Conflict.* Albany: State University of New York Press.

Mohnot, S. M. (1978). Peripheralisation of weaned juveniles in *Presbytis entellus.* In D. J. Chivers and J. Herbert (eds.), *Recent Advances in Primatology,* Vol. 1, London: Academic Press, pp. 87–91.

Moore, J. J. (1984). Age and grooming in langur male bands. In M. L. Roonwal, S. M. Mohnot, and M. S. Rathor (eds.), *Current Primate Researches.* Jodhpur: S. K. Enterprises, pp. 381–387.

Moorhouse, K. (1980). *Social Integration and the Genesis of Male-Male Conflict in a Group of Captive Langur Monkeys.* Ph.D. thesis, University of California, Berkeley.

Oyama, S. (1989). Ontogeny and the central dogma: Do we need the concept of genetic programming in order to have an evolutionary perspective? In M. R. Gunnar and E. Thelen (eds.), *Systems and Development: The Minnesota Symposia on Child Psychology,* Vol. 22. Hillsdale, NJ: Lawrence Erlbaum Associates, pp. 1–34.

Poirier, F. E., and Kanner, M. C. (1989). Cross-specific review of Asian colobine social organization and certain behaviors. In P. K. Seth and S. Seth (eds.), *Perspectives in Primate Biology 3:* 93–115.

Schubert, G. (1982). Infanticide by usurper hanuman langur males: A sociobiological myth. *Biology and Social Life, Soc. Sci. Information (SAGE) 21(2):* 199–244.

Sommer, V. (1993). Infanticide among the langurs of Jodhpur: Testing the sexual selection hypothesis with a long-term record. In S. Parmigiani and F. vom Sall (eds.), *Infanticide and Parental Care.* London: Academia.

van Schaik, C. P., and Dunbar, R. I. M. (1990). The evolution of monogamy in large primates: A new hypothesis and some crucial tests. *Behavior 115:* 30–61.

van Schaik, C. P., and Kappler, P. M. (1992). Lemur and anthropoid societies: Variations on a theme? In *Abstracts, XIVth Cong. Int. Primatol. Soc.,* August 16–21, pp. 25–26.

Taff, M. A. (1990). *Social Dynamics of Langur (Presbytis entellus) All Male Groups: A Captive Study.* Ph. D. thesis, University of California, Berkeley.

Williams, J. B. (1991). *Infanticide in Nonhuman Primates: A Bibliography,* 2nd ed. Primate Information Center Publ. Regional Primate Research Center, University of Washington, Seattle.

Wolfe, K., and Fleagle, J. (1977). Adult male replacement in a group of silvered leaf monkeys (*Presbytis cristata*) at Kuala Selangor, Malaysia. *Primates 18:* 949–955.

*Given that we know natural selection operates on populations, how might we identify an adaptation? Almquist and Matsuda look at alcohol metabolism and alcoholism in search of an example of balanced polymorphisms, like sickle-cell anemia, which could have an adaptive interpretation. They review the history of alcohol use, cross-cultural research on alcoholism, and the physiology and genetics of alcohol metabolism and discover a sexually dimorphic pattern. They discuss how to make the case for the adaptive significance of the nonrandom expression of alcohol metabolism that they have found, providing another example of the "evolutionary perspective as a scientific tool."*

# 11 Good Taste, Good Sense, or Just Plain Good Sex(ual) Differences in the Metabolism of Alcohol

**Alan J. Almquist and David Matsuda,** *Department of Anthropology, California State University, Hayward*

## INTRODUCTION

The fact that natural selection operates on populations is indisputable. From studies of sickle-cell anemia to English peppered moths, selection, its agents, and adaptive values have been demonstrated. The better understood examples of natural selection have almost always involved balanced polymorphisms, such as the well-documented case of sickle-cell anemia heterozygotes providing protection against malaria. Other examples include the recent explanations for the distribution of schizophrenia (Allen and Sarich 1988). Balanced polymorphisms lend themselves well to evolutionary investigations because less fit alleles are maintained in populations at higher frequencies than we would expect. High frequencies of detrimental alleles that often cause disease as recessive homozygotes are clues that selection favors heterozygote combinations. For example, in sickle-cell anemia, the Hb(a) Hb(s) genotype is favored. That we have had only moderate success in elucidating other examples is the result of two factors. First, in the case of sickle-cell anemia, the genetics of the change in the hemoglobin molecule is known and relatively straightforward: one base substitution at position 6 of the beta chain. In most other situations, however, such as schizophrenia, we lack the precise knowledge of the genetics of the disease, thereby making tenuous a convincing argument for selection. Second, better cases for natural selection are made for situations that have only recently emerged. Again, sickle-cell anemia is a good example, as apparently the mutation for Hbs only became frequent in some human populations about 2000 years ago when African agriculturists penetrated tropical rain forests and, thus, came into contact with the malaria-carrying *Anopheles* mosquito. Blood group polymorphisms are other clear examples of balanced situations, but because of the complex nature of the multiple allelic systems that have evolved over millions of years, the adaptive significance of the various genotypes remains mostly hidden.

A second source of examples of natural selection arises as sexually dimorphic differences. Charles Darwin, in his second major book, *The Descent of Man and Selection with Relation to Sex* (1871), elaborated on the concept of sexual selection. Sexual selection, as Darwin envisioned it, involves two levels. The first level concerns competition between members of each sex; the second level involves mate choice and the different reproductive strategies that are employed by males and females, respectively. He viewed sexual selection as that arising from "the advantage which certain individuals have over other individuals of the same sex and species in exclusive relation to reproduction" (1871, Vol. 1: 256).

The consumption of alcohol and alcoholism has been the subject of a substantial literature. In recent years the genetics of alcohol metabolism has been worked out, and a pattern of sexually dimorphic differences have emerged. In this paper we explore these differences, using the perspectives of both natural and sexual selection.

## THE HISTORY OF ALCOHOL USE

Although the consumption of some form of alcohol goes back more than 5000 years, the oldest actual trace of wine, dated to about 3500 B.C., was unearthed as a residue inside an earthen jar from the Sumerian ruins at the site of Godin Tepe, western Iran. The manufacture of beers and other fermented drinks has an equally long history. History records the significance alcohol began to play in society and the problems that could be foreseen from its use. The Sumerian epic of Gilgamesh (circa 3000 B.C.) tells of the enchanted vineyard whose wine was the source of immortality. Hammurabi, king of Babylon around 1700 B.C., decreed laws specific to alcohol consumption, who could imbibe it, and who could not. In Asia, barley beer is thought to have been invented during the reign of the first emperor of the first dynasty. The inventor presented his concoction to the emperor, who was said to have prophesied that the drink would cause great trouble in the empire and subsequently banished the inventor and prohibited beer manufacture (Buckland 1878–79). While we do not intend to summarize the complete history of alcohol consumption in world society, for the purpose of describing an evolutionary model we must set it within a framework of time.

## CROSS-CULTURAL RESEARCH

That consumption of alcoholic drinks has played a significant role in many societies for at least 5000 years is a fact well established in the literature. It was reviewed by the social anthropologist David Mandelbaum, who wrote, "There are a great many substances that men have learned to ingest in order to get special bodily sensation. Of all of them alcohol is culturally the most important by far" (1965: 1). Not only has the use of alcohol been widespread, but as Horton (1943) observed,

> The use of alcohol by man involves a paradox. This paradox is implicit in the fact that for all its dangerous consequences—so dangerous that all societies in which alcohol is used have had to set up more or less stringent and restrictive controls over its use—not even the death penalty has been able to prevent men from using it. (p. 204)

Mac Marshall (1979) began his edited volume by observing the wide cross-cultural variations in behavior as it related to alcohol use:

> The cross-cultural study of alcohol presents a classic natural experiment: a single species (*Homo sapiens*), a single drug substance (ethanol) and a great diversity of behavioral outcomes. (p. 1)

Anthropologists who have studied alcohol use have focused their attention on the manner and meaning of its use (Douglas 1987; Hanna 1976; Heath 1976). Heath (1975, 1986, 1987a, b) has reviewed the data and discussed the relationship of alcohol use within sociocultural systems. He also noted that cultural practices involving alcohol have a wide range, from substantial use to total prohibition and/or abstinence. In the well-known example of heavy drinking found among the Camba of eastern Bolivia, men may participate in recurrent drinking episodes lasting entire weekends. They typically consume so much alcohol that they pass out and after reviving themselves continue to drink once more into unconsciousness (Heath 1958: 31). On the other hand, among Hindu castes certain Brahman communities prohibit the use of alcohol, especially during the worship of certain deities. Also, several states in India prohibit consumption of alcohol to all persons, though prohibition in India has usually been as difficult to enforce as it was in the United States in the 1920s (Jay 1966).

In societies where alcoholic drink is permitted or encouraged, drinking practices may be related to specific cultural themes. For example, in many societies alcohol is used symbolically and is related to ritual practices. Under these circumstances alcohol use is regulated, and drunken behavior is not tolerated. However, notable exceptions can be found among the Aztec (even though nonritualistic drunkenness was punishable by death; see Bunzel 1940: 362), as well as Mayan society and in the Dionysian cults of ancient Greece. In nonritual cases alcohol use often functions as a medium of social exchange. Mandelbaum (1965: 282) observes that the rules for social drinking are well understood by all parties and that the quantity an individual is likely to consume, the circumstances of this consumption, and the consequences of the act are culturally determined before the first drink is poured. This situation Bale (1946) described as "convivial drinking," believing it to symbolize social unity because it acts to facilitate social ease and goodwill.

Another review of the literature makes clear that alcohol use is gender-specific, that is, almost always male-oriented. Agreeing with this, Weibel-Orlando (1986) observes that

> Any way in which comparisons are made across socioeconomic, age, or ethnic categories, findings indicate that

men drink more and more often than women. Women are less likely than men to drink heavily or to experience drinking problems in most cultures and in all modern western societies for which we have data. (p. 165)

A few well-chosen examples illustrate this point. Among the South American Abipone and Choroti, women are totally forbidden to drink alcoholic beverages (Saunders 1980: 67). Reasons given for sex discrimination in alcohol consumption relate the idea that drinking symbolizes male solidarity and becomes part of the definition of maleness. Drinking is recognized as an appropriate mediator for men, who must deal with the problems of society larger than those dealt with by women on the domestic level. While we would like to look at alcohol consumption by men only from the point of view of gender-role reinforcement, we must turn the question around and ask whether, if women don't (usually) drink (much), is it simply because they are prohibited from doing so by drinking's being culturally defined as an exclusive prerogative of men.

Child, Barry, and Bacon (1965: 60) surmise that "the general social role of the sexes make drunkenness more threatening in women than men." Controls on sexuality are numerous and culturally important, and drinking by women is often associated with promiscuity, or at least, a lessening of sexual restraint (Saunders 1980: 68). In this respect, alcohol consumption by women is antithetical to societal goals of sexual regulation. An attitude against female drunkenness may be reinforced by women themselves. Furthermore, in terms of overall health, the deleterious effects of alcohol are not limited to the liver in the form of a cirrhosis. Women who consume excessive amounts of alcohol may also be more prone than men to neuropsychiatric illnesses and to greater deterioration of motor coordination (Schenker and Speeg 1990: 128). These additional factors must be taken into account in any attempt to explain restrictions on the consumption of alcoholic drink placed on women, because, no doubt, observations of "bizarre" behavior by intoxicated women would be incorporated in the folk belief of many societies.

Finally, female alcohol consumption offers dangers to motherhood. Commonly, women in a number of societies observe dietary taboos and precautions during pregnancy. (In some societies men as well as women observe prepartum taboos to ensure a successful delivery and a healthy child.) An important concern is that inappropriate behavior during gestation can have far-reaching consequences for the birth process and the future well-being of the child. In the Judeo-Christian tradition warnings against alcohol use by pregnant mothers can be found in the Old Testament. This caution, addressed to the mother of Samson, was considered sufficiently important that it was repeated three times: "Now therefore beware, I pray thee and drink not wine nor strong drink and eat not any unclean thing" (Judges 13: 4, 7, 14). Certainly one practical consideration, no doubt felt in all societies, is that alcohol consumption by postpartum mothers is incompatible with overall child rearing, and prohibitions exist that recognize this fact (Saunders 1980: 68). Interestingly, prohibitions against alcohol along with a number of other substances are lifted once a woman has passed through menopause (Simic 1983: 76).

From an evolutionary point of view, fetal alcohol toxicity may be a significant agent of natural selection. While the results are still out on the amount of alcohol a pregnant woman can safely consume, some studies show that women who drink even moderately may be harming their unborn children. In the United States, statistics show that 3 out of every 1000 newborns are diagnosed with fetal alcohol syndrome. FAS can result in mental retardation, curvature of the spine, and various facial abnormalities. In the United States, where norms in the recent past have relaxed the sanctions on women who consume alcohol, drinking during pregnancy ranks as one of the major causes of mental retardation. Studies have shown that mothers who had only one or two drinks a day during their first two months of pregnancy gave birth to children who later tested considerably slower in reaction time than children of mothers who refrained completely from drinking during their pregnancies. One of the reasons alcohol can have such long-range effects on newborns is that the fetal liver has little chance to protect itself from the effects of a high concentration of ethanol in the maternal bloodstream, its enzymes activity designed to break down alcohol being only minimally functioning. A better understanding of this situation comes from research on fetuses of the nonhuman primates (Clarren et al. 1992).

While the effects of maternal alcohol consumption postnatally on infants are not well established, animal research suggests that infants may be affected by the alcohol they receive through their mother's milk. Maternal alcohol consumption during breast feeding appears to be unrelated to mental development, but muscle control was significantly lower in those infants exposed to alcohol in breast milk, with the amount of loss directly proportional to the degree of exposure (Little et al. 1989).

Members of early societies, no doubt, recognized the relationship between alcohol-consuming mothers and the physical defects alcohol might have caused in their offspring. But even if health is not an issue, "care of a field may be postponed for a day (due to an over indulgence on alcohol), but care of a child cannot," as Child, Barry, and Bacon observe (1965: 60). Bacon (1976), in a review of the attitudes toward alcohol consumption, found that members of many societies voiced a concern for women and appropriate child care and, as a consequence, approved of restrictions on alcohol consumption by women.

## PHYSIOLOGY OF ALCOHOL METABOLISM

The liver is the primary organ for alcohol (ethanol) metabolism. Through the catalyzing effect of enzymes, the alcohol dehydrogenases convert various alcohol aldehydes. Experiments, however, show that some metabolism of ethanol occurs in the gastrointestinal tract, where it acts as a "first-pass" protection by reducing the amount of ethanol that will enter the bloodstream.

However, in individuals who consume alcohol over a long period of time this enzyme activity in gastric tissue decreases. In alcoholic males this first-pass metabolism is about half that of males who consume only moderate amounts of alcohol. More interestingly, however, experiments in nonalcoholic females showed that the first-pass metabolism is only about one-quarter as effective as it is in nonalcoholic males. In alcoholic females the first-pass metabolism is virtually absent. Clearly, these studies, begun by Frezza et al. (1990), show significant sex differences in alcohol metabolism in gastric tissue. Because females have lower enzyme activity in gastric tissue, more alcohol reaches the bloodstream. Consequently, they are more susceptible to the effects of alcohol after ingesting doses equivalent to those taken by males.

## THE GENETICS OF ALCOHOL METABOLISM

Why is the activity of gastric alcohol dehydrogenase lower in females than in males? And could this difference be genetically related?

Research on the genetics of the human alcohol dehydrogenase (ADH) system indicates a complex, polymorphic situation. This work confirms a model of a three-loci system: ADH1, ADH2, and ADH3. Only the ADH2 and ADH3 loci are, however, polymorphic. At the ADH2 locus, there are two common alleles, ADH 1/2 and ADH 2/2; a third allele is found among American blacks, ADH 3/2. ADH 2/2 is usually found in Asian populations and differs from 1/2 by a single amino acid substitution, that is, arginine to histine at the 47th position. The amino acid substitution between the 1/2 and 3/2 variants is an arginine to cystine at the 369th position. At the ADH3 locus, there are two alleles, ADH 1/3 and ADH 2/3.

The loci ADH 1–3 and their alleles are grouped as class I ADH. This class exhibits high catalytic activity for the oxidation of ethanol. There are two additional classes of ADH, II and III, but they play only a small role in the oxidation of ethanol. Class I ADHs are most abundant in the liver, but they are also found in other tissue. The ADH3 alleles control enzymes found in fetal kidney and fetal and adult gastrointestinal tract tissue. In both sexes testosterone is a allosteric regulator for ADH3, controlling the metabolism of androgens as well.

Class I and II ADH both metabolize neurotransmitters in the liver. For example, dopamine is metabolized by class I ADH: norepinephrine is metabolized by class II ADH, and serotinin is metabolized by ADH of both classes. The suggestion has been made that there may be a relationship among alcoholism, reduced enzyme activity, and the metabolism of these substances.

## THE EVOLUTIONARY PERSPECTIVE

Given the knowledge of the genetics of ethanol metabolism, how do we make a case for natural selection and for the fact that the sexually dimorphic differences in alcohol metabolism are adaptively significant? Additionally, if a case can be made, what sort of an evolutionary model is the most appropriate to use? Donald Symons (1990:429) stated the rules for evolutionary investigations when he wrote about the difference between saying that a trait is adaptive, as opposed to saying that a trait has an evolutionary history. All traits have an evolutionary history, but to demonstrate adaptation one has to be able to explain the how and the why, to show that the trait has some kind of special design that solved a specific problem.

Whatever model is chosen, it must be testable. Our model states that the first-pass enzyme activity in gastric tissue is the result of natural selection favoring males, who may consume ethanol in larger quantities than females consume. However, why males, on average, consume more alcohol than do females in the first place raises another question. Helena Cronin (1992) reviews additional models based on sexual selection that may be pertinent to this issue. The "good taste" model was one proposed by Darwin as part of his theory of female choice. This model was backed up by R. A. Fisher (1930) and elaborated by Dawkins (1986), among others. Fisher argued that female choice based on male attractiveness could be adaptive because an attractive male will have (more than likely) attractive sons. The argument continues that if there is a majority preference for any characteristic, no matter how arbitrary, a female's best strategy is to go along with the fashion. While sons will inherit their father's attractiveness, daughters will inherit their mother's preference for any characteristics, establishing a positive feedback loop. By chance alone, a "runaway" preference for any characteristic can occur that leads to characteristics that are selected for mating success but are a hindrance or even detrimental to a male's survival.

The second model of "good sense" describes sexual selection that results in a male's possessing qualities that may, on the one hand, be a burden but, on the other hand, are indicators of useful qualities, such as apparent good health or an ability to forage successfully. As Cronin remarks (1992: 289), "sensible choice can end up with males looking so defiantly ornamental that the choice appears intuitively to make no sense at all."

Cronin, Fisher, and Dawkins were, of course, using these models to explain such things as male peacock plumage. Do these models of sexual selection help us to elucidate further dimorphic patterns of alcohol metabolism, and, if so, how do they help? In humans, unlike peacocks, mating success is based on a multiplicity of biological and cultural factors. For example, studies of the Aché of Paraguay show that men hunt and gather, but they frequently ignore the high caloric return of plant foods, such as palm, in order to spend their time hunting. Both Aché men and women prefer meat to plant foods, but women rely predominantly on the men to get meat for them. For the males, hunting is certainly a more risky enterprise than gathering palms, and the energy return for their efforts is lower. Why, then, do Aché males hunt? Hawkes (1990, 1991) argues that Aché male hunting can be explained as a mating strategy. The advantage of hunting is that it is variably successful in that some men are better at it than others, and this attracts female sexual favors. Smith (1992) elaborates on this idea.

> This argument explains hunting as a product of sexual selection—a contest, like fighting between stags, a form of "showing off" for sexual reward—rather than optimal foraging in the narrower sense of gaining a livelihood. (p. 24)

There is evidence to support the notion that Aché hunters have higher mean fitness as measured by mating frequencies and offspring survival rates (Kaplan and Hill 1985). In many contemporary urban examples, such as gang warfare, a male puts himself at considerable physical risk that may, in part, be offset by his success at mating. In terms of alcohol consumption using a "good sense" model, a male's ability to drink himself into unconsciousness may appear incredibly nonsensical. But with a particular male's ability to differentially survive such bouts, managing the effects of alcohol may be indicative (at least to the people involved) of his ability to successfully manage other, more important aspects of his society. Also an indicator of healthiness

(at least for the moment, and again for the same audience) could be how fast a male can recuperate from significant alcohol consumption.

The "good taste" model is also potentially useful. If alcohol consumption in some societies makes "good sense" from the point of view of mating success (an issue to be tested), then "good taste" with a "runaway" component explains, to some extent, why in some societies excessive drinking is encouraged, such as in Camban society, while not in others. Aspects of this model relating alcohol consumption and mating success have been indirectly tested by social anthropologists as part of the concept of machismo (Simic 1983). Additional field studies should prove informative.

Timewise, the model is consistent with what we know about the sickle-cell anemia polymorphism. Here protection against infection by the malaria parasite was provided by natural selection favoring a single amino acid substitution on the beta chain of the hemoglobin molecule. By most estimates the hemoglobin mutation became increasingly more common in those populations who came in contact with mosquitoes carrying the parasite, about A.D. 0–500. If it has taken 1500 years or so for this mutation to reach the frequencies it has in various parts of the world, then 5000 years—the approximate date for the beginnings of the production of alcoholic drinks—is sufficient time for the ADH variants to evolve as they appear today.

In terms of the ADH model, however, questions remain as to the specifics of the selective process. Research has singled out the ADH3 locus that produces enzymes that both metabolize ethanol and androgens and are also found in gastrointestinal lining. Because there is more testosterone in males than in females, the amounts of the ADH3 enzyme in the testes to metabolize the androgen excess are larger. As ADH3 operates in a similar manner in both males and females, the difference in activity is only a manner of degree. Selection would have to operate on this differential activity to develop a situation wherein gastric tissue disproportionate enzyme activity would also occur, in this case, for the metabolism of ethanol.

Certainly one test of this model would be to measure enzyme activity in males and females of a species of ape. As there is probably little difference between the sexes in their consumption of naturally fermented food, little difference would be expected in gastric tissue enzyme activity. Measured enzyme activity in the apes should more closely approximate the activity already determined for human females, as alcohol consumption is minimal in both these populations. Among human males, however, we would not expect to find substantial differences in gastric enzyme activity in individuals from different populations, whether or not these populations have had a history of alcohol use. On the other hand, population differences in the effects of alcohol consumption have been observed, most notably among Asians.

The genetic differences exist among human populations and among individuals can be demonstrated in a number of examples. As Mandelbaum (1965: 282) reports, the physiological effects correlated with alcohol use vary extensively among different peoples. He cites Berreman's (1956) observations on alcohol consumption among both the Japanese and Aleut Indians. In these groups Berreman notes that males appeared to become intoxicated after consuming a minimal amount of alcohol. More recent studies by Akutsu et al. (1989) have attempted to confirm this observation. In their research Asian subjects, overall, consumed less alcohol than their Caucasian counterparts. But, as these authors note, the degree of desire to consume does not necessarily reflect an inability to consume.

Drinking usually occurs in social situations; it is important, therefore, to evaluate the effect culture has on drinking behavior. Within traditional belief systems, many Asians regard drinking as immoral, but there is no moral prohibition against drinking in moderation (Singer 1979). However, Asians may disapprove of heavy drinking or drinking alone. Drinking with meals is considered to be appropriate, since alcohol is regarded as food, and drinking is considered to be a phase of eating. However, the negative attributes of alcohol consumption include beliefs in the impairment of sex performance, loss of fertility, and the potential to pass on inherited defects. While Chinese males commonly consume less alcohol overall, men still drink much more frequently and in larger amounts than do females.

On the other hand, a case can be made that differences observed in alcohol consumption between Asians and Caucasians may, in fact, be due to physiological reaction to ethanol rather than to cultural values (Akutsu et al. 1989: 266). Physiological differences do appear. For example, Asians show a significantly higher likelihood to flush after consuming an alcoholic drink than do Caucasians (Johnson et al. 1984). They also exhibit greater dysphoria (Wolff 1972), tachycardia, and a tendency toward higher blood acetaldehyde levels (Ewing et al. 1974). But the nature of the physiological reactivity needs further clarification. One possibility is that the higher incidence of alcohol sensitivity (alcohol flushing) in Asians (50–90%) than in Caucasians (5–10%) could be one linked to the Asian atypical ALDH 2/2 allele of the aldehyde dehydrogenase system, which further oxidizes aldehydes to acetates. It is possible that the higher frequencies of this allele in Asian population than in Caucasian populations provide some protection against Asian's developing alcoholism (Yoshida et al. 1991). It seems, however, that, while different populations show various degrees of sensitivity to alcohol, these differences are not part of the same mechanism that provides for differences between males and females in metabolic activity in the gastrointestinal tract.

## CONCLUSIONS

Sexually dimorphic patterns of alcohol metabolism have been established. Most likely, the ADH3 locus that guides alcohol metabolism in the gastrointestinal lining has been differentially activated by natural selection, which in turn, lends greater protection against alcohol poisoning and, ultimately, alcoholism to the sex that, traditionally, has consumed the most alcohol. We predict that males throughout the world will possess more or less equal gastrointestinal enzyme activity, regardless of whether their societies encourage or prohibit the consumption of alcohol on a regular basis. However, the discovery of significant differences in enzyme activity among individuals in different societies could lead to understanding of the genetic mechanisms involved in alcohol metabolism. We would encourage additional medical studies along these lines. However, while parts to this puzzle are still to be uncovered, we believe that the usefulness of the natural selection model and, perhaps, sexual selection model in the investigation of the alcohol metabolism polymorphism is shown.

## BIBLIOGRAPHY

Akutsu, P. D., Sue. S., Zane, N. W. S., and Nakamura, C. Y. (1989). Ethnic differences in alcohol consumption among Asians and Caucasians in the United States: An investigation of cultural and physiological factors. *J. Studies Alcohol* 50(3): 261–267.

Allen, J. S., and Sarich, V. M. (1988). Schizophrenia in an evolutionary perspective. *Perspectives Biol. Med* 32(1): 132–153.

Bacon, M. K. (1976). Cross-cultural studies of drinking: Integrated drinking and sex differences in the use of alcoholic beverages. In M. W. Everett, J. O. Waddell, and D. B. Heath (eds.), *Cross-cultural Approaches to the Study of Alcohol*. The Hague, Mouton: World Anthropology, pp. 23–33.

Bale, R. F. (1946). Cultural differences in rates of alcoholism. *Quart. J. Studies Alcohol.* 6: 480–499.

Berreman, G. D. (1956). Drinking patterns of the Aleuts. *Quarterly J. Stud. Alcohol* 17: 503–514.

Buckland, A. W. (1878–79). Ethnological hints afforded by the stimulants in use among savages and among the ancients. *J. Royal Anthropol. Inst. 8:* 239–254.

Bunzel, R. (1940). The role of alcoholism in Central American cultures. *Psychiatry* 3: 361–387.

Child, I. L., Barry, H. and Bacon, M. K. (1965). Cross-cultural study of drinking. III. Sex differences. In M. K. Bacon, H. Barry III,

I. L. Child (eds.) *A Cross-Cultural Study of Drinking. Quarterly J. Stud. Alcohol,* Suppl. 3: 49–61.

Clarren, S. K., Astley, S. J., Gunderson, V. M., and Spellman, D. (1992). Cognitive and behavioral deficits in nonhuman primates associated with very early embryonic binge exposures to ethanol. *J. Pediatrics 121* (5): 789–796.

Cronin, H. (1992). Sexual selection: Historical perspectives. In E. Keller and E. Lloyd (eds.), *Keywords in Evolutionary Biology.* Cambridge, MA: Harvard University Press, pp. 286–293.

Darwin, C. (1871). *The Descent of Man and Selection in Relation to Sex.* London: John Murray and Sons.

Dawkins, R. (1986). *The Blind Watchmaker.* New York: Norton.

Douglas, M. (1987). A distinctive anthropological perspective. In M. Douglas (ed.), *Constructive Drinking: Perspectives on Drink from Anthropology.* New York: Cambridge University Press, pp. 3–15.

Ewing, J. A., Rouse, B. A., and Pellizzari, E.D. (1974). Alcohol sensitivity and ethnic background. *Amer. J. Psychiat. 131:* 206–210.

Frezza, M., DiPadova, C., Pozzato, G., Terpin, M., Baraona, E., and Lieber, C. S. (1990). High blood alcohol levels in women: The role of decreased alcohol dehydrogenase activity and first-pass metabolism. *New England J. Med.* 322: 95–99.

Fisher, R. A. (1930). *The Genetical Theory of Natural Selection,* 2nd rev. ed., 1958. New York: Dover Press.

Hanna, J. M. (1976). Ethnic groups, human variation and alcohol use. In M. W. Everett, J. D. Waddell, and D. B. Heath (eds.), *Cross-Cultural Approaches to the Study of Alcohol. World Anthropology.* The Hague: Mouton, pp. 235–242.

Hawkes, K. (1990). Why do men hunt? Some benefits for risky strategies. In E. Cashdan (ed.), *Risk and Uncertainty.* Boulder, CO: Westview Press.

Hawkes, K. (1991). Showing off: Tests of an hypothesis about men's foraging goals. *Ethol. Sociobiol. 12:* 29–54.

Heath, D. B. (1958). Drinking patterns of the Bolivian Camba. *Quart. J. Studies Alcohol 19:* 491–508.

Heath, D. B. (1975). A critical review of ethnographic studies of alcohol use. In R. Gibbons, Y. Israel, H. Kalant, R. Popham, W. Schmidt, and R. Smart (eds.), *Research Advances in Alcohol and Drug Problems,* Volume 2. New York: Wiley, pp. 1–92.

Heath, D. B. (1976). Anthropology perspectives on alcohol: An historical review. In M. W. Everett, J. D. Waddell, and D. B. Heath (eds.), *Cross-Cultural Approaches to the Study of Alcohol. World Anthropology.* The Hague: Mouton, pp. 41–101.

Heath, D. B. (1986). Drinking and drunkeness in transcultural perspective. Parts I and II. *Transcult. Psychiat. Res. Rev.* 23: 7–42, 103–126.

Heath, D. B. (1987). A decade of development in the anthropological study of alcohol use: 1970–1980. In M. Douglas (ed.), *Constructive Drinking: Perspectives on Drink from Anthropology.* New York: Cambridge University Press, pp. 16–69.

Heath, D. B. (1987). Anthropology and alcohol studies: Current issues. *Ann. Rev. Anthropol. 16:* 99–120.

Horton, D. (1943). The functions of alcohol in primitive societies: a cross-cultural study. *Quart. J. Studies Alcohol 4:* 199–320.

Jay, E. J. (1966). Religious and convivial uses of alcohol in a Gond village of middle India. *Quart. J. Studies Alcohol 27*(1): 88–96.

Johnson, R. C., Nagoshi, C. T., Schwitters, S. Y., Bowman, K. S., Ahern, F. M., and Wilson, J. R. (1984). Further investigation of racial/ethnic differences and of familial resemblances in flushing in response to alcohol. *Behav. Genet. 14:* 121–178.

Kaplan, H., and K. Hill (1985). Hunting ability and reproductive success among male Aché foragers: Preliminary results. *Current Anthropology 26:* 131–133.

Little, R. E., Anderson, K. W., Ervin, C. H., Worthingon-Roberts, B., and Clarren, S. K. (1989). Maternal alcohol use during breast-feeding and infant mental and motor development at one year. *New Eng. J. Med. 321:* 425–426.

Mandelbaum, D. G. (1965). Alcohol and culture. *Current Anthropol.* 6: 281–293.

Marshall, M. (1979). *Beliefs, Behaviors and Alcoholic Beverages: A Cross-Cultural Survey.* Ann Arbor: University of Michigan Press.

Saunders, B. (1980). Psychological aspects of women and alcohol. In *Women and Alcohol.* Camberwell Council on Alcoholism. New York: Tavistock, pp. 67–100.

Schenker, S., and Speeg, K. V. (1990). The risks of alcohol intake in men and women. All may not be equal. *New Eng. J. Med. 322:* 127–129.

Simic, A. (1983). Machismo and cryptomatriarchy. Power, affect, and authority in the contemporary Yugoslav family. *Ethos 11*(1/2): 66–86.

Singer, K. (1979). Drinking patterns and alcoholism in the Chinese. In M. Marshall (ed.), *Beliefs, Behaviors and Alcoholic Beverages: A Cross-Cultural Survey.* Ann Arbor: University of Michigan Press, pp. 313–326.

Smith, E. A. (1992). Human behavioral ecology. *Evol. Anthropol. 1:* 20–25.

Symons, D. (1990). Adaptiveness and adaptation. *Ethol. Sociobiol.* 11: 427–444.

Weibel-Orlando, J. C. (1986). Women and alcohol: Special populations and cross-cultural variation. In *Women and Alcohol: Health Related Issues. National Institute of Alcohol Abuse and Alcohol Monograph No. 16.* Rockville, MD, pp. 161–187.

Wolff, P. H. (1972). Ethnic differences in alcohol sensitivity. *Science 125:* 449–450.

Yoshida, A., Hsu, L. C., and Yasunami, M. (1991). Genetics of human alcohol-metabolizing enzymes. *Prog. Nucleic Acid Res. Molecular Biol. 40:* 255–287.

*Washburn felt that evolutionary studies needed to be broader. In fact, he advocates, in this paper, a return to the breadth of Darwin's vision of human evolution, which tried to understand human nature and human evolution in all its complexity and richness. By comparing the anthropology of 100 years ago and of now, he suggests the ways that phylogenetic reconstructions can and must be improved. One hundred years ago, Darwin was trying to convince people that evolution had occurred. Now the new evolutionary synthesis created by the injection of genetics into evolutionary thinking has destroyed most traditional tenets of anthropology: typological thinking, orthogenesis, irreversibility, and the importance of nonadaptive characteristics. During Darwin's time there were not enough fossils to prove or disprove any specific hominid phylogeny. Instead, he argues, it was the climate of opinion that dictated the science as seen in the search for the "missing link," which was based on preconceptions about the size of the brain, the shape of the pelvis, toolmaking, and the singularity of the human lineage. Even now, the fossil evidence is so fragmentary that drawing conclusions is risky in the absence of other supporting evidence.*

*Washburn was the earliest champion, among anthropologists, of the new molecular data. He saw this independent source of information as a way to distinguish among competing hypotheses about the timing of divergences and the nature of the reconstructed phylogenies. He also emphasized how important it was to rephrase traditional problems of reconstructing human evolution in modern form. This would mean recognizing how much our understanding of geological time had changed, replacing typological thinking with an appreciation of adaptive problems which required a consideration of behavior, rejecting origin stories that were about single causes located in restricted times and places, and replacing definitive statements about what happened with probabilistic statements of the likelihood that this or that might have happened. This meant that the traditional physical anthropology of types, orthogenesis, and simplistic phylogenies must be replaced by a biological anthropology that transcends the traditional divisions of knowledge and aims to understand all the dimensions of the lives of our ancestors, as well as the processes that produced the evolutionary changes that resulted in modern humans.*

# 12 One Hundred Years of Biological Anthropology (1968)

**S. L. Washburn**   *Professor of Anthropology, University of California at Berkeley*

Dedicated to the memory of Earnest Albert Hooten

One hundred years take us back into the heart of the Darwinian era. [1] The *Origin of Species* was published in 1859, Huxley's *Man's Place in Nature*, and Lyell's *Age of Man* in 1863. Darwin's *Descent of Man* appeared in 1871,

and we may well start this review with Darwin's view of human evolution. Darwin's object in writing the *Descent of Man* was to consider "whether man, like every other species, is descended from some pre-existing form." [2] The work of the forerunners of Darwin, [3] Darwin's contributions, and the history of the era have been extensively reviewed in numerous symposia and books, many of them celebrating the hundredth anniversary of the *Origin*. Here we are concerned only with Darwin's view of the nature of man and the problem of deriving

J. O. Brew, ed., *One Hundred Years of Anthropology* (Cambridge: Harvard University Press, 1968), pp. 97–115. Reprinted by permission of the publisher. Copyright © 1968 by the President and Fellows of Harvard College.

man from some kind of pre-existing ape. Since very few fossils were known at the time Darwin wrote, the evidences he used were largely indirect and based on still existing forms of life. But Darwin saw the problem of origin in terms of behavior and of the modification of correlated behavior and structure through time. For example, Darwin attributed the reduction of the canine teeth of the male ape and the origin of erect posture to the importance of tools. Further, in the comparison of the mental powers of man and animals, Darwin considered emotion, curiosity, memory, and imagination. He considered language, beauty, and religion, and he pondered on the way natural selection had produced social, moral, intellectual human beings. This breadth of vision tended to be lost and the recent books on human evolution are more limited and tend to be concerned with interpreting the record and the process of evolution. The comparison of the behavior of man and apes was confused both by the state of social science and the lack of reliable accounts of the behavior of nonhuman primates. Today, we can reopen the problem of human nature, of understanding the differences between man and ape, with more effective social science, new evolutionary theory, and major field studies on the behavior of the contemporary monkeys and apes.

The problem of the origin of man is the whole problem of the evolution of human nature. Fossil evidence is essential in charting the course of our evolution, and without genetics there can be no understanding of the process of evolution. But because natural selection operates only through successful behaviors, it is the study of the evolution of behavior that is central to an understanding of the problem of man's origin. In spite of oversimplification, misuse for racist purposes, and misunderstanding, Darwin's view was essentially correct, and the scientific interest in the evolution of behavior has recently revived.[4]

If we accept that the goal of biological anthropology is the understanding of human nature in all its complexity and richness, then we must stress at once that this nature only exists and expresses itself in a social system. Just as the role of the actor is meaningless without the play, so human biology has no meaning without society. For a particular problem in the short run, either biological or social facts may be stressed, but the evolution of man can only be understood as a biosocial problem. Murdock (1945) stressed this in his paper on "The Common Denominator of Cultures."[5] He pointed out that a great deal of culture is universal and the explanation of the universal pattern links all known cultures "simple and complex, ancient and modern."[6] And its explanation can be sought only "in the fundamental biological and psychological nature of man and in the universal conditions of human existence."[7] More

recently, Goldschmidt (1966) in his call for a comparative functionalism has restated the interrelations of biology and society,[8] and Hamburg (1963) has evaluated the emotions of man in the perspective of human evolution.[9] The problems that Darwin raised are being put into modern form, and in this paper I want to consider some of the implications of this transformation.

## THEORY

One hundred years ago scientists were trying to convince people that evolution had taken place and that the general principle applied even to man. Darwin's great contribution was demonstrating a mechanism that could be responsible for the transitions of one form into another. But, in addition, Darwin clearly recognized the need for some theory of genetics, some theory to account for the way the phenotypes of one generation become the phenotypes of the next.[10] Although Mendel's laws were rediscovered in 1900, the full implications of genetics for evolutionary theory developed slowly, and it was not until the 1930's that it became apparent that much of the evolutionary thinking was not compatible with population genetics. The history of the origin of the modern or synthetic theory of evolution has been fully told elsewhere,[11] but for present purposes its origin may be dated by Huxley's book *Evolution, the Modern Synthesis*, which first appeared in 1942. In this country the need for bringing together genetics, paleontology, and systematics was recognized in the 1930's, and a Committee on Common Problems of Genetics, Paleontology, and Systematics was formed, held meetings, and started a journal. This committee's work finally resulted in a symposium which was published under the title *Genetics, Paleontology, and Evolution*.[12] Simpson's *Meaning of Evolution* (1949)[13] made the new synthesis available in simplified form. The new synthesis which was forming in the 1920's and 1930's took shape in the 1940's and became accessible to all by 1950.[14]

Since in anthropology there had been extreme reliance on typological thinking, orthogenesis, irreversibility, and the importance of nonadaptive characters, the synthetic theory devastated most of the structure of traditional anthropological thought. This can be seen most clearly in the study of human races.[15] The majority of physical anthropologists had been busy dividing populations into types, and then manipulating the types in order to reconstitute racial history. Types similar to the existing ones were postulated to have existed hundreds of thousands of years ago; this notion of the fixity of the types of modern man goes along with the theory that modern man is ancient and almost all the fossils represent collateral lines which became extinct. Substitution of the variable Mendelian population for the type (composed of phenotypically similar individuals) simply destroyed the theoretical basis for the vast majority of anthropological thought. Many anthropologists believed in orthogenesis, that evolution proceeds from an internal momentum. The synthetic theory showed that no such process exists, and that trends are due to selection. Also the idea was common that evolution should be traced by nonadaptive characters. This point of view is seen in extreme form in the writings of Wood Jones,[16] who, after giving an excellent comprehensive review of primate anatomy, attempted to determine evolutionary relationships on the basis of a few minor variations in the patterns of sutures. According to the synthetic theory, selection is even more important than Darwin thought, and the explanation of characters should be sought in the understanding of their functions. These theoretical problems were by no means unique to anthropology, but the confusion of typological, pregenetic thinking was extreme in anthropology because of the emphasis on racial types, and the attempt to recreate history without regard to the fossil record.

In summary, the last hundred years may be divided, very approximately, into three major sections. In the first, which lasted to approximately 1900, scientists were primarily interested in proving that evolution had taken place and that the theory applied to man. There were few known fossils and the evidences for evolution of man were primarily indirect from the embryology and comparative anatomy of the living primates. In the second stage[17]—again very approximately 1900 to 1940—attempts were made to reconstruct human evolution in considerable detail. Although some fossils were known, elaborate phylogenetic trees were constructed, still primarily on the basis of indirect evidence. This was an era of extreme typological thinking, and scientists believed many conflicting theories of evolution. By 1940 the implications of genetics had become clear and the synthesis of genetics and paleontology was taking place.

## THE FOSSIL RECORD

In the nineteenth century not enough fossils had been discovered to compel any particular point of view on human evolution. Discoveries of Neanderthal, Java man, and an ape (*Dryopithecus*) were important in helping to prove that man had evolved from some other form of primate, but the main proofs of human evolution came from indirect evidence, the anatomy of the contemporary forms. This evidence is useful in considering the general nature of human evolution, but it gives no information on the precise course of evolution or on the detail of anatomy of the ancestral forms. The idea of a missing link more or less halfway in its structure between ape and man was firmly embedded in the human mind *before* the fossils were found. For example, Neanderthal man was reconstructed walking in a stooped-over position and with a bent-knee gait, and the characteristics of the Neanderthal skeleton were described as apelike, even though in many cases they were ultrahuman! Recent study by Straus and Cave (1957)[18] shows that there is no evidence that the Neanderthals walked differently from the way we do. And now that many fossils are available it is impossible to draw any sharp line of distinction between the Neanderthals and people like ourselves. The populations of ancient men of fifty thousand years ago that were ancestral to us included those which were called Neanderthal (if the term is not restricted to the European forms; if it is, then direct ancestry is still debatable).[19]

The essential point is that, when there are only a few fossils, the climate of opinion may be more important than the fossils in determining how they are regarded. Particularly in the case of human evolution (where feelings are strong and facts are few), it takes repeated discoveries to change the patterns of thought that took form in the period when fossils were few, and when the accepted fossil record included mistakes and even fakes. In the period 1915 to 1940 the most common arrangement of the fossil men of the Middle Pleistocene and later was one which put all the even slightly primitive forms on side lines and which postulated that there had been two separate evolutions in the Pleistocene, one of the ancient forms of man (*Pithecanthropus, Sinanthropus,* Neanderthal, and so forth) and one of the anatomically modern forms (Galley Hill, Piltdown). According to this view, almost all the fossils actually discovered belonged on the side lines and the ancestors were rare indeed. Historically the matter might be put in this way. At the time of the "discovery" of Piltdown man in 1912, there were about as many fossils that appeared to support the early modern man point of view as ones that "proved" that anatomically, modern man was a latecomer. At present there are fewer fossils that can be made to fit the early modern man theory than there were in 1915 and these are mostly fragments. The other point of view is supported by an ever increasing number of well-preserved skulls and skeletons. As Keith put the matter in 1949, "The tide of discovery turned against me."[20] The statement is even truer today than when Keith wrote it.

The view that the populations of ancient men of the Middle Pleistocene and later belonged to one species, that they were at most racially distinct, that interbreeding occurred between them, arose primarily outside of anthropology, and is closely linked to the rise of population genetics and the synthetic theory of evolution. It is no accident that in this country Dobzhansky (1944), Mayr (1950, 1963), and Simpson (1963)[21] (not anthropologists) have been particularly influential in changing the patterns of thought.

If scientists had problems in regarding fossil men, such as Neanderthal, Peking, or Java, as representative of ancestral populations, even greater difficulties were encountered with the small-brained men of the Lower Pleistocene. The first discovery of *Australopithecus* was made in 1924 and numerous subsequent discoveries support Dart's (1925)[22] interpretation of the original specimen. Consideration of these fossils by anthropologists was hindered by four very strong convictions: (1) that the size of the brain proved that the creature could not be close to man, (2) that the pelvis was far too human to be part of such a small-brained creature, and (3) that nothing with such a small brain could have made stone tools, and (4) that only one kind of man could have made even the simplest tools. It is probable that all these assumptions are wrong. In the Lower Pleistocene, several kinds of bipedal hominids made simple tools, and the beginnings of tool-making may be found in prebipedal apes. There was an adaptive radiation of early bipedal human forms with the formation of more than one species, and one of these species evolved into the genus *Homo*, the large-brained men of the Middle Pleistocene. At least one species of *Australopithecus* lived on and was for a time a contemporary of the earliest members of the genus *Homo*.

These small-brained bipeds, no matter how they may ultimately be evaluated, give evidence of a stage in human evolution that is quite different from anything previously anticipated. They indicate that the rates of evolution of the different parts of the body were remarkably different, and that the evolution of large brains was very late in human evolution.[23] They conform very well to the pattern suggested by Darwin—that the evolution of both bipedalism and small canine teeth was the result of the new selection pressures that came with tool using. The evidence suggests a very long stage of the use of simple tools, and then an increase in the rate of cultural evolution synchronous with the evolution of the genus *Homo*.

In contrast to the relative abundance of fossils of *Australopithecus*, the remains of apes (Pongidae) are rare. There is only one relatively well-preserved skull of the genus *Dryopithecus* (*Proconsul*), for example, and most of the fossils are limited to teeth and jaws. And most of these are fragmentary. Probably the earliest monkeys and apes occur in the Oligocene, and it is probable that the two families had separated by the beginning of the Miocene.[24] Although there are only a few postcranial remains, none of those that are preserved has the characteristics of the arm bones of the contemporary great apes.[25] When only the teeth of the fossil apes were known, it was expected that the rest of the skeleton, when discovered, would be apelike. For example, when Gregory wrote the paper entitled "Were the Ancestors of Man Primitive Brachiators?"[26] bones of the contemporary apes were used to illustrate the probable conditions in the ancestral apes. Obviously, no scientist expected that the bones would be identical, but the limb bones of the now-known Middle Miocene forms (*Pliopithecus* and *Limnopithecus, Proconsul*) are more like those of quadrupedal monkeys than those of the contemporary apes.[27] The features of the limb bones that man shares with the gibbons and great apes are not present in the known fossils, and, if the similarities between man (Hominidae) and ape (Pongidae) are to be accounted for by common ancestry, then the ancestral common populations must have been late Miocene or early Pliocene. The climbing-feeding adaptation called "brachiation" was not present in the early apes, and the similarities of man are with the late apes and particularly with the genus *Pan* (chimpanzee and gorilla).

The fossil record is so fragmentary that such conclusions would carry little weight if they were not supported by other lines of evidence, but recent studies of the chromosomes[28] indicate a very close similarity between man and the African apes. Immunological tests give the same result.[29] If the recently devised method of converting immunological distance into time in years is correct,[30] then the time of the populations of ancestral *Pan* is on the order of six to ten million years, or middle Pliocene. This fits very well with the evidence of the limb bones, but, according to Simons and Leakey,[31] the dental evidence suggests a much earlier separation. The matter cannot be settled at this time, and it will probably take more fossils and other chemical investigations to bring about any sort of agreement. But whatever may be the ultimate solution to the apparently very contradictory conclusions based on different lines of evidence, all lines support the traditional point of view expressed by Huxley in 1863[32]—that of the living primates, man is closer to the apes than the apes to the quadrupedal monkeys.

In summary, the continued discovery of actual fossils has slowly changed traditional points of view on human evolution. The minority opinion that fossils of the genus *Homo* represent ancestral populations, rather than extinct side lines, has become the majority opinion. A whole new stage of human evolution is now represented by *Australopithecus* of the Lower Pleistocene. The discovery of quadrupedal fossils and the apparent contradiction between the dental evidence and that of the limb bones on the one hand and immunochemistry on the other has raised new problems on the antiquity of the family of man (Hominidae). It is clear from this discussion that fossil evidence is necessary for the appreciation of human evolution and that, in winning the battle for the acceptance of human evolution on the basis of comparing the living forms, scientists created such fixed notions of what the missing links should be like that the acceptance of the actual evidence has always been delayed.

## TIME

Much of the background for the theory of organic evolution came from geology. The theory that geological formations had been formed over long periods of time by the same processes that can be observed today laid the background for interpreting the history of the creatures whose remains were found in the rocks. In 1778 Buffon speculated that the earth might have cooled from a molten mass and life evolved in a few thousand years. By the end of the nineteenth century Kelvin had suggested that cooling must have taken some thirty or forty million years. On the basis of the amount of salt in the oceans, Jolly estimated that the earth must be one hundred million years old, but scientists were not ready for estimates of this magnitude and Sollas reduced the estimate.

|  | Sollas (1905)[33] | Keith (1931)[34] |
|---|---|---|
| Pleistocene | 350,000 | 200,000 |
| Pliocene | 350,000 | 250,000 |
| Miocene | 460,000 | 450,000 |
| Oligocene | 650,000 | 600,000 |
| Eocene | 1,440,000 | 600,000 |

Keith's estimate gave a total of a little over two million years for the age of mammals. This was a short estimate, and it can be seen at once that, if one is operating with such a frame of time and if seemingly little human evolution occurred in the Pleistocene, it does not appear to take a great extrapolation to divide lineages back into the Miocene. The short estimates of time, plus the view that the duration of the named intervals of time were more or less equal, had a profound effect on evolutionary reconstructions.

In 1947 methods were devised for estimating time from the rate of decay of radioactive minerals.[35] The times were startlingly longer than previous estimates, and the entire age of the earth as estimated by Sollas could easily fit within the age of the mammals (some seventy million years). Life is now estimated to be something on the order of three billion years old and possibly

much older. This time becomes so vast that it can be appreciated only with the aid of an analogy. For example, if we consider a football field as representing, more or less, the five hundred million years of the history of the chordates (vertebrates, the group to which we belong), then the length of all life would be estimated by five or six football fields. The age of the mammals would be on the last fifteen yards of the five football fields and the duration of the genus *Homo* would be on the goal line. It simply would not show on a scale of this size. Certainly one of the great scientific revolutions is the new concept of time—also space and size. The universe is now believed to be large beyond the most extravagant scientific speculations, and it is made of units which are smaller than had ever been imagined. And 4004 B.C. has changed to billions of years.

For anthropology, there are now four very different concepts of time. First there is biological time, the immediately appreciated circadian rhythms.[36] With long jet travel, we feel the upset in these deeply rooted biological rhythms, and the importance of the animal's ability to estimate time can be seen in the field studies of the behavior of monkeys and apes. Regardless of weather conditions, the internal rhythms bring the baboons back to the sleeping trees at the appropriate time, and the rhythms continue during sleep with the alternation of deep sleep and dreaming. It is highly adaptive for the essential activities to be patterned, and the meaning of light sleep (dreaming) as vigilance behavior has been discussed by Snyder (1966).[37] The appreciation of biological time is directly related to physiology reinforced by habit.

A second kind of time is social time, the three to five generations which are important to the social system. But even this amount of time is far more than the human organism usually feels important. Evolution has not adapted the organism to feel strongly about distant times, whether in the future or in the past.

History is still a third kind of time, and interest in recorded events of the last few thousand years is usually an acquired taste. Historians themselves debate the meaning of these events, and nations make the same old mistakes with supreme confidence that what they are doing is right.

And the fourth kind of time—geologic time, scientific time, the time of the atom, or whatever one may wish to call it—is again fundamentally different, and so hard for the human organism to grasp that its meaning can be hinted at only by analogy.

But the essential point I want to make is that the appreciation of time is basically a biological problem. Part of the appreciation is immediate physiology reinforced by habit. Then we learn with more and more difficulty to understand longer periods of time. In the short intervals that have been important in the evolution of the species, we learn easily and may feel strongly. In the longest intervals, even appreciation becomes difficult or perhaps impossible. It becomes necessary to resort to analogies to convey meaning.

The problem of appreciating time brings out a very fundamental principle. What has evolved is not a behavior as such but an ability to learn. Hinde and Tinbergen (1958)[38] refer to the evolution of "the propensity to learn," and Hamburg (1963)[39] has called attention to the same problem under the heading of "ease of learning." At the moment, there is no simple designation for this, but the situation can be described as follows. Through evolution, each species is so constituted that it easily learns those behaviors that are essential for its survival. Man learns to be social, learns to walk bipedally, learns language, and he learns these activities easily, almost inevitably, because of his biological evolution. The whole dichotomy between instinctive and learned behavior is an oversimplification, and there is every gradation from behaviors that are almost completely determined by biology to those that can be learned only with the greatest difficulty. The demonstration that a behavior is learned does not remove its biological foundations or limitations.

For example, monkeys normally learn to be social, and Harlow (1966)[40] has described the stages of this learning and the devastating consequences of social isolation. Gibbons also learn to be social,[41] but they learn a very different social system. It is useless to postulate a social instinct, but the relation of biology of a species, the situations, and the behaviors present a series of problems. Monkeys will learn to work for the sight of another monkey. They will make great efforts to stay with their troop.[42] They make clearly observable efforts to sit near preferred individuals[43] or to touch other individuals, and, in addition to mating behavior, many social behaviors appear to be highly rewarding. One aspect, or more correctly, a number of aspects, of the evolution of man's capacity for culture[44] is the evolution of the biological bases for interpersonal relations. The diversity of cultures in no way alters the fact that in every pattern of culture it is biological organisms which learn human ways, are moved by human emotions, and adjust with human limitations.

## SPACE AND COMING TO THE GROUND

The effect of rephrasing the traditional problems in terms of behavior may be seen by taking the examples of space and of coming to the ground. Traditionally, the utilization of space was not perceived as a problem at all, and our ancestors' coming to the ground was usually accounted for by desiccation, by the reduction in the forests. However, all the nonhuman primates described so far restrict their activities to areas that are, from the human point of view, tiny, a few square miles at most. Probably the vast majority of monkeys spend their entire lives within three or four square miles. Their vision is excellent and they can certainly see rewards (food, water) beyond their habitual ranges, but they do not move long distances. Man is unique not only in his method of locomotion, but in his treatment of space. Man hunts and gathers over hundreds of square miles, and the evolution of human locomotion (the biology) must be seen as an adaptation to this unique use of space, not just to being upright.[45] In 1963, Napier stressed striding as the crucial factor in the human gait, not just being upright. But the point I wish to stress is that the perception that it is advantageous to go long distances probably has been as important in the evolution of locomotion as any other factor. Or, to put it differently, the whole complex of behaviors involving long distances (gathering more extensively, carrying, hunting, seasonal migration)—*all* these would lead to selection for efficient bipedal locomotion. And all these actions involve habits dependent on the learning capacity of the brain, in addition to the locomotor anatomy.

Coming to the ground also is a behavioral problem, and appears very differently if one starts with the behavior of the contemporary primates as a guide. Both the gorilla[46] and the chimpanzee[47] live primarily on the ground. And there is a considerable adaptation for knuckle walking.[48] Gorillas are primarily ground feeders, and chimpanzees eat mostly fruit, knuckle walking from one area of fruiting trees to another.[49] These data point up problems at once. An ape coming to the ground does not necessarily become bipedal, and, second, the ground-living apes are in the forest, not in the savanna. Any reduction of forest would mean a reduction in the number of apes. (This is precisely the reverse conclusion of the desiccation theory.) The larger the forests, the more opportunity for ground living apes. Further, if one argues that the human kind of behavior patterns might have been most likely to evolve on the forest borders, the edge of the forest was much larger when the forests were greater. The Old World forests were much larger and the reduction to the present size took place during the Pliocene, probably due both to the rise of mountains and to the reduction in precipitation. Pilbeam (1967)[50] has shown that, in the early Pliocene and before, forests connected Europe, India, and Africa, and the apes (Pongidae) were widely distributed. There was no necessary separation of the African apes from other forms and *Dryopithecus* (sensu lato, following Simons and Pilbeam) existed all over the area. Similarly, they see *Ramapithecus* as a form similar to *Kenyapithecus*. (The similarity in the dentition is a fact, regardless of whether these forms are ultimately regarded as members of the Pongidae or Hominidae.) The fossils show that the similarity of the African apes to man may be misleading in that the actual ancestral species may have been common to India, the Near East, and Africa. Reduction of the forests led to the separation of Asia and Africa, and to the restriction of our nearest living relatives to Africa. But there is no reason to suppose that the living or extinct African forms are any closer to us than are the extinct ones of India or the Middle East.

In summary, coming to the ground is most likely when forests are extensive and when there are many arboreal species which may make the change. Since the arboreal forms are in the forest, the change is most likely to take place in the forest and along the edges of forests. Knuckle walking is the locomotor adaptation of chimpanzees and gorillas to ground life, and it is probable that our ancestors were knuckle walkers on the forest floor for a long time prior to the emergence of efficient, long-distance bipedalism. The behavior of the living primates shows that merely coming to the ground does not explain human locomotion. The essential question is the nature of the adaptation to ground life, and this may be by quadrupedalism, knuckle walking, or bipedalism.

The problem of coming to the ground illustrates several points in traditional thinking. Origins tended to be considered as due to single causes in relatively restricted times and places. So desiccation might account for ground-living or for domestication around a remaining water hole. But the difference between adaptation and extinction probably depended on many factors over long periods of time. For example, one species of contemporary monkey, *Cercopithecus aethiops,* is distributed over an area some eight thousand miles long. The distance is as great as the distance that separates locations where the fossils of *Ramapithecus* and *Kenyapithecus* have been found. When forests were more extensive, there was no reason why a single species of ape might not have such a distribution. Contemporary chimpanzees have a distribution some three thousand miles long, and the limits appear to be entirely geographical. The transition from ape to man (Pongidae to Hominidae) may have taken place in a highly variable species over some millions of years. The implication of genetics is that there is no "origin" in the typological sense, but hundreds of origins over millions of years. As long as ancestral populations remained part of one species, origin is only localized by the extent of the whole species.

A further aspect of the traditional thinking was to come to conclusions which were stated in a very definite form, rather than as a probability. For example, some stated that man "could not" have been descended

from an ape and others that he "must be" descended from an ape. Since the fossil record is extremely fragmentary, the chances of error are great. It is easy to avoid this kind of statement and the controversies that have stemmed from it. Conclusions can be put in terms of probability. For example, I think that our ancestors of some millions of years ago were knuckle-walking apes, but the evidence is scanty and I think that the betting odds on this might be something like two to one. In other words, I would not be surprised if the conclusion is wrong. I think it is probable that at a still earlier stage our ancestors were apes who had the climbing-feeding complex called "brachiation." The evidence for this point of view is much stronger. I would place the odds in favor at a hundred to one. In other words, I would be very surprised if the conclusion is wrong, but there is a chance that that may be the case. I suspect that many futile controversies might have been avoided if it had been clear that the differing interpretations of human evolution were matters of probability, if the scientists had indicated the degree of certainty with which they held their beliefs.

## CONCLUSIONS

However this may be, the controversies are primarily over the course of evolution, its precise route. There is no debate on the principal ways in which man varies from the other primates and these differences were clear to Darwin and his contemporaries. Man differs in his pattern of locomotion, and this adaptation is more than 2 million years old. Man differs in the size and form of his teeth, and this adaptation shares a comparable antiquity. Both these adaptations may be a consequence of new selection pressures concomitant with the use of tools.

Man differs in the size and structure of his brain, and this (complex of adaptations) came long after the others. The human brain makes the human way of life possible and the brain evolved along with the changing way of life. As we compare the human way to that of the nonhuman primates, as we view the tremendous adaptive success of man's technical and social life, language appears to be the most fundamental adaptive difference. And the later evolution of the brain may have been in a feedback relation with all the complex social patterns which language makes possible.[51]

If this is true, there can be no biological anthropology, in the sense of an independent science, as in the first half of this century. The physical anthropologist can no longer construct an evolutionary history by manipulating types. Nonadaptive characters no longer provide an escape from the study of history and adaptation. Orthogenesis no longer offers a refuge from the study of the actual setting of the evolutionary process. The central evolutionary problem is behavior and, in the case of man, the principal adaptive mechanisms are social and are dependent on the brain and the behaviors that it makes possible, on language, tradition, complex skills, and social change. Clearly, the physical anthropologist cannot deal with all these subject matters. The vision of evolutionary understanding that comes from the synthetic theory, from the union of genetics and paleontology, requires a synthesis of the efforts of many traditional departments. Or, to put the matter differently, the theory that shows why so much of the traditional evolutionary thinking was wrong also shows why the organization of the university is profoundly wrong.[52] The understanding of human behavior is too complicated and too important to be hindered by departmental structures whose origin lies in the nineteenth century. If there is any lesson from a hundred years of biological anthropology, it is that knowledge cannot usefully be divided along the traditional lines and that, perhaps even more than a synthetic theory of evolution, we need a synthetic theory of education. In our universities it should be possible for a student to gain an understanding of man without having to go to a dozen different departments. To understand human evolution we need more fossils, more studies of behavior, more genetics. The technical specialties should be developed. But, beyond these, new academic institutions are needed which are organized around problems and which will share the results of technical specialization with the student. Biological anthropology is concerned with understanding the dimensions of life, the times, places, and conditions under which our ancestors lived; the processes which produced change; the ecological-psychological problems of territory, diet, home base, defense, dentition, and digestion; the social-psychological problems of the group, mother-child, play, the peer group, dominance and order, intelligence, exploration, and religion. However abundant they may be in the fossil record, man did not live by teeth alone, and those who would analyze the fossils must understand the behavior of those who left the bones.

## NOTES

1. Traditional physical anthropology might be defined by the content of Juan Comas, *Manual of Physical Anthropology* (Springfield, 1950) or Ashley Montagu, *An Introduction to Physical Anthropology*, 3rd ed. (Springfield, 1960). The content does not differ essentially from E. A. Hooten's *Up From the Ape* (New York, 1931 and 1946). The content of present-day anthropology is indicated by J. Buettner-Janusch, *Origins of Man* (New York, 1966) and by G. A. Harrison, J. S. Weiner, J. M. Tanner, and N. A. Barnicot, *Hu-*

*man Biology* (Oxford, 1964). It is clear from these and other books that the purposes of phsyical anthropology have always been much broader than the research techniques employed by those scientists labeled "physical anthropologists." In teaching about human evolution, no one would limit himself to anthropological information in the restricted sense, but would include information from many other sciences. I take "biological anthropology" to be even broader, to be the biological element in any anthropological problem.

In limiting this discussion primarily to the question of the origin of man, I do not want to suggest that phsyical anthropology has been limited to this question or that it should be so limited. Physical anthropological technqiues are useful in studies of growth, variation, identification, and constitution. This might have considered race, rather than long-term evolution, as the major theme, and stressed regional variation and adaptation to climate and disease. Either technical advances or theoretical progress could easily fill an entire book, let alone a paper. Likewise, many important scientists are omitted (Coon, Hrdlicka, Krogman, Schultz, Valkis—to mention only a few). A more balanced account is given by J. S. Weiner, "Physical Anthropology: A Survey of Developments," *A Hundred Years of Anthropology*, ed. T. K. Penniman (London, 1965), pp. 285–320. My only essential point is that, with the synthetic theory of evolution, with fossils, and with the study of behavior, there has been major progress, and it is my belief that this progress will continue at a rapidly accelerating rate. The only important conclusion is that social science and biological science are inextricably interwoven in the study of human evolution.

The research for this paper is being carried out under a grant from the U.S. Public Health Service (No. MH 08623). I wish to thank Dr. Phyllis C. Jay for helpful criticism of the manuscript.

2. Charles Darwin. *The Descent of Man and Selection in Relation to Sex* (New York, 1871), p. 390.

3. B. Glass, O. Temkin, and W. L. Straus, Jr., eds. *Forerunners of Darwin, 1745–1859* (Baltimore, 1959).

4. J. Altman, *Organic Foundations of Animal Behavior* (New York, 1966); S. A. Altmann, ed., *Social Communication Among Primates* (Chicago and London, 1967); J. Buettner-Janusch, ed., *Evolutionary and Genetic Biology of Primates* (New York and London, 1963–1964); C. R. Carpenter, *Naturalistic Behavior of Nonhuman Primates* (University Park, 1964); I. DeVore, ed., *Primate Behavior: Field Studies of Monkeys and Apes* (New York, 1965); J. Goodall, "Chimpanzees of the Gombe Stream Reserve," *Primate Behavior: Field Studies of Monkeys and Apes,* ed. I. DeVore (New York, 1965), pp. 425–473; R. A. Hinde, *Animal Behavior* (New York, 1966); P. C. Jay, "Field Studies," *Behavior of Nonhuman Primates,* ed. A. M. Schrier, H. F. Harlow, and F. Stollnitz (New York and London, 1965), pp. 525–591; P. Marler and W. J. Hamilton III, *Mechanisms of Animal Behavior* (New York, 1966); T. E. McGill, *Readings in Animal Behavior* (New York, 1965); J. Napier and N. A. Barnicot, eds., *The Primates* (London, 1963); A. Roe and G. G. Simpson, eds. *Behavior and Evolution* (New Haven, 1958); G. Schaller, *The Mountain Gorilla: Ecology and Behavior* (Chicago, 1953).

5. G. P. Murdock, "The Common Denominator of Cultures," *The Science of Man in the World Crisis* (New York, 1945), pp. 123–142.

6. *Ibid.*, p. 125.

7. *Ibid.*

8. W. Goldschmidt, *Comparative Functionalism* (Berkeley and Los Angeles, 1956).

9. D. A. Hamburg, "Emotions in the Perspective of Human Evolution," *Expression of the Emotions in Man,* P. Knapp, ed. (New York, 1963), pp. 300–317.

10. Charles Darwin, *The Descent of Man and Selection in Relation to Sex* (New York, 1871).

11. E. Mayr, *Animal Species and Evolution* (Cambridge, Mass., 1963); T. H. Huxley, *Man's Place in Nature* (Ann Arbor, 1863). The revolution that the functional point of view of Malinowski and Radcliffe-Brown brought to social anthropology is very comparable to the change which came in biological anthropology with the ad-

vent of the synthetic theory of evolution. In both cases there was a repudiation of reconstructions which had minimum basis in recorded history. In both, interest changed from the description of unrelated items to actual behavior, patttern, and function.

12. G. L. Jepsen, E. Mayr, and G. G. Simpson, eds., *Genetics, Paleontology, and Evolution* (Princeton, 1949).

13. G. G. Simpson, *The Meaning of Evolution* (New Haven and London, 1949).

14. The Cold Spring Harbor Symposium, The Origin and Evolution of Man, organized by Dobzhansky, brought the new human revolutionary synthesis to the attention of all.

15. Darwin believed that the causes of evolution were selection, correlation of parts, sexual selection, and inheritance of acquired characteristics. In modifying his theory to meet criticisms, he reduced the emphasis on natural selection and actually weakened the theory from the modern point of view.

16. F. W. Jones, *Man's Place among the Mammals* (New York, 1929); W. K. Gregory in *Man's Place among the Anthropoids* (Oxford, 1934) criticized Wood Jones, but in retrospect it can be seen that the theoretical arguments could not be settled at that time.

17. This is the era in which physical anthropology took form as a distinct science, and in which degrees were given in physical anthropology. Hooton was trained in classics. Hrdlicka and Keith were medical doctors. The founders of the American Association of Physical Anthropologists were, for the most part, not anthropologists in the restricted sense. The roots of the profession in anatomy and medicine tended to delay progress in both genetics and social science.

18. W. L. Straus, Jr., and A. J. E. Cave, "Pathology and the Posture of Neanderthal Man," *Quarterly Review of Biology*, vol. 32, pp. 348–363.

19. W. W. Howells, *Mankind in the Making* (New York, 1959); "Homo Erectus," *Scientific American*, 215 (1966), 46–53.

20. A. Keith, *A New Theory of Human Evolution* (New York, 1949).

21. T. Dobzhansky, "On Species and Races of Living and Fossil Man," *American Journal of Physical Anthropology* (1944), 251–265; E. Mayr, *Animal Species and Evolution*; G. G. Simpson, "The Meaning of Taxonomic Statements," *Classification and Human Evolution*, ed. S. L. Washburn (New York, 1963), pp. 1–31.

22. R. Dart, "*Australopithecus africanus:* The Man-Ape of South Africa," *Nature*, 115 (1925), 195–199.

23. Clearly anticipating this principle was E. A. Hooton's "The Asymmetrical Character of Human Evolution," *American Journal of Physical Anthropology*, 8 (1925), 125–141.

24. E. L. Simons, "New Fossil Apes from Egypt and the Initial Differentiation of Hominoidea," *Nature*, 205 (1965), 135–139.

25. W. E. L. Clark and D. P. Thomas, *Associated Jaws and Limb Bones of Limnopithecus macinnesi* (London, 1951); J. Napier and P. R. Davis, "The Fore-Limb Skeleton and Associated Remains of *Proconsul africanus*," *Fossil Mammals*, 16 (1959), 1–78; Helmuth Zapfe, "The Skeleton of Pliopithecus (Epipliopithecus) vindobonensis" in *American Journal of Physical Anthropology*, 16 (1958), 441–455.

26. W. K. Gregory, "Were the Ancestors of Man Primitive Brachiators?" *Proceedings of the American Phiolosophical Society*, 67 (1929), 129–150.

27. Since all the recent evidence, reviewed by G. G. Simpson, "The Biological Nature of Man," *Science*, 52 (1966), 472–478, indicates that man's closest relatives are the African great apes, theories that our ancestors were other quadrupedal forms are not considered here, but see W. L. Straus, Jr., ed., "Riddle of Man's Ancestry," *Quarterly Review of Biology*, 24 (1949), 200–223, for an alternative point of view.

28. H. P. Klinger, J. L. Hamerton, D. Mutten, and E. M. Lang, "The Chromosomes of the Hominoidea" in *Classification and Human Evolution* (1963), ed. S. L. Washburn.

29. M. Goodman, "Serological Analysis of the Phyletic Relationships of Recent Hominoids," *Human Biology*, vol. 35, pp. 377–436; A. S. Hafleigh and C. A. Williams, Jr., "Antigenic Correspondence of Serum Albumins among the Primates," *Science*, 151 (1966), 1530–1535.

30. V. Sarich and A. Wilson, "Immunological Time Scale for Hominid Evolution," *Science, 158* (1967), 1200–1202.

31. E. L. Simons, "New Fossil Apes from Egypt and the Initial Differentiation of Hominoidea," *Nature*, pp. 135–138; L. S. B. Leakey, "An Early Miocene Member of Hominidae," *Nature, 212* (1967), 155–163.

32. T. H. Huxley, *Man's Place in Nature.*

33. W. J. Sollas, *The Age of the Earth* (London, 1905).

34. A. Keith, *New Discoveries Relating to the Antiquity of Man* (London, 1931).

35. A. Knopf, "Time in Earth History," *Genetics, Paleontology, and Evolution*, ed. G. L. Jepsen, E. Mayr, and G. G. Simpson, pp. 1–9; "Measuring Geologic Time," *Study of the Earth*, ed. John F. White (Englewood Cliffs, N.J., 1962). The study of time shows the importance of techniques. In spite of great efforts by many competent scientists, it was not until the development of methods based on atomic disintegration that estimates of time became possible. Carbon 14 and potassium-argon have been particularly important in anthropology. Molecular biology gives great promise of the quantification of biological difference. Functional anatomy remains a primitive science, and, even after two hundred years, there is still no agreement as to how structures should be compared or differences evaluated (see Solly Zuckerman, "Myths and Methods in Anatomy," *Journal of the Royal College of Surgeons of Edinburgh*, vol. 11, pp. 87–114). Progress in statistical methods and computer analysis has not been matched by progress in the understanding of things measured.

36. G. E. Folk, Jr., *Introduction to Environmental Physiology* (Philadelphia, 1966).

37. Frederick Snyder, "Toward an Evolutionary Theory of Dreaming," *American Journal of Psychiatry, 123* (1966), 121–142. It is interesting to note that the biology of sleep suggests that the meaning of dreams and their frequency is independent of their content. Here is point of relation between biological and social anthropology. If the social scientist wants to collect dreams without the loss of detail and error that comes with remote recall, the dreamer should be awakened at the end of the Rapid Eye Movement state.

38. R. A. Hinde and N. Tinbergen, "The Comparative Study of Species-Specific Behavior," *Behavior and Evolution*, ed. A. Roe and G. G. Simpson, pp. 251–268.

39. D. A. Hamburg, "Emotions in the Perspective of Human Evolution," *Expression of the Emotions in Man*, ed. P. Knapp, pp. 300–317.

40. H. F. Harlow and M. K. Harlow, "Learning to Love," *American Scientist*, vol. 104, pp. 244–272.

41. C. R. Carpenter, "A Field Study in Siam of the Behavior and Social Relations of the Gibbon (*Hylobates lar*)," *Comp. Psychol. Monogr.*, 16 (1940); J. O. Ellefson, *A National History of Gibbons in the Malay Peninsula* (Doctoral thesis, University of California, Berkeley, 1966).

42. S. L. Washburn and I. DeVore, "The Social Life of Baboons," *Scientific American, 204* (1961), 62–71.

43. D. S. Sade, "Some Aspects of Parent-Offspring and Sibling Relations in a Group of Rhesus Monkeys, with a Discussion of Grooming," *American Journal of Physical Anthropology*, 23 (1965), 1–17; "Ontogeny of Social Relations in a Free-Ranging Group of Rhesus Monkeys" (Doctoral thesis, University of California, Berkeley, 1966).

44. S. M. Garn, eds., *Culture and the Direction of Human Evolution* (Detroit, 1964); J. N. Spuhler, ed., *The Evolution of Man's Capacity for Culture* (Detroit, 1959).

45. J. R. Napier, "The Locomotor Functions of Hominids," *Classification and Human Evolution* (New York, 1963), pp. 178–189.

46. G. Schaller, *The Mountain Gorilla: Ecology and Behavior* (Chicago, 1963).

47. J. Goodall, "Chimpanzees of the Gombe Stream Reserve," *Primate Behavior, Field Studies of Monkeys and Apes,* ed. I. DeVore, pp. 425–473; V. Reynolds and F. Reynolds, "Chimpanzees of the Budongo Forest," *Primate Behavior: Field Studies of Monkeys and Apes* (New York, 1965), pp. 368–424.

48. R. H. Tuttle, "Knuckle-Walking and the Evolution of Hominoid Hands," *American Journal of Physical Anthropology, 26* (1967), 171–206.

49. J. van Lawick-Goodall, *My Friends the Wild Chimpanzees* (Washington, D.C., 1967).

50. P. R. Pilbeam, "Man's Earliest Ancestors," *Science Journal, 3* (1967), 47–53.

51. J. B. Lancaster, "Primate Communication Systems and the Emergence of Human Language," *Patterns of Primate Behavior: Adaptation and Variability* (New York, 1967); E. H. Lenneberg, *Biological Foundations of Language* (New York, 1967).

52. J. Huxley in "The Future of Man—Evolutionary Aspects," *Man and His Future,* ed. G. Wolstenholme (Boston and Toronto, 1963), pp. 1–22, has stated that: "In place of separate subjects each with its own assumptions, methodology and technical jargon, we must envisage networks of co-operative investigation, with common methods and terminology, all eventually linked up in a comprehensive process of enquiry. This, of course, will mean a radical reorganization of scientific teaching and research."

*Zihlman challenges the continuing notion that the "fossils reveal all" and argues for Washburn's position that our ideas about human evolution are most often changed by the application of new methods and the integration of evidence that is independent of the fossil record. In this essay she tackles claims about the status and behavior of* Australopithecus afarensis *by considering how fossil species can be identified and how to interpret the locomotor behavior of our ancestors. She illustrates what it means to use all the data, including a functional anatomy based on behavior, experimental research on the biomechanics of locomotion, and the behavior and taxonomy of living primate species. Their integration produces very different answers about the status and possible locomotor behavior of* A. afarensis *than do assertions based on the fossils alone. Today's new data should, therefore, be placed in an intelligent synthesis of the largest variety of evidence rather than be used selectively and simplistically.*

# 13 Fashions and Models in Human Evolution: Contributions of Sherwood Washburn

## Adrienne L. Zihlman

The how of evolution does not come directly from the record . . . ; progress comes from limiting the alternatives, making the choices narrower. (S. L. Washburn 1972: 350)

### NEWS BULLETIN

When the first complete cranium from Hadar, Ethiopia, appeared as the cover story in *Nature,* the accompanying opinion essay announced two things: that the new fossils "will go a long way to settle some of the most heated controversies surrounding the earliest species in the human lineage" and that "it would now take compelling fossil evidence to start the pendulum of opinion swinging back to the idea that there were several species within the *Australopithecus afarensis* hypodigm" (Aiello 1994: 400). In 1978, this species was designated A. "*afarensis*" based on an aggregate of fossils from localities in northern Ethiopia and from Laetoli, Tanzania, including the 3.7-million-year-old footprints discovered by Mary Leakey (Johanson et al. 1978). Although size variation in the postcranial skeleton was marked, the fossils were interpreted as a single species ancestral to all later hominids. The authors argued that the range of size variation could be accommodated within one highly sexually dimorphic species (Johanson and White 1979). The newly announced fossils allegedly confirm this conclusion. According to

"News and Views" commentator Leslie Aielo, fossils have now settled the controversy of species number, and she maintains that only more fossils can overturn this now unassailable position!

Assertions such as these—that fossils reveal all— have been made numerous times during previous decades only to be revised when the "revelations" proved to be incorrect. Since the recognition of the first human fossils more than a hundred years ago, arguments continue to surround new fossil discoveries (Reader 1988). A close look at this history reminds us that new ideas about human evolution rarely come from the fossils alone. Instead, the interpretation of fossils often changes the light of information from new methods and techniques. Therefore, the basis for selecting one hypothesis over another derives not from the fossils alone but from evidence independent of the fossil record.

As a result of the principles I learned from Sherwood Washburn and conclusions from my own research, I remain skeptical about the claims that have been made for *Australopithecus "afarensis."* In this paper I focus on two issues that illustrate the difficulties of relying too exclusively on the fossils themselves: identification of fossil species and interpretation of locomotor behavior solely from bones. Washburn developed his principles as a result of experiencing the controversies of his day.

When he was a young professor, Piltdown was exposed as an imposter in the human lineage by application of new chemical techniques. Deposing Piltdown cleared the way for seriously considering Raymond Dart's *Australopithecus africanus* as a human ancestor two decades after its discovery (Reader 1988). Although the controversies have changed with new intellectual generations, the principles Washburn developed remain germane.

Washburn's first principle was: *use all the evidence.* Researchers tend to use only part of the easily available information—the part that supports their hypotheses. As Washburn noted, "The basis for selection is by no means clear" (1951a: 155). The disregard for other information, or overreliance on fossil evidence alone, exacerbates current controversies over fossil interpretations. Washburn's second principle was: *use new methods* to decide which facts are important. Washburn pointed out that new methods and experiments would provide objective and replicable information to test hypotheses. Thus it is possible to resolve disputes and thus go beyond personal opinion. Finally, Washburn encouraged the *use of living forms in combination with the fossils rather than either alone* (1951a: 171). These principles provide a solid basis for continuing insight when interpreting fossils.

## A SCIENTIFIC FRAMEWORK FOR EVOLUTION

According to Washburn, a more rigorous, scientific approach to evolution becomes possible when all the evidence is combined, including the application of new methods, consideration of functional complexes rather than isolated traits, and incorporation of discoveries from primate field studies. During the 1940s through the 1980s, Washburn's work continued attempts, begun by Charles Darwin and Thomas Henry Huxley, to bring the study of human origins into a scientific framework. Such a framework first became possible when Charles Darwin proposed that all forms of life descended with modification from previous life forms through the process of natural selection. Although his words in *Origin of Species* (1859) were brief—"Light shall be thrown on man and his origins"—the implications for the human species reverberated widely.

Soon after *Origin* was published, Huxley (1863), in contrast to Darwin's conservatism, directly addressed the implications of the new evolutionary framework. In detailing the anatomical similarities between humans and African apes, he viewed the differences in brain size and locomotion as adaptations to different ways of life. Not until near the end of his life did Darwin document his position on human evolution. Like Huxley, he concluded that humans descended from an ape ancestor with Africa as the most likely place of origin (Darwin 1871).

The hypothesis of African origins was derived almost entirely from comparative anatomy and embryology. It is worth emphasizing that Darwin and Huxley put forth their views in the absence of a fossil record. At that time the only fossil ape known was *Dryopithecus* ("oak ape") from France and the only hominids were Neanderthal remains from Europe that had recently been identified as fossils.

Despite the publication of these ideas, Darwin's conceptual contribution of evolutionary change through the process of natural selection was slow to influence the scientific study of human origins. The idea that humans descended from apes became synonymous with Darwin and natural selection and, consequently, there was outright rejection of Darwinism along with the idea of an ape-human common ancestor (Bowler 1986). Instead, vitalism and directed evolution—orthogenesis—as opposed to the more random process of natural selection, pervaded paleontology as the framework for interpreting the fossil record. Conceptually, the idea of parallel evolution replaced that of common ancestry to explain ape-human similarities (Bowler 1986). Human features such as the large brain and bipedal locomotion—habitual upright walking—were described but not placed into an adaptive framework. As the hominid fossil record expanded to include fossil discoveries such as "Cro-Magnon," "Pithecanthropus" in Southeast Asia, and "Sinanthropus" in China, arguments continued to focus on genealogy and there was a preoccupation with drawing family trees, defining stages of evolution, and emphasizing the human species as distinct from all others. Orthogenesis and the directed pathway toward humans as the pinnacle of evolution remained the goal of evolutionary studies (Bowler 1986).

Darwin's and Huxley's ideas foreshadowed conclusions a century later. With new fossil discoveries combined with new techniques in geochronological dating and in the emerging field of molecular biology, a case for an African origin took shape. Although its significance as a human ancestor was not fully appreciated at the time of its discovery, Raymond Dart's fossil child from Taung, which he named *Australopithecus africanus,* finally located Africa on the human evolutionary map. Later, during the 1960s, new dating techniques confirmed an unexpected antiquity of almost 2 million years for the fossil discoveries from Olduvai Gorge, Tanzania, by Mary Leakey and Louis Leakey (Reader 1988). These fossils shared similarities with the South African hominids, thereby extending the hominid geographic range in Africa. The African connection was to be further supported when humans became linked to African apes genetically.

Today it is difficult to appreciate that the hypotheses regarding human emergence from an African ape ancestor persisted as a *minority view* until the middle of the twentieth century. Washburn contributed to the Darwinian revolution within human evolutionary studies, first by replacing an orthogenetic view with one that focused on natural selection and adaptation, and second, by integrating results from experimental studies. Washburn's perspective brought a wider range of information and new questions—indeed a whole new framework—to bear on evolutionary study.

## THE DARWINIAN AND MOLECULAR REVOLUTIONS: WASHBURN'S CONTRIBUTIONS

By the 1940s, the study of evolution was renewed methodologically and theoretically. The work of Th. Dobzhansky in genetics, Ernst Mayr in systematics, and G. G. Simpson in paleontology, for example, facilitated this transition through the formulation of the new evolutionary synthesis—an integration of classical and population genetics with genetic drift and natural selection (Mayr and Provine 1980; Moore 1993). In anthropology, Washburn (1951b) played a key role in firmly grounding the study of human evolution in the modern synthesis of evolution.

In particular, two aspects of Washburn's work directly impacted the study of evolution: his experimental research and his functional and behavioral approach to whole organisms. As part of the new synthesis, Washburn, along with Simpson (1944), integrated genetics, development, and adaptation to explain structure and its evolution. For example, his experimental findings during the 1940s directly tested the forces that shape bone during an individual's life. He noted that the action of sensory nerves, mechanical forces of muscle action, and growing organs like the eye affect the surrounding bone and can be disrupted by cutting a muscle's insertion or paralyzing the muscle through nerve severance or removing the eye (Washburn 1946a,b). Generalizing from this, Washburn cautioned that morphology of fossil bones may not reflect genetic relationships as much as it might reflect changes that occurred during an individual's lifetime.

Fieldwork in tropical Borneo during the 1937 Asiatic Primate Expedition must have contributed to Washburn's holistic view of primates. Uniquely, he was able to dissect animals, observe muscle-bone-joint relationships, at the same time that he saw the animals moving around their habitat. Later he was to systematically study baboon behavior in Africa (Washburn 1983). Consequently, his emerging research perspective fused an animal's anatomy with its behavior and way of life (Washburn 1973).

Washburn applied this functional perspective in his revolutionary analysis of the order Primates. He viewed the major groups as adaptive radiations, each later in time and less variable than the one preceding (1951a: 158). By relating each radiation to the fossil record, he proposed that the first radiation—primate origins—was based on a locomotor adaptation of climbing by grasping. Correlated anatomical changes such as elongated digits and presence of nails could be incorporated into a functional framework rather than remaining as a list of isolated traits. With the second radiation, the anthropoids emerged through reorganized special senses with emphasis on sight and day living. The apes, as the third radiation, shifted to a hanging-feeding adaptation unlike any of the monkeys and included major modifications in the arms and trunk and in upper limb joint function. Thus primary characters were the basis for functional complexes of bone-joint-muscle patterns rather than secondary or isolated characters based on descriptive measurements.

Applying this approach to human evolution, Washburn (1951a) proposed that bipedal locomotion facilitated life on the ground and became the foundation for the human radiation. Prior to 1950, hominid locomotion had not received a structural/functional or evolutionary analysis. Washburn analyzed locomotor changes comparatively by integrating information based on the fossil pelves of the South African australopithecines along with that based on anatomy and locomotor behavior of monkeys and apes. Human walking utilizes a distinct pattern of one-joint muscle action of hip extensors, gluteus maximus, and the knee extensors, quadriceps femoris; in contrast, quadrupedal runners employ the hamstrings, which move two joints: they extend the hip and flex the knee. Washburn demonstrated that the proportions of muscle groups correlate with locomotor behavior. From this comparison he concluded that because climbing involves one-joint muscles, "climbing is preadaptive for human walking" (1951a: 164). Interestingly, as I discuss later in this essay, more than a decade later, Washburn modified his position in order to incorporate the newly emerging molecular data (1967, 1968). Ironically, his hypothesis that climbing was the precursor to hominid bipedal locomotion gained new popularity decades later while ignoring the molecular findings (e.g., Fleagle et al. 1981; Prost 1980).

Because of the rarity and fragmented australopithecine fossil pelvic and limb bones and the difficulties in fully analyzing them, Washburn concluded that fossils, at best, constitute a limited, though important, source of information; and second, the combination of fossil and living forms offers a fuller understanding of evolution that either one is capable of providing alone (1951a: 170). In this context he emphasized the importance of studying the chimpanzee, not "to prove that it is *the* human ancestor but to understand the kind of organization which may have been characteristic of the ancestral [hominid] forms" (1951a: 171, original emphasis).

In the same way that Washburn argued for an integration of information from living and fossil forms, he embraced and applied the newly emerging discoveries from molecular biology to issues in evolution. Always forward-looking, Washburn invited Morris Goodman, Emil Zuckerkandl, and Harold Klinger to participate in the 1961 conference he organized on Classification and Human Evolution (Washburn 1963). These researchers applied new methods to the study of human-nonhuman genetic relationships.

In the 1960s, immunological studies on proteins and new techniques of protein sequencing began to provide quantitative and replicable results on human-ape relationships (e.g., Goodman 1963; Sarich and Wilson 1967). Several techniques from different laboratories supported the same conclusions: that the African apes were the "closest kin" to humans and were distant from Old World monkeys and that the genetic relationship is so close that the geological time of separation from a common ancestor was estimated at about 5 million years, more recent than those suggesting a 15–20 mya separation. Consequently, from this time forward Washburn emphasized molecular evidence, noting that it places constraints on interpretations of the hominoid fossil record.

Many paleoanthropologists, however, were not as appreciative as Washburn in their assessment of the molecular evidence; consequently, the molecular and paleontological findings were placed in direct competition with each other (Zihlman and Lowenstein 1979). The controversy over which kind of evidence has priority in determining hominid phylogeny is illustrated in one famous case. Here the earliest putative hominid *Ramapithecus*, dated at 15 million years, directly contradicted estimates of hominid origins at 5 million years derived by molecular techniques. This controversy "officially ended" with the discovery of a fossil skull attributed to *Ramapithecus* and resembling an orangutan's; *Ramapithecus* was now accepted as an ape, not a hominid (Pilbeam 1982). However, if the molecular data had not presented another view on the timing of human origins—Washburn's constraints on interpretations of the fossil record—*Ramapithecus* might not have been so critically evaluated.

Immunological techniques and molecular results should have changed the paradigm of human evolution by maintaining that the earliest human ancestors could not have lived before 5 to 8 million years (Sarich 1968). However, the paleoanthropologists cast the new paradigm as a logical outcome of new fossil discoveries, and so continued the tradition of elevating fossils as primary rather than as co-contributers to the study of human evolution.

## WASHBURN AS A TEACHER

As well as informing his own research, Washburn's appreciation of new methods and data provided a non-human primate anatomy and behavioral ecology infused his teaching. Early in my graduate career at Berkeley, with Washburn as my teacher I learned far-reaching lessons in his classroom, during informal discussions, and from his writings. We students listened as he refined his ideas in lectures and in our weekly luncheon discussions. I quickly learned that nonhuman primate data offer insights not obvious when only human populations are studied. The paper I wrote on human blood groups and genetics for my first seminar with Washburn was returned with the question: "What about blood groups in the nonhuman primates?"

Washburn consistently emphasized the need to consider *all* the data, because a single line of evidence could be inconclusive or even misleading, just as a single trait could be. For example, as information emerged from field research during the 1960s on chimpanzees and mountain gorillas, Washburn observed that without direct observations of free-ranging animals, their dietary patterns could not be fully understood even having available information on the dental morphology and masticatory structures. Mountain gorillas rely heavily on herbs and vegetation (Schaller 1963) and chimpanzees on fruit, along with leaves, nuts, and insects and the occasional animal (Goodall 1968). Washburn's point is even more significant in light of recent research on sympatric lowland gorillas and chimpanzees in Gabon, West Africa, that shows similarities between lowland gorilla and chimpanzee diets and differences between lowland and mountain gorilla diets (Tutin and Fernandez 1993; Tutin et al. 1991). In Gabon, diets of gorillas and chimpanzees overlap significantly, with both species relying heavily on fruit and on exploiting many similar species of insects, though using different foraging techniques. Anatomy alone could not have revealed the variability within and between species in dietary composition seasonally and geographically or in foraging methods.

I remember Washburn's applying these dietary insights to human evolution when he sounded a cautionary note regarding a newly published article on fossil hominid diets. John Robinson (1963) proposed that morphological differences between *Paranthropus robustus* and *Australopithecus africanus* could be explained in terms of diet. According to Robinson, *A. (Paranthropus) robustus* was a vegetarian, whereas *A. africanus* was a meat-eating omnivore. Based on the findings of free-ranging chimpanzees and gorillas, as well as other primate species, Washburn doubted the validity of such precise dietary conclusions deduced from fossil dentition.

Washburn was quick to see the significance of information derived from new methods, even when the conclusions were controversial. Unlike most of his colleagues, early on Washburn recognized the importance of the molecular data as well as the implications for human evolution. One example returns to the origin of hominid locomotion. Combining molecular data on the shared ancestry of humans and African apes with field reports, he modified his earlier position and asked a new question: Were human ancestors knuckle-walkers?

Prior to field research, the main issue in the emergence of bipedal locomotion was one of coming to the ground; in other words, the hominoid ancestor either became bipedal in the trees or became bipedal once on the ground. When field studies indicated that chimpanzees and gorillas, although retaining their tree-climbing abilities, also travel on the ground, quadrupedally employing a knuckle-walking hand posture, Washburn (1967, 1968) reasoned that the common ancestor of African apes and humans was likely to have traveled between stands of trees using a quadrupedal knuckle-walking posture similar to that of the chimpanzee and gorilla. Therefore Washburn maintained that hominid ancestors were already on the ground, and research should shift to how the common ancestor became bipedal while on the ground.

Knuckle-walking as a possible ancestral hominid feature was soundly rejected by Washburn's student Russell Tuttle (1969, 1975, 1991), who prefers to view the derivation of hominid locomotion from a small-bodied, arboreal ancestor like the gibbon or siamang. The possibility of knuckle-walking having occurred in the common chimp-human ancestor is being resurrected on the basis of Miocene ape fossils from Hungary (Begun 1992). Similarities in cranial morphology between the ape fossils and chimpanzees have been used to argue that these fossils are the common ancestor of chimpanzees and humans. Here, again, the paleontologists adopt the new paradigm of the 1960s but cast it in terms of the fossil record.

## CURRENT DEBATES IN HUMAN EVOLUTION

Washburn's principles remain relevant to the currently debated issues in human evolution discussed here:

defining fossil hominid species especially that of *Australopithecus "afarensis"* and interpreting locomotion from postcranial remains of *A. "afarensis."* The controversy surrounding these issues mirrors that which Washburn began addressing in the 1940s.

### How Many Fossil Hominid Species?

Defining the boundaries of fossil species is a problem that continually plagues paleoanthropologists. Biologists who study living animals define species based on a combination of information, which, in addition to morphology, includes habitat preference and geographic distribution, behavioral ecology, life history and reproductive patterns, and genetic variation. In contrast, classification of fossil mammalian species relies on diagnostic morphology from dentition or cranial-facial parts, possibly along with postcranial skeletal remains, although usually these parts are isolated from cranial-dental fossils and cannot be assigned to species with any certainty. Fossils of various body parts and assigned to the same species often come from several localities from the same or different time range or even from distantly placed sites, as in the case of *A. "afarensis."* Paleoecological context rarely provides detailed habitat preference of the species in question, and without even a modest sample, there is no way to assess population variation for any morphological feature.

Another limitation in defining paleospecies is that morphological distinctions may occur in body parts not preserved in the fossil record, such as hair pattern and coloration or soft anatomy like gut proportions. Or slight differences in relative limb proportions may occur between species rather than in the morphology of single bones. Or behavioral differences may be diagnostic for assigning species. Using three examples from nonhuman primates, I illustrate how, without several complete skeletons, soft anatomy, or behavior, it would not be possible to distinguish among species of gibbons (*Hylobates*), guenons (*Cercopithecus*), and between the two chimpanzees (*Pan troglodytes* and *Pan paniscus*). Such examples underscore the likelihood of significantly underestimating species number in the early hominid fossil record and the pitfalls of relying too heavily on small samples.

GIBBONS The gibbons comprise approximately nine species, including the siamang (Leighton 1987; Preuschoft et al. 1984). They share a common locomotor-feeding pattern, social organization, and ecology. The nine species include three size ranges (3–5 kg, 5–7 kg, and 8+ kg), and except for size, cranial, dental, and skeletal morphology are very similar. However, gibbon species are distinct in their vocalizations (Marshall and Marshall 1976; Haimoff 1984). In each species, vocalizations of females and males form a species-specific pattern of duetting, and the time and frequency of calling provide further species distinction. When the Marshalls added vocalizations to other information, there was less disagreement on the number of existing species. The molecular data help clarify genetic relationships and evolutionary divergence. Three lineages— siamang, concolor gibbon, and the others—separated some 5 million years ago (Cronin et al. 1984). The largest group of possibly six species apparently radiated about 1 million years ago when sea levels were higher and contributed to isolating the forests and gibbon populations within them.

GUENONS The guenons, or "masked monkeys" (Kingdon 1988), provide another case study of the problem of defining species based on dental and skeletal remains alone. Guenons comprise over 20 species (Napier and Napier 1967). Species are distinguished anatomically by an amazing variety of facial coloration and coat patterns and by small differences in limb proportions, ecologically by slight differences in diet, habitat preference, and geographic distribution, and behaviorally by vocalizations (Gautier 1988; Gautier-Hion et al. 1988, and articles therein). Adolph Schultz noted the comparatively small intergeneric variability in skeleton morphology of all Old World monkeys. He singled out the guenons as having skeletons that are nearly indistinguishable. He concluded that in speciation, characters such as coloration and hair patterns, "are more readily subject to change than the skeleton and dentition" (1970: 48).

CHIMPANZEES The two species of chimpanzee provide a final example of difficulties in distinguishing species on the basis of either the skull or the postcranial skeleton. In the context of this discussion, chimpanzees may be the most compelling example, as opposed to gibbons or guenons, of problems in identification of fossil species because they are most closely related to *Homo sapiens* and therefore to the early hominids.

The two chimpanzee species have different geographic distributions: *Pan troglodytes* ranges from central Africa in Tanzania in its eastern most distribution to western Africa in Senegal, whereas *Pan paniscus* is confined to the Zaire River Basin. *Pan paniscus* was first proposed as a distinct species of *Pan* around 1930. The basis for Coolidge's conclusion (1933) that *P. paniscus* was a distinct species of chimpanzee derived from a few skulls and one adult skeleton. As recently as 1986, Groves questioned whether these two chimpanzees were distinct species and argued instead that size could account for the variation.

There are now considerable data to support species distinction. For example, the molecular data indicate that the two species separated 2–2.5 million years ago (e.g., Miyamoto et al. 1988; Ruvolo et al. 1991). Field research also documents significant differences in geographic distribution, habitat preference, and behavioral ecology (Kano 1992). Substantial anatomical evidence for two species emerged initially from cranial-facial features based on a large sample of 60 individuals. Cramer (1977) found differences in facial robusticity, mandibular size, average cranial capacity, and canine and postcanine dental size. Only mandibular length discriminated between the two species because this measurement formed two distinct ranges and did not overlap.

The two species overlap almost completely in body weight; joint morphology is nearly identical, and length and robusticity of the long bones overlap completely. Several features distinguish the two species statistically: (1) the longer clavicle, (2) wider ilium, and (3) proportions of the upper and lower limbs (the intermembral index) (Zihlman and Cramer 1978). *Pan troglodytes* has a higher intermembral index (a relatively longer upper limb), and *P. paniscus* a lower one. These proportions seem to be a species character that is not affected by body size (Morbeck and Zihlman 1989).

From the point of view of sex differences, *P. paniscus* illustrates another cautionary note. Although sex differences cannot be demonstrated in any skeletal feature— and only slightly in canine breadth—body weight differences between females and males is moderate, with females about 80% of male body weight (Cramer and Zihlman 1978). The chimpanzee examples underscore the importance of having both complete skeletons of known sex *and* a reasonable sample size that can be studied statistically in order to demonstrate significance.

SPECIES NUMBER AMONG EARLY HOMINIDS With regard to the interpretation of the early hominid fossil record, and in particular to the alleged species designation of A. "afarensis," the relationship between morphology and species distinctions among nonhuman primates demonstrates the hazards involved in too much lumping. Differences between species, as well as sex within species, can only be demonstrated with several complete individuals of the species in question.

Keep in mind the conditions of the fossil record. Complete body parts and complete individuals are almost nonexistent, much less a minimal sample of individuals (more than 1 or 2) or complete bones. For example, the cranium assigned to A. "afarensis" (AL 444-2) (Kimbel et al. 1994) dated to ~3 myr is the first reasonably complete cranium covering an approximate 1 million year period between 4 and 3 million years.

The species designation A. "afarensis" includes fossils widely separated in time (1 million years) and space (northern Ethiopia to Laetoli, Tanzania). On the basis of canine size this cranium is diagnosed as male. However, once again the chimpanzee example serves as a relevant caution. Except for the larger canine teeth of *Pan troglodytes,* the dental morphology is similar in the two chimpanzee species, though differing in size, with *Pan paniscus* smaller. If cranial fragments of either *Pan* species were found as fossils, it would be easy, even logical, to accept the two species as one species having considerable variation. For example, in a fossil bone assemblage the large canines of *P. troglodytes* could be interpreted as male and the smaller canines of all the *P. paniscus* as female.

Another claim for the Hadar cranium is that it demonstrates the existence of one species morphologically stable for a million years. The evidence for this claim is a previously discovered fragmentary frontal bone from another locality estimated at 3.9 my (Clark et al. 1984). The long history of erroneous paleontological interpretations should promote skepticism about assigning AL 444 to the same species as a fragmentary frontal bone dated several hundred thousand years earlier. Furthermore, this skepticism may be warranted in light of an even older species, *Australopethecus anamensis,* at 4.0 myr from Kenya (Leakey et al. 1995).

The postcranial skeleton is even more problematic in assigning isolated bones to a particular sex or species. The two species of *Pan* may be sorted statistically on the basis of limb proportions, provided that the sample is composed of known sex and species. It would seem quite impossible to draw conclusions about either sex or species number on the basis of limb bones, even complete ones. For example, in each of two published accounts of A. "afarensis," the humerus is put forth as significant evidence of one species with marked sexual dimorphism. In Kimbel et al. (1994), the similar morphology is noted, and, unlike the humerus from Maka (White et al. 1993), estimated length measurement is provided in the report.

The humerus (AL 137-50) when compared to the one from AL 288—"Lucy"—is given as 24% greater (295 vs. 238 mm) (Kimbel et al. 1994). I extend this comparison to include the African apes and use average lengths. For example, the average humerus length of a small sample of mountain gorillas (from Jungers and Susman 1984) is 21% greater than females (434.6 mm vs. 357.8 mm). Therefore the variation in A. "afarensis" may even exceed that between male and female mountain gorillas. Between female mountain gorillas and male *Pan troglodytes* (mean = 320 mm, Schultz 1969), female gorillas are only 18% longer in humeral length, less than the difference from *within* gorillas.

These figures suggest the possibility that in the instance of similar morphology, size is a significant factor in differentiating between species. Therefore differences in bone lengths in these two hominid fossils (AL 137-50 and AL 288) might, on the basis of size, indicate the presence of two species, even though the morphology is similar.

Recognizing a tendency to underestimate species number, several researchers (e.g., Tattersall 1992), in reassessing fossil hominids, propose increased numbers of species, for example, *Homo rudolfensis* and *Homo ergaster,* in addition to *H. habilis* and *H. erectus* (Wood 1992a). Recently there has been reevaluation and a proliferation of species for all groups of human evolution, including resurrecting the genus *Paranthropus* for hominids between 1 and 2 million years (Wood 1992b). What is curious is the absence in the literature of applying such criteria to A. "afarensis."

Data from nonhuman primates, including the new information on the chimp-human common ancestor, cast a stronger light on this issue of species characters and raise significant questions. For example, is the degree of sexual dimorphism as supposedly illustrated on the basis of the two fossil humeri—which is more extreme than seen in gorillas—likely to have existed in early hominids? Applying the nonhuman primate perspective to early hominid fossils supports the conclusion that the hominid population between 3 million and 4 million years ago consists of more, rather than fewer, species.[1]

## Locomotor Behavior of Lucy

The discovery of the partial skeleton of AL 288 from Hadar, Ethiopia, popularly known as "Lucy" and assigned to the new species of *Australopithecus* "afarensis" extended the controversy over locomotor behavior of early hominids. The first fossil pelvic and limb bones from the South African caves during the 1940s formed the basis for Washburn's functional analysis in 1951, but over the years as more bones were uncovered and more different approaches used there has been little agreement on how to interpret them (summarized in Zihlman and Brunker 1979). The pelvic and limb bones from Hadar, Ethiopia, including AL 288, and the Laetoli footprints fueled these debates.

In the past decade interpretations of A. "afarensis" locomotor behavior have centered around two camps

---

[1] It is important to note that on several other grounds, including cranial and postcranial evidence of the fossils themselves, several researchers argue that there is more than one species of A. "afarensis" and that sexual dimorphism is insufficient to account for this variation (e.g., Falk 1990; Hager 1991, 1993; Senut 1992; Zihlman 1985).

that return to themes first addressed by Washburn: (1) that *Australopithecus* and AL 288 were well-adapted bipeds in the sense of modern humans, in spending virtually all their time on the ground (e.g., Latimer et al. 1987; Lovejoy 1981, or (2) that early hominid locomotion included a significant component of arboreality. (Stern and Susman 1983; Tuttle 1981). These divergent and somewhat conflicting positions are both based on the same fossil remains. Greater mobility of the foot and ankle like that of the apes and unlike humans has been stressed by Christie (1977); Susman et al. (1984) and Lewis (1989), whereas Latimer et al. (1987) describe the ankle as fully adapted to a bipedalism equivalent to that of *Homo sapiens.* Curved phalanges of the hands and feet and an angled glenoid fossa of the scapula are other features presented as evidence for australopithecine arboreality. (Susman et al. 1984). Foot bones from Sterkfontein also emphasize hominid arboreality (Clarke and Tobias 1995).

It is not surprising that the same bones are interpreted in opposite ways. The problem is that body structures are a combination of function and the constraints of evolutionary history. Structure can be directly related to function, that is, to behaviors that the hominids actually performed or had the potential to perform during their lives. Or specific anatomical features of fossil bones might be due to evolutionary history, that is, to the adaptation of previous ancestors. More likely, structure is a combination of both function and evolutionary history, and there is no way to select among these possibilities by studying only fragmentary fossil bones and skeletons.

In these two camps, knuckle-walking is either implicitly or explicitly rejected as part of the behavioral profile of the ancestral ape. Admittedly we are trapped by language (Zihlman 1990). Nature does not compartmentalize behavior, so that in labeling African ape locomotion as "knuckle-walking" or "arboreal," we lose sight of the total motor repertoire. Washburn (1967) noted that the entire locomotor profile of African apes is made up of varied activities, including climbing, hanging, swinging, leaping, standing, and bipedal walking. When he reevaluated the origin of bipedal locomotion on the basis of ape field studies and of molecular data, Washburn did not specifically reject climbing, but instead suggested that the ancestral ape might have also knuckle-walked.

Washburn's prescience in the 1960s takes on greater significance in the 1990s in light of the newest evidence from molecular, field, and laboratory studies. First, since 1984, numerous studies on DNA, both mitochondrial and nuclear, continue to pile up evidence for a closer relationship between chimpanzees and humans, with gorillas more distantly related (e.g., Miyamoto et al. 1988; Ruvolo et al. 1991; Sibley and

Ahlquist 1984). This common ancestry—combined with the acknowledged similarities between the earliest hominids and chimpanzees, for example, in cranial capacity—should compel a reconsideration of the common ape-human ancestor. The emergence of new species and the development of new adaptations—in this case bipedal locomotion—take place within the constraints of the ancestors. If the common ancestor had knuckle-walking in its locomotor repertoire, this should be a point of discussion when speculating about early hominid locomotion.

Second, field studies that specifically focus on posture and locomotion indicate that the locomotor repertoire of gorillas and chimpanzees include knuckle-walking, climbing, and hanging (Doran 1989; Hunt 1989; Remis 1994). For example, in a study on Tai Forest chimpanzees (*Pan troglodytes*) in the Ivory Coast, Doran (1989) found that of all locomotor behavior, 84% was terrestrial knuckle-walking. The remaining 16% was arboreal locomotion of which 14% was climbing up and down trees to feed or rest, and 2% hanging, swinging and leaping, and quadrupedal behavior in trees. In calculating locomotor activity as a percentage of locomotor time, chimpanzees knuckle-walked 87% of the time. During feeding, chimpanzees arm hang on the smallest branches, a posture most common when chimpanzees feed on fruit. It is in this feeding posture that the hand is used as a hook (Hunt 1989).

Finally, laboratory studies clarify the biomechanical underpinnings for the tendency of apes to exhibit bipedal posture and bipedal running. Rather than distribute body weight evenly over four limbs, during quadrupedal locomotion chimpanzees actively shift body weight to the hind limbs. This minimizes compressive forces on the forelimbs; the result is hind limb–dominated quadrupedal locomotion (Kimura et al. 1979; Reynolds 1985a,b). Because of its extreme mobility, the hominoid shoulder joint allows climbing and hanging but is not very suitable for accommodating compressive forcing during quadrupedal locomotion. It is this evolutionary history that predisposes ancestral hominids for becoming bipedal.

What is clear from the past 10 years of arguments about the hominid fossil bones from Hadar is that all the available and relevant information is not brought into the discussion. As a result, the two camps simply go back and forth and reassert their positions.

One way to interpret bipedal behavior of early hominids is to approach locomotor behavior broadly, as part of a way of life essential for survival, through travel and avoiding predators, and feeding for finding mates and raising offspring (Zihlman 1992). Washburn (1960) pointed out that bipedal locomotion was part of a whole way of life and an adaptation for covering long distances. With information from field studies we can now begin to evaluate what exactly is meant by "long distances" and how efficiency relates. The average distance traveled each day is one measure of distance. For example, chimpanzees from the Tai Forest, Ivory Coast, and Gombe, Tanzania, cover an average distance 2 kilometers for females with infants, 3 kilometers for other females, and 3–5 kilometers for males (Doran 1989; Goodall 1986). Extending this to hominids, one might suppose, for example, that bipedal behavior allowed them to travel at least 6 kilometers a day, on average. The ability of early hominids to range farther on a daily basis than documented for either chimpanzees or gorillas could enhance survival through exploiting a wider variety of resources (Zihlman 1993) and therefore could promote morphological changes for greater locomotor efficiency (Zihlman and Brunker 1979). This kind of approach provides a basis for sounder speculation that encourages consideration of entire animals and their way of life. In this way discussion can move beyond narrow arguments about the function of one or another joint or about climbing trees versus terrestrial walking.

## CLOSING THOUGHTS

In a real way, history repeats itself. New data, today as 50 years ago, too often are used selectively. In pointing this out and moving beyond with his encompassing perspective, Washburn brought physical anthropology onto a more modern, more scientific track. The controversy over locomotion, like that over species number, derives from failing to consider all available data, data that could hold important clues to reconstructing the earliest phase of human evolution. Washburn's principles continue to be relevant: Use all the evidence; use new methods; and use information from living species in combination with the fossils rather than either alone. Information from nonhuman primates integrated with the fossil record will help contribute to resolution of some debates—for example, about chimp-human relationships, species identification among living primates, comparative anatomy and biomechanics, and field studies on locomotor behavior. It is not a matter of having the "right" answer but coming to the best available synthesis of the data from all disciplinary views and having an open, honest and thorough debate.

## ACKNOWLEDGMENTS

My thanks to Donald Lindburg, Shirley Strum, and David Hamburg for putting the volume together. I enjoyed my discussions with and benefited from the comments of Ted Grand, Jerry Lowenstein, Robin McFarland, and Kim Nichols. In presenting S. L. Washburn's ideas and work to my students, I have been enlightened by our exchanges during courses in Anthropology 101, 109, and 194. The University of California, Santa Cruz, Committee on Research and the Social Sciences Division, has supported my research, for which I am grateful.

## BIBLIOGRAPHY

Aiello, L. C. (1994). Variable and singular. *Nature 368:* 399–400.

Begun, D. (1992). Miocene fossil hominids and the chimp-human clade. *Science 257:* 1929–1933.

Bowler, P. (1986). *Theories of Human Evolution. A Century of Debate 1844–1944.* Oxford: Blackwell.

Christie, P. (1977). Form and function of the Afar ankle. *Amer. J. Phys. Anthrop. 47:* 123 (abstract).

Clark, J. D., Asfaw, B., Assefa, G., Harris, J. W. K., Kurashina, H., Walter, R. C., White, T. D., and Williams, M. A. J. (1984). Palaeoanthropological discoveries in the Middle Awash Valley, Ethiopia. *Nature 307:* 423–428.

Clarke, R. J., and Tobias, P. V. (1995). Sterkfontein member 2 foot bones of the oldest South African hominid. *Science* 269:521–524.

Coolidge, H. (1933). *Pan paniscus.* Pygmy chimpanzee from south of the Congo River. *Amer. J. Phys. Anthrop. 18*(1): 1–57.

Cramer, D. L. (1977). Craniofacial morphology of *Pan paniscus:* A morphometric and evolutionary appraisal. In *Contributions to Primatology,* Vol. 10. Basel: Karger.

Cramer, D. L., and Zihlman, A. L. (1978). Sexual dimorphism in the pygmy chimpanzee, *Pan paniscus.* In D. J. Chivers and K. A. Joysey (eds.), *Recent Advances in Primatology.* Vol. 3, *Evolution.* London: Academic Press, pp. 487–490.

Cronin, J. E., Sarich, V. M., and Ryder, O. (1984). Molecular evolution and speciation in the lesser apes. In H. Preuschoft et al. (eds), *The Lesser Apes.* Edinburgh: Edinburgh University Press, pp. 467–485.

Darwin, C. (1859). *The Origin of Species.* London: John Murray.

Darwin, C. (1871). *The Descent of Man and Selection in Relation to Sex.* London: John Murray.

Doran, D. (1989). Chimpanzee and pygmy chimpanzee positional behavior: The influence of environment, body size, morphology and ontogeny, locomotion and posture. Ph.D. dissertation, State University of New York, Stony Brook.

Falk, D. (1990). Brain evolution in Homo: The "radiator" theory. *Behav. Brain Sci. 13:* 333–344.

Fleagle, J. G., Stern, J. T., Jungers, W. L., Susman, R. L., Vangor, A. K., and Wells, J. P. (1981). Climbing: A biomechanical link with brachiation and with bipedalism. *Symp. Zool. Soc. Lond. 48:* 359–375.

Gautier, J. P. (1988). Interspecific affinities among guenons as deduced from vocalizations. In A. Gautier-Hion et al. (eds.), *A Primate Radiation. Evolutionary Biology of the African Guenons.* Cambridge: Cambridge University Press, pp. 194–226.

Gautier-Hion, A., Bourliere, F., Gautier, J.-P., and Kingdon, J. (1988). *A Primate Radiation. Evolutionary Biology of the African Guenons.* Cambridge: Cambridge University Press.

Goodall, J. (1968). The behaviour of free-ranging chimpanzees in the Gombe Stream Reserve. *Animal Behaviour Monographs 1:* 165–311.

Goodall, J. (1986). *The Chimpanzees of Gombe.* Cambridge, MA: Harvard University Press.

Goodman, M. (1963). Man's place in the phylogeny of the primates as reflected in serum proteins. In S. L. Washburn (ed.), *Classification and Human Evolution.* Chicago: Aldine, pp. 204–234.

Groves, C. P. (1986). Systematics of the great apes. In *Comparative Primate Biology.* Vol. 1, *Systematics, Evolution and Anatomy.* New York: Alan R. Liss, pp. 187–217.

Hager, L. D. (1991). The evidence for sex differences in the hominid fossil record. In D. Walde and N. D. Willows (eds.), *The Archaeology of Gender*. Calgary: University of Calgary Archaeological Association, pp. 46–54.

Hager, L. D. (1993). Sex determination in the australopithecines and early Homo. Paper presented at "Four Million Years of Hominid Evolution in Africa," International Conference in honor of Mary D. Leakey, Arusha, Tanzania.

Haimoff, E. H. (1984). Acoustic and organizational features of gibbon songs. In H. Preuschoft et al. (eds.), *The Lesser Apes*. Edinburgh: Edinburgh University Press, pp. 333–353.

Hunt, K. D. (1989). Positional behavior in *Pan troglodytes* at the Mahale Mountains and the Gombe Stream National Parks, Tanzania. Ph.D. dissertation, University of Michigan.

Huxley, T. H. (1863). Evidence as to Man's Place in Nature.

Johanson, D. C., White, T. D., and Coppens, Y. (1978). A new species of the genus *Australopithecus* (Primates: Hominidae) from the Pliocene of eastern Africa. *Kirtlandia 28:* 1.

Johanson, D. C., and White, T. D. (1979). A systematic assessment of early African hominids. *Science 202:* 321.

Jungers, W. L., and Susman, R. L. (1984). Body size and skeletal allometry in African apes. In R. L. Susman (ed.), *The Pygmy Chimpanzee*. New York: Plenum Press, pp. 131–177.

Kano, (1992). *The Last Ape. Pygmy Chimpanzee Behavior and Ecology.* Palo Alto, CA: Stanford University Press.

Kimbel, W. H., Johnson, D. C., and Rak, Y. (1994). The first skull and other new discoveries of *Australopithecus afarensis* at Hadar, Ethiopia. *Nature 368:* 449–451.

Kimura, T., Okada, M., and Ishida, H. (1979). Kinesiological characteristics of primate walking: Its significance in human walking. In M. E. Morbeck, H. Preuschoft, and N. Gomberg (eds.), *Environment, Behavior, and Morphology: Dynamic Interactions in Primates*. New York: Gustav Fisher, pp. 297–311.

Kingdon, J. (1988). What are face patterns and do they contribute to reproductive isolation in guenons? In A. Gautier-Hion et al. (eds.), *A Primate Radiation. Evolutionary Biology of the Guenons.* Cambridge: Cambridge University Press, pp. 227–245.

Latimer, B., Ohman, J. C., and Lovejoy, C. O. (1987). Talocrural joint in African hominoids: Implications for *Australopithecus afarensis*. *Amer. J. Phys. Anthrop. 74(2):* 155–175.

Leakey, M. G., Feibel, C. S., McDougall, I., and Walker, A. (1995). New four-million-year-old hominid species from Kanopoi and Allia Bay, Kenya. *Nature 376:* 565–571.

Leighton, D. R. (1987). Gibbons: Territoriality and monogamy. In B. Smuts et al. (ed.), *Primate Societies*. Chicago: University of Chicago Press, pp. 135–145.

Lewis, O. J. (1989). *Functional Morphology of the Evolving Hand and Foot.* Oxford, England: Clarendon Press.

Lovejoy, C. O. (1981). The origin of man. *Science 211:* 341–350.

Marshall, J. T., and Marshall, E. R. (1976). Gibbons and their territorial songs. *Science 193:* 235–237.

Mayr, E., and Provine W. B. (1980). *An Evolutionary Synthesis*. Cambridge, MA: Harvard University Press.

Miyamoto, M. M., Slightom, J. L., and Goodman, M. (1988). Phylogenetic relations of humans and African apes from DNA sequences in the globin region. *Science 238:* 369–373.

Moore, J. (1993). *Science as a Way of Knowing*. Cambridge, MA: Harvard University Press.

Morbeck, M. E., and Zihlman, A. L. (1989). Body size and proportions in chimpanzees, with special reference to *Pan troglodytes schweinfurthii* from Gombe National Park, Tanzania. *Primates 30(3):* 369–382.

Napier, J. R., and Napier, P. H. (1967). *A Handbook of Living Primates. Morphology, Ecology and Behaviour of Nonhuman Primates.* London: Academic Press.

Pilbeam, D. R. (1982). New hominoid skull material from the Miocene of Pakistan. *Nature 295:* 232–234.

Preuschoft, H., Chivers, D. J., Brockelman, W. Y., and Creel, N. (1984). *The Lesser Apes. Evolutionary and Behavioural Biology.* Edinburgh: Edinburgh University Press.

Prost, J. (1980). Origin of bipedalism. *Amer. J. Phys. Anthrop. 52:* 175–189.

Reader, J. (1988). *Missing Links*. London: Penguin.

Remis, M. J. (1994). Feeding ecology and positional behavior of western lowland gorillas (*Gorilla gorilla gorilla*) in the Central African Republic. Ph.D. Dissertation, Yale University.

Reynolds, T. R. (1985a). Mechanics of increased support of weight by the hindlimbs in primates. *Amer. J. Phys. Anthrop. 67:* 335–349.

Reynolds, T. R. (1985b). Stresses on the limbs of quadrupedal primates. *Amer. J. Phys. Anthrop. 67:* 351–362.

Robinson, J. T. (1963). Adaptive radiation in the Australopithecines and the origin of man. In F. C. Howell and F. Bourliere (eds.), *African Ecology and Human Evolution.* Chicago: Aldine, pp. 385–416.

Ruvolo, M. (1994). Molecular evolutionary processes and conflicting gene trees: The hominoid case. *Amer. J. Phys. Anthrop. 94:* 89–113.

Ruvolo, M., Disotell, T. R., Allard, M. W., Brown, M. W., and Honeycutt, R. L. (1991). Resolution of the African hominoid trichotomy by use of a mitochondrial gene sequence. *Proc. Natl. Acad. USA 88:* 1570–1574.

Sarich, V. M. (1968). The origin of the hominids: An immunological approach. In S. L. Washburn and P. C. Jay (eds.), *Perspectives on Human Evolution*. Vol. I. New York: Holt, Rinehart and Winston, pp. 94–121.

Sarich, V. M., and Wilson, A. C. (1967). Immunological time scale for hominid evolution. *Science 158:* 1200–1203.

Schaller, G. (1963). *The Mountain Gorilla*. Chicago: University of Chicago Press.

Schultz, A. H. (1969). *The Skeleton of the Chimpanzee. The Chimpanzee.* Basel: S. Karger, Vol. 1, pp. 50–103.

Schultz, A. H. (1970). The comparative uniformity of the Cercopithecoidea. In J. H. Napier (ed.), *Old World Monkeys*. New York: Academic Press, pp. 39–51.

Senut, B. (1992). The French contribution to the study of human origins: The case of *Australopithecus afarensis*. *Hum. Evol. 7:* 15–24.

Sibley, C. G., and Ahlquist, J. E. (1984). The phylogeny of the hominoid primates, as indicated by DNA–DNA hybridization. *J. Mol. Evol. 20:* 2–15.

Simpson, G. G. (1944). *Tempo and Mode in Evolution*. New York: Columbia University Press. Reprint. 1982.

Stern, J. T., and Susman, R. L. (1983). The locomotor anatomy of *Australopithecus afarensis*. *Amer. J. Phys. Anthrop. 60:* 279–318.

Susman, R. L., Stern, J. T., and Junger, W. L. (1984). Arboreality and bipedality in the Hadar hominids. *Folia Primat. 43:* 113–156.

Tattersall, L. (1992). Species concepts and species identification in human evolution. *J. Hum. Evol. 22:* 341–349.

Tutin, C. E. G., and Fernandez, M. (1993). Composition of the diet of chimpanzees and comparisons with that of sympatric lowland gorillas in the Lope Reserve, Gabon. *Amer. J. Primat. 30:* 195–211.

Tutin, C. E. G., Fernandez, M., Rogers, M. E., Williamson, E., and McGrew, W. E. (1991). Foraging profiles of sympatric lowland gorilla and chimpanzees in Lope Reserve, Gabon. *Phil. Trans. Roy. Soc. London B334:* 179–186.

Tuttle, R. H. (1969). Knuckle-walking and the problem of human origins. *Science 166:* 953–961.

Tuttle, R. H. (1975). Parallelism, brachiation and hominoid phylogeny. In P. Luckett and F. Szalay (eds.), *Phylogeny of the Primates.* New York: Plenum Press, pp. 447–480.

Tuttle, R. H. (1981). Evolution of hominid bipedalism and prehensile capabilities. *Phil. Trans. Roy. Soc. London B292:* 89–94.

Tuttle, R. H., Webb, D. M., and Tuttle, N. I. (1991). Laetoli footprint trails and the evolution of hominid bipedalism. In Y. Coppens and B. Senut (eds.), *Origine(s) de la Bipedie chez Les Hominides*. Paris: CNRS, pp. 187–198.

Washburn, S. L. (1946a). The effect of facial paralysis on the growth of the skull of rat and rabbit. *Anat. Rec. 94*(2): 163–168.

Washburn, S. L. (1946b). The effect of the removal of the zygomatic arch in the rat. *J. Mammal. 27*(2): 169–172.

Washburn, S. L. (1951a). Analysis of primate evolution with particular reference to the origin of man. *Cold Spring Harbor Symp. Quant. Biol. 15:* 67–78.

Washburn, S. L. (1951b). The new physical anthropology. *Trans. N.Y. Acad. Sci. 13*(7): 298–304.

Washburn, S. L. (1960). Tools and human evolution. *Sci. Amer. 203*(3): 63–75.

Washburn, S. L., ed. (1963). *Classification and Human Evolution.* Chicago: Aldine.

Washburn, S. L. (1967). Behaviour and the origin of man. The Huxley Memorial Lecture 1967. Ireland: Proc. Roy. Anthrop. Inst. Gt. Brit., pp. 21–27.

Washburn, S. L. (1968). One hundred years of biological anthropology. In J. O. Brew (ed.), *One Hundred Years of Anthropology.* Cambridge, MA: Harvard University Press, pp. 97–115.

Washburn, S. L. (1972). Human evolution. In T. Dobzhansky, M. K. Hecht, and W. C. Steere (eds.), *Evolutionary Biology,* Vol. 6. New York: Appleton Century Crofts, pp. 349–361.

Washburn, S. L. (1973). Primate studies and human evolution. In *Nonhuman Primates and Medical Research.* New York: Academic Press, pp. 467–485.

Washburn, S. L. (1983). Evolution of a teacher. *Ann. Rev. Anthrop. 12:* 1–24.

White, T. D., Suwa, G., Hart, W. K., Walter, R. C., WoldeGabriel, G., deHeinzelin, J., Clark, J. D., Asfaw, B. and Vrba, E. (1993). New discoveries of Australopithecus at Maka in Ethiopia. *Nature 366:* 261–265.

Wood, B. (1992a). Origin and evolution of the genus *Homo. Nature 355:* 783–790.

Wood, B. (1992b). Early hominid species and speciation. *J. Hum. Evol. 22:* 351–365.

Zihlman, A. L. (1985). *Australopithecus afarensis:* Two sexes or two species? In P. V. Tobias (ed.), *Hominid Evolution: Past Present and Future.* New York: Alan R. Liss, pp. 213–220.

Zihlman, A. L. (1990). Knuckling under: Controversy over hominid origins. In G. Sperber (ed.), *From Apes to Angels: Essays in Anthropology in Honor of P. V. Tobias.* New York: Wiley-Liss, pp. 185–196.

Zihlman, A. L. (1992). Locomotion as a life history character: The contribution of anatomy. *J. Hum. Evol. 22:* 315–325.

Zihlman, A. L. (1993). Small steps for humankind; a giant step for paleoanthropology. Paper presented at "Four Million Years of Hominid Evolution in Africa," International Conference in honor of Mary D. Leakey, Arusha, Tanzania.

Zihlman, A. L., and Brunker, L. (1979). Hominid bipedalism: Then and now. *Yrbk. Phys. Anthrop. 22:* 132–162.

Zihlman, A. L., and Cramer, D. L. (1978). Skeletal differences between pygmy (*Pan paniscus*) and common chimpanzee (*Pan troglodytes*). *Folia Primat. 29:* 86–94.

Zihlman, A. L., and Lowenstein, J. M. (1979). False start of the human parade. *Natural History 88*(7): 86–91.

*Turner and Weiss illustrate Washburn's position that genetic techniques should help us understand the process of primate evolution and human variation essential to better phylogenetic reconstructions. They turn to Old World monkeys, not for insights about the emergence of hominids as in the early days of the new physical anthropology, but as models for the microevolutionary processes that contributed to the later differentiation of human populations. Since the 1960s, thousands of primates have been sampled as part of the study of nonhuman primate genetics. Turner and Weiss highlight the limitations and advantages of genetic data for evolutionary reconstructions. In particular, the chapter summarizes what is known about the genetic variation in three genera of Old World monkeys,* Macaca, Papio, *and* Cercopithecus. *The species selected share some important characteristics; they are distributed widely across a diversity of ecological zones and have populations whose groups exchange members but are still divisible into larger evolutionary units, or "races." The authors conclude that the considerable work on nonhuman primate genetics, as illustrated by these species of Old World monkeys, has only partly answered the key questions about the origins and maintenance of variation. This may be because of inadequacies in sampling, insufficient knowledge about the relationship of the social unit to the reproductive unit, and/or inadequate assessment of the "flexibility" of a species' behavior patterns. Despite these shortcomings, macaques, baboons, and vervets offer important insights about the evolutionary dynamics of polymorphic, polytypic, widely distributed primate species that are particularly relevant to understanding another such primate species,* Homo sapiens.*

# 14 Genetics of Old World Monkeys: One Aspect of the "New" Physical Anthropology

**T. R. Turner**  *Department of Anthropology, University of Wisconsin-Milwaukee*

**M. L. Weiss**  *Department of Anthropology, Wayne State University*

In 1951, Sherwood L. Washburn published "The New Physical Anthropology" in which he characterized the older physical anthropology as "primarily a technique . . . the measurement of external form with calipers," whereas "the new physical anthropology is primarily an interest, the desire to understand the process of primate evolution and human variation by the most efficient techniques available." These techniques would, in many cases, come from the study of genetics. In fact, the theoretical underpinnings for this new physical anthropology arise from the integration of genetic concepts into a Darwinian view of life. Washburn felt that this "must be more than the adoption of a little genetic terminology."

During the intervening years, physical anthropology moved in the direction that Washburn pointed. Molecular genetic and molecular biological approaches for deciphering primate evolution have revolutionized our views. Physical anthropologists have come to use "the most efficient techniques available." Our view of the human place in nature and human evolution have undergone major reevaluation. DNA and protein evidence point to the close relationships between humans and the great apes (Goodman et al. 1983; Ruvolo et al. 1991; Sarich and Wilson 1967). Nucleic acid techniques have been applied to primate evolution and taxonomy (e.g., Melnick et al. 1993), areas long of interest to physical anthropologists. Ironically, the new approaches result in a view of hominoid relationships reminiscent of one held by primate anatomists at the start of the twentieth century (Mann and Weiss 1996).

The other central interest identified by Washburn was "human races." Human variation, or "races," in Washburn's time, "must be based on the study of populations. . . . It is not enough to state that races should be based on genetic traits; races which cannot be reconciled with genetics should be removed from consideration." Rather than focusing on classification as a goal, Washburn proposed that the goal should be the explanation of the origin and maintenance of diversity through the application of knowledge of evolutionary processes. Achieving this goal would be advanced by use of an experimental approach, for "the literature is already too full of uncontrolled speculation."

In this area too there has been movement. Classification of "races" is no longer a goal. In fact, the American Association of Physical Anthropologists recently adopted a statement on the lack of utility of the concept. Yet, in many ways, we may not have moved as far here as we have in our appreciation of primate evolution. In large measure this may result from the enormous pressure that the social construct of race exerts on our scientific framework.

In keeping with Washburn's imperative to apply experimental procedures to the understanding of primate evolution and human diversity, researchers began studying primates that had a wide geographic distribution and lived in an environment in which early humans may have lived. These animals were looked to as models for the evolution of the human lineage. In this essay we present an examination of genetic variation among some cercopithecines that have been presented as a model for understanding human diversity and evolution.

## OLD WORLD MONKEYS AS MODELS

Old World monkeys have often been proposed as models for studying the processes that have affected human evolution, including the differentiation of human populations. The broad distribution, the diversity of ecological zones, and the social structures and behaviors of Old World monkeys have all been compared to the hominid condition. Studies of Old World monkeys have taken multiple forms, including long-term behavioral observation of a single species (e.g., Strum 1987; Whitten 1983), analysis of sympatric populations and their use of the environment (e.g., Struhsaker and Leland 1979), and the genetic structure of primate populations (e.g., Dracopoli et al. 1983; Melnick et al. 1984). All of these types of studies have been used to help elucidate

human evolution (Fedigan 1982; Strum 1987). In addition, they have highlighted nonhuman primates as subjects of particular interest in their own right. Primates, especially the Old World monkeys, are prime examples of large, long-lived, slow-breeding organisms. Their distribution and patterns of speciation can illuminate the process of evolution in general. In recent years, however, instead of concerning themselves with primates as models for earlier human populations, primate geneticists have been concerned with microevolutionary processes in selected populations of organisms (Ober et al. 1978, 1980; Rogers and Kidd 1993; Scheffrahn et al. 1993; Turner 1981) conservation and conservation genetics (Morin et al. 1994; Pope 1992), and the relationship between genetics and behavior (Inoue et al. 1993; Pereira and Weiss 1991; de Ruiter and van Hooff 1993; de Ruiter et al. 1992).

This shift can be traced in part to theoretical advances in evolutionary theory, such as models of punctuated equilibrium, which decoupled speciation and adaptation, and sociobiology, which looked for genetic explanations for behavior. Twenty-some years ago the justification for the study of the genetics of primate populations in the wild always included a statement that indicated the study of microevolution in a specific population would help elucidate the process of speciation and also the evolution of human populations. With the advent of punctuated equilibrium, the necessity of explaining speciation as part of a microevolutionary study lessened. It became possible to talk about the subtle microevolutionary changes in populations, for example, troop structure and male migration (Dracopoli et al. 1983; Melnick et al. 1984), the evolution of genes themselves (e.g., Rogers et al. 1992), and paternal investment in offspring (de Ruiter and van Hoof 1993) in primates without focusing back on humans and the process of speciation in this single lineage.

## THE QUESTIONS

The interest in nonhuman primate genetics had its real beginnings in the 1960s. Since then, thousands of primates have been sampled. The earliest work relied on samples from primates held in captivity and provided reports on, for example, the existence of hemoglobin variants in baboons (Barnicot et al. 1966) and transferrin variants in macaques (Goodman et al. 1965). Very few animals were sampled. These studies indicated, however, that the same types of genetic variation found in humans also existed in nonhuman primates. For example, the types of variation found in the transferrin or hemoglobin loci in humans also existed in nonhuman primates. The existence of the variation allowed for the possibility of population genetics and systematic studies of primates.

The next stage in the study of primate genetics took advantage of this genetic variation. Large-scale surveys of various species of primates from multiple locations were designed and executed. Provenance of these animals was only roughly estimated. For instance, in some of the earlier work by Darga et al. (1975), Weiss and Goodman (1971), and others, animals were described as being from the general region of Kuala Lampur, Malaysia. Such minimal descriptions resulted from the need to rely on information provided by local trappers who captured the animals for export. These studies began to document genetic differences in frequency of alleles among species and among populations of widely distributed species.

Studies of macaques and baboons indicated that genetic differences among groups could help elucidate some evolutionary processes. However, researchers recognized that it was important to know the precise location of animals and the troop structure and demography to document microevolutionary change fully. At that time, it was believed that the study of microevolutionary processes would ultimately lead to an understanding of speciation. The next group of studies were designed specifically to understand these microevolutionary processes by sampling animals from known local populations. These studies were conducted by researchers who trapped the animals themselves and obtained genetic and demographic data; they included those conducted by Jolly and Brett (1973), Olivier, et al. (1974), Ober et al. (1978, 1980), Byles and Sanders (1981), Olivier, et al. (1986), and Rogers and Kidd (1993) on baboons; Nozawa et al. (1982) on *Macaca fuscata*, and Turner (1981) and Dracopoli et al. (1983) on vervet monkeys. The final stage of large-scale genetic surveys attempted to combine genetic, demographic, and long-term behavioral observation. These included studies by Melnick and Kidd (1983) and Melnick et al. (1984) on *M. mulatta* and de Ruiter et al. (1992) on *M. fascicularis* and Phillips-Conroy et al. (1992) on baboons.

Recent studies on population genetics have concentrated on the meaning of local fluctuations of gene frequencies and have utilized protein, nuclear, and microsatellite loci (Melnick 1988; Nozawa et al. 1991; Turner et al. 1996). Genetic studies have also become the standard for determining systematic relationships. Systematics addresses the relationship between species and subspecies. Some of these relationships in Old World monkeys have been examined by the use of mitochondrial DNA (Disotell et al. 1992; Melnick et al. 1993). In addition, some recent studies have been conducted to answer questions in evolution and sociobiology—

specifically, what is a high-ranking male's contribution to subsequent generations, what is the differential behavior of specific males toward young, and how is female choice accomplished?

## THE DATA

In order to understand the utility of the Old World monkey data both as an analogy for genetic variability in human populations and for the elucidation of the evolutionary process, we first need to understand the amount and kind of data available. We have conducted an extensive survey of published accounts of genetic variation in cercopithecoids for the last 30 years. Virtually all the information is limited to three genera, *Macaca*, *Papio*, and *Cercopithecus*. Within the latter, information is almost exclusively available for *C. aethiops*.

Our investigation of the available data highlights some limitations that need to be recognized in order to effectively draw conclusions about the three genera, the meaning of local variation in gene frequencies, sociobiology, and primate evolution. These limitations apply primarily to the sampling process.

### Number of Animals Surveyed

Nearly 11,000 macaques, 3000 baboons, and 750 vervets have been surveyed over the past 30 years (see Figure 1). Although these numbers may seem substantial, they give only a gross picture of the pattern of surveying. There are several species of macaques widely distributed over Asia. However, almost all of the work on the genus has concentrated on four species. There have been 3800+ *M. fascicularis*, 3500+ *M. fuscata*, 2000+ *M. mulatta*, and 1000+ *M. nemestrina* surveyed for genetic variation. Of the *M. mulatta* surveyed, over 500 were from Cayo Santiago, an island off the coast of Puerto Rico where a seminaturalistic population of rhesus macaques was started over 40 years ago. *M. fuscata*, found only in Japan, has one of the narrowest distributions, whereas *M. fascicularis* and *M. mulatta* are widely distributed, found in several countries throughout Asia.

The number of animals surveyed, where they are located, and available demographic data are all important considerations for the study of microevolutionary processes. For *M. fascicularis*, there is what we call "high-quality data" for about 420 animals, or approximately 11% of the total number of samples for the species. "High-quality data" refers to samples where the trappers knew, at a minimum, what troop the animals were from and the precise geographic location of the troops. The best data sets include also the demographic structure of the troop and the ages of the individuals trapped.

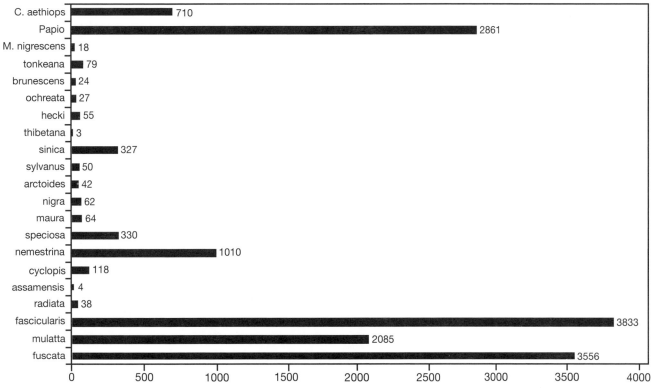

FIGURE 1. *Sample Sizes by Species. Number of animals sampled in each species.*

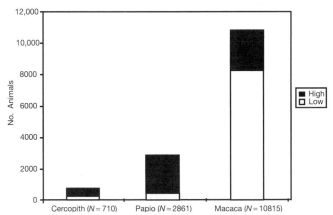

FIGURE 2. *Quality of Data by Genus. All data with high-quality data are shaded.*

Figure 2 shows the total number of animals sampled for the different genera and the number of high-quality samples. We also present a series of maps that display the location of animals sampled for genetic information and graphically represent the difference in overall sampling and quality of data sets. The first series of maps concentrates on protein polymorphism. The locations of all samples and samples with high-quality data are presented for macaques (Figure 3), baboons (Figure 4), and vervets (Figure 5).

For *M. mulatta*, there are high-quality data for about 870 animals, or 42% of the total. However, 79% of that information comes from Cayo Santiago. It is difficult to assess the *M. fuscata* information. The locations of almost all of the samples are documented. Only the provisioned populations have information on troop structure or demography. Thus provenance and troop membership are included, but demographic data and age structure are not. Although only a few *M. sylvanus* have been sampled, that data give location and demographic information. Additionally, 55% of the total of 181 samples of *M. sinica* have good information.

The situation in *Papio* and *C. aethiops* is actually the reverse for the macaques. Although the total number of animals sampled is substantially less, the animals consisted of known troops with demographic information. Eighty-four percent of the baboon information has good data regarding provenance and demographics. Seventy-three percent of the vervet data also has high-quality information on provenance and age structure of the populations. So, whereas the information on baboons and vervets may not be as extensive in terms of

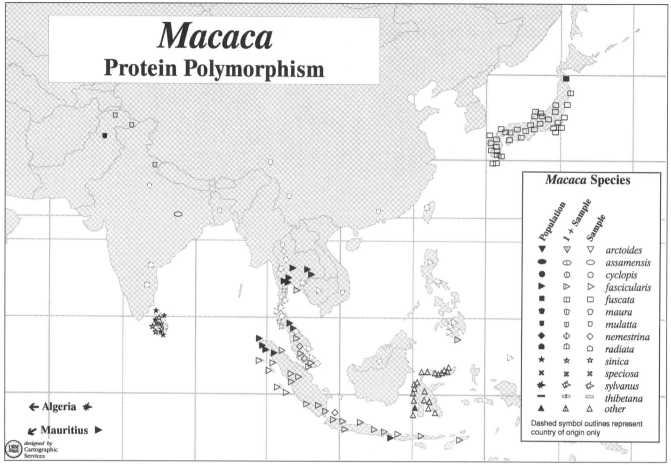

FIGURE 3. Macaca *Protein Polymorphism. Location of study sites by species; high-quality data are shaded.*

number or geography as that for macaques, it is extremely valuable in determining the pattern of evolutionary change in these species.

## Types of Genetic Data Available

The earliest data were largely on ABO blood group and allozyme variation. Information based on electrophoresis of blood proteins still remains the largest single body of genetic data. Beginning in the 1980s, researchers started to compile information detected by other techniques, including mitochondrial DNA (mtDNA), restriction fragment length polymorphism (RFLP), unique sequence nuclear genes, and mini- and microsatellites. The techniques used to elucidate these systems require the extraction of DNA from cells. These techniques have been available for over a decade, but their use in primates has been limited.

Only 22% of the macaques examined have been observed with a system other than protein electrophoresis, most of which utilized isoelectric focusing (see

Figure 6). Sixty-six percent of the baboons and 65% of the vervets have information on systems other than allozyme variation. However, the great majority of this additional information is on the ABO blood group system (see Figures 7 and 8). In almost all cases, when data are available for specific animals for IEF or ABO blood groups, allozyme data are also available for the same animals. In some samples of baboons and vervets, there is usually a comparison of ABO and allozyme data. In macaques, especially *fuscata*, the preponderance of data is generated most often by IEF and allozyme information. With data that require DNA extraction, this is not the case. If DNA data are available from any animals, electrophoretic data usually are not available for the same animals; however, there are exceptions to this.

As yet, there have been almost no comparisons of results from allozyme- and DNA-derived information. Melnick et al. (1993) have compared allozyme and mtDNA information for rhesus macaques. Turner et al. (1997a) have compared allozyme and microsatellite data on a series of vervet troops in Kenya. We expect more information of this type to be coming from *M. fus-*

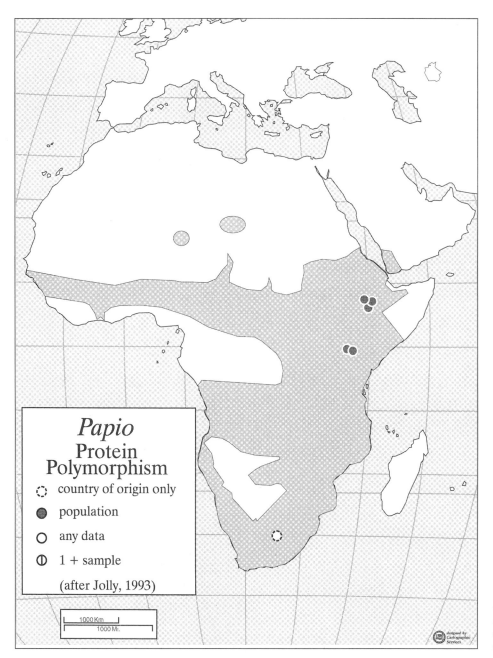

*Papio*
Protein
Polymorphism

- ◌ country of origin only
- ● population
- ○ any data
- ◍ 1 + sample

(after Jolly, 1993)

1000 Km
1000 Mi.

*FIGURE 4.* Papio *Protein Polymorphism. Location of study sites; high-quality data are shaded.*

*cata.* Most of the Japanese macaques have been examined for a variety of systems. No comparative information has yet been published.

## BEGINNINGS OF THE ANSWERS

### Amount of Genetic Variation

*M. fascicularis* is a widely distributed species with populations living on both the mainland and on islands off the mainland. There seems to be greater genetic variability in mainland populations than in island populations (first noted in Weiss and Goodman 1971). A similar reduction of variation is noted when another island species, *M. fuscata,* is compared to *M. mulatta,* the mainland ancestral species (Weiss et al. 1971). This reduction in variation may reflect past bottlenecks that the island populations have passed through, either during their inception or during more recent glacial events (Melnick 1988).

The baboon populations sampled represent animals in only a small part of the total range of the species. One of the populations in the Awash is at the edge of the

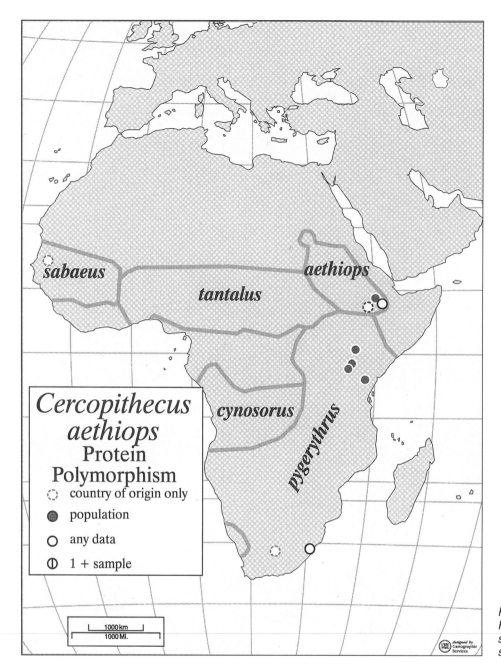

FIGURE 5. Vervet Protein Polymorphism. Location of study sites; high-quality data are shaded.

*anubis* range and form a hybrid zone with hamadryas baboons (Phillips-Conroy and Jolly 1986). This population has been followed extensively for 20 years and should provide interesting data about the nature of subspecific hybridization. Other baboon populations examined are in Kenya (Byles and Sanders 1981; Ober et al. 1978; Olivier et al. 1974, 1986) and Tanzania (Rogers and Kidd 1993). These populations are more central to the range of baboons, yet they are still located in a fairly narrow corridor of the total range of the species. This same problem is found in vervet monkey populations. The Ethiopian vervet monkeys (Turner 1981) may also be on the edge of the species range. The

Kenyan animals (Dracopoli et al. 1983) are more central. However, they do represent only the smallest fraction of the total distribution of the species.

A very general but frequently used indicator of genetic diversity in populations is average heterozygosity ($\overline{H}$), which calculates the frequency of heterozygote individuals in a population. The higher the proportion of heterozygotes, the more variable the population. In macaques, $\overline{H}$ for electrophoretic data ranges from 0.02 in *cyclopis* and *speciosa* to 0.20 in *mulatta* and mainland *fascicularis*. In baboons the range is 0.019 to 0.096, and in vervets it is 0.02 to 0.05. This may indicate that for electrophoretic data, macaques are more variable than

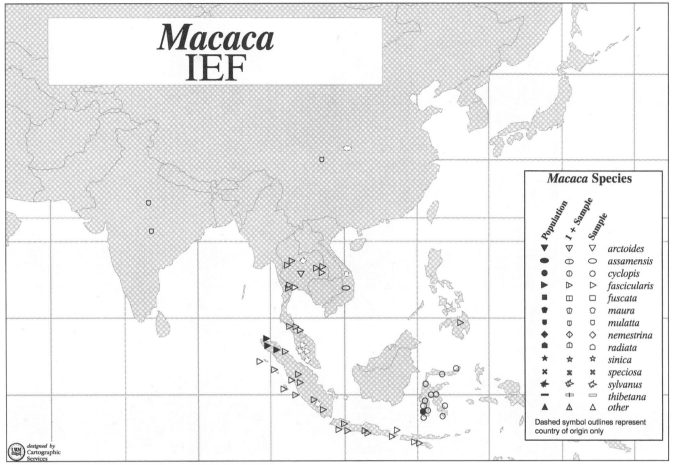

*FIGURE 6.* Macaca *Isoelectric Focusing. Location of study sites; high-quality data are shaded.*

baboons, which are more variable than vervets. To date, there are no published accounts comparing the three genera for other types of systems.

## Local Populations and Gene Flow

Another indicator of diversity in populations is seen from an examination of Nei's (1973) analysis of gene diversity in subdivided populations. $H_T$ is an indicator of the overall genetic heterogeneity. In several species of macaques, $H_T$ is about 0.08 (Melnick 1988); in vervets, it is about 0.03. This difference may also be the result of the evolutionary history of these organisms. Low overall heterogeneity and reduced diversity among disparate groups of organisms result for several reasons, including subspeciation by subdivision, or recent time since subdivision, or high levels of gene flow.

Several conclusions have been proposed to help explain the pattern of allozyme variation in nonhuman primates where most of the variation is found in the local population and less in troops at a site or between sites. The most often cited explanation concerns a single sex migrating to mate (Melnick 1988). The pattern of

migration in the three genera of Old World monkeys is similar: The males leave their natal group and migrate to another group to mate. Although this pattern describes migration, there is another factor present in vervet populations that may influence genetic variation. Vervet males migrate to groups where their brothers or half-brothers have migrated before them. Vervet males need to establish coalitions in order to mate (Whitten, personal communication). These coalitions seem to be kin-based, although only a genetic analysis can determine this precisely. This pattern of nonrandom dispersal of males may lead to an increased lack of differentiation among groups.

## Paternity

For the past dozen years, researchers have actively sought the answers to the questions of whether the highest ranking male has primary access to estrus females and whether males behave preferentially toward their own young. These questions have been notoriously difficult to answer. Allozymes were often not sufficiently variable to permit determination of paternity

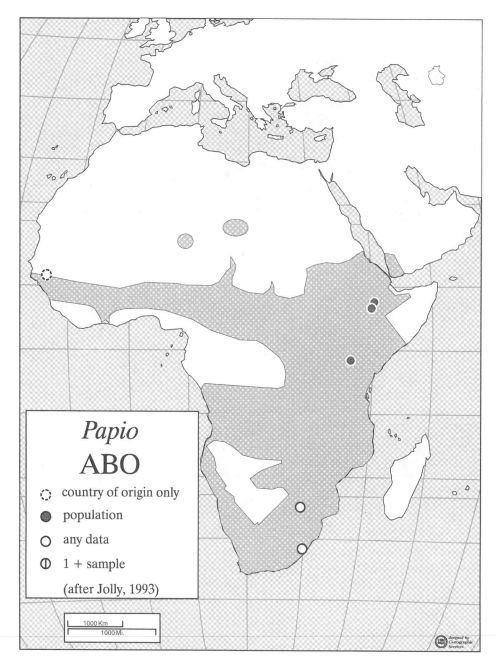

*FIGURE 7.* Papio *ABO data. Location of study sites; high-quality data are shaded.*

(note Smith 1980, as an exception). The use of mini- and microsatellite variation alleviated that problem. Also, because of male migration, it was often difficult to sample all potential fathers. The best designed paternity studies should be prospective. Animals should be sampled at the beginning of a multiyear study. Thus males who may be fathers but who may have moved are sampled. Two studies are of note: Inoue et al. (1993) on Japanese macaques and de Ruiter et al. (1992) on *fascicularis.* Inoue's results indicate that higher ranking males do have some preferential access to estrus females

and de Ruiter's results indicate that males do act preferentially toward their offspring.

## CONCLUSIONS

Considerable work has been done on nonhuman primate genetic variation, but many of the questions remain only partly answered. We know there is considerable variation in primate species and population. But why is there so much more in some than in others?

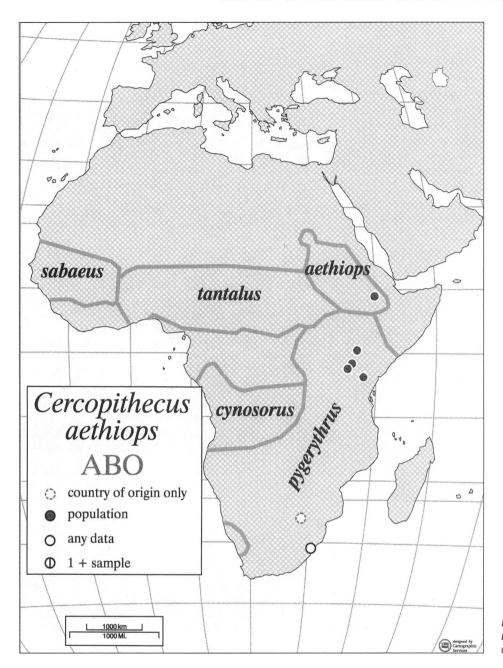

*FIGURE 8.    Vervet ABO data. Location of study sites; high-quality data are shaded.*

What part do social relationships and social structure play in defining these patterns? What are the different levels of variation in different systems? Do these correlate with social structure? Does one find the same type of patterning in animals living in different parts of the species range? Do these animals have any utility as analogy for human evolution?

Answering these questions will rely on more complete data sets that allow us to determine the relative effects of general "rules" and patterns and the roles of specific conditions affecting a particular group of animals. For example, mainland populations of primates are generally more variable genetically than island populations. However, the phylogenetic history and the local history of groups can interact with the social structure to determine the level of variability observed. Because genetic and behavioral parameters are in part determined by particularistic conditions, one needs data sets that are comprehensive and include the behavior, demography, ecology, endocrinology, and the genetics of several groups.

It is often the case that a species is known from only one or two, sometimes ill-defined, locations. To give a truer picture of a species of primates, data sets from multiple locations with differing conditions need to be examined. At least in some cases, the social unit in *toque* macaques may not be identical to the reproductive unit (Keane et al. 1997), but we do not know the degree to which this is a general feature of the species. Likewise, there is no single vervet pattern of genetic or morphological variation (Turner et al. 1997b), for example; there are a number of patterns reflecting different local conditions. It is only by examining an array of populations over a wide variety of conditions that we will be able to begin to answer questions about primate patterns. This is fully in keeping with the admonition of Washburn et al. (1965), when writing of primate behavior studies, to "sample behavior in several habitats to gain an understanding of the flexibility of the built-in behavior patterns of a species."

It is through an examination of widely distributed species that primates may serve as models for interpreting human evolution. The Old World monkeys may not be the obvious models for early hominid evolution. However, they may give us information about the later stages of hominid evolution. *Homo sapiens* is the most widely distributed primate, living in an enormous array of environmental and ecological conditions. Modern humans are highly polymorphic; they exchange members between local groups, yet they are divisible into larger clusters. They exhibit a wide array of social structures. So do three Old World monkey genera. Macaques, baboons, and vervets are also polymorphic, polytypic, and widely distributed. They exchange members between groups but still are divisible into larger units, or "races." The parallels between Old World monkeys and modern humans may be the real grounds for analogies between the two and may provide models for interpreting the distribution and patterning of human populations.

This approach is fully in keeping with Washburn's goal of applying experimental procedures to the understanding of primate and human diversity and illustrates the continuing validity of the new physical anthropology.

## REFERENCES

Barnicot, N. A., Huehns, E. R., and Jolly, C. J. (1966). Biochemical studies on hemoglobin variants of the *irus* macaque. *Proc. Royal Soc. Lond.* 165: 224–244.

Byles, R. H., and Sanders, M. F. (1981). Intertroop variation in the frequencies of ABO alleles in a population of olive baboons. *Int. J. Primatol.* 2: 35–46.

Darga, L. L., Goodman, M., Weiss, M. L., Moore, G. W., Prychodko, W., Dene, H., Tashian, R., and Koen, A. (1975). Molecular systematics and clinal variation in macaques. In C. L. Markert (ed.), *Isozymes.* Vol. 4, *Genetics and Evolution.* New York: Academic Press.

Disotell, T. R., Honeycutt, R. L., and Ruvolo, M. (1992). Mitochondrial DNA phylogeny of the Old-World monkey tribe *Papionini. Mol. Biol. Evol.* 9: 1–13.

Dracopoli, N. C., Brett, F. L., Turner, T. R., and Jolly, C. J. (1983). Patterns of genetic variation in the serum proteins of the Kenyan vervet monkey (*Cercopithecus aethiops*). *Am. J. Phys. Anthropol.* 61: 39–49.

Fedigan, L. M. (1982). *Primate Paradigms.* Montreal: Eden Press.

Goodman, M., Braunitzer, G., Stangl, Z., and Schrank, B. (1983). Evidence on human origin from haemoglobins of African apes. *Nature (London)* 303: 546–548.

Goodman, M., Kulkarni, A., Poulik, E., and Riklys, E. (1965). Species and geographic differences in transferrin polymorphism of macaques. *Science* 147: 384–446.

Inoue, M., Mitsunaga, R., Nozaki, N., Ohsawa, H., Takenada, A., Sugiyama, Y., Siomizu, D., and Takenaka, O. (1993). Male dominance rank and reproductive success in an enclosed group of Japanese macaques: With special reference to post conception mating. *Primates* 34: 503–512.

Jolly, C. J. (1993). Species, subspecies, and baboon systematics. In W. H. Kimbel and L. B. Martin (eds.), *Species, Species Concepts, and Primate Evolution.* New York: Plenum Press.

Jolly, C. J., and Brett, F. L. (1973). Genetic markers and baboon biology. *J. Med. Primatol.* 2: 85–99.

Keane, B., Dittus, W. P. J., and Melnick, D. J. (1997). Paternity assessment in wild groups of toque macaques *Macaca sinica* at Polonnaruwa, Sri Lanka using molecular markers. *Mol. Ecol.* 6: 267–282.

Mann, A., and Weiss, M. (1996). Hominoid phylogeny and taxonomy: A consideration of the molecular and fossil evidence in an historical perspective. *Mol. Phylog. Evol.* 5: 169–181.

Melnick, D. J. (1988). The genetic structure of a primate species: Rhesus macaques and other cercopithecine monkeys. *Int. J. Primatol.* 9: 195–231.

Melnick, D. J., Hoelzer, G. A., Absher, R., and Ashley, M. V. (1993). mtDNA diversity in rhesus monkeys reveals overestimates of divergence time and paraphyly with neighboring species. *Mol. Biol. Evol.* 10: 282–295.

Melnick, D. J., Jolly, C. J., and Kidd, K. K. (1984). The genetics of a wild population of rhesus monkeys (*Macaca mulatta*). I. Genetic variability within and between social groups. *Am. J. Phys. Anthropol.* 63: 341–360.

Melnick, D. J., and Kidd, K. K. (1983). The genetic consequences of social group fission in a wild population of rhesus monkeys (*Macaca mulatta*). *Behav. Ecol. Sociobiol.* 12: 229–236.

Melnick, D. J., Pearl, M. C., and Richard, A. F. (1984). Male migration and inbreeding avoidance in wild rhesus monkeys. *Am. J. Primatol.* 7: 229–243.

Morin, P. A., Moore, J. J., Chakraboraty, R., Jin, L., Goodall, J., and Woodruff, D. S. (1994). Kin selection, social structure, gene flow and the evolution of chimpanzees. *Science* 265: 1193–1201.

Nei, M. (1973). Analysis of gene diversity in subdivided populations. *Proc. Natl. Acad. Sci. USA* 70: 3321–3323.

Nozawa, K., Shotake, T., Kawamoto, Y., and Tanabe, Y. (1982). Population genetics of Japanese monkeys. II. Blood protein polymorphisms and population structure. *Primates* 23: 252–271.

Nozawa, K., Shotake, T., Minezawa, M., Kawamotot, Y., Hayasaka, K., and Kawamoto, S. (1991). Population genetics of Japanese monkeys. III. Ancestry and differentiation of local populations. *Primates* 32: 411–435.

Ober, C., Olivier, T. J., and Buettner-Janusch, J. (1978). Carbonic anhydrase heterozygosity and F_{st} distributions in Kenyan baboon troops. *Am. J. Phys. Anthropol.* 48: 95–100.

Ober, C., Olivier, T. J., and Buettner-Janusch, J. (1980). Genetic aspects of migration in a rhesus monkey population. *J. Human Evol.* 9: 197–203.

Olivier, T. J., Buettner-Janusch, J., and Buettner-Janusch, V. (1974). Carbonic anhydrase isoenzymes in nine troops of Kenya baboons, *Papio cynocephalus* (Linneaus 1766). *Am. J. Phys. Anthropol. 41:* 175–190.

Olivier, T. J., Coppenhaver, D. H., and Steinberg, A. G. (1986). Distributions of immunoglobulin allotypes among local populations of Kenya olive baboons. *Am. J. Phys. Anthropol. 70:* 29–38.

Pereira, M., and Weiss, M. L. (1991). Female mate choice, male migration, and the threat of infanticide in ringtailed lemurs. *Behavioral Ecology and Sociobiology 28:* 141–152.

Phillips-Conroy, J. E., and Jolly, C. J. (1986). Changes in the structure of the baboon hybrid zone in the Awash National Park, Ethiopia. *Am. J. Phys. Anthropol. 71:* 337–350.

Phillips-Conroy, J. E., Jolly, C. J., Nystrom, P., and Hemmalin, H. A. (1992). Migration of male hamadryas baboon into *anubis* groups in the Awash National Park, Ethiopia. *Int. J. Primatol. 13:* 455–476.

Pope, T. R. (1992). The influence of dispersal patterns and mating system on genetic differentiation within and between populations of the red howler monkey (*Alouatta seniculus*). *Evolution 46:* 1112–1128.

Rogers, J., and Kidd, K. K. (1993). Nuclear DNA polymorphisms in a wild population of yellow baboons (*Papio hamadryas cynocephalus*) from Mikumi National Park, Tanzania. *Am. J. Phys. Anthropol. 90:* 477–486.

Rogers, J., Ruano, G., and Kidd, K. K. (1992). Variability in nuclear DNA among nonhuman primates: Application of molecular genetic techniques to intra- and inter-species genetic analyses. *Am. J. Primatol. 27:* 93–105.

de Ruiter, J. R., Scheffrahn, W., Trommelen, G. J. J. M., Uitterlinden, A. G., Martin, R. D., and van Hooff, J. A. R. A. M. (1992). Male social rank and reproductive success in wild long-tailed macaques. Paternity exclusion by blood protein analysis and DNA fingerprinting. In R. D. Martin, A. F. Dixson, and E. J. Wickings (eds.), *Paternity in Primates.* Basel: Karger.

de Ruiter, J. R., and van Hooff, J. A. R. A. M. (1993). Male dominance rank and reproductive success in primate groups. *Primates 34:* 513–524.

Ruvolo, M., Disotell, T. R., Allard, M. W., Brown, W. M., and Honeycutt, R. L. (1991). Resolution of the African hominoid trichotomy by the use of a mitochondrial gene sequence. *Proc. Natl. Acad. Sci. USA 88:* 1570–1574.

Sarich, V. M., and Wilson, A. C. (1967). Rates of albumin evolution in primates. *Proc. Natl. Acad. Sci. USA 58:* 142–148.

Scheffrahn, W., Menard, N., Vallet, D., and Gaci, B. (1993). Ecology, demography and population genetics of Barbary macaques in Algeria. *Primates 34:* 381–394.

Smith, D. G. (1980). Paternity exclusion in six captive groups of rhesus monkeys (*Macaca mulatta*). *Am. J. Phys. Anthropol. 53:* 243–249.

Struhsaker, T. T., and Leland, L. (1979). Socioecology of five sympatric monkey species in the Kibale Forest, Uganda. *Adv. Study Behav. 9:* 159–228.

Strum, S. (1987). *Almost Human.* New York: Random House.

Turner, T. R. (1981). Blood protein variation in a population of Ethiopian vervet monkeys. (*Cereopithecus aethiops aethiops*). *Am. J. Phys. Anthropol. 55:* 225–232.

Turner, T. R., Rosinsky, B., Weiss, M. L., and Jolly, C. J. (1996). Microsatellite variation in four populations of vervet monkeys (*Cercopithecus aethiops*) in Kenya. *Am. J. Phys. Anthropol. Supplement 22:* 231.

Turner, T. R., Weiss, M. L., and Gray, J. P. (1997a). The uses of stored samples for genetic analysis: Recycled field studies. *Am. J. Phys. Anthropol. Supplement 24:* 230.

Turner, T. R., Anapol, A., and Jolly, C. J. (1997b). Growth, development and sexual dimorphism in vervet monkeys. (*Cercopithecus aethiops*) at four sites in Kenya. *Am. J. Phys. Anthropol. 103:* 19–335.

Washburn, S. L. (1951). The new physical anthropology. *Transactions of the New York Academy of Science Series II 13:* 298–304.

Washburn, S. L., Jay, P. C., and Lancaster, J. B. (1965). Field studies of Old World monkeys and apes. *Science 150:* 1541–1547.

Weiss, M. L., and Goodman, M. (1971). Genetic structure and systematics of some macaques and men. In A. B. Chiarelli (ed.), *Comparative Genetics in Monkeys, Apes and Man.* London: Academic Press, pp. 129–151.

Weiss, M. L., Goodman, M., Prychodko, W., and Tanaka, T. (1971). Species and geographic distribution patterns of the macaque prealbumin polymorphism. *Primates 12:* 75–80.

Whitten, P. L. (1983). Diet and dominance among vervet monkeys. *Am. J. Primatol. 5:* 139–159.

*Lowenstein summarizes the recent history of the dramatic changes in techniques that have allowed the exploration of the molecular fossil record. Despite the initial controversy about the use of molecular methods in dating the divergence of species, Lowenstein's history shows that Washburn's faith in the power and promise of the molecular data was correct. In recent years, the consistency of the evidence and the addition of new techniques have made this a valuable source of independent evidence. In fact, the great agreement about molecular family trees among different laboratories stands in marked contrast to the continuing disagreements about phylogenies among those who rely solely on morphological data. Lowenstein uses molecular data to solve the mystery of which ape was used in the Piltdown hoax and suggests ways that molecular methods could advance our understanding of archaeological and paleontological remains, determine the sex of skeletons, and interpret patterns of migration and colonization during human evolution. The future of the molecular evidence will likely prove Washburn's assertion that controversies in science are usually resolved by better techniques and methods of analysis.*

# 15 Evolutionary Information from Fossil Molecules

## Jerold M. Lowenstein

### OF DNA AND DINOSAURS

The movie *Jurassic Park,* and the book by Michael Crichton on which it was based, propelled into the public consciousness a new scientific discipline that has been growing and gathering strength for several decades—the study of fossil molecules. In the book and movie, dinosaurs are reconstructed from the DNA of dinosaur blood in the stomachs of mosquitos preserved in amber, dating to the Jurassic era. When the book was published in 1990, no DNA molecules had been retrieved that were anywhere near Cretaceous age, but so quickly does nature imitate art these days that the sequencing of DNA from a 120-million-year-old weevil in amber was accomplished in 1993 by Cano et al.

All living organisms contain enormous numbers of long, chainlike molecules, particularly DNA and proteins, that may be recoverable from fossil sediments and from specially preserved specimens like insects in amber. These molecules contain valuable genetic and phylogenetic information that is the invisible counterpart of that found in macroscopic fossil skeletal material.

The recovery and analysis of molecular genetic information from fossils have been progressing rapidly in the past decade as a result of improved techniques, such as the polymerase chain reaction (PCR) and methods for the rapid sequencing of DNA and proteins (Eglinton and Curry 1991). In this essay, I summarize the background and highlights of this fast-moving exploration of the molecular fossil record, which has emerged as one of the latest scientific disciplines of our molecular century.

### THE MOLECULAR CENTURY

At the beginning of the twentieth century, the world was perceived as being a lot younger and smaller than it is today. In 1900, the age of the earth was thought to be less than 100 million years and the age of mammals less than 3 million years. Our knowledge of the universe was limited to the Milky Way, for the existence of other galaxies had not yet been recognized.

As we approach the end of the twentieth century and look back at its beginning, we can see two unifying themes running through the great advances in our understanding of the physical and biological worlds we live in. The first theme is evolution: evolution of the universe from a hot big bang about 10 billion years ago; evolution of the solar system by nuclear and gravitational processes during the past 4.6 billion years; evolution of the earth by plate tectonics; and the rise and evolution of life on earth from bacterialike organisms 4 billion years ago to the millions of complex life forms that swim, crawl, walk, and fly today.

The second theme is the atomic and molecular structure of all matter in our universe, nonliving and living. So pervasive now is the atomic and molecular basis for physics, chemistry, biology, and medicine that it's hard to realize that when the century dawned, many if not most prominent scientists did not believe in the reality of atoms and molecules.

The tide of opinion did not turn decisively until 1905, when the young Albert Einstein showed by his mathematical analysis of Brownian motion that the effects of molecules on microscopic particles could be observed and the number of molecules in a solution calculated (Pais 1982). This episode illustrates a point that Sherwood Washburn has made repeatedly. Controversies in science are usually not settled by logical arguments in which reasonable people disagree but by improved techniques and methods of analysis. The reality of atoms had been debated for 2000 years, since the atomic structure of matter was proposed by Democritus and denied by Aristotle, but the issue wasn't settled until Einstein revealed that almost anyone could do simple experiments and come up with numerical results.

Quantum mechanics in the mid-1920s united physics and chemistry. Linus Pauling (1940) in particular used the new knowledge to clarify the nature of the chemical bond and gain insights into protein structure, molecular medicine, and molecular evolution. Finally, the unification of biology and chemistry was achieved in 1953, when James Watson and Francis Crick discovered the double-helical structure of DNA, the molecular spring of life on earth.

Thus the first half of the twentieth century can be viewed as a progressive amalgamation of the disjunct disciplines of physics, chemistry, biology, evolution, and medicine within the unifying framework of molecular science. Radioactive dating revealed that the earth was 4.6 billion years old and that life had existed here for nearly 4 billion of those years. The universe was expanding at a rate that suggested it was about 10 billion years old.

## MOLECULAR METHODS IN EVOLUTION

During the first half of the century, there was no agreement among anthropologists as to which primates were most closely related to humans or as to the timing of primate evolution (Washburn 1973, 1978, 1985). New molecular methods for determining phylogenies and divergence times have helped to resolve these questions. Washburn's 1963 symposium volume on *Classification in Human Evolution* included pioneer work in molecular evolution by Emil Zuckerkandl (1963) and Morris Goodman (1963).

Zuckerkandl, working with Linus Pauling (1962), derived phylogenies by comparing the hemoglobin molecules of different species and came up with the concept of "molecular clocks" to time divergence. Goodman's immunodiffusion comparisons of primate serum proteins showed such close relations among humans, chimpanzees, and gorillas that he suggested classifying these three as members of the same family, the Hominidae.

Vincent Sarich, a chemistry major turned anthropologist, worked with evolutionary biochemist Allan Wilson in further defining primate relationships by means of the microcomplement fixation test (MC'F), a more quantitative method than Goodman's. In 1967, Sarich and Wilson set off a huge debate when they used the molecular clock concept to propose that humans, chimpanzees, and gorillas had diverged from a common African ape ancestor only 5 million years ago, not 25 million, as supposed by most paleontologists.

Darwin and Huxley had suggested that humans were most closely related to the African apes, and other comparative anatomists had been debating the matter for the past hundred years, naming just about every known primate as the putative human ancestor and giving estimates of the time of the human-ape divergence as anywhere from 2 million to 50 million years ago. Instead of converging on a consensus, anatomists were in greater disagreement than they had been a century earlier. Washburn commented (1991), "A molecular biochemist in a few afternoons can provide solutions to the problems of human ancestry which are more likely to be correct and useful than all the studies of comparative anatomy."

Many noted paleontologists assailed Sarich and Wilson. The chief obstacle to the 5 my ape-human divergence, in the minds of the fossil hunters, was a 15-my-old hominoid known then as *Ramapithecus,* represented mainly by a fragmentary upper jaw and palate from the Siwalik Hills of pre-partioned India, later Pakistan. Some paleontologists were certain that *Ramapithecus* was a hominid, in the direct human lineage, based on its dentition but lacking limb bones and pelvis. The reconstructed creature was routinely displayed in the Time-Life parade of evolving humans, striding upright between *Australopithecus* and *Dryopithecus* (Zihlman and Lowenstein 1979).

Obviously, if *Ramapithecus* was a hominid 15 mya, the pongid-hominid split couldn't have taken place 5 mya. The battle raged on for another decade, until limb bones of *Ramapithecus* were discovered that seemed to belong to a tree-living ape, not a bipedal hominid. Nowadays *Ramapithecus,* submerged in the genus *Sivapithecus,* is considered an orangutan ancestor, based on the same kind of morphological comparisons that were mistakenly used for so long to classify it as a human ancestor (Pilbeam 1982).

## MOLECULAR STUDIES ON FOSSILS

If immunological tests on the proteins of living primates could reveal their family relationships, why couldn't the same thing be done with fossil primates? I asked myself this question in 1976 and started a new line of investigation to search for the answer.

Medical researchers had been using the technique of radioimmunoassy (RIA), which employs radioactively labeled antibodies or antigens, to detect millionths or billionths of grams of specific proteins. It seemed that this approach could be used to detect collagen, the main structural protein of bones and teeth, or albumin, the most abundant serum protein, in fossil bone and teeth.

As it happened, the RIA method earned the Nobel Prize in Medicine or Physiology in 1977 for Rosalyn Yalow, a physicist specializing in nuclear medicine. In her acceptance speech in Stockholm, Dr. Yalow related that her first report on RIA, which she had used to measure insulin levels in the blood of diabetics and others, was rejected by a prominent medical journal, because her results did not agree with the preconceptions of the reviewer (Yalow 1978).

Prior to RIA, there was no technique sensitive enough to quantitate insulin levels in blood. Subsequently, RIA revolutionized biology and medicine by making it possible to measure precisely the blood and tissue levels of many hormones, drugs, and physiologically important molecules that had previously been undetectable. The RIA method adopted for fossil research was a variant known as a solid-phase double-antibody technique. It could detect microgram quantities of collagen and distinguish among the collagens of closely related species like humans, apes, and monkeys, as well as those of distant species like salmon, nematode, and sea anemone. In a series of human fossils ranging from a 900-year-old burial to a 1.9-million-year-old australopithecine (Figure 1), the assay revealed decreasing but measurable amounts of human collagen (Lowenstein 1980, 1981).

In 1979, the RIA technique was applied to detecting albumin in the tissues of a 40,000-year-old frozen Siberian mammoth. We demonstrated that after 40 millennia

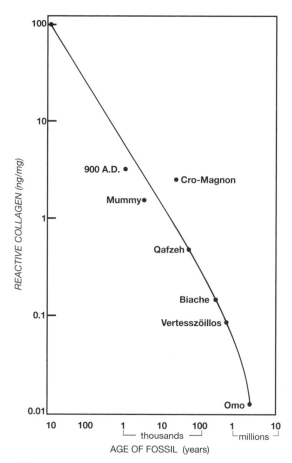

FIGURE 1. *Extractable collagen vs. age of human fossil. Extracts of fossil bones were tested by radioimmunoassay (RIA) for their ability to bind antiserum to human collagen. The series includes bones of* Homo sapiens, Neanderthal, Homo erectus, *and* Australiopithecus. *Immunoreactivity decreased with fossil age but was still detectable in the nearly 2-million-year-old australopithecine.*

in the permafrost, albumin from mammoth tissue was immunologically virtually identical to the albumins of the extant African and Asian elephants (Lowenstein et al. 1981; Prager et al. 1980).

Within a few years we were able to make a similar analysis of proteins in the bones of two more extinct species, the American mastodon (*Mammut americanum*) (Shoshani et al. 1985) and Steller's sea cow (*Hydrodamalis gigas*) (Rainey et al. 1984). Elephants and sea cows are related, so it was possible for the first time to make a molecular family tree that included three extinct species.

## MOLECULAR STUDIES ON THE EXTINCT QUAGGA

While morphologists did not seem to be able to agree on evolutionary relationships, molecular analysis of living species done in different laboratories generally gave the same results. Would this also prove to be true of fossils? The extinct quagga provided a test case of this thesis.

The South African quaggas, equines striped on their front half like a zebra and chestnut-toned on their hindquarters like horses, roamed in huge herds for much of the nineteenth century until they were wiped out like the plains bison of North American by over-hunting and habitat destruction. The last quagga died in a zoo about 100 years ago. Morphologists came up with three different theories of quagga relationships: (1) Its nearest relative was the domestic horse, *Equus caballus;* (2) its nearest relative was the plains zebra, *Equus burchelli;* (3) it was equally related to the three African zebra species.

The questions of whether molecular relationships could be done on fossil material, and if so whether two different sets of investigators would agree, was put to the test. Proteins from a 150-year-old quagga skin were compared immunologically to those of other equids (Lowenstein and Ryder 1985). Russell Higuchi, working in Allan Wilson's laboratory (Higuchi et al. 1984, 1987), extracted mitochondrial DNA from quagga tissue, the first time fossil DNA had been identified, and compared the DNA sequence of the quagga to those of other equids.

Higuchi and I, not knowing each other's results, were invited to present our findings at a meeting of the Carnegie Institution of Washington. Fortunately for this embryonic field of research, our different techniques—RIA of fossil proteins and sequencing of mitochondrial DNA—led us to identical conclusions: that the quagga was so closely related to the plains zebra (Figure 2) that it could be considered a subspecies.

The identification of quagga DNA was front-page news throughout the world and encouraged widespread speculation in the press that it might be possible to resurrect extinct species. Unfortunately, the DNA recovered was only a tiny fraction of the quagga genome, less than one-tenth of 1 percent.

These results have, however, inspired a breeding program in South Africa intended to "retrieve" quaggas from the still-abundant plains zebras. Plains zebras vary considerably in their striping pattern, and a selected group that closely resemble the quaggas have been trucked to a breeding farm north of Cape Town. If the quagga was in fact merely a subspecies of the plains

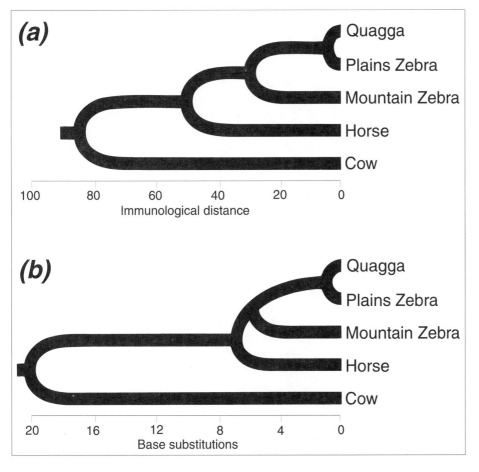

FIGURE 2. *Comparison of immunological (RIA) and DNA phylogenies derived from quagga skin. Both (a) RIA analysis of quagga skin proteins and (b) mitochondrial DNA show the quagga to be much closer to the plains zebra than to any other living equid. In contrast, morphologists have suggested that three different phylogenies: the one supported here, a quagga-horse pairing, and the quagga equidistant from the three zebras.*

zebra and not a distinct species, the animals bred in this experiment should be very close replicas, both genetically and morphologically, of the extinct quaggas.

## WHICH APE WAS USED IN THE PILTDOWN HOAX?

Three-quarters of a century after the "discovery," the famous Piltdown hoax continues to stir heated controversy. Books propounding new theories appear annually, speculating endlessly as to whether Charles Dawson, the finder of Piltdown, acted alone or in collaboration with any one of 20 or 30 other prominent contemporaries, including Teilhard de Chardin, Arthur Conan Doyle, and Arthur Keith.

Speculation also abounded as to whether the Piltdown jaw was that of a chimpanzee or an orangutan, and whether the canine tooth, on which the fossil's original designation as a hominid partly depended, was that of a human, a chimp, or an orangutan. The hoaxer or hoaxers had so thoroughly distorted the anatomy of the original parts by filing, boiling, breaking, and discoloring them that those crucial elements of the Piltdown mystery couldn't be resolved.

Sherwood Washburn suggested to me that molecular testing of Piltdown might help to resolve these issues. When extracts of tiny fragments of the Piltdown jaw and canine were tested by RIA with antisera to the collagens of humans, chimpanzees, gorillas, orangutans, and gibbons, both the jaw and tooth reacted like orangutan (Lowenstein et al. 1982). Let the conspiracy theorists fit these small pieces of the Piltdown puzzle into their complicated schemes.

## BIOMOLECULAR PALEONTOLOGY

A few years ago, being able to extract molecular genetic information from a 40,000-year-old mammoth was a major achievement. Nowadays, it seems that every issue of *Nature* or *Science* reports findings of older and older DNA sequences.

As related earlier, the first fossil DNA sequence to be recovered was from a 150-year-old quagga skin (Higuchi et al. 1984). Next, Pääbo (1985) extracted mitochondrial DNA sequences from a 2400-year-old Egyptian mummy. Rogers and Bendich (1985) reported DNA from plant tissues 44,600 years old.

Skipping three orders of magnitude and electrifying the scientific world, Golenberg et al. (1990) obtained chloroplast DNA from a 17-million-year-old magnolia leaf preserved in a Miocene lake bed in Clarkia, Idaho. A 770-base-pair segment of a chloroplast gene was am-

plified using the polymerase chain reaction (PCR), sequenced, and compared with sequences from several different plant species. The fossil DNA was most like that from *Magnolia macrophylla* and varied from it by only 17 nucleotide substitutions. Here we have a direct calibration of a molecular clock, ticking at one substitution per million years!

Lindahl (1993) has protested that it is theoretically impossible for DNA to survive in fossils for more than a few thousand years, but this biochemical bumblebee continues to fly nevertheless and to swarm in ever-increasing numbers, especially in the jewelled environs of amber.

Insects in amber are a special case. Not only is the three-dimensional creature itself preserved for posterity, but the DNA seems to survive particularly well. De-Salle et al. (1993) extracted mitochondrial DNA from a 30-million-year-old termite, *Mastotermes darwiniensis*, thought by some scientists to be the "missing link" between cockroaches and termites. The fossil DNA sequence related this species to other termites and did not support the hypothesized cockroach connection. Molecular resolution of the disputed phylogenetic relations of a 30-million-year-old insect would have been unimaginable only a few years ago.

Cano et al. (1993) turned the fiction of *Jurassic Park* into at least partial scientific plausibility when they amplified DNA from a 120-million-year-old weevil in amber, an insect that lived in the age of the dinosaurs. If weevils had only dined on dinosaurs, the investigators could have looked for dino DNA in this specimen's gastrointestinal tract. Pressing even closer to the Hollywood scenario, Woodward et al. (1994) were able to extract mitochondrial DNA fragments from 80-million-year-old bones presumed to be those of dinosaurs, from a Utah coal mine. Unfortunately, this stretch of DNA did not match with the mitochondrial DNA of birds, generally thought to be the closest surviving dinosaur relatives, or indeed with the DNA of any living creature. For the moment, this molecular fossil remains a mystery.

It is already clear, though, that the study of fossil molecules can potentially add a fourth dimension—time—to our understanding of the genetic relationships of the myriad organisms that have lived on earth and become extinct.

## HUMAN EVOLUTION AND THE MOLECULAR FOSSIL RECORD

Genetic analysis of archaeological and paleontological remains could obviously clarify and expand our knowledge of the human past and contribute vital information to our understanding of human ancestry, evolution, migration, diet, and the domestication of plants and animals. Such analyses are now in their infancy but doubtless will burgeon rapidly in the next few years (Brown and Brown 1994).

Loy (1983) reported identification of bloodstains from prey species on ancient stone weapons by hemoglobin recrystallization. This method has been criticized because it depends on the hemoglobin structure being precisely preserved for thousands of years. Radioimmunoassay, on the other hand, can detect and identify fragments of large proteins such as albumin even after they have undergone extensive breakdown. This method was used to identify bloodstains on a series of stone spear points 3000 years old from British Columbia (Lowenstein and Scheuenstuhl 1991).

Sex determination on archaeological skeletal remains is a commonly encountered problem. Pelvic anatomy provides reasonable discrimination in well-preserved specimens, but sex determination becomes difficult and controversial when dealing with fragmentary remains and ancestral forms such as *Homo erectus*, *Homo habilis*, and *Australopithecus*, for which the type and degree of sexual dimorphism are a matter of speculation.

Because the X and Y chromosomes have different DNA sequences, male and female are routinely identified with modern DNA. Sexing of archaeological bone has proved more difficult, but several groups have reported success with DNA from tooth enamel (Nakahori et al. 1991).

Migration and colonization from Southeast Asia to the islands of Melanesia and Polynesia have been tracked by comparing the mitochondrial DNA from fossil bones with that of living individuals (Hagelberg and Clegg 1993). Previous linguistic and archaeological studies have suggested at least two waves of migration, the first (about 40,000 years ago) into Melanesia, and the second, much more recently (about 3600 years ago), into Polynesia. Polynesians and Southeast Asians but not Melanesians were found to share a 9-base-pair deletion of the mitochondrial genome, permitting the reconstruction of the pattern of these migrations.

Perhaps the most heated controversy in human evolution during the past few years has been the dispute between proponents of a recent (about 200,000 years) African origin of *Homo sapiens* (Cann et al. 1987) and the multiregional hypothesis proposing that *Homo sapiens* evolved simultaneously on several continents over the past million years (Wolpoff et al. 1984).

The "out-of-Africa" scenario is based on the finding that mitochondrial DNA of Africans is more diverse than that of Orientals or Caucasians, implying that Africans have been evolving longer. But the degree of sequence difference between geographic groups is so small as to suggest a common ancestor in Africa about 200 millennia ago.

This dispute could potentially be resolved by detailed comparisons of the fossil DNA of various human populations throughout the world. The African-origin theory predicts that *Homo sapiens* DNAs would converge to a common genotype in Africa at about 200,000 years before the present and that the DNAs of *Homo sapiens* on different continents would be more like each other than like those of the regional *Homo erectus* populations. The multiregional theory, alternatively, predicts a much older convergence and greater congruence between *Homo sapiens* and *Homo erectus* in each geographic region.

In coming years we will be looking more and more to the molecular fossil record as well as the macroscopic morphological record for vital evolutionary and phylogenetic information. It will be a long time, if ever, before we can re-create dinosaurs in the fashion of *Jurassic Park*. But it may not be too much to hope that we can solve some of the mysteries of dinosaur as well as human evolution by studying ancient DNA and proteins. As the decade of the 1990s comes to a close, we can add the new discipline of biomolecular paleontology to the many unifying scientific insights of our molecular century.

## REFERENCES

Brown, T. A., and Brown, K. A. (1994). Ancient DNA: Using molecular biology to explore the past. *BioEssays 16:* 719–726.

Cann, R. L., Stoneking, M., and Wilson, A. C. (1987). Mitochondrial DNA and human evolution. *Nature 325:* 31–36.

Cano, R. J., Poinar, H. D., Pieniazek, N. J., Acra, A., and Poinar, G. O. (1993). Amplification and sequencing of DNA from a 120–125-million-year-old-weevil. *Nature 363:* 536–538.

DeSalle, R., Gatesy, J., Wheeler, W., and Grimaldi, D. (1993). DNA sequences from a fossil termite in Oligo-Miocene amber and their phylogenetic implications. *Science 257:* 1933–1936.

Eglinton, G., and Curry, G. B., eds. (1991). *Molecules Through Time: Fossil Molecules and Biochemical Systematics.* London: Royal Society.

Golenberg, E. M., Giannassi, D. E., Clegg, M. T., Smiley, C. J., Durbin, M., Henderson, D., and Zurawski, G. (1990). Chloroplast DNA sequence from a Miocene *Magnolia* species. *Nature 344:* 656–658.

Goodman, M. (1963). Man's place in the phylogeny of the primates as reflected in serum proteins. In S. L. Washburn (ed.), *Classification and Human Evolution.* Chicago: Aldine, pp. 204–234.

Hagelberg, E., and Clegg, J. B. (1993). Genetic polymorphisms in prehistoric Pacific Islanders determined by analysis of ancient bone DNA. *Proc. Royal Society of London*, Series B 252: 163–170.

Higuchi, R., Bowman, B., Friedberger, M., Ryder, O. A., and Wilson, A. C. (1984). DNA sequences from the quagga, an extinct member of the horse family. *Nature 312:* 282–284.

Higuchi, R., Wrischnik, L. A., Oakes, E., George, M., Tong, B., and Wilson, A. C. (1987). Mitochondrial DNA of the extinct quagga: Relatedness and extent of post-mortem change. *J. Mol. Evol. 25:* 283–287.

Lindahl, T. (1993). Instability and decay of the primary structure of DNA. *Nature 362:* 709–715.

Lowenstein, J. M. (1980). Species-specific proteins in fossils. *Naturwissenschaften 67:* 343–346.

Lowenstein, J. M. (1981). Immunological reactions from fossil material. *Phil. Trans. Royal. Soc. London B292:* 143–149.

Lowenstein, J. M., Molleson, T., and Washburn, S. L. (1982). Piltdown jaw confirmed as orang. *Nature 299:* 294.

Lowenstein, J. M., and Ryder, O. A. (1985). Immunological systematics of the extinct quagga (Equidae). *Experientia 41:* 1192–1193.

Lowenstein, J. M., Sarich, V. M., and Richardson, B. J. (1981). Albumin systematics of the extinct mammoth and Tasmanian wolf. *Nature 291:* 409–411.

Lowenstein, J. M., and Scheuenstuhl, G. (1991). Immunological methods in molecular paleontology. *Phil. Trans. Royal Soc. London B333:* 375–380.

Loy, T. H. (1983). Prehistoric blood residues: Detection on tool surfaces and identification of species of origin. *Science 1269:* 1271.

Nahori, Y., Takenaka, O., and Nakagome, Y. (1991). A human X-Y homologous region encodes "amelogenin." *Genomics 9:* 264–269.

Pääbo, S. (1985). Molecular cloning of ancient Egyptian mummy DNA. *Nature 314:* 644–645.

Pais, A. (1982). *Subtle Is the Lord: The Science and the Life of Albert Einstein.* Oxford: Oxford University Press.

Pauling, L. (1940). *The Nature of the Chemical Bond.* Ithaca, NY: Cornell University Press.

Pilbeam, D. (1982). New hominoid skull material from the Miocene of Pakistan. *Nature 295:* 232–234.

Prager, E. M., Wilson, A. C., Lowenstein, J. M., and Sarich, V. M. (1980). Mammoth albumin. *Science 209:* 287–289.

Rainey, W. E., Lowenstein, J. M., Sarich, V. M., and Magor, D. M. (1984). Sirenian molecular systematics—including the extinct Steller's sea cow (*Hydrodamalis qigas*). *Naturwissenschaften 71:* 586–588.

Rogers, S. O., and Bendich, A. J. (1985). Extraction of DNA from milligram amounts of fresh, herbarium, and mummified plant tissues. *Pl. Mol. Biol. 5:* 69–76.

Sarich, V. M., and Wilson, A. C. (1967). Immunological time scale for hominid evolution. *Science 158:* 1200–1203.

Shoshani, J., Lowenstein, J. M., Walz, D. A., and Goodman, M. (1985). Proboscidean origins of mastodon and woolly mammoth demonstrated immunologically. *Paleobiology 11:* 429–437.

Washburn, S. L., ed., (1963). *Classification and Human Evolution.* Chicago: Aldine.

Washburn, S. L. (1973). The evolution game. *J. Hum. Evol. 2:* 557–561.

Washburn, S. L. (1978). The evolution of man. *Scientific American 239:* 194–208.

Washburn, S. L. (1985). Human evolution after Raymond Dart. In N. J. Pines (ed.), *Raymond Dart Lectures.* Johannesburg: Witwatersrand University Press.

Washburn, S. L. (1991). Biochemical insights into our ancestry. In M. Robinson and L. Tiger (eds.), *Man and Beast.* Washington, DC: Smithsonian Institution Press.

Wolpoff, M. H., Xinzhi, W., and Thorne, A. G. (1984). In F. H. Smith and F. Spencer (eds.), *The Origins of Modern Humans: A World Survey of the Fossil Evidence.* New York: Alan R. Liss.

Woodward, S. R., Weyand, N. J., and Bunnell, M. (1994). DNA sequence from Cretaceous Period bone fragments. *Science 266:* 1229–1232.

Yalow, R. S. (1978). Radioimmunoassay: A probe for the fine structure of biologic systems. *Med. Phys. 5:* 247–257.

Zihlman, A. L., and Lowenstein, J. M. (1979). False start of the human parade. *Natural History 88:* 86–89.

Zuckerkandl, E. (1963). Perspectives in molecular anthropology. In S. L. Washburn (ed.), *Classification and Human Evolution.* Chicago: Aldine, pp. 243–272.

Zuckerkandl, E., and Pauling, L. (1962). Molecular disease, evolution, and genic heterogeneity. In M. Kasha and B. Pullman (eds.), *Horizons in Biochemistry.* New York: Academic Press, pp. 189–225.

*Washburn was always concerned about the nature of science and the practice of science. Almost every paper of his included some comment about the problems of doing science and suggested remedies that might improve both the framework for science and its practice. In this paper he formalizes his position in a slightly different way. Washburn, in "Human Evolution: Science or Game," suggest that we would make more progress if we approached the study of human evolution as a game rather than as a science. This is because the old ways of doing science are no longer appropriate; modern science no longer fits traditional categories or traditional ways of thinking. The study of evolution seems a good place to start the type of reorganization that is necessary to escape the constraints of the past since the evolutionary perspective must integrate a number of disciplines. In addition, given the paucity of data and the amount of speculation, it would be better to treat it as a game. Rather than a commitment to one theory, which always results in controversy, multiple alternative scenarios with attached probabilities would be better. There are two benefits of this approach. First, the probabilities give readers a better sense of the speculative nature of much of reconstruction of human evolution. Second, by admitting this and not claiming black and white truths, scientists may be more willing to change their positions as new evidence comes to light. In this scheme, the more evidence upon which scenarios are based, the higher the probabilities or the certainty. Playing the game of human evolution would require both explicit rules and all the players to agree to the same rules. Washburn points out that in the study of human evolution we seem to be lacking both. He proposes that the rules should include playing with many kinds of evidence, keeping possibilities open, avoiding the illusion that we can reach a "final" conclusion, and attaching probabilities to each "theory" of human evolution based on the robustness of the evidence. A games approach is one way to improve the way we think about the study of human evolution. Washburn also advocates Huxley's networks of cooperative investigation in place of separate disciplines as the way to move forward in the future.*

# 16 Human Evolution: Science or Game?

**S. L. Washburn**  *Department of Anthropology, University of California*

It might be useful to view the study of human evolution as a game, rather than as a science. This thought comes from two quite different sources. First, the reality of evolution was in the behaviors of populations now long extinct. Success, or failure, depended on complex conditions only dimly reflected in the fossil record, and it is not possible to bring the past into the laboratory. No one can see a walking *Australopithecus.* Second, the stress on science leads to a form of conclusion which creates unnecessary controversy, and frequently slows the progress of understanding. If, instead of defending one theory, several theories were normally compared in

terms of probability, it might be much easier to change. Once very definite positions have been taken in public, an individual becomes emotionally involved, and change becomes difficult.

For example, at present many of us think that man originated in Africa, a point of view which has been vigorously defended. But suppose that the ancestral apes occupied an area extending from India to Africa and that the apes in India or the Near East evolved into men and the African apes into chimpanzee and gorilla. This would fit the facts just as well; the closest living relatives of man would still be the African apes, as suggested in numerous papers in the symposium on molecular biology.

With the game approach, the question of whether the australopithecines were restricted to Africa might

*Yearbook of Physical Anthropology* 17 (1973): 67–70. Reprinted by permisssion of Wiley-Liss, Inc., a division of John Wiley & Sons, Inc.

become: the more they were bipedal, stone tool-using, hunting, and savanna-living, and the longer they lasted, the less likely they were to have been restricted to one geographical area.

Consider the old problem of the antiquity of anatomically modern man and the evolutionary events in a short, traditional Pleistocene. Quite a few years ago it seemed certain (scientifically proven) that there were at least three kinds of men at the beginning of the Pleistocene. These were represented by: Java man, the Galley Hill skull, and Piltdown. If this is accepted as fact, then none of these can be ancestral to the others because they were all alive at the same time, and common ancestors must be postulated much further back. Although this was vigorously defended by many competent scientists, it was not accepted by others (Weidenreich, for example). Since both sides were convinced that they were making scientific judgments, the pros and cons were never discussed freely and easily at our meetings. The experts gave their scientific opinions, almost all of which have proved to be wrong.

If one looks at the history of these points, each was resisted strenuously by leaders in the study of human evolution. It was claimed that the australopithecines were apes, not closely related to man; that the pelvis could not belong to the same species as the skull; that no creature with such a small brain could have made tools; that hunting was impossible with pebble tools. My point is not to judge who was right or who was wrong, but that the illusion of science led to conclusions which slowed progress in the understanding of human evolution. Testing a variety of interpretations would, in the long run, have been far more useful for everyone.

Now the consensus of opinion is at the opposite extreme from that of Keith or Hooton. It follows the pattern, outlined by Weidenreich, in which all forms of fossil men are regarded as ancestral to anatomically modern man. My guess is that this will prove to be wrong, that the change from ancient populations to modern took place in one large area, and that there was considerable extinction among the groups which had not evolved the capacity for language—that is, language as we know it today. Again, I stress I am not concerned with proof, with who is right at the present time, but with keeping at least three different models in mind. One is the model which stresses the concept of separation of the races for a very long time (essentially Keith, Hooton, Coon). Another stresses the contributions from all populations of ancient man to the gene pool of modern man (Weidenreich from a typological point of view, Dobzhansky from a genetic point of view). The third suggests that there was a great change in the era 45,000–35,000 years ago, and that the change to modern man took place only in one area

(such as India, plus the Near East). At the moment, I would guess that game plan one is very improbable; that the odds might be two-to-one against plan two, and two-to-one in favor of game three. Obviously there are intermediate positions, and this is no place to go into detail. But, by outlining three ways of looking at the information, the issues are kept open. Preferences may be stated without insisting that there is only one correct way of interpreting the evidence.

But what if everyone agrees? Then isn't there only one conclusion? Not necessarily. For example, everyone regarded the Pliocene as several times as long as the Pleistocene, beginning some 10 or 12 million years ago. But the evidence has recently been reviewed by Van Couvering ('72), and the Pliocene probably began considerably less than 6 million years ago. If the Pleistocene is regarded as beginning 3 million years ago, then Pleistocene and Pliocene are of comparable length (as Keith thought more than 40 years ago!), and the combined epochs amount to only a third of the Miocene. Obviously, when more radiometric dates are available, it will not be necessary to use the old terms at all. But the point at the moment is simply that the argument that we "know" that the human lineage separated from that of the apes in the Miocene and, therefore, we "know" that the separation "must" have been more than 12 million years ago does not necessarily hold. One game plan might be separation of $8 \pm 2$ million years, a late Miocene separation played against twice that, an early Miocene divergence.

But, if we want to play the game of early separation versus late separation of the human lineage, there needs to be some discussion of the rules of the game. At the present time, there is not only no agreement on the rules, but little discussion of the basis for comparisons and conclusions. I think one advantage of a games approach is that it forces a discussion of rules at once. For example, Kurtén ('72: 44–45) dismisses all comparisons of contemporary forms as "not really historical." His view that man must have separated from other primates more than 35 million years ago is based primarily on teeth and on the conviction that the course of evolution may be determined from very fragmentary evidence. Playing the evolution game by those rules places an enormous burden on parallel evolution, because much of what man shares with the apes had not evolved 35 million years ago. The interpretation of parallel evolution at the morphological level has proven an exceedingly difficult problem. But how probable is parallel evolution at the level of DNA? Is it conceivable that close similarity in DNA is the result of anything except close genetic relation?

The evolution game played with molecular information, immunochemistry, functional anatomy, and behavior is a very different game than one which is limited to fossils—especially when the record is as fragmentary as is the case of the primates.

It is interesting to look at the possibility that man's ancestors were knuckle-walkers from a game point of view. In the first place, the idea depends on the field studies. Traditionally, knuckle-walking was viewed as a makeshift action used by arboreal animals on the ground. The field studies show that this mode of locomotion is normal for chimpanzees and gorillas, and that it is effective and used for moving long distances. Before the field studies, there was no reason to consider such a locomotor stage in human evolution, or to see how it might change thoughts on coming to the ground, origins of object-using, and the beginnings of bipedalism. At the moment, the scientific reply to this suggestion is that it is wrong because we do not have some of the anatomical features related to this mode of progression found in the chimpanzee and gorilla (Tuttle, '69). Since it was Tuttle's work which called my attention to the problem, what we are really disagreeing on is the way we play with the facts, not on the descriptive information. In traditional comparative anatomy, dissections were made and conclusions were drawn from the resulting comparisons. The controversies between Clark and Zuckerman give a vivid picture of the kind of continuing disagreements which will come from this approach to the problems of human evolution.

But in the games approach, all players know that they are likely to be wrong. If man's ancestors ever were knuckle-walkers, they have not been so for some millions of years. Chimpanzees and gorillas have continued this kind of locomotion, and so it is not surprising that the contemporary African apes have adaptations which man does not have. It would take nearly complete skeletons of the ancestral forms to prove this speculation one way or the other. Although the fossils needed to settle the matter do not exist, the fossil record might be interpreted to give some support to this notion. For example, the hand from Olduvai does show many features of a knuckle-walker (Tuttle, '67). Man may assume the position under special circumstances, and this illustrates a general point. If a contemporary creature can actually perform a behavior, its ancestors may have performed it at a higher frequency. One may not conclude that an action is impossible, if it is, in fact, performed (even if very rarely). The orang may knuckle-walk (Tuttle, '72), showing that apes may do it, without any of the specialized anatomy of the African forms. In the symposium on molecular evolution, Hoyer suggested that, according to the DNA comparisons, the order of branching may have been: gorilla, chimpanzee, and man. If chimpanzee and man shared a common ancestor after the gorilla had branched off, this would make a knuckle-walking ancestor for all three far more probable. But I think that no one would claim that it has been proven that there was a knuckle-walking stage in human ancestry. In 1968 I guessed that the odds on such a stage might be two-to-one. Now, with the new information noted above, I'd raise the odds to four- or five-to-one in favor. Hopefully, this way of putting the matter makes it clear that the opposite point of view is reasonable, that the matter is not settled one way or the other, and that more evidence is needed. The point of regarding the study of evolution as a game is to keep possibilities open, to play with many kinds of evidence, and to avoid the illusion that there is so much information that very definite final conclusions are possible.

Much of the discussion at the symposium and in the recent literature seems to me to show that people are playing the evolution game with very different rules. For example, how certain can one be about the interpretation of the fragmentary bits of face called *Ramapithecus*? It is quite possible that these forms were human ancestors, but the evidence for such factors as ground feeding, nature of the food, and weight, seems very speculative. Our tradition of presentation in this sort of situation is to propose reasonable conclusions and then to attempt to destroy alternative interpretations (Pilbeam, '72: 91–98). The game plan I am suggesting is that alternative suggestions should always be kept in mind, and that a scholar gives some indication of what he thinks is most probable. In the present case, one might ask how complete a fossil record has it taken to settle the problems of the relations in other groups of mammals? Whether one considers elephants, horses, pigs, or camels, I think it is clear that it required a great many fossils, including most of the skeleton, to determine even the major outlines of the history of the groups. Surely, ground feeding cannot be determined from a whole skeleton of a contemporary monkey or ape. Even the orang comes to the ground much more than has been presumed (Horr, personal communication). The field studies suggest that many primates are quite variable in their behaviors, adapting to local opportunities and conditions. Perhaps one rule for interpretations of the fossils is that they should not go beyond what is possible with contemporary forms.

Perhaps a rule might be that the more fragmentary the evidence, the more room should be left for alternative explanations. *Ramapithecus* may be ancestral to *Australopithecus*, but it is striking that, at the moment, there is more agreement on *Ramapithecus* than on *Australopithecus*, even though there is vastly more information on the latter. With *Australopithecus* (in the widest sense, all forms called "australopithecines"), there is disagreement among competent scientists on the number of species, the patterns of locomotion, diet, distribution, and evolutionary relationships. Each speaks, or writes, as if definite scientific conclusions were now possible. A games approach suggests that this is not the case, that several interpretations are possible, and that over-emphasis on the importance of final conclusions keeps the study of human evolution unnecessarily and unprofitably in turmoil.

The reason that the games approach is so important at the present time is the great progress which is being made in a wide variety of kinds of evidence. The discovery of fossils is limited only by financial support. Many rocks can now be dated by radiometric methods, and the age of the fossils determined accurately. Amino acid dating methods may make possible direct dating of bones (Turekian and Bada, '72). The field studies of behavior are forcing new ways of classifying behavior, setting limits on dietary reconstruction, and I think that they will be one of the factors in leading to a far more useful functional anatomy. The many chemists who are becoming interested in evolutionary problems are bringing with them great technical and human resources. The extensive use of primates in medical research has increased an interest in evolutionary problems. To take advantage of these opportunities, anthropologists need a way of welcoming the new. There is no use in opposing biochemical clocks until they have had a chance to run. This is the reason to insist that the study of human evolution is a game and that we must discover the rules. It will keep anthropology open. Moreover, it will avoid the illusion that the problems which were discussed at the symposium can be settled at this time by any one person or any one kind of evidence. This situation is not at all limited to anthropology or to the study of human evolution. Modern science does not fit into the traditional categories, nor can it be mastered by any single individual. Particularly in a synthetic study, such as human evolution, many sciences and many individuals have much to offer. Huxley ('63) has stated the issue in the following way. "In place of separate subjects, each with its own assumptions, methodology, and technical jargon, we must envisage networks of cooperative investigation, with common methods and terminology, all eventually linked up in a comprehensive process of inquiry. This,

of course, will mean a radical reorganization of scientific teaching and research." By its very nature, the study of evolution is a useful place to start this reorganization, and a games approach is one way to escape from the limitations of the past, to welcome change from any quarter, and to make progress in the understanding of human evolution.

## ACKNOWLEDGMENTS

The author wishes to thank Dr. Michael H. Crawford for the invitation to make some opening remarks at the symposium. This paper was written after the symposium and includes some comments on the papers presented there. The great differences of opinion presented at the symposium strengthened my conviction that a different style of presentation is desirable. My research is supported by NSF Grant No. G-S-3194X which is gratefully acknowledged. I wish also to thank Mrs. Alice Davis for her editorial assistance.

## LITERATURE CITED

Horr, D. Personal communication.

Huxley, J. 1963. The future of man—evolutionary aspects. In *Man and his Future*, ed. by G. Wolstenholme. Little, Brown and Company, Boston. 1–22.

Kurtén, B. 1972. *Not from the Apes.* Pantheon Books, New York.

Pilbeam, D. 1972. *The Ascent of Man.* The Macmillan Company, New York.

Turekian, K. K., and J. L. Bada. 1972. The dating of fossil bones. In *Calibration of Hominoid Evolution*, ed. by W. W. Bishop and J. A. Miller. Scottish Academic Press, Edinburgh. 171–186.

Tuttle, R. H. 1967. Knuckle-walking and the evolution of hominoid hands. *Amer. J. Phys. Anthrop., 26:* 171–206.

——— 1969. Knuckle-walking and the problem of human origins. *Science, 166:* 953–961.

Tuttle, R. H., and B. B. Beck. 1972. Knuckle walking hand postures in an orangutan (*Pongo pygmaeus*). *Nature, 236:* 33–34.

Van Couvering, J. A. 1972. Radiometric calibration of the European neogene. In *Calibration of Hominoid Evolution,* ed. W. W. Bishop and J. A. Miller. Scottish Academic Press, Edinburgh. 247–271.

Zuckerman, S. 1966. Myths and methods in anatomy. *J. Roy. Coll. Surg.* Edinburgh, *11:* 87–114.

*Washburn emphasized the provisionality of ideas and of knowledge about human evolution. He frequently revised his assessment of the state of our understanding of human origins, treating each version as a work in progress. He was also very concerned about the psychology of science: what makes scientists select one theory over its competitor or hold on to theories in the face of contradictory evidence. Lee addresses the current controversy about science in anthropology caused by the rise of postmodernism. Constructivism, as Lee calls the position that knowledge is socially constructed, is the foundation of the postmodernist critique of cultural, social, and biological anthropology. Lee explores the challenges of constructivism using the study of hunter-gatherers. His critique of deconstructionism ends with a proposal for the reconciliation of the radically different cultures now embedded in anthropology in which the claims of the constructivists can be subjected to investigation using sound methods, thereby making constructivism a useful complement to science. The answer to the controversy, according to Lee, is to continue the search for methods that can assess the merits of competing explanations both of human evolution and of anthropology. In the process, we will enlarge our sphere of knowledge by creating an anthropology that is both critical and empirical, an agenda that Washburn would recognize and support.*

# 17 Science and Constructivism: Notes Toward a Reconciliation[1]

**Richard B. Lee**  *University of Toronto*

Throughout the 1980s and 1990s, the centrality and legitimacy of science have come under increasing scrutiny in the discipline of anthropology. The current soul-searching is symptomatic of a much broader series of social, political, and technological shock waves that are transforming human society. To say we are living in an age of crisis is to state the obvious. Far more difficult to comprehend is how the crisis manifests itself across the academic disciplines. Cultural and social anthropology have been particularly hard-hit by the epochal and cataclysmic events of the late twentieth century. With the accelerating expansion of the capitalist world system into the remotest corners of the globe, anthropology has had to witness its traditional objects of study—non-Western, pre-class societies—disappearing with the speed of light, as one after another has been "pacified," settled, and put to work in the farms and factories of the new world order. As a result, the question of what constitutes knowledge of the "other" and how it is produced has become particularly troubling for social anthropologists.

In anthropology these current trends have brought to the surface long-standing ambiguities lying at the very root of the discipline, not the least of which revolves around the much debated concept of the "primitive," the rubric under which non-Western, pre-class societies have long been lumped. Many would agree with the late Stanley Diamond (1974: 118) that the "search for the primitive" is the heart of anthropology's unique role in the human sciences. Much of the history of anthropology is linked to our multifaceted understandings of the primitive in Diamond's sense, as the quest for origins and fundamentals, or in what Levi-Strauss terms anthropology's deeper purpose "to bear testimony to future generations of the ingeniousness, diversity, and imagination of our species" (1968: 349).

For evolutionary anthropologists the quest for origins and fundamentals is a given, but for *some* contemporary cultural anthropologists this focus is regarded as an anachronism. In a world where all work for wages and watch the same TV programs what constitutes the primitive? For some critics the primitive is thus an illusion, an arbitrary construction of the dis-embodied "other" divorced from history and context (e.g., Clifford 1983; Sperber 1985; Wagner 1981). Of these, some "postmodernists" would even find anthropology's preoccupation with the primitive an embarrassment, and as a consequence one raison d'etre of anthropological inquiry becomes moot (Wilmsen 1989: xi–xviii; 1–6).

This period of soul-searching in social anthropology arises in tandem with the ascendance of one of the most influential current theories in the human sciences: the view that knowledge is socially constructed. Within this framework, theories are seen as "master narratives" arising from "discourses" that are themselves strongly influenced by dominant beliefs and power relations of the wider society (Berger 1980; Foucault 1976a,b).

The impact of constructivism has been both positive and negative. The constructivist position has had a number of salutary effects on the disciplines of anthropology and archaeology by drawing attention to the social context in which science is conducted and how wider beliefs about class, race, and gender affect the scholar's search for objective reality (Gero and Conkey 1991; Haraway 1989; Wylie 1992a). But there is a downside: By focusing on the way that knowledge is put together, constructivist views appear to render irrelevant the claims to empirical validity, implicitly absolving the analyst of the responsibility of evaluating the truth claims on which their assertions are based. Thus what had been the touchstone of anthropological scholarship for a century—the testing of theory against evidence and the search for better explanatory frameworks (however defined)—is thrown into question.

Drawing on recent debates in ethnography, this essay will explore the challenge to "normal science" posed by constructivism, employing examples from recent debates in the study of hunters and gatherers. Does constructivism change the ground rules so fundamentally that the rules of evidence, hypothesis formation, confirmation and disconfirmation no longer apply? Or is constructivism better viewed as an useful adjunct that complements but does not supersede the continuing necessity for some form of science?

## GETTING TO THE BOTTOM ... OF WHAT?

Constructivism, known by a variety of terms, has been an extremely influential mode of thought since its emergence in the 1970s and 1980s (Berger 1980; Derrida 1976, 1978; Foucault 1976a,b). It has functioned largely as a critique of the ideological suppositions that underlie, indeed permeate, many branches of scholarship. It

has shown the ways in which power relations of the wider society affect and shape the questions asked and the conclusions reached. But rarely addressed is the question of what, if any, relation exists between social construction and empirical reality. Some analysts have seen the explication of the social forces behind a given theory as an end in itself, as if once the social context is given, the task of evaluation is done. But theories do not stand or fall entirely on the extent to which they make explicit and transcend the social/political assumptions on which they are based. Other criteria of validity are indispensable in this process, and it is the lack of awareness of these other criteria that constitutes a conspicuous blind spot for the social constructivists.

One curious aspect of the whole affair is that some of the ideas underlying constructivism have been around for a long time. Over a long career in physical anthropology, Sherwood Washburn emphasized the provisionality of knowledge of human evolution and put his convictions to the test by writing, every few years, a paper reviewing the state of human evolutionary studies. He argued that knowledge of this complex, multifaceted subject is always fragmentary, based on an infinitesimally small percentage of the total data; therefore our understandings are of necessity provisional. He offered these syntheses as work in progress and issued pleas to avoid ego investment in the defense of one or another school of interpretation, pleas that fell largely on deaf ears (for a sampling, see Washburn 1978, 1982; Washburn and Avis 1958; Washburn and Lancaster 1968). He also took pains to understand what he called the psychology of human evolutionary studies: what made people favor one theory over another and cling to outmoded theories in the face of contradictory evidence (1961, 1973).[2]

Washburn was more perceptive than many of his contemporaries about another area of ambiguity, about the nature of the anthropological enterprise itself. Since its establishment in the 1870s and 1880s, anthropology has never declared itself unequivocally on whether it is a particularizing, historical discipline interested in understanding unit cultures, or whether it is a generalizing, nomothetic science searching for the broadest possible explanatory frameworks. Whereas evolutionary anthropologists have adhered in the main to the latter vision, the founders of "modernist" social and cultural anthropology—all of whom did important research on hunters and gatherers—had vigorous adherents of both tendencies, with Boas (1936, 1966) and Kroeber (1925) exemplifying the first, and Steward (1936, 1938) and Radcliffe-Brown (1922, 1931) the second (see also Harris 1979).[3] If we are to understand constructivism, we have to look at the deeper roots in classical anthropology.

## TWO CULTURES, OR THREE, OR FOUR?

As a starting point it might be helpful to recall C. P. Snow's famous essay "The Two Cultures" (1959) in which he explored the eternal conflict between two irreconcilable academic subcultures: the *humanistic* and the *scientific*.[4] In the first, scholarship was devoted to the study of meanings and interpretations in great works of art and literature. In the second, research was dedicated to systematic and rigorous investigation of the laws and general principles governing the natural and human worlds.

Anthropology is an apt example of a discipline that finds itself straddling the boundaries of Snow's two cultures. Within the discipline today there is a powerful current moving toward the view of anthropology as essentially a humanistic, even literary, discipline, where truth, apart from the poetic variety, is unattainable. It is here that constructivism has been most influential. But an equally strong current moves in the opposite direction, embracing the promise and moral authority of science, and strengthening its commitment to improved techniques of data collection and measurement, coupled with more (not less) rigorous application of theory. The first sees itself as modeled after literature and literary criticism; and the second draws its inspiration from theoretical biology and evolutionary ecology as well as an updated and recharged structural functionalism.

In ethnography, the struggles and contradictions between the humanistic and scientific cultures are played out in a number of ways. While the scientists are gathering data for the construction of mathematical models of predator-prey behavior, the humanists, working sometimes among the same people, are collecting life histories of elders and recording and interpreting cosmologies and religious beliefs.

But there is a third culture embedded in current anthropological practice. This school sees neither humanistic nor scientific discourses as adequate to account for the past, present, and future of anthropological subjects. Raising issues of context and history, and placing societies in regional systems, some scholars focus on the overriding issue of the relations of the "other" with the world system. I will call this the "culture" of *political economy*.

The first anthropological perspective draws its inspiration from the interpretivist, structuralist, and hermeneutic traditions of Clifford Geertz (1973), Claude Levi-Strauss (1961), Mary Douglas (1966), Victor Turner (1969), and James Clifford (1988; Clifford and Marcus 1986); the second from the positivist and adaptationist current of Julian Steward (1936, 1938), Lew Binford (1980), and others (e.g., Harris 1979), and the third from the critical Marxist tradition in which Eric Wolf and Sidney Mintz are situated (Wolf 1982; Mintz 1985; Leacock 1981; see also Patterson and Gailey 1987; Roseberry 1988). Each approach has a distinctive methodological stance and each has made important contributions to contemporary anthropology. In fact, however much one may profess allegiance to one or another of the three cultures, in practice most of us employ elements of all three approaches in our work (for a classic example of synthesis directed to a key argument about hunter-gatherers, see Sahlins 1968).

However, before one can evaluate the contributions to the production of knowledge from each of the anthropological traditions, a prior question must be addressed, an issue that poses a challenge to the entire collective enterprise so fundamental that to ignore it would be to fiddle while Rome burns. Following the lead of Foucault, Derrida, and the French poststructuralists, several anthropologists have carried constructivism to the *n*th degree and have declared primitive societies a noncategory, a construction of observers mired in one or another brand of romantic idealism. The claims of this group are so far-reaching and so ill-contained within the paradigm space of the three cultures that they could be said to constitute a fourth culture rendering irrelevant large parts of the other three.

One manifestation of this fourth culture has been called "revisionism," an expression of constructivism that has been particularly active in hunter-gatherer studies (Wilmsen 1989; cf. Solway and Lee 1990). Combining *some* elements of political economy with *some* elements of poststructuralism, revisionism presents a fundamental challenge to the way that anthropologists have looked at hunters and gatherers for the past 30 years. It posits that they are not what they appear to be; and it proposes a drastic rethinking of our subject.

There are two strands to the revisionist critique: what I will call the historical and the poststructuralist. The first argues (see, e.g., Headland and Reid 1989; Myers 1988: 262–264) that past ethnographers have treated societies as more bounded, more isolated, and more pristine than they actually were. They counter that foraging societies have been integrated into larger regional or even international structures of power and exchange for so long that they can tell us nothing about the antecedent ways of life (Flanagan 1989; Price and Brown 1985; Le Gros 1985).[5] These critiques raise important issues, yet in terms of method, the argument remains on familiar terrain: One examines the historical, archaeological, or other data and tests the merits of competing hypotheses against these data. Were the peoples in question isolated? What does archaeology reveal? What is the most parsimonious explanation for the observed facts?[6]

Elsewhere I have considered *historical* revisionism in greater depth (Lee 1992). Here I wish only to examine that branch of revisionism that arises directly from constructivism. And for that we need to address the radical skepticism that lies at the heart of poststructuralist criticism. This view argues that there is no truth, only regimes of truth and power, and that all anthropology is powerfully shaped by the cultural constructions of the observer. Thus ethnographic writing has more in common with the historical novel and other works of fiction than it has with a scientific treatise. The task of ethnography then becomes immeasurably more problematic; truth is at best partial, flawed, obscured, and above all *relative*.[7]

This argument has radical implications for methodology. The production of knowledge has left the realm of empirical investigation, and analytical methods of the past can no longer be relied upon. One can no longer utilize, for example, the etic/emic distinction because science, after all, is really only "Western emic" (Marcus and Fischer 1986: 180–181). The use of Ockham's razor or the law of parsimony to choose between the merits of two competing explanations is no longer admissible because all are "true" at some level.

What are the specific impacts of this strand of revisionism on the study of the hunters and gatherers and other pre-class, non-Western societies? Poststructuralists have argued the extraordinary proposition that the natives are "us" and have put into question the assumption that the "primitives," whatever they may be, represent the "other." They argue that because anthropologists, like everyone else, are prisoners of their own ideology, as a consequence they can see in the "other" only a flawed perception of themselves. The "other" is thus declared a noncategory.

Practically speaking, this declaration of "non-otherness" has the effect of cutting away large portions of what had been anthropological subject matter. For example the category "indigenous people" disappears, because in some versions of revisionism, no one is any more "indigenous" than anyone else.

One would expect that acceptance of this position would bring empirical investigation to a crashing halt. But this has not happened; in effect, there has been a reprieve. Investigation continues, but it is now the scientists, their times and social milieux that become the objects of study. What led them to write what they did is sought in the social conditions under which the knowledge was produced, and not in the nature of the phenomena under study.

There are a number of ironies in the revisionist stance. First, closer examination reveals that even while declaiming the inadequacies of empiricism, revisionist scholars make liberal use of conventional empirical evidence, a point we return to later. Second, its practitioners tend to apply their critical perspective to all theoretical positions but their own. But the beauty of social constructivism is that it cuts both ways; revisionism can be subjected to the same type of analysis to which it subjects others.

What does constructivism look like under the lens of a constructivist analysis? I see the extreme form of constructivism and its close cousin, anthropological revisionism, both as peculiar expressions of the intellectual culture of "late capitalism." Both spring from a major tenet of contemporary Western thought: the proposition that *nothing is real*.

## NOTHING IS REAL

We live in an era in which the line between real and nonreal has become dangerously blurred. What is real has become a scarce commodity, and the pursuit of the "real" sometimes becomes a desperate search. Under capitalism, as Marshall Berman (quoting Marx) titles his book, "all that is solid melts into air" (1983). We don't have to search far for evidence of this proposition. The Disney corporation produces and disseminates in a single fiscal year, perhaps in a single week, more fantasy material to more people than entire archaic civilizations could produce in a century. States of the left, right, and center and their bureaucracies also produce prodigious volumes of fantasy, and through advertising and other media, elites deploy enormous manipulative power (Anderson 1991; Ewen 1976). A recent ad for Winston's cigarettes (typical of the thousands that bombard North Americans daily) has a picture of a carefully posed professional model, turned out as a fashion photographer, pretending to photograph another professional model herself posing, surrounded by other posed models in postures of forced gaiety. The caption: "Real People/Real Taste."

To protect the psyche from this type of assault, consumers and citizens in the West (and East) can be forgiven for erecting a shell of cynicism as a survival strategy under conditions of extreme debasement of the currency of reality. In fact, it is hard to imagine keeping one's sanity by any other means. This position of cool detachment and ironic distanciation has been considered the hallmark of the "postmodern condition" (Jameson 1984; Lyotard 1984; Sloterdijk 1987).

The world of scholarship has not escaped these massive social and psychological forces. In *The Invention of Tradition* (1983), Hobsbawm and Ranger and others show how allegedly hallowed customs handed down from the past are in fact the product of recent history. In his method of deconstruction, Derrida has argued that history is akin to a literary text and like all texts is ultimately unknowable (1976, 1978). It seems a short step to transposing a critical and debunking discourse to all anthropological subjects.

But along the way there has been a slippage. The tools of deconstruction, developed to debunk and call into question the high and mighty, are now being applied to the powerless. Where the invention of tradition perspective was initially deployed to deconstruct the public rituals of the nineteenth-century British monarchy or pomp and circumstance in colonial India, it was now being generalized to question the claims to authenticity of small peoples. In his influential work "The Predicament of Culture," James Clifford (1988) shows how the Mashpee Indians construct their identity de novo in order to meet the exigencies of a court case. Similar arguments, but with less sympathy for the subalterns, have been made for the Maori by Hanson (1989) and for the ancient Hawaiians by Bergendorff, Hasager, and Henriques (1988; see also the reply by Sahlins 1989).[8]

The situation within anthropology is paralleled by the impact of poststructuralism on the broad front of the social sciences. Foucault's famous dictum (1976a,b) that there is no truth, only regimes of truth and power, was originally intended as a critique of arbitrary power, but by showing the fragility of all truth-claims it has had the effect of undermining the legitimacy as well of oppositional movements for justice against these same powers (Habermas 1987; Taylor 1984).

Of course there is a kernel of validity to the idea that all societies in the world are products of interaction with other societies and world society. Modern ethnography grew out of the Enlightenment and is a form of practice in which members of our academic subculture observe the other; and as the late Kathleen Gough (1968, 1993) reminded us, anthropology is a child of imperialism. And then there are cases like the Philippine Tasaday, where a perfectly reasonable Southeast Asian semi-hunter-gatherer group, of which many examples exist, was seized on by the *National Geographic* and other media and popularized as the "Lost Stone Age" find of the century. Their recent exposure and the media circus surrounding them certainly fuels the cynicism that is itself the source of postmodernist sensibilities (Lee 1992b; see also Berreman 1991; Duhaylungsod and Hyndman 1992; Dumont 1988).

Nevertheless to succumb to the enticements of the poststructuralist/revisionists would be a disaster. Where I part company with the poststructuralists is the view that our knowledge of the other, being filtered through perceptions, language, and culture, is so suspect that subjects can only be provisionally and arbitrarily constructed.[9] I do not believe that anthropologists are nearly so powerless before the awesome task of representing the other's reality, or that the ethnography of the 1960s or 1970s was so flawed that it has to be discarded. Adam Kuper, in a recent critique of postmodernism, points out that the methodologies of the 1960s were not so very different from those of the present,[10] and that their results were subjected to the critical scrutiny of peer review and comparative evidence. Kuper argues, and I would agree, that the view that ethnographic writing is more akin to fiction than it is to science does not accord with the history of the discipline. If the ethnographers of that not-so-distant era had passed their fiction off as science, their readership and their peers would not have stood for it (Kuper 1993). (For other critiques of "postmodernism" that attempt to reconstruct the "realist" foundations of social science epistemologies, see Gellner 1988; Lovibond 1989; Mascia-Lees, Sharpe, and Cohen 1989; Roth 1989; Sangren 1988; Soper 1991; see also Bhashkar 1979, 1986).

## NOTES TOWARD A RECONCILIATION

How can we sort out the conflicting claims of the poststructuralist/revisionists and those whose views they criticize? One of the most useful of the recent discussions of constructivism in anthropology and archaeology is by the Canadian philosopher of science Alison Wylie, based at the University of Western Ontario. In a series of important papers (1992a, 1992b, in press), Wylie presents a sympathetic account of the constructivist position, documenting its salutary influence in exposing the ideological assumptions underlying archaeological research, particularly in the area of gender. Her sympathies, however, are neither unqualified nor unlimited. In important ways, she argues, empirical evidence remains crucial, *undermining* the constructivist position, because it is a property of certain kinds of evidence to resist appropriation:

> No matter how irresistible these [constructivist] arguments may seem in the abstract, they are often subverted by the very contingencies that they mean to bring into view. However much a construct archaeological evidence may be, however inextricable from the power relations that constitute the thoroughly cultural enterprise of its production, *it does routinely resist appropriation; . . . In fact, this is a feature of archaeological practice that the critics of ethnocentric, androcentric and nationalistic bias in archaeology regularly exploit.* Time and again they make good use of recalcitrant evidence—evidence that resists appropriation in any of the terms compatible with dominant views or assumptions about the past—to expose the deeply political nature of the discipline (in press, p. 12; emphasis added)

How is it possible for certain knowledge sets to resist appropriation? The answers Wylie offers are complex, hinging on technical arguments about "theory-ladenness" in the philosophy of science (in press, pp. 14–17; see also Hacking 1983; Kosso 1988, 1989).

Basically, Wylie argues, all constructivists are (and must be) empiricists; all address data; all sift and weigh evidence. After they have placed an interpretation in its social context, how else can they demonstrate its constructedness except by evaluating how well it accounts or fails to account for a body of evidence? And by presenting alternate (and better) interpretations, the constructivist critic lays bare the arbitrariness of the earlier interpretation. Looked at it this way, the constructivist project functions in ways rather similar to the methods of the very object of its criticism: conventional science!

A case in point is North American archaeology's conventional views of the origin of agriculture. Wylie notes that scenarios of male centrality in the process of domestication of plants and animals have dominated theories for decades in spite of considerable collateral evidence for the importance of women's contributions. She illustrates this point by referring to Watson and Kennedy's feminist critique (1991) of male-centered arguments for the transition from foraging to agriculture in the eastern woodlands of North America.

Critical theorists like Watson and Kennedy are able to carry out these analyses because, as Wylie asserts, though the conduct of research can be constrained in many ways, at least some empirical findings do "resist theoretical appropriation"; and this property is used by even the most ardent constructionists to counter/refute/expose arguments that they see as politically inspired or shaped by the prevailing ethos.

Given the enormous load of ideology in anthropology, along with other branches of scholarship, the work of Wylie and others does offer some relief from the bleak vision of the poststructuralists that knowledge is simply what the powerful say it is. Therefore it is worthwhile to reiterate a plea for the importance of empirical evidence; I am as much opposed to mindless empiricism as anyone, but without the constraints imposed by empirical evidence, constructivism could disintegrate into an ideological parlor-game for cynics (Palmer 1990; Sloterdijk 1987).

What is urgently needed in this era of disillusionment is the middle path: a working discipline that sees science, humanism, and critical reflection as three components of a single field; scholars need empiricism tempered by reflexivity and a dialectic between the two. All of this should be framed within a sense of history and political economy to ensure that a scholar's situated history and the relationship between scholar and subject are not lost. Scholars must interrogate assumptions as the poststructuralists suggest, but after that I for one would like to get on with it.

To return to the question originally posed: What is the status of the claim that the so-called primitive peoples are simply like the rest of us, their cultures shaped and molded, as are ours, by the titanic forces of late capitalism? There is an ample body of evidence to evaluate that proposition. If sound methods demonstrate, for example, that hunter-gatherers or pastoralists are historically serfs or proletarians, then so be it. But the current crop of revisionist arguments are dubious, to say the least.[11] The task of situating the hundreds of non-Western, pre-state societies historically has barely begun and there remains a great deal of scope for archaeological, ethnographic, and ethnohistoric investigations to resolve the questions raised by the revisionists.[12] I also suggest that answering these questions will motivate the production of the kinds of knowledge that will be used by future generations, sifted and resifted long after the debates of this decade fade into the past.

Donna Haraway (1989), a noted constructivist, makes the case that one of the master narratives constructed (in part) from anthropological data has been the story of human nature and life in the "state of nature"—who we are as a species, our past, and by implication our future. But herein lies the rub: The poststructuralist project focuses our attention so exclusively on the "constructedness" of these narratives that we lose sight of another equally valid dimension. Just because they are constructed doesn't mean that they have no claim to empirical validity or that the search for knowledge of the past is an illegitimate enterprise. Haraway herself does not deny the possibility of "objective knowledge," but she would insist that it be a "situated objectivity," reflexively aware of the circumstances of its making.

All this highlights the critical need for maintaining and enlarging the sphere of knowledge—in both archaeology and ethnography—that transcends the ideological battles of each era: the need for a version of anthropology that is both critical and empirical (cf. Carrithers 1990; O'Meara 1989).

Perhaps the most significant contribution to this development in social anthropology is the emergence of indigenous peoples speaking to us in their own voices, for example, the Canadian Innu, Lubicon, and Teme-Augama, among others (see Richardson 1989). The Gitksan and Wet'suet'en people of British Columbia are good examples of indigenous peoples who have made excellent use of anthropological knowledge, generated by sympathetic scholars to address the larger public directly in a variety of voices including the courts (People of 'Ksan 1980; Sterritt 1989; Wa and Uukw 1989).

On this new and expanded political terrain an interesting question is how the former subjects of anthropological inquiry themselves regard anthropology. In a minority of situations, the anthropologist is seen as part of the problem, an appropriator of culture. But this is by no means the only scenario. There is a growing sensitivity on the part, for example, of archaeologists to the legitimate concerns of indigenous peoples, particularly on the issue of repatriation of cultural materials and human remains. Another manifestation is the cultural renaissance underway in many native communities; it has generated considerable interest in native language, "traditional" ethos and worldview, governance, subsistence, arts, crafts, ethnobotany, and healing. For these and other spheres of knowledge, the elders are the primary sources; however, anthropological texts have played and continue to play a significant roles as sources of information.[13]

## CONCLUSION

This essay has delineated the crisis of representation in the anthropology of pre-class societies and has attempted to comprehend its underlying epistemiological and ideological roots. The field has been undergoing a series of transformations, and the original raison d'etre has required reassessment. Yet despite the fundamental challenges of the "revisionists," it can be argued that a core of relevance to both scholarly and indigenous peoples' agendas remains. That the field is responding to this challenge is indicated by the shift away from simplistic evolutionary arguments toward more nuanced, historically sensitized, and critical understandings. In this respect the altered contours of anthropological studies of the "primitive" represent a successful "incursion" by humanists and political economists on a terrain that had been largely dominated by natural science–oriented methods and philosophies.

Almost all of humanity lives today in highly organized bureaucratized societies of enormous scale and systematic inequalities. Hunters and gatherers, in spite of the inducements (or threats?) to become incorporated, choose for whatever reasons to resist and to live lives very different from that of the majority. The pace is slower, technology simpler, numbers smaller, inequality less, and the relationship to land and resources—the sense of place—is on a radically different basis.

If indigenous peoples want to adopt a Western (or Russian) way of life, the door is open; in fact, the pressures to conform are immense. The fact that this has not happened, that some foragers still pursue alternative lifeways not in isolation but in full awareness of the wider world, is a persuasive argument that the "system" is not all-powerful and that Western-capitalist reality is not the only reality. Pockets of resistance persist and show us that even in this hard-bitten "postmodern"

age other ways of being are possible. These alternate ways exist; they are not simply constructions of Western social scientists' fertile imaginations.

Despite its complex history of involvement with the colonial order, anthropology has produced much knowledge that counters the interests of the established order and which has in Wylie's terms resisted theoretical appropriation. The commitment to reflect reality as accurately as possible and in ways that are sympathetic to the subaltern marks the best research in anthropology for most of its hundred-year history. Although they at times appear to imply it, the practitioners of social constructionism did not invent the moral high ground, nor do they hold a monopoly on it today. Although its impact has been profound, social constructionism is better viewed as one important tool of social analysis among several rather than as a paradigm that overthrows all existing understandings. If anthropology is not to fall into a hyperrelativist universe, the search for methods for resolving the merits of competing explanations will continue to be an essential component of our work.

## NOTES

1. As a social anthropologist, I hesitated to join a project that would bring together so many distinguished physical anthropologists and evolutionists. Hopefully this modest contribution can be encompassed under the expanded and generous umbrella that has been Sherry Washburn's view of science. Portions of this paper are adapted from Lee 1992. I would like to thank Victor Barac, Irven DeVore, Peter Fitting, Fred Jameson, Michael Lambek, Gavin Smith, Ted Chamberlin, Alison Wylie, and students in the University of Toronto graduate anthropology seminar on research methods (1992–1994) for useful input on earlier versions of this paper. None of the above would necessarily endorse the positions adopted here.

2. Washburn's intellectual relativism may have anticipated postmodernism, but in other ways he was resolutely (and refreshingly) modernist—for example, in his uncompromising stand against theories he regarded as racist (Washburn 1965).

3. Malinowski's enduring popularity within the discipline may have something to do with the fact that he sat on the fence in the nomothetic/ideographic debate.

4. Snow's position in turn can be traced back to a nineteenth-century critical Romanticism that saw science as providing an ideological basis for the spread and destructive effects of capitalism. (I thank Victor Barac for this observation.)

5. For a thoughtful and balanced discussion of this issue, see Paynter 1989.

6. This is what Jacqueline Solway and I did in a *Current Anthropology* article titled "Foragers, Genuine or Spurious" (1990), meeting the issues raised by revisionists with empirical data that refuted their position (see also Lee and Guenther 1993).

7. For a late conversion to relativism, see Leach 1989; on the fallacy of "hyperrelativism," see Trigger 1989.

8. In his widely cited "revisionist" study of the Kalahari San, Wilmsen uses the Hobsbawm and Ranger thesis to the same effect in a section of his book entitled "The Invention of 'Bushmen'" (1989: 24–26).

9. Mascia-Lees, Sharpe, and Cohen, in a now classic paper (1989), note that it is striking how the largely male, white, and Western poststructuralists are proclaiming the death of the subject, precisely at the moment when alternative voices—women, people of color, and Third World and aboriginal peoples—are struggling to constitute themselves as subjects of history, as the makers of their own history (see also Spivak 1988).

10. As a case in point, Wilmsen, after stating that his "book is . . . not an ethnography" and proclaiming the end of "the ethnographic era of anthropology" (1989: xii), then goes on to devote several hundred pages to the presentation of "ethnographic" data on the San in the form of ethnohistory, genealogies, demography, economic anthropology, and subsistence ecology.

11. For a critique of revisionist historiography in the Kalahari, see Lee and Guenther 1991, 1993, in press.

12. For two excellent examples of how this can be done, see Trigger 1990 and Hunn 1990.

13. For example, the Nimkish band of the Kwagiuthle of Alert Bay, British Columbia, played host in 1986 in a potlatch for the descendants of Franz Boas, on the occasion of the centenary of Boas's first visit to the community. Boas's surviving grandchildren were feasted and given titles. Similar celebrations have been held in other communities for other scholars and their descendants.

# REFERENCES

Bergendorff, S., Hasager, U., and Henriques, P. (1988). Mythopraxis and history: On the interpretation of the Makahiki. *Journal of the Polynesian Society* 97: 391–408.

Berger, P. (1980). *The Social Construction of Reality,* 2nd ed. New York: Anchor.

Berman, M. (1983). *All That Is Solid Melts into Air.* New York: Simon & Shuster.

Berreman, G. (1991). The incredible "Tasaday": Deconstructing the myth of a "Stone-Age" people. *Cultural Survival Quarterly* 15(1): 3–46.

Bhaskar, R. (1979). *The Possibility of Naturalism: A Philosophical Critique of the Human Sciences.* Brighton: Harvester Press.

Bhaskar, R. (1986). *Scientific Realism and Human Emancipation.* London: Verso.

Binford, L. R. (1978). *Nuniamiut Ethnoarchaeology.* New York: Academic Press.

Boas, F. (1935). Kwakiutl culture as reflected in mythology. *Memoirs of the American Folklore Society 28.*

Boas, F. (1966). *Kwakiutl Ethnography,* ed. H. Codere. Chicago: University of Chicago Press.

Carrithers, M. (1990). Is anthropology art or science? *Current Anthropology* 31: 263–282.

Chomsky, N. (1989). *Necessary Illusions: Thought Control in Democratic Societies.* The Massey Lectures. Montreal: CBC Enterprises.

Clifford, J. (1983). On ethnographic authority. *Reflections 1:* 118–145.

Clifford, J. (1988). *The Predicament of Culture: Twentieth Century Ethnography, Literature and Art.* Cambridge, MA: Harvard University Press.

Clifford, J., and Marcus, G., eds. (1986). *Writing Culture: The Poetics and Politics of Ethnography.* Berkeley: University of California Press.

Derrida, J. (1976). *Of Grammatology.* Baltimore: Johns Hopkins University Press.

Derrida, J. (1978). *Writing and Difference.* Chicago: University of Chicago Press.

Dews, P. (1987). *Logics of Disintegration: Post-structuralist Thought and the Claims of Critical Theory.* London: Verso.

Diamond, S. (1974). *In Search of the Primitive: A Critique of Civilization.* New Brunswick, NJ: Transaction Books.

Douglas, M. (1966). *Purity and Danger.* New York: Praeger.

Duhaylungsod, L., and Hyndman, D. (1992). Creeping resource exploitation in the Tboli homeland: Political ecology of the Tasaday hoax. In T. Headland (ed.), *The Tasaday Controversy: Assessing the Evidence.* Washington, DC: American Anthropological Association, pp. 59–75.

Dumont, J. P. (1988). The Tasaday, which and whose? Towards the political economy of an ethnographic sign. *Cultural Anthropology* 3(3): 261–275.

Ewen, S. (1976). *Captains of Consciousness: Advertising and the Social Roots of Consumer Culture.* New York: McGraw-Hill.

Flanagan, J. (1989). Hierarchy in simple "egalitarian" societies. *Annual Review of Anthropology* 18: 245–266.

Foucault, M. (1976a). Truth and Power. In C. Gordon (ed.), *Power/Knowledge.* New York: Pantheon.

Foucault, M. (1976b). *The Archaeology of Knowledge.* New York: Harper & Row.

Geertz, C. (1973). *The Interpretation of Cultures: Selected Essays.* New York: Basic Books.

Gellner, E. (1988). The stakes in anthropology. *American Scholar* 57: 17–32.

Gero, J., and Conkey, M., eds. (1991). *Engendering Archaeology: Women and Prehistory.* Cambridge: Basil Blackwell.

Gough, K. (1968). Anthropology and imperialism. *Monthly Review* 19(11): 12–27.

Gough, K. (1993). "Anthropology and Imperialism" revisited. In R. Lee and K. B. Sacks (eds.), *Anthropology, Imperialism and Resistance: The Work of Kathleen Gough.* Special Issue *Anthropologica* 35(2): 279–290.

Habermas, J. (1987). Modernity—An incomplete project. In P. Rabinow and W. M. Sullivan (eds.), *Interpretive Social Science: A Second Look.* Berkeley: University of California Press, pp. 141–156.

Hacking, I. (1983). *Representing and Intervening: Introductory Topics in the Philosophy of the Natural Sciences.* Cambridge: Cambridge University Press.

Hanson, A. (1989). The making of the Maori: Cultural invention and its logic. *American Anthropologist* 91: 890–902.

Haraway, D. (1989). *Primate Visions: Gender, Race and Nature in the World of Modern Science.* New York: Routledge, Chapman, Hall.

Harris, M. (1979). *Cultural Materialism: The Struggle for a Science of Culture.* New York: Vintage.

Headland, T., and Reid, L. (1989). Hunter-gatherers and their neighbors from prehistory to the present. *Current Anthropology* 30: 43–66.

Hobsbawm, E., and Ranger, T. O., eds. (1983). *The Invention of Tradition.* Cambridge: Cambridge University Press.

Hunn, E. (1990). *Nch'i-Wana, The Big River: Mid-Columbian Indians and Their Land.* Seattle: University of Washington Press.

Jameson, F. (1984). Postmodernism, or the cultural logic of late capitalism. *New Left Review* 146: 53–92.

Kosso, P. (1988). Science and objectivity. *British Journal of Philosophy* 86: 245–257.

Kroeber, A. L. (1925). *Handbook of the Indians of California.* Bureau of American Ethnology Bulletin No. 78.

Kuper, A. (1993). On ethnographic practice. *Social Anthropology* 1(2).

Leach, E. (1989). Review of Geertz, *Works and Lives. American Ethnologist* 16(1): 137–141.

Leacock, E. (1982). *Myths of Male Dominance.* New York: Monthly Review Press.

Lee, R. (1979). *The !Kung San: Men, Women and Work in a Foraging Society.* Cambridge: Cambridge University Press.

Lee, R. (1992a). Art, science or politics: The crisis in hunter-gatherer studies. *American Anthropologist 90:* 14–34.

Lee, R. (1992b). Making sense of the Tasaday: Three discourses. In T. Headland (ed.), *The Tasaday Controversy: Assessing the Evidence.* Washington, DC: American Anthropological Association, pp. 167–171.

Lee, R. (in press). Autonomy and dependency in non-hierarchical societies: The case of the Ju/'hoansi. Paper presented at the Symposium on Khoisan Studies, Tutzing, Germany, July 1994.

Lee, R., and DeVore, I., eds. (1968). *Man the Hunter.* Chicago: Aldine.

Lee, R., and Guenther, M. (1991). Oxen or onions: The search for trade (and truth) in the Kalahari. *Current Anthropology 32*(5): 592–601.

Lee, R., and Guenther, M. (1993). Problems in Kalahari historical ethnography and the tolerance of error. *History in Africa 20:* 185–235.

LeGros, D. (1985). Wealth, poverty, and slavery among 19th century Tutchone, Athapaskans. *Research in Economic Anthropology 7:* 37–64.

Levi-Strauss, C. (1963). *Structural Anthropology.* New York: Basic Books.

Levi-Strauss, C. (1968). The concept of primitiveness. In R. Lee and I. DeVore (eds.), *Man the Hunter.* Chicago: Aldine, pp. 349–352.

Lovibond, S. (1989). Feminism and postmodernism. *New Left Review 178:* 5–28.

Lyotard, J. F. (1984). *The Postmodern Condition: A Report on Knowledge.* Minneapolis: University of Minnesota Press.

Marcus, G., and Fischer, M. (1986). *Anthropology as Cultural Critique: An Experimental Moment in the Human Sciences.* Chicago: University of Chicago Press.

Mascia-Lees, F., Sharpe, P., and Cohen, C. B. (1989). The post-modernist turn in anthropology: Cautions from a feminist perspective. *Signs 15*(1): 7–33.

Mintz, S. (1985). *Sweetness and Power: The Place of Sugar in Modern History.* New York: Viking Press.

Myers, F. (1986). The politics of representation: Anthropological discourse and Australian Aborigines. *American Ethnologist 13:* 430–447.

Myers, F. (1988). Critical trends in the study of hunter-gatherers. *Annual Review of Anthropology 17:* 261–282.

O'Meara, T. (1989). Anthropology as empirical science. *American Anthropologist 91:* 354–369.

Palmer, B. (1990). *Descent into Discourse: The Reification of Language and the Writing of Social History.* Philadelphia: Temple University Press.

Patterson, T., and Gailey, C., eds. (1987). *Power Relations and State Formation.* Washington, DC: American Anthropological Association.

Paynter, R. (1989). The archaeology of equality and inequality. *Annual Review of Anthropology 18:* 369–399.

People of 'Ksan. (1980). *Gathering What the Great Nature Provided: Food Traditions of the Gitksan.* Vancouver: Douglas and McIntyre.

Price, T., and Brown, J., eds. (1985). *Prehistoric Hunter-Gatherers: The Emergence of Social Complexity.* Orlando, FL: Academic Press.

Radcliffe-Brown, A. R. (1922). *The Andaman Islanders.* Cambridge: Cambridge University Press.

Radcliffe-Brown, A. R. (1931). The Social organization of Australian tribes. *Oceania Monographs 1.*

Richardson, B., ed. (1989). *Drumbeat: Anger and Renewal in the Indian Country.* Toronto: Summerhill Press/Assembly of First Nations.

Roseberry, W. (1989). *Anthropologies and Histories: Essays in Culture, History, and Political Economy.* New Brunswick, NJ: Rutgers University Press.

Roth, P. A. (1989). Ethnography without tears. *Current Anthropology 30:* 555–569.

Sahlins, M. (1968). Notes on the original affluent society. In R. Lee and I. DeVore (eds.), *Man the Hunter.* Chicago: Aldine, pp. 85–89.

Sahlins, M. (1989). Captain Cook at Hawaii. *Journal of the Polynesian Society 98:* 371–423.

Sangren, S. (1988). Rhetoric and the authority of ethnography: "Postmodernism" and the social reproduction of texts. *Current Anthropology 29:* 405–435.

Schrire, C. (1984). *Past and Present in Hunter-gatherer Studies.* Orlando, FL: Academic Press.

Sloterdijk, P. (1987). *Critique of Cynical Reason.* Minneapolis: University of Minnesota Press.

Snow, C. P. (1959). *The Two Cultures and the Scientific Revolution.* Cambridge: Cambridge University Press.

Solway, J., and Lee, R. (1990). Foragers, genuine or spurious: Situating the Kalahari San in history. *Current Anthropology 31:* 109–146.

Soper, K. (1991). Postmodernism, subjectivity and the question of value. *New Left Review 186:* 120–128.

Sperber, D. (1985). *On Anthropological Knowledge.* New York: Cambridge University Press.

Spivak, G. C. (1988). Can the subaltern speak? In C. Nelson and L. Grossberg (eds.), *Marxism and the Interpretation of Culture.* Urbana: University of Illinois Press, pp. 271–313.

Sterritt, N. J. (1989). Gitksan and Wet'suwet'en: Unflinching resistance to an implacable invader. In B. Richardson (ed.), *Drumbeat: Anger and Renewal in the Indian Country.* Toronto: Summerhill Press/Assembly of First Nations, pp. 265–294.

Steward, J. (1936). The economic and social basis of primitive bands. In R. H. Lowie (ed.), *Essays in Anthropology in Honor of A. L. Kroeber.* Berkeley: University of California Press, pp. 331–350.

Steward, J. (1938). *Basin-Plateau Aboriginal Sociopolitical Groups. Bureau of American Ethnology Bulletin No. 120.* Washington, DC: Smithsonian Institution.

Taylor, C. (1984). Foucault on freedom and truth. *Political Theory 12*(2): 152–183.

Trigger, B. (1989). Hyperrelativism, responsibility and the social sciences. *Canadian Review of Sociology and Anthropology 26*(5): 776–797.

Trigger, B. (1990). Maintaining economic equality in opposition to complexity: An Iroquoian case study. In S. Upham (ed.), *The Evolution of Political Systems.* Cambridge: Cambridge University Press, pp. 109–146.

Turner, V. (1969). *The Ritual Process.* Chicago: Aldine.

Wa, G., and Uukw, D. (1989). *The Spirit in the Land: The Opening Statement of the Gitksan and Wet'suwet'en Hereditary Chiefs in the Supreme Court of British Columbia.* Gabriola, BC: Reflections Press.

Wagner, R. (1981). *The Invention of Culture.* Chicago: University of Chicago Press.

Washburn, S. L. (1961). *The Social Life of Early Man.* New York: Viking Fund.

Washburn, S. L. (1963). The study of race (presidential address). *American Anthropologist 65:* 521–531.

Washburn, S. L. (1973). The evolution game. *Journal of Human Evolution 2*(6): 557–561.

Washburn, S. L. (1978). Human behavior and the behavior of other animals. *American Psychologist 33:* 405–418.

Washburn, S. L. (1982). Fifty years of study of human evolution. *Bulletin of the Atomic Scientists 38:* 37–43.

Washburn, S. L., and Avis, V. (1958). Evolution and human behavior. In A. Roe and G. G. Simpson (eds.), *Behavior and Evolution.* New Haven, CT: Yale University Press.

Washburn, S. L., and Lancaster, C. S. (1968). The evolution of hunting. In R. B. Lee and I. DeVore (eds.), *Man the Hunter.* Chicago: Aldine, pp. 293–303.

Watson, P. J., and Kennedy, M. C. (1991). The development of horticulture in the eastern woodlands of North America: Women's role. In J. Gero and M. Conkey (eds.), *Engendering Archaeology: Women and Prehistory.* Cambridge: Basil Blackwell, pp. 255–275.

Wilmsen, E. (1989). *Land Filled with Flies: A Political Economy of the Kalahari.* Chicago: University of Chicago Press.

Wolf, E. R. (1982). *Europe and the People Without History.* Berkeley: University of California Press.

Wylie, A. (1992a). The interplay of evidential constraints and political interests in recent archaeological research on gender. *American Antiquity 57:* 15–34.

Wylie, A. (1992b). On heavily decomposing red herrings: Scientific method in archaeology and the ladening of evidence with theory. In L. Embree (ed.), *Metaarchaeology.* Boston Studies in the Philosophy of Science, pp. 269–288.

Wylie, A. (in press). Evidential constraints: Pragmatic empiricism in archaeology. In L. McIntyre and M. Martin (eds.), *Readings in the Philosophy of Social Science.* Cambridge, MA: MIT Press.

*It was Washburn's deep conviction that science can be used to build a better future based on evidence rather than prejudice. He epitomized the image of the socially responsible scientist but he also brought a unique framework to bear on specific issues. Early in his career he tackled the issue of "race" (see Appendix), then the questions of aggression and conflict in the modern setting (see Appendix) and latterly the problems of learning and education in the modern context. In each case he used the evolutionary perspective as a scientific tool and treated the behavior within its adaptive context, offering insights into the modern dilemma. In some cases, this perspective and the new evidence also provided suggestions for how to remedy the problem. "Evolution and Learning" is just one in a series of papers concerned with current problems in American schools. Here Washburn contrasts modern schools and the modern form of learning with "primitive" hunter-gatherers and more recent folk society. He contrasts each of these with what we know about primate learning to conclude that biology determines what we are capable of learning, but the social system determines what we actively learn. However, the motivation to learn is crucial because learning is not inevitable. Some things are easily learned and all learning is easier if there are appropriate rewards and appropriate models. Learning in traditional societies approximates more closely the normal conditions of primate learning than does what happens in modern schools. Washburn suggests that today in our schools, what is learned and how it is taught are out of step with our underlying primate biology. As a result, schools often create bored and alienated primates. He uses the perspective of animal behavior and primate evolution to offer some hints about how to change schools and improve the learning experience. Washburn also reminds us that the aims of education remain the same today as in the past. The challenge, however, is much greater: to help people learn how to live intelligently in a changing world.*

# 18  Evolution and Learning: A Context for Evaluation (1975)

### S. L. Washburn

Today, living as we do in the United States, the necessity of schools seems so obvious that our efforts go into improvement of the curriculum or educational reform. It is easy to forget that through most of human history, people learned languages, complex social systems, and elaborate technology without schools. In preagricultural societies, people learned the local flora and fauna, geography, economic practices, social customs, religion, folklore—a whole complex way of life. It is not at all certain that the graduate of a modern high school has learned as much as an uncivilized, primitive hunter.

*Principal* 54 (1975): 4–10. Reprinted with permission. Copyright © 1975 National Association of Elementary School Principals. All rights reserved.

The high school graduate has learned different things than the hunter learned, but the modern student has the enormous handicap that what he has been asked to learn does not seem to fit into any easily visible way of life. In the folk society, learning is motivated by identification, emotion, and clear goals. From an evolutionary point of view, these motivations are seen as the necessary conditions of learning. What may be learned depends on biology, but what actually *is* learned depends on the social system.

The act of throwing may make the issues clear. It is easy for people to learn to enjoy throwing. Note the form of that statement: it is *easy* for people to *learn.* Many games include throwing, and skill requires an enormous amount of practice. From an evolutionary point of view, throwing has been an important skill in the survival of the species. It was important in hunting and in warfare, and practice in play ensured the development of the necessary skill.

Chimpanzees are one of the very few animals that also throw. They have the anatomy that permits throwing either underhand or overhand, anatomy shared only with the other apes and man. But chimpanzees do not practice. A chimpanzee does not make a pile of rocks and then throw them at a selected target. Other chimpanzees do not watch and call encouragement. In man, however, the act must be embedded in a social system of sports, so that the years of repetition necessary to develop a high level of skill are fun. Skills take years to develop, and the pressure of play is the biological solution to the motivation of learning.

The learning of skills has been so important in human evolution that selection has incorporated the basis for skills in the structure of the brain. The part of the human brain most closely related to hand movements is very large. Proportionately, it is far larger in human beings than in any other primate. In other words, a much larger part of the human brain is related to skills—practiced, integrated movements. But just because there is a biological basis for learning skills does not mean that the skills will be learned. For learning to occur, there must also be a social system that puts the learning into an acceptable form and that clearly shows the learner the utility of the skill in adult life. In a folk society dependent on the spear in both hunting and war, the games of childhood were direct preparation for clearly perceived adult actions.

Learning of skills is affected by rewards, but the nature of the animal greatly affects the kind of reward that is appreciated. In the matter of hunting and fishing, human beings, especially males, will spend many hours and make great efforts for the most minimal success. For many people, catching a fish is a reward far beyond the possible economic value of the food. Many states have departments of fish and game that spent millions of dollars to provide fish and game for hunters long before lunches for hungry school children were even considered. Clearly, there is something about hunting that is remarkably rewarding to human beings. The importance of hunting in our evolutionary history has built a human biology that makes hunting *easy to learn*, and very little compensation is enough to motivate very substantial efforts. The pleasure of hunting makes people willing to work hard, practice the necessary skills, and devote much time and expense for a minimal reward.

The education of uncivilized people was successful without schools because learning was motivated by identification, emotion, and clear goals and because evolution (through natural selection) had produced a species for whom classes of learning were natural.

Clearly, the need for schools and the problems of the schools come from three quite different sources. First, there is no longer any folk society, any highly visible system of human behavior that can be easily appreciated by the participants. Second, many of the skills needed in modern complex society take years to acquire, and, so far, no one has succeeded in making the intermediate goals—the steps between elementary science and being a chemist, for example—exciting and adequately rewarding. Third, the necessary ways of life in complex society no longer bear any simple relation to human nature. For example, in all folk societies, basic learning is completed by maturity, and shortly thereafter people live as adults. But in our society, education may continue more than a dozen years after maturity. The institutional framework of the graduate school is merely an extension of the elementary school; there are still courses and marks, teachers and children. To live as an adult, a person must drop out of school.

Perhaps the most fundamental difference between folk learning and modern education is that under folk conditions, most people did the same things. There was a division of labor between men and women, but aside from that, there were not many different kinds of jobs. Boys played with spears because all men would use spears in hunting and warfare.

In marked contrast, very few students who take biology today become biologists. The situation in which most students do not think they are going to use what they learn is a new one. Lacking the fundamental human desire to learn what will be useful, students become bored, and the school resorts to discipline to maintain the process of education. But discipline is no substitute for play and internal motivation—and examinations are no substitute for life. A species that tries to substitute discipline for pleasure has given up its whole biological heritage, the whole relation of learning and life. Human beings are not pigeons who may be taught to peck out the solutions to futile problems. People are the most creative, imaginative, social, empathetic beings that exist. But schools may reduce youth to bored and alienated primates, people who have been educated out of their natural desires to learn and separated from the larger society in which they must ultimately live.

The distinction between learning and the schools is most clearly illustrated in the first few years of life. In monkeys, excellent observational and experimental studies show the importance of early learning. In a natural setting, the mother and infant are together constantly. The infant learns from its mother, or from other animals in close proximity. Long before the infant is weaned, for example, it has tried the kinds of foods its mother is eating, often spitting them out in distaste. But by the time it is weaned, the young monkey has learned what is edible and what is not. Separation of mother and infant leads to profound and lasting psychological disturbances. In extreme cases the infant may die, even though there is plenty of food easily available. These animal studies suggest the great importance of early experience, strong social bonds, and an enriched environment for learning. The emotional situation is a critical factor in learning, and a deprived infant ceases to learn.

If we turn to man with this kind of information in mind, we cannot say that early experience must be important simply because this is the case with our nearest relatives. Human behavior is not reduced to that of other primates, but there is, nevertheless, the strongest indication that events that take place before the nervous system has fully matured are somehow, incorporated in a way that is different from the incorporation of later events. What the animal studies do suggest is that learning in the first years of human life should be examined with the greatest care.

At birth, humans are far less mature than any of the nonhuman primates. After only a few days, an infant monkey can walk independently, and almost from the first day of life, it actively helps in the interaction with its mother. The human mother has a much greater responsibility, one that lasts over years, rather than months. Judging from the animal studies, we should expect to find that man is unique in the importance of early learning. A number of studies clearly show that this is the case. The most important events in human learning take place before formal schooling begins. In our culture almost no attention is paid to this critical period, and there is no education for effective mothering. Behavior in the family is regarded as a private concern; people may beat their children if they want to, and the state only intervenes if the child is battered to a degree considered criminal.

The schools receive the products of these critical early years, and it is an illusion to suppose that a single teacher in a large class can overcome the deficits of each child's early experience. In both monkey and man, early learning takes place in an environment of few individuals and strong emotions. It takes place over many hours each day, and there is enormous pleasurable repetition. A few hours a day in a large class, well disciplined and without strong emotional bonds, cannot possibly provide the biosocial setting for effective early learning.

As a monkey grows older, much of its time is spent in a play group. Learning from peers gradually replaces learning from mother, although the attachment to mother may last for years. In the play group, the monkey learns social skills, the forms of adult behavior, and these are practiced every day. At a later stage, juvenile females play with infants and become skilled mothers before the birth of their own infants. With time, the play of juvenile males becomes much rougher, and they practice the aggressive behaviors that will be essential in later life. Both sexes learn the behaviors that are essential for life in the social group, and these behaviors may differ from one group to the next, especially with the kinds of food and dangers of predators.

From an evolutionary point of view, much of the behavior of human children is similar to that of other primates, but the time of maturation, learning, and practice is greatly prolonged. The slowing of maturation is costly from a biological point of view. Young primates are likely to be injured or killed, which suggests that prolonging youth must have been so important that it was favored by selection in spite of the risks involved. The delay of maturation took place long before the discovery of agriculture, so the explanation of the delay must lie in the life of the hunter-gatherers. These people led complicated lives that were quite different from those of the nonhuman primates. The biological delay of maturation appears to be directly related to the evolution of a nervous system that could learn the technical and social complexities of the uniquely human way of life. Both brain and way of life are evolved in a feedback relationship with each other. Learning lies at the core of being human, and this was the case many thousands of years before there were any schools. Peers played an essential role in that learning.

From a biological point of view, perhaps the most fundamental change that could be made in the schools is to give back the role of teacher to the peers. From a practical point of view, this would mean that slightly older children would do *some* of the teaching of the younger children. This would have three results. First, it would increase the number of teachers, so that much of the teaching could be done in the small, informal, emotionally supporting groups that are natural for man. Second, it would provide satisfactory social roles for many children, roles in which they could be proud of their accomplishments, work for which they could be praised. Third, to teach successfully, the peer teachers would have to really learn the subject matter.

I have tried peer teaching with college seniors teaching freshmen, and I have no doubt that the quality of college education could be greatly increased tomorrow by the careful use of student teachers. But the essential point is that the slightly older peer can have a very different relationship with the pupil. The point of teaching by peers is to restore the conditions of learning that are natural for man, the kind of situations in which the human brain evolved. Just as many sports continue natural situations of maturing and learning, situations that are pleasurable and socially rewarding even if one has to practice long and hard, so peer teaching could be used to create intellectual situations that would be pleasurable and rewarding even if one had to practice long and hard.

Peer teaching provides two kinds of motivations. First, the learner sees that someone just older than he can do the required tasks, and as a result, the tasks no longer seem impossible or irrelevant. Second, the peer teacher has an important social position in the life of the school, just as the successful athlete does. A peer teacher might spend up to one-fifth of his or her schooltime helping peers. Given the many different subject matters, most children might be teachers at least occasionally, and all would have the opportunity to be helped by peers. In the past, without schools, human beings were able to master complex social tasks in ways that were in accord with human nature. Surely, with modern knowledge, science, and a whole profession of educators, we should not do worse.

•

To summarize what we have been saying so far, the study of animal behavior and evolution suggests that early learning takes place primarily from the mother, closely associated people, or substitutes (as in the kibbutz). It involves countless repetitions in a warm, emotional environment. This early learning is critical in preparing the child for learning in school. In our society, there is no substitute for parents talking, reading, and playing with their children. As the child grows older, peers become more and more important, but the attitudes and actions of the home remain of great importance. Children play with peers, and this is a fundamental setting for learning, but their games reflect the actions and values of their adult community. It is only recently, for special reasons, that a separate institution (the school) has become necessary for teaching the young, and its problems arise from the loss of the traditional folk learning situation in which learning depends on identification, emotion, and clearly visible goals.

But even if early learning is successful, and even if peers help in creating a social situation for elementary learning, the problem of goals remains. How can the years in school be made to seem important to the developing human being? The answer is very simple: they have to be important in ways that a young person can understand. Many children do not enjoy learning, simply because they do not believe that what they are required to learn is practical and important. And many of us older people are skeptical of what is required because we, too, doubt that what is taught in the schools—

beyond the basic skills—is necessary. Take Latin, for example. Latin was taught because it was the language of scholarship, international learning, and religion. But when it ceased to have these functions, it was still taught for "mind training," because of its supposed superior quality, and because it was required for college entrance. Latin is essential if one is to understand the classics and much of European history. Probably too few people master it today. But it is a lasting blot on the history of education that millions of hours were spent learning a language that was, for most people, useless; that was justified on the basis of spurious reasons; and that was used to prevent many from going to college.

The motivation of the older student requires support and understanding in the home and in the community. The student needs visible, important goals, as was the case in the folk society. As long as the school is considered a separate institution insisting on tasks that bear no relation to life, it will fail in its most important intellectual functions. Since the motivation for learning comes from family, peers, and society, the isolated school has minimized its chances to teach.

The ultimate aims of education should be to give the student some understanding of the nature of man, the world we live in, intellectual fun, and preparation for jobs. These matters have become technical problems, and so we need to have an institution designed to deal with them. The simple folk explanations of human nature are no longer enough. We are living in the world of DNA, modern biology, and complicated medicine of incredible possibility. The small, flat world, the center of the universe, has been replaced by a universe of temporal and spatial dimensions that would have been totally incomprehensible to our ancestors. Music, art, and literature are available in forms and quantity that the kings of years ago could not have commanded. Even as late as 1900, most of the jobs in the United States were on farms, and the sheer variety of careers now open to young people is something entirely new in human history.

If these technical problems were simple ones, they could be managed in the home, just as learning was for countless thousands of years. They are not simple, however, and they are changing all the time. But human beings are not changing. If we are still evolving, it is at a rate too slow to be of practical importance. The biology that evolved under the conditions of gathering and hunting—human biology—is the nature with which we must learn to live in the modern technical world. This is a new problem. On the one hand, the system of education must consider the nature of the youth being educated. And it must consider the social, emotional, and biological conditions of the system itself, as well. But the schools must also show how to deal with the new problems arising from the rapid change in the technical sciences.

Fortunately, many of the problems facing the world today do not fit into the traditional departments of educational categories. Population, energy, and crime, for example, involve many different sciences. Each has a history. Each involves trends. The daily newspaper provides numerous examples of problems whose solution will not come from any one branch of knowledge. The educated citizen in a democracy today should be able to see what kinds of information are actually useful in moving toward better solutions of the real problems that face us all. For example, the theory of continental drift provides understanding of earthquakes, mountains, volcanoes, and distributions of ancient life. Why the drift theory was opposed gives insights into the scientific enterprise and into some very human scientists. Studying carefully selected cases of this sort would make it possible for students to see the importance of what they are doing and the interrelations of different kinds of knowledge. And it could help them to develop intellectual habits that would last long after their formal education was over.

This is, after all, the fundamental issue. To live intelligently in a changing world, new information is necessary, and the purpose of the schools should be to help people learn how to live. The educated person should both have more fun and be more useful. Or, to put it more accurately, the educated person should be more likely to lead a satisfying, useful life.

The test for the schools comes in the actual behavior of their graduates. How do they approach problems? What resources do they bring? Are they innovative, cooperative? Do they know where to look for knowledge and how to ask for advice? It is not easy to test for these important abilities, and again, the biology suggests some of the complications. For example, those abilities that are measured by IQ tests are not changed by massive damage to the frontal lobes of the brain, a fact that was used as a defense of frontal brain operations. Yet this part of the brain is composed of billions of cells, both the number and complexity of which have increased in primate evolution, and especially in the later phase of human evolution. Since such increase is due to natural selection, we know that the frontal region must be important. Its probable functions are foresight, insight, planning, persistence, and originality—what are thought of as the higher mental functions. Not only is the so-called IQ greatly affected by the child's environment, but it does not measure the most important human abilities. Tests of performance clearly show the disastrous results of frontal brain operations, and the implications of this fact for testing are clear. Human beings are much too complicated to be evaluated by

pencil-and-paper tests, which can be quickly administered to groups. People are more important than tests. What counts in life is performance, which is based on both biology and experience. For example, in modern science most projects are cooperative. In real life, the ability to work creatively with others is of the utmost importance. Yet the educational system minimizes cooperation and forces the student to work in isolation. The desire to grade a paper (how will we know who did the work?) forces immediate and trivial emphasis on individual work, which, in effect, discourages learning the complex personal and intellectual complications of cooperation. Yet performance in cooperative projects that lead toward problem solution is probably a far more useful measure of ability than the usual tests.

The problem of grading may be illustrated by writing and spelling. If the goal is the ability to express oneself in useful ways, the student needs to be encouraged to engage in the repetition necessary to master these skills. But if the student is penalized too much for misspelling, the whole task becomes distasteful. This is particularly the case if difficult words are introduced merely to find out who are the best spellers. Again, animal behavior clearly shows that creatures who are repeatedly discouraged give up the task. Conversely, success leads to repeated performance and to the development of skills. If the classroom, through frequent testing and grading, becomes the symbol of discouragement, students can only protect themselves by withdrawal in one form or another. From a biological point of view, the classroom should be a place of encouragement, and students should run into class as joyfully as they run out into the play yard.

In a recent issue of *Daedalus*, devoted to higher education, many authors mentioned the importance of discipline and the learning of a foreign language. As teachers, they seemed to feel no guilt that many of the problems are in the culture of the schools. Surely teachers should be among the first to urge the use of simplified spelling, the metric system, a rational typewriter keyboard, and the calculator. Children should not be blamed for difficulties that arise from irrational behavior of adults. The issues can be most clearly seen in the problem of learning a foreign language. As noted earlier, mastery of a second language was not a problem when there was no school and the child was in a situation in which learning two languages was useful. Years of study in school may accomplish much less. Perhaps a minimum standard for evaluating a school might be that it not do worse than was easily achieved without a school. Certainly, experience shows that learning a language is easy if the process begins early; if it is done with a native speaker; and if it is perceived to be useful. A child may have a good start on a language but then forget it if he feels there is no reason to continue. Why it is useful to learn a language will depend on the time and place. For example, in California today, there are millions of Spanish-speaking people. This is the foreign language most likely to be useful to citizens of that state. Accordingly, many California schools should offer Spanish, not for magic or mind training, but because it is useful. Spanish-speaking children could be the peer teachers, and many hours would be devoted to games, texts, and tapes. This would change the position of the Spanish-speaking child in the school, and it might even prepare the way for better understanding between the cultures. Later, Spanish history would be studied, and the problems of Latin America would be contrasted with those of the United States. Finally, every effort would be made to show all the different kinds of careers in which it is an advantage to speak both Spanish and American English. The aim of such a program would be useful mastery of the language, and every aspect of it would be different from learning a soon-to-be-forgotten smattering of a scholarly language.

Of course, there will be problems in any changes in the schools. As Jerrold Zacharias has remarked, "Instant educational reform is wish fulfillment for the naive." But, at least occasionally, it is fun to be naive, to think how different it all might be. Perhaps evolution and animal behavior do give some hints for change. After all, as a recent presidential candidate orated, "Our future lies ahead of us," and that should give encouragement to those who see the schools as the place to start "the human use of human beings."

*Although species conservation was not part of the agenda of Washburn's new physical anthropology, Lindburg's topic and his research can be seen as a natural extension of both the scientific framework and the application of science and an evolutionary approach to the concerns of modern life. This essay discusses a controversial new conservation technique, captive propagation of endangered species, or ex situ care. Lindburg argues that regardless of its deficiencies, the technique is an important stopgap given the current biodiversity crisis. However each step of ex situ propagation is plagued with difficulties: how and which animals to put in captivity, how to increase their reproduction, and, finally, how to return surplus animals back to the wild. He demonstrates, using case studies of five species, the need for scientific criteria that are based on an evolutionary understanding of the species' adaptation. Lindburg's own work with captive breeding of cheetahs and lion-tailed macaques shows the advantage of taking a broad, biobehavioral approach rather than applying simplistic frameworks and selective data. Just as with the study of primate and human evolution, ex situ issues would benefit from the infusion of more evidence in a multidisciplinary framework that integrates information from a larger variety of sources, including information from wild populations and a better understanding of intraspecies diversity. Lindburg, like Washburn, also recognizes the importance of biopolitics in determining how decisions are made about the value of science and of an evolutionary perspective in solving problems of current social concern.*

# 19 Zoos as Arks: Issues in Ex Situ Propagation of Endangered Wildlife

**Donald G. Lindburg**   *Zoological Society of San Diego*

## INTRODUCTION

Captive propagation of wildlife as a conservation strategy is controversial. Issues of wise use of conservation resources, product quality, and ethics related to the captive experience leave all who value wildlife divided on approaches. Whether or not single option efforts on behalf of a particular taxon, that is, in situ conservation, will suffice is beyond the scope of this discussion. Although it is limited in effectiveness, the author takes the position that we lack sufficient foresight to close out captive breeding as one among several strategies. This view stems in part from the fact that several species owe their survival to a stint in captivity. It is reinforced by the concern that trends in human population growth and consequent habitat loss cannot be arrested overnight (Reid and Miller 1989), leaving little doubt that increasing numbers of vanishing wildlife will ulti-

mately exist only under captive conditions. Although there are hopeful developments in some areas (see, e.g., Western 1989), few will doubt that extinctions on an unprecedented scale will occur within the next few decades (Myers 1987; Wilson 1985). Ranking highly among the difficulties in ordering captive efforts is the sheer enormity of the task and, therefore, the rendering of decisions (as well as the decision-making process) that will provide the best possible return. The objective of this essay is to review some of the thinking that has been invoked in attempts to guide ex situ propagation of endangered forms.

Ex situ propagation, in simplest terms, is propagation of animal populations away from their natural habitat. It is single-species propagation, in the absence of natural ranging, predators, food shortages, thermal stress, and numerous other factors that impact on wild populations. Ex situ propagation entails three activities:

(1) capture and removal of brood stock from wild to captive facilities, (2) holding in captivity for purposes of breeding up the numbers, and (3) the return of captive-bred individuals to protected wild habitat. As laid out by conservationists in the 1980s (Soulé et al. 1986), this effort may be compared to the biblical story of Noah, who saved species from imminent destruction by taking them into an ark until the threat to their survival had passed. Thus modern-day zoos are often characterized as "arks," which, in this instance, will save wildlife from the overpopulation of our planet by humankind (the "demographic winter").

The first of these steps, capturing wildlife for captive breeding, is rarely practiced today, given the potential for negative impact on wild populations and the very tightly regulated traffic in international transport of live animals. Having recognized in addition that their own future as zoological institutions is in jeopardy through loss of this source of animals (see, for example, Benirschke 1986), zoos have readily lent their existing brook stock to the conservation effort. Therefore the stock that forms the basis for captive breeding is, for the most part, descended from ancestors that were brought into captivity for the more traditional reasons of entertainment and education. In terms of founders, propagation potential (effective population size), and long-term preservation of gene pool diversity, it is necessary to make do with the brood stock already in hand. Notable exceptions in the recent past are the California condor, the black-footed ferret, and the Sumatran rhinoceros, for which further removals from wild stock have been undertaken.

Breeding up the numbers in the captive sector such that there is a surplus that can theoretically be returned to the wild is cited as a major raison d'etre of modern zoos. This is a process that is constrained, unfortunately, by lack of knowledge about reproductive function, limitations in staff expertise, and limited resources. Nevertheless, in a growing number of cases, the disposition of individuals that are surplus to the breeding endeavor looms as a serious problem (Lacy 1995; Lindburg 1991; Lindburg and Lindburg 1995).

Returning captive-reared individuals to protected habitat is the most daunting of all the steps in ex situ propagation, for it is rather like attempting to reassemble Humpty-Dumpty. Several recent evaluations of the success of reintroduction efforts (Beck et al. 1994) raise doubts among conservationists as to its viability as a way of saving increasingly imperiled wildlife from extinction. However, success seemingly has reduced prospects of occurring as long as repatriation is viewed as the strategy of last resort (Conway 1989). There is some evidence to support the notion that waiting too long to plan for reintroductions (Griffith et al. 1989) is a key factor in their failure. Not only does a long so-journ in captivity enhance the need for retraining in basic survival tasks, but it often requires greater effort in the protection and/or restoration of a viable ecosystem for the animals that are to be released.

In buttressing the case for captive breeding, zoos often point to instances where the remnants of once vast wild populations survive today only in their facilities. The Przewalski's horse, for example, was last seen in the wild in 1968, but in captivity has grown from a base of 13 individuals to its present size of over 700 (Benirschke and Kumamoto 1991). The last of China's Pere David's deer were consumed by hungry soldiers during the Boxer Rebellion in 1900, but fortunately 18 individuals that had been sent to Western zoos and parks were collected at Woburn Abbey as the only survivors, and today this captive population numbers more than 1,000 individuals (Cherfas 1984). A more current example is that of the California condor, which, in 1987, had the last member of a wild population that once covered most of the western United States and south into portions of Mexico brought into captivity, to add to a small but growing population of captive fledged birds (Toone and Risser 1988). Not only have captive-born condors reproduced in captivity, but by early 1992 the population had reached sufficient numbers to permit the first releases of captive-reared birds to wild habitat in southern California (Toone and Wallace 1994). Although more species could be added to this list, the cases cited provide a corpus of information on the values and shortcomings of ex situ propagation and offer a basis for further development of strategies that may have to be increasingly employed in future decades.

Among the questions that are posed in designing ex situ efforts, perhaps the most fundamental is this: Out of the great diversity found in nature, how shall we make decisions about which entities shall be the beneficiaries of our efforts? And once this has been decided, how then do we best manage these populations, given their smallness, their greatly varied living requirements, and their different life histories? We may ask as well which manipulations in the form of technological advances can be applied to achieving or maintaining their viability. Finally, because it is unlikely that we can operate in an arena devoid of political considerations, the story would be incomplete if this aspect were left out. After reviewing each of these points, I then cite some case histories to illustrate the more pressing issues in ex situ conservation.

## THE SMALL POPULATION PARADIGM

Having previously attempted to define ex situ propagation, it may be instructive to outline some of the parameters within which these efforts are implemented. In many ways, they are not very different from those that apply to the conservation of certain wild populations.

First, ex situ propagation is the propagation of *small* populations. This derives from the fact that there is limited space available in captivity—far less than will likely be required to meet future efforts. According to Conway (1989), about 500,000 spaces exist in zoos today, and there is little prospect that their number will increase appreciably in the future. A modest allocation of 250 slots to each species or subspecies to be preserved would provide room for only 2000 taxa. If we hedge our bets against the stochastic processes, genetic and demographic, that threaten the extinction of small populations and increase the slots per taxon, an obvious result is that fewer taxa can be accommodated. Allocation of such finite resources among taxa deemed to benefit from captive propagation inevitably limits the amount available to any one.

Most wild populations are losing ground to the forces that destroy their habitat, leaving in situ efforts to the conservation of what is left of once vastly greater distributions. In addition, fragmentation of once contiguous ranges results in genetic isolation of demes, with increased prospects of inbreeding and local extinctions. The disconnected patches of rain forest that now prevail throughout the range of lion-tailed macaques provide one of but dozens of examples that could be cited. According to Kumar (1987), the available rain forest today covers approximately 1 percent of its original land area, and nearly half of the wild population ($<$ 5000 total) lives in isolated patches that are less than 20 square kilometers in size. Not only were captive populations small from the outset, but their dispersal among cooperating zoos resembles patchy habitats insofar as gene flow is concerned, a need that is met by the expensive and often risky transfer of individuals between institutions. Translocation is not yet routine for any wild population, but will increasingly become a part of wild population management in the future (Strum and Southwick 1986).

Finally, in both captive and natural milieux, there is lack of certainty about the "rules of the game." This is seen, for instance, in the models developed for the maintenance of genetic diversity. Recognizing that most of our knowledge comes from domestic species in which the goal has been to eliminate genetic diversity in favor of commonly shared traits, the proposition that genetic diversity in rare wildlife should be retained for an indefinite number of generations represents a major challenge. In 1984, experts attending a symposium on the genetic management of small captive populations reasoned that, because no one can crystal-ball the future with great certainty, a reasonable goal for ex situ propagation would be the retention of 90% of the original genetic diversity for a period of 200 years (Soulé

et al. 1986). Quite obviously, for a given species the parameters of generation time, effective population size, and numbers of founders would be implicated in attaining this goal.

In addition to uncertainties about long-term demographic trends, the difficulty in working toward such distant goals is that we must work with rules having only provisional reality. That is, no data on 200 years of genetic management exist, particularly for forms having longer generation times, that would fully corroborate our assumptions. Yet, to wait for the acquisition of empirical data before proceeding is to succumb to what Soulé (1986) has aptly termed the "Nero dilemma." Starting from the premise that conservation biology is best described as a crisis discipline, Soulé likens the situation to a battlefield in which a soldier observes a group of armed men stealthily approaching his lines. It would be reasonable to assume that these are in fact enemy forces (a good working hypothesis), and taking precautionary action is therefore justified. However, there are alternative hypotheses to be considered: (1) these are one's own troops returning from a mission, (2) they belong to a third force that may be either neutral or friendly, or (3) they are illusory manifestations of hysteria. To await confirming data on their identity may be, like Nero, to fiddle indefinitely with such ideas until it is too late. As Soulé concludes, "Dithering and endangering are often linked." In neither arena, captive or wild, does sufficient empirical backing exist that would provide confidence in outcomes, but inaction is to court unacceptable risk.

## WHAT TO SAVE?

How do we decide which populations to select for ex situ propagation? The answer entails two levels of decision making. First, because we are forced to capitalize on the brood stock already on hand in the captive sector, we inescapably rely on criteria previously used by zoos in selecting animals for their collections. In former times, perhaps the most important criterion in acquisition was potential for revenue generation, but opportunistic availability was also a factor. Revenue generation meant that animals were often chosen that today are commonly referred to as "charismatic megavertebrates"—elephants, tigers, giraffes, gorillas—animals that have a high profile as public favorites. Not only are these taxa represented in captivity today without regard to conservation requirements but, in the missions of modern zoos, continue to be favored in attracting program support for research and captive breeding. As a rule, then, a cheetah will be preferred over a hairy-nosed wombat. But, if a zoo or its director has had a past association with hairy-nosed wombats, they might find at least one privileged spot in the sun. To be sure, other criteria such as degree of endangerment, uniqueness as an evolutionary lineage, and prospects for survival and breeding success in captivity, are increasingly affecting decisions about ex situ propagation.

The second level of selection concerns within-species diversity. At a meeting in Philadelphia in 1985, a small group of zoo planners discussed the "subspecies dilemma" (Conway 1985; see also Ryder 1986). About five years earlier, zoos had embarked on a program of national cooperation in breeding and managing targeted species in what eventually came to be known as a "Species Survival Plan," or SSP (Hutchins and Wiese 1991). By 1985, there were some 30 SSPs in existence, but already a number of troublesome questions about identification of the biological entity to be conserved had arisen. For example, although differences in morphology and known or suspected provenance had long constrained zoos to maintain Bornean and Sumatran orangutans as separate populations in captivity, with the discovery of an inversion involving the second pair of chromosomes (Seuánez et al. 1979), a simple and highly reliable test for differentiation of the two forms became available. Application of this test led to the definitive identification of 88 Bornean/Sumatran hybrids living in zoos. What should be their fate in future breeding programs? Asian lions are subspecifically differentiated from African lions, and are on the verge of extinction. Should a breeding plan be formed, along with the allocation of precious captive space, to save a subspecies of an otherwise fairly abundant mammal? And what of the 40% or so of zoo-held animals that are listed by trinomials? Must all of slightly variant forms be given equal attention? The dimensions of natural diversity present in almost any taxon, measured against the limited numbers that can be held in captivity, raised grave questions about sampling of nature's diversity in propagation efforts.

Not surprisingly, the search for answers to these vexing questions led to yet more fundamental questions—for example, the amount of diversity within a species and how it is distributed across remaining habitat. For zoo propagators, the conclusion was reached, whether justified or not, that traditionally defined subspecies may not be suitable for propagation as a valid biological entity. This led to the birth of the "evolutionarily significant unit" (ESU), a "definable, hence, unique, genetically coherent population of a subspecies which may be accorded SSP status" (Conway 1985). Its boundaries may or may not be congruent with present subspecies classifications.

In practice, defining an ESU would rely on traditional criteria such as provenance and phenotypic variation, but would also add a number of genetic ones to those traditionally used and would search for congruence among them. Where congruence is not found, it is not clear how decisions would be made. Seemingly, decisions would then be based in the first instance on genetic criteria, that is, if significant genetic differences exist, even in monomorphic populations, the road to be followed will be determined genetically. But if genetic differences are trivial, then phenotypic and even political criteria will affect the result. An interesting case is that of the American bobwhite, an avian taxon that met ESU criteria. But when southern bobwhites were introduced into northern states, the effort failed because the southern forms had livers too small to enable them to store the quantities of vitamin A needed to survive in northern winters (Ellis and Serafin 1977).

Rendering the decision-making process even more vexing is that relatively few species can be said to have been genetically characterized, most certainly not throughout the extent of their natural geographic ranges. To this can be added concern for the genetic makeup of brood stock that has resulted from long-term captive breeding of dealer-supplied animals of uncertain provenance. Genetic knowledge often becomes available, therefore, long after critical decisions about what to propagate have already been made.

## CAPTIVE MANAGEMENT

Implicit is the need for enlightened management, once decisions have been rendered about the entity to be propagated. In the past, management concerns entailed nutrition, disease, configuration of living quarters, and the like. The formation of species' survival plans, however, depends on interinstitutional cooperation of unprecedented degree, and the treatment of dispersed members of an SSP taxon as one population. Master planning in these instances calls upon zoos to cooperate in maximizing the number of founders and to take precautions to avoid inbreeding. This is achieved through carefully planned redistributions of individuals of known pedigree within the population. Although it would follow that these redistributions should be taken in ways compatible with the social and behavioral requirements of species, unfortunately, genetic criteria prevail to the point that a strongly bonded female primate, for example, may be treated in similar fashion to a solitary tigress. In addition, redistribution often follows upon the failure of given individuals to reproduce in their present circumstances, based on the unverified assumption that a "change of scenery" will be of benefit. Personal awareness of a number of these cases indicates that exchanges not based on scientifically valid reproductive criteria merely subject relocated brood stock to needless stress.

## BIOTECHNOLOGY

Hand in hand with the development of master plans is the growing application of artificial techniques to preserve or enhance biological diversity. These approaches are subsumed under the rubric of "biotechnology." In the broadest sense, nearly all aspects of the captive existence are artificial. A list of biotechnical aspects would be a long one, indeed, embracing such innovations as the creation of artificial swamps and simulated rainstorms. Double clutching and puppet rearing of chicks are techniques that have been a boon to the California condor recovery program (Toone and Risser 1988), and chasing a mechanical lure by the cheetah represents an attempt to compensate for the absence of hunting and to maintain good body condition (Lindburg 1998).

It is in the field of reproduction, however, that we find approaches that truly excite the imagination, perhaps because they often carry an aura of being at the portals of a "brave, new world." As an example, founder representation has the potential for being enhanced through transfer of embryos from rare taxa to more commonly available surrogates, as in the case of the Indian gaur embryo successfully transferred to the womb of a Holstein cow (Stover et al. 1981). The rates at which rare species can be propagated are theoretically enhanced by this technique, and the harvesting and cryopreservation of embryos from females unable to reproduce naturally may also enhance its value as a conservation tool.

Given that genetic diversity is lost with each act of reproduction, in small populations having short generation times, diversity will be lost at a more rapid rate than in species having a generation time of, say, 20 years. One scenario, therefore, envisions artificial manipulation of generation times through cryopreserved germ plasm coupled with temporary suspension of reproduction. Another scenario envisions the transfer of cryopreserved sperm or embryos to wild-living dams when other factors preclude their being united with preferred sires for natural mating (Conway 1989).

Although these are the kinds of extraordinary manipulations that draw the attention of the media and excite the general public, they have as yet made relatively little impact on captive propagation of endangered wildlife. Whether they ever will, or even whether they should, have application in any but the most unusual cases is very much a matter of debate (Lasley and Anderson 1991; Wildt et al. 1992). The known certainty is that intervention at such advanced technological levels dramatically increases the cost of reproduction and, equally likely, until it becomes economically feasible to do so, we shall continue to read about these rare successes in the daily newspapers.

## BIOPOLITICS

It seems reasonable to suggest that biopolitics, defined simply as the interaction of political and biological factors in the conservation of world resources, should be considered in ex situ propagation along with biodiversity and biotechnology. Interestingly, although these other "bios" are indexed in the seminal book *Conservation for the Twenty-first Century* (Western and Pearl 1989), "biopolitics" is not, nor is "politics." Yet it would seem that all else is of little consequence in conservation efforts if the empowerment of even the most carefully reasoned decisions is lacking. Political considerations, not surprisingly, enter at every level, as we see, for example, in the reluctance of host countries to buy into global conservation efforts if their own populations are not to be propagated as biologically "pure" entities. And, despite their potential to focus international attention and rally public support for conservation of wild habitat, reintroduction schemes often face incredible political obstacles. A recent account of the history of North American reintroduction efforts provides a sad litany of the politics of conservation, inevitably to the detriment of the wild forms these efforts would conserve (De Blieu 1991).

Ex situ propagation as an enterprise is itself disdained by those who argue that conservation is better served by rechanneling resources from ex situ to in situ efforts (see, e.g., Karanth 1992). Cost comparisons in the two locales are often used to indicate how much further conservation dollars will go in promoting in situ conservation, particularly in the Third World. However, there is also an implication that zoos are consuming funds that would otherwise be available for these efforts. Those who make such comparisons assume that compassion for wildlife conservation on the part of the zoo-going public approaches their own. Even more to the point, over 70% of North American zoos are wholly or largely supported by city or county governments (Boyd 1994), which view the local zoo as a resource for use by the community which sustains it. Seen in this light, Hutchins et al. (1995) are undoubtedly correct in stating that even if all zoos were to close tomorrow, it is most unlikely that additional funding would become available for saving endangered species or habitats. The financial resources of a zoo, in sum, are realized from the local educational and entertainment programs of the institution itself, and the funding of in situ projects through zoos is likely to occur only if these are strongly coupled to zoo-based conservation efforts.

It would be misleading to suggest that ex situ advocates are unimpeded by political contentiousness within their ranks. The journal *Zoo Biology* in 1995 devoted an entire issue to the discussion of various levels of strategic planning (e.g., institutional, regional, global), revealing the existence of significant polarization in how to proceed (see Hutchins et al. 1995 and accompanying commentary from national and international authorities). Also, in 1995, publication of the volume *Ethics on the Ark* (Norton et al.) brought into sharp focus the deep divisions within the zoo community on such issues as the disposal of surplus animals and repatriation to wild habitat. Biopolitics clearly affects in adverse ways the common goal of saving wildlife from extinction, both within the ex situ and in situ camps and between them.

## CASE STUDIES

In the case studies that follow, I will attempt to show how the points reviewed in the previous sections have application to ex situ conservation efforts.

### Tigers

Being very big and very high on the charismatic scale, it is a foregone conclusion that tigers would be among those species favored for ex situ propagation. This was true long before the severe threat to wild populations brought tigers to the cover of *Time* magazine in 1994. All considerations about value of a species aside, the issue I want to consider in this case is "which tiger?"

Tigers have been divided by traditional criteria into eight subspecies (Table 1), of which three are most certainly extinct. Another, *P. t. amoyensis* from China, is believed to number less than 100 individuals, of which about half are in Asian zoos. It may well be that *amoyen-*

*sis* will shortly follow the route of the Caspian, Balian, and Javan tiger to extinction. Originating in the Lower Pleistocene, tigers once had a more or less continuous distribution from Iran in the westernmost part of its range to the tip of Siberia in the former USSR and throughout southern Asia as far as the island of Bali (Hemmer 1987). Like all species with large geographic ranges, the distribution today is disjunct, and subspecies as they are traditionally defined correspond roughly to surviving geographic isolates. All are considered endangered, and in the wild the Bengal subspecies, with 5000 to 6000 surviving, is the most numerous.

Tigers provide a good example of the problem in deciding the amount of natural diversity that might be preserved through ex situ efforts. An answer to this question hinges on at least two givens regarding captive propagation, namely, the revelation through surveys that the available space set aside for tiger propagation is about 1000 slots and that 90% of the population on hand consists of the Siberian and Bengal subspecies and hybrids of these two (Maguire and Lacy 1990).

The five extant subspecies of tigers reveal only modest phenotypic differences, and in some cases within-population variability in such overt features as the pelage makes differentiation difficult, even by the experts. Morphometric studies suggest that *amoyensis* (the Chinese subspecies) is the most divergent, and could be a relict population of primitive tigers (Herrington 1987). However, as noted earlier, this race is on the verge of extinction and has not been seriously considered as a potential beneficiary of captive efforts. Recent electrophoretic analysis of blood proteins from captive individuals indicates that the remaining four subspecies differ very little genetically, that is, "less than one-third the divergence seen among human social groups and less than half the separation among African lion populations" (O'Brien et al. 1987a).

These findings give rise to the conventional wisdom which holds that captive efforts should emphasize the preservation of those subspecies least likely to survive in the wild, as such losses mean that a portion of the

**TABLE 1.  Subspecies of *Panthera tigris***

| Taxon | Common Name | Provenance | Population Status (Wild/Captive) |
|-------|-------------|------------|----------------------------------|
| *P. t. virgata* | Caspian | Iran | Extinct |
| *P. t. tigris* | Bengal | India | 5600/1000 |
| *P. t. corbetti* | Corbett's | Vietnam | 2500/20 |
| *P. t. sumatrae* | Sumatran | Sumatra | 650/170 |
| *P. t. sondaica* | Javan | Java | Extinct |
| *P. t. balica* | Balian | Bali | Extinct |
| *P. t. amoyensis* | South China | China | 40/40 |
| *P. t. altaica* | Siberian | North Korea | 250/700 |

SOURCE:  Maguire and Lacy 1990.

species' genetic heritage will irretrievably vanish. As articulated by Herrington (1987), "We cannot truly claim to have 'preserved' a species unless we preserve its naturally occurring variability as well." Following this logic, captive efforts should be focused on the Chinese, Sumatran, and Vietnamese subspecies. Having already given up on China's *amoyensis* as a lost cause, the Tiger SSP in fact decided to allocate 250 spaces in zoos to each of the four remaining subspecies.

Armed with additional data on electrophoretically determined genetic variance in tigers, Maguire and Lacy (1990) recommended that the ESU of tigers should consist of 550 Bengals and 150 each of the three remaining subspecies. In their view, "Maintaining the most variable subspecies in captivity (vis., Bengals) preserves greater genetic diversity for the species as a whole than allocating space to the less diverse subspecies." Yet another alternative would be to select the Bengal subspecies as *the* tiger of the future, since it is the most genetically variant of the subspecies and seems to be maintaining viability in the wild.

If we grant that these scenarios are genetically sound, they nevertheless raise serious biopolitical questions, namely, the fate of some 550 Siberian tigers in captivity that would suddenly be declared surplus, and the need for an influx of 150 Vietnamese tigers, 130 of which would have to come from the wild. Many will question whether such a proposal can be taken seriously. In effect, the proposals that have been given consideration to date have one element in common, and that is the separate perpetuation of modestly variant subpopulations as subpopulations forevermore. No gene flow is prescribed. The extremes in genetic management would be (1) a situation in which no alleles are shared by the four subspecies (in which case they seemingly cease being merely subspecies); or (2) a situation in which all subspecies are genetically identical. A species having a measure of between-subspecies divergence of only 0.073 ($F_{ST}$, blood protein electrophoresis) tells us that tigers are in fact very close to the second extreme (O'Brien et al. 1987a). Yet the merging of these four subpopulations into a single captive breeding population (i.e., a generic tiger) is not discussed as an option (but see Vrijenhoek 1995 for a recent exception). Considered by the majority of conservationists to be a radical, because irreversible, step, merging of these slightly variant subspecies into one breeding entity would increase the number of founders and the size of the effective breeding population. In addition, one could predict a decrease in the effects of inbreeding and drift and a lessening of the risk of loss through stochastic demographic processes. Yet few are prepared to assign priority to species preservation over and above the maintenance of "pure" racial variants, or to ac-

knowledge that gene flow between and among demes (hybridization) is also a natural evolutionary process.

The difficulty in making choices in this case is readily apparent. Overriding the biological facts as they are known is the unlikely prospect that all or even most of the tiger's natural diversity can be preserved away from its natural habitat.

## Lions

Although still fairly plentiful, lions once had a much greater distribution, extending from Africa through the Middle East and into South Asia as far as central India. Unfortunately, with the advent of firearms, the Asian lion (*Panthera leo persica*) was eventually exterminated over most of its range. Some readers will be familiar with attempts by the Gujarat state government (India) to conserve lions in the Gir Forest and in captivity, particularly in the Sakkarbaug Zoo.

The zoo profession decided several years ago to focus captive breeding efforts on Asian lions, assuming on the basis of provenance that they were subspecifically differentiated from the more common African form. Accordingly, an SSP was established for Asian lions by North American zoos in the early 1980s. Suspicions of hybridization with lions of African origin subsequently emerged, however, particularly in the Delhi and Trivandrum zoo populations from which all North American stock was descended. This concern led to a number of investigations of both morphology and genetics.

From a phenotypic standpoint, a detailed examination of extant Asian lions and of 47 published photographs led Joslin (1986) to conclude that presence of an abdominal skin fold approached 100% in both sexes. By contrast, in 72 published photos of African males, only 7% had a noticeable fold, and only one of 88 photos of females showed this feature. A second, often cited phenotypic difference is in the mane, described as being somewhat fuller in the African subspecies. However, after examining 148 photographs, Joslin concluded that 80% of African and Asian males were indistinguishable by this criterion. Other differences, such as in skull morphology and in a sex-based difference in roaring, have been described (see Joslin 1986 for details).

Genetic studies initiated in 1985 revealed that African and Asian lions are only modestly divergent. According to O'Brien et al. (1987c), the results indicate the sharing of a common ancestry between 50,000 and 200,000 years ago. This difference is equivalent to that found between lions from southern and eastern Africa. Genetic analysis of the captive population indicated that 72% of the presumed Asian forms were in fact hybrids, including all but four aged individuals in North

American zoos (O'Brien et al. 1987b). The world population of "pure" Asian lions was thus set at about 250 wild individuals and less than 70 captives, nearly all residing in Indian zoos. Failing to obtain "pure" brood stock from India, the North American program for ex situ propagation of Asian lions no longer exists.

Although it would seem in this case that Asian lions as an ESU failed the test, the argument to devote space and other resources to their perpetuation as a separate biological entity could be advanced on biopolitical grounds. The long history of geographic separation and the importance of lions to India's impoverished fauna are compelling aspects for many. India lost the cheetah in 1967, when the last known individual died at the Mysore Zoo (Krishne Gowda 1983). India appears to have brought the Bengal tiger back from a low of 1800 individuals in 1972 to a population estimated to number more than 6000 today (O'Brien et al. 1987c). Perhaps preservation of the Asian lion would be a more critical test of India's resolve to take significant strides in conserving its rapidly declining wildlife.

## Rhinoceroses

Yet another case of interest, because it has a different set of contingencies, is that of the African rhinoceroses. For the black rhinoceros (*Diceros bicornis*), Groves (1967) recognized seven subspecies (Table 2), of which *D. b. ladoensis* is believed to be extinct. Two additional subspecies, *D. b. brucii* and *D. b. longipes,* are either extinct or very close to it. The serious decline in the numbers of all rhinoceros taxa, primarily as a result of poaching, is common knowledge.

A question of relevance to this case is whether the remaining wild population of blacks should be maintained as one population, despite subspecific designations, for breeding purposes. Perpetuation as small, isolated entities imposes risks to the survival of these isolates in the form of disease epidemics, inbreeding depression, genetic drift, and random demographic processes. But before moving to relocate some of the

75 or so scattered fragments to a smaller number of relatively safe sanctuaries, it was deemed necessary to explore the range of genetic diversity in this taxon.

Results from a recent survey of mtDNA polymorphisms in the two most numerous subspecies, *michaeli* and *minor,* indicated that they are very close genetically: "Mitochondrial DNA divergence . . . was estimated to be only 0.29%" (Ashley et al. 1990). The authors of this report concluded that relocation of scattered isolates to a smaller number of relatively safe sanctuaries should be seriously considered as an option for increasing the survival prospects of black rhinos.

Another example is that of the white rhinoceros, which exists in Africa in two subspecies, the Southern (*Ceratotherium simum simum*) and the Northern (*C. s. cottoni*), which exists as a single population of less than 30 individuals in Zaire (Smith and Smith 1991). These two taxa have been completely separate during historic times, and a preliminary analysis using molecular data suggests a separation of less than 2 million years (George et al. 1991). Despite heroic efforts, one may wonder if recovery of the Northern subspecies from such a small population base, even if given adequate protection, is likely. This case has significance for captive efforts, since about a dozen Northern whites are currently maintained in zoos at Dvur Králové in eastern Europe, and at the San Diego Wild Animal Park (Svitalsky et al. 1991). Despite the decision to propagate the Northern subspecies as a separate entity, no births in captivity have occurred since 1989.

These examples are of interest as commentary on how we use data on biological diversity in making decisions about ex situ propagation. It appears that the investigative process leads inevitably to the separate perpetuation of modestly variant entities, never to their merger. In some cases, separate propagation can be pursued only through inbreeding of small numbers of founders, at great material cost. It seems appropriate to ask at what point and by what criteria do we finally conclude that conservation is best served by merging the miniscule fragments of once abundant and interbreeding populations into a single, more viable entity. When, in other words, do we conclude that no amount of data collection will be of any consequence because other factors tell us it is already too late? Given that hybridization is a natural process (Vrijenhoek 1995), must we invariably cling to concepts that would be reasonable only were we living in a more pristine world?

If the confirmation of even small amounts of intrapopulation variation consistently commits us to its preservation, we exacerbate the problem of overtaxed resources for ex situ efforts. The findings on the black rhinoceros are instructive because, apparently, this is a rare and perhaps initial instance of a recommendation

**TABLE 2.   Subspecies of the African Black Rhinoceros (*Diceros bicornis*)**

| Subspecies | Provenance | Population Size |
|---|---|---|
| *D. b. ladoensis* | Kenya, Uganda, Sudan | 0 (?) |
| *D. b. brucii* | Ethiopia, Somalia | 0 (?) |
| *D. b. longipes* | Cameroon, Chad (?) | 0 (?) |
| *D. b. chobiensis* | Angola | <100 |
| *D. b. bicornis* | Namibia | <100 |
| *D. b. machaeli* | Kenya, Tanzania | 500–1000 |
| *D. b. minor* | Kenya to South Africa | 2500 |

SOURCES:  Groves (1967); Ashley et al. (1990).

that fragmented wild populations be merged into a smaller number of more viable entities. Such advocacies do not discount the importance of intrapopulation diversity but rather question how that information can best be applied, including the captive sector, in a world where conservationists' options are in decline.

## Cheetahs

The cheetah (*Acinonyx jubatus*) affords an example of a species said to have unusual potential for benefitting from the application of biotechnological advances. Cheetahs have achieved a certain notoriety as having unusually low genetic diversity (O'Brien et al. 1983). In a summary article covering several lines of investigation, O'Brien et al. (1986) stated that skin transplants between unrelated cheetahs were not rejected, even though those between cheetahs and domestic cats were, and that on the basis of electrophoretic analysis of blood proteins cheetahs apparently passed through a major population bottleneck perhaps 10,000 years ago, resulting in contemporary cheetahs that are as similar as "inbred strains of laboratory mice" (see Merola 1994 for an opposing view). Cheetahs were further characterized as being highly susceptible to disease, especially viral infections that produce only modest levels of mortality in other exotic felids, and as being under threat of extinction from the combined burdens of high infant mortality and low reproductive rates. The documentation of poor quality sperm, particularly the occurrence of high rates of teratospermia in samples collected by electroejaculation (Wildt et al. 1983), led to the positing of a linkage between low genetic diversity (inbreeding), reproductive failure in captivity, and decline of the species in the wild (O'Brien et al. 1986). Cheetahs have long had a reputation for being difficult to breed in captivity. Marker and O'Brien (1989) drew upon studbook records to show that of approximately 200 individuals alive at the end of 1985, less than 20% had ever reproduced. Their analysis, although failing to identify the basis for the cheetah's poor reproductive performance in captivity, led them to speculate that genetic homogeneity was the primary cause.

Following on these reports, the North American cheetah SSP approved a series of investigations into reproductive physiology, behavior, genetics, and disease problems. A widely held belief was that further sampling would demonstrate a positive correlation between poor sperm quality and low male fertility. Females, similarly, would be subjected to a battery of tests, including visual scrutiny of reproductive organs (laparoscopy), hormonal challenge, and blood chemistry analysis, designed to separate the breeders from the nonbreeders. Completion of this work failed to demonstrate the predicted correlations (Wildt et al. 1993) and left unresolved the relationship of purported genetic deficiencies to poor reproductive performance. One response to these results was to advocate the broader application of high technology programs such as artificial insemination, in vitro fertilization, and embryo transfer as ways of overcoming the cheetah's failure to reproduce naturally.

A competing hypothesis is that husbandry factors rather than inherent defects in the animals themselves, namely, management deficiencies (Lindburg et al. 1993, 1994; Lindburg and Millard 1997), would better explain the failure of ex situ propagation efforts. A factor that received only limited attention was the purported reticence of males to engage in mating activity when in the presence of estrous females. Anecdotal information on these motivational deficiencies led to hormonal screenings of testosterone levels in an unsuccessful attempt to identify the cause of males' sexual lassitude (see Wildt et al. 1983, 1993).

In 1981, I was unexpectedly handed the task of resolving breeding problems in the cheetah population being maintained at the San Diego Wild Animal Park. An early discovery was that a high frequency of nonconceptive matings, as would be predicted if males of the species were in fact subfertile, did not occur. In addition, it appeared that if given the opportunity to investigate olfactorily the living quarters of estrous females prior to pairing for mating, the libidos of cheetah males were unquestionably intact. After approximately 10 years of effort, it was shown that despite species-typical levels of teratospermia (c. 70%), 10 of 12 males in the San Diego sample produced offspring (Lindburg et al. 1993). Further experimentation with intersexual communication provided documentation of the importance of allowing males to become behaviorally primed for mating through olfactory stimulation before being directly exposed to estrous females (Lindburg and Fitch-Snyder 1994; Lindburg and Millard 1997). Stated another way, the deficient libidos of cheetah males were found to be entirely attributable to management regimes that failed to provide for activation of the sensory modality used by cheetahs to detect the receptive state of females.

In retrospect, it now appears that the early focus on male inadequacies was focused on the wrong sex. It remains the case that the majority of cheetah females fail to experience spontaneous episodes of estrus, but only in the captive population. The alacrity with which females in wild habitat reproduce (Laurenson et al. 1993) leaves little doubt that some condition in captivity is having a suppressing effect on females' reproductive physiology. Studies underway that utilize fecally derived reproductive and stress hormones to measure physiological function under varied social and physical arrangements hold promise of resolving this issue (Czekala et al. 1994; Jurke et al. 1997). Thus biotechnology may yet play a significant role in ex situ efforts, but not to overcome inherent defects in the animals themselves, as originally posited.

## Lion-Tailed Macaques

A final illustration of salient management issues in ex situ propagation is provided by the lion-tailed macaque (*Macaca silenus*), an endangered monkey native to the tropical rain forests of southern India. Believed to number under 5000 surviving in the wild, this species, never numerous, has been a longtime favorite of zoos for exhibition. In contrast to cheetahs, lion-tails in recent decades have had no difficulty reproducing in captivity (Lindburg and Forney 1992). A doubling of the size of the North American population between 1979 and 1988 has produced numbers in excess of the zoo space available for the species, necessitating the implementation of measures to reduce the rate of reproduction (Lindburg and Gledhill, 1992).

Demographic analysis of the North American population by the author in 1989, in connection with the preparation of a species' master plan, revealed a total of 243 lion-tails distributed among 24 institutions in numbers ranging from 2 to 37. As can be seen from Figure 1, 75% of the participating institutions held collections averaging about 6 individuals, including 10 to 15 fully adult males that were being singly housed to preclude intermale aggression. This distribution may be said to reflect historical accident, space limitations, and institutional preferences more so than awareness of and interest in species' well-being. In the distribution shown in Figure 1, the largest social group was found to be 16 individuals, but when adjusted for the singly housed adult males, group size in the majority of zoos averaged about 5 individuals. This compares with a mean size of 20.8 individuals per group for 8 multimale groups censused by Kumar (1987) over 4 to 5 years in a south Indian rain forest. Kumar's data further revealed that wild living groups contained, on the average, 9.6 immature individuals.

A concern arising from maintenance of a captive population with atypical, that is, overly small, social units is that some offspring would inevitably have limited contact with peers during early development. It is well known that peer deprivation leads to a degree of developmental retardation in other macaques (see Mitchell 1970 for a review), and the presence of several older but behaviorally deficient males in the existing population may be the legacy of a time when many zoos engaged in the "postage-stamp" approach to exhibitry, that is, built their programs around a single adult pair. Although groups today may be somewhat larger than in the past, social units that remain overly small may yet contribute to developmental deficiencies.

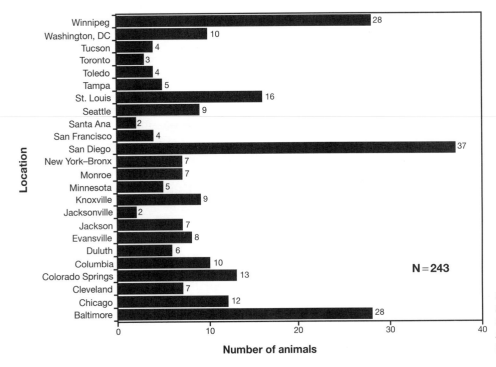

FIGURE 1. Master plan document indicating the distribution of lion-tailed macaques across 24 North American zoo collections in 1989.

Concern with adequate socialization is exacerbated by the need to contracept a portion of the existing breeders in order to limit population growth. This requirement leads to the selection, on an annual basis, of about 20 genetically least represented females, distributed over as many as 11 or 12 institutions, for breeding. Allowing for infant mortality and for emphasis on breeding those females whose high priority ranking genetically ensues from past failure to contribute to the gene pool, it is expected that only about 10 offspring born in a given year will themselves reach reproductive age (see Table 3). It follows, therefore, that a number of zoos are designated to have no reproduction in certain years, whereas the majority of those assigned breeding will have only single immatures in a given age cohort. Alleviation of this problem can be realized only through a redistribution of the species across institutions. Because overall population size is limited by available spaces to about 200 individuals, fewer collections with larger groupings in each would reduce the probabilities of single-offspring rearing. This requirement in turn mandates the construction of more spacious exhibits and attendant support facilities than zoos have traditionally allocated to individual species.

A final factor in enlightened management of lion-tails concerns the movement of breeders between institutions in order to fulfill genetic objectives. As earlier noted, gene flow between collections can be realized only through the exchange of individuals. Given the intensely social and highly xenophobic nature of macaques, including lion-tails, it should be readily apparent that management of gene flow cannot be achieved in the same fashion as for tigers or elands. Introduction of a newly arrived female lion-tail into an established group carries high probability of failure, perhaps even mortal wounding. In addition, the translocation of females contributes to periodic social upheaval and to the fostering of groups lacking the matrilineal structure known to be characteristic of this macaque (Birky 1993). Alternatively, movement of breeder males between institutions emulates the process by which gene flow occurs in nature, and is a less traumatic and more socially preferable way of addressing genetic requirements in the captive population (see Lindburg et al. 1997).

**TABLE 3. Annually Sanctioned Reproduction for Lion-Tailed Macaque Females in Relation to Available Space in North American Zoos**

| | |
|---|---:|
| Number of available spaces | 200 |
| Annual recruitment rate (births) needed to maintain steady state | 10 |
| Number of females designated to breed annually, to offset reproductive failures estimated at 50% | 20 |

Without question, genetic management has been the driving force in devising survival plans for zoo-living animals (Foose et al. 1985; Read and Harvey 1986). Only recently have social requirements begun to receive the attention they deserve (Hutchins and Wiese 1991; Thompson 1993). As the lion-tailed macaque example indicates, the management of highly social primates requires a significant departure from the ways in which zoos have maintained their collections in the past. Improved conditions for socialization and reduction in trauma related to interinstitutional exchanges are but two of the more obvious adjustments needed. It seems likely that further benefits in the form of increased expression of species-typical behaviors and psychologically enhanced living will follow from management plans that are sensitive to the unique requirements of individual species.

## CONCLUSIONS

What are the lessons to be drawn from these experiences that will be of benefit to ex situ conservation efforts?

Additional information on the status of wild populations that are today represented in the captive sector would serve a number of purposes. Census and demographic data would assist in focusing efforts, a point that can be made by considering members of the genus *Macaca*. Species such as *M. pagensis, M. ochreata, M. thibetana,* and *M. cyclopis* all have populations in captivity but not as parts of widely supported preservation efforts. Information leading to the reclassification of such forms in terms of endangerment would help to foster such efforts.

Increased understanding of the extent and distribution of intraspecific diversity would give guidance to decision making in the captive sector. If we can say that we have been truly enlightened by the studies of diversity in tigers or rhinoceroses, then how might such efforts with these and other species, both in captive and wild settings, be illuminating? Although many conservationists shrink from advocating the hybridization of modestly varying entities, lack of knowledge in the past on the provenance of zoo animals or intraspecies diversity may already have led to the creation of *generic* captive populations. In the absence of genetic assessments of the wild population of lion-tailed macaques, for example, or of the origin point of captured individuals during several decades of importation to Western zoos, we may have representatives of but a small portion of the gene pool in captivity or a homogenized lion-tail that is the result of years of randomized breeding.

There is also the need for more rationally determined allocations of space for ex situ propagation. On the one hand, we have noted cases in which the treatment of captive populations as a single breeding population, regardless of subspecific designations, would be a more judicious use of limited resources. In some instances, however, biopolitical considerations may be relevant. In a related vein, the reassignment of space now held by animals having admitted educational and entertainment value to those most in need of captive propagation may be required. This reallocation should include the reevaluation of efforts to house and propagate genetic novelties such as white tigers.

Finally, the need for more scientifically based management programs is urgent. Zoos today are in many ways prisoners of their pasts, placing local interests ahead of species' welfare, or lacking in comprehension of the diversity of nature, on the one hand, and the creation of viable living environments in captivity, on the other. As earlier noted, some of the best minds in the fields of molecular and population genetics have been utilized in the formulation of captive management plans, whereas the expertise from other academically relevant disciplines remains largely untapped and unheeded.

## LITERATURE CITED

Ashley, M. V., Melnick, D. J., and Western, D. (1990). Conservation genetics of the black rhinoceros (*Diceros bicornis*). I. Evidence from the mitochondrial DNA of three populations. *Cons. Biol. 4: 71–77.*

Beck, B. B., Rapaport, L. G., Stanley Price, M. R., and Wilson, A. C. (1994). Reintroduction of captive-born animals. In P. J. S. Olney, G. M. Mace, and A. T. C. Feistner (eds.), *Creative Conservation: Interactive Management of Wild and Captive Animals.* London: Chapman & Hall, pp. 265–286.

Benirschke, K. (1986). *Primates: The Road to Self-Sustaining Populations.* New York: Springer-Verlag.

Benirschke, K., and Kumamoto, A. (1991). Mammalian cytogenetics and conservation of species. *J. Hered. 82: 187–191.*

Birky, W. A. (1993). *Female-Female Social Relationships in a Captive Group of Lion-Tailed Macaques (Macaca silenus).* MSc. thesis, California State University, Northridge.

Boyd, L. J., ed. (1994). *Zoological Parks and Aquariums in the Americas, 1994–1995.* Bethesda, MD: American Zoo and Aquarium Association.

Cherfas, J. (1984). *Zoo 2000: A Look Beyond the Bars.* London: British Broadcasting Corporation.

Conway, W. (1985). *The SSP Subspecies Dilemma: A Report of an Exploratory Meeting of the AAZPA Species Survival Plan Subcommittee (SSPC) of the Wildlife Management and Conservation Committee.* Ogleby Park, WV: American Association of Zoological Parks and Aquariums.

Conway, W. (1986). The practical difficulties and financial implications of endangered species breeding programs. *Int. Zoo Yb. 24/25: 210–219.*

Conway, W. (1989). The prospects for sustaining species and their evolution. In D. Western and M. C. Pearl (eds.), *Conservation for the Twenty-first Century.* New York: Oxford University Press, pp. 199–209.

Czekala, N. M., Durrant, B. S., Callison, L., Williams, M., and Millard, S. (1994). Fecal steroid hormone analysis as an indicator of reproductive function in the cheetah. *Zoo Biol. 13: 119–128.*

De Blieu, J. (1991). *Meant to Be Wild: The Struggle to Save Endangered Species Through Captive Breeding.* Golden, CO: Fulcrum.

Ellis, D. H., and Serafin, J. A. (1977). A research program for the endangered masked bobwhite. *Wd. Pheasant Assoc. J. 2: 16–33.*

Foose, T. J., Seal, U. S., and Flesness, N. R. (1985). Conserving animal genetic resources. *IUCN Bull. 16: 20–21.*

George, M. Jr., Chemnick, L. G., Cisova, D., Gabrisova, E., Stratil, A., and Ryder, O. A. (1991). Genetic differentiation of white rhinoceros subspecies: Diagnostic differences in mitochondrial DNA and serum proteins. In O. A. Ryder (ed.), *Rhinoceros Biology and Conservation: Proceedings of an International Conference.* San Diego, CA: Zoological Society of San Diego, pp. 105–113.

Griffith, B., Scott, J. M., Carpenter, J. W., and Reed, C. (1989). Translocation as a species conservation tool: Status and strategy. *Science 245: 477–480.*

Groves, C. P. (1967). Geographic variation in the black rhinoceros *Diceros bicornis* (L., 1758). *Z. Saugtierkunde 32: 267–276.*

Hemmer, H. (1987). The phylogeny of the tiger (*Panthera tigris*). In R. L. Tilson and U. S. Seal (eds.), *Tigers of the World: The Biology, Biopolitics, Management, and Conservation of an Endangered Species.* Park Ridge, NJ: Noyes, pp. 28–35.

Herrington, S. J. (1987). Subspecies and the conservation of *Panthera tigris:* Preserving genetic heterogeneity. In R. L. Tilson and U. S. Seal (eds.), *Tigers of the World: The Biology, Biopolitics, Management, and Conservation of an Endangered Species.* Park Ridge, NJ: Noyes, pp. 51–61.

Hutchins, M., and Wiese, R. J. (1991). Beyond genetic and demographic management: The future of the Species Survival Plan and related AAZPA conservation efforts. *Zoo Biol. 10: 285–292.*

Hutchins, M., Willis, K., and Wiese, R. J. (1995). Strategic collection planning: Theory and practice. *Zoo Biol. 14: 5–25.*

Joslin, P. (1986). *Distinguishing Characteristics of the Asiatic Lion (Panthera leo persica) and Its Distribution Within Historical Time.* Chicago: Chicago Zoological Society.

Jurke, M. H., Czekala, N. M., Lindburg, D. G., and Millard, S. E. (1997). Fecal corticoid metabolite measurement in the cheetah (*Acinonyx jubatus*). Zoo Biol. 16: 133–147.

Karanth, U. K. (1992). Conservation prospects for lion-tailed macaques in Karnataka, India. *Zoo Biol. 11: 33–41.*

Krishne Gowda, C. D. (1983). Racing to extinction. *Gnu's Letter 1: 18–22.*

Kumar, A. (1987). *The Ecology and Population Dynamics of the Lion-Tailed Macaque (Macaca silenus) in South India.* Ph.D. dissertation, Cambridge University.

Lacy, R. (1995). Culling surplus animals for population management. In B. G. Norton, M. Hutchins, E. F. Stevens and T. L. Maple (eds.), *Ethics on the Ark: Zoos, Animal Welfare, and Wildlife Conservation.* Washington, DC: Smithsonian Institution Press, pp. 187–194.

Lasley, B. L., and Anderson, G. B. (1991). Where does biotechnology fit in captive breeding programs? *Zoo Biol. 10: 195–196.*

Laurenson, M. K., Caro, T. M., and Borner, M. (1993). Female cheetah reproduction. *Natl. Geogr. Res. Explor. 8: 64–75.*

Lindburg, D. G. (1991). Zoos and the "surplus" problem. *Zoo Biol. 10: 1–2.*

Lindburg, D. G. (1998). Enrichment of captive mammals through provisioning. In D. Shepherdson, J. Mellen, and M. Hutchins (eds.), *Second Nature: Environmental Enrichment for Captive Animals.* Washington, DC: Smithsonian Institution Press, pp. 262–276.

Lindburg, D. G., Durrant, B. S., Millard, S. E., and Oosterhuis, J. (1993). Fertility assessment of cheetah males with poor quality semen. *Zoo Biol. 12: 97–103.*

Lindburg, D. G., and Fitch-Snyder, H. (1994). Use of behavior to evaluate reproductive problems in captive mammals. *Zoo Biol. 13: 433–445.*

Lindburg, D. G., and Forney, K. A. (1992). Long-term studies of captive lion-tailed macaques. *Primate Rep. 32:* 133–142.

Lindburg, D. G., and Gledhill, L. (1992). Captive breeding and conservation of lion-tailed macaques. *End. Species Update 10*(1): 1–4, 10.

Lindburg, D. G., Iaderosa, J., and Gledhill, L. (1997). Steady-state propagation of captive lion-tailed macaques in North American zoos: A conservation strategy. In *Primate Conservation: The Role of Zoological Parks,* Janette Wallis (ed.), American Society of Primatologists, Special Topics in Primatology, Vol. 1, pp. 131–149.

Lindburg, D. G., and Lindburg, L. L. (1995). Success breeds a quandary: To cull or not to cull. In B. G. Norton, M. Hutchins, E. F. Stevens, and T. L Maple (eds.), *Ethics on the Ark: Zoos, Animal Welfare, and Wildlife Conservation.* Washington, DC: Smithsonian Institution Press, pp. 195–208.

Lindburg, D. G., and Millard, S. E. (1997). Behavioral issues in reproductive management of cheetahs, with implications for the giant panda. *Proc. Second Int. Conf. Env. Enrich.* Copenhagen: Copenhagen Zoo, pp. 251–259.

Maguire, L. A., and Lacy, R. C. (1990). Allocating scarce resources for conservation of endangered species: Partitioning zoo space for tigers. *Cons. Biol. 4:* 157–166.

Marker, L., and O'Brien, S. J. (1989). Captive breeding of the cheetah (*Acinonyx jubatus*) in North American zoos (1871–1986). *Zoo Biol. 8:* 13–16.

Merola, M. (1994). A reassessment of homozygosity and the case for inbreeding depression in the cheetah, *Acinonyx jubatus:* Implications for conservation. *Cons. Biol. 8:* 961–971.

Mitchell, G. (1970). Abnormal behavior in primates. In L. A. Rosenblum (ed.), *Primate Behavior: Developments in Field and Laboratory Research,* Vol. 1. New York: Academic Press, pp. 195–249.

Myers, N. (1987). The extinction spasm impending: Synergisms at work. *Cons. Biol. 1:* 14–21.

Norton, B. G., Hutchins, M., Stevens, E. F., and Maple, T. E., eds. (1995). *Ethics on the Ark: Zoos, Animal Welfare, and Wildlife Conservation.* Washington, DC: Smithsonian Institution Press.

O'Brien, S. J., Collier, G. E., Benveniste, R. E., Nash, W. G., Newman, A. K., Simonson, J. M., Eichelberger, M. A., Seal, U. S., Bush, M., and Wildt, D. E. (1987a). Setting the molecular clock in Felidae: The great cats, *Panthera.* In R. L. Tilson and U. S. Seal (eds.), *Tigers of the World: The Biology, Biopolitics, Management, and Conservation of an Endangered Species.* Park Ridge, NJ: Noyes, pp. 10–27.

O'Brien, S. J., Joslin, P., Smith, G. L. III, Wolfe, R., Schaffer, N., Heath, E., Ott-Joslin, J., Rawal, P. P., Bhattacharjee, K. K., and Martenson, J. S. (1987b). Evidence for African origins of founders of the Asiatic lion Species Survival Plan. *Zoo Biol. 6:* 99–116.

O'Brien, S. J., Martenson, J. S., Packer, C., Herbst, L., de Vos, V., Joslin, P., Ott-Joslin, J., Wildt, D. E., and Bush, M. (1987c). Biochemical genetic variation in geographic isolates of African and Asiatic lions. *Natl. Geog. Res. 3:* 114–124.

O'Brien, S. J., Wildt, D. E., and Bush, M. (1986). The cheetah in genetic peril. *Sci. Amer. 254:* 84–92.

O'Brien, S. J., Wildt, D. E., Goldman, D., Merril, C. R., and Bush, M. (1983). The cheetah is depauperate in genetic variation. *Science 221:* 459–462.

Read, A. F., and Harvey, P. H. (1986). Genetic management in zoos. *Nature 322:* 408–410.

Reid, W. V., and Miller, K. R. (1989). *Keeping Options Alive: The Scientific Basis for Conserving Biodiversity.* Washington, DC: World Resources Institute.

Ryder, O. A. (1986). Species conservation and systematics: The dilemma of subspecies. *Trends Ecol. Evol. 1:* 9–10.

Seuánez, H. M., Evans, H. J., Martin, D. E., and Fletcher, J. (1979). An inversion in chromosome 2 that distinguishes between Bornean and Sumatran orangutans. *Cytogen. Cell Gen. 23:* 137–140.

Smith, K., and Smith, F. (1991). Conserving rhinos in Garamba National Park. In O. A. Ryder (ed.), *Rhinoceros Biology and Conservation: Proceedings of an International Conference.* San Diego, CA: Zoological Society of San Diego, pp. 166–177.

Soulé, M. E. (1986). Conservation biology and the "real world." In M. E. Soulé (ed.), *Conservation Biology: The Science of Scarcity and Diversity.* Sunderland, MA: Sinauer Associates, pp. 1–12.

Soulé, M. E., Gilpin, M., Conway, W., and Foose, T. (1986). The millennium ark: How long a voyage, how many staterooms, how many passengers? *Zoo Biol. 5:* 101–113.

Stover, J., Evans, J., and Dolensek, E. P. (1981). Inter species embryo transfer from the gaur to domestic Holstein. *Ann. Proc. Amer. Assoc. Zoo Vets. 1981:* 122–124.

Strum, S. C., and Southwick, C. H. (1986). Translocation of primates. In K. Benirschke (ed.), *Primates: The Road to Self-Sustaining Populations.* New York: Springer-Verlag, pp. 949–957.

Svitalsky, M., Vahala, J., and Spala, P. (1991). Breeding experience with Northern white rhino (*Ceratotherium simum cottoni*) at Dvur Králové. In O. A. Ryder (ed.), *Rhinoceros Biology and Conservation: Proceedings of an International Conference.* San Diego, CA: Zoological Society of San Diego, pp. 282–286.

Thompson, S. (1993). Zoo research and conservation: Beyond sperm and eggs toward the science of animal management. *Zoo Biol. 12:* 155–159.

Toone, W. D., and Risser, A. C., Jr. (1988). Captive management of the California condor. *Int. Zoo Yb. 27:* 50–58.

Toone, W. D., and Wallace, M. P. (1994). The extinction in the wild and reintroduction of the California condor (*Gymnogyps californianus*). In P. J. S. Olney, G. M. Mace, and A. T. C. Feistner (eds.), *Creative Conservation: Interactive Management of Wild and Captive Animals.* London: Chapman & Hall, pp. 411–419.

Vrijenhoek, R. (1995). Natural processes, individuals, and units of conservation. In B. G. Norton, M. Hutchins, E. F. Stevens, and T. L. Maple (eds.), *Ethics on the Ark: Zoos, Animal Welfare, and Wildlife Conservation.* Washington, DC: Smithsonian Institution Press, pp. 74–92.

Western, D. (1989). Population, resources, and environment in the twenty-first century. In D. Western and M. C. Pearl (eds.), *Conservation for the Twenty-first Century.* New York: Oxford University Press, pp. 11–25.

Western, D., and Pearl, M. C. (eds.) (1989). *Conservation for the Twenty-first Century.* New York: Oxford University Press.

Wildt, D. E., Bush, M., Howard, J. G., O'Brien, S. J., Meltzer, D., Van Dyk, A., Ebedes, H., and Brand, D. J. (1983). Unique seminal quality in the South African cheetah and a comparative evaluation in the domestic cat. *Biol. Reprod. 29:* 1019–1025.

Wildt, D. E., Brown, J. L., Bush, M., Barone, M. A., Cooper, K. A., Grisham, J., and Howard, J. G. (1993). Reproductive status of cheetahs (*Acinonyx jubatus*) in North American zoos. *Zoo Biol. 12:* 45–80.

Wildt, D. E., Monfort, S. L., Donoghue, A. M., Johnston, L. A., and Howard, J. G. (1992). Embryogenesis in conservation biology—or, how to make an endangered species embryo. *Thereoginol. 37:* 161–184.

Wilson, E. O. (1985). The biological diversity crisis. *BioSci. 35:* 700–706.

*Anthropology dawned on Washburn "as a pleasant surprise." In this paper he recounts his first and subsequent encounters with issues and with the important people in the field during his career. Along the way we see the evolution of the man and his simultaneous progress in physical anthropology. From retirement he offers his suggestions about how to teach a course on human evolution today, revising the usual class structure to reflect what we know that we didn't know before and what we don't know that we thought we knew.*

# 20 Evolution of a Teacher

**Sherwood L. Washburn**  *Department of Anthropology, University of California, Berkeley*

Anthropology dawned on me as a pleasant surprise. I had never heard of it before going to college, and I only took an introductory course because it was taught by Professor Tozzer. He was my freshman adviser and an old friend of my family. Here was a mixture of biological evolution, archaeology, and cultural anthropology which appealed to me. At that time I had been considering majoring in zoology and, possibly, going to medical school, but I quickly changed the plan to a major in anthropology with the idea of choosing a career later on. I never went back to the earlier plans.

During vacations from school I had done volunteer work in the Harvard Museum of Comparative Zoology for which eventually I was paid 25 cents an hour. This was the depth of the Great Depression, and any pay was appreciated. Although my major was anthropology, friends in the MCZ were very important in my life. Glover Allen, then Curator of Mammals, not only supervised my first job and advised me over many years, but finally served on my oral examinations. I took his course on mammals and wrote my undergraduate honors thesis in his department. Barbara Lawrence, Allen's assistant and later successor, was a great help, guiding me through the problems of classification. The Director of the MCZ, Thomas Barbour, was an encouraging friend, and Harold Coolidge helped me and later included me in his research plans. I stress this network of old friends in the Museum because over a number of years they provided guidance and escape from a number of anthropological errors which were common at that time.

*Annual Review of Anthropology* 12 (1983): 1–24. Copyright © 1983 by Annual Reviews, Inc. All rights reserved.

The late E. A. Hooton was my principal professor and his teaching strongly influenced my interests. *Up From the Ape* was the bible for physical anthropologists for a number of years, and that, plus the one-year laboratory course, formed the basis of the physical anthropology program. People have often asked me about Hooton and about the reasons for his success as a teacher. Hooton was enthusiastic, imaginative, and helpful. These qualities, plus his sense of humor, came across very clearly in the introductory course. The advanced laboratory course had only 10 to 12 people, so we got to know Hooton very well. He was an impressive person. I think his students were lucky people. They could not have received a better education in physical anthropology at that time, the 1930s. The great breadth of his interests can be seen in his popular books, or even by just glancing at the table of contents in *Up From the Ape*.

But the 1930s were a time of great change in the study of evolution. Genetics had begun to exert a profound influence on the way scientists looked at evolution, and problems and methods changed radically with the events which led to the synthetic theory. Hooton's research methods, unfortunately, were not compatible with genetics. All of Hooton's major studies depended on the statistical validation of typologies and his advanced teaching was simply incorrect. Hooton thought that he was right and that it was bias, particularly in social science, which led people to reject his views. He stated that his popular books and articles were designed to skip the professionals and reach the intelligent layman. Naturally, he was particularly upset when some of his own students disagreed with his conclusions and the methods on which they were based. Hooton believed that the world's problems were fundamentally biological, and that improvement would only come when the breeding of the biologically inferior was controlled. He considered the environment, but minimized its importance. These views, coupled with the concept of pure races (Nordic, for example) in the 1930s and 40s led to severe criticism, and it was very difficult for many to see that a Hooton student might appreciate his undergraduate teaching, his support of evolutionary studies, and his interest in behavior, but repudiate his concept of race, research methods, and his applications of physical anthropology.

I have always been grateful that my background in the Museum of Comparative Zoology helped me to appreciate the best of Hooton but stay removed from his research methods and some conclusions. The complications of being a Hooton student are well illustrated by my first meeting with Theodosius Dobzhansky. When I dropped in on him at Columbia he asked me if I was not a Hooton student. "Yes," I replied. He then said, "I do not understand the method of finding several racial types in one population." I answered that "I do not believe in types and think that it is populations which should be compared." He beamed, shook my hand, and there began a very pleasant friendship.

My first graduate year was highlighted by courses in comparative anatomy and paleontology with A. S. Romer. The efficiency with which he managed human evolution without biometry impressed me and reinforced an uneasy feeling that there was very little communication among anthropology, paleontology, and zoology. Starting in the summer of 1936, a series of events ensued which laid the background for my scientific career. Harold Coolidge had planned an expedition to Thailand to make collections for the Museum of Comparative Zoology. Several people were involved, but as far as I was concerned, the principals were A. H. Schultz to collect primates and C. R. Carpenter to study primate behavior. In both cases gibbons were the main objectives, and Coolidge invited me to assist Schultz and Carpenter. Needless to say, I was eager to go and a Sheldon Traveling Fellowship made it possible to accept. But the participants were not meeting until 1937 in Singapore, and I had six months in the summer and fall which were spent studying human anatomy at Michigan and Oxford. As it worked out, the plan could not have been better.

At Michigan the medical anatomy class met at 8 in the morning for a lecture and then worked in the laboratory until 5 in the afternoon. The work was traditional and intensive with excellent laboratory assistants. One of them, W. T. Dempster, was very interested in locomotion and the work of some of the German anatomists. He explained to me how the body works, and showed me how it was necessary to combine an understanding of the joints with the lengths of the bones to produce the functional system. Here was the key to the limitations of biometry—no joints—but also the way to relate it to a vastly broader functional anatomy. Laboratory teaching basically gives the time for what amounts to individual tutorials, and Dempster checked the dissections and then showed how the meaning of what was seen depended on a broad understanding, a philosophy of anatomy.

After the summer at Michigan I went to Oxford as a special student for the fall quarter. LeGros Clark's lectures were superb. He combined the information usually taught in several different courses and gave elegant lectures which were polished essays. He liked to take long walks on weekends, discussing whatever was on his mind. He asked me to accompany him on some, and we had many discussions on these and over tea. He saw evolution as changes in patterns, and he believed that much of the confusion in the study of human evolution came from reliance on isolated "facts." The patterns came from experience and intuition, and Clark never made it clear how one knows where a pattern begins and ends. It was the intuitive element that left Clark's evolutionary conclusions open to Zuckerman's attacks. A medical student and I helped in one of Zuckerman's endocrine projects, and Zuckerman gave me monkey material to dissect. This enabled me to make comparisons with the humans in the laboratory, but overwhelmingly the most important part of my few weeks at Oxford was becoming acquainted with the personality and lectures of LeGros Clark.

After Oxford I spent a month in Ceylon making a small collection for the MCZ, then on to Singapore where Coolidge's expedition was gathering. In a few weeks we were all camped on a mountain in northern Thailand. Coolidge's plans were excellent and the hunters he had hired and local people brought in gibbons almost daily. Schultz would measure and record any point of special interest. My job, preparation of the skeletons, enabled me to spend almost every day dissecting, and gave me the great opportunity of having unlimited, unembalmed material to study. Every day was a seminar with Schultz, supplemented by applying Dempster's ideas and LeGros Clark's notion on the importance of patterns. I worked very rapidly, stressing one part on one gibbon and a different area on another. Monkeys were not at all common in the vicinity, but a few were collected, and I could compare them with the gibbons. How human the gibbons appeared! In point after point human and gibbons were basically the same and very different from the monkeys. My experience was essentially the same as that of Sir Arthur Keith, and the conclusions were the same.

Carpenter found that it was impossible to study behavior from the same camp used for the collecting. He moved to an area some miles away where gibbons were even more abundant. I spent a few weeks making observations for Carpenter. The gibbons, hanging-feeding, walking bipedally on big limbs and swinging under smaller ones, and diving from one tree to the next gave a vivid view of their anatomy in action. It also contrasted with the quadrupedal monkeys progressing through the same tree. The social behavior of the gibbons, each group consisting of a female-male pair and their young, contrasted with the much larger groups of langurs and macaques in the same area. In a very short time Carpenter had collected the information for his monograph on gibbon behavior. Excellent visibility at the end of the dry season, the number of gibbons, and the simplicity of the social group all worked together so that the information for a major work could be collected in a short period of time.

Collections for the MCZ were completed in May and Coolidge, Schultz and I headed back to Singapore and then on to Borneo. It took a week from Singapore to Borneo, and the freight boat stopped nearly every day. The weather was beautiful and I spent my time on the deck reading Conrad's *Victory.* We stopped at many of the ports described in the book, and I found, much to my surprise, that the descriptions which I had assumed to be imaginative were almost photographic. British North Borneo was the last of the chartered companies, and one could still buy stock in it (although we were strongly advised not to do so). Coolidge had made arrangements for transportation to Abai on the Kinabatangan River. We brought materials with us and a small house was constructed in three days. The area was rich in primates. Every morning two or three hunters would leave at sunrise and return with three or four specimens by midmorning. Then Schultz would measure them and make notes. The notes were illustrated with pen and ink drawings of remarkable quality. He drew rapidly and beautifully, many of the figures in the notes being suitable for publication without alteration.

The work at Abai was much more intense than the earlier collecting in Thailand. Most of the time Schultz and I were the only scientists there, and we worked all day every day. I skinned and dissected specimens and supervised the local helpers who cleaned skeletons. The routine in the camp was always the same, but the hunters brought in proboscis monkeys, orangutans, two kinds of macaques and three kinds of leaf monkeys.

The opportunities for study were amazing, far more than I could fully utilize. We talked about almost nothing but anthropology. Adolph informed me on the problems of the field, and urged me to stick to problems of biometry, growth, and variation. I soon found that he had little interest in muscles, joints, or behavior. The remarkable variety of specimens gave me the opportunity of seeing what a master did superlatively well. It also made vivid the limitations of anthropometry.

Most unfortunately, Harold Coolidge had been ill, and so he could not take part in the Borneo collecting as he had planned. He did come to the Abai camp briefly and approved the collections soon to be headed for the MCZ. His approval was a relief to me because I thought that he might have wanted more general collecting rather than the emphasis on primates.

Schultz was very considerate of me, suggesting that there were plenty of problems with the small monkeys for a thesis for me while he wrote on the gibbons, orangutans, and proboscis monkeys. He was never critical, even when I grew a beard. Only when I shaved it off he remarked, "It is a great improvement." Adolph left camp a few weeks before I did. This had been planned all along, but it did come shortly after we had run out of gin. I'll never forget Adolph raising a glass of warm coconut milk and the last of the gin and saying, "Sherry, the best drink in the world is Drambuie!"

On arrival back in the USA I received a telegram asking me to be the teaching assistant in Professor Tozzer's introductory course. I was delighted, even though there were seven sections and a short quiz every week. One hundred and forty papers to correct! The teaching convinced me that that was what I wanted to do, and I found I learned far more teaching than I had as a student. One session I took the class to see the exhibits in the Museum of Comparative Zoology. I knew every one of those stuffed primates, and ended my demonstration saying that they did not have to remember them all but should get an idea of the variation. I heard a Radcliffe woman comment, "They all look just the same to me!" No truer words were ever spoken.

Finally the crates with all the Asiatic Primate Expedition specimens arrived. Each skeleton had to be cleaned. After a few tests Gabriel Lasker and I set up an assembly line for the macerations. At one time we had over 90 skeletons in various stages of preparation. The cleaning was routine and Lasker and I discussed anthropology constantly. He helped me to understand why the genetics of populations replaced typology, and the nature of Boas's contributions to biometry.

Lasker's experiences in China and his interests in genetics and migration ideally supplemented my background, and he clearly saw the social importance of anthropology. Our long discussions were an important part of my education, and helped later on in planning the Viking Fund summer seminars on physical anthropology.

In the fall of 1938, Dr. Hooton asked me to teach a course on primates. It was to be a joint course, but Hooton was very busy and turned the whole course over to me. Hooton and Coolidge came to all the lectures, and we used specimens from the MCZ. I stressed that all the major families of primates could be seen as adaptive radiations, but Hooton was sure that the families should be defined by nonadaptive characters. This was an issue we never settled. It has been reopened by the neutral theory and by evidence that changes at the molecular level occur at surprisingly constant rates.

S. R. Detwiler offered me a job in anatomy in his department at Columbia. It sounded fascinating, especially when Dr. Detwiler said the job would pay $2400. "Are you married?" he asked. "Yes." "Then I'll make it 25." What a contrast with all the searches and mechanics of hiring today! A recommendation from Dr. Wislocki of the Harvard Medical School, a word from Dr. Hooton, and Detwiler was free to act as he chose.

The Harvard years had been fun and useful, but I had a feeling that what I had been taught was already out of date. Surely anthropometry was much too limited a technique for functional or evolutionary problems. In thinking back (always a risky business), I discovered that the three books which influenced me most were Bridgman's *Logic of Modern Physics*, Ogden and Richards' *The Meaning of Meaning*, and Malinowski's *Argonauts of the Western Pacific*. Bridgman's operationalism gave clear guides to the relations of technique to analysis. Ogden and Richards helped one to see the nature of words and avoid at least some of the most common errors. Malinowski read like a great novel, after courses in which little was stressed beyond descriptions and distribution.

Today none of these have the impact they did many years ago. Times have changed but the basic issues have not. Biometry was designed to describe bones and its exclusive use brings the limitations of death to the study of the living. Words must stand for clearly defined referents. Human behavior cannot be reduced to trait lists.

The Columbia Medical School was a complete change from anything I had known before. The research on all sides convinced me that what I had learned was mostly out of date. The head of the anatomy department, Dr. Detwiler, was doing fascinating experiments on amphibian embryos. I asked him about the relation of the orbit and the eye. He replied, "Let's find out." So he put the eye of a large form into the developing orbit of a much smaller form. The eye displaced the orbital structures, making an orbit 140% of normal. What was to become hard bone was greatly influenced by the soft tissue, and I remembered LeGros Clark's remark that bone was, next to the blood, the most plastic tissue in the body. I wrote a paper, applying the results of the experiment to anthropological problems. Of course, it was turned down by the American Journal of Physical Anthropology. After some correspondence and considerable revision, it was accepted—but I had learned my lesson. Anyone trying to use experimental methods in anthropology was going to have a hard time.

At the time I thought that the basic issue was simple. I still think it is! The form of the traditional question in comparative anatomy or physical anthropology is: describe with words and measurement, compare and draw conclusions. Little attention is paid to what is being compared or to a discussion of the conclusions. While there was no doubt in Detwiler's study that the large species of salamanders had larger orbits, one could not tell how much this was the result of the form of the skull or how much the form of the skull was adapting to the size of the eyes. The experiments showed that the developing eyes were very important in determining the form of the orbit. Generalizing from this one case, the traditional form of comparisons was: describe, compare, and speculate. The modified form is: choose what is to be compared on the basis of some clearly defined important problem; compare; speculate; then devise experiments to determine the probability of the speculations. The main research effort should be in the experimental analysis.

Over the next few years at Columbia, I devised a series of experiments designed to help in understanding the factors which influence the form of the mammalian skull. Newborn rats are exceedingly immature and are readily available and inexpensive to maintain. I learned to operate through very small incisions using a dissecting microscope. The role of individual muscles, nerves, and bones was investigated, and it soon became apparent that the experiments revealed anatomical patterns. For example, removal of the temporal muscle altered the mandible, occlusion, temporal line, and nuchal crest. But these were described in different chapters of the standard anatomy textbooks. The results did not lend themselves to description, either bone by bone or area by area. The growth in a suture was not characteristic of a bone, but depended on the particular suture as well as on the adjacent bones and muscles. Early closure of the sagittal suture in human beings makes the skull grow long and changes the length, breadth, and height of the skull. In cases which cause extreme deformation, the neurosurgeon opens the suture by operation and the skull then returns to normal form.

The diagram gives a first approximation of the relatively independent areas of the jaw (Figure 1). It can be seen at once that the chin is the result of the core bone projecting farther forward than the tooth-supporting bone. This condition is characteristic of modern humans.

In people living on soft foods that do not cause wear on the teeth, the upper incisors bite over the lower ones and act like an orthodontist's band. This makes the chin more prominent. Male hormone stimulates the growth of the basic core bone and so accentuates the chin. The chin then is the result of a number of factors, including culture through the preparation of food. For the purposes of research, one must study the nature of face and jaw, not the chin.

Changes in form and function during growth frequently provide information closely paralleling what is obtained from experiments. Figure 2 shows the skull of a young baboon compared to that of an adult. Note that not only has the face grown larger, but it has changed in fundamental ways. The buttress of bone between the cheek bone and the tooth-supporting bone is above the first molar tooth in the juvenile and behind the third molar in the adult. As the face grows the relation of cheek bone and teeth changes from before first molar to after third molar, a distance of more than 5 centimeters.

In growth one sees not only the changing relations but sees that they are related to changes in the face. In

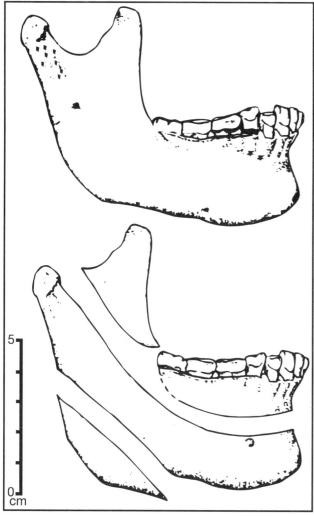

FIGURE 1.    The human lower jaw divided into some of its principal parts. These may vary remarkably independently. The basis for defining the parts depends on: experiments, growth, comparisons, and pathology.

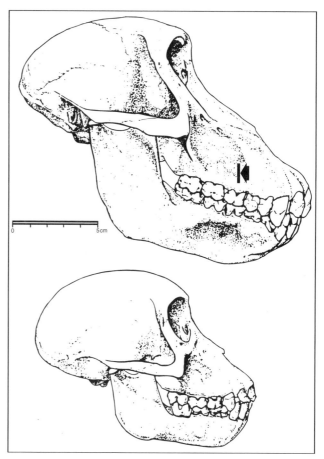

FIGURE 2.    Skulls of adult female and juvenile baboons. Note that the face migrates forward relative to the cheek bones. The cheek bone is over the first permanent molar in the juvenile and behind the third in the adult. The line and arrow mark where the cheek bone was when the adult was a juvenile. The canine fossa is full of developing teeth in the juvenile and become large in the adult. The same is the case for the mandibular fossa which is not present at all in the juvenile. There are no fixed points but only patterns of changing relations.

classification or the study of fossils, the relation of the buttress to a tooth is often taken as a "fact," something to use in classification, not as a symptom, something to be understood in terms of the pattern of growth of the face.

Also, the juvenile has a very small canine fossa, while the adult has a very large one, as shown in the figure. The fossa is caused by an area of very thin bone being surrounded by the buttress, alveolar bone, and thick bone, as noted in the figure. Presence or absence of a fossa is not an independent fact but the result of the relations of the main parts of the face. In the juvenile the developing teeth fill the area which will become thin bone later on.

The same principle may be seen in the lower jaw. In the juvenile the developing teeth fill the mandible. As they erupt and the tooth-supporting bone is separated from the core bone along the base of the mandible, the outer table of bone is resorbed and a fossa appears.

To generalize the situation, almost all the traditional anthropological measurements and observations are composite. Biometry is a science of symptoms, not of the biological factors that lie behind the symptoms and cause them.

All the measurements are composite, suitable for description but not analysis. For example, reduction in the size of the canine tooth may change the shape of the palate, of the jaw, of the nose, of muscles and their bony origins. If the reduction of the tooth is the result of aggressive behavior being based on tools rather than teeth, then much of the evolution of the human face is the result of culture.

This may seem obvious and it was not new, but the implications are profound. The words and measurements used in the study of human evolution are useful for preliminary description but not for analysis. The logic of traditional physical anthropology is: describe with words and measurements, compare, and draw conclusions. The operations are so simple that anyone can learn them in a few hours, and no knowledge of modern biology is required. A different way of looking at the situation is that the descriptions result in a set of problems and the problems must be analyzed before the conclusions are very useful.

These issues are so obvious today that the reader may have difficulty seeing how important they were. Weidenreich's descriptions of Peking man, for example, have been recognized as probably the most useful descriptions of fossil humans. This is fortunate because the originals are lost. Yet the lower jaws, teeth, and skull were described in different monographs. This not only leads to a very large amount of repetition, but makes it difficult to determine the morphological patterns. Weidenreich was exceedingly generous with the fossils in his possession. I remember visiting him at the American Museum. The skull of Java man was on the table and Weidenreich said, "Pick it up. Pick it up. It is the original!" I will never forget Weidenreich at the Physical Anthropology annual meeting receiving the first Viking Fund medal for physical anthropology. Krogman was president at the time and he towered over Weidenreich as he presented the medal and check. With tears pouring down his cheeks, Weidenreich said, "It is not the medal. It is not the money. It is that you have made me welcome."

I saw Weidenreich a number of times at the American Museum of Natural History, and he was always eager to discuss the fossils. He asked about what I was doing, and I explained the experimental work. "But," he said, "what have rats to do with anthropology?" It seemed obvious to me that they play the same role they do in medical research. They help in solving problems, and the solutions help human beings. Just as fruit flies helped in laying a basis for human genetics, so experimental anatomy can lay a basis for understanding human form.

During the war years the Army sent groups of surgeons for special training. The anatomy department gave quick reviews to plastic and orthopedic, neuro- and maxillo-facial surgeons. The courses were intensive, and the content was adjusted to each group of specialists. In addition, the Army sent the first-year medical students to Columbia at the beginning of the summer, although the regular medical courses did not start until fall. Anatomy was offered in the summer, and this gave me the opportunity of altering the course. One of the main problems with anatomy as taught at Michigan or Oxford was that one area was dissected in detail before its functions could be appreciated. For example, the plexus of nerves that go from the spinal cord to the arms was studied in detail before the arms were studied. In the summer, when changes were possible, arms and legs were dissected at the same time, one side superficially and the other in depth. Then the orthopedic anatomy of the whole being was demonstrated and discussed.

New York is a remarkable city because of its range of resources. For someone like myself, employed in an anatomy department, there was also the American Museum and evening meetings of the Ethnological Society and the anthropology section of the New York Academy of Sciences. Even more important, from my point of view, was the Viking Fund (later the Wenner-Gren Foundation for Anthropological Research). Paul Fejos, an M.D., was the founder and director. He asked me to come to his office and explain my research. I brought the skull of a rat whose parietal bone had been removed on day 2 and had then lived for some two months. I showed the skull to Dr. Fejos, explained the operation and the reasons for some experiments in anthropology. His immediate reaction was, "It is magic. How much will it cost to finish the experiment?" "Eighteen hundred dollars," I replied. "Ask for it, ask for it," he said.

Paul Fejos was a dramatic person. He enjoyed the new. When he heard of Carbon 14 he flew to Chicago, discussed the technique with Willard Libby, and arranged for a grant of $25,000. That was the way he enjoyed operating. He saw the importance of encouraging the new in physical anthropology and partially supported the summer seminars in physical anthropology. He encouraged me, on many occasions invited me to the Foundation, and sent me on my first trip to Africa.

Fejos was very interested in international anthropology and took advantage of the Foundation's tenth anniversary to promote a major conference. The 52 papers were published in a volume nearly 1000 pages long. This conference was a major success, giving the Foundation an assured position in the world of anthropology. Fejos, typically, was not satisfied with the conference; he had hoped it might lead to more suggestions of change. Alfred Kroeber, who was president of the congress, pointed out that anthropology was small enough so that most of the major parts could be represented at the meeting. Today the profession is some ten times as large and much more diversified. The conference marked the end of an era, a time in which anthropologists could know most other anthropologists. Kroeber asked me to chair the final dinner, and I remember looking over the room and seeing that I knew the majority of people who were there. Many were friends who had helped me with my career.

In the summers of 1946, '47, and '48, seminars for physical anthropologists were held at the New York headquarters of the Viking Fund. As secretary of the American Association of Physical Anthropologists, it seemed to me that the profession was handicapped by being too small, too restricted in interests, and too conservative. Also, it had been greatly disrupted by the war. Fejos aided the seminars and courses were arranged at Columbia to help in the financing. Gabriel Lasker founded the *Yearbook* to expand the possibilities of publication, and the *Yearbook* carried accounts of the seminars. The second seminar had 34 participants, and 69 people attended at least some of the sessions. I think the seminars performed a very useful function in accelerating progress in physical anthropology. With the aid of the *Yearbook*, the seminars certainly provided a greatly expanded vision of the scope of the field and of the diversity of problems and techniques.

For some years Fejos planned dinners at the Foundation for groups of anthropologists. There was a talk and discussion, and this enabled him and the staff of the Foundation to sample anthropology in an effective,

first-hand way. Most of the dinners centered around an anthropological specialty, and the guests too were specialists in the same area. Fejos invited me to many of the dinners, and this was a major factor in my keeping up to date in anthropology although employed in anatomy.

The American Anthropological Association had no requirements for membership except the dues. There were many interested members who were not trained, and Julian Steward thought that the AAA should be reorganized with the professional business being managed by a new class of fellows who were to have professional qualifications. The rapid expansion of anthropology after the war made some changes necessary, but there were strong differences of opinion as to what they should be. Ralph Linton, then president of the Association, appointed a committee of nine to draw up a plan for change and present it to the Association at the annual meeting at Chicago in 1946. It was a very interesting committee, and, as the youngest member, I was fascinated to hear the views of Julian Steward, Ralph Linton, Pete Murdock, Dunc Strong, and many others.

It was lucky that I had paid very close attention to the discussions because less than an hour before the business meeting was to start Murdock came to me and said that the committee had decided that I was to present their recommendations. After recovering from my surprise, I asked for the report. Murdock replied, "Actually there isn't one—but you have a way of putting things." So I made a few notes and then addressed the business meeting, stating the main arguments for change. Fortunately, the motion passed, but I have rarely felt so on the spot as I did presenting a nonexistent report to a highly critical audience.

Later the same day Sol Tax told me that Bill Krogman was leaving Chicago and going to Pennsylvania and that I was being considered as a possible replacement. I had very mixed feelings because the experiments I had under way at Columbia needed about two years for completion, but good jobs in physical anthropology were rare and the Chicago department was one of the best. The formal offer included the promise of space in the anatomy department, and this made it ideal from my point of view.

The anthropology department at Chicago was a powerful institution. Fred Eggan, Bob Redfield, and Sol Tax formed the core, old friends who had been highly influenced by A. R. Radcliffe-Brown. The British tradition of social anthropology was reinforced by visitors such as I. A. Schapera, Raymond Firth, Meyer Fortes, E. E. Evans-Pritchard and others. Departmental meetings were held in a small room at the faculty club. They were mostly general discussion; business was disposed of quickly. Particularly when a visitor was present, the business lunches were more like seminars than business meetings. Shortly before I went to Chicago the curriculum had been revised. It then consisted of a three-quarter introduction to ethnology, organized by Eggan, a three-quarter introduction to social anthropology, organized by Tax, and a three-quarter introduction to human evolution and archeology, organized by Bob Braidwood. Much of the teaching was joint and there were frequent visitors. I think that the department functioned as smoothly as it did because there was a very high level of understanding among the members.

Redfield inspired many students. As one student remarked, "It was not just the way he said it, it was what he said too." Redfield thought in typologies, ideal types. These were clear and were used to make important general points. But the link between the type and the ethnological fact was a subjective leap. Exciting as this mode of thought was, it provided no guide for research, and this, in my opinion, is why so few students finished graduate programs under Redfield's guidance. Eggan not only commanded a remarkable number of ethnological facts, but illustrated how data and theory are interrelated and how this guides research. Tax always had students involved in some project, frequently close to the university. His desire to involve native Americans in applied projects led students to understand the practical problems from the native point of view. The combination of ideal type, action anthropology, and Philippine ethnology, plus the heritage of Radcliffe-Brown and the social anthropology visitors, made a rich and challenging program.

The most interesting part of Braidwood's course was on the origins of agriculture and the Near East. The origins of civilization was treated with the aid of visitors from the Oriental Institute. In retrospect, the most important aspect of the course was the joint teaching, discussion, and having visitors. Almost inevitably, the content of the course was modified from year to year far more than if it had been taught by any one person. The biases of Robert Maynard Hutchins' educational reforms exerted a strong influence on the anthropology program and courses. It was quite impossible to be a physical anthropologist in the traditional sense. As the years went by, my part of the course stressed behavior more and structure less.

The department and teaching were very satisfactory, but the anatomy department had withdrawn its offer of space for research, and the space finally assigned to physical anthropology was most unsatisfactory. Over the years, several students made heroic efforts to maintain our experimental animals. The principal research was on the growth of the skull as shown by intravital dyes.

In the spring of 1948 I went to South Africa and Uganda, a trip planned with Dr. Fejos and supported by the Viking Fund. In Johannesburg I called on Professor Raymond Dart. He was most cordial, welcoming me to his laboratory and showing me his specimens. A paper was on his desk and he complained bitterly that it had just been turned down. He reminisced about how he had always had problems getting his ideas published. I urged him to send the paper to the *American Journal of Physical Anthropology*. Dale Stewart had recently become editor, and I know that he was short on papers. Dart's paper was accepted, and this started a long series of papers, not only from Dart, but from other South African scientists.

Dart drove me over to Pretoria on the occasion when Robert Broom was to receive his Commemorative Volume. Typically, Broom gave the major speech himself. He remarked, after mentioning many of the troubles he had had, that "God was on my side, or at least I was on the side of God." Days later, I visited Broom's laboratory and saw the remarkable specimens. The pelvis and vertebrae of *Australopithecus* were still largely in the rock. On the shelves were numerous specimens, the best collection of the man-apes at that time.

Broom took great pleasure in showing the specimens and discussing his problems. A geologist walked past the door of the lab, and Broom's voice boomed out, "There goes my worst enemy. Do you have enemies like that?" He showed me a skull bone which was indented, probably by a blow, and added, "That wouldn't surprise you coming from Chicago, would it?" Broom was a remarkable old man, energetic, difficult, and a great collector. He revived the search for fossil man in South Africa which had been stalled for some years.

In South Africa I spent my time in museums in Johannesburg, Kimberley, and Cape Town. Then I flew to Uganda. In Kampala I stayed with Alexander Galloway, Dean of the Makerere Medical School. Galloway was interested in my research on monkeys and helped in obtaining animals, assistants, and working space. I collected data on the relations of muscle size to behavior and skull form, and devised a method of preparing the skeletons which took less than half of the time spent on previous collections.

At that time Uganda was a beautiful peaceful country. In the game reserves one got images of what it must have been like before the expansion of human populations. We went from Butiaba to Murchison Falls by boat. For hours hippos were constantly in sight and there were great crocodiles on the banks. At the falls we disembarked and walked around to the top. There the whole Nile dashed through a gap only 14 feet wide. In the trees watered by the spray were black and white colobus. Elephants browsed leisurely a few hundred yards away. One could see the great importance of big game for human hunters.

The time in Africa had been varied, rich, and rewarding. I had seen australopithecine fossils, studied Bush and Bantu skeletons, collected monkeys, and met fascinating people. But on my way back to Chicago, as I pondered the diversified experiences, I realized that I needed a much more explicitly stated point of view to bring it all together. At the time I looked to the biological sciences and Malinowski's social anthropology for a synthetic theory. I now see, following Misia Landau's ideas, that what I was really doing was trying to assemble information for making a consistent story on human evolution and supporting it with facts wherever possible.

The factual side of the story of human evolution was brought together in a major symposium, organized by Th. Dobzhansky with some help from me. The Cold Spring Harbor Symposium of 1950 was designed to bring genetics into a working relationship with physical anthropology. At that time physical anthropology was still such a small field that most of the major American scientists were participants.

Of the 18 anthropologists presenting papers, 11 were students of the late E. A. Hooton. This gives a measure of his influence, and although one of the main purposes of the conference was to stress the importance of thinking in terms of populations, typology continued to be used by a number of the participants. Population vs type was probably too fundamental an issue to be discussed usefully in a public meeting. Three of the contributors—Dobzhansky, Ernst Mayr, and George Simpson—made, and have continued to make, contributions which have exerted major influences on the study of human evolution.

A Pan African Congress was held in Livingstone in 1955. This was organized by J. Desmond Clark, and the papers and discussions showed that he was the leader in the study of African prehistory. Raymond Dart exhibited a collection of bones, illustrating the osteo-donto-keratic culture. Louis Leakey remarked of them, "Just ordinary veldt bone." One of the reasons for regarding the bones as the product of hunters was that the distribution of the kinds of bones was not random. A few weeks later I collected bones in the Wankie Game Reserve and found that the kinds of bones on the surface were not randomly preserved, but the frequencies agreed with the ones exhibited by Dart. Some bones are preserved much more frequently than others, and for middle-size game, preservation appeared to be a function of edibility. Ribs and other easily eaten parts go first, jaws and teeth last. Here was an explanation of the preservation of fossil primates. It is not just that teeth are hard; teeth and jaws are the least edible parts of the animal.

After the Congress, with Desmond Clark's help, I arranged for a small collection of baboons. But much more importantly, as it turned out, there were troops of baboons close to the Victoria Falls Hotel where I was staying.

The supply of baboons was irregular, and I spent any extra time watching the local troops. This was so much more rewarding that I closed out the collecting and spent my time watching the tame baboons. The troop next to the hotel must have been the tamest in Africa; one could walk between the animals. The next troop would let one come close, but not between troop members. The third troop out would not permit a close approach. Almost at once the animals ceased to be just baboons; they became personalities. There was only one large dominant male. He got the best of everything. Later he was displaced by a much younger male from the next troop. I did not see the fight, but the wounds were apparent the next day, and the new dominant male was constantly making the old one move. There was no doubt of the change of power. The local people threw rocks at the baboons, and the animals could judge the necessary escape distance precisely. I never saw one get hit, even when stealing mangoes from the hotel garden.

In order to see baboons under much more natural conditions, I made a trip to the Wankie Game Reserve. Along with marvelous views of buffalo, eland, and lions, there were numerous troops of baboons. I was impressed by how each troop seemed to be an independent social system. One day I was watching a mixed group of impala and baboons when three cheetahs came along. The impala and baboons looked at the cheetahs as they approached, but showed no signs of fear. Suddenly one big male baboon started toward the cheetahs and gave a warning bark. The cheetahs turned and trotted off. This demonstrated that one function of the troop was protection, and the ease with which one baboon drove off three large carnivores, and the fact that the impala knew they were in no danger as long as they were with the baboons, was very impressive. The functions of the troop could be observed, and Malinowski's functional theory probably works more usefully for monkey than for human beings. Language adds a new dimension and complicates everything. Radcliffe-Brown's analogies are quite unnecessary when studying nonhuman primates.

The 1955 trip had been most rewarding in learning about prehistory, distributions of bones, baboon anatomy, and behavior. Thinking over the experiences, I realized that a much more behavioral approach to human evolution would be useful. Emphasis on behavior was a necessary consequence of the synthetic theory of evolution. The opportunity for considering a fundamental change in emphasis in my thinking came in 1956–57 at the Center for Advanced Study in the Behavioral Sciences. During that year we ran a seminar which interested about half of the Fellows, a little more than 20 people, who represented numerous social sciences and biology. Uniquely, at least in my experience, everyone seemed interested in new ideas, and everyone was free from the normal pressures of academic life. The seminar was the kind of activity the director, Ralph Tyler, had hoped might take place, and it certainly marked a high point in my academic experiences.

In January, David Hamburg arrived at the Center and became a major contributor to the seminar. Hamburg was interested in evolution and the primates and eventually was an important spokesman in explaining these topics to the medical profession. He contributed his strong interest in learning and emotions.

Theodore McCown invited me to lunch at Berkeley, and there we discussed evolution and the problems of teaching physical anthropology. After a time McCown said that the department at Berkeley was considering adding a second physical anthropologist and asked me whom I recommended. I said, "Me." He said, "Will you come if we make the offer?" "Yes." In retrospect, I think that there was a variety of reasons for wanting to leave Chicago. The decision could be explained in terms of climate, the chance to keep monkeys, the opportunity of having my own introductory course (after being in other people's courses for 19 years). But I think the main reason was just that I had been in Chicago for 11 years and the time at the Center had made me see the need for a change.

Irven DeVore and his family spent the year 1958–59 studying baboons as a part of our Ford Foundation-financed project on primate behavior and human evolution. I, together with my wife Henrietta and younger son Stanley, joined them in the summer. Irv had been studying the baboons in the Nairobi Park and introduced us to the tamest troop and showed us the social system. After the animals had been studied for some months, Irv used small amounts of food to work out the hierarchy. If a bit of food was tossed between two or three animals, one would take it. With careful application this simple method let one see which animal was dominant. My bias is that after several months in which the animals are disturbed as little as possible, experiments are necessary to make sure the social system is analyzed correctly. We saw baboons catch and eat hares, but found that meat formed a very small part of their diet. The compact nature of the troop was an especially interesting feature. A year was not an adequate amount of time to understand the baboon troop. In the short run it seemed independent and inbred, but longer studies have shown that males generally leave the troop when three or four years old.

After a few weeks in Nairobi, we went to the Amboseli Game reserve. Here were much larger troops of baboons than in the Nairobi Park, and they had been far less disturbed. These troops varied in size from a little over a dozen to nearly 200. Animals with broken limbs or animals carrying dead infants were not rare. Injured animals made every effort to keep up with the troop, and this reinforced our feelings from Victoria Falls and Nairobi that baboons are very social; fearing the dangers of separation, they make every effort to stay with the troop.

Amboseli, with its elephants, rhinos, and numerous ungulates, was an exciting place. On an average day, watching baboons mostly near waterholes, we would see some 1500 head of game. It was not unusual to see gazelle, impala, giraffe, zebra, elephant, rhino, warthog, and baboons all at the same time. The animals usually paid no attention to each other or to us. The human idea of "wild" is the result of hunting disturbing the animals. It is likely that until our ancestors became hunters, they were of as little interest to other animals as those around the waterholes.

We paid particular attention to kills, both to see the distribution of bones and to see how much might be left over for a primate. Scavenging has been much discussed in the literature as a possible stage in human evolution, but actually the carnivores eat most of the animal, and the kill is a dangerous place until they have left. While carnivores can and do scavenge, scavenging is an unpredictable source of food. A minimum of hunting would provide an early human with more food than could be obtained by scavenging. The primary killers (lions, leopards, cheetahs, hyenas) are rare compared to the primates. It was estimated that there were some 40 lions and 400 baboons in Nairobi Park. Except under most unusual circumstances, most groups of primates will only rarely be near a kill.

We returned to Nairobi, and DeVore directed some motion pictures on baboon behavior. Later the movie won a prize, and it has been available for more than 20 years.

The 1960s were a very busy time. There was great scientific progress and political turmoil. I was elected president of the American Anthropological Association, and it is hard to believe now how calm the academic scene was in 1962. The executive board looked for indications of needed changes but found no discontent. At one meeting a resolution on race was discussed. In an effort to make the resolution accurate, it became more and more qualified until Steve Boggs, the executive secretary, said, "If that is the board's resolution, I resign as of now." This shocked the board and there was a keen discussion, but it was not heading for a solution. Joe Casagrande suddenly turned to me and said, "Sherry, you can get us out of this." "How?" "If you give your presidential address on race, we will accept that as the board's position." So that is how I happened to talk on race rather than on primate behavior.

Field studies on primate behavior expanded rapidly in the late 1950s and 1960s. In marked contrast to a decade earlier, there were plenty of studies, so an assessment seemed in order. Dave Hamburg and I, with the aid of Ralph Tyler and Preston Cutler, organized a meeting and a year-long study group for the Center for Advanced Study in the Behavioral Sciences. The purpose of this project was to produce a book. The result was *Primate Behavior,* edited by Irven DeVore, published in 1965. The 18 chapters included papers on the behaviors of monkeys, apes, and the implications of the field studies. The group at the Center was enthusiastic, and there was a strong feeling that a useful first step had been taken and the next few years would see the establishment of a science of primatology. In reality, the expansion in terms of scientists, societies, and journals has been far greater than any at the Center expected.

Paul Fejos regarded American anthropology as being much too provincial. To overcome this difficulty, he thought that the Foundation should have an international center where conferences could be held. With this in mind, he purchased a castle, Burg Wartenstein, located a few miles south of Vienna. Fejos asked me to help in the organization of a conference on the "Social Life of Early Man," and in 1961 the results were published in a volume of the same name. Primate studies were included, especially through the contributions of Ernest Caspari, DeVore, and Hamburg. A much more integrated conference followed on "Classification and Human Evolution," and this was published in 1963. Evolution was treated as the guiding principle, uniting classification, structure, behavior, and psychology. At the conference there was enough agreement for useful discussion and enough disagreement to keep the session lively. No conference with Louis Leakey and Bill Straus could be dull! Before the end, Leakey had challenged Mayr's views on classification, and Anne Roe and George Simpson had stationed themselves one on each side of Straus to limit his contributions. The main unresolved conflict was between Morris Goodman and Emile Zuckerkandl, stressing the importance of molecular anthropology, and the more traditional but no less important views of Simpson and Mayr.

Paul Fejos died in 1963. As director of the Wenner-Gren Foundation, he had been remarkably successful, supporting many new developments such as Carbon 14. He was one of the most imaginative and creative people I have ever known and his death brought a great sense of personal loss. His wife, Lita Osmudsen, suc-

ceeded him as director, and she has continued many of his policies down to the present.

One of the first conferences at Burg Wartenstein under Osmundsen's direction was on primate behavior. This was organized by Phyllis Jay (now Dolhinow) and the results published in 1968. The 19 papers formed a useful introduction to what was then known about primate behavior and its implications for the understanding of human evolution. Primate studies were now moving so rapidly that Dolhinow published a second edited volume in 1972. The influence of the 1962–63 year at the Center for Advanced Study of the Behavioral Sciences remained strong.

In the fall of 1964 many Berkeley students refused to obey the university regulations controlling activities both on and off the campus. Students occupied the administration building and were arrested. Many students struck, and there was a long series of demonstrations. That fall there were some 1200 students in the introductory physical anthropology course, and all of the teaching assistants in that course went on strike. There was confusion at every level. The university was not prepared for violent action, and a small part of the student body eagerly promoted violence at every opportunity. I spent a considerable amount of time listening to the speeches and watching the riots. I learned two things almost at once. The university had been trying to treat the situation as local, but the issues were national—the civil rights movement and the threat of the draft. The issues could not be settled locally, so the efforts of both students and administration were largely beside the point. The apparent chaos of the riots was actually highly structured.

In Berkeley most students live away from campus. They will assemble at noon and listen to speeches. If enough is going on, a march may then take place. But if the crowd loses interest, there will be no riot. At Stanford, by contrast, students mostly live on campus and the activity is after dinner, a time of peace at Berkeley.

During those Berkeley riots, when the police were called on to control the students as they advanced, most students would retreat. But there were some who seized tear gas canisters and threw them back at the police. Other students would shake their hands or clap them on the back, and they received immediate public acclaim for their actions. In this way the crowd has a life of its own with great rewards which have nothing to do with the reasons for the strike. Burton Benedict and I watched several of the student-police confrontations. It was clear what the reward was—the crowd's recognition of personal risk and aggressive courage. In almost no time the protection of free speech became a very rough game which intensified feelings but did nothing to solve the issues.

The first phase of the strike ended with students going back to classes. Jane Lancaster told me that the teaching assistants and other students were expecting me to discuss the situation, not just continue with the course. I tried to give a speech showing the interrelations of biology and social science in understanding the situation on the Berkeley campus. It was the most difficult talk I ever gave and it was greeted with a standing ovation. Lancaster, my liaison with the teaching assistants throughout the strike, reported success. For my own part, I realized the possibility of a much more useful relationship between behavior, bones, and baboons. The strike had shaken me out of my academic rut, and my introductions to human evolution were never quite the same again.

In spite of the political unrest, the anthropology department at Berkeley expanded rapidly in the 1960s. Frank Beach had started a center for the study of animal behavior, so when Phyllis Dolhinow joined the department in 1966, she had a place to keep live monkeys. The animals constituted the basis for the teaching and research. When her students went to the field they were trained in methods of observation and were familiar with monkeys. It was a great improvement over what I had been able to do before.

Since the Wenner-Gren conference on classification in 1962, I had been looking for someone in molecular anthropology. The main contributors to the field were not anthropologists, but we were fortunate to be able to employ Vincent Sarich, an anthropologist who had trained in Allan Wilson's biochemical laboratory at Berkeley.

Ted McCown died in 1969. For many years he had done all the teaching in physical anthropology. He had strongly supported the expansion and diversification of the program. After a careful search, Clark Howell was appointed to continue the work in paleoanthropology. But the program in human evolution depended on much more than physical anthropology. We received strong support from other departments, and from Desmond Clark and Glynn Isaac in archeology. I note that my most frequent luncheon companions have been Burton Benedict, Elizabeth Colson, and George Foster—all social anthropologists. I audited the graduate introduction to social anthropology on several occasions, and Benedict and I have done considerable joint teaching. He has been a great help in evaluating the possible contributions of the primate studies to social science.

In looking back over this manuscript, I see that I have omitted the best organized symposium I ever attended—*Behavior and Evolution,* the volume edited by Anne Roe and George Simpson, 1958. Also, the Ciba Foundation conference on aggression and my Huxley lecture might be mentioned. But these events which influenced me so much were only important because they led to constant modifications in teaching. Over the years I supervised some 40 doctoral programs, and the students did their research in a wide variety of techniques. I think that all of the thesis committees had members from other departments. There were no fixed course requirements for the advanced work; everyone got some exposure to anatomy, paleontology, genetics, and some behavioral science. Much of the best education came from the discussions among the students. My role was to open up the subject of human evolution at an elementary level and then encourage students to pursue their own kinds of anthropology.

After all, physical anthropology is not defined by a technique as it once was, but is given cohesion by its goals, the understanding of human evolution. At an elementary level such understanding might well be a part of everyone's education. But the evidence for human evolution has become much more complex. This means that there are many different kinds of anthropologies and this trend to increasing specialization will itself increase. This situation is by no means confined to anthropology; it is a fundamental problem in modern science. It is intensified in anthropology because the technical aspects of human evolution relate differently to archeology, linguistics, and social anthropology.

I retired in 1979. Looking back over 50 years of studying human evolution I have a feeling of satisfaction. The number of physical anthropologists has increased tenfold, from a little over 100 scientists to well over 1000. Fifty years ago few departments had one physical anthropologist. Now many departments have several, allowing for diversification in problems and techniques.

Over the last few years there have been major changes in biology. In general these have been resisted in anthropology. As I see the matter, the relations between the contemporary mammals may be more accurately assessed by molecular methods (analysis of DNA, order of amino acids in proteins, immunology, electrophoresis) than by the traditional anatomical methods. After 100 years of study, scientists could not agree whether humans were closely related to the African apes, or even if there had been an ape-like form in human ancestry.

Molecular biology settles this problem (Figure 3). Humans are very closely related to the African apes and much less closely related to the Asiatic apes. Paleontology and comparative anatomy tell about the events of the past (when humans evolved large brains, for example), but these methods were unable to produce agreement among scientists.

The usual course on human evolution starts with the events of time long past. But that is where knowledge

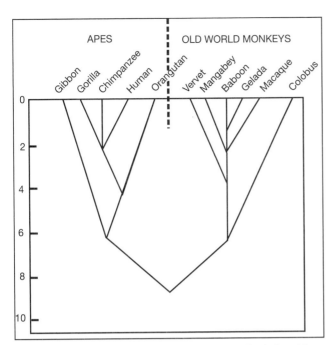

FIGURE 3.   *A single set of determinations of relationships by the method of DNA hybridization effectively settles the debates over the position of humans among the primates. The conclusions are supported by immunology and other molecular methods. The whole history of human evolution would have been very different if modern methods had been available. Today we should be going with the new and not repeating the errors of the past.*

is least certain. Molecular biology has not only brought new techniques, but also the interest and competence of far more scientists than are directly involved in the study of human evolution. If I were offering a course on human evolution today, I would start with now, what is known of the molecular biology, behavior, and experimental biology of contemporary forms. Then I would go back to the fossils, seeing the variety and the order of events of the past.

Suggesting a course of this nature is just a teacher's way of saying that the balance of methods and conclusions which give meaning to the study of evolution have changed, and changed radically. The techniques which give the basis for the study of evolution now include the molecular methods as well as the traditional ones. The synthetic theory of the 1940s is now being modified by the discovery of vast amounts of variation, stochastic factors, and the neutral theory. The view of evolution as necessarily gradual is being modified to an unknown extent by the theory of the punctate origin of species.

Teachers of human evolution have been immersed in the past. The problems, methods, and theories have all been continuations of the nineteenth century. But starting in the 1960s, a new approach to human evolution became possible. Time and relationships could both be accurately measured. This combination offers a new setting for the interpretation of the fossils, for the study of behavior, and for a new attempt to understand the meaning of human evolution.

## ACKNOWLEDGMENTS

The writing of this article was supported by the University of California faculty research funds. I wish to thank Mrs. Alice Davis for editorial assistance on this and many other manuscripts.

*Theodore Grand presents Washburn's contribution to the revolution in physical anthropology, as well as the impact of Washburn, the man and the teacher, on Grand's own intellectual development. In this history, as in Washburn's, change and environment also play a role. The intertwining of the story of changes in scientific perspectives and the interaction of teacher and student during their careers have remarkable parallels to the evolutionary process they both chose to study.*

# 21 Sherry Washburn and the Revolution in Functional Anatomy

**Theodore I. Grand**  *Departments of Pathology and Zoological Research, National Zoological Park, Washington, D.C.*

Sherry Washburn is one of the central figures in the revolutionary advance of physical anthropology since 1950. His "experimental" approach to muscle-bone interaction and his "functional" approach to the reconstruction of fossils have revitalized human paleontology and invigorated primate anatomy. Since his vision influenced my own research career, I explore our teacher-student interaction, the roles of accident and environment in my intellectual development, and some trends in anatomy that are extensions of Washburn's methods of problem identification and problem solving.

> The present is rich in three great vital dimensions which dwell together . . . , whether they will or no, linked . . . , and perforce, because they are different, in essential hostility. . . . For some, "today" is the state of being twenty, for others forty, and for still another group, sixty; and this, the fact that three such different ways of life have the same "today," creates the dynamic drama, the conflict, and the collision which form the background of historic material.[1]

I am an anatomist, taught by skilled anatomists. One of them, Sherry Washburn, was influenced by William King Gregory, who studied with Henry Fairfield Osborne, himself a student of Thomas Henry Huxley. This, my "shield of ancestors," strengthens my links with the past, conveys an historic inevitability, and confers upon my life in research an unsought legitimacy. Nonetheless, one must ask: "(Had) the Book of Destiny . . . been written up in full from the beginning of time?"[2] No, said Lawrence of Arabia after he crossed the Nefud: "Nothing is written."

## I BECOME SHERRY'S STUDENT

"Wie es eigentlich gewesen ist"
(How things actually happened)[3]

### The Role of Chance

We met by accident, and this is how it happened. The last weekend of my junior year at Brown—the morning after the night before—I staggered into the university refectory for breakfast. I was thinking about food, not my future, when a classmate asked me to drive with him to Detroit after final exams. I jumped at the chance for adventure: two Jersey boys crossing upper New York State and lower Ontario, hunting down midwestern classmates, and fishing up a storm in Lake Michigan. When a professor of mine heard about the trip, he urged me on to Chicago to meet one S. L. Washburn, a friend of his and a "great biologist," teaching anthropology(?) at the university. Well, I *was* bound for graduate school *in biology,* but I duly set up the appointment and met him. What first struck me about Washburn's office was that it was filled with (sealed) boxes; obviously he was going somewhere. He began with something like: "I suppose Bill wanted me to give you a pep talk about coming here, but I can't do that. I'm leaving next week for Berkeley." Since going west to study anthropology was the farthest thing from my mind, I sat back, relaxed but fascinated, while he told me about his experiments in anatomy, their relevance to the interpretation of human origins, his plans for his next field trip. He was crystal clear, dynamic, sweeping in vision—vintage Washburn.

It behooves me, at this point, to try and capture his *presence* for those who haven't known him. He is slightly below average height, lean and wiry rather than skinny. A story I heard much later concretizes his vitality and strength. While Washburn was an undergraduate at Harvard, William Sheldon included him in his study of body types. These have come down to us as endomorph, mesomorph, and ectomorph. Sheldon made him a skinny ectomorph *until* he found out that Washburn was on the wrestling team, whereupon Sheldon reclassified him as a muscular mesomorph. He told the story to poke fun at Sheldon's (non-) methodology, but I thought no: I would not have looked forward to meeting him on the wrestling mat. Another illumination: Washburn's brother Bradford is a mountaineer, so revered that Mt. Washburn in Alaska is named for him. Since they were the sons of a distinguished Harvard theologian, socializing them must have been akin to wrapping fissionable material in newspaper.

In any event, throughout my senior year at college, I kept doing instant replays of our single conversation. I was convinced that I wanted to study with Washburn, even if that meant physical anthropology at Berkeley.

## The Role of the Environment

WOODS HOLE  During the summer between graduation and departure for California, I took the embryology course at the Marine Biological Laboratory (MBL) on Cape Cod. It was to be my farewell to life beyond the primates (happily, it wasn't), and definitively, the end of my interest in developmental biology (happily, it wasn't). But that was OK. For the moment, I inhaled the "mystique of place": the MBL was the *sanctum sanctorum*, the holy of holies, the oldest laboratory of its kind in the United States, and history seeped from its walls. Here, generations of distinguished biologists had cut their intellectual canines and returned year after year to sharpen them. (I was unaware of the profundity of this metaphor until I saw more of the world of science.) In those bygone days the MBL was doubly distilled, the concentrated essence of science *qua* curiosity. The library with its vast journal collection was open 24 hours a day and one felt the historic waves of thought that buoyed us and carried us along. Fortunately, after the course was over, a few of us stayed on to continue our research. I shared a lab with Dick Whittaker, a graduate student from Yale, now my lifelong friend and alter ego in the Scientist's Survival Plan (or

SSP). For each of us, that summer at the MBL helped to crystallize our scientific identities.

Access to the library also provided the opportunity to read many of Washburn's papers in the original. His classic experiments with Samuel Detweiler on the eye and orbital bone of salamanders (Washburn and Detweiler 1943) signaled his break with the descriptive tradition of primate anatomy. He demonstrated that skull shape was the result of complex developmental processes and not of simple, measurable traits. He proposed that experiments could settle many long-standing arguments: "The views of Hrdlicka and Weidenreich are as far apart today as were those of Virchow and Fick in 1859" (Washburn 1943: 172). Sherry then designed a range of experiments to isolate other determinants of cranial and mandibular form: paralysis of the facial and masticatory musculature (Washburn 1947), removal of the zygomatic arch (Washburn 1946a), feeding Alizarin dye to developing animals (Mednick and Washburn 1956). He once told me (only after I had pointedly asked him) how difficult it had been to publish those first papers because the experimental animals had been rabbits, rats, and piglets rather than primates. Not relevant!

In another series of papers he took on the problem of sexing human pelves (Washburn, 1948, 1949; Washburn and Hanna 1953). Hitherto, anthropologists had depended for evaluation upon several features (angulation of the greater sciatic notch, the shape of the pelvic outlet, the shape of the obturator foramen, etc.). Washburn reasoned that since the female pubic bone grew at puberty under the influence of estrogen, why not (simply) use a ratio of the length of pubis to ischium to separate male and female? The growth of the female pubis caused the other differences. Adjusted for various ethnic groups, the predictive success of the ischiopubic index was extremely high. Suffice to say, the force and clarity of each of these papers primed me for Berkeley.

The irony, of course, was that while I was reading Washburn the anatomist, he was in Africa formulating a revolution in the study of primate social behavior.

BERKELEY  Despite the quantum shift in his own research, Washburn was still magical with a box of bones: scapula, femur, skull—it never mattered what bone or what animal. He would pick it up, clothe it in muscle, reconstruct the entire animal before our eyes, and make it jump (or climb or brachiate) straight off the table and into the canopy!

During that first year I took human gross anatomy from another wonderful teacher, Herb Srebnik, a warm friend and confidant to many Washburn students. This class went full-bore for the entire year, an historic curiosity in these days when gross anatomy is crammed into the period between Labor Day and Christmas. Herb's exams were tremendously challenging and I used to wonder: What can he throw at us this time? The year I took the class a student ran screaming from our midterm exam and never returned. Me? I loved the logic of design as Srebnik and *Grant's Method of Anatomy* presented it and just came back for more. After we had finished the eye and the orbit, I stayed in Berkeley over a vacation just to dissect the other eye.

Thursday was the day that Washburn scheduled brown-bag lunches in his office in order to discuss current research as well as recent publications. Our first professional talks were practiced over lunch. He insisted on clarity and strong visual aids. For 15- or 20-minute presentations, we might make only one or two points; for a 30-minute paper, three points, possibly four. He thoroughly disapproved of the shotgun approach: throw up the data, shut your eyes, and blast away. Since his own presentations were so compelling, many of us took this advice deeply to heart.

## I BECOME A SCIENTIST

> The young man finds himself caught in (the) world at twenty-five, and throws himself into living in it on his own account, that is to say, he too takes his place in world making. But as he meditates on the world in force (the world of the men who in his time are mature), his thesis, his problems, his doubts, are very different from those which these mature men felt when in their own youth they in turn meditated on the world of those who were then mature (men who are now very old), and so on backwards.[4]

For the record, during my time in Berkeley, Washburn suggested repeatedly that I do a primate field study where he could get me plenty of money. However, for reasons only a few of which I could specify, my synapses had already closed; I was going to be an anatomist.

### The "Functional Complex"

This, for me, was the single most intriguing concept in Washburn's anatomical philosophy (1951a, b). His experiments had clearly shown the interrelation of tissues (skin, muscle, bone, cartilage, nerve) and that a change in one component changed the others. Thus the fulcrum of physical evolution was not the single bone or separate muscle, but the underlying functional-structural complex in which each was embedded. Variants of this conception may be found in W. K. Gregory, Le Gros Clark, and Dullemeijer. I began to explore this in my thesis on the chimpanzee shoulder and then, working in Oregon, on the ankle and foot

of *Nycticebus*, the limbs of *Alouatta*, and the hip joint of *Tarsius*. Through my friendship with Matt Maberry, chief veterinarian at the Portland Zoo, I extended my study materials to nonprimates; associations with John Eisenberg and Ted Reed at the National Zoo expanded my species sensibilities even more. This shift in attention was beneficial. Primate anatomy seemed to me anemic, the stepchild of Keith and Weidenreich's human anatomy, and not very comparative, isolated as it was from the anatomy of other mammals. In due course, my reading moved to Wood Jones, Böker, Slijper, and Brazier Howell, anatomists to whom I had not been exposed. Ultimately, my research curiosity turned to South American porcupines, the didelphids of French Guyana, the kangaroos, and the East African bovids.

### Body Structure and the Locomotor Repertoire

The level of resolution of my research also expanded from one- and two-joint mechanisms to the whole body and to body composition. Despite the fact that I was swimming against a reductionist tide (microscopic analysis, early molecular anthropology), my field experiences (Madagascar, Sri Lanka, Panama, Venezuela) convinced me that the behavior and structure of whole animals should remain the core of my attention. I am sure that fieldwork was also a touchstone for Washburn—that is, What are the real selection pressures being applied to the behavioral repertoire? My answers connected to locomotor and feeding skills: feeding at the ends of branches, moving across the open ground, the role of upper body agility in climbing and feeding. Occasionally, ethologist colleagues taunted me that I was not studying real behavior, certainly not on a par with social organization, feeding, or reproduction. My wry counterargument was that skin and the musculoskeletal system of mammals account for more than two-thirds (60–70%) of body weight, a significant investment in carrying the brains, gastrointestinal tract, and gonads from place to place. Thus, without locomotor evolution, mammals would simply be sessile, if hairy plants. This has always seemed to quiet them.

Parenthetically, Washburn seemed pragmatic about defining an adaptation. If it worked, use it. This strategy (or attitude) troubled some people who carped about "scientific rigor" and the "perils of subjectivity." On the other hand, his pragmatism struck me as a lot healthier than the naive worship of induction. Needless to say, such criticisms seemed not to faze him, and when hypothetico-deductive reasoning was unveiled as a legitimate form of knowing, we like-thinkers were comforted.

## THE VISIONARY AS TEACHER

One hundred and fifty years of musical history can be reconstructed from the life histories of individual composers: young Mozart (1756–1791) sounds like middle period Haydn (1732–1809) as he should, since Wolfgang studied with Poppa; young Beethoven (1770–1827) sounds like later Haydn and late Mozart; and young Brahms (1833–1897) sounds like popular Beethoven, not the inaccessible Beethoven of the late quartets. Each man transmuted what he learned of orchestral technique and thematic development to serve his own emotive and aesthetic needs.

### The Teacher-Student Dialectic

Washburn's vision and impatience were occupational hazards for his students, a subset of the universal teacher-student dialectic. If you caught his attention, his laser-beam intellect split the problem open so that you could chew on and swallow morsels of appropriate size without choking. If, however, you put to him the wrong question, you got a less helpful response. (Did he want to choke you?)

Once I asked him about de Beer's *Embryos and Ancestors*, that fascinating synthesis of developmental process with evolutionary result. He got a funny look on his face and just changed the subject. Since I have returned to the interrelation of ontogeny to phylogeny out of serendipity, *not* Freudian cussedness, it is instructive to speculate on his lack of interest in the problem.

### Growth and Evolution

Many biologists since Von Baer in 1828 have remarked on the remarkable physical transformation from birth to adulthood in various species. I first confronted this with newborn and adult macaques. Newborns were and are wholly different organisms—aside from the fact that they do not move with much skill (always significant to a locomotor specialist). That is why I began applying to neonates the methods (segmental distribution of body mass, body composition, regional disposition of muscle) I used for adults. I wanted to describe just how different they were. At the time, John Eisenberg remarked that I was (finally) adding a time dimension to locomotor adaptation.

Colleagues encouraged this expansion so that I would study "their" species: Karl Kranz introduced me to the African bovids, Miles Roberts to the red pandas, Nan Muckenhirn to the Callitrichidae, Marty Fujita, Pete August, and Holly Stack to the bats. I consider it good fortune that I entered the study of growth through the backdoor. In that way I was free of disciplinary constraints and boundaries and could read whatever I wanted. In retrospect, I think I was simply trying to quantify the anatomy of species across major taxonomic divides.

### Altricial and Precocial Mammals

My model of the altricial and precocial continuum was based on the levels of development of the brain and the musculature. Retarded species such as the red pandas have low prenatal neural and muscular development and at birth are extremely dependent on their parents. Advanced species such as the wildebeest have relatively high levels of development of the brain and muscle and their neonates are the most independent. To be sure, the latter are also tied to their mothers and the herd and subjected to entirely different locomotor demands. Primates, with large brains and underdeveloped musculature, lie somewhere in the middle. Here was a method of quantative anatomical evaluation, not simply a verbal description of behavioral capacity.

Another fact about neonates repeatedly strikes most observers and has done so for centuries: Regardless of adult size, the young of kindred species bear a strong resemblance to one another. Once we lost a bongo calf and I had to call the local museum to see if they wanted the skeleton. The answer came back that no, the skeletons of newborn bovids were too much alike and therefore too confusing to keep in the collection. Since I wanted the animal for my own studies, I bit my tongue and did not say: *That* is precisely what makes them interesting! In Oregon I had witnessed a most instructive error. I had dissected and cleaned the skull of a newborn chimpanzee, which I then put into a museum case for the edification of staff and visitors. When Father Jean Frisch, the great expert on pongids, came to visit, he proclaimed the skull that of a gorilla! Since postnatal heterochronic growth is part of the machinery of diversification, I have always wondered about Washburn's dismissal of the investigation of growth in relation to evolution. Why didn't he pass the problem on to us?

### The Cycles of History

Washburn overlapped at Columbia (circa 1940) with Thomas Hunt Morgan, arguably the most celebrated American biologist of his time. Early in his own career, Morgan had studied ontogeny and phylogeny under W. K. Brooks, but concluded that the rediscovered genes offered far more promise as the proximate controls of development. In a series of lectures in the mid-1930s he baldly stated that evolution had little to say about development, and vice versa!

It seems to me that Washburn bought Morgan's judgment (and why not?). His own experiments on the skull and mandible and the eye-orbit interaction were precisely of the same order, analyses of proximate causal forces. Besides, anthropological studies of growth at the time were descriptive and nonfunctional. Basically, they led nowhere. In fact, Washburn (1946b) had written about growth (the sequence of epiphyseal union) in order to show *how* metrical studies ought to be designed, but these recommendations seemed to fall on sterile ground. Other students of growth (Bolk, Starck, Len Friedmann) were concerned with paedomorphism and neoteny, headed down other terminological alleys, arguing over strings of (anatomically) undefined terms, which Washburn judged unpromising.

Lita Osmundsen, herself a major force in anthropology and a great friend of Washburn's, told me a Gregory Bateson story that I have altered only slightly for rhetorical purposes. A cat was being tested in a maze-learning experiment and bypassed the tunnel that had led to a reward on the previous test. Had the cat forgotten? No, said Bateson, the cat had already eaten that mouse (and thus "knew" that success, another mouse, was unlikely on the next try). So it may have been with Washburn; he had already eaten that (ontogenetic-phylogenetic) mouse.

The historic peaks of interest in development and evolution (Von Baer in the 1820s; Haeckel and Brooks from the 1870s through the 1890s; Bolk in the 1920s; and de Beer and Portmann in the 1960s) have been driven partly by the teacher-student interactions I have been describing: X thinks the paradigm fruitful, Y thinks it saturated and unprofitable, Z sees a way through the impass. This chemical dynamic fuels many of the curves in the history of science. When we encourage (or discourage) a line of questioning, it is because our experience and intuition help us to see, possibly, where a well-framed question leads. In this way, we teach others to read the signposts of history. Thus, on the one hand, Washburn's legacy as an anatomist has been revolutionary and concrete; on the other hand, even though he might not have been interested in particular problem areas, his training of students in the identification and solution of problems, the interaction of accident with environment, have had unpredictable effects, just like evolution itself.

And to make an end is to make a beginning.
The end is where we start from.

We shall not cease from exploration
And the end of all our exploring
Will be to arrive where we started
And know the place for the first time.[5]

## ACKNOWLEDGMENTS

John Jerome, Lita Osmundsen, Barbara Questad, Butch Rommel, Herb Srebnik, Dick Whittaker, and Adrienne Zihlman have commented on these reminiscences. For the first but not the last time, I thank Jack Aubrey, R.N., for his invaluable editorial advice.

## NOTES

1. J. Ortega y Gasset, *Man and Crisis.* New York: Norton, 1958, p. 42.
2. G. Ryle, *Dilemmas.* Cambridge: University Press, 1966, pp. 15–16.
3. Attributed to Leopold Von Ranke
4. Ortega y Gasset, *Man and Crisis,* pp. 40–41.
5. T. S. Eliot, from "Little Gidding."

## REFERENCES TO WASHBURN'S PAPERS

Mednick, L. W., and Washburn, S. L. (1956). The role of the sutures in the growth of the braincase of the infant pig. *Am. J. Phys. Anthrop.* 14: 175–192.

Washburn, S. L. (1946a). The effect of removal of the zygomatic arch in the rat. *J. Mamm.* 27: 169–172.

Washburn, S. L. (1946b). The sequence of epiphysial union in the opossum. *Anat. Rec.* 95: 353–364.

Washburn, S. L. (1947). The relation of the temporal muscle to the form of the skull. *Anat. Rec.* 99: 239–248.

Washburn, S. L. (1948). Sex differences in the pubic bone. *Am. J. Phys. Anthrop.* 6: 199–207.

Washburn, S. L. (1949). Sex differences in the pubic bone of Bantu and Bushman. *Am. J. Phys. Anthrop.* 7: 425–432.

Washburn, S. L. (1951a). The new physical anthropology. *Trans. NY Acad. Sci. II.* 13: 298–304.

Washburn, S. L. (1951b). The analysis of primate evolution with particular reference to the origin of man. *Cold Spring Harbor Symposia on Quantitative Biology* 15: 67–78.

Washburn, S. L., and Detweiler, S. R. (1943). An experiment bearing on the problems of physical anthropology. *Am. J. Phys. Anthrop.* 1: 171–190.

Washburn, S. L., and Hanna, R. E. (1953). The determination of the sex of skeletons, as illustrated by a study of the Eskimo pelvis. *Hum. Biol.* 25: 21–27.

# The New Physical Anthropology: Science, Humanism, and Critical Reflection

## S. C. Strum

Ideally, the epilogue to this book should discuss the fate of the new physical anthropology. The task would be manageable if the book was a conference proceedings and the conference itself had provided the participants the opportunity to discuss the "state" of the field. Alternatively, a trained historian could do a scholarly and intellectually rigorous assessment using the primary literature. Instead, I will make a few personal remarks, leaving it to others to agree or disagree, to add or fill in the gaps and, eventually, to do the real history of what has happened.

There is no "Center for the New Physical Anthropology." By some standards of science, this means that Washburn's project failed. I disagree. This book demonstrates how much the new physical anthropology (NPA) survives in the minds and work of Washburn's students and their descendants (only a small segment of whom are represented here). However, it may be that part of the explanation for the current "fate" of NPA is that it was simply ahead of its time. Many areas of science are only now taking up Washburn's suggestions. These projects, despite originating from a variety of sources, demonstrate the utility of the framework that the new physical anthropology proposed. Equally far-reaching and innovative, the new physical anthropology self-consciously tried to combine science, humanism, and critical reflection. It is no surprise that these efforts made only modest headway. The currently raging "science wars" illustrate the difficulty and uniqueness of such an undertaking for scientists and science critics alike (Gross and Levitt 1994; Huber 1991; Nader 1996; New York Academy of Sciences 1996).

Let me illustrate what I mean with a few examples.

COMPLEXITY   A major challenge for the NPA was to discard the old simplistic approaches to the study of primate and human evolution and develop ways (theory, methods, models) that recognized the complex interaction of biology, behavior, and environment. This meant both considering multiple processes of adaptation and discarding the widely held idea that the links between elements in adaptive complexes were simple. NPA actually embraced the possibility of nonlinear dynamics in evolutionary interactions, although it lacked the recently developed formal language and concepts to bolster this position (Bak and Chen 1991; Feldman 1989; Nicolis and Prigogine 1989; Waldrop 1992). NPA was concerned to find patterns and principles that could explain both the emergence of higher level phenomena and their historicity (see Wertsch 1985; McClelland et al. 1986; Elman et al. 1996; and Hutchins 1995 for comparable recent "moves"). Recognizing this, the new physical anthropologists were urged to bring together the multiple relevant disciplines in, to use Huxley's words, "networks of cooperative investigation" in order to understand primate and human adaptation in a new and different (and better) way. The NPA papers from the 1950s and 1960s fit well with the modern study of complexity as epitomized in the work promoted by the Sante Fe Institute (Stein 1989). Both projects recognize that the successful exploration of complexity is crucially dependent upon forging new connections, new links aimed at the integration of multiple fields of knowledge.

BRAIN, MIND AND BEHAVIOR   With the influence of "behaviorism" on the wane, "mind," not just "brain," has recently become a legitimate topic of scientific investigation (Gardner 1985; Ristau 1990). Washburn had long insisted that there were two entities, brain and mind, and that neither could be understood independently from the other. A major premise of the NPA was that any behavior, whether of the body or the brain, must be studied in relationship to its underlying biology and, conversely, any aspect of biology must be seen in the context of the behavior that it motivated. Equally provocative was the insistence on an evolutionary framework for both brain and mind. The human brain (like the brains of all animals) was seen as an organ of adaptation specifically suited to some circumstances

233

and not to others. Today's brain and mind scientists are embracing these ideas, acknowledging that the phenomena they are investigating are part of an interconnected complex of biology and behavior that has a relevant evolutionary history (Barkow et al. 1992; Tooby and Cosmides 1990). Despite this convergence of principles, Washburn would strongly disagree with the often simplistic formulations of current attempts precisely because they violate the "complexity" principal (Wright 1994).

**MOLECULAR GENETICS** For NPA, the potential of the molecular data lay in its ability to improve phylogenetic reconstructions. And initially, Washburn was the only senior scientist in the field supporting the new approach. Today molecular techniques and data are routinely used in biological anthropology. The growth of genetic projects outside of anthropology has been even more remarkable. But there is convergence between the two. For example, the proliferating "genome" projects are beginning to think in terms of adaptive complexes and to base their evolutionary interpretations on at least rudimentary comparisons between species (Kahn 1994; Kelves and Hood 1992). However, modern projects still lag behind NPA in some respects. Their insufficient attention to variation could easily lead to fallacious "typological" thinking and conclusions (see discussion in Haraway 1997).

**SCIENCE STUDIES** Critical reflection about science was a remarkable characteristic of the work that Washburn did as part of the NPA, a stance that influenced many of his descendants. He claimed that science was deeply immersed in a particular European history and that this "past" (in its culture, its theory, its methods, and its traditional divisions of knowledge) limited the potential of science. He sought ways to break out of traditional thinking and advocated new cross-disciplinary and multidisciplinary links and networks as one solution. In addition, Washburn recognized and emphasized the probabilistic nature of our evidence, always arguing that today's science will be tomorrow's superstition. For him, facts are only as good as the methods that produced them. The corollary was that facts were bound to change as methods changed. Washburn's "science studies" deconstructed science in order to reconstruct it in ways that made science better. In this light, his suggestion that the scientific study of human evolution should be treated as a game (1973) was not an attempt to deride science. Instead it was an effort to make us see science realistically by building into practice a recognition of the limitations of the data, methods, and theory at any moment in time. Practitioners in the new field of science studies, and amal-

gam and reworking of philosophy, history, sociology, and anthropology of science, would be pleasantly surprised by Washburn's stance, which is rare among "scientists," then or now. A growing cohort of science scholars is currently pursuing these issues (e.g., Haraway 1989; Latour 1987; Shapin 1994).

**SCIENCE AND SOCIETY** Today, science is being closely scrutinized by society and, partly in response, by scientists themselves. What is at stake is not only the definition of what science is but how it is and should be embedded in society. Regardless of how the current controversy resolves itself, both sides share a growing concern about the relevance of scientific knowledge to solving major social problems. Here, too, Washburn's personal commitment to making science useful to society was prescient. He pushed anthropologists to take cognizance of a number of urgent social issues, many of which are still at the heart of the dilemmas of the 1990s. Race (Haraway 1989; Stocking 1993; UNESCO 1952) was the first of these (see Appendix). NPA tried to change arguments about race by using a different evolutionary framework (Haraway 1989: 186–250) and giving scientific legitimacy to an alternative way to think about human nature (see further discussion in Haraway 1997). The next issue under scrutiny for Washburn and his students was aggression and conflict (see Appendix). The future of the human species seemed in doubt after World War II and in the context of the cold war (Haraway 1989). The NPA argued that we could not understand modern human aggression without an evolutionary perspective. This perspective combined data from other primate species and the fossil evidence to suggest an alternative view of human nature that was a counterpoint to the very pessimistic and deterministic vision of instinctive aggression then popular (see Lorenz 1966). In the NPA argument about aggression are claims about behavior that are only now gaining wider currency. For example, Washburn argued (in collaboration with David Hamburg) that aggression (or any behavior) was adaptive but not inevitable, that it depended on a biology, but biology created an "ease of learning," not destiny. Certain aspects of the modern world made life difficult for humans because old ways of behavior, adapted to the past, were slow to change and not suited to our modern lifestyles. The complexity of interactions, themselves placed in a variable and complex context of biology and behavior, provided a different kind of scientific model of behavior. At the same time it offered some hope that humans, if they wanted to, could mold a different future, not by naive idealism but by recognizing that evolutionary history built obstacles into any effort to change human behavior.

An evolutionary perspective on human behavior was also applied to the problems of the faltering American public school system. Using the NPA framework, Washburn rethought the problem. He reasoned that a major source of the difficulty was that humans were no longer learning the way that primates had for more than 50 million years of evolution. The new ways were not only different, they seemed to violate the basic rules of successful primate learning: Make it fun, have a strong social attachment to your learning partner or teacher, play is best, be allowed to make mistakes without paying the price. From this evolutionary vantage point, it was easy to see what was wrong with formal education systems as well as how we might change them for the better.

We have yet to resolve the problems of race, conflict, and education. The challenge to the many agencies, institutions, and actors (both scientific and nonscientific) remains how to break out of past ways of thinking about the issues and find new solutions. The NPA and Washburn offered a perspective for reflection that generated concrete suggestions about how to change what we didn't like, if only we were brave enough to both understand our history and act on that knowledge.

RADICAL AGENDAS Many of the central tenets of the NPA have become part of a diverse number of radical initiatives both within and outside of science. These include the claim that the social cannot be understood without reference to the biological (and vice versa); that emotions are evolutionarily important aspects of the lives of many species, and that the discovery of truth is not a given but the result of our (human) evolutionary history. Equally revolutionary is the insistence on a comparative perspective based on the assumption that we cannot understand or make interpretations about something without multiply situating it. The "situatedness of knowledge" is currently a hotly contested concept (Clifford and Marcus 1986; Nader 1996), primarily because many science critics, unlike Washburn, deconstruct our past ways of creating knowledge without reconstructing better ways of doing so.

## The Future of the New Physical Anthropology

Latour (in press) has suggested that what distinguishes good from bad science (not truth from falsehood) is the ability to make many new links, to entangle, to articulate in ways that reconfigure our knowledge of the world, the way we do science and perhaps even the way we do society. This has been the central concern of the new physical anthropology from the start. The enterprise was unique because of Sherwood Washburn's personal vision and his quest to create a science that recognizes the inappropriateness of past, traditional ways of thinking and of doing science and that is able to move on, to forge a science "not limited by the past." To the extent that the new physical anthropology has succeeded, it may be one of the first examples of a postmodern or a-modern science (Latour 1993), at least in its founding principles.

Because there is no "institute" devoted to the new physical anthropology, its future will depend, as has its past, on its practitioners, individuals who were trained in its precepts and who are now scattered all over the world. Each one continues to work through these agendas in his or her own fashion. But one indication of the success of the project may be that many "new physical anthropologists" work in association with "outsiders." This suggests that networks of cooperative collaboration have been created that cross and combine disciplines in pursuit of the five goals of the new physical anthropology:

1. Diagnose evolutionary complexes.
2. Describe variations in adaptations.
3. Determine the underlying biology and genetics of each adaptive complex.
4. Identify the conditions that would have selected for the adaptation.
5. Improve the quality of phylogenetic reconstructions and do so with better methods, better theory and with social responsibility.

I gained a fresh sense of my own history and of the joint endeavor called the new physical anthropology by putting this book together. What surprised me the most was the remarkable unity of vision expressed in the diversity of our work. Unity does not mean simplicity. On the contrary, it is the complexity of the framework offered by the new physical anthropology that has allowed each of us to take very different routes, explore divergent topics, and still be part of the same enterprise. It was only when the seminal papers of Sherwood Washburn were brought together with this range of independent research could I appreciate the extent to which the new physical anthropology is still a vibrant field and a living practice.

## SELECTED BIBLIOGRAPHY

Bak, P. and Chen, K. (1991). Self-organized criticality. *Scientific American*, January. 46–53.

Barkow, J., Cosmides, L., and Tooby, J. eds. (1992). *The Adapted Mind: Evolutionary Psychology and the Generation of Culture.* New York: Oxford University Press.

Clifford, J. and Marcus, G. E. (1986). *Writing Culture: The Poetics and Politics of Ethnography.* Berkeley: University of California Press.

Elman, J., Bates, L., Johnson, M., Karmiloff-Smith, A., Parisi, D., and Plunkett, K., eds. (1996). *Rethinking Innateness: Connectionism in a Developmental Framework*. Cambridge, MA: MIT Press.

Feldman, M.S. (1989). *Order Without Design.* Berkeley: University of California Press.

Gardner, H. (1985). *The Mind's New Science: A History of the Cognitive Revolution*. New York: Basic Books.

Gross, P. R., and Levitt, N. (1994). *Higher Superstition: The Academic Left and Its Quarrels with Science*. Baltimore: Johns Hopkins University Press.

Haraway, D. (1989). *Primate Visions: Gender, Race and Nature in the World of Modern Science*. New York: Routledge.

Haraway, D. (1997). *Modest_Witness@Second_Millennium*. New York: Routledge.

Hutchins, E. (1995). *Cognition in the Wild*. Cambridge, MA: MIT Press.

Huber, P. W. (1991). *Galileo's Revenge: Junk Science in the Courtroom*. New York: Basic Books.

Kahn, P. (1994). Genetic Diversity Project tries again. *Science 266:* 720–722.

Kelves, D., and Hood, L. (1992). *The Code of Codes: Scientific and Social Issues in the Human Genome Project*. Cambridge, MA: Harvard University Press.

Latour, B. (1987). *Science in Action*. Cambridge, MA: Harvard University Press.

Latour, B. (1993). *We Have Never Been Modern*. Cambridge, MA: Harvard University Press.

Latour, B. (in press). A well-articulated primatology: Reflections of a fellow traveler. In S. C. Strum and L. M. Fedigan (eds.), *Primate Encounters: Models of Science, Gender, and Society*. Chicago: University of Chicago Press.

Lorenz, K. (1966). *On Aggression*. New York: Harcourt, Brace and World.

McClelland, J., Rumelhart, D., and the PDP Group, eds. (1986). *Parallel Distributed Processing: Explorations in the Microstructure of Cog-nition*. Vol. 2, *Psychological and Biological Models*. Cambridge, MA: MIT Press.

Nader, L., ed. (1996). *Naked Science: Anthropological Inquiry into Boundaries, Power and Knowledge*. New York: Routledge.

New York Academy of Sciences. (1996). *The Flight from Science and Reason*. New York.

Nicolis, G. and Prigogine, I. (1989). *Exploring Complexity*. New York: Freeman.

Ristau, C., ed. (1990). *Cognitive Ethology: The Minds of Other Animals*. Hillsdale, NJ: Lawrence Erlbaum Associates.

Shapin, S. (1994). *The Social History of Truth: Civility and Science in Seventeenth-Century England*. Chicago: University of Chicago Press.

Stein, D. L., ed. (1989). *Lectures in the Sciences of Complexity*. Sante Fe Institute Studies in the Sciences of Complexity, Vol. 1. Redwood City, CA: Addison-Wesley.

Stocking, G., Jr. (1993). The turn-of-the-century concept of race. *Modernism/Modernity 1:* 4–16.

Tooby, J., and Cosmides, L. (1990). The past explains the present: Emotional adaptations and the structure of ancestral environments. *Ethology and Sociobiology 11:* 375–421.

UNESCO. (1952). *The Race Concept: Results of an Inquiry*. Paris.

Waldrop, M. M. (1992). *Complexity*. New York: Simon & Schuster.

Washburn, S. L. (1973). Human evolution: Science or game? *Yearbook of Physical Anthropology 17:* 67–70.

Washburn, S. L., and Hamburg, D. A. (1968). Aggressive behavior in Old World monkeys and apes. In P. C. Jay, (ed.), *Primates: Studies in Adaptation and Variability*. New York: Holt, Rinehart and Winston, pp. 458–478.

Wertsch, J. (1985). *The Social Formation of Mind*. Cambridge, MA: Harvard University Press.

Wright, R. (1994). *The Moral Animal: Evolutionary Psychology and Everyday Life*. New York: Pantheon.

*Washburn's presidential address to the American Anthropological Association in 1962 identified race as an emotional and confusing topic that, nonetheless, was of great interest to both scientists and society. Washburn argues that changes in the way we understand evolution as the result of the "new synthesis" fundamentally alter the way we should study race and interpret its importance. An emphasis on evolution at the species level and on the important evolutionary processes of migration, drift, and selection demonstrates the shortcomings of previous typological thinking, particularly as applied to racial categories. Instead, Washburn recognized that race is a "flexible" category whose configuration relies on the ultimate purpose of the argument. Washburn illustrates the difference between the old and new ways of thinking about race and charts the future of scientific investigations. A pivotal proposition that Washburn puts forward is that no race evolved in the modern technical cultural context and therefore no race has any special preadaptation to current circumstances. He ends with a consideration of the costs of social discrimination, the nature of a democratic society, and the relative contribution of nature and nurture—all points that continue to be salient to this day.*

# The Study of Race

**S. L. Washburn**  *University of California, Berkeley*

The Executive Board has asked me to give my address on the subject of race, and, reluctantly and diffidently, I have agreed to do so. I am not a specialist on this subject. I have never done research on race, but I have taught it for a number of years.

Discussion of the races of man seems to generate endless emotion and confusion. I am under no illusion that this paper can do much to dispel the confusion; it may add to the emotion. The latest information available supports the traditional findings of anthropologists and other social scientists—that there is no scientific basis of any kind for racial discrimination. I think that the way this conclusion has been reached needs to be restated. The continuation of antiquated biological notions in anthropology and the oversimplification of facts weakens the anthropological position. We must realize that great changes have taken place in the study of race over the last 20 years and it is up to us to bring our profession into the forefront of the newer understandings, so that our statements will be authoritative and useful.

This paper will be concerned with three topics—the modern concept of race, the interpretation of racial dif-

Delivered as the Presidential Address at the annual meeting of the American Anthropological Association, November 16, 1962, in Chicago. Reprinted from *American Anthropologist* 65, No. 3 (June, 1963), pp. 521–531.

ferences, and the social significances of race. And, again, I have no illusion that these things can be treated briefly; I shall merely say a few things which are on my mind and which you may amplify by turning to the literature, and especially to Dobzhansky's book, *Mankind Evolving.* This book states the relations between culture and genetics in a way which is useful to social scientists. In my opinion it is a great book which puts the interrelations of biology and culture in proper perspective and avoids the oversimplifications which come from overemphasis on either one alone.

The races of man are the result of human evolution, of the evolution of our species. The races are open parts of the species, and the species is a closed system. If we look, then, upon long-term human evolution, our first problem must be the species and the things which have caused the evolution of all mankind, not the races, which are the results of local forces and which are minor in terms of the evolution of the whole species. (A contrary view has recently been expressed by Coon in *The Origin of Races.* I think that great antiquity of human races is supported neither by the record nor by evolutionary theory.)

The evolution of races is due, according to modern genetics, to mutation, selection, migration, and genetic drift. It is easy to shift from this statement of genetic theory to complications of hemoglobin, blood groups or other technical information. But the point I want to stress is that the primary implication of genetics for anthropology is that it affirms the relation of culture and biology in a far firmer and more important way than ever in our history before. Selection is for reproductive success, and in man reproductive success is primarily determined by the social system and by culture. Effective behavior is the question, not something else.

Drift depends on the size of population, and population size, again, is dependent upon culture, not upon genetic factors as such. Obviously, migration depends on clothes, transportation, economy, and warfare and is reflected in the archeological record. Even mutation rates are now affected by technology.

Genetic theory forces the consideration of culture as the major factor in the evolution of man. It thus reaffirms the fundamental belief of anthropologists that we must study man both as a biological and as a social organism. This is no longer a question of something that might be desirable; it must be done if genetic theory is correct.

We have, then, on the one hand the history of genetic systems, and on the other hand the history of cultural systems, and, finally, the interrelation between these two. There is no evolution in the traditional anthropological sense. What Boas referred to as evolution was orthogenesis—which receives no support from modern genetic theory. What the geneticist sees as evolution is far closer to what Boas called history than to what he called evolution, and some anthropologists are still fighting a nineteenth-century battle in their presentation of evolution. We have, then, the history of cultural systems, which you may call history; and the history of genetic systems, which you may call evolution if you want to, but if you use this word remember that it means selection, migration, drift—it is real history that you are talking about and not some mystic force which constrains mankind to evolve according to some orthogenetic principle.

There is, then, no possibility of studying human raciation, the process of race formation, without studying human culture. Archeology is as important in the study of the origin of races as is genetics; all we can do is reconstruct as best we can the long-term past, and this is going to be very difficult.

Now let me contrast this point of view with the one which has been common in much of anthropology. In the first place, anthropology's main subject, the subject of race, disregarded to an amazing degree the evolution of the human species. Anthropologists were so concerned with the subdivisions within our species and with minor detailed differences between small parts of the species that the physical anthropologists largely forgot that mankind is a species and that the im-

portant thing is the evolution of this whole group, not the minor differences between its parts.

If we look back to the time when I was educated, races were regarded as types. We were taught to go to a population and divide it into a series of types and to re-create history out of this artificial arrangement. Those of you who have read *Current Anthropology* will realize that this kind of anthropology is still alive, amazingly, and in full force in some countries; relics of it are still alive in our teaching today.

Genetics shows us that typology must be completely removed from our thinking if we are to progress. For example, let us take the case of the Bushmen. The Bushmen have been described as the result of a mixture between Negro and Mongoloid. Such a statement could only be put in the literature without any possible consideration of migration routes, of numbers of people, of cultures, of any way that such a mixing could actually take place. The fact is that the Bushmen had a substantial record in South Africa and in East Africa and there is no evidence that they ever were anywhere els˜ except in these areas. In other words, they are ₌ r which belongs exactly where they are.

If we are concerned with history let us consider, on the one hand, the ancestors of these Bushmen 15,000 years ago and the area available to them, to their way of life, and, on the other hand, the ancestors of Europeans at the same time in the area available to them, with their way of life. We will find that the area available to the Bushmen was at least twice that available to the Europeans. The Bushmen were living in a land of optimum game; the Europeans were living close to an ice sheet. There were perhaps from three to five times as many Bushmen ancestors as there were European ancestors only 15,000 years ago.

If one were to name a major race, or a primary race, the Bushmen have a far better claim in terms of the archeological record than the Europeans. During the time of glacial advance more than half of the Old World available to man for life was in Africa. The numbers and distributions that we think of as normal and the races whose last results we see today are relics of an earlier and far different time in human history.

There are no three primary races, no three major groups. The idea of three primary races stems from nineteenth-century typology; it is totally misleading to put the black-skinned people of the world together—to put the Australian in the same grouping with the inhabitants of Africa. And there are certainly at least three independent origins of the small, dark people, the Pygmies, and probably more than that. There is no single Pygmy race.

If we look to real history we will always find more than three races, because there are more than three major areas in which the raciation of our species was taking place.

If we attempt to preserve the notion of three races, we make pseudo-typological problems. Take for example, again, the problem of the aboriginal Australian. If we have only three races, either they must be put with the people of Africa, with which they have nothing in common, or they must be accounted for by mixture, and in books appearing even as late as 1950, a part of the aboriginal Australian population is described as European, and listed with the Europeans, and the residue is listed with the Africans and left there.

The concept of race is fundamentally changed if we actually look for selection, migration, and study people as they are (who they are, where they are, how many they are); and the majority of anthropological textbooks need substantial revision along these lines.

Since races are open systems which are intergrading, the number of races will depend on the purpose of the classification. This is, I think, a tremendously important point. It is significant that as I was reviewing classifications in preparing this lecture, I found that almost none of them mentioned any purpose for which people were being classified. Race isn't very important biologically. If we are classifying races in order to understand human history, there aren't many human races, and there is very substantial agreement as to what they are. There are from six to nine races, and this difference in number is very largely a matter of definition. These races occupied the major separate geographical areas in the Old World.

If one has no purpose for classification, the number of races can be multiplied almost indefinitely, and it seems to me that the erratically varying number of races is a source of confusion to student, to layman, and to specialist. I think we should require people who propose a classification of races to state in the first place why they wish to divide the human species and to give in detail the important reasons for subdividing our whole species. If important reasons for such classification are given, I think you will find that the number of races is always exceedingly small.

If we consider these six or nine geographical races and the factors which produced them, I think the first thing we want to stress is migration.

All through human history, where we have any evidence of that history, people have migrated. In a recent ANTHROPOLOGIST there is a suggestion that it took 400,000 years for a gene that mutated in China to reach Europe. We know, historically, that Alexander the Great went from Greece into Northern India. We know that Mongol tribes migrated from Asia into Europe. Only a person seeking to believe that the races are very separate could possibly believe such a figure as that cited.

Migration has always been important in human history and there is no such thing as human populations which are completely separated from other human populations. And migration necessarily brings in new genes, necessarily reduces the differences between the races. For raciation to take place, then, there must be other factors operating which create difference. Under certain circumstances, in very small populations, differences may be created by genetic drift, or because the founders are for chance reasons very different from other members of the species.

However, the primary factor in the creation of racial differences in the long term is selection. This means that the origin of races must depend on adaptation and that the differences between the races which we see must in times past have been adaptive. I stress the question of time here, because it is perfectly logical to maintain that in time past a shovel-shaped incisor, for example, was more efficient than an incisor of other forms and that selection would have been for this, and at the same time to assert that today this dental difference is of absolutely no social importance. It is important to make this point because people generally take the view that something is always adaptive or never adaptive, and this is a fundamental oversimplification of the facts.

Adaptation is always within a given situation. There is no such thing as a gene which has a particular adaptive value; it has this value only under set circumstances. For example, the sickle-cell gene, if Allison and others are right, protects against malaria. This is adaptive if there is malaria, but if there is not malaria it is not adaptive. The adaptive value of the gene, then, is dependent on the state of medicine and has no absolute value. The same is true of the other characteristics associated with race.

I would like to go over some of the suggestions which have been made about the adaptive values of various structures in human beings, because I think these need to be looked at again.

I have stressed that the concept of race which comes from population genetics is compatible with what anthropologists have thought. I think that this concept represents great progress. But when I read the descriptions of the importance of adaptive characteristics, I am not sure that there has been any progress since the nineteenth century.

In this connection I should like to speak for a moment on the notion that the Mongoloids are a race which are adapted to live in the cold, that these are arctic-adapted people.

In the first place, in marked contrast to animals which are adapted to live in the arctic, large numbers of Mongoloids are living in the hot, moist tropics. Altogether unlike animal adaptation, then, the people who are supposed to be adapted to the cold aren't living under cold conditions, and I think we should stress this. For thousands of years the majority of this group have not been living under the conditions which are supposed to have produced them. They are presumed, as an arctic-adapted group following various laws, to have short extremities, flat noses, and to be stocky in build. They are, we might say, as stocky as the Scotch, as flat-nosed as the Norwegians, and as blonde as the Eskimos. Actually, there is no correlation, that is, one that has been well worked out, to support the notion that any of these racial groups is cold-adapted.

Let me say a few more words on this lack of correlation. If one follows the form of the nose, in Europe, as one moves north, narrow noses are correlated with cold climate; in Eastern Asia low noses are correlated with cold climate. In neither case is there the slightest evidence that the difference in the form of the nose has anything whatsoever to do with warming the air that comes into the face. Further, if we look at these differences expressed in this way, we see that they are posed in terms of nineteenth-century notions of what a face is all about.

Let us look at it differently. The nose is the center of a face. Most of a face is concerned with teeth, and bones, and muscles that have to do with chewing. The Mongoloid face is primarily the result of large masseter muscles and the bones from which these muscles arise (malar and gonial angles). This is a complex structural pattern related to the teeth, and a superficially very similar pattern may be seen in the Bushman, whose facial form can hardly be attributed to adaptation to cold.

The face of the Neanderthal man has recently been described also as cold-adapted, though it does not have the characteristics of the Mongoloid face. We are told that the blood supply to the Neanderthal face was greatly increased because the infraorbital foramen was large, bringing more blood to the front of the face. In actual fact, most of the blood to our face does not go through that artery. The artery that carries most of the blood to the face comes along the outside, and even our arteries are far too large to go through the mental or infraorbital foramen of Neanderthal man. This kind of statement, as well as the statement that the maxillary sinus warmed the air and that the function of a large orbit was to keep the eyes from freezing, seems to me an extraordinary retrogression to the worst kind of evolutionary speculation—speculation that antedates genetics and reveals a lack of any kind of reasonable understanding of the structure of the human face.

The point I wish to stress is that those who have spoken of the cold-adaptation of the Mongoloid face and of the Neanderthal face do not know the structure of the human face. We have people writing about human faces who are anatomically illiterate. I am genetically illiterate; I do not know about the hemoglobins. I am not asserting that all of us should be required to be literate in all branches of physical anthropology. As Stanley Garn points out, the field has become complicated, but people who are writing about the structure of the human face should learn the elements of anatomy.

The adaptive value of skin color has been repeatedly claimed, but recently Blum has indicated that the situation is more complicated than it appeared. In the first place, he points out the melanin in the skin doesn't do what anthropologists have said it has done. The part of the skin which mainly stops ultraviolet light, the short-wave length light, is a thickened *stratum corneum,* rather than melanin.

Again, the chimpanzee and the gorilla live in precisely the same climatic conditions in Uganda, but the gorilla has one of the blackest, most deeply pigmented skins of the primates and the chimpanzee has a very light skin. It simply is not true that skin color closely parallels climate. The point here is that racial classification tells us very little. The classification poses problems; it does not solve them.

In scientific method, as I see it, one looks at relevant data and when these data are laid out, as in, say, the classification of races, one may then find a correlation which is helpful. But after that, one has to do an experiment; one has to do something that shows that the correlation has validity. And it's no use continuing to correlate nose-form or skin color with climate. The crude correlations were made many years ago, and to advance the study of race requires new methods and more sophisticated analyses.

When I was a student, there were naive racial interpretations based on the metrical data. When these became unacceptable politically the same people used naive constitutional correlations to reach the same conclusions of social importance. Today we have naive concepts of adaptation, taking the place of the earlier interpretations, and a recrudescence of the racial thinking.

All along the line there have been valid problems in race, valid problems in constitution, and valid problems in adaptation. What I am protesting against strongly is the notion that one can simply take a factor, such as a high cheek-bone, think that it might be related to climate, and then jump to this conclusion without any kind of connecting link between the two elements—without any kind of experimental verification of the sort of material that is being dealt with. If we took really seriously this notion that a flat face with large maxillary sinuses, deep orbits, and big brow ridges is cold-adapted, it is clear that the most cold-adapted animal in the primates is the gorilla.

Race, then, is a useful concept only if one is concerned with the kind of anatomical, genetic, and structural differences which were in time past important in the origin of races. Race in human thinking is a very minor concept. It is entirely worth while to have a small number of specialists, such as myself, who are concerned with the origin of gonial angles, the form of the nose, the origin of dental patterns, changes in blood-group frequencies, and so on. But this is a very minor, specialized kind of knowledge.

If classification is to have a purpose, we may look backward to the explanation of the differences between people—structural, anatomical, physiological differences—and then the concept of race is useful, but it is useful under no other circumstances, as far as I can see.

When the meaning of skin color and structure is fully understood, it will help us to understand the origin of races, but this is not the same thing as understanding the origin of our species. It will help in the understanding of why color was important in time long past, but it will have no meaning to modern technical society.

I turn now to a brief statement on the influence of culture upon race. Beginning with agriculture and continuing at an ever-increasing rate, human customs have been interposed between the organism and the environment. The increase of our species from perhaps as few as five million before agriculture to three billion today is the result of new technology, not of biological evolution. The conditions under which the races evolved are mainly gone, and there are new causes of mutation, new kinds of selection, and vast migration. Today the numbers and distribution of the peoples of the world are due primarily to culture. Some people think the new conditions are so different that it is better no longer to use the word race or the word evolution, but I personally think this confuses more than it clarifies.

All this does not mean that evolution has stopped, because the new conditions will change gene frequencies, but the conditions which produced the old races are gone. In this crowded world of civilization and science, the claim has been made repeatedly that one or another of the races is superior to the others. Obviously, this argument cannot be based on the past; because something was useful in times past and was selected for under conditions which are now gone, does not mean that it will be useful in the present or in the future.

The essential point at issue is whether the abilities of large populations are so different that their capacity to participate in modern technical culture is affected. Remember in the first place that no race has evolved to fit the selective pressures of the modern world. Technical civilization is new and the races are old. Remember also that all the species of *Homo* have been adapting to the human way of life for many thousands of years.

Tools even antedate our genus, and our human biological adaptation is the result of culture. Man and his capacity for culture have evolved together, as Dr. Dobzhansky has pointed out. All men are adapted to learn language—any language; to perform skillful tasks—a fabulous variety of tasks; to cooperate; to enjoy art; to practice religion, philosophy, and science.

Our species only survives in culture, and, in a profound sense, we are the product of the new selection pressures that came with culture.

Infinitely more is known about the language and culture of all the groups of mankind than is known about the biology of racial differences. We know that the members of every racial group have learned a vast variety of languages and ways of life. The interaction of genes and custom over the millennia has produced a species whose populations can learn to live in an amazing variety of complex cultural ways.

Racism is based on a profound misunderstanding of culture, of learning, and of the biology of the human species. The study of cultures should give a profound respect for the biology of man's capacity to learn. Much of the earlier discussion of racial inferiority centered on the discussion of intelligence; or, to put the matter more accurately, usually on that small part of biological intelligence which is measured by the IQ. In the earlier days of intelligence testing, there was a widespread belief that the tests revealed something which was genetically fixed within a rather narrow range. The whole climate of opinion that fostered this point of view has changed. At that time animals were regarded as primarily instinctive in their behavior, and the genes were supposed to exert their effects in an almost mechanical way, regardless of the environment. All this intellectual climate has changed. Learning has proved to be far more important in the behavior of many animal species, and the action of the complexes of genes is now known to be affected by the environment, as is, to a great degree, the performance that results from them. For example, Harlow has shown that monkeys learn to learn. Monkeys become test wise. They become skillful in the solution of tests—so monkeys in Dr. Harlow's laboratories are spoken of as naive or as experienced in the use of tests. To suppose that humans cannot learn to take tests is to suppose that humans are rather less intelligent than monkeys.

Krech and Rosenzweig have shown that rats raised in an enriched environment are much more intelligent and efficient as maze-solvers than rats that have been given no opportunity to learn and to practice before the testing. To suppose that man would not learn through education to take tests more efficiently, is to suppose that our learning capacities are rather less than those of rats.

The human is born with less than a third of the adult brain capacity, and there is tremendous growth of the cortex after birth. There is possibly no mammalian species in which the environment has a longer and more direct effect on the central nervous system than man. We should expect, then, that test results are going to be more affected by the environment of man than in the case of any other animal. Deprivation studies of monkeys and chimpanzees and clinical investigations of man show that the lack of a normal interpersonal environment may be devastating to the developing individual.

Today one approaches the study of intelligence expecting to find that environment is important. The intellectual background is very different from that of the '20's. The general results on testing may be briefly summarized as follows:

> The average IQ of large groups is raised by education. I believe the most important data on this are the comparisons of the soldiers of World War I and of World War II. More than 80 per cent of the soldiers tested in World War II were above the mean of those tested in World War I. This means a wholesale massive improvement, judged by these tests, in the sons of the people who fought in World War I.

In the states where the least educational effort is made, the IQ is the lowest. In fact, as one looks at the review in Anastasi, it is exceedingly difficult to see why anyone ever thought that the IQ measured innate intelligence, and not the genetic constitution as modified in the family, in the schools, and by the general intellectual environment.

I would suggest that if the intelligence quotients of Negroes and Whites in this country are compared, the same rules be used for these comparisons as would be used for comparisons of the data between two groups of Whites. This may not seem a very extreme thing to suggest, but if you look at the literature, you will find that when two groups of Whites differ in their IQ's, the explanation of the difference is immediately sought in schooling, environment, economic positions of parents, and so on, but that when Negroes and Whites differ in precisely the same way the difference is said to be genetic.

Let me give you but one example of this. Klineberg showed years ago in excellent studies that the mean test scores of many Northern Negro groups were higher than those of certain groups of Southern Whites. When these findings were published, it was immediately suggested that there had been a differential migration and the more intelligent Negroes had moved to the North. But the mean of Northern Whites test results is above that of Southern Whites. Are we to believe that the intelligent Whites also moved to the North?

There is no way of telling what the IQ would be if equal opportunity were given to all racial and social groups. The group which is sociologically classified as Negro in the United States, about one-third of whose genes are of European origin, might well test ahead of the Whites. I am sometimes surprised to hear it stated that if Negroes were given an equal opportunity, their IQ would be the same as the Whites'. If one looks at the degree of social discrimination against Negroes and their lack of education, and also takes into account the tremendous amount of overlapping between the observed IQ's of both, one can make an equally good case that, given a comparable chance to that of the Whites, their IQ's would test out ahead. Of course, it would be absolutely unimportant in a democratic society if this were to be true, because the vast majority of individuals of both groups would be of comparable intelligence, whatever the mean of these intelligence tests would show.

We can generalize this point. All kinds of human performance—whether social, athletic, intellectual—are built on genetic and environmental elements. The level of all kinds of performance can be increased by improving the environmental situation so that every genetic constitution may be developed to its full capacity. Any kind of social discrimination against groups of people, whether these are races, castes, or classes, reduces the achievements of our species, of mankind.

The cost of discrimination is reflected in length of life. The Founding Fathers were wise to join life, liberty, and the pursuit of happiness, because these are intimately linked in the social and cultural system. Just as the restriction of social and economic opportunity reduces intelligence so it reduces length of life.

In 1900 the life expectancy of White males in the United States was 48 years, and in that same year the expectancy of a Negro male was 32 years; that is a difference of 50 per cent, or 16 years. By 1940 the difference had been reduced to ten years, and by 1958 to six. As the life expectancy of the Whites increased from 48 to 62 to 67 years, that of the Negroes increased from 32 to 52 to 61 years. They died of the same causes, but they died at different rates.

Discrimination, by denying equal social opportunity to the Negro, made his progress lag approximately 20 years behind that of the White. Somebody said to me, "Well, 61, 67, that's only six years." But it depends on whose six years it is. There are about 19 million people in this country sociologically classified as Negroes. If they die according to the death rate given above, approximately 100 million years of life will be lost owing to discrimination.

In 1958 the death rate for Negroes in the first year of life was 52 per thousand and for Whites 26. Thousands of Negro infants died unnecessarily. The social conscience is an extraordinary thing. A lynching stirs the whole community to action, yet only a single life is lost. Discrimination, through denying education, medical care, and economic progress, kills at a far higher rate. A ghetto of hatred kills more surely than a concentration camp, because it kills by accepted custom, and it kills every day in the year.

A few years ago in South Africa, the expectation of life for a Black man was 40 years, but it was 60 at the same time for a White man. At that same time a White woman could expect 25 more years of life than a Black woman. Among the Blacks the women lived no longer than the men. People speak of the greater longevity of women, but this is only because of modern medicine. High birth rates, high infant mortality, high maternal mortality—these are the hallmarks of the history of mankind.

Of course there are biological differences between male and female, but whether a woman is allowed to vote, or the rate that she must die in childbirth, these are a matter of medical knowledge and of custom. Biological difference only expresses itself through the social system.

Who may live longer in the future—Whites or Negroes? There's no way of telling. Who may live longer in the future—males or females? There is no way of telling. These things are dependent on the progress in medical science and on the degree to which this progress is made available to all races and to both sexes.

When environment is important, the only way genetic difference may be determined is by equalizing the environment. If you believe in mankind, then you will want mankind to live on in an enriched environment. No one can tell what may be the ultimate length of life, but we do know that many people could live much longer if given a chance.

Whether we consider intelligence, or length of life, or happiness the genetic potential of a population is only realized in a social system. It is that system which gives life or death to its members, and in so doing

changes the gene frequencies. We know of no society which has begun to realize the genetic potential of its members. We are the primitives living by antiquated customs in the midst of scientific progress. Races are products of the past. They are relics of times and conditions which have long ceased to exist.

Racism is equally a relic supported by no phase of modern science. We may not know how to interpret the form of the Mongoloid face, or why Rh° is of high incidence in Africa, but we do know the benefits of education and of economic progress. We know the price of discrimination is death, frustration, and hatred. We know that the roots of happiness lie in the biology of the whole species and that the potential of the species can only be realized in a culture, in a social system. It is knowledge and the social system which give life or take it away, and in so doing change the gene frequencies and continue the million-year-old interaction of culture and biology. Human biology finds its realization in a culturally determined way of life, and the infinite variety of genetic combinations can only express themselves efficiently in a free and open society.

## REFERENCES

Anastasi, Anne. 1958. *Differential Psychology: Individual and Group Differences in Behavior.* New York, The Macmillan Company.

Blum, Harold F. 1961. Does the melanin pigment of human skin have adaptive value? *The Quarterly Review of Biology* 36:50–63.

Coon, Carleton S. 1962, *The Origin of Races.* New York, Alfred A. Knopf.

Dobzhansky, Theodosius. 1962. *Mankind Evolving: The Evolution of the Human Species.* New Haven and London, Yale University Press.

Dublin, Louis I., Alfred J. Lotka, and Mortimer Spiegelman. 1949. *Length of Life: A Study of the Life Table.* (Revised Edition.) New York, The Ronald Press Company.

Klineberg, Otto. 1935. *Race Differences.* New York and London, Harper & Brothers.

Krech, David, Mark R. Rosenzweig, and Edward L. Bennett. 1962. Relations between brain chemistry and problem-solving among rats raised in enriched and impoverished environments. *Journal of Comparative and Physiological Psychology:* 55:801–807.

*This paper was part of the proceedings of a conference that brought together experts on the hunting way of life, past and present. Washburn and cultural anthropologist Lancaster look at hunting and gathering from an evolutionary perspective. They argue that hunting by humans is different from hunting by other mammals and that it is a complex way of life that has both dominated and molded human evolution. Although the changes during the last 6000 years of human history have been dramatic, the evolutionary legacy of hunting is much greater. It is written into the biological unity of humans as well as being the source of unique features that separate humans from other primates. Washburn and Lancaster discuss the nature of human hunting and its social, biological, and psychological consequences. They focus on salient features like cooperation between males, the ability to plan, an intensification of the division of labor, sharing of food, economic reciprocity, new technical skills, and a new social organization, arguing that evolution builds a relationship among biology, psychology, and behavior. The evolution of the brain, handedness, language, loss of estrus, and aggression are examined from this perspective. Gathering and the role of females are briefly considered. The "man the hunter" model helped to explain many features of human behavior and created a context for improved evolutionary reconstructions. It was subsequently criticized for its emphasis on hunting, to the detriment of gathering, and on the role of men, rather than women, in human evolution.*

# The Evolution of Hunting

## Sherwood L. Washburn and C. S. Lancaster

It is significant that the title of this symposium is Man the Hunter for, in contrast to carnivores, human hunting, if done by males, is based on a division of labor and is a social and technical adaptation quite different from that of other mammals.[1] Human hunting is made possible by tools, but it is far more than a technique or even a variety of techniques. It is a way of life, and the success of this adaptation (in its total social, technical, and psychological dimensions) has dominated the course of human evolution for hundreds of thousands of years. In a very real sense our intellect, interests, emotions, and basic social life—all are evolutionary products of the success of the hunting adaptation. When anthropologists speak of the unity of mankind, they are stating that the selection pressures of the hunting and gathering way of life were so similar and the result so successful that populations of *Homo sapiens* are still fundamentally the same everywhere. In this essay we are concerned with the general characteristics of man that we believe can be attributed to the hunting way of life.

Perhaps the importance of the hunting way of life in producing man is best shown by the length of time hunting has dominated human history. The genus *Homo*[2] has existed for some 600,000 years, and agriculture has been important only during the last few thousand years. Even 6,000 years ago large parts of the world's population were nonagricultural, and the entire evolution of man from the earliest populations of *Homo erectus* to the existing races took place during the period in which man was a hunter. The common factors that dominated human evolution and produced *Homo sapiens* were preagricultural. Agricultural ways of life have dominated less than 1 per cent of human history, and there is no evidence of major biological changes during that period of time. The kind of minor biologi-

Richard B. Lee and Irven DeVore, eds., *Man the Hunter* (New York: Aldine de Gruyter), pp. 292–303. Reprinted with permission. Copyright © 1968 by the Wenner-Gren Foundation for Anthropological Research, Inc.

[1] This paper is part of a program on primate behavior, supported by the United States Public Health Service (Grant No. 8623) and aided by a Research Professorship in the Miller Institute for Basic Research in Science at the University of California at Berkeley. We wish to thank Dr. Phyllis C. Jay for her helpful criticism and suggestions about this paper.

[2] The term *Homo* includes Java, Pekin, Mauer, etc., and later forms.

cal changes that occurred and which are used to characterize modern races were not common to *Homo sapiens*. The origin of all common characteristics must be sought in preagricultural times. Probably all experts would agree that hunting was a part of the social adaptation of all populations of the genus *Homo*, and many would regard *Australopithecus*[3] as a still earlier hominid who was already a hunter, although possibly much less efficient than the later forms. If this is true and if the Pleistocene period had a duration of three million years, then pre-*Homo erectus* human tool using and hunting lasted for at least four times as long as the duration of the genus *Homo* (Lancaster, MS.). No matter how the earlier times may ultimately be interpreted, the observation of more hunting among apes than was previously suspected (Goodall, 1965) and increasing evidence for hunting by *Australopithecus* strengthens the position that less than 1 per cent of human history has been dominated by agriculture. It is for this reason that the consideration of hunting is so important for the understanding of human evolution.

When hunting and the way of life of successive populations of the genus *Homo* are considered, it is important to remember that there must have been both technical and biological progress during this vast period of time. Although the locomotor system appears to have changed very little in the last 500,000 years, the brain did increase in size and the form of the face changed. But for present purposes it is particularly necessary to direct attention to the cultural changes that occurred in the last ten or fifteen thousand years before agriculture. There is no convenient term for this period of time, traditionally spoken of as the end of the Upper Paleolithic and the Mesolithic, but Binford and Binford (1966a) have rightly emphasized its importance.

During most of human history, water must have been a major physical and psychological barrier and the inability to cope with water is shown in the archeological record by the absence of remains of fish, shellfish, or any object that required going deeply into water or using boats. There is no evidence that the resources of river and sea were utilized until this late preagricultural period, and since the consumption of shellfish in particular leaves huge middens, the negative evidence is impressive. It is likely that the basic problem in utilization of resources from sea or river was that man cannot swim naturally but to do so must learn a difficult skill. In monkeys the normal quadrupedal running motions serve to keep them afloat and moving quite rapidly. A macaque, for example, does not have to learn

any new motor habit in order to swim. But the locomotor patterns of gibbons and apes will not keep them above the water surface, and even a narrow, shallow stream is a barrier for the gorilla (Schaller, 1963). For early man, water was a barrier and a danger, not a resource. (Obviously water was important for drinking, for richer vegetation along rivers and lakeshores, and for concentrating animal life. Here we are referring to water as a barrier prior to swimming and boats, and we stress that, judging from the behavior of contemporary apes, even a small stream may be a major barrier.)

In addition to the conquest of water, there seems to have been great technical progress in this late preagricultural period. Along with a much wider variety of stone tools of earlier kinds, the archeological record shows bows and arrows, grinding stones, boats, houses of much more advanced types and even villages, sledges drawn by animals and used for transport, and the domestic dog. These facts have two special kinds of significance for this symposium. First, the technology of *all* the living hunters belongs to this late Mesolithic era at the earliest, and many have elements borrowed from agricultural and metal-using peoples. Second, the occasional high densities of hunters mentioned as problems and exceptions at the symposium are based on this very late and modified extension of the hunting and gathering way of life. For example, the way of life of the tribes of the Northwest Coast, with polished stone axes for woodworking, boats, and extensive reliance on products of the river and sea, should be seen as a very late adaptation. Goldschmidt's distinction (1959, pp.185–93) between nomadic and sedentary hunting and gathering societies makes this point in a slightly different way. He shows the social elaboration which comes with the settled groups with larger populations.

The presence of the dog (Zeuner, 1963) is a good index of the late preagricultural period, and domestic dogs were used by hunters in Africa, Australia, and the Americas. Among the Eskimo, dogs were used in hunting, for transportation, as food in time of famine, and as watchdogs. With dogs, sleds, boats, metal, and complex technology, Eskimos may be a better example of the extremes to which human adaptation can go than an example of primitive hunting ways. Although hardly mentioned at the symposium, dogs were of great importance in hunting, for locating, tracking, bringing to bay, and even killing. Lee (1965, p.131) reports that one Bushman with a trained pack of hunting dogs brought in 75 per cent of the meat of a camp. Six other resident hunters lacked hunting packs and accounted for only 25 per cent of the meat. Dogs may be important in hunting even very large animals; in the Amboseli Game Reserve in Kenya one of us saw two small dogs bring a rhinoceros to bay and dodge repeated charges.

---

[3] Using the term to include both the small *A. africanus* and large *A. robustus* forms. Simpson (1966) briefly and clearly discusses the taxonomy of these forms and of the fragments called *Homo habilis*.

With the acquisition of dogs, bows, and boats it is certain that hunting became much more complex in the last few thousand years before agriculture. The antiquity of traps, snares, and poisons is unknown, but it appears that for thousands of years man was able to kill large game close in with spear or axe. As Brues (1959) has shown, this limits the size of the hunters, and there are no very large or very small fossil men. Pygmoid hunters of large game are probably possible only if hunting is with bows, traps, and poison. It is remarkable that nearly all the estimated statures for fossil men fall between 5 feet 2 inches and 5 feet 10 inches. This suggests that strong selection pressures kept human stature within narrow limits for hundreds of thousands of years and that these pressures relaxed a few thousand years ago, allowing the evolution of a much wider range of statures.

Gathering and the preparation of food also seem to have become more complex during the last few thousand years before agriculture. Obviously gathering by nonhuman primates is limited to things that can be eaten immediately. In contrast, man gathers a wide range of items that he cannot digest without soaking, boiling, grinding, or other special preparation. Seeds may have been a particularly important addition to the human diet because they are abundant and can be stored easily. Since grinding stones appear before agriculture, grinding and boiling may have been the necessary preconditions to the discovery of agriculture. One can easily imagine that people who were grinding seeds would see repeated examples of seeds sprouting or being planted by accident. Grinding and boiling were certainly known to the preagricultural peoples, and this knowledge could spread along an Arctic route, setting the stage for a nearly simultaneous discovery of agriculture in both the New and Old Worlds. It was not necessary for agriculture itself to spread through the Arctic but only the seed-using technology, which could then lead to the discovery of seed planting. If this analysis is at all correct, then the hunting-gathering, adaptation of the Indians of California, for example, should be seen as representing the possibilities of this late preagricultural gathering, making possible much higher population densities than would have been the case in pregrinding and preboiling economy.

Whatever the fate of these speculations, we think that the main conclusion, based on the archeological record, ecological considerations, and the ethnology of the surviving hunter-gatherers, will be sustained. In the last few thousand years before agriculture, both hunting and gathering became much more complex. This final adaptation, including the use of products of river and sea and the grinding and cooking of otherwise inedible seeds and nuts, was worldwide, laid the basis for the discovery of agriculture, and was much more effective and diversified than the previously existing hunting and gathering adaptations.

Hunting by members of the genus *Homo* throughout the 600,000 years that the genus has persisted has included the killing of large numbers of big animals. This implies the efficient use of tools, as Birdsell stressed at the symposium. The adaptive value of hunting large animals has been shown by Bourlière (1963), who demonstrated that 75 per cent of the meat available to human hunters in the eastern Congo was in elephant, buffalo, and hippopotamus. It is some measure of the success of human hunting that when these large species are protected in game reserves (as in the Murchison Falls or Queen Elizabeth Parks in Uganda), they multiply rapidly and destroy the vegetation. Elephants alone can destroy trees more rapidly than they are replaced naturally, as they do in the Masai Amboseli Reserve in Kenya. Since the predators are also protected in reserves, it appears that human hunters have been killing enough large game to maintain the balance of nature for many thousands of years. It is tempting to think that man replaced the saber-toothed tiger as the major predator of large game, both controlling the numbers of the game and causing the extinction of Old World saber-tooths. We think that hunting and butchering large animals put a maximum premium on cooperation among males, a behavior that is at an absolute minimum among the nonhuman primates. It is difficult to imagine the killing of creatures such as cave bears, mastodons, mammoths—or *Dinotherium* at a much earlier time—without highly coordinated, cooperative action among males. It may be that the origin of male-male associations lies in the necessities of cooperation in hunting, butchering, and war. Certainly butchering sites, such as described by F. Clark Howell in Spain, imply that the organization of the community for hunting large animals goes back for many, many thousands of years. From the biological point of view, the development of such organizations would have been paralleled by selection for an ability to plan and cooperate (or reduction of rage). Because females and juveniles may be involved in hunting small creatures, the social organization of big-game hunting would also lead to an intensification of a sexual division of labor.

It is important to stress, as noted before, that human hunting is a set of ways of life. It involves divisions of labor between male and female, sharing according to custom, cooperation among males, planning, knowledge of many species and large areas, and technical skill. Goldschmidt (1966, p. 87 ff.) has stressed the uniqueness and importance of human sharing, both in the family and in the wider society, and Lee (personal communication) emphasizes orderly sharing as fundamental to human hunting society. The importance of seeing human hunting as a whole social pattern is well illustrated by the old idea, recently revived, that the way of life of our ancestors was similar to that of wolves rather than that of apes or monkeys. But this completely misses the special nature of the human adaptation. Human females do not go out and hunt and then regurgitate to their young when they return. Human young do not stay in dens but are carried by mothers. Male wolves do not kill with tools, butcher, and share with females who have been gathering. In an evolutionary sense the whole human pattern is new, and it is the success of this particularly human way that dominated human evolution and determined the relation of biology and culture for thousands of years. Judging from the archeological record, it is probable that the major features of this human way, possibly even including the beginnings of language, had evolved by the time of *Homo erectus*.[4]

## THE WORLD VIEW OF THE HUNTER

Lévi-Strauss urged that we study the world view of hunters, and, perhaps surprisingly, some of the major aspects of world view can be traced from the archeological record. We have already mentioned that boats and the entire complex of fishing, hunting sea mammals, and using shellfish was late. With this new orientation, wide rivers and seas changed from barriers to pathways and sources of food, and the human attitude toward water must have changed completely. But many hundreds of thousands of years earlier, perhaps

[4] In speculations of this kind, it is well to keep the purpose of the speculation and the limitation of the evidence in mind. Our aim is to understand human evolution. What shaped the course of human evolution was a succession of successful adaptations, both biological and cultural. These may be inferred in part from the direct evidence of the archeological record. But the record is very incomplete. For example, Lee (personal communication) has described, for the Bushmen, how large game may be butchered where it falls and only meat brought back to camp. This kind of behavior means that analysis of bones around living sites is likely to underestimate both the amount and variety of game killed. If there is any evidence that large animals were killed, it is probable that far more were killed than the record shows. Just as the number of human bones gives no indication of the number of human beings, the number of animal bones, although it provides clues to the existence of hunting, gives no direct evidence of how many animals were killed. The Pleistocene way of life can only be known by inference and speculation. Obviously, speculations are based on much surer ground when the last few thousand years are under consideration. Ethnographic information is then directly relevant and the culture bearers are of our own species. As we go farther back in time, there is less evidence and the biological and cultural difference becomes progressively greater. Yet it was in those remote times that the human way took shape, and it is only through speculation that we may gain some insights into what the life of our ancestors may have been.

with *Australopithecus*, the relation of the hunters to the land must also have changed from an earlier relationship which may be inferred from studies of contemporary monkeys and apes. Social groups of nonhuman primates occupy exceedingly small areas, and the vast majority of animals probably spend their entire lives within less than four or five square miles. Even though they have excellent vision and can see for many miles, especially from tops of trees, they make no effort to explore more than a tiny fraction of the area they see. Even for gorillas the range is only about fifteen square miles (Schaller, 1963), and it is on the same order of magnitude for savanna baboons (DeVore and Hall, 1965). When Hall tried to drive a troop of baboons beyond the end of their range, they refused to be driven and doubled back into familiar territory, although they were easy to drive within the range. The known area is a psychological reality, clear in the minds of the animals. Only a small part of even this limited range is used, and exploration is confined to the canopy, lower branches, and bushes, or ground, depending on the biology of the particular species. Napier (1962) has discussed this highly differential use of a single area by several species. In marked contrast, human hunters are familiar with very large areas. In the area studied by Lee (1965), eleven waterholes and 600 square miles supported 248 Bushmen, a figure less than the number of baboons supported by a single waterhole and a few square miles in the Amboseli Reserve in Kenya. The most minor hunting expedition covers an area larger than most nonhuman primates would cover in a lifetime. Interest in a large area is human. The small ranges of monkeys and apes restrict the opportunities for gathering, hunting, and meeting conspecifics, and limit the kind of predation and the number of diseases. In the wide area, hunters and gatherers can take advantage of seasonal foods, and only man among the primates can migrate long distances seasonally. In the small area, the population must be carried throughout the year on local resources, and natural selection favors biology and behavior that efficiently utilize these limited opportunities. But in the wide area, natural selection favors the knowledge that enables a group to utilize seasonal and occasional food sources. Gathering over a wide and diversified area implies a greater knowledge of flora and fauna, knowledge of the annual cycle, and a different attitude toward group movements. Clearly one of the great advantages of slow maturation is that learning covers a series of years, and the meaning of events in these years become a part of the individual's knowledge. With rapid maturation and no language, the chances that any member of the group will know the appropriate behavior for rare events is greatly reduced.

Moving over long distances creates problems of carrying food and water. Lee (1965, p.124) has pointed out that the sharing of food even in one locality implies that food is carried, and there is no use in gathering quantities of fruit or nuts unless they can be moved. If women are to gather while men hunt, the results of the labors of both sexes must be carried back to some agreed upon location. Meat can be carried away easily, but the development of some sort of receptacles for carrying vegetable products may have been one of the most fundamental advances in human evolution. Without a means of carrying, the advantages of a large area are greatly reduced, and sharing implies that a person carries much more than one can use. However that may be, the whole human pattern of gathering and hunting to share—indeed, the whole complex of economic reciprocity that dominates so much of human life—is unique to man. In its small range, a monkey gathers only what it itself needs to eat at that moment. Wherever archeological evidence can suggest the beginnings of movement over large ranges, cooperation and sharing, it is dating the origin of some of the most fundamental aspects of human behavior—the human world view. We believe that hunting large animals may demand all these aspects of human behavior which separate man so sharply from the other primates. If this is so, then the human way appears to be as old as *Homo erectus*.

The price that man pays for his high mobility is well illustrated by the problems of living in the African savanna. Man is not adapted to this environment in the same sense that baboons or velvet monkeys are. Man needs much more water, and without preparation and cooking he can only eat a limited number of the foods on which the local primates thrive. Unless there have been major physiological changes, the diet of our ancestors must have been far more like that of chimpanzees than like that of a savanna-adapted species. Further, man cannot survive the diseases of the African savanna without lying down and being cared for. Even when sick, the locally adapted animals are usually able to keep moving with their troop; and the importance to their survival of a home base has been stressed elsewhere (DeVore and Washburn, 1963). Also man becomes liable to new diseases and parasites by eating meat, and it is of interest that the products of the sea, which we believe were the last class of foods added to the human diet, are widely regarded as indigestible and carry diseases to which man is particularly susceptible. Although many humans die of disease and injury, those who do not, almost without exception, owe their lives to others who cared for them when they were unable to hunt or gather, and this uniquely human caring is one of the patterns that builds social bonds in the group and permits the species to occupy almost every environment in the world.

A large territory not only provides a much wider range of possible foods but also a greater variety of potentially useful materials. With tool use this variety takes on meaning, and even the earliest pebble tools show selection in size, form, and material. When wood ceases to be just something to climb on, hardness, texture, and form become important. Availability of materials is critical to the tool user, and early men must have had a very different interest in their environment from that of monkeys or apes. Thus, the presence of tools in the archeological record is not only an indication of technical progress but also an index of interest in inanimate objects and in a much larger part of the environment than is the case with nonhuman primates.

The tools of the hunters include the earliest beautiful manmade objects, the symmetrical bifaces, especially those of the Acheulian tradition. Just how they were used is still a matter of debate, but, as contemporary attempts to copy them show, their manufacture is technically difficult, taking much time and practice and a high degree of skill. The symmetry of these tools may indicate that they were swung with great speed and force, presumably attached to some sort of handle. A tool that is moved slowly does not have to be symmetrical, but balance becomes important when an object is swung rapidly or thrown with speed. Irregularities will lead to deviations in the course of the blow or the trajectory of flight.

An axe or spear to be used with speed and power is subject to very different technical limitations from those of scrapers or digging sticks, and it may well be that it was the attempt to produce efficient high-speed weapons that first produced beautiful, symmetrical objects.

When the selective advantage of a finely worked point over an irregular one is considered, it must be remembered that a small difference might give a very large advantage. A population in which hunters hit the game 5 per cent more frequently, more accurately, or at greater distance would bring back much more meat. There must have been strong selection for greater skill in manufacture and use, and it is no accident that the bones of small-brained men (*Australopithecus*) are never found with beautiful, symmetrical tools. If the brains of contemporary apes and men are compared, the areas associated with manual skills (both in cerebellum and cortex) are at least three times as large in man. Clearly, the success of tools has exerted a great influence on the evolution of the brain, and has created the skills that make art possible. The evolution of the capacity to appreciate the product must evolve along with the skills of manufacture and use, and the biological capacities that the individual inherits must be developed in play and practiced in games. In this way, the beautiful, symmetrical tool becomes a symbol of a level of human intellectual achievement, representing far more than just the tool itself.

In a small group like the hunting band, which is devoted to one or two major cooperative activities, the necessity for long practice in developing skills to a very high level restricts the number of useful arts, and social organization is relatively simple. Where there is little division of labor, all men learn the same activities, such as skill in the hunt or in war. In sports (like the decathlon) we take it for granted that no one individual can achieve record levels of performance in more than a limited set of skills. This kind of limitation is partially biological but it is also a matter of culture. In warfare, for example, a wide variety of weapons is useful only if there are enough men to permit a division of labor so that different groups can practice different skills. Handedness, a feature that separates man from ape, is a part of this biology of skill. To be ambidextrous might seem to be ideal, but in fact the highest level of skill is attained by concentrating both biological ability and practice primarily on one hand. The evolution of handedness reflects the importance of skill, rather than mere use.

Hunting changed man's relations to other animals and his view of what is natural. The human notion that it is normal for animals to flee, the whole concept of animals being wild, is the result of man's habit of hunting. In game reserves many different kinds of animals soon learn not to fear man, and they no longer flee. James Woodburn took a Hadza into the Nairobi Park, and the Hadza was amazed and excited, because although he had hunted all his life, he had never seen such a quantity and variety of animals close at hand. His previous view of animals was the result of his having been their enemy, and they had reacted to him as the most destructive carnivore. In the park the Hadza hunter saw for the first time the peace of the herbivorous world. Prior to hunting, the relations of our ancestors to other animals must have been very much like those of the other noncarnivores. They could have moved close among the other species, fed beside them, and shared the same waterholes. But with the origin of human hunting, the peaceful relationship was destroyed, and for at least half a million years man has been the enemy of even the largest mammals. In this way the whole human view of what is normal and natural in the relation of man to animals is a product of hunting, and the world of flight and fear is the result of the efficiency of the hunters.

Behind this human view that the flight of animals from man is natural lie some aspects of human psychology. Men enjoy hunting and killing, and these activities are continued as sports even when they are no longer economically necessary. If a behavior is important to the survival of a species (as hunting was for man throughout most of human history), then it must be both easily learned and pleasurable (Hamburg, 1963). Part of the motivation for hunting is the immediate pleasure it gives the hunter, and the human killer can no more afford to be sorry for the game than a cat can for its intended victim. Evolution builds a relation between biology, psychology, and behavior, and therefore, the evolutionary success of hunting exerted a profound effect on human psychology. Perhaps, this is most easily shown by the extent of the efforts devoted to maintain killing as a sport. In former times royalty and nobility maintained parks where they could enjoy the sport of killing, and today the United States government spends many millions of dollars to supply game for hunters. Many people dislike the notion that man is naturally aggressive and that he naturally enjoys the destruction of other creatures. Yet we all know people who use the lightest fishing tackle to prolong the fish's futile struggle, in order to maximize the personal sense of mastery and skill. And until recently war was viewed in much the same way as hunting. Other human beings were simply the most dangerous game. War has been far too important in human history for it to be other than pleasurable for the males involved. It is only recently, with the entire change in the nature and conditions of war, that this institution has been challenged, that the wisdom of war as a normal part of national policy or as an approved road to personal social glory has been questioned.

Human killing differs from killing by carnivorous mammals in that the victims are frequently of the same species as the killer. In carnivores there are submission gestures or sounds that normally stop a fatal attack (Lorenz, 1966). But in man there are no effective submission gestures. It was the Roman emperor who might raise his thumb; the victim could make no sound or gesture that might restrain the victor or move the crowd to pity. The lack of biological controls over killing conspecifics is a character of human killing that separates this behavior sharply from that of other carnivorous mammals. This difference may be interpreted in a variety of ways. It may be that human hunting is so recent from an evolutionary point of view that there was not enough time for controls to evolve. Or it may be that killing other humans was a part of the adaptation from the beginning, and our sharp separation of war from hunting is due to the recent development of these institutions. Or it may be simply that in most human behavior stimulus and response are not tightly bound. Whatever the origin of this behavior, it has had profound effects on human evolution, and almost every human society has regarded killing members of certain other human societies as desirable (D. Freeman, 1964). Certainly this has been a major factor in man's view of the world, and every folklore contains tales of culture heroes whose fame is based on the human enemies they destroyed.

The extent to which the biological bases for killing have been incorporated into human psychology may be measured by the ease with which boys can be interested in hunting, fishing, fighting, and games of war. It is not that these behaviors are inevitable, but they are easily learned, satisfying, and have been socially rewarded in most cultures. The skills for killing and the pleasures of killing are normally developed in play, and the patterns of play prepare the children for their adult roles. At the conference Woodburn's excellent motion pictures showed Hadza boys killing small mammals, and Laughlin described how Aleuts train boys from early childhood so that they would be able to throw harpoons with accuracy and power while seated in kayaks. The whole youth of the hunter is dominated by practice and appreciation of the skills of the adult males, and the pleasure of the games motivates the practice that is necessary to develop the skills of weaponry. Even in monkeys, rougher play and play fighting are largely the activities of the males, and the young females explore less and show a greater interest in infants at an early age. These basic biological differences are reinforced in man by a division of labor which makes adult sex roles differ far more in humans than they do in nonhuman primates. Again, hunting must be seen as a whole pattern of activities, a wide variety of ways of life, the psychobiological roots of which are reinforced by play and by a clear identification with adult roles. Hunting is more than a part of the economic system, and the animal bones in Choukoutien are evidence of the patterns of play and pleasure of our ancestors.

## THE SOCIAL ORGANIZATION OF HUMAN HUNTING

The success of the human hunting and gathering way of life lay in its adaptability. It permitted a single species to occupy most of the earth with a minimum of biological adaptation to local conditions. The occupation of Australia and the New World was probably late, but even so there is no evidence that any other primate species occupied more than a fraction of the area of *Homo erectus*. Obviously, this adaptability makes any detailed reconstruction impossible, and we are not looking for stages in the traditional evolutionary sense. However, using both the knowledge of the contemporary primates and the archeological record, certain important general conditions of our evolution may be reconstructed. For example, the extent of the distribution of the species noted above is remarkable and gives the strongest sort of indirect evidence for the adaptability of the way of life, even half a million years ago. Likewise all evidence suggests that the local group was small. Twenty to fifty individuals is suggested by Goldschmidt (1959, p.187). Such a group size is common in nonhuman primates and so we can say with some assurance that the number of adult males who might cooperate in hunting or war was very limited, and this sets limits to the kinds of social organizations that were possible. Probably one of the great adaptive advantages of language was that it permits the planning of cooperation between local groups, temporary division of groups, and the transmission of information over a much wider area than that occupied by any one group.

Within the group of the nonhuman primates, the mother and her young may form a subgroup that continues even after the young are fully grown (Sade, 1965, 1966; Yamada, 1963). This grouping affects dominance, grooming, and resting patterns, and, along with dominance, is one of the factors giving order to the social relations in the group. The group is not a horde in the nineteenth-century sense, but it is ordered by positive affectionate habits and by the strength of personal dominance. Both these principles continue into human society, and dominance based on personal achievement must have been particularly powerful in small groups living physically dangerous lives. The mother-young group certainly continued and the bonds must have been intensified by the prolongation of infancy. But in human society, economic reciprocity is added, and this created a wholly new set of interpersonal bonds.

When males hunt and females gather, the results are shared and given to the young, and the habitual sharing between a male, a female, and their offspring becomes the basis for the human family. According to this view, the human family is the result of the reciprocity of hunting, the addition of a male to the mother-plus-young social group of the monkeys and apes.

A clue to the adaptive advantage and evolutionary origin of our psychological taboo on incest is provided by this view of the family. Incest prohibitions are reported universally among humans and these always operate to limit sexual activity involving subadults within the nuclear family. Taking the nuclear family as the unit of account, incest prohibitions tend to keep the birth rate in line with economic productivity. If in creating what we call the family the addition of a male is important in economic terms, then the male who is added must be able to fulfill the role of a socially responsible provider. In the case of the hunter, this necessitates a degree of skill in hunting and a social maturity that is attained some years after puberty. As a young man grows up, this necessary delay in his assumption of the role of provider for a female and her young is paralleled by a taboo which prevents him from prematurely adding unsupported members to the family. Brother-sister mating could result in an infant while the brother was still years away from effective social maturity. Father-daughter incest could also produce a baby without adding a productive male to the family. This would be quite different from the taking of a second wife which, if permitted, occurs only when the male has shown he is already able to provide for and maintain more than one female.

To see how radically hunting changed the economic situation, it is necessary to remember that in monkeys and apes an individual simply eats what it needs. After an infant is weaned, it is on its own economically and is not dependent on adults. This means that adult males never have economic responsibility for any other animal, and adult females do only when they are nursing. In such a system, there is no economic gain in delaying any kind of social relationship. But when hunting makes females and young dependent on the success of male skills, there is a great gain to the family members in establishing behaviors which prevent the addition of infants, unless these can be supported.

These considerations in no way alter the importance of the incest taboo as a deterrent to role conflict in the family and as the necessary precondition to all other rules of exogamy. A set of behaviors is more likely to persist and be widespread, if it serves many uses, and the rule of parsimony is completely wrong when applied to the explanation of social situations. However, these considerations do alter the emphasis and the conditions of the discussion of incest. In the first place, a mother-son sexual avoidance may be present in some species of monkeys (Sade, 1966) and this extremely strong taboo among humans requires a different explanation than the one we have offered for brother-sister and father-daughter incest prohibitions. In this case, the role conflict argument may be paramount. Second, the central consideration is that incest produces pregnancies, and the most fundamental adaptive value of the taboo is the provision of situations in which infants are more likely to survive. In the reviews of the incest taboo by Aberle and others (1963) and Mair (1965), the biological advantages of the taboo in controlling the production of infants are not adequately considered, and we find the treatment by Service (1962) closest to our own. In a society in which the majority of males die young, but a few live on past forty, the probability of incest is increased. By stressing the average length of life

rather than the age of the surviving few, Slater (1959) underestimated the probability of mating between close relatives. Vallois (1961, p. 222) has summarized the evidence on length of life in early man and shows that "few individuals passed forty years, and it is only quite exceptionally that any passed fifty."

That family organization may be attributed to the hunting way of life is supported by ethnography. Since the same economic and social problems as those under hunting continue under agriculture, the institution continued. The data on the behavior of contemporary monkeys and apes also show why this institution was not necessary in a society in which each individual gets its own food.[5] Obviously the origin of the custom cannot be dated, and we cannot prove *Homo erectus* had a family organized in the human way. But it can be shown that the conditions that make the family adaptive existed at the time of *Homo erectus*. The evidence of hunting is clear in the archeological record. A further suggestion that the human kind of family is old comes from physiology; the loss of estrus is essential to the human family organization, and it is unlikely that this physiology, which is universal in contemporary mankind, evolved recently.

If the local group is looked upon as a source of male-female pairs (an experienced hunter-provider and a female who gathers and who cares for the young), then it is apparent that a small group cannot produce pairs regularly, since chance determines whether a particular child is a male or female. If the number maturing in a given year or two is small, then there may be too many males or females (either males with no mates or females with no providers). The problem of excess females may not seem serious today or in agricultural societies, but among hunters it was recognized and was regarded as so severe that female infanticide was often practiced. How grave the problem of imbalance can become is shown by the following hypothetical example. In a society of approximately forty individuals there might be nine couples. With infants born at the rate of about one in three years, this would give three infants per year, but only approximately one of these three would survive to become fully adult. The net production in the example

---

[5] The advantage of considering both the social group and the facilitating biology is shown by considering the "family" in the gibbon. The social group consists of an adult male, an adult female, and their young. But this group is maintained by extreme territorial behavior in which no adult male tolerates another, by aggressive females with large canine teeth, and by very low sex drive in the males. The male-female group is the whole society (Carpenter 1941: Ellefson, 1966). The gibbon group is based on a different biology from that of the human family and has none of its reciprocal economic functions. Although the kind of social life seen in chimpanzees lacks a family organization, to change it into that of a man would require far less evolution than would be required in the case of the gibbon.

would be one child per year in a population of forty. And because the sex of the child is randomly determined, the odds that all the children would be male for a three-year period are 1 in 8. Likewise the odds for all surviving children being female for a three-year period are 1 in 8. In this example the chances of all surviving children being of one sex are 1 in 4, and smaller departures from a 50/50 sex ratio would be very common.

In monkeys, because the economic unit is the individual (not a pair), a surplus of females causes no problem. Surplus males may increase fighting in the group or males may migrate to other groups.

For humans, the problem of imbalance in sex ratios may be met by exogamy, which permits mates to be obtained from a much wider social field. The orderly pairing of hunter males with females requires a much larger group than can be supported locally by hunting and gathering, and this problem is solved by reciprocal relations among several local groups. It takes something on the order of 100 pairs to produce enough children so that the sex ratio is near enough to 50/50 for social life to proceed smoothly, and this requires a population of approximately 500 people. With smaller numbers there will be constant random fluctuations in the sex ratio large enough to cause social problems. This argument shows the importance of a sizable linguistic community, one large enough to cover an area in which many people may find suitable mates and make alliances of many kinds. It does not mean either that the large community or that exogamy does not have many other functions, as outlined by Mair (1965). As indicated earlier, the more factors that favor a custom, the more likely it is to be geographically widespread and long lasting. What the argument does stress is that the finding of mates and the production of babies under the particular conditions of human hunting and gathering favor both incest taboo and exogamy for basic demographic reasons.

Assumptions behind this argument are that social customs are adaptive, as Tax (1937) has argued, and that nothing is more crucial for evolutionary success than the orderly production of the number of infants that can be supported. This argument also presumes that, at least under extreme conditions, these necessities and reasons are obvious to the people involved, as infanticide attests. The impossibility of finding suitable mates must have been a common experience for hunters trying to exist in very small groups, and the initial advantages of exogamy, kinship, and alliance with other such groups may at first have amounted to no more than, as Whiting said at the conference, a mother suggesting to her son that he might find a suitable mate in the group where her brother was located.

If customs are adaptive and if humans are necessarily opportunistic, it might be expected that social roles would be particularly labile under the conditions of small hunting and gathering societies. At the conference, Murdock (Chapter 1, this volume) pointed out the high frequency of bilateral kinship system among hunters, and the experts on Australia all seemed to believe that the Australian systems had been described in much too static terms. Under hunting conditions, systems that allow for exceptions and local adaptation make sense and surely political dominance and status must have been largely achieved.

## CONCLUSION

While stressing the success of the hunting and gathering way of life with its great diversity of local forms and while emphasizing the way it influenced human evolution, we must also take into account its limitations. There is no indication that this way of life could support large communities of more than a few million people in the whole world. To call the hunters "affluent" (Sahlins, Chapter 9b, this volume) is to give a very special definition to the word. During much of the year, many monkeys can obtain enough food in only three or four hours of gathering each day, and under normal conditions baboons have plenty of time to build the Taj Mahal. The restriction on population, however, is the lean season or the atypical year, and, as Sahlins recognized, building by the hunters and the accumulation of gains was limited by motivation and technical knowledge, not by time. Where monkeys are fed, population rises, and Koford (1966) estimates the rate of increase on an island at 16 per cent per year.

After agriculture, human populations increased dramatically in spite of disease, war, and slowly changing customs. Even with fully human (*Homo sapiens*) biology, language, technical sophistication, cooperation, art, the support of kinship, the control of custom and political power, and the solace of religion—in spite of this whole web of culture and biology—the local group in the Mesolithic was no larger than that of baboons. Regardless of statements made at the symposium on the ease with which hunters obtain food some of the time, it is still true that food was the primary factor in limiting early human populations, as is shown by the events subsequent to agriculture.

The agricultural revolution, continuing into the industrial and scientific revolutions, is now freeing man from the conditions and restraints of 99 per cent of his history, but the biology of our species was created in that long gathering and hunting period. To assert the biological unity of mankind is to affirm the importance of the hunting way of life. It is to claim that, however much conditions and customs may have varied locally, the main selection pressures that forged the species were the same. The biology, psychology, and customs that separate us from the apes—all these we owe to the hunters of time past. And, although the record is incomplete and speculation looms larger than fact, for those who would understand the origin and nature of human behavior there is no choice but to try to understand "Man the Hunter."

# REFERENCES

Aberle, David F., Urie Bronfenbrenner, Eckard H. Hess, Daniel R. Miller, David M. Schneider, and James N. Spuhler. 1963. The incest taboo and the mating patterns of animals. *American Anthropologist* (n.s.), 65:253–65.

Binford, Lewis R., and Sally R. Binford. 1966a. The predatory revolution: a consideration of the evidence for a new subsistence level. *American Anthropologist* (n.s.), 68(2), pt. 1:508–512.

Bourlière, François. 1963. Observations on the ecology of some large African mammals. In F. C. Howell and F. Bourlière (Eds.), *African ecology and human evolution*. Chicago: Aldine Publishing Company.

Brues, Alice. 1959. The spearman and the archer, an essay on selection in body build. *American Anthropologist* (n.s.), 61:457–69

Carpenter, Clarence R. 1941. *A field study in Siam of the behavior and social relations of the Gibbon (Hylabates lar)*. Baltimore: Johns Hopkins Press.

DeVore, Irven, and K.R.L. Hall. 1965. Baboon ecology. In I. DeVore (Ed.), *Primate behavior*. New York: Holt, Rinehart, and Winston.

DeVore, Irven, and Sherwood L. Washburn. 1963. Baboon ecology and human evolution. In F. C. Howell and F. Bourlière (Eds.), *African ecology and human evolution*. Chicago: Aldine Publishing Company.

Ellefson, J.O. 1966. *A natural history of gibbons in the Malay Peninsula*. Unpublished doctoral dissertation, University of California, Berkeley.

Freeman, Derek. 1964. Human aggression in anthropological perspective. In J. D. Carthy and F. J. Ebling (Eds.), *The natural history of aggression*. New York: Academic Press.

Goldschmidt, Walter R. 1959. *Man's way: a preface to the understanding of human society*. New York: Henry Holt.

———1966. *Comparative functionalism: an essay in anthropological theory*. Berkeley and Los Angeles: University of California Press.

Goodall, Jane. 1965. Chimpanzees on the Gombe Stream reserve. In I. DeVore (Ed.), *Primate behavior*. New York: Holt, Rinehart and Winston.

Hamburg, David A. 1963. Emotions in the perspective of human evolution. In P.H. Knapp (Ed.), *Expression of the emotions in man*. New York: International Universities Press.

Koford, Carl B. 1966. Population changes in rhesus monkeys: Cayo Santiago, 1960–1964. *Tulane Studies in Zoology*, 13:1–7.

Lee, Richard B. 1965. *Subsistence ecology of !Kung Bushman*. Unpublished doctoral dissertation, University of California, Berkeley.

Lorenz, Konrad Z. 1966. *On aggression*. Trans. by Marjorie K. Wilson. New York: Harcourt, Brace and World.

Mair, Lucy. 1965. *An introduction to social anthropology*. Oxford: Clarendon Press.

Napier, John R. 1962. Monkeys and their habitats. *New Scientist*, 15: 88–92.

Sade, Donald S. 1965. Some aspects of parent-offspring and sibling relations in a group of rhesus monkeys, with a discussion of grooming. *American Journal of Physical Anthropology* (n.s.), 23(1):1–17.

———1966. *Ontogeny of social relations in a group of free ranging Rhesus monkeys (Macaca mulalla Zimmerman)*. Unpublished doctoral dissertation, University of California, Berkeley.

Schaller, George B. 1963. *The mountain gorilla: ecology and behavior*. Chicago: University of Chicago Press.

Service, Elman R. 1962. *Primitive social organization: an evolutionary perspective*. New York: Random House.

Simpson, George Gaylord. 1966. The biological nature of man. *Science*, 152(3721): 472–78.

Slater, Miriam K. 1959. Ecological factors in the origin of incest. *American Anthropologist* (n.s.), 61: 1042–59.

Tax, Sol. 1937. Some problems of social organization. In Fred Eggan (Ed.), *Social anthropology of North American tribes*. Chicago: University of Chicago Press.

Vallois, Henri V. 1961. The social life of early man: the evidence of skeletons. In S. L. Washburn (Ed.), *Social life of early man*. Chicago: Aldine Publishing Company.

Yamada, Munemi. 1963. A study of blood-relationship in the natural society of the Japanese macaque. *Primates (Journal of Primatology)*, 4: 43–66.

Zeuner, F. E. 1963. *A history of domestic animals*. New York: Harper and Row.

*This article from* Scientific American, *although written for a popular audience, clearly illustrates a range of connected arguments embedded in the new physical anthropology framework. The focus is on how knowledge of baboons in their natural habitat helps us understand human evolution. A basic assumption is that social behavior has played a crucial role in biological evolution. This being the case, archaeological information is not enough because most aspects of behavior don't fossilize. We need alternative sources of information if we want to understand the evolution of behavior and improve evolutionary reconstructions. Washburn and his graduate student, DeVore, articulate both the rationale for selecting baboons and the "baboon model," as it has come to be known. The baboon model not only set up expectations about the behavior of the earliest humans but also about other nonhuman primates. Baboons are used to discuss such key topics as what holds a group together, the role of males, the importance of male dominance hierarchy, the challenge of being a ground-living primate, the adaptive value of socialness, and its ontogeny. Methodological issues are also considered. These range from how groups are selected for study to the importance of naturalistic data for the interpretation of experimental results from captive studies. Finally, Washburn and DeVore emphasize the similarities between baboons and humans in fundamental social patterns and trace the unique features of human social behavior (such as large home range, food sharing, and defensive territoriality) to the human hunting adaptation. Together, the baboon model and the "man the hunter" model span critical periods of human evolution and demonstrate the utility of using a comparative approach to evolutionary reconstructions.*

# The Social Life of Baboons

## S. L. Washburn and Irven DeVore

The behavior of monkeys and apes has always held great fascination for men. In recent years plain curiosity about their behavior has been reinforced by the desire to understand human behavior. Anthropologists have come to understand that the evolution of man's behavior, particularly his social behavior, has played an integral role in his biological evolution. In the attempt to reconstruct the life of man as it was shaped through the ages, many studies of primate behavior are now under way in the laboratory and in the field. As the contrasts and similarities between the behavior of primates and man—especially preagricultural, primitive man—become clearer, they should give useful insights into the kind of social behavior that characterized the ancestors of man a million years ago.

With these objectives in mind we decided to undertake a study of the baboon. We chose this animal be-

cause it is a ground-living primate and as such is confronted with the same kind of problem that faced our ancestors when they left the trees. Our observations of some 30 troops of baboons, ranging in average membership from 40 to 80 individuals, in their natural setting in Africa show that the social behavior of the baboon is one of the species' principal adaptations for survival. Most of a baboon's life is spent within a few feet of other baboons. The troop affords protection from predators and an intimate group knowledge of the territory it occupies. Viewed from the inside, the troop is composed not of neutral creatures but of strongly emotional, highly motivated members. Our data offer little support for the theory that sexuality provides the primary bond of the primate troop. It is the intensely social nature of the baboon, expressed in a diversity of interindividual relationships, that keeps the troop together. This conclusion calls for further observation and experimental investigation of the different social bonds. It is clear, however, that these bonds are essential to compact group living and that for a baboon life in the troop is the only way of life that is feasible.

Many game reserves in Africa support baboon populations but not all were suited to our purpose. We had to be able to locate and recognize particular troops and their individual members and to follow them in their peregrinations day after day. In some reserves the brush is so thick that such systematic observation is impossible. A small park near Nairobi, in Kenya, offered most of the conditions we needed. Here 12 troops of baboons, consisting of more than 450 members, ranged the open savanna. The animals were quite tame; they clambered onto our car and even allowed us to walk beside them. In only 10 months of study, one of us (DeVore) was able to recognize most of the members of four troops and to become moderately familiar with many more. The Nairobi park, however, is small and so close to the city that the pattern of baboon life is somewhat altered. To carry on our work in an area less disturbed by humans and large enough to contain elephants, rhinoceroses, buffaloes and other ungulates as well as larger and less tame troops of baboons, we went to the Amboseli game reserve and spent two months camped at the foot of Mount Kilimanjaro. In the small part of Amboseli that we studied intensively there were 15 troops with a total of 1,200 members, the troops ranging in size from 13 to 185 members. The fact that the average size of the troops in Amboseli (80) is twice that of the troops in Nairobi shows the need to study the animals in several localities before generalizing.

A baboon troop may range an area of three to six square miles but it utilizes only parts of its range intensively. When water and food are widely distributed, troops rarely come within sight of each other. The ranges of neighboring troops overlap nonetheless, often extensively. This could be seen best in Amboseli at the end of the dry season. Water was concentrated in certain areas, and several troops often came to the same water hole, both to drink and to eat the lush vegetation near the water. We spent many days near these water holes, watching the baboons and the numerous other animals that came there.

On one occasion we counted more than 400 baboons around a single water hole at one time. To the casual observer they would have appeared to be one troop, but actually three large troops were feeding side by side. The troops came and went without mixing, even though members of different troops sat or foraged within a few feet of each other. Once we saw a juvenile baboon cross over to the next troop, play briefly and return to his own troop. But such behavior is rare, even in troops that come together at the same water hole day after day. At the water hole we saw no fighting between troops, but small troops slowly gave way before large

ones. Troops that did not see each other frequently showed great interest in each other.

When one first sees a troop of baboons, it appears to have little order, but this is a superficial impression. The basic structure of the troop is most apparent when a large troop moves away from the safety of trees and out onto open plains. As the troop moves the less dominant adult males and perhaps a large juvenile or two occupy the van. Females and more of the older juveniles follow, and in the center of the troop are the females with infants, the young juveniles and the most dominant males. The back of the troop is a mirror image of its front, with less dominant males at the rear. Thus, without any fixed or formal order, the arrangement of the troop is such that the females and young are protected at the center. No matter from what direction a predator approaches the troop, it must first encounter the adult males.

When a predator is sighted, the adult males play an even more active role in defense of the troop. One day we saw two dogs run barking at a troop. The females and juveniles hurried, but the males continued to walk slowly. In a moment an irregular group of some 20 adult males were interposed between the dogs and the rest of the troop. When a male turned on the dogs, they ran off. We saw baboons close to hyenas, cheetahs and jackals, and usually the baboons seemed unconcerned—the other animals kept their distance. Lions were the only animals we saw putting a troop of baboons to flight. Twice we saw lions near baboons, whereupon the baboons climbed trees. From the safety of the trees the baboons barked and threatened the lions, but they offered no resistance to them on the ground.

With nonpredators the baboons' relations are largely neutral. It is common to see baboons walking among topi, eland, sable and roan antelopes, gazelles, zebras, hartebeests, gnus, giraffes and buffaloes, depending on which ungulates are common locally. When elephants or rhinoceroses walk through an area where the baboons are feeding, the baboons move out of the way at the last moment. We have seen wart hogs chasing each other, and a running rhinoceros go right through a troop, with the baboons merely stepping out of the way. We have seen male impalas fighting while baboons fed beside them. Once we saw a baboon chase a giraffe, but it seemed to be more in play than aggression.

Only rarely did we see baboons engage in hostilities against other species. On one occasion, however, we saw a baboon kill a small vervet monkey and eat it. The vervets frequented the same water holes as the baboons and usually they moved near them or even among them without incident. But one troop of baboons we observed at Victoria Falls pursued vervets on sight and attempted, without success, to keep them out of certain

| | ECOLOGY | | | ECONOMIC SYSTEM | |
| --- | --- | --- | --- | --- | --- |
| | Group Size, Density and Range | Home Base | Population Structure | Food Habits | Economic Dependence |
| | Groups of 50–60 common but vary widely. One individual per 5–10 square miles. Range 200–600 square miles. Territorial rights, defend boundaries against strangers. | Occupy improved sites for variable times where sick are cared for and stores kept. | Tribal organization of local, exogamous groups. | Omnivorous. Food sharing. Men specialize in hunting, women and children in gathering. | Infants are dependent on adults for many years. Maturity of male delayed biologically and culturally. Hunting, storage and sharing of food. |
| | 10–200 in group. 10 individuals per square mile. Range 3–6 square miles. No territorial defense. | None; sick and injured must keep up with troop. | Small, inbreeding groups. | Almost entirely vegetarian. No food sharing, no division of labor. | Infant economically independent after weaning. Full maturity biologically delayed. No hunting, storage or sharing of food. |

fruit trees. The vervets easily escaped in the small branches of the trees.

The baboons' food is almost entirely vegetable, although they do eat meat on rare occasions. We saw dominant males kill and eat two newborn Thomson's gazelles. Baboons are said to be fond of fledglings and birds' eggs and have even been reported digging up crocodile eggs. They also eat insects. But their diet consists principally of grass, fruit, buds and plant shoots of many kinds; in the Nairobi area alone they consume more than 50 species of plant.

For baboons, as for many herbivores, association with other species on the range often provides mutual protection. In open country their closest relations are with impalas, while in forest areas the bushbucks play a similar role. The ungulates have a keen sense of smell, and baboons have keen eyesight. Baboons are visually alert, constantly looking in all directions as they feed. If they see predators, they utter warning barks that alert not only the other baboons but also any other small animals that may be in the vicinity. Similarly, a warning bark by a bushbuck or an impala will put a baboon troop to flight. A mixed herd of impalas and baboons is almost impossible to take by surprise.

Impalas are a favorite prey of cheetahs. Yet once we saw impalas, grazing in the company of baboons, make no effort to escape from a trio of approaching cheetahs. The impalas just watched as an adult male baboon stepped toward the cheetahs, uttered a cry of defiance and sent them trotting away.

The interdependence of the different species is plainly evident at a water hole, particularly where the bush is thick and visibility poor. If giraffes are drinking, zebras will run to the water. But the first animals to arrive at the water hole approach with extreme caution. In the Wankie reserve, where we also observed ba-

boons, there are large water holes surrounded by wide areas of open sand between the water and the bushes. The baboons approached the water with great care, often resting and playing for some time in the bushes before making a hurried trip for a drink. Clearly, many animals know each other's behavior and alarm signals.

A baboon troop finds its ultimate safety, however, in the trees. It is no exaggeration to say that trees limit the distribution of baboons as much as the availability of food and water. We observed an area by a marsh in Amboseli where there was water and plenty of food. But there were lions and no trees and so there were no baboons. Only a quarter of a mile away, where lions were seen even more frequently, there were trees. Here baboons were numerous; three large troops frequented the area.

At night, when the carnivores and snakes are most active, baboons sleep high up in big trees. This is one of the baboon's primary behavioral adaptations. Diurnal living, together with an arboreal refuge at night, is an extremely effective way for them to avoid danger. The callused areas on a baboon's haunches allow it to sleep sitting up, even on small branches; a large troop can thus find sleeping places in a few trees. It is known that Colobus monkeys have a cycle of sleeping and waking throughout the night; baboons probably have a similar pattern. In any case, baboons are terrified of the dark. They arrive at the trees before night falls and stay in the branches until it is fully light. Fear of the dark, fear of falling and fear of snakes seem to be basic parts of the primate heritage.

Whether by day or night, individual baboons do not wander away from the troop, even for a few hours. The importance of the troop in ensuring the survival of its members is dramatized by the fate of those that are badly injured or too sick to keep up with their fellows.

| | SOCIAL SYSTEM | | | COMMUNICATION | | |
| Organization | Social Control | Sexual Behavior | Mother-Child Relationship | Play | |
| --- | --- | --- | --- | --- | --- |
| Bands are dependent on and affiliated with one another in a semiopen system. Subgroups based on kinship. | Based on custom. | Female continuously receptive. Family based on prolonged male–female relationship and incest taboo. | Prolonged; infant helpless and entirely dependent on adults. | Interpersonal but also considerable use of inanimate objects. | Linguistic community. Language crucial in the evolution of religion, art, technology and the co-operation of many individuals. |
| Troop self-sufficient, closed to outsiders. Temporary subgroups are formed based on age and individual preferences. | Based on physical dominance. | Female estrus. Multiple mates. No prolonged male-female relationship. | Intense but brief; infant well developed and in partial control. | Mainly interpersonal and exploratory. | Species-specific, largely gestural and concerned with Immediate situations. |

APES AND MEN are contrasted in this chart, which indicates that although apes often seem remarkably "human," there are fundamental differences in behavior. Baboon characteristics, which may be taken as representative of ape and monkey behavior in general, are based on laboratory and field studies; human characteristics are what is known of preagricultural Homo sapiens. The chart suggests that there was a considerable gap between primate behavior and the behavior of the most primitive men known.

Each day the troop travels on a circuit of two to four miles; it moves from the sleeping trees to a feeding area, feeds, rests and moves again. The pace is not rapid, but the troop does not wait for sick or injured members. A baby baboon rides its mother, but all other members of the troop must keep up on their own. Once an animal is separated from the troop the chances of death are high. Sickness and injuries severe enough to be easily seen are frequent. For example, we saw a baboon with a broken forearm. The hand swung uselessly, and blood showed that the injury was recent. This baboon was gone the next morning and was not seen again. A sickness was widespread in the Amboseli troops, and we saw individuals dragging themselves along, making tremendous efforts to stay with the troop but falling behind. Some of these may have rejoined their troops; we are sure that at least five did not. One sick little juvenile lagged for four days and then apparently recovered. In the somewhat less natural setting of Nairobi park we saw some baboons that had lost a leg. So even severe injury does not mean inevitable death. Nonetheless, it must greatly decrease the chance of survival.

Thus, viewed from the outside, the troop is seen to be an effective way of life and one that is essential to the survival of its individual members. What do the internal events of troop life reveal about the drives and motivations that cause individual baboons to "seek safety in numbers"? One of the best ways to approach an understanding of the behavior patterns within the troop is to watch the baboons when they are resting and feeding quietly.

Most of the troop will be gathered in small groups, grooming each other's fur or simply sitting. A typical group will contain two females with their young offspring, or an adult male with one or more females and juveniles grooming him. Many of these groups tend to persist, with the same animals that have been grooming each other walking together when the troop moves. The nucleus of such a "grooming cluster" is most often a dominant male or a mother with a very young infant. The most powerful males are highly attractive to the other troop members and are actively sought by them. In marked contrast, the males in many ungulate species, such as impalas, must constantly herd the members of their group together. But baboon males have no need to force the other troop members to stay with them. On the contrary, their presence alone ensures that the troop will stay with them at all times.

Young infants are equally important in the formation of grooming clusters. The newborn infant is the center of social attraction. The most dominant adult males sit by the mother and walk close beside her. When the troop is resting, adult females and juveniles come to the mother, groom her and attempt to groom the infant. Other members of the troop are drawn toward the center thus formed, both by the presence of the protective adult males and by their intense interest in the young infants.

In addition, many baboons, especially adult females, form preference pairs, and juvenile baboons come together in play groups that persist for several years. The general desire to stay in the troop is strengthened by these "friendships," which express themselves in the daily pattern of troop activity.

Our field observations, which so strongly suggest a high social motivation, are backed up by controlled experiment in the laboratory. Robert A. Butler of Walter Reed Army Hospital has shown that an isolated monkey will work hard when the only reward for his labor is the sight of another monkey [see "Curiosity in Monkeys," by Robert A. Butler; *Scientific American,* February, 1954]. In the troop this social drive is expressed in strong individual preferences, by "friendship," by interest in the infant members of the troop and by the attraction of the dominant males. Field studies show the adaptive value of these social ties. Solitary animals are far more likely to be killed, and over the generations natural selection must have favored all those factors which make learning to be sociable easy.

The learning that brings the individual baboon into full identity and participation in the baboon social system begins with the mother-child relationship. The newborn baboon rides by clinging to the hair on its mother's chest. The mother may scoop the infant on with her hand, but the infant must cling to its mother, even when she runs, from the day it is born. There is no time for this behavior to be learned. Harry F. Harlow of the University of Wisconsin has shown that an infant monkey will automatically cling to an object and much prefers objects with texture more like that of a real mother [see "Love in Infant Monkeys," by Harry F. Harlow; *Scientific American,* June, 1959]. Experimental studies demonstrate this clinging reflex; field observations show why it is so important.

In the beginning the baboon mother and infant are in contact 24 hours a day. The attractiveness of the young infant, moreover, assures that he and his mother will always be surrounded by attentive troop members. Experiments show that an isolated infant brought up in a laboratory does not develop normal social patterns. Beyond the first reflexive clinging, the development of social behavior requires learning. Behavior characteristic of the species depends therefore both on the baboon's biology and on the social situations that are present in the troop.

As the infant matures it learns to ride on its mother's back, first clinging and then sitting upright. It begins to eat solid foods and to leave the mother for longer and longer periods to play with other infants. Eventually it plays with the other juveniles many hours a day, and its orientation shifts from the mother to this play group. It is in these play groups that the skills and behavior patterns of adult life are learned and practiced. Adult gestures, such as mounting, are frequent, but most play is a mixture of chasing, tail-pulling and mock fighting. If a juvenile is hurt and cries out, adults come running and stop the play. The presence of an adult male prevents small juveniles from being hurt. In the protected atmosphere of the play group the social bonds of the infant are widely extended.

Grooming, a significant biological function in itself, helps greatly to establish social bonds. The mother begins grooming her infant the day it is born, and the infant will be occupied with grooming for several hours a day for the rest of its life. All the older baboons do a certain amount of grooming, but it is the adult females who do most. They groom the infants, juveniles, adult males and other females. The baboons go to each other and "present" themselves for grooming. The grooming animal picks through the hair, parting it with its hands, removing dirt and parasites, usually by nibbling. Grooming is most often reciprocal, with one animal doing it for a while and then presenting itself for grooming. The animal being groomed relaxes, closes its eyes and gives every indication of complete pleasure. In addition to being pleasurable, grooming serves the important function of keeping the fur clean. Ticks are common in this area and can be seen on many animals such as dogs and lions; a baboon's skin, however, is free of them. Seen in this light, the enormous amount of time baboons spend in grooming each other is understandable. Grooming is pleasurable to the individual, it is the most important expression of close social bonds and it is biologically adaptive.

The adults in a troop are arranged in a dominance hierarchy, explicitly revealed in their relations with other members of the troop. The most dominant males will be more frequently groomed and they occupy feeding and resting positions of their choice. When a dominant animal approaches a subordinate one, the lesser animal moves out of the way. The observer can determine the order of dominance simply by watching the reactions of the baboons as they move past each other. In the tamer troops these observations can be tested by feeding. If food is tossed between two baboons, the more dominant one will take it, whereas the other may not even look at it directly.

The status of a baboon male in the dominance hierarchy depends not only on his physical condition and fighting ability but also on his relationships with other males. Some adult males in every large troop stay together much of the time, and if one of them is threatened, the others are likely to back him up. A group of such males outranks any individual, even though another male outside the group might be able to defeat any member of it separately. The hierarchy has considerable stability and this is due in large part to its dependence on clusters of males rather than the fighting ability of individuals. In troops where the rank order is clearly defined, fighting is rare. We observed frequent bickering or severe fighting in only about 15 percent of the troops. The usual effect of the hierarchy, once relations among the males are settled, is to decrease disruptions in the troop. The dominant animals, the males in particular, will not let others fight. When bickering breaks out, they usually run to the scene and stop it. Dominant males thus protect the weaker animals against harm from inside as well as outside. Females and juveniles come to the males to groom them or just to sit beside them. So although dominance depends ultimately on force, it leads to peace, order and popularity.

Much has been written about the importance of sex in uniting the troop, it has been said, for example, that "the powerful social magnet of sex was the major impetus to subhuman primate sociability" [see "The Origin of Society," by Marshall D. Sahlins; *Scientific American,* September, 1960]. Our observations lead us to assign to sexuality a much lesser, and even at times a contrary, role. The sexual behavior of baboons depends on the biological cycle of the female. She is receptive for approximately one week out of every month, when she is in estrus. When first receptive, she leaves her infant and her friendship group and goes to the males, mating first with the subordinate males and older juveniles. Later in the period of receptivity she goes to the dominant males and "presents." If a male is not interested, the female is likely to groom him and then present again. Near the end of estrus the dominant males become very interested, and the female and a male form a consort pair. They may stay together for as little as an hour or for as long as several days. Estrus disrupts all other social relationships, and consort pairs usually move to the edge of the troop. It is at this time that fighting may take place, if the dominance order is not clearly established among the males. Normally there is no fighting over females, and a male, no matter how dominant, does not monopolize a female for long. No male is ever associated with more than one estrus female; there is nothing resembling a family or a harem among baboons.

Much the same seems to be true of other species of monkey. Sexual behavior appears to contribute little to the cohesion of the troop. Some monkeys have breeding seasons, with all mating taking place within less than half the year. But even in these species the troop continues its normal existence during the months when there is no mating. It must be remembered that among baboons a female is not sexually receptive for most of her life. She is juvenile, pregnant or lactating; estrus is a rare event in her life. Yet she does not leave the troop even for a few minutes. In baboon troops, particularly small ones, many months may pass when no female member comes into estrus; yet no animals leave the troop, and the highly structured relationships within it continue without disorganization.

The sociableness of baboons is expressed in a wide variety of behavior patterns that reinforce each other

and give the troop cohesion. As the infant matures the nature of the social bonds changes continually, but the bonds are always strong. The ties between mother and infant, between a juvenile and its peers in a play group, and between mother and an adult male are quite different from one another. Similarly, the bond between two females in a friendship group, between the male and female in a consort pair or among the members of a cluster of males in the dominance hierarchy is based on diverse biological and behavioral factors, which offer a rich field for experimental investigation.

In addition, the troop shares a considerable social tradition. Each troop has its own range and a secure familiarity with the food and water sources, escape routes, safe refuges and sleeping places inside it. The counterpart of the intensely social life within the troop is the coordination of the activities of all the troop's members throughout their lives. Seen against the background of evolution, it is clear that in the long run only the social baboons have survived.

When comparing the social behavior of baboons with that of man, there is little to be gained from laboring the obvious differences between modern civilization and the society of baboons. The comparison must be drawn against the fundamental social behavior patterns that lie behind the vast variety of human ways of life. For this purpose we have charted the salient features of baboon life in a native habitat alongside those of human life in preagricultural society. Cursory inspection shows that the differences are more numerous and significant than are the similarities.

The size of the local group is the only category in which there is not a major contrast. The degree to which these contrasts are helpful in understanding the evolution of human behavior depends, of course, on the degree to which baboon behavior is characteristic of monkeys and apes in general and therefore probably characteristic of the apes that evolved into men. Different kinds of monkey do behave differently, and many more field studies will have to be made before the precise degree of difference can be understood.

For example, many arboreal monkeys have a much smaller geographical range than baboons do. In fact, there are important differences between the size and type of range for many monkey species. But there is no suggestion that a troop of any species of monkey or ape occupies the hundreds of square miles ordinarily occupied by preagricultural human societies. Some kinds of monkey may resent intruders in their range more than baboons do, but there is no evidence that any species fights for complete control of a territory. Baboons are certainly less vocal than some other monkeys, but no nonhuman primate has even the most rudimentary language. We believe that the fundamental contrasts in our chart would hold for the vast majority of monkeys and apes as compared with the ancestors of man. Further study of primate behavior will sharpen these contrasts and define more clearly the gap that had to be traversed from ape to human behavior. But already we can see that man is as unique in his sharing, cooperation and play patterns as he is in his locomotion, brain and language.

The basis for most of these differences may lie in hunting. Certainly the hunting of large animals must have involved co-operation among the hunters and sharing of the food within the tribe. Similarly, hunting requires an enormous extension of range and the protection of a hunting territory. If this speculation proves to be correct, much of the evolution of human behavior can be reconstructed, because the men of 500,000 years ago were skilled hunters. In locations such as Choukoutien in China and Olduvai Gorge in Africa there is evidence of both the hunters and their campsites [see "Olduvai Gorge," by L. S. B. Leakey; *Scientific American*, January, 1954]. We are confident that the study of the living primates, together with the archaeological record, will eventually make possible a much richer understanding of the evolution of human behavior.

## BIBLIOGRAPHY

*Behavior and Evolution.* Edited by Anne Roe and George Gaylord Simpson. Yale University Press, 1958.

*A Study of Behaviour of the Chacma Baboon, Papio Ursinus.* Niels Bolwig in *Behaviour,* Vol. 14, No. 1–2, pages 136–163; 1959.

*Taxonomy and classification are old practices predating modern evolutionary theory. In this paper Washburn tries to make sense of primate classification by injecting a new evolutionary reality. He hopes that this will cut through many controversies, including which animals to classify as similar or distinct and which characteristics are most appropriate to use in a taxonomy. Natural adaptive complexes must be our guide.*

*The emphasis on adaptation inevitably leads to a consideration of behavior before structure, and it certainly argues against any interpretation of structure in isolation—a radical departure from the standard taxonomic practices of that time. Here, as elsewhere, Washburn highlights the need for functional interpretations of anatomy. This approach provides special benefits for understanding primate classification since it replaces the vague, hard to define, generalized features of primates with specific characteristics that distinguish primates from other mammals and from each other. As in other writings, Washburn insists on considering as many kinds of evidence as possible, along with an assessment of the importance of specific characteristics in the evolution of primate species. This approach will replace the nonevolutionary thinking that biases our existing taxonomies.*

*We also have another problem: we treat humans differently from other primate species. The closer we get to humans in the classification, the smaller are the differences we allow as distinguishing features. By implication, if we used the same criteria and "distance" for hominids as for other species, we might end up with a very different primate taxonomy, as Washburn tries to illustrate. On the other hand, paying attention to behavior could serve to focus classifications on the most important behaviors that might distinguish hominids as primates.*

*Washburn's conclusions about the timing and important events in human evolution run contrary to the wisdom of the time, but they have found support in the evidence accumulated over the past 40 years. Modern interpretations appear remarkably similar to what Washburn was suggesting.*

# Behavior and Human Evolution

## S. L. Washburn

The interest in human classification and evolution has been so great that it has produced a bewildering quantity and variety of terms and theories. Yet, in spite of the diversity, the major groups of primates recognized today were familiar to the scholars of the 19th century. The groups which seemed "natural" to the pre-evolutionary zoologist remain central in the thinking of the modern student of human evolution, and the purpose of this paper is to suggest reasons why this is the case. My thesis will be that the principal groups of the living primates are adaptive and that the characters by which they have been recognized are structures which are closely related to the behavior of the groups. With the addition of the evolutionary point of view, the contemporary groups are seen as the ends of adaptive radiations but the groups are the same. If this is the case, the referents of the names should be the adaptive groups. The most useful taxonomic characters will be those closely correlated with the basic adaptation. And "splitters" will be scientists who divide "natural," that is adaptive, groups.[1]

[1] Classifications are made by human beings with varied training and interests, and there is no reason why a particular classification should seem equally reasonable to different people. I am not suggesting that this is the only way to look at the primates, but that emphasis on behavior and adaptation is a great aid in understanding the groups which have been described and in the evaluation of the characters used in classification.

In S. L. Washburn, ed., *Classification and Human Evolution* (New York: Wenner Gren, Viking Fund Publications in Anthropology, 1963), pp. 190–203.

Some illustrations of these points will be given before proceeding to a discussion of the Hominidae.

The primates have been found hard to define, and generalized features tend to be mentioned. Yet the order is characterized by the adaptation of climbing by grasping which is a complex specialization, separating the primates from other living mammals. It is fully developed in the prosimians and was present in the Eocene, as shown by *Notharctus*. Observation of the *quadrumana* was a factor in the recognition of the primates as a natural group, and the fundamental adaptation of elongated digits, flattened terminal phalanges with nails, and specialized palms and soles is basic to the locomotor and feeding patterns of monkeys and apes. Climbing-by-grasping is the adaptation which separates primate arboreal life from that of the tree-shrews which climb with claws. The adaptation is carried farthest in the Lorisidae and has numerous consequences. For example, in jumping primates (Tarsiidae, Galagidae) elongation is in the tarsal bones, rather than the metatarsals which is the situation in other jumping mammals. This is because the first toe must be able to oppose the others and elongation in the metatarsals would destroy the grasping adaptation of the foot.

According to this view, the basic adaptation of the primates is a way of climbing, the structure which permits that mode of locomotion, and this complex separates the order from all other groups of living mammals. Naturally, there must have been intermediate forms between tree-shrews and primates in the Paleocene, and hands and feet have evolved. But, if one compares *Notharctus* and *Homo*, it is remarkable how little the hands have changed compared to other parts of the body. In the vast majority of the living primates the original, basic locomotor adaptation of the group is still present. If this view of the primates is correct, there is no intellectual problem in defining the order which may be done by the locomotor pattern, which is easily studied in the living forms. However, in fossils reconstruction of locomotor patterns is difficult, unless large parts of the skeleton are preserved, and emphasis will continue to be on the teeth and skull. All available evidence should be utilized, in order to get as full an understanding as possible of the earliest primates and of the trends in primate evolution. However, emphasis on behavior suggests that a locomotor specialization is the basic adaptation and that the primates cannot be understood without an appreciation of this way of locomotion and its consequences.

If a special way of locomotion is the basic adaptation of the primates, then locomotor characters must be emphasized in the definition of the order. Characters of the teeth and skull will be useful for identification, to determine parallelism or convergence, and to estimate the multiplicity and relations of fossil forms. But emphasis must be on locomotion.

Emphasis on behavior does give a way of evaluating structure, and this can be illustrated by comparing three pairs of taxa which have often been classed as subfamilies: Galaginae and Lorisinae, Cercopithecinae and Colobinae, Hylobatinae and Ponginae. Galagoes differ from lorises in almost every feature of their postcranial anatomy. In locomotion the galagoes and lorises represent extremely different adaptations. The Colobinae are similar to other Old World monkeys in general structure, but differ profoundly in their viscera. The gibbons differ in no fundamental way from other members of the Pongidae. Locomotor and visceral adaptations are the same, and there is nothing to suggest that they represent a major adaptive radiation distinct from that of the other apes. From the point of view of behavior, it is convenient to regard the galagoes and lorises as comprising two very distinct families (Galagidae and Lorisidae), each containing many genera and species. The many structural-behavioral similarities of the Old World monkeys suggest that a single family, divided into two sub-families to express the differing visceral adaptation, is appropriate. But the gibbons may be treated as a single genus composed of several species, which are small apes but not fundamentally different from other members of the Pongidae.

Starting with three pairs of sub-families, it has been suggested that emphasis on adaptation and behavior suggests that the degree of difference is very unequal in the three cases. The adaptive situation would be more conveniently indicated by the terms: Galagidae and Lorisidae, Cercopithecine and Colobinae, and *Hylobates*. There is nothing novel about this suggestion. The names are the same as Simpson, 1945, with the exception that the contemporary gibbons are treated as a single genus which was a common opinion. All that is suggested is that the emphasis on adaptation helps in the evaluation of the classification. Further, emphasis on adaptation forces a consideration of the biology of the groups in question. It is necessary to consider many kinds of evidence and the importance of characters depends on an estimate of their importance in evolution.

These three pairs of taxa were picked to illustrate the fact that, the closer man is approached in classification, the smaller the differences which will be accepted as important. Further, these pairs were picked to suggest that emphasis on adaptation offers a way of estimating this bias, at least to some extent. The families and sub-families of Old World primates are groups which are distinguished by major adaptations, except in the case of the Pongidae which is subdivided in a way which does not conform to any major adaptive divisions.

The Pongidae are characterized by a way of climbing which sharply distinguishes the living forms from other primates. This mode of locomotion is clearly reflected in the skeleton and many bodily proportions, and, judging from the very fragmentary fossil limb bones, this locomotor pattern probably evolved in the Miocene. If this is correct, the dentition of the apes had evolved its characteristic pattern long before the locomotor adaptation was complete, and the structure of the arm and trunk which man shares with the apes was not evolved until the Pliocene. This view is shown in Figure 1.

The diagram is intended to suggest that the *Dryopithecus* pattern was established in the Oligocene and the separation of Pongidae and Cercopithecidae had taken place at that time. During the Miocene the apes evolved their distinctive locomotor pattern, and parallel evolution appears to have gone on in several distinct lines of brachiators. Obviously, with so few fossils such a view is only speculation, and the actual situation was much more complicated.

The locomotor pattern of the apes has been called brachiation, meaning swinging below the branches rather than walking on top as the monkeys do. This term has been widely misunderstood, partially because of the lack of behavioral data and partially because the term applies to only a small part of the locomotor pattern of the Pongidae. Apes also walk quadrupedally on the ground. None of the Pongidae, not even the gibbons, swing under branches most of the time. But in a recent study in which examples of all the living Pongidae and many kinds of the Cercopithecidae were run across the same branches, all the apes brachiated and no monkey did. (Avis, "Brachiation," *Southwestern Journal of Anthropology*, 18:119–148, 1962). Old World monkeys will consistently "choose" to cross a small branch quadrupedally while the apes (Pongidae) will swing below. But, if the branch is large and stable, the apes will stay on top and move quadrupedally (*Pan, Pongo, Gorilla*) or bipedally (*Hylobates*). In a restricted sense "brachiation" applies to only a small part of ape locomotion, and, if apes are referred to as brachiators, it must be remembered that is much less descriptive of what they do than "quadrupedalism" is for monkeys.

Apes are brachiators in the sense that, in particular situations, they all swing below branches, and Old World monkeys are not brachiators in the sense that, given comparable situations, none of them swing under the branch. But for brachiation to be very useful in the description of ape behavior it must be descriptive of a much wider range of actions. These might be described as climbing and eating by reaching, a pattern of slow feeding and moving in the ends of small branches. Apes will hang by one arm and feed with the other, or

hold a branch with one hand and lean out, and stretch the other hand out as far as possible to pluck food. Positively, brachiation is emphasis on long, highly mobile arms with powerful flexor muscles. Negatively, it is the reduction in importance of the lower back in locomotion. In the living Pongidae the full structural emphasis on arms may be seen and the great reduction of back motion as an essential part of locomotion. In some of the New World monkeys there appears to be a partial parallelism, both in the acquisition of brachiating structural-behavioral mechanisms and in the reduction in the back. When these are studied in more detail, they should provide a much fuller understanding of the nature of brachiation and aid in the reconstruction of the locomotor patterns of the formative apes (*Limnopithecus, Pliopithecus*) as these forms may have been in a behavioral stage very similar to that of *Ateles*.

The climbing-feeding adaptation of the Pongidae is reflected in many simple actions and postures, and these can readily be observed in zoos. For example, apes stretch by putting the arms to the side as far as possible; sit on a shelf with legs handing down; cross arms or put one hand on the opposite upper arm; cross one leg over the other; lie flat on the back, especially with knees separated and elbows apart and hands above head. It will be noted that the positions of the chimpanzee look human, and that in the list of postures, every one characteristic of the Pongidae is also characteristic of man. There is a profound similarity in the motions of the arms of man and apes, and on any playground one can see humans brachiating from bars, hanging by one hand, and exhibiting a variety of motions and postures which are similar to those of the apes. Man still is a brachiator. He is simply the one who is least frequently in the situation which calls forth this behavior. Our legs are too heavy and our arms are too weak for efficient brachiation but, when we climb, we climb like apes and not like monkeys.

The structural basis for the motions and postures which are shared by man and ape is complex, and the following listing of characters which man and ape share gives only a partial idea of the degree of similarity. Only those features are included which are importantly related to the functioning of the arms and in each case comparison is to the condition in the Cercopithecidae. The order of comparison starts with the sternum and proceeds along the arm to the fingers. In man and ape the sternum is wide, the sterno-clavicular joint stable, the clavicle long, and a large part of the pectoralis major muscle arises from the clavicle. At the shoulder, the acromion process is large and the deltoid muscle is large, permitting powerful abduction. The coracoid process of the scapula is large and the glenoid fossa nearly flat with a small supraglenoid tubercle.

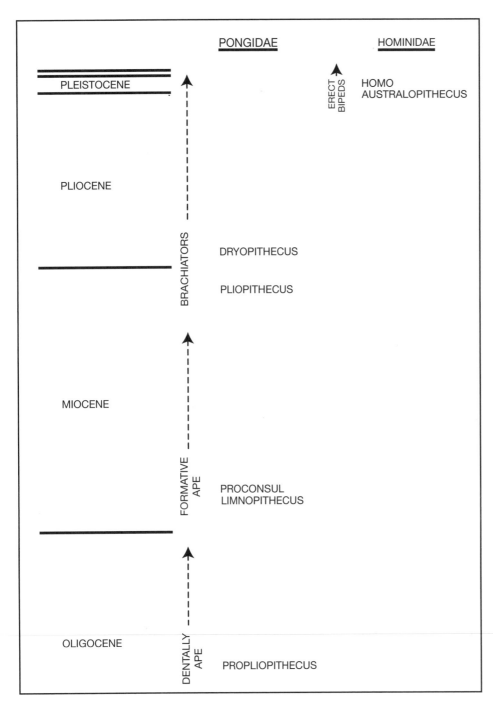

PONGIDAE       HOMINIDAE

PLEISTOCENE

ERECT BIPEDS — HOMO / AUSTRALOPITHECUS

PLIOCENE

BRACHIATORS

DRYOPITHECUS

PLIOPITHECUS

MIOCENE

FORMATIVE APE

PROCONSUL
LIMNOPITHECUS

OLIGOCENE

DENTALLY APE

PROPLIOPITHECUS

*FIGURE 1*

Trepezius is very thick in the central part, correlated with the long spines of lower cervical and upper thoracic vertebrae. The head of the humerus is more rounded, and the bicipital groove is narrow with no extension of the articular surface into it. Flexor muscles are large relative to the extensors. Taken together these structures permit the wide range of lateral and flexor movements which are the basis of brachiation.

In the elbow and forearm are a series of adaptations which allow powerful flexor action in any part of a much greater range of pronation and supination. These are, on the humerus, a wide trochlea with a lateral ridge and a fully rounded capitulum. The proximal end of the ulna is wide, olecranon very short and the head of the radius is round. The stability of the joint depends almost entirely on the ulna-trochlea fit, and the deep olecranon fossa permits full extension so hanging is possible with a minimum of muscular effort.

In the wrist, the ulna does not articulate with the carpal bones, and this allows freer abduction and adduction necessary in swinging, where the whole force of the swing is taken in the wrist.

The hand is specialized for flexion and the sesamoid bones are lost. Compared to trunk, the hand is always long.

The structural-functional similarity of the arm of man and ape is related to less obvious similarities in the viscera and trunk. Lumbar vertebrae are few in number and the lumbar region is short. The back is not flexed in locomotion and the deep back muscles are small. In correlation with the structure of the shoulder and lumbar region, the trunk is short, wide, and shallow. This means that the viscera cannot be arranged as in the long, narrow, and deep trunks of the quadrupedal monkeys. Certainly much of the similarity in the arrangement of the thoracic and abdominal viscera is secondary to the locomotor adaptations in the form of the trunk. Even the similarity in the branching from the aortic arch and the number of rings in the trachea may be secondary.

It seems most improbable that this detailed structural-functional similarity could be due to parallelism. Certainly the fact that many other lines of evidence suggest that man and ape are related makes explanation by parallelism most unlikely. Furthermore, parallelism means that animals resemble each other because similar groups have adapted in similar ways but that the lines are genetically independent. To suggest that man evolved the structure of a brachiator by parallelism and not brachiating is to misunderstand the nature of parallel evolution.

The functioning and structure of the arm and trunk show the similarity of Pongidae and Hominidae. They are alike because of common ancestry and having lived a particular kind of arboreal life for millions of years. The divergence of the Hominidae appears to be based on a new adaptive complex in which tools and erect bipedalism are basic. Large brains and small faces followed long after the Hominidae were distinct from the apes. The earliest part of the adaptive radiation of the Hominidae now known is in the Lower Pleistocene (Upper Villafranchian). It has become customary to indicate the human line as diverging from the Pongidae at least as far back as the Miocene. But most of the differences between man and ape seem to have evolved within the Pleistocene. Probably the only bone by which an ancestor of *Australopithecus* with a large canine tooth could be distinguished from an ape is the ilium and, possibly, the bones of the foot. The brain was not larger than that of the living apes. The hand shows many intermediate features. The ischium is ape-like, and it is tools, dentition, and ilium and foot which suggest similarity to *Homo* and the first stage in human behavior. There were at least two species of *Australopithecus* (*A. africanus* and *A. robustus*), and probably more.

The genus seems to have lasted at least 500,000 years, and possibly more than three times that. Stratigraphy and associated fossils suggest a rapid rate of evolution, but the absolute dates from the Berkeley potassium-argon laboratory suggest a much longer period. The accuracy of the method and dates is under discussion. The genus *Homo* is characterized by lower limb bones which are characteristic of modern man. It appears that the human adaptation of erect bipedalism evolved in two stages, the first of which involved primarily the ilium and the second the femur and ischium. It is possible that the first stage was primarily an adaptation to erect running, and it is only with the second stage that fully erect, long-distance walking evolved. With *Homo* appear large brains, complicated tools made by clearly defined traditions, and, probably, language. The adaptations of the genus *Homo* were so effective that these forms spread over all the Old World, except into the very cold regions and to islands where boats were needed. Conquest of the Arctic and the oceans awaited *Homo sapiens*.

It has been debated whether psychological characters should be used in classification. However, if one is interested in adaptation, there is no choice in the matter. The adaptation of the genus *Homo* is based on technical skills, language, and many attributes of mind (memory, planning, etc.), and, if complex tools and intelligence account for the radiation, they must be used in classification.

If emphasis is on behavior, it is convenient to divide the Hominidae into two genera, *Australopithecus* and *Homo*. They are distinct in locomotor adaptation, brain size, and capacity for tool making.[2] At least two species of *Australopithecus* are known, and probably there were several more, especially if the long estimates of Lower Pleistocene time are correct.

With the advent of *Homo* (possibly in the first interglacial or second glacial some 400,000 to 500,000 years ago) the human adaptation was so effective that further

---

[2] Dr. Phillip V. Tobias writes: "If generic separation between *Australopithecus* and *Paranthropus* is justified, then I feel *Zinjanthropus* is more likely to prove a third separate genus; however, I have serious doubts whether generic distinction is indeed justified between the first two forms. I am increasingly inclining to the view that the distinctions, dental and otherwise, between the two forms have been overrated and that all the South African Australopithecines should be lumped into a single genus. If this were accepted, then it seems clear that '*Zinjanthropus*' belongs in the same single genus (*Australopithecus*). My study of the '*pre-Zinjanthropus*' is not yet sufficiently advanced for me to draw any firm conclusions about its status; at the present, my *interim view* is that the scanty remains available are not incompatible with those of an australopithecine with a somewhat bigger brain than the specimens hitherto assessed; its dental features would seem to place it rather closer to *Australopithecus* (in Robinson's sense) than to *Paranthropus*, but I do not think I have yet seen any features which, individually or collectively, place it outside the probable range for *Australopithecus sensu lato*." (Personal communication)

speciation may have stopped. The presence of the same kinds and sequence of tools in Africa, India, and Europe is evidence that there was migration over all this area during the Middle Pleistocene. The Far East appears to have been culturally distinct, and there is too little skeletal evidence to decide whether there was a distinct species of man in the Far East in the early Middle Pleistocene. At a later time, the similarity of Mapa, Solo, Rhodesian, and Neanderthal remains suggests no more than racial distinction.

## DISCUSSION

The emphasis on behavior may be defended on theoretical grounds. If the direction of evolution is due primarily to natural selection, the taxa which are recognized today should be the ends of adaptive radiations. However, there are numerous practical difficulties in the application of the point of view. There are few behaviorally oriented studies. There is no agreement on the meaning of the terms, such as brachiation. The most important parts may not fossilize so that the dangers of reconstruction and speculation are *greatly* increased.

These points may be illustrated with reference to bipedal locomotion. When human bipedalism is under discussion, reference is usually made to other bipeds (birds, dinosaurs, and various jumping mammals). But human bipedalism is structurally unique, and it is not even mechanically convergent with these other forms of bipedalism. Human bipedalism is a gait which is carried on while the trunk is erect, and walking is dependent on a unique form of ilium and a pattern of muscles found in no other animal. In mammals the ischium is normally long and the main propulsion comes from pulling the leg back, primarily by the hamstring muscles. Two-joint muscles are the most important. In man the ischium is short, quadriceps extensor femoris is larger than the hamstrings, and one-joint muscles are large. A pattern of walking based on large gluteus maximus, quadriceps, and soleus is uniquely human, as is the importance of the first toe in the structure of the foot.

Considering *Australopithecus* from the point of view of behavior, it will be seen that the ilium is constantly described but the ischium is not, although both are essential to the analysis of gait. The use of the word "biped" does not distinguish the kind of bipedalism, whether like a bird, a galago, or gibbon, or recent man. And an estimate of locomotion has to contain a personal opinion on how the muscles should be reconstructed. Emphasis on behavior forces the consideration of a range of problems which are minimally considered at present. What sort of a sequence of behavioral events

might lead to the ilium (and presumably the hip musculature) evolving to nearly the condition seen in *Homo* while the ischium remained almost as seen in the living Pongidae? One theory which will fit the facts is that bipedal running preceded efficient, long-distance, bipedal walking. In this stage of locomotor evolution the ischium was long (fact) and the hamstrings were relatively large (guess). From the point of view of evolution, this mean that *Australopithecus* may have been able to run as fast as *Homo*. Since even some of the living apes can run faster than man, there may never have been a stage of slow, partial bipedalism. Whatever the truth proves to be, emphasis on behavior leads to making a distinction between bipedal running and walking, to postulating running as essential in the ape-to-man transition, and to see fully-erect, long-distance, bipedal walking as later. Casts of the foot from Olduvai were shown to the conference by Drs. Leakey and Napier. It appears to be even more like that of modern man than the ilium of the South African representatives of *Australopithecus*. This foot strongly supports the notion that bipedal locomotion is the adaptation which separated the Hominidae from the Pongidae.

With these behavioral distinctions in mind, it is easy to select measurements which will distinguish the Pongidae, *Australopithecus,* and *Homo*. In the Pongidae the distances from anterior superior iliac spine to the acetabulum and from the acetabulum to the origin of the hamstrings on the ischial tuberosity are both long. In *Australopithecus* the iliac measurement is short and the ischial one long. In *Homo* both are short. The dimensions may be measured in various ways and indices which identify the groups are easily constructed. But direct comparison is the most revealing. The iliac distance in a small gibbon is absolutely as long as in *Homo*, and the ischial distance in the gibbon is much longer than in man, Figure 2.

These dimensions in man are so short that they may be duplicated, or surpassed, in an ape of 1/10 the body size. Correlated with the unique locomotor pattern of *Homo*, several dimensions of the pelvis are unique and not duplicated in other living primates. In *Australopithecus* the ilium approaches the condition in *Homo* but the ischium is long, and it is suggested that this unique structure was correlated with a form of locomotion characteristic of no living primate. The interest in behavior leads to measuring the pelvis in new ways and to reaching conclusions which are different from those in the literature. The pelvis is not a structural unit, and it is very misleading to refer to the pelvis of *Australopithecus* as human. The form of the pelvis is a compromise between several sets of functional requirements, and the different sets may evolve with a considerable degree of independence.

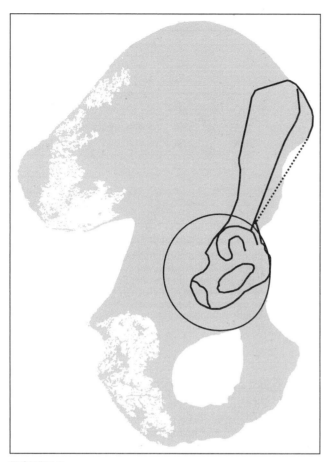

*FIGURE 2*

Interest in function leads to seeing some of these complexes.

The pelvis of *Australopithecus* has been used as an example to show that interest in behavior leads to an analysis in which the emphasis is different from that in the literature. Similarity to ape or man is used to reconstruct behavior *first*, then the position of the reconstructed stage in the evolution of man is evaluated. A model of the method is: comparison of data, reconstruction of behavior, evolutionary conclusion.

In my opinion this emphasis really makes a large difference from the traditional anthropological model in which structures are compared and conclusions drawn directly from the comparison. The importance of the difference may be illustrated by the problem of counting vertebrae. Traditionally vertebrae have been counted by the presence or absence or ribs. Using these criteria, the numbers of vertebrae in the primates have been thoroughly explored. Counted in this way, there is a gradation in the numbers of vertebrae between Cercopithecidae, Pongidae, and Hominidae.

But the vertebrae may be compared in quite a different way. The motions of the vertebrae are correlated with their joints and muscles. In rapidly-moving quadrupedal primates the back is flexed in locomotion, and sacrospinalis is large, rectus abdominis is large and long, and the lumbar region is long and composed of many vertebrae. If the vertebrae are divided by counting all vertebrae as lumbar which have facets allowing primarily flexion and extension, quadrupedal monkeys normally have seven cervical, ten thoracic, and nine lumbar vertebrae. Compared to the traditional method, two vertebrae have been added to the lumbar region. In Table 1, counting by ribs is compared to counting by facets.

When counts are made by ribs, it will be seen that many gibbons and monkeys have twelve or thirteen ribs and six lumbar vertebrae are present in many gibbons and some monkeys. There appears to be little evolution in the numbers of vertebrae. But when the counting is done by facets, a very different picture emerges. Gibbons have twelve or thirteen thoracic vertebrae and five or six lumbars, with rare exceptions. Monkeys have ten thoracics and nine lumbars, with little variation, and there is no overlapping between monkeys and gibbons in either region in even the exceptional cases (Table 1).

But even counting by facets underemphasizes the functional differences because, in the monkeys, all the lumbar characteristics are more pronounced. The neural spines are longer and the anticlinal vertebra is more pronounced. The facets fit more closely and limit motion more. The centra are longer. The transverse processes are larger. In short, correlated with large muscles, all muscular processes are larger, and the lumbar region is approximately twice the length of the thoracic. In gibbons, the opposite is the case and the thoracic region is approximately twice the length of the lumbar. The short, stocky trunk of the brachiator is not flexed and extended in locomotion as is the long, narrow trunk of the quadrupedal monkey. The number of ribs does not differ greatly between gibbons and monkeys, but the functional lumbar complex of the gibbon is approximately one-half that of a monkey of comparable weight. The condition in the monkey is primitive and part of a generalized quadrupedal complex, while the structure of the gibbon is specialized.

The specializations in the human back are basically similar to those of the gibbon, and show none of the primitive quadrupedal features seen in monkeys.

The question of the significance of the numbers of vertebrae has been elaborated because it illustrates both the importance of relating structure and behavior and the difficulty of doing so. Counting by ribs obscures the differences between Cercopithecidae and Pongidae and that hides the close similarity of Pongidae and Hominidae. If the aim is to see the relation of

**TABLE 1**

| | Species | No. | | | | Thoracic Vertebrae | | | Lumbar Vertebrae | | | | | |
|---|---|---|---|---|---|---|---|---|---|---|---|---|---|---|
| | | | | | | 12 | 13 | 14 | 4 | 5 | 6 | 7 | | |
| Ribs | Hylobates lar, | 159 | | | | 3 | 143 | 13 | 5 | 116 | 38 | | | |
| | C. aethiops, | 60 | | | | 56 | 4 | | | 8 | 52 | | | |
| | Papio, | 11 | | | | 2 | 9 | | | 11 | | | | |
| | | | 9 | 10 | 11 | 12 | 13 | 14 | 5 | 6 | 7 | 8 | 9 | 10 |
| Facets | Hylobates lar, | 159 | | | | 60 | 97 | 2 | 59 | 99 | 1 | | | |
| | C. aethiops, | 60 | 4 | 56 | | | | | | | | 3 | 54 | 3 |
| | Papio, | 11 | 1 | 9 | 1 | | | | | | | | 11 | |

The number of thoracic and lumbar vertebrae in a sample of gibbons, vervets, and baboons, counted by the traditional method (ribs) and by the structure of the articulations (facets). This is part of a study on vertebrae started with the help of research funds provided by the University of California through its Committee on Research and continued under Grant No. G-17954 from the National Science Foundation. The writer is deeply indebted to Ralph Holloway for help in collecting the data. The gibbons were collected in one locality in Thailand on the Asiatic Primate Expedition organized by Harold Coolidge. The *Cercopithecus* monkeys were collected in Uganda under a grant from the Wenner-Gren Foundation and with the help of Dr. A. Galloway. The baboons were collected in Northern Rhodesia with the help of Dr. Desmond Clark. The gibbon collection was loaned by the Museum of Comparative Zoology of Harvard Univeristy.

brachiation to the evolution of the back, the vertebrae must be counted in functional groups, but, if that is done, the counts are not comparable to those in the literature, and this is an immense loss. This then, is a general problem when interest shifts from traditional categories to behavior. I think that the following statement will be correct, but much additional material would have to be examined to prove it. Vertebral regions are most clearly defined and stable when they are important in the locomotor pattern. The Galagidae are at one extreme and the Lorisidae at the other. In the Cercopithecidae, the regions are more sharply defined and much more stable than in the Pongidae. The situation in the Hominidae is derived from that of the Pongidae, but with bipedal locomotion lumbar length has become important again. There is strong selection against a sixth lumbar vertebra, over 95 per cent of humans are at the norm, and bipedalism is so new that there has not been time for a structurally efficient lower lumbar region to evolve.

From the point of view of classification, a functional view of the vertebrae fits the traditional categories. It suggests a much greater separation of Cercopithecidae and Pongidae than counting by ribs. It offers support for the derivation of Hominidae from Pongidae.

It has become traditional to date the separation of the Hominidae from the Pongidae to the Miocene. Earlier and later separations have been suggested, but early Miocene appears to be the commonest opinion. This view is usually diagrammed approximately as shown in the accompanying Figure 3A. It will be noted that the Pleistocene appears nearly as long as the Pliocene. In Figure 3B the time scale is corrected, and it will be seen at once that all known fossils of the Hominidae are well within the Pleistocene and that a separate line has been postulated which has twenty times the duration of the known record. When Gregory and Keith pictured the separation of man and ape much as in Figure 3A, they thought that Miocene apes were essentially like living ones, that the Pliocene was little longer than the Pleistocene, and that *H. sapiens* had existed for a very long time. Figure 3A is a natural representation of this view. But now it appears that the distinctive size of the human brain evolved at the end of the Lower or beginning of the Middle Pleistocene. In the Lower Pleistocene, the ischium is long and ape-like; the ilium and hand do not yet have the full characteristics of *Homo*. Most of the characteristics of *Homo* seem to have evolved well within the Pleistocene, and there is no need to postulate an early separation of man and ape.

From the point of view of behavior, a major question is whether *Australopithecus* represents a stage of long duration, a relatively stable adaptation, or a transitional form evolving rapidly under the new selection pressures which came with the use of tools. My guess is that the second of these alternatives is correct and that tool use caused a rapid change in selection which separated the Hominidae from the Pongidae, possibly entirely within the Pleistocene.

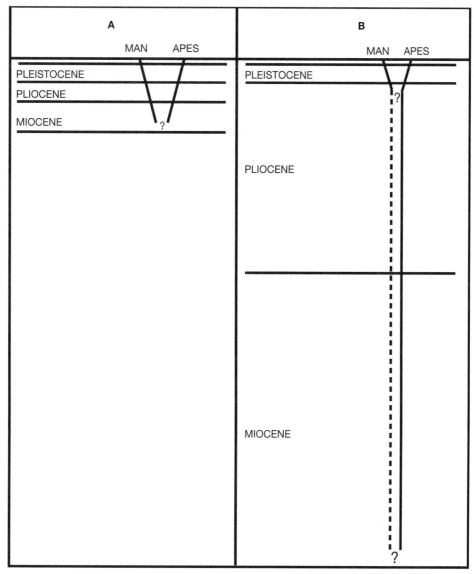

FIGURE 3     APPROXIMATE DURATION:    PLEISTOCENE   1,000,000 YEARS
                                                   PLIOCENE     10,000,000 YEARS
                                                   MIOCENE      15,000,000 YEARS

## CONCLUSIONS

It has been suggested that the "natural" groups of primates are adaptive radiations. The main adaptations were recognized by the early students of the primates, and this accounts for the agreement concerning many groupings.

Emphasis on adaptation helps in the evaluation of the structures which are used in classification, and the constant emphasis on function and behavior frequently leads to the reinterpretation of descriptive data.

*What can we understand about conflict in modern human societies when we assume that humans are primates and that primates are mammals? The evidence on aggression in mammals was still very rudimentary when Washburn wrote this paper. Naturalistic data on aggression in nonhuman primates was almost nonexistent. Nonetheless, he argued that we should consider several important points. First, aside from predation, interspecies conflict is rare and evolutionarily unimportant. By contrast, intraspecies conflict is frequent, meaning that aggression should be seen as part of an adaptive complex that functions to space individuals in relationship to each other and to resources, and ultimately orders the group. Although aggression and conflict are adaptive, they are expressed as part of species-specific patterns molded by the ecological context.*

*Washburn draws out the implications for understanding the evolution of aggression and conflict among humans. Unlike for other primates, the rate of social and cultural change means that humans are adapted to a past that no longer exists, and even worse, that biological evolution has not been able to keep pace. Humans are thus saddled with emotions and behaviors which were adaptive in the past but may have untoward consequences today. Washburn suggests some features that might create problems, such as the dominance-seeking, aggressive nature of males, or emotions geared to small social groups but unable to cope with larger ones, or a sense of time that does not comprehend history, which produces a disregard for events that are remote in space and time. Thus evolutionary biology has created fundamental problems for all human societies, as well as for people who might try to create something as anomolous as "world peace." Washburn warns that the success of humans in the future will depend on how well they appreciate the evolutionary "peculiarities and limitations" of human actors in the modern world.*

# Conflict in Primate Society

**S. L. Washburn**   *Department of Anthropology, University of California, Berkeley*

Aggression and conflict are very widely distributed throughout the vertebrates. In modern human society conflict is usually regarded as undesirable, as a response to frustration, and as maladaptive, something that should be avoided. But the frequency and complexity of aggressive behaviours show that selection must have favoured them in many groups of vertebrates over vast periods of time. In his classic study of aggressive behaviour, Collias[1] concluded that the function of a great deal of conflict was the control of food and reproduction through the control of territory and the maintenance of a hierarchy within groups, and that males were responsible for most of the aggression. Scott,[2,3] while agreeing with Collias' main conclusions, stressed the importance of learning in mammals; success in fighting is a powerful agent in reinforcing learn-

In *Conflict in Society* (London: Ciba Society, 1966), pp. 3–15.

ing, and fear is easily learned and hard to extinguish. Wynne Edwards[4,5] has stressed social behaviour through control of territory, hierarchy and reproduction as the mechanism of distributing the species and controlling its population size.

It is my belief that these main conclusions will be shown to apply to primates in general, including man. Within the group, order is normally maintained by a hierarchical organization. Between groups, space is divided by habit and conflict. The aggressive individual is the essential actor within the social system and the competing group is necessary for the distribution of the species and the control of local populations.

There are not enough data at present to prove these points, and conclusions about the behaviour of primates are guides to research rather than facts. In Scott's 1962 review on aggression in animals, the only major accounts of the behaviour of free-ranging primates were Carpenter's studies[6] of the gibbon (made in 1940) and howling monkey (1934). In Hall's 1964 review[7] of aggression in monkey and ape societies almost all the data are drawn from references as recent as 1962 or later. Few scientists have studied free-ranging primates, and the combination of laboratory, experimental and naturalistic study, which has been so successful in the study of the behaviour of birds, has hardly begun in primatology. With this major qualification, this paper will consider conflict in primate behaviour.

## INTERSPECIFIC CONFLICT OF MONKEYS AND APES

From the human point of view, the point of view of a hunter in the modern, crowded world, it is remarkable how little conflict there is between species of mammals, with the exception of carnivores and their prey. At African water holes near the end of the dry season a wide variety of species come to feed and drink without engaging in interspecific aggressive actions. In the Amboseli Game Reserve in Kenya there are frequently several species around a water hole at the same time. It is not uncommon to see baboons, vervet monkeys, warthogs, impala, gazelle of two species, zebra, wildebeest (gnu), giraffe, elephant and rhino near a water hole at the same time, especially in the late afternoon. Although eating the same food and drinking from very limited water the different kinds of animals walk past each other and feed beside each other without apparent conflict. The same general situation seems to be true in the forest, although there observation is more difficult. Carpenter[6] (1940 study) saw gibbons feeding in trees with langurs and macaques. I remember seeing two kinds of vervets (*Cercopithecus aethiops* and *C. nictitans*), mangabeys and black and white colobus monkeys in the same trees at the same time in western Uganda. The general impression is of a very wide range of tolerance for other species.[7,8]

There are exceptions. Goodall[9] saw chimpanzees hunt red colobus. DeVore has seen baboons catch and eat vervets. I have seen baboons try to drive vervets from fruit trees without success, because the vervets are much more active climbers and simply went to the next tree by way of very small branches, and later returned. Both chimpanzees[9] and baboons[10] may occasionally hunt and eat small mammals, particularly young ones. But the overwhelming majority of interspecific encounters among the primates appear to be neutral, eliciting neither attack nor retreat.

Monkeys and apes certainly take aggressive action against enemies. Baboons drive off cheetahs, and Hall[7] and Jay[8] have reviewed the aggressive behaviour of

monkeys and apes towards predators. The reaction to carnivores of a large troop of baboons is an impressive sight. There was a troop of more than 180 in the Amboseli Reserve. One day two Masai dogs ran barking toward the troop. The females and young hurried a little and this left an irregular line of nearly 30 big adult males between the dogs and the bulk of the troop. The dogs turned and ran. Jackals and even carnivores as large as big hyenas (*Crocuta*) do not seem to provoke any reaction from the baboons. Lions were the only animals from which the baboons fled.

One kind of aggressive behaviour which appears to be limited to primates and is characteristic of many species of monkeys and apes is the use of objects in agonistic display. Many kinds of monkeys and apes drop objects from the trees in the direction of enemies.[11] This use of objects thrown in defence has not yet been observed in other orders of animals. The displays of gorillas[12,13] and of chimpanzees[9] are particularly impressive, and include breaking off branches and throwing stones, in the case of chimpanzees. In most cases these objects are only dropped or tossed in the air but sometimes they are unquestionably aimed at the intruder.

It is very difficult to estimate the amount of predation on primate troops. Haddow[14] describes a male colobus monkey climbing up towards and threatening an eagle while the rest of the group dropped to lower branches. Obviously, human observers are rarely in a position to see such interactions. In captivity, macaques of several species react much like the free-ranging baboons. Gorillas will display against human beings and attack under special circumstances,[12] and there is no reason to suppose that these reactions are different from those directed against other predators. Probably the males of many different kinds of monkeys and apes will defend themselves against predators. Agonistic display and bluffing by baboons is carried out even against lions.[15,16]

## INTRASPECIFIC CONFLICT

In very marked contrast to the usually pacific or at least neutral relations between different species of primates and associated mammals, reactions between groups of the same species range from avoidance to agonistic display and even to violence. This is well illustrated when baboons are crowded into a small area near water holes at the end of the dry season.[10] Impala, gazelle, warthogs and other ungulates might be mixed among the baboons, but if two baboon troops are at the water hole at the same time, they remain separate. No mixing occurs, and if a large troop comes to the hole, a smaller troop will move slowly away, feeding as it goes. Calm avoidance is the rule, but sometimes there are agonistic displays and the males move to the side nearest the other troop. It is probable that the calm avoidance takes place between troops that know each other and the agonistic display between troops that are strangers. This conjecture is strengthened by the reaction of troops to released strangers and by the similar reaction of captive monkeys. DeVore and I released four baboons near a troop in the Nairobi Park; the troop immediately chased the strangers. Our group of *Macaca irus* at Berkeley has violently attacked newly introduced animals, and attempts to add two adult males of the same species to the group peacefully have failed over a three-month period, even though the animals have been caged next to each other in plain sight. Ceylon grey langurs (*Presbytis entellus*) attack other troops of the same species but do not attack macaques or purple-faced langurs in the same area.[17,18] Male gibbons defend territory (Carpenter's study[6] in 1940; J. O. Ellefson, personal communication, 1965).

It is my belief that territorial behaviour in primates has been underestimated for three reasons. First, studies so far have concentrated on understanding the social behaviour within a group; this has meant that observers have not been looking for situations in which intergroup conflict might be seen. Secondly, groups are normally spaced well apart; the observer sees the results of avoidance, not the events causing it. Thirdly, learning is very important in monkeys and apes, and the pattern of inter-troop relations has been learned; in the short run the observer sees order, not the events that led to the orderly spacing of the groups. Carpenter[6] has reviewed this question, calling special attention to the role of sounds in spacing groups without conflict.

The maximum intergroup conflict reported so far is for rhesus monkeys living in a temple in India.[19] Here, the areas that three troops occupied overlapped to such an extent that groups frequently came in contact and intergroup fights occurred. This situation involved an aggressive species in an overcrowded locality and a habitat that prevented separation. It should be stressed that even under such circumstances agonistic display is much more common than actual fighting. Since conflict is normally between adjacent groups that know each other and have had prior experience of each other's fighting potential, calls, displays and agonistic gestures are usually adequate to keep groups apart without fighting.

## CONFLICT WITHIN THE GROUP

The members of a group of monkeys or apes are usually arranged in a hierarchy and normally this results in peace and order within the group. The most dominant animals in the hierarchy are also the ones that are most likely to defend the group. This simple picture is complicated because position in the hierarchy may depend on the joint action of two or three animals; thus the rank of some depends on their relation to the others. It is further complicated by species differences. For example, hierarchy is far less developed in langurs than it is in baboons and macaques,[20,21,8] In chimpanzees there is no group in the sense of a localized aggregation of animals that know each other and are consistently in association.[9,22] Even in this extremely fluid situation some animals are more dominant than others.

Conflict between individuals within the local group or temporary aggregation is far more frequent than are intergroup or interspecific conflicts. It is impossible to watch monkeys and apes for any long period of time without seeing conflict over food or interpersonal relations. In the absence of speech the adjustment of individual to individual is often made by agonistic gesture, and it is my belief that language has been one of the most important factors in reducing agonistic gestures and interpersonal conflict. As Scott[2] has pointed out, aggressive behaviour is greatly increased by being rewarded. In non-human primate society, which lacks language, aggressive action is constantly rewarded and one of the most important functions of language in society may be to offer a way of constant adjustment without recourse to conflict. Actual fighting is rare because the animals know each other, and their positions are determined by habit. It is further reduced by gestures, displays and pursuits. Normally, these are enough to settle differences without the occurrence of actual biting, but fights do occur and can be severe.

Learning is important in establishing hierarchy. Yamada[23] and Sade[24] have shown that the infants of dominant females are more likely to be dominant. Not only do these infants grow up with the more dominant animals in the heart of the troop, but also the mother supports her offspring in aggression, even when a son is fully mature. But ultimately hierarchy depends on force. For example, a baboon which changed to a different troop defeated the old dominant male of the new troop and became first in the hierarchy as a result of a single fight in which the old leader was severely beaten.

## THE EVOLUTION OF CONFLICT

Whether conflict is between species, between groups of the same species, or between individuals in a group, the actual interactions are carried out by individuals. Individual animals must be fitted for this social role as for the others they are destined to play, and evolution through selection builds an interrelated complex of structure, temperament and social behaviour. Just as selection for greater speed involves muscles, nervous control and physiology, so selection for fighting involves structure, skill and temperament.

## Aggression

The males of many species of monkeys have large canine teeth which are used in fighting. To use these weapons the animal must have specialized features of the jaws, skull and neck. The skilful use of the fighting complex must be learned in play and the animal's temperament must be such that aggressive behaviour may be elicited by the proper stimuli. Differences in the aggressive behaviour of males and females are rooted in a complex biology, developed through differing patterns of play, and elicited by differing stimuli. This structural–behavioural complex of aggression forms an important part of the adaptation of the species, and a comparison of the behaviour of different species may make clear some of the reasons for aggression. Within the normally arboreal genus *Cercopithecus* one species, *C. aethiops*, frequently feeds on the ground, and in this species aggression is high in interpersonal situations. In the closely related but much more arboreal species *C. nictitans* (*ascanius*) and *C. mitis* there is much less aggression and the structural basis for fighting (teeth, jaws, etc.) is less developed. These differences may be seen in free-ranging animals; they are well known to those who handle animals in captivity; and they are deeply embedded in the structure of the species. For example, an adult male *C. aethiops* has a temporal muscle that weighs approximately 45 g., whereas a *C. nictitans* of comparable size has a muscle weighing only from 10 to 12 g.; the far more arboreal *C. nictitans* simply lacks the structure which would make effective aggression possible.

A further example of such a contrast is that between baboons and patas monkeys. Hall[7] has described how patas monkeys escape some dangers by freezing in the grass while the adult male runs away, luring the predator from the vicinity of the group. Under comparable conditions the much larger baboons rely on the defensive action of the adult males acting in concert.

Aggression may be viewed as part of the species-specific pattern of adapting behaviours. It is complex, expressing itself in actions against other species and against other individuals of the same species; it is rooted in the biology of the species. In a given species the nature of the biology of aggression is adapted to the way of life of that species. Langurs run under conditions where baboons fight. In mixed groups, macaques dominate langurs.[20] The species-specific patterns of aggression are persistent, biologically based and only partially modified by individual experience. Since this biology of aggression is the result of the long-term evolution of the species it is adapted to the conditions under which the species existed in the past. It is adaptive in the present only if the conditions of the present are the same as those under which the behaviour evolved. If change is rapid the behavioural-structural pattern of aggression may not be adaptive under the new conditions.

The situation can be illustrated by the behaviour of domestic animals. The normal aggressive behaviour patterns of wild species make them exceedingly difficult to manage and domestication involved, among other things, selection for amenable strains. Probably, the beginnings of such selection were achieved simply by killing the most aggressive individuals, but the end results are domestic breeds that are less aggressive, less intelligent and biologically very different from their wild counterparts. Even with considerable control of breeding it took thousands of years for the domestic breeds to become adapted to their new environment, although this certainly could have been done more rapidly with a modern knowledge of genetics.

Throughout most of human evolution man was adapted to ways of life radically different from those of today and there has been neither the time nor the control of breeding to change the biology of human aggression from what was adaptive in the past to what is adaptive now. Throughout most of human history, society has depended on young adult males to hunt, to fight and to maintain the social order with violence. Even if co-operation were present, the individual role could only be executed by extremely aggressive action, which was socially approved, learned in play, and personally gratifying. Until recently the kings of the most civilized countries took part in individual combat for personal and national glory. The basis for the majority of contemporary sports was the preparation for war, and the purpose of the sports was to render the individuals taking part in them physically and psychologically tough, so that they would be capable of and would enjoy the physical destruction of other human beings. We still inherit the biology of aggression that was adaptive in the past. This aggressive nature is nurtured by many customs, and individuals thus equipped by nature and rewarded by society are then loosed on the complex, crowded world of modern science.

In the other primates, evolution has progressed slowly enough for the balance between the species-specific structures and the social behaviours to be maintained. But, in the case of man, culture and social behaviour have changed at an unprecedented rate. There has been no comparable biological evolution, and the human actor is not fitted to take part in modern life in the same sense that a baboon or patas monkey is adapted to its way of life.

For the modern, crowded, scientific world, the human actor, particularly the male,[2] is too dominance-seeking and too aggressive. These attributes are frequently rewarded in play and encouraged by the existence of antiquated customs. In the past and in simpler societies the customs and values of the adult world are clear to the child and the patterns of play build appropriate skills and temperament. This is no longer the case.

The adaptation of human biology to conditions long past is shown in two other ways that are very important in the consideration of conflict. Our ancestors lived in very small groups, and we have evolved to feel strongly about only a very small number of people. It is emotions which move people to action, and the basis for social emotions which was adequate among small groups of hunter-gatherers is entirely inadequate for the societies of today. Practically, this means that those trying to move people to action use the vocabulary of the small group in which the emotions are real. It also means that people respond to a leader; the top of the hierarchy is still followed, and he is blamed for war or peace, good or evil. The complex forces of history are of little or no interest to the average actor in human society and it comes as a repeated surprise that changes in the leaders do not change the world.

Further, man was adapted to the violent, unpredictable world of time past by being optimistic beyond reason and by being emotionally concerned with a very short period of time. The lessons of the past were quickly forgotten and the long-term future was not a matter of concern. Even as recently as the First World War, the war was described as "a war to end war" and many nations disarmed, in spite of every lesson of history and the evidence of German rearmament. This lack of concern with events remote in space or time that is a characteristic of the human species was adaptive in the past, but this aspect of human biology presents profound problems to those who would plan for peace on a worldwide, long-term basis.

Hamburg[25] has developed this theme much more fully in his paper "Emotions in the Perspective of Human Evolution". The essence of his argument is that every species is adapted to a way of life. Structure, physiology, emotions and mental abilities are all integrated and make possible the species-specific behaviour. Particularly in mammals the kinds of learning on which survival depends are also built into the species by evolution. Just as it is easy for man to learn speech or tool-use because the basis for these abilities has been built into the brain by selection and evolution, so it is easy for man to learn to be aggressive and to glory in conflict. This does not mean that this kind of behaviour in man is inevitable, but it does mean that it is very probable. It does mean that aggression will easily appear whenever it is rewarded, even if only minimally. It does mean that young males will feel joy in conflict whenever the social system provides opportunity for and approval of conflict.

In summary, the data on the behaviour of primates living under natural conditions are limited. They are compatible with the conclusion that, leaving predation aside, conflict between species is rare and of little importance. But within a species conflict is frequent and forms the basis for spacing the social groups. The social hierarchy, based ultimately on force, keeps order in the group. To survive in this kind of society the males must enjoy aggression, and, when all the means of bluffing fail, must be equipped to fight. In spite of great social changes, man still inherits the biology which adapted him to live in a small society in which many forms of conflict were highly rewarded. This biology will present fundamental problems to all human societies, and planning for the future should be based on an appreciation of the peculiarities and limitations of the actors.

## ACKNOWLEDGMENTS

This paper is a part of a programme on the Analysis of Primate Behaviour, supported by Grant MH-08623 of the United States Public Health Service. The point of view on the evolution of emotion has been developed in conversations with David A. Hamburg, M.D., of Stanford University. I particularly want to thank Mrs. Jane B. Lancaster for advice and help in the preparation of this paper.

## BIBLIOGRAPHY

1. Collias, N. E. (1944). *Physiological Zoology,* **17,** 83–123.
2. Scott, J. P. (1958). *Aggression.* Chicago: University of Chicago Press.
3. Scott, J. P. (1962). In *Roots of Behavior,* pp. 167–178, ed. Bliss, E. L. New York: Harper.
4. Wynne-Edwards, V. C. (1962). *Animal Dispersion in Relation to Social Behaviour.* Edinburgh: Oliver and Boyd and New York: Hafner.
5. Wynne-Edwards, V. C. (1965). *Science,* **147,** 1543–1548.
6. Carpenter, C. R. (1964). In *Naturalistic Behavior of Nonhuman Primates,* pp. 3–92 (1934 Study) and pp. 145–271 (1940 Study), author and ed. Carpenter, C. R. University Park, Pennsylvania: Pennsylvania State University Press.

7. Hall, K. R. L. (1964). In *The Natural History of Aggression*, pp. 51–64, ed. Carthy, J. D., and Ebling, F. J. London and New York: Academic Press.

8. Jay, Phyllis (1965). In *Behavior of Nonhuman Primates*, pp. 525–591, ed. Schrier, A. M., Harlow, H. F., and Stollnitz, F. New York: Academic Press.

9. Goodall, Jane (1965). In *Primate Behavior*, pp. 425–473, ed. DeVore, I. New York: Holt, Rinehart and Winston.

10. DeVore, I., and Hall, K. R. L. (1965). In *Primate Behavior*, pp. 20–52, ed. DeVore, I. New York: Holt, Rinehart and Winston.

11. Hall, K. R. L. (1963). *Current Anthropology*, **4**, 479–494.

12. Schaller, G. B. (1963). *The Mountain Gorilla*. Chicago: University of Chicago Press.

13. Schaller, G. B. (1965). In *Primate Behavior*, pp. 324–367, ed. DeVore, I. New York: Holt, Rinehart and Winston.

14. Haddow, A. J. (1952). *Proceedings of the Zoological Society of London*, **122**, 297–394.

15. DeVore, I., and Washburn, S. L. (1962). Film: Baboon Behavior. Berkeley, California: The University of California Extension Division.

16. Hall, K. R. L., and DeVore, I. (1965). In *Primate Behavior*, pp. 53–110, ed DeVore, I. New York: Holt, Rinehart and Winston.

17. Ripley, Suzanne (1965). In *Social Interactions among Primates*, ed. Altmann, S. A. Chicago: University of Chicago Press.

18. Ripley, Suzanne (1965). The Ecology and Social Behavior of the Ceylon Gray Langur. Doctoral Thesis, University of Calfornia, Berkeley.

19. Southwick, C. H., Beg, M. A., and Siddiqi, M. R. (1965). In *Primate Behavior*, pp. 111–159, ed. DeVore, I. New York: Holt, Rinehart and Winston.

20. Jay, Phyllis (1963). The Social Behavior of the Langur Monkey. Doctoral Thesis, University of Chicago.

21. Jay, Phyllis (1965). In *Primate Behavior*, pp. 197–249, ed. DeVore, I. New York: Holt, Rinehart and Winston.

22. Reynolds, Vernon and Reynolds, Frances (1965). In *Primate Behavior*, pp. 368–424, ed. DeVore, I. New York: Holt, Rinehart and Winston.

23. Yamada, Munemi (1963). *Primates* **4**, 43–65.

24. Sade, D. S. (1965). Paper presented at annual meeting of Southwestern Anthropological Association, University of California, Los Angeles, April 1965.

25. Hamburg, D. A. (1963). In *Expression of the Emotions in Man*, pp. 300–317, ed. Knapp, P. H. New York: International Universities Press.

# BIBLIOGRAPHY OF S. L. WASHBURN

1936    (with Barbara Lawrence). A new eastern race of Galago demidovaii. *Occasional Papers of the Boston Society of Natural History* 8:255–266.

1941    (abstract)
        Observations on certain langurs. *American Journal of Physical Anthropology* (Suppl. 1) 18:6.

        (abstract)
        Technique in primatology. *American Journal of Physical Anthropology* 28:12.

1942    (abstract)
        Sequence of epiphysial union in Old World monkeys. *American Journal of Physical Anthropology* (Suppl. 2) 29:318.

        Skeletal proportions of adult langurs and macaques (abridged version of doctoral dissertation, Harvard University, 1940). *Human Biology* 14:444–472.

        Technique in primatology. *Anthropological Briefs* 1:6–12; 2:29–32.

1943    (with S. R. Detwiler). An experiment bearing on the problems of physical anthropology. *American Journal of Physical Anthropology,* n.s., 1:171–190.

        The sequence of epiphysial union in Old World monkeys. *American Journal of Anatomy* 72:339–360.

        Technique in primatology. *Anthropological Briefs* 3:9–17.

        Glover Morrill Allen, 1879–1942. *Journal of Mammology* 24:(3):301–302.

1944    The genera of Malaysian langurs. *Journal of Mammalogy* 25:289–294.

        Review of Mankind So Far, by W. W. Howell. *American Anthropologist,* n.s., 46:548–549.

        Thinking about race. *Science Education* 28:65–76.

        Review of Chimpanzees: A Laboratory Colony, by R. M. Yerkes. *American Journal of Physical Anthropology,* n.s., 2:224.

1945    (abstract)
        The experimental approach of anthropological problems. *American Journal of Physical Anthropology,* n.s., 3:219.

        Review of Anatomy as the Basis for Medical and Dental Practice, by Donald Mainland. *American Journal of Physical Anthropology,* n.s., 3:213–214.

1946    The effect of facial paralysis on the growth of the skull of rat and rabbit. *The Anatomical Record* 94:163–168.

        The effect of removal of the zygomatic arch in the rat. *Journal of Mammalogy* 27:169–172.

        Experimental anthropology. *Transactions, New York Academy of Science* 8:186–187.

        The sequence of epiphysial union in the opossum. *The Anatomical Record* 95:353–364.

        (abstract)
        Thoracic viscera of the gorilla. *American Journal of Physical Anthropology,* n.s., 4:262.

1947    (abstract)
The biological basis of measurement. *American Journal of Physical Anthropology,* n.s., 5:237.

Review of The South African Fossil Ape-Men: The Australopithecinae, by R. Broom and G. W. Schepers. *American Anthropologist* 49:296–297.

The effect of the temporal muscle on the form of the mandibles. *Journal of Dental Research* 26:174.

Review of Human Genetics, by R. R. Gates. *American Anthropologist* 49:488–489.

The relation of the temporal muscle to the form of the skull. *The Anatomical Record* 99:239–248.

1948    Review of Outline of Anthropology, by M. Jacobs and B. J. Stern, *American Journal of Physical Anthropology,* n.s., 6:111–112.

1949    (abstract)
The determination of the sex of skeletons. *Anatomical Record* 103:516.

Review of Robert Broom Commemorative Volume, by A. L. Dutoit, ed. *American Anthropologist* 51:649–651.

Review of A New Theory of Human Evolution, by Sir Arthur Keith. *American Journal of Physical Anthropology,* n.s., 7:263–266.

Sex differences in the pubic bone of Bantu and Bushman. *American Journal of Physical Anthropology,* n.s., 7:425–432.

(with Davida Wolffson). *The Shorter Anthropological Papers of Franz Weidenreich Published in the Period 1939–1948.* New York: The Viking Fund.

1950    (abstract)
The analysis of facial growth. *American Journal of Physical Anthropology,* n.s., 8:271.

Review of Genetics, Paleontology, and Evolution, by G. L. Jepsen, E. Mayr, and G. G. Simpson, eds. *American Journal of Physical Anthropology,* n.s., 8:245–247.

Thoracic viscera of the gorilla. In W. K. Gregory, ed., *The Anatomy of the Gorilla,* Part 3. New York: Columbia University Press, pp. 189–195.

(letter to the editor)
Constitutional types and physical anthropology. *American Anthropologist* 52:437.

1951    (abstract)
The analysis of anatomical difference. *American Journal of Physical Anthropology,* n.s., 9:235.

The analysis of primate evolution with particular reference to the origin of man. In *Cold Spring Harbor Symposia on Quantitative Biology* 15:67–78, Origin and Evolution of Man.

Review of The Human Species: A Biology of Man, by Anthony Barnett. *American Sociological Review* 15:576:577.

Review of Unraveling Juvenile Delinquency, by S. and E. Glueck. *American Anthropologist* 53:572–574.

(with B. Patterson). Evolutionary importance of the South African 'man-apes.' *Nature* 167:650–651.

(with H. H. Strandskov). Genetics and physical anthropology. *American Journal of Physical Anthropology,* n.s., 9:261–263.

The new physical anthropology. In *Transactions of the New York Academy of Sciences,* Series II, 13:298–304.

Review of The New You and Heredity, by Amram Scheinfeld. *American Sociological Review* 16:577–578.

(abstract)
On the interpretation of differences in the form of the skull. *Anatomical Record* 109:355.

Review of Varieties of Delinquent Youth: An Introduction to Constitutional Psychiatry, by W. H. Sheldon. *American Anthropologist* 53:561–563.

1952    Carelton Stevens Coon, Viking Fund Medalist for 1951. *American Journal of Physical Anthropology,* n.s., 10:227–228.

(abstract)

(with J. Buettner-Janusch). The definition of thoracic and lumbar vertebrae. *American Journal of Physical Anthropology,* n.s., 10:251.

(with F. Clark Howell). On the identification of the hypophysial fossa of Solo man. *American Journal of Physical Anthropology,* n.s., 10:13–22.

(with J. A. Gavan and P. H. Lewis). Photography: An anthropometric tool. *American Journal of Physical Anthropology,* n.s., 10:331–353.

The strategy of physical anthropology. Presented at Wenner-Gren Foundation International Symposium on Anthropology, New York, 1952.

(with R. J. Havighurst, A. Keys, and P. A. Weiss). The study of growth and its meaning to mankind, II: The human implications. *The University of Chicago Round Table,* No. 765.

Reviews of Essay on the Cerebral Cortex, by G. von Bonin; Frontal Lobotomy and Affective Behavior, by J. F. Fulton; The Cerebral Cortex, by W. Penfield and T. Rasmussen. *American Anthropologist,* 54:402–403.

1953     (with R. E. Hanna). The determination of the sex of skeletons, as illustrated by a study of the Eskimo pelvis. *Human Biology* 25:21–27.

The Piltdown hoax. *American Anthropologist* 55:759–762.

Editorial. *American Anthropologist* 55:157–158.

1954     An old theory is supported by new evidence and new methods. *American Anthropologist* 56:433–441.

(abstract)
On the antiquity of anatomically modern man. *American Journal of Physical Anthropology* 12:285.

1955     Review of The Fossil Evidence for Human Evolution, by W. LeGros Clark. *American Journal of Physical Anthropology* 13:545–547.

Human evolution. In J. R. Newman, ed., *What Is Science?* New York: Simon & Schuster, pp. 321–322.

Review of Evolution as a Process, by Julian Huxley, et al. *American Journal of Physical Anthropology* 13:162–164.

1956     Anthropologic difference between man and the rat. In S. J. Fomon, ed., *Report of the 17th Ross Pediatric Research Conference,* Columbus, Ohio, pp. 45–46.

The relationship of form and function of the masticatory apparatus. In S. J. Fomon, ed., *Report of the 17th Ross Pediatric Research Conference,* Columbus, Ohio, pp. 53–58.

(with L. W. Mednick). The role of the sutures in the growth of the braincase of the infant pig. *American Journal of Physical Anthropology,* n.s., 14:175–191.

1957     Australopithecines: The hunters or the hunted? *American Anthropologist* 59:612–614.

Ischial callosities as sleeping adaptations. *American Journal of Physical Anthropology* 15:269–276.

1958     Review of Body Measurements and Human Nutrition, by J. Brozek, ed. *American Anthropologist* 60:207.

Review of History of the Primates, by W. LeGros Clark. *American Anthropologist* 60:610–611.

Review of Bones for the Archeologist, by I. W. Cornwall. *American Anthropologist* 60:406.

(with V. Avis) Evolution of human behavior. In A. Roe and G. G. Simpson, eds., *Behavior and Evolution.* New Haven: Yale University Press, pp. 421–436.

Review of Skeletal Age Changes in Young American Males, by T. W. McKern and T. D. Stewart. *American Antiquity* 24:198–199.

Review of Traite de Paleontologie, Tome VII, by J. Piveteau. *American Journal of Physical Anthropology* 16:493–494.

1959     Review of the Evolution of the Speech Apparatus, by E. L. Du Brul. *American Anthropologist* 61:918.

Speculations on the interrelations of the history of tools and biological evolution. *Human Biology* 31:21–31.

1960      Cultural determinants of brain size. *American Journal of Physical Anthropology* 18:349.

(with F. Clark Howell). Human evolution and culture. In Sol Tax, ed., *Evolution after Darwin*, Vol. II. Chicago: University of Chicago Press, pp. 33–56.

(with I. DeVore). K. Imanishi, social organization of subhuman primates in their natural habitat. *Current Anthropology* 1:405.

Tools and human evolution. *Scientific American* 203:63–75.

(with I. DeVore). Baboon Behavior, 16mm. sound, color film. Motion Picture Production Department, Berkeley: University of California.

1961      (with T. D. McCown). Review of The Prehistory of Southern Africa, by J. D. Clark. *American Antiquity* 26:445.

(abstract)
The genus *Australopithecus. American Journal of Physical Anthropology*, n.s., 19:97.

Review of Man, Race and Darwin. Papers read at a joint conference of the Royal Anthropological Institute and the Institute of Race Relations. *American Anthropologist* 63:1154.

Review of Introduction to Physical Anthropology: Third Edition, by M. F. Ashley Montagu. *American Anthropologist* 63:452–453.

(with I. DeVore). Social behavior of baboons and early man. In S. L. Washburn, ed., *Social Life of Early Man*, Viking Fund Publications in Anthropology, No. 31. New York: Wenner-Gren Foundation for Anthropological Research, pp. 91–105.

(with I. DeVore). Social life of baboons. *Scientific American* 204:62–71.

(ed.). *Social Life of Early Man.* Viking Fund Publications in Anthropology, No. 31. New York: Wenner-Gren Foundation for Anthropological Research, and Chicago: Aldine Publishing Company.

1962      (with I. DeVore). Ecologie et Comportement des Babouins. *La Terre et la Vie* 109:133–149.

1963      (with I. DeVore). Baboon ecology and human evolution. In F. Clark Howell and F. Bourliere, eds., *African Ecology and Human Evolution*, Viking Fund Publications in Anthropology, No. 36. New York: Wenner-Gren Foundation for Anthropological Research, pp. 335–367.

Behavior and human evolution. In S. L. Washburn, ed., *Classification and Human Evolution*, Viking Fund Publications in Anthropology, No. 37. New York: Wenner-Gren Foundation for Anthropological Research, pp. 190–203.

(ed.). *Classification and Human Evolution.* Viking Fund Publications in Anthropology, No. 37. New York: Wenner-Gren Foundation for Anthropological Research, and Chicago: Aldine Publishing Company.

Comment on The Essential Morphological Basis for Human Culture, by A. L. Bryan. *Current Anthropology* 4:304–305.

Review of The Origin of Races, by C. S. Coon. *American Scientist* 51:168A–170A.

The curriculum in physical anthropology. In D. G. Mandelbaum et al., eds., *The Teaching of Anthropology.* Berkeley: University of California Press, pp. 39–47.

Review of The Mountain Gorilla: Ecology and Behavior, by G. B. Schaller. *American Scientist* 51:438A.

The study of race (presidential address, American Anthropological Association, 1962 Meeting, Chicago). *American Anthropologist* 65:521–532.

Tool-using performances as indicators of behavioral adaptability. *Current Anthropology* 4:492.

1964      Racial differences in skin color. *American Anthropologist* 66:1173–1174.

Review of A Suggested Case of Evolution by Sexual Selection in Primates, by C. Jolly. *Man* 64:91.

The origin of races: Weidenreich's opinion. *American Anthropologist* 66:1165–1167.

Race, racism and culture. *Princeton University Magazine* 5:6–8.

Review of Naturalistic Behavior of Nonhuman Primates, by C. R. Carpenter. *American Scientist* 53:468A–470A.

1965      (with D. A. Hamburg). The implications of primate research. In I. DeVore, ed., *Primate Behavior.* New York: Holt, Rinehart and Winston, pp. 607–622.

Introduction. In S. Elmerl and I. DeVore, eds., *The Primates*. New York: Time, Inc., p. 7.

(with D. A. Hamburg). The study of primate behavior. In I. DeVore, ed., *Primate Behavior,* New York: Holt, Rinehart and Winston, pp. 1–13.

(with P. Jay and J. B. Lancaster). Field studies of Old World monkeys and apes. *Science* 150:1541–1547.

An ape's eye view of human evolution. In *The Origin of Man*. Wenner-Gren Conference, Chicago, pp. 89–96.

Review of the naturalistic behavior of nonhuman primates. *American Scientist* 53:468a–470a.

1966    Conflict in primate society. In *Conflict in Society*. London: Ciba Society, pp. 3–15.

Double projection. *American Anthropologist* 68:504–505.

(with J. B. Lancaster). Psychology and the evolution of man. *Harvard Educational Review* 36:333–335.

What is a primate? *Primate News* 4:6–7. Beaverton: Oregon Regional Primate Center.

1967    (with J. Shirek). Human evolution. In J. Hirsch, ed., *Behavior-Genetic Analysis.* New York: McGraw-Hill, pp. 10–21.

Perspectives and prospects. *American Journal of Physical Anthropology* 27:367–373.

Review of Social Communication Among Primates, by S. A. Altmann. *Science* 158:481–482.

Review of Men and Apes, by D. Morris. *Quarterly Review of Biology* 42:559.

Review of Processes of Organic Evolution, by G. L. Stebbins. *American Journal of Physical Anthropology* 27:224–225.

(with P. C. Jay). More on tool use among primates. *Current Anthropology* 8:253–257.

1968    Behavior and the origin of man. *Proceedings of the Royal Anthropological Institute of Great Britain and Ireland, 1967,* pp. 17–21.

Franz Weidenreich. In *International Encyclopedia of the Social Sciences*. New York: Macmillan, pp. 502–503.

Speculations on the problems of man's coming to the ground. In B. Rothblatt, ed., *Changing Perspectives on Man*. Chicago: University of Chicago Press, pp. 191–206.

The study of human evolution. *Condon Lectures*. Eugene: University of Oregon Press.

One hundred years of biological anthropology. In J. O. Brew, ed., *One Hundred Years of Anthropology*. Cambridge: Harvard University Press, pp. 97–115.

(with D. A. Hamburg). Aggressive behavior in Old World monkeys and apes. In P. C. Jay, ed., *Primate Behavior: Studies in Adaptation and Variability*. New York: Holt, Rinehart and Winston, pp. 458–478.

(with C. Lancaster). The evolution of hunting. In R. B. Lee, ed., *Man the Hunter*. Chicago: Aldine, pp. 293–303.

(with J. B. Lancaster). Human evolution. *International Encyclopedia of the Social Sciences*. New York: Macmillan, pp. 215–221.

On Holloway's "Tools and Teeth." *American Anthropologist* 70:97–101.

(ed. with P. C. Jay). *Perspectives on Human Evolution,* Vol. 1. New York: Holt, Rinehart and Winston.

Review of Evolution and Human Behavior, by A. A. Alland, Jr. *American Journal of Physical Anthropology* 29:105.

Review of Man-Apes or Ape-Men? The Story of Discoveries in Africa, by W. E. LeGros Clark. *American Anthropologist* 70:639–640.

Review of Social Organization of Hamadryas Baboons: A Field Study, by H. Kummer. *Man* 3:665.

Review of Race and Modern Science: A Collection of Essays by Biologists, Anthropologists, Sociologists, and Psychologists, by R. E. Kuttner, ed. *American Anthropologist* 70:1035–1037.

Review of Man and Aggression, by M. F. A. Montagu. *New York Times Book Review* (October 6, 1968).

Review of The Apes: The Gorilla, Chimpanzee, Orang-utan, and Gibbon: Their History and Their World, by V. Reynolds. *Man* 3:661–662.

Review of Olduvai Gorge, by P. V. Tobias. *Quarterly Review of Biology* 43:318.

1969    The evolution of human behavior. In J. D. Roslansky, ed., *The Uniqueness of Man*. Amsterdam: North Holland Publishing Company, pp. 167–189.

Review of Men in Groups, by L. Tiger. *New York Times Book Review* (July 27, 1969).

1970    (with R. S. O. Harding). Evolution of primate behavior. In F. O. Schmitt, ed., *The Neurosciences: Second Study Program*. New York: Rockefeller University Press, pp. 39–47.

(with R. S. O. Harding). The selection of nonhuman primates in biological research. In R. S. Harris, ed., *Feeding and Nutrition of Nonhuman Primates*. New York: Academic Press, pp. 1–13.

Origin of aggressive behavior. In *Behavior Sciences and Mental Health*. Chevy Chase: National Institute of Mental Health, pp. 54–71.

Comment on A possible evolutionary basis for aesthetic appreciation in men and apes, by J. S. Bleakney. *Evolution* 24:477–479.

(with R. S. O. Harding). Review of Evolutionary Trends in Fossil and Recent Hominids, by J. Nemeskeri and G. Dezso, eds. *Quarterly Review of Biology* 45:224.

Review of Naked Ape or Homo Sapiens? by J. Lewis and B. Towers. *American Anthropologist* 72:955–956.

Review of The Life of Primates, by A. H. Schultz. *Man* 5:314–315.

1971    On the importance of the study of primate behavior for anthropologists. In M. L. Wax, S. Diamond, F. O. Gearing, eds., *Anthropological Perspectives on Education*. New York: Basic Books, pp. 91–97.

On understanding man. *Rehovot* 6:22–31.

Review of the Human Animal, by H. Hass. *American Anthropologist* 73:1425.

(with J. B. Lancaster). Comment on On the Origins of Language, by L. Carini. *Current Anthropology* 12:384–385.

Comment on Assumption and Inference on Human Origins, by C. Quigley. *Current Anthropology* 12:533–535.

1972    (ed. with P. Dolhinow). *Perspectives on Human Evolution,* Vol. 2. New York: Holt, Rinehart and Winston.

(with P. Dolhinow). Introduction. In S. L. Washburn and P. Dolhinow, eds., *Perspectives on Human Evolution,* Vol. 2. New York: Holt, Rinehart and Winston, pp. 1–13.

(with S. Strum). Concluding comments. In S. L. Washburn and P. Dolhinow, eds., *Perspectives on Human Evolution*. New York: Holt, Rinehart and Winston, pp. 469–491.

Human evolution. In T. Dobzhansky, M. Hecht, W. Steere, eds., *Evolutionary Biology,* Vol. 6. New York: Appleton-Century-Crofts, pp. 349–360.

Man: On the origin of species. *California Monthly* (June/July) 82(8):12–13.

Aggressive behavior and human evolution. In G. V. Coelho and E. A. Rubinstein, eds., *Social Change and Human Behavior*. Rockville: National Institute of Mental Health, pp. 21–32.

(with E. R. McCown). Evolution of human behavior. In R. H. Osborne, ed., *Social Biology* 19:163–170.

1973    Primate studies in human evolution. In G. H. Bourne, ed., *Nonhuman Primates and Medical Research*. New York: Academic Press, pp. 467–485.

The promise of primatology. *American Journal of Physical Anthropology* 38:177–182.

Primate field studies and social science. In L. Nader and T. W. Maretzki, eds., *Cultural Illness and Health*. Anthropological Studies Series No. 9. Washington, DC: American Anthropological Association, pp. 128–134.

The evolution game. *Journal of Human Evolution* 2:557–561.

(with E. R. McCown). The new science of human evolution. In *1974 Britannica Yearbook of Science and the Future*. Chicago: Encyclopedia Britannica, pp. 32–49.

(with M. J. Raleigh). Human behavior and the origin of man. *Impact of Science on Society* 23:5–14.

Review of Not from the Apes, by B. Kurten. *American Journal of Physical Anthropology* 39:319–320.

Comment on Primate Communication and the Gestural Origin of Language, by G. W. Hewes. *Current Anthropology* 14:18.

1974    (with R. Moore). *Ape into Man*. Boston: Little, Brown.

Evolution and education. *Daedalus* 103:221–228.

Human evolution: Science or game? *Yearbook of Physical Anthropology 1973*, 17:67–70.

(with R. L. Ciochon). Canine teeth: Notes on controversies in the study of human evolution. *American Anthropologist* 76:765–784.

(with D. A. Hamburg and N. H. Bishop). Social adaptation in nonhuman primates. In G. V. Coelho, D. A. Hamburg, J. E. Adams, *Coping and Adaptation*. New York: Basic Books, pp. 3–12.

Human evolution. In H. Boardman and S. A. Ross, eds., *Biology in Human Affairs*. Washington DC: Voice of American Forum Series, pp. 223–232.

Review of The Predatory Behavior of Wild Chimpanzees, by G. Teleki. *American Anthropologist* 76:687–688.

Review of God or Beast, by R. Claiborne. *American Scientist* 63:476.

1975    (with R. S. O. Harding). Evolution and human nature. In D. A. Hamburg and H. K. H. Brodie, eds., *American Handbook of Psychiatry*, Vol. VI. New York: Basic Books, pp. 3–13.

Evolution and learning: A context for evaluation. *Principal* 54:4–10.

Comment on Ecology and Australopithecine Taxonomy. *American Anthropologist* 77:618.

Comment on Evolution of the Brain and Intelligence, by H. J. Jerison. *Current Anthropology* 16:412.

1976    The war between words: Biological versus social evolution and some related issues. *American Psychologist* 31:353–355.

Comment in Section 1, Biological versus Social Evolution. *American Psychologist* 31:353–355.

Foreword. In R. B. Lee and I. DeVore, eds., *Kalahari Hunter-Gatherers*. Cambridge: Harvard University Press, pp. xv–xvii.

The extinction of dinosaurs. *American Anthropologist* 78:902.

Comment on Sociobiology. *Reviews in Anthropology* 3:558–559.

Foreword. In W. Montagna, *Nonhuman Primates in Biomedical Research*. Minneapolis: University of Minnesota Press, pp. ix–xi.

(with R. L. Ciochon). The single species hypothesis. *American Anthropologist* 78:96–97.

1977    Postscript: Physical anthropology at Berkeley. *Kroeber Anthropological Society Papers* 50:121–122.

The fun of human evolution. In R. K. Wetherington, ed., *Colloquia in Anthropology*, Vol. I. Fort Burgwin Research Center, Taos, New Mexico.

Beyond the basics: Some future uses of the past. *Principal* 57:33–38.

Field studies of primate behavior. In G. H. Bourne, ed., *Progress in Ape Research*. New York: Academic Press, pp. 231–242.

Discussion. *Yearbook of Physical Anthropology 1976* 20:466–467.

1978    Animal behavior and social anthropology. In Gregory et al., eds., *Sociobiology and Human Nature*. San Francisco: Jossey-Bass, pp. 53–74.

The evolution of man. *Scientific American* 239:194–208.

Human behavior and the behavior of other animals. *American Psychologist* 33:405–418.

What we can't learn about people from the apes. *Human Nature* 1:70–75.

(with E. R. McCown). Human evolution and social science. In S. L. Washburn and E. R. McCown, eds., *Human Evolution: Biosocial Perspectives.* Menlo Park, California: Benjamin/Cummings, pp. 285–295.

(with F. C. Howell and R. L. Ciochon). Relationship of *Australopithecus* and *Homo. Journal of Human Evolution* 7:127–131.

(abstract)
Reflections on the development of studies of primate behavior. *American Journal of Physical Anthropology* 48(3):446.

1979    Ethnologists do not study human evolution. *Behavioral and Brain Sciences* 2:49.

(letter)
Montezuma's zoo. *New York Review of Books* 26:52.

(letter with B. Benedict)
Non-human primate culture. *Man* 14:163–164.

(letter)
The Piltdown hoax: Piltdown 2. *Science* 203:955–958.

1980    A view of the primates. In S. S. Kalter, A. Hellman, and J. Gruber, eds., *Primates and Human Cancer.* Department of Health, Education and Welfare Publication No. (NIH) 79-1889, pp. 3–9.

Back to back. *New York Review of Books* (May 29) 27:49–50.

(letter)
Ape language. *Psychology Today* 13:5.

(with Ruth Moore). *Ape into Human: A Study in Human Evolution.* Boston: Little, Brown.

(comment)
On Brace's review of Origins. *American Anthropologist* 82:392–394.

(with J. M. Lowenstein). Species specific proteins in fossils. *Naturwissenschaflen* 67:343–346.

1981    (letter)
Ape language, or more on ape talk. *New York Review of Books* (April 2) p. 43.

Review of Human Nature and History: A Response to Sociobiology, by Kenneth Bock. *New York Review of Books* (April 6) 28:6.

(letter)
Reagan on Evolution. *San Francisco Chronicle.* (October 14, 1981).

Statement on Human Evolution. Prepared at the request of the American Anthropological Association for the annual meeting, December 1980.

Language and the fossil record. In L. L. Mai, ed., *The Perception of Evolution: Papers Honoring Joseph Birdsell.* Los Angeles: University of California Monographs in Anthropology.

Review of Who Brought Home the Bacon? by F. Dahlberg, ed. In Woman the gatherer. *New York Review of Books* (September 24, 1981).

William King Gregory, 1876–1970. *American Journal of Physical Anthropology* 56:393–395.

Longevity in primates. J. L. McGaugh and S. B. Kiesler, eds., *Aging: Biology and Behavior.* New York: Academic Press, pp. 11–29.

A defense of Father Teilhard de Chardin: A reply to the Piltdown Conspiracy by Stephen Gould. *Natural History* 90:12–31.

1982    Human biology and social science. In E. A. Hoebel, R. Currier, and S. Kaiser, eds., *Crisis in Anthropology: View from Spring Hill, 1980.* New York: Garland Publishing, pp. 321–332.

Fifty years of studies on human evolution. *Bulletin of the American Academy of Arts and Sciences* 35:25–39.

Human evolution. In *Perspectives in Biology and Medicine* 25:583–602. Chicago: University of Chicago Press.

(with J. M. Lowenstein). Piltdown jaw confirmed as orangutan. *Nature* 229:294.

Gabriel Ward Lasker. *Human Biology* 54:171–173.

1983    Human origins. Essay Prepared at the request of Committee on Basic Research in the Behavioral and Social Sciences of the National Research Council.

(with P. Dolhinow). Comparison of human behaviors. In D. W. Rajecki, ed., *Comparing Behavior: Studying Man Studying Animals.* Erlbaum Publishing, pp. 27–43.

Human nature. *AnthroQuest* 26:9.

Evolution of a teacher. *Annual Review of Anthropology* 12:1–24.

1984    A comment on Feldesman's Analysis of the Distal Humerus. *American Journal of Physical Anthropology* 63:85–89.

Review of History of American Anthropology, by F. Spencer. *Human Biology* (May 1982) 56:393–410.

1985    Human evolution after Raymond Dart. In P. Tobias, ed., *Hominid Evolution: Past, Present and Future.* New York: Liss Inc., pp. 3–18.

1993    Evolution and education. In A. Almquist and A. Manyak, eds., *Milestones in Human Evolution.* Prospect Heights, Illinois: Waveland Press, pp. 223–240.